AF600526

The Cartulary-Chronicle of St-Pierre of Bèze

Medieval Academy Books, No. 116

The Cartulary-Chronicle of St-Pierre of Bèze

Edited by
Constance Brittain Bouchard

Published for the Medieval Academy of America by
University of Toronto Press 2019

University of Toronto Press
Toronto Buffalo London
utorontopress.com

ISBN 978-1-4875-0615-5

Library and Archives Canada Cataloguing in Publication

Title: The cartulary-chronicle of St-Pierre of Bèze / [edited by]
Constance Brittain Bouchard.
Names: Bouchard, Constance Brittain, editor. | Medieval Academy
of America, issuing body.
Series: Medieval Academy books ; no. 116.
Description: Series statement: Medieval Academy books ; no. 116 | This volume is an edition of St-Bénigne's chronicle, with in addition an abbreviated transcription of Bèze's cartulary-chronicle, reprinted from the seventeenth-century edition. | Includes bibliographical references and indexes. | Text in English and Latin.
Identifiers: Canadiana 20190117230 | ISBN 9781487506155 (hardcover)
Subjects: LCSH: Abbaye Saint-Pierre de Bèze (Burgundy, France) – Charters. | LCSH: Benedictines – France – Burgundy – History – To 1500 – Sources. | LCSH: Monasticism and religious orders – France – Burgundy – History – To 1500 – Sources. | LCSH: Burgundy (France) – Church history – Sources.
Classification: LCC BX2615.B87 C37 2019 | DDC 271/.10444—dc23

University of Toronto Press acknowledges the financial assistance to its publishing program of the Canada Council for the Arts and the Ontario Arts Council, an agency of the Government of Ontario.

CONTENTS

PREFACE

The cartulary-chronicle of Bèze is both a history of the monastery and a collection of its charters (some summarized and some in integral form), from its seventh-century foundation until the middle of the twelfth century. One of the oldest monasteries in Burgundy, Bèze was a Benedictine house whose history included at least six incidents of sacking and destruction, from all of which it recovered, and according to its twelfth-century chronicler it always came back stronger than ever. Combining the history of Burgundy and Francia with the history of his house, John, the chronicler, created a past for Bèze as he wanted it to be remembered. The cartulary-chronicle is here published in full for the first time.

This edition was begun during the year I was a Visitor at the Institute for Advanced Study in Princeton. There cannot be a better place to be a medieval historian. I would like to thank the archivists at the Archives départementales of Côte-d'Or and Haute-Marne for their assistance in finding documents of Bèze. An especial thank you goes to the *conservateurs* at the Bibliothèque nationale de France, who let me consult the original manuscript of the cartulary-chronicle even though, officially, no one is supposed to handle it. The Medieval Academy of America has been very tolerant of a historian who wants to keep on producing cartulary editions, making Medieval Academy Books her own.

ABBREVIATIONS

AASS	*Acta Sanctorum*
BnF	Paris, Bibliothèque nationale de France
GC	*Gallia christiana*
MGH	Monumenta Germaniae historica
	DD *Diplomata*
	Epp. *Epistolae*
	Form. *Formulae*
	SS *Scriptores*
	SSRM *Scriptores rerum Merovingicarum*
PL	*Patrologia cursus completus*, Series Latina
RHGF	*Recueil des historiens des Gaules et de la France*

The Cartulary-Chronicle of St-Pierre of Bèze

Map 1 The region around Bèze

INTRODUCTION

The monastery of St-Pierre of Bèze, located some twenty-five kilometres northeast of Dijon, has always suffered in the shadow of the much better-known monastery of St-Bénigne of Dijon. The cartulary-chronicle of Bèze, originally composed around 1120 by a monk named John, includes extensive sections copied more or less verbatim from the mid-eleventh-century chronicle of St-Bénigne but also 331 charters dating from the seventh century to the first half of the twelfth (two additional documents from this period survive as originals).

The volume through which most modern scholars know Bèze's cartulary-chronicle (if they know it at all) is the Bougaud-Garnier version published in 1875. This volume is an edition of St-Bénigne's chronicle, with in addition an abbreviated transcription of Bèze's cartulary-chronicle, reprinted from the seventeenth-century edition.[1] Probably because the chronicle aspect of the cartulary-chronicle is so derivative, scholars have ignored Bèze, in spite of its over 300 documents surviving from before 1150, and there is no modern secondary literature on the house.[2] The present edition gives for the first time a critical edition of the complete text of the cartulary-chronicle of Bèze, bringing Bèze out of the shade cast by its better-known neighbour and giving one of the oldest Burgundian monasteries its proper due.

1 *Chronique de l'abbaye de Saint-Bénigne de Dijon, suivie de la Chronique de Saint-Pierre de Bèze*, ed. E. Bougaud and Joseph Garnier, pp. 231–503. The chronicle of St-Bénigne is on pp. 1–229.

2 The only exceptions are brief discussions of Bèze's five Merovingian-era documents: their authenticity (or lack thereof) and the question of whether the dukes mentioned in those documents might fit into the family tree of the so-called Etichonen – which assumes those documents' authenticity.

THE MONASTERY OF BÈZE

Bèze was one of several Benedictine monasteries in the diocese of Langres with roots in the sixth and seventh centuries. Moûtier-St-Jean, St-Seine, and St-Bénigne of Dijon were slightly older. All of these Merovingian-era houses, including Bèze, grew and prospered during the initial spread of Frankish monasticism.[3] By the late ninth century Molosmes, St-Michel of Tonnerre, and Pouthières had also all been founded in the diocese, though on the opposite side of the diocese from Bèze. St-Étienne of Dijon, originally a basilica, acquired a body of secular canons who were transformed into canons regular during the High Middle Ages.

The monastery of St-Pierre of Bèze was founded near the source of the small river Bèze, which emerges below a limestone cliff, already wide and swiftly flowing. The river wanders southeast some twenty-five kilometres (in a straight line, longer following the meanders) until it joins the Saône. Originally the monastery was called Fons Besua, the Fountain of Bèze, and later simply Bèze. Although the chronicler John confidently asserted that the house was founded in 600, the monastery probably dated from the middle decades of the seventh century. The year 600 may have been chosen in part because the chronicle of the monastery of Flavigny, in the adjacent diocese of Autun, written not long before John set to work at Bèze, dated that monastery's foundation to 606,[4] and John wanted precedence.

The monastery of Bèze, according to the chronicler John, had been devastated no fewer than six times between its foundation and the eleventh century. First its property and title deeds were stolen by "perfidious" Christians; then it was sacked by the Vandals; in the early eighth century it was sacked again by the Saracens; then in the late eighth century the Carolingians gave the house and its possessions to a laywoman. Bishop Alberic of Langres re-established the house with its possessions and a regular life for monks and had his refoundation confirmed by Louis the Pious in 830. But later in the ninth century Bèze was sacked by the Vikings; in 889 King Odo confirmed this *monasterium* to the bishop of Langres as part of his see's possessions in the aftermath of its destruction.[5] Bèze's monks shortly returned, but the monastery was sacked again in the tenth century by the Magyars. Only at the end of the tenth century,

3 Jamie Kreiner connects this spread to a linking of secular and sacred power at this time; *Social Life of Hagiography in the Merovingian Kingdom*, pp. 195–201.

4 Hugh of Flavigny, "Chronicon," MGH SS 8:323.

5 *Cartulaire du chapitre cathédral de Langres*, ed. Hubert Flammarion, p. 342, no. 339.

after the house had stood vacant for two generations, was it refounded again, finally giving it the prosperity John felt it had always deserved.[6]

During the eleventh and early twelfth centuries, when according to John Bèze grew to fifty or sixty monks, they created close ties with the petty nobility of their northern Burgundy region. The dukes and the counts of Burgundy, however, made only extremely rare appearances in their documents. The most important local authorities were the lords of Beaumont and of Fouvent, related by marriage; both had asserted the title of count in the early eleventh century but settled, after the rise of ducal power, for being castellans. Most of the monastery's friends were castellans or knights or small landowners, who might appear repeatedly as donors or as witnesses, often over several generations. The monks of Bèze, as much as can be determined, tended to come from the same rather narrow geographic area as their donors.

In this corner of Burgundy, the monastery of Bèze, along with St-Seine and St-Bénigne of Dijon, was the primary recipient of secular generosity in the eleventh century. In 1075 the monastery of Molesme was founded in the diocese, yet it was relatively far away and initially attracted little attention from the local lords and knights who had long patronized Bèze. But in 1098 Cîteaux was founded, a short distance south of Dijon, and in the next two generations a wave of Cistercian houses was established, a great many in the diocese of Langres: Morimond, Auberive, Beaulieu, Longué, La Crête, and Quincy. Bèze and many of the other older houses found themselves outcompeted. The abbot of Cîteaux appears in a document from Bèze for the first time in 1112/13.

With the Cistercians receiving most of the attention in the middle and later years of the twelfth century, Bèze – like other older Benedictine houses – received far fewer gifts than the monks had earlier. In 1772 the monks set out to copy into a register all the twelfth-century documents not already copied into the cartulary-chronicle,[7] but they could find extremely few such charters, only five of them, even though the cartulary did not extend into the second half of the twelfth century. The eighteenth-century register was left with a number of blank pages intended for twelfth-century documents that did not exist – although they *did* find and copy a large number of charters from the thirteenth and later centuries. This drastic drop in numbers of documents, from hundreds issued in the eleventh and early twelfth centuries to essentially none from the

6 See also Bouchard, "High Medieval Monks Contemplate Their Merovingian Past," p. 55.

7 Dijon, Archives départementales, 3 H 1 (cart. 130). This register is sometimes referred to as "le cartulaire vert" because of its green cover. The register states at the beginning that it was created "pour servir de continuation à la Chronique, depuis l'an 1100 jusque à l'an 1500."

period between the 1140s and the early thirteenth century, indicates a monastery being forgotten.

The monastery of Bèze rarely appears in the records of other monasteries, even those closest. It appears in the records of St-Bénigne only twice – which seems odd, given that in the early eleventh century the two monasteries had the same abbot. The two monasteries made an exchange of property in 827, and in 1066 a synod was held at Bèze to deal with the abbot of St-Bénigne's complaints that his exclusive wine ban was being violated by one of the duke's men. Curiously, although the original record of the synod's decision survives among St-Bénigne's records, it does not even mention the abbot or monks of Bèze, in whose monastery the decision was reached.[8]

THE CARTULARY-CHRONICLE OF BÈZE

The monk John set out, probably shortly before 1120, to tell the history of his monastery, embedded within a broader history of Burgundy and Francia, studded with both paraphrased and integrally copied charters from his house's archives. John's epitaph was added to his cartulary-chronicle by later scribes, along with a remarkably long list of books he had copied. His epitaph speaks of him, a lifelong monk of Bèze, as improving the monastery's written record at the same time Abbot Stephen was restoring its property and regular life.

John had worked closely with Abbot Stephen (d. 1120), so his work should be seen as part of an effort to organize and stabilize the monastery's possessions. A great admirer of the abbot, John said that under Stephen's rule the abbey expanded from maybe twenty monks to fifty or sixty, or as many as one hundred if one counted those in dependent cells. The abbots of a number of other monasteries, he added, began as monks of Bèze. In addition, the house's property greatly expanded. Thus he set out to tell a story of 500 years of challenges and setbacks culminating in regularity, honour, and prosperity.

For the broader history in which he placed Bèze, John relied principally on the chronicle of St-Bénigne, written two or three generations earlier and itself compiled from earlier chronicles. He continued his work until around 1130. Other scribes added additional charters in the following decades, as well as giving John's epitaph and a poem on the subject of Jerusalem. John's continuators, however, made no effort to continue the chronicle.

Although clearly attempting to organize the materials in his monastery's archives and to put them into context, John was not attempting to create what

8 *Chartes et documents de Saint-Bénigne de Dijon*, 2:122–125, no. 344.

might be called a legal dossier. His paraphrases of many documents indicate that he was more interested in the fact that property had been given to his monastery by a certain donor than in the actual wording. Indeed, as he went on he tended more and more to paraphrase and summarize, although he might still copy a dating formula or witness list.

The latter part of the manuscript was added after John had completed his work. A number of different hands copied charters primarily dating from the abbacy of Girard (1125–1142). Because the hands change almost with every charter, it is most likely that they were copied into the volume individually, shortly after being issued. These later documents were generally copied integrally, rather than being summarized, though the scribes might abbreviate the witness lists. Only two documents (both of which are dated 1159–1164 because they mention Abbot Geoffrey) were copied into the codex after the 1140s.

John's original manuscript, with the additions of the following decade, is in Paris, Bibliothèque nationale de France (BnF, MS lat 4997).[9] It is written on parchment in brown ink in John's neat twelfth-century book hand and that of his continuators. The folios measure 27.5 centimetres high and 17 centimetres wide. The written area, measuring 22 by 13 centimetres, is ruled in drypoint, for 25 or 26 lines (there is some variation). There are frequent red initials and rubrics, clearly added slightly later, because there is often not enough room for the rubrics, which generally ended up in the margins.

There are 22 gatherings of 8 folios each, except for the eighteenth gathering, which has only 4 folios. The first 18 most likely correspond to John's original work, up through document 262. The first 17 gatherings are numbered consecutively in the lower margin on the last page, with the exception of the third gathering, which is numbered on the front. The folios are numbered in Roman numerals in an early modern hand; there are two folios mistakenly numbered 83 and two numbered 139 (the second of each is now designated as *bis*), so the folio numbering goes up through 170, even though there are 172 folios. Although John originally completed his work with the eighteenth gathering, the nineteenth gathering begins with what appear to be later additions that he made, through document 268. The rest of the volume is a series of later additions in a variety of hands. A few were earlier documents that John must have missed while copying, but most were later.

On folio 1r, which may have been intended as a title page, some late twelfth-century charters were later copied – now faded and essentially

9 It is also described on the website of the BnF, http://archivesetmanuscrits.bnf.fr/ark:/12148/cc136298 (accessed 1 August 2014).

illegible. There are three blank pieces of parchment at the beginning and three at the end, doubtless added during binding; they are not numbered. The binding is eighteenth-century red leather, carrying the royal court of arms, three fleurs de lys surmounted by a crown. On its spine the codex reads "IOANNIS MONACHI CHRONICO BESUENSI."

None of the documents copied into the twelfth-century cartulary-chronicle survived the French Revolution and the dissolution of the monastery, although some later manuscripts and registers still exist. The codex itself survived because it had, by the seventeenth century, ended up in the French royal library, rather than being at the monastery. In the sixteenth century, it had formed part of the library of Philippe Hurault de Cheverny, grand chancellor of France, and it was from his library that it passed in the early seventeenth century to the royal library. The eighteenth-century monks of Bèze knew of its existence and were able to consult it in the library, but it was no longer in their hands.

BÈZE'S MEROVINGIAN-ERA DOCUMENTS

One of the most vexing issues of editing the monk John's work has been determining the accuracy of its Merovingian-era history, specifically its earliest documents. The new Monumenta Germaniae historica (MGH) edition of the documents of the Merovingian kings has declared them all forgeries; the editor, Theo Kölzer, had indeed published an earlier study in which he closely analysed them and concluded that none were authentic.[10] I would not however be quite so dismissive. Certainly one cannot accept at face value John's narrative account of his house's foundation by a duke, uncle of a sainted bishop, in the year 600, and of the duke's son serving as abbot for close to a century. But one also cannot accuse John of blithely fabricating documents; he appears rather to have been trying to create explanations for documents, already in his house's archives, that he found anomalous. The monastery had by the early twelfth century recovered its regularity, independence, and to a large extent its property. Now it was time to remember everything properly.

My own conclusion is that Bèze actually did have a few Merovingian-era royal charters, as well as some other charters from the same period. These I believe were reworked at least to some extent in the ninth century, at the time the house was refounded and reformed by the bishop of Langres, but they retained most of what had originally been in them. This reworking would have doubtless taken place when the papyrus originals were copied onto parchment.

10 Kölzer, *Merowingerstudien II*, pp. 1–17.

Two of Bèze's supposed Merovingian-era documents do, however, seem to be complete fabrications, probably created at the same time to fill in what the monks saw as serious gaps.

John's account of his monastery's origins gives the founder as Amalgarius, a duke and father of the first abbot, as well as father of one Duke Adalricus.[11] The monks did not simply invent this "founder," for there really was a Frankish Duke Amalgarius active in the Burgundy region in the seventh century. The chronicler Fredegar mentioned Amalgarius several times for the period between about 628 and 642. Amalgarius carried out King Dagobert I's orders to kill a rival, acted as royal ambassador to the Goths, and fought the Gascons. He last appears plotting to kill a patrician under King Clovis II.[12] If the monks were just seeking a name for a fictional founder, it seems unlikely that they would have chosen this rather bloodthirsty royal functionary; after all, the chronicler John knew Fredegar's account through the chronicle of St-Bénigne. When the bishop of Langres issued a confirmation of Bèze's possessions in 830 (document 9), he cited Amalgarius as the house's founder. Thus, it is possible that Amalgarius really was involved in some capacity in the early history of Bèze, even if not as founder.

According to John, Amalgarius originally founded a house of monks with his son Waldalenus as the first abbot and a house of nuns with his daughter as first abbess, but within a short time the two merged under the son's leadership. This is a straightforward story – and John even seems to have known that the Merovingian era had had double houses, where both men and women lived under a common superior. But the charter on which John appears to have based this account does not actually say that this is what happened. Its differences from John's explanation suggest that it was, at base, an authentic charter with which he had to deal, not simply his own confection.

This charter in question was the first that John copied, one that he took as the equivalent of a foundation charter (document 1).[13] A woman named Adalsinda

11 Yaniv Fox takes John's account as accurate and builds a picture of a powerful seventh-century family of the Jura largely on the basis of it and the vita of Columbanus; *Power and Religion in Merovingian Gaul*, pp. 99–108.

12 Fredegar, *Fourth Book of the Chronicle with Its Continuations*, pp. 48, 62, 65, 77–78, chapters 4.58, 73, 78, 90. An Amalgarius also appears in a charter of Theoderic III, a document that still exists as an original; MGH DD *regum francorum e stirpe Merovingica*, ed. Theo Kölzer, pp. 319–320, no. 126. This document, however, most likely dates to 682, a generation too late for the Amalgarius in Fredegar. The Amalgarius in this document calls himself son of Gaeltramnus.

13 See also Bouchard, "High Medieval Monks," pp. 50–51.

issued it in 658. She called herself the daughter of Amalgarius and Aquilina and added that she had a brother named Adalricus. The charter did not call Adalricus a duke, even though John used the title in his own account.[14] The timing would be right for Adalsinda to be the daughter of the Duke Amalgarius known from Fredegar. In this charter she gave the little monastery of St-Martin of Brégille to the abbot of Bèze. St-Martin, she said, had been founded by her parents. This house was located some seventy kilometres from Bèze, on the outskirts of Besançon. Due to vaguely specified injuries and adversities, Adalsinda said that she and her brother could no longer live regularly there. Thus, they had decided to relocate to St-Pierre of Bèze and give St-Martin to that monastery.

John's efforts to create a family for the first abbot of his house led him to add some explanatory material and creatively misread a word or two, but the charter's text remains markedly different from what he said it said. To begin with, the charter itself never names the abbot of Bèze, even though the rubric calls him Waldalenus. It is also worth noting that although Adalsinda calls this abbot "brother" (*frater*), he is specifically her brother *in Christo* and thus not a blood relative, as is her *germanus* Adalricus.[15] The charter also does not explicitly say that Adalsinda was an abbess – although again she is so named in the rubric. (Her charter was signed by a nun, a *monacha*, who said that she signed at the orders of her *domna*, which must be the source of John's belief that she was an abbess.) It does not even say that St-Martin was a nunnery; indeed, it might be more accurately described as a cell, as there is no indication of other inhabitants besides the brother and sister and the *monacha*. John's suggestion that Adalricus became a duke, like his father, appears to be contradicted by this charter, which shows him living under monastic discipline.

14 A certain Duke Adalricus was the founder of the powerful "Etichonen" clan, perhaps a generation later; Bouchard, *Rewriting Saints and Ancestors*, pp. 181–185. John may have seen a reference to this Duke Adalricus and assumed he was the same man as the son of his house's founder. The Adalricus of the 658 charter, son of Amalgarius, would however be hard to identify with the ancestor of the Etichonen, who is generally assumed to be son of one Leudesius by most of those who attempt to trace the family tree earlier than Adalricus; for example, Vollmer, "Die Etichonen," pp. 143–145. In contrast, Hans J. Hummer suggests that Adalricus, founder of the Etichonen, might have been son of Amalgarius's son Adalricus; *Politics and Power in Early Medieval Europe*, pp. 46–47. He is followed by Fox, *Power and Religion in Merovingian Gaul*, pp. 99, 103. For the Etichonen, the basic studies remain those of Vollmer and of Christian Wilsdorf, "Les Etichonides aux temps carolingiens et ottoniens."

15 Scholars, however, have generally followed the chronicle in assuming that the first abbot of Bèze was the founder's son; for example, Susan Wood, *Proprietary Church in the Medieval West*, p. 136; and Fox, *Power and Religion in Merovingian Gaul*, p. 103.

Adalsinda's charter begins by referring to Amalgarius and Aquilina as "my" parents. Since she is acting with her brother Adalricus, it is not surprising that she should also refer to them as "our" parents, as indeed she does. And yet twice the charter, at least as copied into the cartulary, calls them "your" parents, that is the parents of Waldalenus. Here John either accidentally misread *noster* and *nostri* as *uester* and *uestri* – easy enough to do, as the abbreviations are identical except for the extremely similar letters *n* and *u* – or else misread the words deliberately, as making Amalgarius father of Waldalenus. On the basis of this charter, therefore, John created the story of Amalgarius founding two monasteries, a nunnery where Adalsinda ruled and a male monastery under Waldalenus, which were then merged.

John further embellished the story by making Bishop Donatus of Besançon (627–658), who is referenced in Adalsinda's charter as the current bishop, into a virtual cousin. There were two dukes in Burgundy, John said, implying though not actually saying that they were brothers, named Waldalenus and Amalgarius.[16] Waldalenus was the father of Bishop Donatus of Besançon, and Amalgarius the father of Abbot Waldalenus. Indeed Bishop Donatus really was the son of a Waldalenus, information given by the vita of St Columbanus,[17] so when John saw this name he knew that duke must be related to the first abbot of his house, also named Waldalenus.[18]

The differences between John's account and what document 1 actually says thus should clear him of the charge of having fabricated it. The only really anachronistic aspect of Adalsinda's charter is that it is dated both by the year of the incarnation and by the regnal year of Chlothar III, whereas a genuine Merovingian-era document would not normally include the year of the incarnation. In addition, the two dates given do not match: the former gives 652, the latter 658. If one removes the year of the incarnation, however – doubtless added later by a scribe making his best guess as to the regnal years of King Chlothar – as well as the implication that Adalsinda was the abbot's sister, then there is every reason to believe that this charter is, at base, authentic.

16 Fox suggests without evidence that Amalgarius was son-in-law (rather than brother) of this Waldalenus; *Power and Religion in Merovingian Gaul*, pp. 99–100, 185.

17 Jonas, "Vita Columbani" 1.14, MGH SSRM 4:79.

18 Columbanus referred in his own letters to a Waldalenus who might make good leadership material; "Epistola" 4, pp. 165–167. John doubtless assumed that this Waldalenus was the first abbot of his house, helping explain his foundation date of 600. However, it would be very difficult to identify this man either with the (putative) abbot of Bèze or with the father of Bishop Donatus; Fox, *Power and Religion in Merovingian Gaul*, pp. 105–106.

John followed Adalsinda's document with another which also may have been somewhat reworked but which still seems essentially authentic (document 2). Again, John appears to have elaborated what was in it. His introductory comments state that "perverse men" took Bèze's foundation documents and that Sichelm – who succeeded Duke Amalgarius, the monastery's founder, as duke of Burgundy – obtained a confirmation from King Chlothar, restoring what had been taken. Abbot Waldalenus is very much a part of the story in John's summary of the events.

The actual document from 663 gives a slightly different account. Here Sichelm is not called a duke; he is not given any title at all. Waldalenus is not mentioned. Rather, Sichelm addresses mayors of the palace, asking them to go to the king and request him to confirm the monks of Bèze in their possessions, taken from them by evildoers who also took their charters. He does say that Duke Amalgarius had founded Bèze, which might be a later addition, although referring to the duke as *illustris uir* is certainly the correct Merovingian-era term. The names given for the mayors of the palace are the names of a real mayor of a palace and of two men who appeared with him in a charter of 654, a charter that still survives. Sichelm himself appeared in a different authentic royal charter in 654; neither 654 charter involved Bèze. This extra step, of having someone approach the mayor(s) of the palace rather than going directly to the king, is unlikely to have occurred to an outright forger.

Other than perhaps calling Amalgarius Bèze's founder, this document thus appears authentic. The same, however, cannot be said of the following one (document 3). Here King Chlothar, responding to Sichelm's request, confirms Bèze in all its possessions. If Sichelm's document were real, then the monks of Bèze would have expected to see the royal charter he had sought, and if it were not in their archives, they would have created it. In this charter, which does not mention the mayors of the palace, the king recalls that Amalgarius, here called a duke, founded Bèze with his wife Aquilina, and that Waldalenus is abbot, directing a house that follows the Rules of Columbanus and Benedict. This sort of detail suggests a later writer who knows his house's history, and it also is highly reminiscent of Adalsinda's charter. This purported royal charter, again dated both by the incarnation and by the king's regnal year, with dates that do not match, also spells out in great detail the monk's property holdings, including property the monks are known to have had only substantially later. Here the doubt that has been cast on Bèze's early charters appears entirely justified.

But it is interesting to note that the idea that King Chlothar approved of Amalgarius and his wife founding the monastery with their son as first abbot was not simply created in the High Middle Ages. When the bishop of Langres refounded the house in 830 (document 9), he referred to that king as playing a role in Bèze's foundation. Even if document 3 was confected in the eleventh or twelfth century, it was based on a far older tradition. Indeed, the reworking of those Merovingian-era documents from Bèze that have authentic elements may perhaps be dated to the time of the house's refoundation.

At the end of document 3 is a mention of Gengulf as *aduocatus* of the monastery. The following charter (document 4) explains that St Gengulf was given this office by the king in 667. Now Gengulf was a local saint who had owned property at Véronnes, not far from Bèze. His vita, probably nearly contemporary, says that he was assassinated in 670 at his wife's instigation because he reproached her for her adultery. This mention of advocacy, common in the eleventh and early twelfth centuries but not known in the Merovingian era, suggests that the whole purpose of the charter was to tie Bèze to a local saint.

And yet the following charter from 679 (document 5) once again suggests an authentic charter in the monastery's archives. Here, Theoderic III gives some goods of a rebellious Duke Adalricus to Bèze.[19] Unlike documents 1 and 2, this charter names Waldalenus as abbot in the text itself, as opposed to in the rubric. It was doubtless on the basis of this charter that John decided that Adalricus, supposed brother of his house's first abbot, was a duke, in spite of his appearance as a religious recluse in document 1. Indeed, it would have made good sense in the twelfth century that the brother of the founding abbot, the son of the secular founder, would have made an attempt to reclaim property his family gave to the church.

Although there are anomalies in document 5, such as characterizing the scribe as *notharius*, a scribe with the same name (Glybertus or Aghliberthus) is also found as having written another charter of Theoderic III in the same year, this one for St-Denis, a charter for which the original still exists; this suggests that Bèze's document was, at base, real. The abbreviation used for *subscripsit* as copied into the cartulary is the normal Merovingian-era abbreviation, although there is also what appears to be a Carolingian-style monogram. One might also wonder if the king really would give all of a duke's property to a monastery, but the appearance here of Duke Adalricus as a rebellious lord, when earlier he had been the monastic brother of Abbot Waldalenus in the house's narrative of its history, again suggests that no one at Bèze decided to create a charter to explain his role in the story but rather shaped the story as suggested by the charters. And here the very unspecific description of Adalricus's possessions indicates that no one was trying to give later property holdings an earlier origin.

19 This Adalricus may in fact be identical with the ancestor of the Etichonids.

All in all then, although it seems very unlikely that Bèze was founded in 600 with Waldalenus as first abbot, an office he still held as late as 679, there seems little reason to doubt that it really was a seventh-century house and that aristocrats and kings helped it establish its property holdings. It was already in existence by the 650s and apparently prospered, if as a small, rather obscure house, in the following generations. John commented that under Pippin the Short and Charlemagne the regular life of the house was lost, and indeed the house has no existing documents from the eighth century.[20] At the time when Remigius (Pippin's half-brother) was bishop of Langres, he gave the house to a noblewoman named Angela or Angla, according to the chronicler, and its subsequent history is a blank for some seventy-five years, until a document issued in 816 (document 6). Here the local count determined the borders of the monastery's property, presumably because the house was being restored to regularity. The full restoration of the religious life, however, appears to have taken another dozen years or more, until Louis the Pious confirmed its restoration and its possessions.

THIS EDITION

The cartulary-chronicle of Bèze has never been edited in its entirety before. The only previous edition, which accidentally missed three of the house's documents and deliberately skipped over all the sections which John copied more or less verbatim from the chronicle of St-Bénigne, was that of Luc d'Achery, done in the seventeenth century.[21] His edition was simply reprinted by J.-P. Migne[22] and, perhaps surprisingly, in the Bougaud-Garnier edition of 1875. According to an editorial note (p. 230), the latter edition was supposedly based on a transcription from the original manuscript by M. de l'Epinois, with notes by Joseph Garnier, archivist of Côte-d'Or. And yet a comparison with the d'Achery edition shows that M. de l'Epinois transcribed not from the manuscript but from the earlier edition. His misreadings, slips, efforts to classicize the Latin, and decisions on where to abbreviate the chronicle sections are precisely those of d'Achery. Although he does seem to have glanced at the original manuscript itself – he knew the correct shelf number in Paris and noted in a few places where the manuscript reproduced a monogram – the only genuinely

20 The same was true of a number of other Burgundian houses; Bouchard, *Rewriting Saints and Ancestors*, pp. 156–171.

21 D'Achery, *Spicilegium*, 2:400–463. The original edition was published in 13 volumes, 1665–1677.

22 PL 162:862–1006.

new part of this edition is Garnier's footnotes. Some individual charters from the cartulary-chronicle have been published by the MGH – primarily those of the Merovingian kings – using the original manuscript, but in most cases previous editions of Bèze's charters have simply reprinted them from d'Achery's edition.

The cartulary-chronicle includes 331 documents, dating from the seventh century to the 1140s. Some are integral copies, some briefer paraphrases. With the exception of the five Merovingian-era documents, there is no reason to doubt the authenticity of any of them. This edition also includes, in an appendix, the only two surviving documents from the period of the cartulary-chronicle not to have been copied into it. John's manuscript is written in a clear twelfth-century book hand and presents few transcription challenges. The only place where reading offers any difficulty is the first folio, which is worn away at the edges. Here I have provided d'Achery's reading in brackets where the manuscript is missing a word or words, in the assumption that it was not so badly worn 350 years ago.

In editing, I have retained the spelling of the manuscript, which, like most Latin of the twelfth century, is not entirely classical. For example, it is common to find *abere* for *habere*, *nichil* for *nihil*, or *auctum* for *actum*, and the same person may be called Aribertus, Charibertus, or Haribertus even in the same charter. The text will vary between *ca-* and *cha-*, or between *-cio* and *-tio* even within a few lines. Twelfth-century Latin in fact was probably more classical than that of Gregory of Tours and Fredegar, the ultimate sources for the early part of the chronicle. The scribes often used the "e-cedilla" for both the *-ae-* and *-oe-* diphthongs (ę), but they also used a simple *-e-*.

Because all previous printed editions of any of the monks' charters have been based on BnF lat 4997, generally via d'Achery, I have not bothered to enumerate the differences between those editions and mine, which would only be pointing out misprints or efforts to classicize the Latin. Abbreviations have been silently expanded, and capitalization has been normalized. In most cases I have followed modern conventions of punctuation, though trying to follow the scribes in their sense of where sentences should stop and start. I have begun new paragraphs wherever the scribe indicated the beginning of a new section by a large capital, and also in a few places where it is necessary to break up very long sections.

Dating many of the charters is a challenge, because John typically omitted any dating formula that might have been found in the original.[23] For the first

23 Bèze is not unusual here. For the challenge, see Gervers, ed., *Dating Undated Medieval Charters*. For Merovingian-era charters, I have relied on the royal dates worked out by Wood, *Merovingian Kingdoms*.

three or four centuries of the house's history, he copied charters approximately where he believed they fell within his broader narrative, but he made no effort to maintain more than a general chronology for the numerous eleventh- and twelfth-century charters. When the name of the abbot is given, the date can be placed within a range, but for many charters it is impossible to be more precise than, for example, "early twelfth century," based on the context of surrounding charters. Specific information about dating is given in the notes for a number of individual documents, and a chronological cross-listing of the documents follows this introduction.

I have identified all important individuals found in the charters (counts, bishops, and the like). Sometimes this becomes repetitive, as the same people are often found acting in a succession of charters that John copied together, but I thought it best to have all identification both for people and places there with the documents, because those consulting this edition may well be interested in only one of them.

Most of the places mentioned in the documents are still there today, generally located within thirty-five kilometres or less of the monastery. Place names have changed very little over the centuries; for example, the *Belmons* of the twelfth century is the modern Beaumont, and medieval *Domnus Petrus* is modern Dampierre. Especially useful was Alphonse Roserot's 1924 study, tracing place names of the Côte-d'Or and their modifications over the last ten centuries.[24] Joseph Garnier's notes to the 1875 edition of the cartulary-chronicle were also helpful, especially for places that have vanished in the last century and a half. For places with very similar names, it is usually straightforward to distinguish them by reference to other places in the same document. I identify places in the notes and give their location, usually by direction (north, south, etc.) and distance from Bèze. This seems less anachronistic than the normal French convention of identifying places by canton and arrondissement, as well as making it easier to locate them on a map.

I have felt it important to present the entire text of Bèze's cartulary-chronicle, including the sections derived from the chronicle of St-Bénigne. John, after all, did not simply copy the whole thing directly. Rather, even while reproducing large sections, he rearranged and altered as he went so that the text better served his own purposes. For example, he abbreviated or eliminated sections focusing specifically on St-Bénigne, and he made Abbot William, who had been abbot of both houses, principally the abbot of Bèze. Thus John's text, while not telling us anything new about Burgundian history in general, is extremely revelatory

24 Roserot, *Dictionnaire topographique du département de la Côte-d'Or*.

of his views about what was important in the past and the position of his own monastery in the world.

Nonetheless, I know that this edition will be consulted primarily for the documents in it. Since modern cartulary editors always number the individual charters within them for ease in reference, I have numbered the charters here as well. The edition may well give an unusual effect, blocks of chronicle interrupted by editions of charters, but it seemed the best way to preserve John's original intent. I certainly did not want to do what has been done, for example, with the materials from Le Mans, where the chronicle is printed in one volume and the charters that had been embedded within it were taken out and printed separately.[25]

For the individual documents, I indicate if they have been printed separately before (for example, by the MGH). Because generations of scholars of medieval Burgundy have used the Bougaud-Garnier edition, I also note where individual charters were printed in that volume. Unless otherwise indicated, one can assume that all previous editions of the individual charters were transcribed from d'Achery, *Spicilegium*.

In contrast to the charters, my annotations of the chronicle portions of the text are deliberately light. After all, John drew almost everything from the chronicle of St-Bénigne, although with some additions and changes, primarily to assert the importance of the monastery of Bèze where the chronicler of St-Bénigne was giving precedence to his own house; I have noted the most significant of these changes. The chronicler of St-Bénigne in turn drew almost all events before the eleventh century from earlier chronicles, especially Fredegar for the pre-Carolingian era, and then a variety of Carolingian-era sources, including Einhard and the *Miracula* of St-Benoît-sur-Loire.[26] As a third-hand account, Bèze's chronicle will not be useful for historians wanting to know what happened in early medieval Francia. Thus, I have kept identifications of people and places minimal, putting more emphasis on noting where John condensed or altered his source.

25 Weidemann, ed., *Geschichte des Bistums Le Mans*.

26 The chronicle of St-Bénigne itself deserves a study of its sources and its use of these sources, because its author deliberately condensed and, on occasion, reordered the material he used for Burgundy's early history. Because this volume focuses on Bèze, however, I do not go into detail on the sources of the Bèze chronicler's own source, that is, the chronicle of St-Bénigne.

CHRONOLOGICAL LIST OF DOCUMENTS

997–1016	53	c. 1031–c. 1055	85
1008	43	c. 1031–c. 1055	86
c. 1008	42	c. 1031–c. 1055	87
1008–1016	45	c. 1031–c. 1055	88
c. 1008–1016	44	c. 1031–c. 1055	89
c. 1008–1016	47	c. 1031–c. 1055	90
c. 1010–1016	57	c. 1031–c. 1055	91
c. 1016	46	c. 1031–c. 1055	92
1018	58	c. 1031–c. 1055	93
1018	60	1032	66
1019	59	1034	71
c. 1019	61	c. 1034	73
1023	62	1036	72
1024	63	1036	74
1026–1031	50	c. 1040	84
1026	67	1043	77
1026	68	c. 1043	81
c. 1026	69	1044	75
c. 1026	70	c. 1045	76
1027	64	mid-11th c.	103
1027	65	mid-11th c.	104
early 11th c.	48	mid-11th c.	105
early 11th c	49	mid-11th c.	106
early 11th c.	54	mid-11th c.	107
early 11th c.	55	mid-11th c.	108
early 11th c.	101	mid-11th c.	110
early 11th c.	102	mid-11th c.	111
1031–c. 1040	83	mid-11th c.	112
1031–c. 1055	78	mid-11th c.	113
1031–c. 1055	82	mid-11th c.	114
c. 1031–c. 1055	79	mid-11th c.	115
c. 1031–c. 1055	80	mid-11th c.	116

mid-11th c.	117	mid-11th c.	155
mid-11th c.	120	mid-11th c.	160
mid-11th c.	121	mid-11th c.	161
mid-11th c.	122	mid-11th c.	162
mid-11th c.	123	mid-11th c.	163
mid-11th c.	125	mid-11th c.	164
mid-11th c.	126	mid-11th c.	165
mid-11th c.	127	mid-11th c.	166
mid-11th c.	128	mid-11th c.	167
mid-11th c.	129	mid-11th c.	168
mid-11th c.	130	mid-11th c.	169
mid-11th c.	131	mid-11th c.	170
mid-11th c.	132	mid-11th c.	171
mid-11th c.	134	mid-11th c.	172
mid-11th c.	135	mid-11th c.	173
mid-11th c.	136	mid-11th c.	174
mid-11th c.	137	mid-11th c.	176
mid-11th c.	138	mid-11th c.	177
mid-11th c.	139	mid-11th c.	178
mid-11th c.	140	mid-11th c.	179
mid-11th c.	141	mid-11th c.	180
mid-11th c.	142	mid-11th c.	181
mid-11th c.	143	mid-11th c.	182
mid-11th c.	144	mid-11th c.	183
mid-11th c.	145	1051	94
mid-11th c.	146	c. 1055–c. 1065	95
mid-11th c.	147	c. 1055–c. 1065	97
mid-11th c.	150	c. 1055–c. 1065	98
mid-11th c.	151	c. 1055–c. 1065	99
mid-11th c.	152	c. 1055–c. 1065	100
mid-11th c.	153	c. 1055–c. 1065	109
mid-11th c.	154	c. 1055–c. 1065	118

c. 1055–c. 1065	119	1098	193
c. 1055–c. 1065	133	1099	194
c. 1055–c. 1065	148	1099–1108	200
c. 1055–c. 1065	149	1100	207
c. 1055–c. 1065	156	c. 1100	230
c. 1055–c. 1065	157	1101	192
c. 1055–c. 1065	158	early 12th c.	197
c. 1055–c. 1065	159	early 12th c.	201
c. 1055–c. 1065	175	early 12th c.	202
1057–c. 1065	96	early 12th c.	204
1059	124	early 12th c.	212
c. 1070–1088	272	early 12th c.	216
1076	187	early 12th c.	217
1080	184	early 12th c.	218
c. 1080	185	early 12th c.	219
1083	186	early 12th c.	220
1084–1087	188	early 12th c.	221
1084–1087	255	early 12th c.	222
1088–1091	191	early 12th c.	226
1088–1102	205	early 12th c.	233
1088–1102	206	early 12th c.	243
1088–1105	189	early 12th c.	247
1088–1108	223	early 12th c.	251
1088–1114	203	early 12th c.	252
1088–1120	319	early 12th c.	254
late 11th c. (?)	195	early 12th c.	265
late 11th c. (?)	196	early 12th c.	266
late 11th c. (?)	198	early 12th c.	274
late 11th c. (?)	199	early 12th c. (?)	208
late 11th c. (?)	256	early 12th c. (?)	209
late 11th c. (?)	257	early 12th c. (?)	210
1093	190	early 12th c. (?)	211

early 12th c. (?)	213	1114	261
early 12th c. (?)	214	1114–1120	262
early 12th c. (?)	215	1119	275
early 12th c. (?)	224	1119	277
early 12th c. (?)	225	c. 1119	278
early 12th c. (?)	227	c. 1120	270
early 12th c. (?)	228	c. 1120	271
early 12th c. (?)	229	1125–1130	267
early 12th c. (?)	231	c. 1125–1130	273
early 12th c. (?)	232	1125–1136	279
early 12th c. (?)	234	1125–1142	280
early 12th c. (?)	235	1125–1142	281
early 12th c. (?)	236	1125–1142	282
early 12th c. (?)	239	1125–1142	283
early 12th c. (?)	240	1125–1142	284
early 12th c. (?)	241	1125–1142	285
early 12th c. (?)	244	1125–1142	286
early 12th c. (?)	246	1125–1142	287
early 12th c. (?)	248	1125–1142	288
early 12th c. (?)	249	1125–1142	289
early 12th c. (?)	250	1125–1142	290
early 12th c. (?)	253	1125–1142	292
early 12th c. (?)	258	1125–1142	293
early 12th c. (?)	259	1125–1142	294
early 12th c. (?)	260	1125–1142	295
early 12th c. (?)	263	1125–1142	299
early 12th c. (?)	264	1125–1142	302
1105	238	1125–1142	305
1109	237	1125–1142	306
1112/13	245	1125–1142	307
1113	242	1125–1142	309
1113–1120	276	1125–1142	313

1125–1142	320
c. 1125–1142	291
c. 1125–1142	297
c. 1125–1142	301
c. 1125–1142	308
1127–1142	304
1127–1142	329
1129–1142	298
c. 1130	268
c. 1130–c. 1140	269
1131	332
1134	296
1134	333
1134–1142	300
1138	310
1139–c. 1145	322
1139–c. 1150	323
c. 1142	303
c. 1142	311
1142–c. 1145	312
1142–c. 1145	314
1142–c. 1145	316
1142–c. 1145	318
1142–c. 1145	321
1142–c. 1145	324
1142–c. 1145	327
1142–c. 1145	328
c. 1145	315
c. 1145	317
c. 1145	325
c. 1145	326
1159–1164	330
1159–1164	331

INCIPIT LIBER MEMORABILIUM RERUM SEU ETIAM CARTARUM

Antiquorum[1] huius saeculi sapientium laudabile ac ideo imitandum fuit studium, ut non solum ea quę acciderent in diebus eorum, sed etiam fortia priscorum facta heroum ad memoriam posterorum traderent monimentis scripturarum. Quę utilis res et eis extitit materia humanę laudis et futuris hęc legentibus uel audientibus exemplum incitamentumque ęmulationis. Talia considerantes nos Besuenses sacri monasterii a paruulo habitatores et amatores, ne forte nobis iuste succenseant nostri successores, sic et nos de incuria merito culpamus nostros antecessores, aggrediemur cum adiutorio Dei describere, licet rusticana et minime polita narratione, quę de prefati loci antiquitate, seu deuotorum Deo fidelium eidem donata sunt largitione, uidelicet regum, pontificum, ducum, comitum, ac illustrium uirorum potuimus ad[dicer]e ueraci relatione. Quatinus et honori sit cœnobio [nostro] possessionum ipsi collatarum, et memorandarum [rerum] in eodem gestarum descriptio, et cum diuinę lau[dis de]bito ex optanda benefactoribus eius cęlestis [glori]ę remuneratio.

[Primo igitur] prosequenda nobis est eorum [Chro]nica qui regnauerunt in Francia atque Burgun[dia] usque ad Chlotarium, Chilperici filium.[2] Cuius uidelicet [tem]pore monasterium istud Besuense edificatum est ab Amalgario duce optimo et uxore eius Aquilina nomine, largissimeque de rebus propriis ditatum, anno ab incarnatione Domini sexcentesimo, indictione tertia, presidente sancte Romane ęcclesię Sancto Gregorio Papa, Mauricio uero Cesare imperante in

1 The first page is worn on the outer edge, so I have supplied missing words in brackets, relying on the d'Achery edition.

2 Although the King Chlothar of Bèze's documents, insofar as they have authentic elements, would have been Chlothar III (657–673), the chronicler assumes he was instead Chlothar II (584–629).

republica, Beato uero Columbano commorante in Burgundia.[3] Siquidem[4] ad cognoscendas abbatum successiones qui per diuersa hic prefuerunt tempora et quę sub uniuscuiusque illorum regimine huic loco conlata sunt fidelium largitione. Episcopos quoque Lingonice ęcclesię qui circa hunc locum munificos se exibuerunt nominatim singulos curabimus ostendere, et quid ab uno quoque illorum conlatum sit in aucmentatione huius domus Dei, singillatim demonstrare.

Igitur[5] Childerico rege Francorum defuncto, Chlodoueus filius eius[6] succedit in regnum, uir bellicosus et in armis strenuus. Anno quinto regni eius, Siagrius filius Egidii, patricius Romanorum qui in Galliis habitabant, in Suessionis ciuitate[7] quam pater eius tenuerat residebat, super quem Chlodoueus cum exercitu uenit atque deuicirt. Siagrius fugiens ad Alaricum regem Gothorum Tholosa aliquandiu habitauit.[8] Chlodoueus legatos ad Alaricum misit ut eum redderet, alioquin nouerit sibi bellum illaturum. At ille metuens, Siagrium uinctum legatis tradidit, quem Chlodoueus custodie mancipauit, regnumque eius acceptum et omnia quę illius fuerant sue potestati subegit, eumque gladio trucidari precepit, atque ex illo die a dominatione imperii sublata est Gallia.

Anno x regni sui Chlodoueus commoto exercitu sibi Toringiam prouinciam subiugauit.[9] Inde Gundebaudi regis Burgundionum neptem, uidelicet fratris sui Chilperici filiam quem gladio interfecerat nomine Chrotildem,[10] pulchram satis puellam et uere Christianissimam, interueniente Aureliano consiliario ac legatario suo in coniugem sumpsit. Nuptie Cauilonno[11] preparantur.

Venientes cum celeritate Franci Chrothildem a Gundebaudo acceptam leuantes in basterna, cum multis thesauris ad Chlodoueum dirigunt. Postea

3 Pope Gregory the Great (590–604), the Byzantine emperor Maurice (582–602), and the monastic reformer St Columbanus (d. 615). The author added these names to emphasize what he considered the date of his house's foundation, 600.

4 At this point, the chronicler begins following the chronicle of St-Bénigne essentially word-for-word; in the printed edition of that chronicle he begins on p. 16.

5 At this point, the chronicle of St-Bénigne and the chronicle of Bèze which follows it begin taking their material from Fredegar, *Chronica*, ch. 3.15, p. 98 in the MGH edition. They thus skipped Fredegar's early material on the history of the world from Adam. Fredegar in turn drew from Gregory of Tours (although he heavily condensed), here at chapter 2.27, as well as other sources. For Fredegar's sources and the surviving manuscripts, none of which can now be identified as the one used by the eleventh-century chronicler at Dijon, see Collins, *Die Fredegar-Chroniken*.

6 Clovis I (481–511), son of Childeric.

7 Soissons.

8 Alaric II, king of the Visigoths, had his capital at Toulouse.

9 Thuringia.

10 Clotildis, daughter of King Chilperic II of Burgundy, niece of King Gundebaud.

11 Chalon-sur-Saône.

penitens Gundebaudus recordatus quod patrem Chrothilde matremque ac fratres interfecisset, dirigit protinus post eam exercitum, qui consequentes thesauros et basternam cuncta retentant, Chrothildis uero leuata in equum a Francis ad Chlodoueum euasit. Quam regali honore assumens in matrimonium perfecto amore dilexit.

Habebat iam tunc Chlodoueus filium de concubina, nomine Theodoricum.[12] Interea Godegisilus Gundebaudi regis frater contra eundem germanum suum machinans dolum, per legatos petit auxilium a Chlodoueo cum eum comperisset fortissimum in preliis, promittens si posset eicere Gundebaudum a regno per eius adiutorium, tributum se illi soluere paratum.[13]

Gundebaudus uero ignorans dolum, ab eodem fratre instigatus preparat exercitum copiosum ad pugnam. Chlodoueus cum Francis aduersus duos reges uenit, ingenti multitudine uallatus, initum est bellum super Oscaram fluuium, secus castrum quod Diuion dicitur.[14] Godegisillus Chlodoueo coniungitur, uterque exercitus Gundebaudi populum adterit. At ille sentiens dolum fratris, terga uertit, Rodani ripam percurrens Auinionem urbem ingreditur,[15] et postea per Aridium consiliarium pacem a Chlodoueo expeciit. Chlodoueus uero cum preda maxima et Francorum exercitu ad propria est reuersus, relictis cum Godegisilo quinque milia Francis. Godegisilus obtenta uictoria promissa Chlodoueo ex parte implens, Viennam[16] post Gundebaudum dirigit. Exiens Gundebaudus de Auinione resumptis uiribus, Godegisilum Vienna circumdat, per aque ductum in ciuitatem ingrediens Godegisilum interfecit, Francos adgregatos in unam turrim ferro trucidauit, nichil postea Chlodoueo reddere disponens.

Postea Chlodoueus mittens legatum, nomine Paternum, uirum industrium, ad Alaricum regem Gothorum de amicitie inter eos conditione mandauit. Alaricus uero cum per Paternum uellet Chlodoueum decipere, a Paterno exploratis que circa eum erant, et thesauris eius ingenio subarratis, illusus est. Igitur Chlodoueus aduersus Alaricum arma commouit, et in campania Moglotinse[17]

12 Theoderic, oldest son of Clovis.

13 Curiously, the chronicler of St-Bénigne, who condenses Fredegar as he goes, entirely skipped chapter 3.21 with the account of the baptism of Clovis.

14 Dijon is on the Ouche river.

15 Avignon is on the lower Rhône.

16 Vienne, the capital of the early medieval kingdom of Burgundy.

17 The Chronicle of St-Bénigne reads, more correctly, "Voglanense." There is debate about this location, somewhere outside of Poitiers, where Clovis defeated the Visigoths under Alaric in 507 and, according to modern French historiography, founded France. The major contenders are Voulon and Vouillé. The account originated with Gregory of Tours. See Mathisen and Shanzer, eds., *Battle of Vouillé*, and Carol Symes, "Middle Ages between Nationalism and Colonialism," p. 37.

decimo ab urbe Pictaui miliario Alaricum interfecit, plurima manu Gothorum trucidata. Regnum eius a mari Tirreno Ligereque fluuio, et montibus Pirenesis usque oceanum mare a Chlodoueo occupatum est, et thesauros eius a Tolosa auferens, secum Parisius duxit.

Per idem tempus ab Anastasio imperatore codicellos Clodoueus rex pro consulatu accepit, cum quibus codicellis etiam illi Anastasius coronam auream misit gemmis decoratam et tunicam blatteam. Ex illo die consul et augustus est appellatus.[18] Post hec mortuus est Clodoueus rex in pace, et sepultus est in basilica Sancti Petri quam ipse et regina sua edificauerunt. Mortuus est autem anno v postquam cum Alarico rege Gothorum pugnauit. Regnauit uero annis xxx, fiunt a transitu Sancti Martini usque ad obitum Chlodouei anni cxii.[19]

Mortuo Clodoueo rege quattuor filii eius, id est Theodericus, Clodomeris, Childebertus, Chlotharius, regnum eius aequo ordine inter se diuiserunt. Sortitus est sedem Theodericus Mettis, Chlodomeris Aurelianis, Childebertus Parisius, et Chlotharius Suessionis.[20] Theodericus habebat iam filium nomine Theodebertum,[21] utilem et strenuum. Amalricus filius Alarici sororem eorum in matrimonium accepit. Dani euectu nauale Gallias appetunt, in regno Theoderii irruunt, a Teodeberto filio Theoderici superantur, omnemque predam et uitam amiserunt.

Gundebaudi filius Sigismundus apud Genuensem urbem uilla Quadruuio[22] iussu patris sublimatur in regno, habens uxorem filiam Theoderici regis Italie, unde habebat filium nomine Sigiricum. Eadem mortua aliam duxit uxorem, filium suum quem ex priore coniuge habebat nouerce insidiis iussit interfici. Vnde postea penitentiam agens, monasterium sanctorum Agaunensium[23] miri operis construxit, et alia plurima monasteria edificauit. Chrotildis assidue filios ammonebat mortem patris matrisque uel fratrum ulcisci. Quam ob causam illi Burgundias appetunt. Sigismundum et Godomarem Gundebaudi fratrem in prelio uincunt. Clodomeris Sigismundum ad monasterium sanctorum dum

18 Although Gregory of Tours, from whom this detail derives, was doubtless overstating what Emperor Anastasius (491–518) granted Clovis, he still gave him significant recognition; Wood, *Merovingian Kingdoms*, pp. 48–49.

19 Clovis died in 511.

20 Clovis's four sons divided his realm between them, Theoderic I (511–533) taking Metz as his capital, Chlodomer (511–524) taking Orléans, Childebert I (511–558) Paris, and Chlothar I (511–561) Soissons.

21 Theodebert I (533–548), son of Theoderic I.

22 Le Carré, near Geneva, according to the MGH. Sigismund succeeded his father Gundobad as king of the Burgundians in 516. He was defeated and executed in 524 by Clovis's sons and later considered a saint.

23 St-Maurice of Agaune.

fugeret captum, cum uxore et liberis Aurelianis adducit. Godomaris terga uertens latuit, postea resumptis uiribus regnum Burgundie tenet. Clodomeris iterum aduersus Godomarem exercitum mouet, Sigismundum cum uxore et liberis interfecit. Clodomeri ab Auito abbate predictum est, quod fecerat Sigismundo ipsum itidem passurum.

Cumque Veserontia[24] Franci cum Burgundionibus bellum inissent, Clodomeris capite truncatus est, deceptus ab auxiliis Theoderici, qui filiam Sigismundi habebat uxorem. Franci uero in ipso prelio resumptis uiribus, Burgundionibus superatis et ad internetionem perductis, patriam eorum deuastant. Clotarius uxorem Clodomeris, nomine Gundiocham, uxorem duxit, filios uero eius tres his nominibus, Teodoaldu, Gunthariu, Clodoaldu, Chrotechildis alebat. Clotarius et Childebertus fugato Godomare Burgundias occupant. Theodoricus filio suo Theodeberto cuiusdam regis filiam desponsauit, Wisegardam nomine. Theodericus xxiii regni sui anno moritur, regnum eius Theodebertus assumpsit, magnum se in omnibus et bonitate pręcipuum ostendit.

Post hęc Childebertus et Chlotarius ut diximus Hipanias appetunt, easque parte maxima depopulati sunt. Amalricum regem Barcinona[25] interficiunt, sororemque suam auferunt. Cesaraugusta[26] ciuitas orationibus et ieiuniis liberatur. Theodericus Italie rex sororem Clodouei in matrimonium habuit, ex qua filiam unam cum matre reliquit. Cum mater ei regis filium sociandum prouideret, a seruo nomine Traquila accipitur. Traquila cum exercitu a matre puelle capitur, et capite truncatur, acceptam filiam mater disciplinam ei ingerens secum duxit. Filia matrem ueneno interficit. Theodatus regnum Theoderici adeptus, filiamque in matre parricida extiterat, balneo uehementer succenso iussit includi, ibique comburitur. Vnde causa compositionis quinquaginta milia solidorum Childeberto, Clothario, et Teodeberto transmissa sunt. Quod Childebertus et Teodebertus inter se diuidentes, nichil exinde Clothario dederunt. Theodato defuncto, Totila successit in regnum. Quem Narsis patricius interfecit, regnumque Gothorum in Italia destructum est.

Narses a Romanis per inuidiam acusatus apud Iustinum[27] et coniugem eius Sophiam quod seruitio premeret Italiam. Timens secessit Neapoli campanie, et scripsit genti Langobardorum ut uenirent et possiderent Italiam. Theodebertus rex cum exercitu Italiam ingressus, eam maritimis terminis depopulatus, Narsetem patricium fuga uersum. Postea Bucellinus dux iussu Theodeberti

24 Besançon.
25 Barcelona.
26 Saragossa.
27 The emperor Justinian (527–565). His wife was named Theodora, not Sophia. The generals Narses and Belisarius helped Justinian reestablish imperial rule in Italy.

Siciliam occupauit, totamque Italiam dominatus est, magna felicitas in his omnibus fuit.

Chlotharius de Ingundę Guntharium, Childericum, Aribertum, Guntrannum, Sigibertum, et Chlodesindam filiam habuit, de Arigunde sorore Ingundis Chilpericum, et de Vnxina habuit Chrannum.[28] Bucellinus in Italia apud Belisarium et Narsetem patricios sepius fortiter dimicans, eos in fugam uertit, eorumque exercitum proterit. Tandem infirmatus a profluuio uentris, exercitusque suus ea infirmitate adtritus, Belisario iam interfecto, a Narsete superatur et interficitur. Theodobaldus filius Theodeberti Walderatam duxit uxorem, fuit ualde iniquus suis. Secundo anno regni sui Theodobaldus obiit, regnumque eius Clotharius accepit, copulans Walderatam sibi uxorem.[29]

Eo anno rebellantes Saxones Clotharius commoto exercitu maximam eorum partem deleuit, Toringiam uastans quod eis auxiliari presumpsissent. Nec multo post tempore denuo Saxones rebellantes Clotharius mouet exercitum aduersus eos. Saxones offerentes cuncta emendare que male gesserant, et dimidiam partem ex omnibus rebus suis exceptis uxoribus et liberis, in compositione promittunt dare. Quod Franci accipere despicientes, sed omnes uolentes interficere, inito certamine, tanta strages a Saxonibus de Francis facta est, ut mirum fuisset. Childebertus rex apud Parisius obiit, basilica Sancti Vincentii quam ipse construxerat sepultus est. Cuius thesauros et regnum Clotharius accepit. Chlotharius pro suis peccatis quę gesserat aut negligenter egerat, ad limina Beati Martini confessoris properat, exinde Compendio uilla ueniens, anno li regni sui uexatus a febre obiit.[30]

Chilpericus occupatis thesauris Chlotharii patris sui in uilla Brennaco, sedem Childeberti Parisius occupauit, sed mox exinde repellitur. Aribertus, Guntrannus, Chilpericus, et Sigibertus regnum patris diuidunt. Dedit sors Ariberto regnum Childeberti, Parisius sedem abens, Guntranno uero regnum Chlodomeris, sedem habens Aurelianis, Chilperico regnum Chlotharii, cathedram habens Suessionas, Sigiberto quoque regnum Theoderici, sedem habens

28 Chlothar I, originally king only of the small kingdom of Soissons when Clovis's realm was divided, became the ancestor of all the Merovingian kings who ruled after the middle of the sixth century. By various queens and consorts, especially Ingund and her sister Arigund, he had Kings Charibert I of Paris (561–567), Guntram of Orléans (561–592), Sigibert I of Reims (561–575), and Chilperic of Soissons (561–584), as well as sons Gunthar, Childeric, and Chramn and at least one daughter, Chlodesindis.

29 Waldrada, Chlothar's sixth wife, had originally been the wife of his great-nephew, King Theobold of Reims (548–555).

30 Chlothar had been king for fifty years when he died at Compiègne, on his way to Tours. The divison of his realm among his sons followed the original division of Clovis's realm among Chlothar and his brothers.

Mettis. Eodem tempore Chuni[31] Gallias appetunt, contra quos Sigibertus mouet exercitum, eosque uicit atque fugauit, postea cum eis pacem iniuit.

Guntrannus in Burgundia regnans fuit rex bonus, timens Deum, elemosinam pauperibus largiter tribuens, tanta prosperitate regnum tenuit ut omnes etiam uicine gentes ad plenitudinem laudes de ipso canerent. Accepit primum concubinam nomine Venerandam, de qua habuit filium nomine Gundebaudum. Post accepit Marchitrudem filiam Magnacharii, que postquam de Guntranno habuit filium, ueneno Gundebaudum prioris coniugis filium interfecit. Ipsa iudicio Dei filium quem habebat perdidit, et odium regis per saginam incurrit. Ea dimissa, Austrichildem cognomento Boibilane Guntrannus uxorem accepit, de qua duos filios habuit his nominibus, Chlotharium et Glodomere.[32] Guntrannus instituit Celsum patricium in locum Auricolanis, uirum in uerbis paratum et ad omnia promptissimum.

Gens Langobardorum comitante fame et mortalitate omnem inuasit Italiam, ipsamque Romanam uastatrix obsidet urbem, quibus tempore illo rex erat Albuinus. Hic Clotharii regis filiam nomine Chlodesindam habuit uxorem. Mortuo Albuino, Langobardi regem nomine Clip super se elegerunt. Haribertus rex, frater Guntranni, accepit uxorem nomine Ingobergam, qua relicta Merofledam Ianarii filiam accepit, et aliam pastoris ouium filiam, nomine Theudichildam, duxit uxorem, ex qua habuit filium, sed protinus moritur.

Porro Sigibertus cum uideret fratres suos uiles uxores accipere, Gogonem maiorem domus causa legationis ad Anagildum regem direxit, petens ut ei filiam suam Brunam nomine coniugio traderet.[33] Quam Anagildus cum multis thesauris Sigiberto ad matrimonium transmisit. Ad nomen eius ornandum est auctum ut uocaretur Brunichildis. Quam cum multa lęticia atque iocunditate Sigibertus accepit uxorem. Que ipsum Gogonem continuo apud Sigibertum fecit odiosum, ac post eadem instigante interfecit. Tanta mala et effusiones sanguinum Brunichildis consilio in Francia facte sunt, ut prophetia Sibille impleretur, dicentis, "Veniens Bruna de partibus Hispanię, ante cuius conspectum gentes peribunt."[34] Hęc uero equitum calcibus disrumpetur. Chilpericus Gachilisindam sororem eius habuit uxorem, relinquens Fredegundem et alias quas habuerat uxores. Postea transcendens sacramentum quem Gothorum legatis dederat, ne umquam eam de culmine regni degradaret, ipsam sugillare

31 The Huns.

32 In spite of having at least four sons, Guntram had no grandsons. The same was true, as the chronicler notes below, of Charibert.

33 Brunhild was daughter of Athanagild, king of the Visigoths. Her sister Galswinth married Sigibert's brother Chilperic I, as noted below, but she was mother of none of his children.

34 The source of this supposed Sibylline prophecy remains unidentified.

fecit. Post cuius mortem Fredegundem denuo accepit uxorem. Habebat Chilpericus de priore regina Audouera tres filios, Theodebertum, Meroueum, et Clodoueum. Sigibertus precepit Aruernis ciuibus Arelatam occupare.[35] Iubente Guntranno a Celso patricio Aruerni trucidati sunt. Anathagildo rege Hispanie defuncto, Leuua cum Leuildo fratre regnum adsumunt. Moritur Leuua, Leuildus integrum Hispanię regnum tenet, habens Gadsuindam matrem Brunichilde uxorem.

Eodem tempore defuncto Constantinopoli Iustiniano imperatore, Iustinus ambiuit imperium, uir iniquus et cupidus.[36] Ad quem Sigibertus legatos Warnacharium, Francum, et Firminum comitem direxit, qui pacem cum imperatore facerent, qui secundo anno sunt reuersi. Defuncto Ariberto, Sigibertus regnum eius obtinuit. Prorumpentibus Langobardis in Galliis, Amatus patricius ab ipsis interficitur, de Burgundionibus multe ibidem strages facte sunt. Post Amatum Mummolus patriciatum adsumpsit. Irruentibus iterum Langobardis in Galliis, Mummolus contra eos fortiter dimicauit, et usque ad internetionem oppressit. Pauci ex eisdem Italiam repedantur.

Saxones quos Teodebertus in Italiam miserat in Galliis prorumpunt, apud Stuplonem castra ponentes, multe strages per uicina loca ab ipsis perpetrantur, qui a Mummolo superantur, et in Italia fugaciter reuertuntur, amissis omnibus quę predauerant. Iterum Saxones cum uxoribus et liberis in Galliis properant, ut a Sigiberto rege recepti in locum unde exierant redirent. Venientes in territorio Auennico, Mummolus protinus obuiam ueniens, eis Rodanum transire non permittebat. Postea acceptis muneribus transire eos permisit. Ad Sigibertum pergentes, in loco unde prius egressi fuerant, sunt stabiliti. Postea defuncto Clyp, Langobardorum duces Chamo, Zaban, et Rodanus Gallias inruperunt. Quibus obuiam Mummolus cum exercitu uenit, et hos tres duces cum exercitu eorum usque ad internetionem deleuit. In alio anno Mummolus cum exercitu Turonos et Pictauos, iubente Guntranno, de potestate Chilperici abstulit, et ad partem Sigiberti restituit. Multi ibidem de exercitu Chilperici et ipsi Pictauenses sunt gladio trucidati. Taloardus et Vncio duces Langobardorum per Hoscola in Sedunensi territorio cum exercitu sunt ingressi, ad monasterium sanctorum Agaunensium usque accesserunt. Nimia strage Baccis uilla,[37] non procul ab ipso monasterio, duces eorum exercitus a Violico et Theoderico ducibus Guntranni sunt interfecti, xl tantum ex illis fugaciter Italiam remearunt.

Postea Chilpericus et Sigibertus ineuntes consilium, ambo mouerunt exercitum, uolentes Guntrannum interficere regnumque eius adsumere. Sed

35 The Auvergne and Arles.

36 After the death of Emperor Justinian in 565, the empire was headed by his nephew Justin II.

37 Bex is in the Alps, in modern-day Switzerland, on the eastern banks of the Rhône.

uoluntate Dei mutato consilio, Sigibertus super Chilpericum inruit, iam eius exercitus ad propria festinans longe aberat. Cum hęc cognouisset Chilpericus, terga uertens Tornacum[38] peruenit. Sigibertus post tergum eius uenit Parisius, ibique Sanctum ac Beatissimum Germanum Parisiorum urbis[39] episcopum Sigibertus cum uidisset, hęc ab eodem uerba prophetię audiuit, "Si germanum tuum ita persequi cogitas, ut eum interficere disponas, et regnum eius auferre, scriptum est, Foueam quam fratri tuo paras, in eam cades" [cf. Ps. 7:15]. Cuius castigationem nolens audire cogitabat cepta perficere. Cumque Victuriaco[40] accessisset, omnes Neptrasii[41] se sue ditioni subiecerunt. Ansoaldus tantum cum Chilperico remansit. Fredegundis duobus pueris dolo transmissis Sigibertum interficiunt, et ipsi interfecti sunt. Resumptis uiribus Chilpericus suum regnum recepit. Brunichildis cum filio suo Childeberto Parisius sub custodia tenebatur. Sed factione Gundoaldi ducis, Childebertus in pera positus, per fenestram demissus, a puero Mettis solus exibitus est, ibique a Gundoaldo uel Austrasiis in regno patris sublimi. Brunichildis iussu Chilperici exilium Rotomago[42] truditur. Sigibertus in ęcclesia Sancti Medardi sepultus est, etate quadragenaria, anno regni sui xiiii.[43]

Eo tempore Sanctus Germanus Parisiorum episcopus transiit. Mummolus patricius Guntranni contra Clodoueum et Desiderium ducem Chilperici bellum gessit, eosque superauit. Chilpericus enim filium suum Clodoueum transmiserat, qui et ultra Ligerim ciuitates Childeberti peruaderet. Cesa sunt a Mummolo exercitus l milia, a Desiderio uero xx milia. Chilpericus tres filios suos iam adultos ab infirmitate dissenterii uno anno perdidit, quos de Fredegunde habebat. Restiterat adhuc Chlodoueus filius eius, quem postea instigante Fredegunde uinctum custodia retrusit, ibique factione Fredegunde cultro percussus obiit. Chilpericus denuo ut filius sibi nasceretur, iubet omnes carceratos relaxare.

Guntrannus rex duos Magnacharii filios gladio interemit, instigante Austrichilde regina, facultates eorum fisco redigit. Filii Guntranni duo continuo moriuntur. Guntrannus Childebertum adoptauit in filium. Anno quoque tercio Childeberti regis, qui erat Chilperici et Guntranni xvi, eo anno stella in medio lune fulgens uisa est. Childebertus rex Ingundem sororem suam Erminigildo Leouigildi regis Wisigothorum tradidit filio, qui hortatione Leandri Hispalensis

38 Tournai.

39 St Germanus, bishop of Paris, to whom St-Germain-des-Prés is dedicated.

40 There are many places in France called Vitry; this is probably the one near Arras.

41 This is probably intended as a reference to Neustria.

42 Rouen.

43 Sigibert died in 575, after fourteen years as king, and was buried at St-Medard of Soissons.

episcopi et sue coniugis ad fidem Catholicam conuersus est. Anno v Childeberti regis tantę lues per uniuersas regiones facte sunt, ut omnibus mirum fuisset, et uniuersa flumina terminos quos nunquam excesserant preterierunt. Childebertus rex Italiam intrauit et Langobardi eius se ditioni commendant. Gloriose exinde Childebertus reuertitur. Acceperat prius a Mauricio imperatore[44] l milia solidorum auri, ut Langobardos de Italia expugnaret. Sed non solum eis non nocuit, uerum amiticias cum ipsis iniuit.

Guntrannus[45] rex Francorum cum iam anno xxiii regnum Burgundię feliciter regeret, uedens sibi liberos non superesse, cepit thesauros suos in elemosinis pauperum distribuere, monasteria et loca sancta ex ipsis thesauris ditare.[46]

Igitur legati Chilperici Ansoaldus et Domegilesus qui ad conspiciendam dotem in Spania missi fuerant sunt reuersi. His diebus Leobildus rex contra Erminigildum filium suum in exercitu residebat, quem paruo transacto tempore interfecit. Eius uero uxor uolens reuerti Franciam, una cum filio capta atque Siciliam perducta est, ibi usque ad mortem exulauit. Chilpericus et Fredegundis filiam suam cum magnis thesauris et multa familia in eius obsequium Hispaniam direxunt. Quam filius Leopildi uxorem accepit. Nec post mora extante Chilpericus ueniens ad uillam Calensem,[47] quę distat ab urbe Parisius quasi centum stadiis, illic uenationem exercebat. Quadam uero die regressus de uenatione iam sub obscura nocte, dum de equo suscipieretur, et unam manum super scapulam pueri teneret, adueniens quidam nomine Falco, qui missus a Brunichilde fuerat, cum cultro sub ascellam percussit, iteratoque ictu uentrem eius perforat. Statimque fluente copia sanguinis tam per os quam per aditum uulneris, spiritum fudit.

Cumque Guntranno perlatum fuisset hoc quod frater suus Chilpericus esset interfectus, perrexit Parisius, ibique Fredegundem cum filio Chilperici Clothario ad se uenire precepit. Quem Riolo uilla[48] baptizare iubet, et eum de sancto lauacro excipiens in regnum patris firmauit. Anno xxv regni sui exercitus Guntranni Hispaniam ingręditur, sed loci infirmitate grauatus protinus ad propria reuertitur. Anno xxvi eiusdem regni Leudiscus a Guntranno patricius partibus Prouincię ordinatur. Childeberti regis filius Teodebertus natus fuisse nunciatur. Eo anno nimia inundatio fluminum in Burgundia fuit, ita ut solitum

44 The emperor Maurice (582–602).

45 This is the beginning of Book 4 of Fredegar.

46 At this point (fol. 8r) the chronicler of Bèze skipped a long section from the Chronicle of St-Bénigne (pp. 29–33 in the printed edition) in which the earlier chronicler had detailed Guntram's gifts to that monastery.

47 Chelles, located east of Paris.

48 Rueil, just west of Paris.

terminum nimium transcenderent. Ipsoque anno Leupildus rex Hispanię moritur, et obtinuit regnum Richaredus filius eius. Anno xxvii regni domni Guntranni alius filius Childeberti, nomine Teodericus, natus nunciatur.

Langobardorum gens quemadmodum tributa xii milia solidorum dicioni Francorum annis singulis desoluebant, referam, uel quo ordine duas ciuitates Agusta et Siusiu cum territorio ad partem Francorum cassauerant, dicam. Defuncto Clyp principe, duces Langobardorum xii annos sine regibus transegerunt, ipsoque tempore sicut suprascriptum legitur per loca in regnum Francorum proruperunt. Pro hac presumptione in compositione Agustam et Siusium ciuitates, cum integro illorum territorio et populo partibus Guntranni tradiderunt. Post hęc legationem ad Mauricium imperatorem dirigunt. Hi xii duces singuli legatos dirigunt, pacem et patrocinium imperii petentes. Idemque et alios legatores xii ad Guntrannum et Childebertum destinant, ut patrocinium Francorum et defensionem habentes, xii milia solidos annis singulis his duobus regibus in tributa implerent, uallem cui nomen Ametegis partibus Guntranni cassantes. His legatis ubi plus congruebat patrocinium sibi firmarent. Post hęc integra deuocione patrocinium eligunt Francorum. Nec mora post permissu Guntranni et Childeberti et Clotharii ducem super se Langobardi sublimunt in regnum. Alius Autharius itemque dux cum integro suo ducatu se dicioni imperii tradidit, ibique permansit. Autharius uero rex tributa, que ad partem Francorum spoponderat, annis singulis reddidit. Post eius discessum filius eius Ago in regnum sublimatus, similiter implesse dinoscitur.

Anno xxxii regni Guntranni, ita a mane usque ad mediam diem sol minoratus est, ut tertia pars ex ipso uix appareret. Anno xxxiii regni Guntranni, v kalendas Aprilis, ipse rex moritur, sepultus est in ęcclesia Sancti Marcelli, in monasterio quod ipse construxerat.[49] Regnum eius Childebertus adsumpsit, quod tenuit annis quattuor. Anno iii Childeberti regnantis in Burgundia, multa signa in celo ostensa sunt, et stella cometes apparuit. Anno iiii, postquam Childebertus regnum Guntranni acceperat defunctus est regnumque eius filii sui Teodebertus et Teodricus adsumunt. Theodebertus sortitus est Austru, sedem habens Mettis. Tęodericus accepit regnum Guntranni in Burgundia, sedem habens Aurelianis.[50]

---

49 The basilica of St-Marcel of Chalon does indeed seem to have acquired monks under King Guntram, even though the foundation charter attributed to him in the monastery's cartulary is a forgery. *The Cartulary of Saint-Marcel-lès-Chalon*, ed. Bouchard, pp. 31–32, no. 7. Guntram died in 592.

50 Childebert II had been adopted by his uncle Guntram, as noted above. He ruled in Burgundy for only four years (592–596), before being succeeded by his sons, King Theodebert II in Austrasia (596–612), with his capital at Metz, and King Theoderic II in Burgundy (596–613), with his capital at Orléans.

Anno iiii regni Theoderici clades glandolaria Massiliam et reliquas Prouintię ciuitates grauiter uastauit.[51] Eo anno aqua calidissima in lacu Dunense, in quem Arola fluuius influit,[52] sic ualide ebulliuit, ut multitudinem piscium coxisset. Anno v Theuderici regni, iterum signa que anno superiore uisa fuerant, globi ignei per celum currentes, et ad instar multitudinem astarum ignearum ad occasum apparuerunt. Ipsoque anno Theodebertus et Theodericus reges contra Clotarium mouent exercitum, et super fluuium Aroanna, nec procul a Doromello uico prelium confligentes, iunxerunt. Ibique exercitus Clotharii regis grauissime trucidatus est, ipsumque cum ipsis qui remanserant in fugam uersum pagos et ciuitates in ripa Sequane, qui se Clothario tradiderunt, depopulantur et uastant. Plurimi captiui ab exercitu Theodeberti et Theoderici abducuntur. Clotharius oppressus, uellet nollet, per pactionis uinculum firmauit, ut inter Sequanam et Ligerim usque mare Oceanum et Brittanorum limitem Theodericus haberet,[53] et per Sequanam et Isaram ducatum Denteleni integrum usque Oceanum mare Theodebertus recepit,[54] xii tantum pagi inter Isaram et Sequanam et mare Oceanum Chlotario remanserunt.

Anno vi regni Theoderici natus est ei filius de concubina nomine Sigibertus. Eo anno Teudebertus et Teodericus exercitum contra Wascones direxerunt, ipsoque Deo auxiliante deuictos in sua dominatione redigunt et tributarios faciunt. Eodem anno corpus Sancti Victoris, qui Salodoro cum Sancto Vrso passus fuerat, a beato Econio pontifice Mauriennense inuenitur.[55] Viderat namque in uisu ut surgens protinus iret ad ecclesiam quam Sedeleuba regina in suburbano Genauense[56] construxerat, et in medio ęcclesię designatum locum ubi sanctum corpus iacebat. Cumque Genaua perexisset cum beatis Rustico et Patricio episcopis, triduanum ieiunium faciens, lumen per noctem splendidum ubi gloriosum illud corpus erat, apparuit. Quod cum silentio hii tres pontifices cum lacrimis et orationibus, eleuato lapide in archa argentea inuenerunt sepultum. Cuius faciem rubentem quasi uiueret, reperiunt. Ibi Theodericus rex presens aderat, qui multis muneribus ecclesiam ipsam ditauit, et maximam partem ex facultatibus Warnacharii ibidem contulit. Eo anno Eucherius episcopus Lugdunensis[57] obiit, ordinatur loco ipsius Secundinum episcopus. Eodem anno

51 The disease that ravaged Marseille and other cities of Provence was the plague of the late sixth century.

52 The lake Thun, in modern-day Switzerland, empties into the Aare river.

53 Theoderic's territory between the Seine and the Loire reached to Brittany and the Atlantic.

54 The Oise joins the Seine west of Paris. The region west of the Oise, reaching to the Atlantic, includes the territory later called Normandy.

55 Maurienne, in the French Alps (Savoy).

56 Geneva.

57 The chronology seems confused here. St Eucherius, bishop of Lyon, died c. 450.

Focas dux et patricium reipublice uictor a Persis rediens, Mauricium imperatorem interfecit, et in loco ipsius imperium assumpsit.[58]

Anno vii regni Theoderici de concubina nascitur ei filius nomine Childebertus. Eo anno sol obscuratus est. Anno quoque viii regni Theoderici nascitur ei filius de concubina nomine Corbus. Eodem tempore Bertoaldus genere Francus maior domus palacii erat Teoderici, moribus mensuratus, sapiens et cautus, in prelio fortis, fidem omnibus conseruans. Defuncto Wandalmaro duce in pago Vltra Iurano et Scutengorum,[59] Protadius ordinatur patricius, instigatione Brunichilde, et ut Bertoaldus interiret, eum ripa Sequane usque Oceanum mare per pagos et ciuitates fiscum inquirendum dirigunt.

Bertoaldus a Theoderico missus cum trecentis tantum uiris, illis partibus properauit. Hęc comperiens Clotarius filium suum Meroueum et Landericum maiorem domus cum exercitu ad opprimendum Bertoaldum direxit, et maximam partem inter Sequanam et Ligerim pagos et ciuitates de regno Theoderici presumpsit contra pactum preuadere. Cum Theodericus comperisset quod a Clotario pars regni sui contra ius fuerat prerepta, protinus cum exercitu Stampas[60] super fluuium Loaperuenit. Ibique obuiam Meroueus filius Clotharii regis cum Landerico et magno exercitu uenit. Cum esset arduus transitus ille ubi Loa fluuius transmeatur, uix tercia pars exercitus Theoderici transierat, initum est bellum. Ibi Meroueus filius Clotharii capitur, Landericus in fugam uersus est, nimia multitudo exercitus Clotarii in eo prelio trucidata est. Theodericus rex uictor Parisius ingreditur. Postea pacem Theodericus cum Clotario Conpendio uilla[61] iniuit, utriusque exercitus redit ad propria.

Anno x regni Theoderici cum Brunichildis auia eius et Protadius maior domus assidue instigarent eum ut contra Teodebertum fratrem suum moueret exercitum, tandem iussu Theoderici exercitus coadunatus loco nomine Caraciaco castra metasset, orabatur a leudibus suis ut cum Teudeberto pacem inirent. Protadius singulos ortabatur ut prelium committerent. Teodebertus non procul exinde cum exercitu residebat. Tunc omnis exercitus Theoderici inuenta occasione supra Protadium irruunt, dicentes melius esse unum hominem mori, quam totum exercitum in periculum mitti. Interfecto Protadio Teodericus confusus et coactus cum Theodeberto pacem iniuit, et illesus uterque exercitus ad propria recessit. Anno xii regni sui Teodericus Aridium episcopum Lugdunensem,[62] Rocconem et Eborinum comitem stabuli, ad Betericum regem Hispanię

58 In 602 the general Phocas overthrew the emperor Maurice and replaced him on the throne.

59 The Jura region.

60 Étampes, southwest of Paris.

61 Compiègne.

62 Bishop Aridius of Lyon (603–615).

direxit, ut filiam eius Hermenbergam matrimonio sibi iungendam adducerent. Qui datis sacramentis ne unquam a regno degradaretur, accipientes eam Theoderico Cabillonno presentant. Quam ille gaudens suscepit, factione uero auię suę Brunichilde non eam cognouit, et in tantum odiosa facta est, ut post annum expoliatam thesauris Hispaniam retransmitteret. Eo anno Theodericus persuasione auię suę Brunichildis, et consilio Aridii Lugdunensis episcopi utens, Sanctum Desiderium episcopum Viennensem[63] de exilio regressum lapidare precepit. Ad cuius sepulchrum mire uirtutes actenus fiunt.[64]

Anno xii regni Theoderici natus est ei filius de concubina nomine Meroueus, quem Clotharius de sancto lauacro suscepit. Eo tempore fuit Ysidorus doctor Spalensis episcopus.[65] Eodem anno mortuo Beterico, Sisebodus successit in regnum Hispanię, uir sapiens et tota Hispania laudabilis, ualde pietate plenus. Nam et aduersus rempublicam fortiter dimicauit, et prouinciam Cantabriam Gothorum dicioni subegit. Dux Francio nomine, qui Cantabriam in tempore Francorum rex erat, tributa Francorum regibus multo tempore impleuerat. Sed cum a parte imperii fuerat Cantabria reuocata, a Gothis preoccupatur, et plures ciuitates ab imperio Romano Sisebodus littore maris abstulit, et usque ad fundamenta destruxit.

Anno xiii regni Theoderici habebat Teudebertus rex uxorem Belichildem nomine, quam Brunichildis a negociatoribus mereauerat, et cum esset Belchildis utilis et a cunctis Austrasiis uehementer diligeretur, simplicitatem Teudeberti honeste comportans, nichiloque seminorem a Brunichilde esse cerneret, et sepius Brunichildem per legatos despiceret, dum ab ipsa improperaretur quod ancilla eius fuisset. Tandem cum his et aliis uerbis legatis discurrentibus, ab inuicem uexarentur, placitum inter Colerence et Suentense consistitur, ut has duas reginas pro pace inter Theoderium et Teodebertum coniungerent ad loquendum. Sed Belichildis consilio Austrasiorum inibi uenire distulit.

Eo tempore Beatus Columbanus,[66] cuius fama sanctitatis creuerat iam passim per uniuersas Gallię et Germanię prouincias, erat omnium rumore laudabilis, in omni cultu religionis uenerabilis, in tantum ut Theodericus rex ad eum sepe Luxouium[67] ueniret, et orationum suarum suffragia omni cum humilitate

63 Desiderius, bishop of Vienne (d. 607). He is considered a martyred saint.

64 At this point the chronicler of St-Bénigne added a long section on the bishops of Langres and the abbots of his monastery (pp. 39–43 in the printed edition), skipped by the chronicler of Bèze.

65 Isidore of Seville.

66 Columbanus (d. 615), the Irish monastic leader who heavily influenced Frankish monasticism. For his influence, see, most recently, Fox, *Power and Religion in Merovingian Gaul*.

67 The monastery of Luxeuil.

posceret. Cumque sepissime ad eum ueniret, cepit uir Dei cum increpare, cur concubinarum adulteriis misceretur, et non potius legitime coniugis solamine frueretur, ut regalis proles ex honorabili regina procederet, et non potius ex lupanaribus uideretur emergi. Et cum iam ad uiri Dei imperium rex obtemperaret, et se omnibus inlicitis segregare responderet, mentem Brunichildis auię, secundę ut erat Iezabelis, antiquus anguis adiit, eamque contra uirum Dei stimulis superbię incitat, quia cernere uiro Dei Theodericum obedire. Verebatur enim ne si abiectis concubinis reginam aule preficeret, dignitatis atque honoris sui modum amputasset.

Euenit ergo ut quadam die Beatus Columbanus ad Brunichildem ueniret. Erat enim tunc apud Brucariacum uillam. Cumque illa eum in aula uenire cerneret, filios Theoderici quos de adulterinis permixtionibus habebat, ad uirum Dei adducit. Quos cum uidisset, sciscitatur quid sibi uellent. Brunichildis ait, "Regis filii sunt, tu eos benedictionibus robora." At ille ait, "Nequaquam, inquid, istos regalia sceptra suscepturos scias, quia de lupanaribus emerserunt." Illa furens paruulos abire iubet. Egrediens uir Dei regiam aulam, dum limitem transiret, fragor subito exortus est, qui totam quatiens domum omnibus terrorem incussit, nec tamen miserę feminę furorem compescuit. Paratque deinde insidias molire, ortatur proceres, aulicos, obtimatesque omnes, ut regis animum contra uirum Dei perturbent. Episcopos quoque sollicitare adgressa est, ut de eius religione detrahendo, statum regulę quam suis custodiendam monachis indiderat macularent. Obtemperantes igitur, auligeri persuasionibus miserę reginę, regis animum perturbant, cogentes ut accederet ad locum ac religionem probaret.

Abactus itaque rex ad uirum Dei Luxouio uenit, conquestusque cum uiro Dei, cur ab conprouincialium moribus disscisseret, et intra septa secretiora omnibus Christianis aditus non pateret. Beatus uero Columbanus his ei aliis uerbis auditis, ut erat audax animo, obicienti regi respondit, "Si ob hanc causam tu in hunc locum uenisti, ut seruorum Dei cœnobia destruas, et regularem disciplinam macules, scito tuum regnum funditus ruiturum, et cum omni propagine regia dimersurum." Quod postea rei probauit euentus. Iam temerario conatu, rex refectorium ingressus fuerat. His ergo territus dictis, foris celer rapedat. Duris post hęc uiri Dei increpationibus rex urguebatur. Contraque Theodericus ait, "Martirii coronam me tibi illaturam speras." Deinde dixit non esse tantę dementię se, ut hoc tantum facinus patraret, sed pocioris consilii se agere utilia paraturum, ut qui ab omnium more disciscat, quo uenerat ea uia repedare studeat. At quia longum est uniuersa gesta percurrere, quas insidias regine, quę exilia et tribulationes pertulit recitare, succinte finem rei explicemus. Vir Dei deputatis custodibus a Theoderico, qui quousque dicionis sue regno pelleretur, non eum relinquerent, Namnetis[68] usque perrexit. Moratus ergo ibi paululum, sciens non placerę diuinę maiestati ut patriam rediret, post ad Clotarium Chilperici regis filium, qui Neustrasiis Francisque regnabat extrema Gallia ad Oceanum positis pergit.

Chlotarius porro audierat quantis qualibusue iniuriis uirum Dei Brunichildis ac Theodericus fatigauerant. Quem cum uidisset, uelut celestę munus suscepit. Tenuit ergo eum Chlotarius quantis potuit penes se diebus. Erat enim Clotarius pollens in amore sapientię. Beato uero Columbano morante apud Clotarium, lis oritur inter duos fratres Teodebertum et Theodericum, disceptantibus utrisque de regni terminis. Anno igitur xv regni sui uterque ad Clotarium legatos dirigit, uterque aduersus parem auxilium postulat. Quod Clotharius beato uiro insinuare procurat, consulens ut si uideretur eius consilii se uni consentiendo, contra alium dimicaret. Ad quem ille repletus spiritu prophetico ait, "Neutri te fore pariturum scias conuenire consiliis, tuaque intra trienni tempus in ditione utrorumque regna uenire." Videns Clotarius a uiro Dei talia sibi prophetico ore dici, neutri parere uoluit, sed promissum sibi tempus fideliter expectans, potitus est triumphum uictorię.

Anno xvi regni sui Teodericus mouet exercitum, et Lingonis de uniuersis regni sui prouintiis mense Maio exercitus adunatur. Dirigensque per Andalaum, Nasio castrum super Ornam fluuium situm cepit, et inde Tullum ciuitatem perrexit.[69] Ibi Theodebertus cum Austrasiorum exercitu obuiam uenit, Tullensi campania confligunt, Theodericus superat Theodebertum, eiusque prostrauit exercitum. Cesa est eodem prelio nimia mulitudo uirorum fortium. Theodebertus terga uertens per territorium Mettense, transita Vosago Coloniam fugaciter peruenit. Theoderius cum exercitu post tergum insequens, Aruenna transiens peruenit Tulbiaco. Theodebertus, Saxones, Toringos, uel ceteras gentes trans Renum uel undecumque poterat adunare contra Theodericum, Tulbiaco perrexit. Ibique denuo commissum est bellum a Francis ceterisque gentibus, tantaque ibi strages ab utroque exercitu facta est, ubi Falanges in congressu certaminis preliabantur, ut cadauera occisorum undique non haberent qua ruere possent, sed stabant mortui, ac si uiuerent stricti inter ceteros. Auxiliante Deo iterum Theodericus Theodebertum superat, et a Tulbiaco usque Coloniam exercitus eius gladio trucidatus, oram terrę cooperuit.

Eo igitur in tempore uir Dei Columbanus in heremo morabatur, contentus tantum unius ministri solatio. Ea ergo hora, qua apud Tulbiacum commissum est bellum, supra querci putrefacti truncum sedebat, legens librum, quem

68 Nantes.

69 Andelot, Nançois-sur-Ornain, and Toul, in what is now Lorraine.

subitus sopor oppressit, et quid inter duos reges ageretur uidit. Mox excitatus ministrum uocat, cruentamque regum pugnam indicat, multum humanum sanguinem fundi suspirat. Persequutus est ergo Theodebertum Theodericus, et suorum proditione captum ad auiam Brunichildem Cabillonno direxit. Quem illa cum recepisset, quia Theoderici partibus magis fauebat, furens Theodebertum fieri clericum rogauit, ac non multo post impie nimis perimi iussit.

Anno xvii regni sui Theodericus exercitum de Austrasiis et Burgundia moueri precepit, uolens super Clotarium inruere. Iamque exercitus adgrediebatur, et Theodericus Mettis ciuitate pro fluuio uentris inter flagrantis urbis incendia mortuus est. Exercitus protinus redit ad proprias sedes. Brunichildis filium eius Sigibertum in regno patris suffecit. Clotarius collecto exercitu, fines regni quę sue ditioni debebantur conatur recipere. Contra quem Sigibertus cum hostium cuneis pugnaturus aduenit, quem Chlotarius captum fraude suorum peremit, fratresque eius quinque Theoderici filios cum Brunichilde proauia eorum cepit, pueros separatim peremit, Brunichildis pestifere uidens cumulum malorum[70] eius cœlum usque pertingere, uindictam publicam decommuni hoste facere statuit, ueniensque ad eam quasi facturus coniugium, cum se illa prepararet ad conubiale conuiuium, coacta est bibere quod regnis et populis propinauerat poculum. Nam camelo superpositam girari fecit per exercitum, quam cum omnes in clamando horruissent, uelut sub carnis uelamine Zabulum. Iterum iussit reduci et inter equos quattuor indomitos ligari. Ad quorum prima erumpentium fugam, partibus rupta, postea igne combusta, cum satellitio peccatorum ab ipsis inferioribus est inmersa. Funditus ergo radicitusque deleta Theoderici stirpe, Clotarius potitus est trium regnorum monarchia solus. Anno xxx regni sui Clotharius Burgundie et Austrasiorum regnum adeptus est.[71]

De constructione huius loci

Igitur quoniam monasterium istud Besuense Clotharii regis tempore ab Amalgario duce fundatum fuisse prelibauimus, paulo latius nobis uisum est prosequendum, qualiter ab eo et ubi fuerit constructum, et quibus rebus ab eo primum ditatum ac deinceps a ceteris Deum timenentibus, imo diligentibus largissimis facultatibus amplificatum. Fuerunt[72] siquidem illis temporibus duo duces in

70 Here the chronicler of Bèze's wording is different from that of the chronicler of St-Bénigne, which is itself different from that of Fredegar.

71 At this point the chronicler stops following Fredegar and begins the history of Bèze proper on fol. 14r. For a discussion of this section, see the introduction.

72 This section of the chronicle, down through "Quid plura? Waldalenum abbatem ibi prefecit," is printed in GC 4, instr. col. 128, no. 3; dated 600.

Burgundia, quorum unus Waldalenus nomine, gentes quę intra Alpium septa et Iurani saltus arua incolunt regebat. Erat huic uxor nomine Flauia de qua cum nullius heredis habuisset gaudia, cui suarum opum et honorum post se reliquisset amplissima subsidia, per Beati Columbani, qui Luxouio[73] preerat, Deo digna precamina filium susceperunt, et ei illum de sacro fonte leuandum sicut ipse quesierat obtulerunt. Itaque eum sanctus uir baptizauit, Donatumque nomen imposuit, qui postea in eodem monasterio sapientia imbutus, Bisontine sedis archiepiscopatum clarissime gubernauit. Alter uero dux harum duarum partium circumquaque latissimus dominator, Amalgarius nomine, habens uxorem nomine Aquilinam, habuit ex ea filios, quorum uni Audalrico nomine ducatus sui regimina post se dereliquit. Habuit et alium Waldalenum nomine, quem offerre Deo a quo eum acceperat cupiens per manus Beati Columbani eum ipsi in predicto Luxouiensi monasterio, quod tunc precipue preceteris Galliarum atque Burgundie monasteriis religione florebat, educandum contradidit. Habuit iterum filiam Adalsindam nomine, quam etiam Deo offerendam ac diuino cultui mancipandam adiudicauit.

Dum itaque hii duo in scola Christi erudiuntur, uidelicet Waldalenus et Adalsinda, pater Amalgarius excogitat ubi religioni eorum edificet loca conuenientia, et si qui postea cum eis Deo militare uoluerint unde habeant uictus ac uestitus sufficientia. Cum igitur in ducatu suo duo Christi construere uellet ouilia, et ouibus, quas ibi Deus aggregaret utriusque sexus, ex illis quos sibi dederat Deus pueris pastores preficere, uidelicet Waldalenum uiris et Adalsindam feminis, inter cetera ducatus sui loca, duo inuenit speciosissima, atque ad id non parum conuenientia. Est locus inter fluuium qui dicitur Araris et Sagunna et fluuium quem Tylam uocant,[74] ab emergente ibidem fonte non modico qui Besuus dicitur,[75] dictus et ipse Besua. Fons est ipse limpidissimus, ad potandum habilis, ac multimoda piscium copia fertillissimus, nec sicut alii fontes qui plurimi decurrendo et augmentando nomen accipit fluuii, sed ibidem ubi oritur pre magnitudine flumen dicitur.[76] Nascuntur in eo diuersi generis herbę, quę si frugum alimonia minus habundauerit pauperibus subsidium prebeant uitę. Sicque fons iste tocius sui irrigans confinia, ad omnia quęcumque ibi seruntur uel coluntur confouenda, loca reddit habilia. Terra satis optima, et nisi desit qui laboret frugum feracissima. Prata prope sunt habunde, quibus possunt nutriri peccora, et suppleri alia queque priuata necessaria. Siluas habet

73 St Columbanus (d. 615) and his monastery of Luxeuil.

74 The monastery is located between the Saône and the Tille rivers.

75 The Bèze river, at whose source the monastery that took its name was established, is a tributary of the Saône.

76 John is correct; the Bèze is a river from the moment it bubbles from the ground.

in procinctu locus et contiguas, quę ad construenda edificia, seu ad omnia quę generi humano necessaria sunt sufficiant.

Talem igitur locum Amalgarius dux Deo et sanctis eius apostolis Petro et Paulo dignum duxit offerre et sub manu filii sui Waldaleni monachos qui ibi Deo et sanctis eius deseruirent sub regula Beati Columbani studuit aggregare. Quid plura? Waldalenum abbatem ibi prefecit, locum ut prediximus Deo et Sancto Petro et Paulo liberrime cum omnibus appenditiis suis obtulit, cum terris et edificiis, cum siluis et accessibus omnibus, cum mancipiis et colonis et seruientibus. Denique quidquid ibi habere uidebatur, totum liberrime et integerrime, nec sibi nec cuiquam aliquid ex illis retinens.

Et quoniam locum omni adnisu uoluit extollere et amplificare, uisum est ei ex aliis rebus et appenditiis eum ditare. Dedit itaque Vetusuineas cum appenditiis suis et siluis, Tilerias, Beriam,[77] Tregias, Cypetum, Buxatellum, et Vendoueram.[78] Item Auxiliacum cum adiacentiis suis et siluis et colonicis, Blaniacum,[79] Berlariam, Baymam, et Viriacum,[80] et Attiuiacum, et Nouiliacum et uillam Calatunnam et Curtem Mulinensem.[81] Marcenniacum[82] com [*sic*] uineis xii, et uinitoribus, et colonicis qui excolere uidentur. Apud Cocheiacum[83] uineas non minime quantitatis. Dedit etiam in pago Belnensi[84] uineas octo cum uinitoribus et colonicis. In uilla quę Vaona dicitur,[85] uineas et terras cum seruis et ancillis excolentibus eas. Tradidit etiam com [*sic*] ceteris rebus Sancto Petro terras quas habebat in Diuione et in fine Domni Petri et Longouico et in Canauis, et in Arzilirias, et Tremoldo, et Prouiso, et Disto.[86] Dedit et in Gibriaco[87] uinearum non modicam quantitatem, cum uinitoribus et colonicis et siluis

77 Viévigne, 4 km southwest of Bèze; Tilchâtel, 9 km northwest of Bèze; and Beire, 8 km southwest of Bèze. This list of property is the same as that given in document 3.

78 Treige is now the name of a farm 7 km southwest of Bèze, and Spoy is 6 km southwest of Bèze. According to Roserot, *Dictionnaire topographique du département de la Côte-d'Or*, Buteau is a now-ruined village near Viévigne. Véronnes is 7 km north-northwest of Bèze.

79 Oisilly, 9 km southeast of Bèze; and Blagny, 8 km east-southeast of Bèze.

80 Joseph Garnier suggests that Berlaria may be Berthaut, which was a hamlet in the commune of Fontaine-Française. The next two places are unidentified.

81 Athée, 27 km east-southeast of Bèze; Neuilly, 7 km southeast of Dijon; unidentified; and Crimolois, 9 km southeast of Dijon.

82 Marsannay, 7 km southwest of Dijon.

83 Couchey, 8 km south-southwest of Dijon.

84 The pagus of Beaune, south of Dijon.

85 Vosne, 19 km south-southwest of Dijon.

86 Dijon; Dampierre, 7 km east-northeast of Bèze; Longvic, 4 km southeast of Dijon; Chenôve, 5 km southwest of Dijon; Aisery, 20 km southeast of Dijon; Trimolois, a former hamlet between Chenôve and Dijon; Prenois, just outside Dijon; and Daix, 5 km northwest of Dijon.

87 Gevrey, 12 km southwest of Dijon.

et pratis et omnibus adiacentiis, cum seruis et ancillis, omnia omnino liberrime, et prorsus ab omni consuetudinali reclamatione aliena. Item in uilla et in Chaciaco[88] quidquid habebat. In uilla quę Patriniacus dicitur[89] mansum unum optimum cum appenditiis suis. Cumque his omnibus dedit uillam Maiescum[90] et adiacentia sua predicto monasterio, et datis his, factaque epistola propria manu consignata, in perpetuum possidenda contradidit.

His ita digestis, descriptaque Besuensis monasterii constructione, quoniam de alio loco superius fecimus mentionem, quem in ducatu suo Amalgarius edificauit, ubi et filiam suam Adalsindam sanctimonialibus abbatissam prefecit, dicendum equum putamus ubi sit locus et quis uocatus quibus appenditiis ditatus, ut ibi Deo seruientibus uictus non defuerit atque uestitus. Est locus haut longe a Vesontiensi ciuitate super fluuium Dubium apellatum,[91] ipsius fluuii intercursu tantum a ciuitate se iunctus, ex alia uero parte habens montem uocatum Wandalenum a nomine Wandalorum qui ibi castrum habuerunt ut antiqui incole dicunt. Dornatiacus dicitur, qui et Virzillias,[92] in honorem Sancti Martini consecratam habens ecclesiam, quem Amalgarius dux filię suę Adasinde donauit, et ut sub eius regimine regulariter ibi uiuerent, congegationem sanctimonialium constituens, de propriis rebus donationem fecit. Villam scilicet quę Assona uocatur, uillam Parnatiacum, uillam Potentiacum, et medietatem quam in Balatunna[93] possidere uidebatur. De uilla uero Montaniaco[94] similiter. Sed cum his omnibus qualiter praefatus locus Dornatiacus ęcclesię Besuensi donatus atque coniunctus postea fuerit, in sequentibus et ubi congruum uidebitur inseremus.

Anno[95] xxxiiii regni Clotharii Warnarium, quem maiorem domus in Burgundia instituerat cum uniuersis pontificibus Burgundię seu et Burgondefaronis, Bonogello uilla ad se uenire precepit. Ibique cunctis illorum iustis peticionibus annuens, preceptionibus roborauit.

Anno xxxviii regni Clotharii Dagobertum filium suum consortem regni facit,[96] eumque Austrasiis regem instituit, retineus sibi quod Ardenna et Vosagus[97] uersus Neustriam et Burgundiam excludebat.

---

88 Cessey-sur-Tille, 21 km south-southwest of Bèze.

89 Perrigny, 7 km south-southwest of Dijon.

90 Maâtz, 30 km north-northeast of Bèze.

91 Besançon is on the river Doubs, 62 km east-southeast of Bèze.

92 The church is St-Martin of Brégille, 2 km east of Besançon, across the river.

93 Auxonne is 32 km south-southeast of Bèze; the subsequent places are unidentified.

94 Probably Montagney, 36 km southeast of Bèze.

95 At this point, at the bottom of fol. 16r, the chronicle begins again to copy the text of the chronicle of St-Bénigne from where he left off, beginning from p. 48 of the printed edition. The chronicler of St-Bénigne was in turn continuing to follow Fredegar.

96 Chlothar II associated his son Dagobert I with him in Austrasia in 623.

97 The Ardennes forest and the Vosges mountains.

Anno xlii regni Clotharii Dagobertus cultu regio ex iussu patris honeste cum leudibus Chilppiaco[98] procul Parisius uenit, ibique germanam Sichildis regine nomine Gomatrude, in coniugium accepit. Transactis nuptiis die tertio inter Clotharium et eius filium Dagobertum grauus orta est contentio, eo quod Dagobertus cuncta que ad regnum Austrasiorum pertinebant sue ditioni uellet recipere, quod Clotharius uehementer denegabat, eidem nichil ex hoc uolens concedere. Electi sunt ab his duobus regibus xii ex Francis iudices, ut eorum disceptacione fineretur intentio, inter quos et domnus Arnulfus pontifex Mettensis[99] cum reliquis episcopis eligitur, ut benignissime ut sua erat sanctitas inter patrem et filium pro pacis loqueretur concordia. Tandem a pontificibus uel sapientissimis uiris proceribus, pater pacificatur cum filio, reddens ei solidatum quod adspexerat ad regnum Austrasiorum. Hoc tantum exinde quod citra Ligerim uel Prouincię partes situm erat suę ditioni retinuit.

Anno xlv regni sui Clotharius moritur, et suburbano Parisius in ecclesia Sancti Vincentii sepelitur.[100] Dagobertus cernens genitorem suum defunctum, uniuersis leudibus quos regebat in Austrasia iubet exercitum promouere, missos in Burgundia et ceteris regni partibus direxit, ut suum regimen eligerent. Cumque Remis uenisset, Suessionis peraccedens, omnes pontifices et leudi de regno Burgundie inibi se Dagoberto tradidisse noscuntur, sed et Neustrasii pontifices et procerum plurima pars regnum Dagoberti uisi sunt expetisse. Aribertus frater eius nitebatur si posset regnum adsumere, sed eius uoluntas pro simplicitate parum sortitur effectum. Cumque regnum omne a Dagoberto fuisset preoccupatum, et thesauri eius ditioni redacti, tandem misericordia motus et sapientum usus consilio, citra Ligerim et limitem Hispanię et Wasconie, seu et montes Pireneos, pagos et ciuitates, fratri suo Ariberto concessit, id est Tolosam, Caturcimam, Agenenssem, Petrogoricum, et Santonicum, uel quod ab his uersus Pireneos montes excluditur.[101] Quod et per pactionis uinculum firmauit. Aribertus sedem Tolosanam eligens, regnat in partibus Prouincię et Aquitanię. Post annos tres quam regnare cepisset, totam Wasconiam superans, largiorem fecit regni sui spacium.[102]

98 Clichy, near Paris.

99 St Arnulf of Metz, Charlemagne's putative ancestor.

100 Chlothar II died in 629, after forty-four years as king. His son Dagobert I, already king in Austrasia since 623, became king of Neustria and Burgundy as well (629–639).

101 Dagobert's brother Charibert II became king of Aquitaine (629–632). The region is described here as lying between the Loire and the borders of Spain and Gascony, up to the Pyrenees, including Toulouse, Cahors, Agen, Poitiers, and Saintes.

102 At this point the chronicler of Bèze skipped a paragraph in the chronicle of St-Bénigne (on p. 50 of the printed edition), which detailed some gifts to that monastery.

Dagobertus anno vi regni sui Burgundias ingreditur, tanto uero timore pontifices et proceres et cunctos in regno Burgundie consistentes aduentus Dagoberti concusserat, ut omnibus esset mirandus pre timore iusticię quam pauperibus faciebat. Veniens ergo ciuitatem Lingonas et inde Diuion adgressus ac Latona[103] residens aliquantis diebus, tantam intentionem iudicandi iusticiam uniuerso populo regni sui habebat, ut huius benignitatis desiderio nec somnum oculis posset capere, nec cibo saciabatur, intentissime cogitans ut omnes cum iusticia accepta a conspectu suo remearent.

Quia[104] igitur per successiones regum ad tempora usque Dagoberti regis narrationem protulimus, dignum esse putauimus huic loco miserere, quid ipse Dagobertus huic nostro Besuensi monasterio beneficii contulerit, et quibus appenditiis locum hunc augmentauerit, atque sui precepti auctoritate firmauerit, ut quod ipse Deo et sanctis apostolis eius Petro et Paulo offerebat perpetualiter inconuulsum permaneret. Audiens enim bonam famam Waldaleni abbatis, de quo supra meminimus, qui tunc preerat huic sacro monasterio, donationem fecit per manum ipsius Deo et ecclesię Besuensi, de uilla quę dicitur Artasia, cum terris et appenditiis suis, quę uilla sita est in fine Campolimicensi.[105] Dedit etiam uillam quę Monasteriolus uocatur,[106] nec longe a supradicta Artasia et in eosdem fines. Crescente itaque huius loci religione, Amalgarius dux, fundator huius sancti monasterii, terras quas acceperat ab ipso Dagoberto rege in beneficium contulit huic ecclesię, uillam scilicet Alteriacum cum adiacentiis suis, uillam quę dicitur Boensis[107] cum omnibus appenditiis suis, omnia dedit ad integrum cum consensu et precepto ipsius Dagoberti regis. Item dedit uillam Ginceniacum et uillam Talamarum[108] cum omnibus ubique ab ea pertinentibus.

Die[109] quadam Dagobertus rex a Latona Cabillono[110] properare deliberans, priusquam lucesceret balneum ingrediens, Brunulfum auunculum fratris sui Ariberti interficere iussit. Qui ab Amalgario et Arneberto ducibus et Wilbado patricio interfectus est. Dagobertus rex post hęc Cabillono pergit, iusticię amore quam ceperat perficiende. Post Augustiduno inde Autisiodoro pergens,

103 Langres, Dijon, and St-Jean-de-Losne.

104 This paragraph is an addition to the chronicle of St-Bénigne. There is no existing charter of Dagobert for Bèze, either authentic or forged.

105 Joseph Garnier identified Artasia as Vars, 20 km northeast of Bèze and 9 km south of Champlitte.

106 Garnier identified this as a priory near Neuville, which is 4 km southeast of Champlitte.

107 Autrey, 17 km east-northeast of Bèze; and Bouhans, 2 km southeast of Autrey.

108 Jancigny, 14 km southeast of Bèze; and Talmay, 18 km southeast of Bèze.

109 Having detailed gifts to Bèze, the chronicler returns to the chronicle of St-Bénigne where he left off (p. 50 of the printed edition).

110 Chalon-sur-Saône.

de hinc Senonas ciuitatem, indeque Parisius uenit.[111] Gomatrudem reginam Romiliaco uilla ubi matrimonium acceperat relinquens, Nantildem unam ex puellis de ministerio eius accipiens, reginam sublimauit.[112]

Anno vii regni sui cum Austrasiam regio cultu circuiret, quandam puellam nomine Ragnitrudem stratu suo adsciuit, de qua eo anno habuit filium nomine Sigibertum. Aribertus Aurelianis ueniens, Sigibertum de sancto lauacro excepit. Anno viii Dagoberti Haribertus rex moritur,[113] relinquens filium paruulum nomine Chilpericum, qui nec post mora defunctus est, fertur factione Dagoberti fuisse interfectus.

Anno x regni Dagoberti cum ei nunciatum fuisset exercitum Winidorum Toringa fuisse ingressum, cum exercitu de regno Austrasiorum de Mettis urbe promouens, transita Ardenna Magontiam adgreditur, disponens Renum transire, scalam de electis uiris fortibus de Neustria et Burgundia cum ducibus et grafionibus secum habens. Saxones missos ad Dagobertum dirigunt, petentes ut eis tributa quas fisci ditionibus dissoluebant indulgeret, promittentes se Winidis resistere, et Francorum limitem de illis partibus custodire spondentes. Quod Dagobertus consilio Neustrasiorum prestitit. Saxones qui huius postulationis legati fuerant, sacramentis, ut eorum mos erat, super arma pro uniuersis Saxonibus firmant. Sed postmodum sicut in ceteris mendaces apparuerunt. Tamen Saxones tributum quod a Clothario seniore censiti annis singulis quingentas uaccas inferendalis reddere consueuerant, preceptione Dagoberti habent indultum. Eo tempore legati Dagoberti quos ad Heraclium imperatorem direxerat,[114] his nominibus Seruatus et Paternus, sunt reuersi, nuntiantes pacem perpetuam cum Heraclio firmasse.

Anno xi regni Dagoberti cum Winidi fortiter seuirent, et sepe transgresso eorum limite regnum Francorum uastando Toringiam et reliquos pagos insisterent, Dagobertus Mettis urbem ueniens cum concilio pontificum et procerum, seu et omnibus primatibus regni sui consentientibus, Sigibertum filium suum in regnum sublimauit, sedemque Mettis ciuitate habere permisit.[115] Chunibertum

111 Autun, Auxerre, Sens, and Paris.

112 The chronicler obtained from Fredegar, via the chronicle of St-Bénigne, the information about Dagobert's itinerary, his decision while taking his bath to kill Brunulf – carried out by Duke Amalgarius and others – and his leaving his first wife at Reuilly to marry a chambermaid; Fredegar, *Fourth Book of the Chronicle with Its Continuations* 58, pp. 48–49.

113 Charibert II died in 632, having been godfather to his nephew Sigibert III. Charibert left no descendants.

114 The Byzantine emperor Heraclius (610–641).

115 Sigibert III, son of Dagobert I, was made king of Austrasia at Metz in 632, at a very young age.

Colonię urbis pontificem et Anchisum ducem instituit gubernare palacium et regnum,[116] thesaurum quod sufficeret filio tradidit, condigne ut decuit in culmine regni sublimauit, et quodcumque eidem largitus fuerat, singillatim preceptionibus roborandum decreuit. Deinceps Austrasiorum regnum et fines regni Francorum contra Winidos utliter defensare noscuntur.

Cumque anno xii regni Dagoberti eidem filius nomine Clodoueus de Nantilde regina natus fuisset, consilio Neustrasiorum, et admonitione principum suorum, per pactionis uinculum firmasse dignoscitur, ut Neptreco et Burgundia ad regnum Clodouei, post Dagoberti discessum aspiceret, Austrasia uero eo quod et populo et spacio coequalis esset, ad regnum Sigiberti pertinere deberet.[117] Et quicquid ad regnum Austrasiorum iam olim pertinuerat, hoc Sigibertus rex sue dicioni subdiceret et perpetuo dominandum haberet, excepto ducatu Denteleni quod ab Austrasiis separatum fuerat, ne iterum ad Neustriam iungeretur et Clodouei regimini subderetur. Sed has pactiones Austrasii terrore Dagoberti coacti uellent nollent firmasse uisi sunt, quod post mortem eius filiis regnum administrantibus dissolutum fuisse constat.

Eodem tempore quid Hispanie partibus a regibus eorum gestum sit dicendum est. Defuncto Sisebodo rege clementissimo, Sentila succussit [*sic*] in regnum anno uno. Cum esset Sentila nimium iniquus in suos, omnium principum regni sui odium incurrit. Quapropter Sisenandus quidam ex proceribus cum consilio ceterorum Dagobertum expeciit, ut ei cum exercitu auxiliaretur qualiter Sentilam pelleret regno.[118] Huius beneficii reconpensatione missorium aureum ex thesauris Gothorum quem Torsimodus rex ab Egecio patricio susceperat, Dagoberto dare promisit, pensantem auri libras quinquaginta. Quo audito Dagobertus ut erat cupidus exercitum in auxilium Sisenandi totum regnum Burgundie bannire precepit. Cumque Hispania diuulgatum fuisset exercitum Francorum auxiliando Sisenando Hispaniam ingredi, omnis Gothorum exercitus ditioni eius se tradidit, habundantius et uenerandus cum exercitu Tolosano tantum usque Cesaraugustam ciuitatem cum Sisenando accesserunt. Ibique omnes Gothi de regno Hispanie Sisenandum sublimant in regnum. Duces predicti cum exercitu remeant ad proprias sedes muneribus honorati. Dagobertus legatos ad Sisenandum regem Amalgarium ducem et Venerandum dirigit, ut missorium quem promiserat eidem dirigeret. Cumque a Sisenando missorius ille legatariis fuisset traditus, a Gothis per uiam tollitur, nec eum exinde

116 Cunibert, bishop of Cologne (c. 623–663), and Duke Anchisus, the father of Pippin of Herstal.

117 Dagobert I's son Clovis II (639–657) was designated as king of Burgundy and Neustria.

118 Sisenand became king of the Visigoths with Dagobert's assistance. For these events, see Wood, *Merovingian Kingdoms*, pp. 65, 174.

permiserunt auferri. Postea discurrentibus legatis, ducenta milia solidorm quod adpreciatum est missorium, Dagobertus a Sisenando accepit.

Anno xiii regni Dagoberti cum Wascones fortiter rebellarent et multas predas in regno Francorum, quod Aribertus tenuerat, facerent, Dagobertus de uniuerso regno Burgundie exercitum promoueri iubet, statuens ei caput exercitus Adoindum referendarium, qui temporibus Theoderici regis quondam in multis preliis probatus est strenuus, cui duces x et exercitus eorum adiunxit. Fuerunt autem hii, Arembertus, Amalgarius, Leudebertus, Wandalmarus, Waldericus, Hermendricus, Barontus, Airardus ex genere Francorum, Ramelenus ex genere Romano, Willibadus patricius ex genere Burgundionum, Aighinus ex genere Saxonum, exceptis comitibus plurimis qui ducem super se non habebant. Qui cum in Wasconiam cum exercitu perrexissent, et tota prouincia Wasconię ab exercitu Burgundię fuisset repleta, Wascones de montium latebris egressi properant ad bellum. Cumque preliari cepissent, ut eorum mos est terga uertentes dum cernerent se esse superandos, in fauces uallium montis Pirenei latebram dantes, se locis tutissimis per rupes eiusdem montis collocant. Exercitus post tergum eorusm insequens, plurimos interficiunt, multitudinem captiuorum abducunt, omnes domos eorum incendio tradunt, peculiis et rebus expoliant.

Tandem Wascones obpressi seu perdomiti ueniam et pacem petunt promittentes se glorię et conspectui Dagoberti regis presentaturos et sue dicioni traditos cuncta ab eo iniuncta inplecturos. Exercitus patrata uictoria redeunt ad propria sani. Sed Arembertus dux post agmen custodiam exercitus agens, in ualle Subola a Wasconibus est interfectus, cum principibus et nobilioribus de suo exercitu.

Dagobertus residens Clippiaco mittit nuncios in Brittaniam, ut Brittones quę male gesserunt in fines regni Francorum uelociter emendarent et sue ditioni se traderent. Alioquin exercitus Burgundię qui in Wasconia fuerant, de presenti in Brittanias deberent inruere. Quod audiens Iudaicale rex Brittonum Clippiaco ad Dagobertum uenit cum multis muneribus, cuncta que sui in leudibus Francorum inlicite perpętrauerant emendandum spondet, et semper se et regnum Brittanię subiectum dicioni Dagoberti et Francorum regibus esse promisit, indeque Iudaicale rex Dagoberto uale dicens in Brittania repedauit, condigne tamen a rege muneribus honoratur.

Anno xv regni Dagoberti Wascones omnes seniores terrę illius cum Amando duce ad Dagobertum Clippiaco uenerunt. Ibi regio timore perterriti confugerunt in ecclesia Sancti Dionisii, clementia Dagoberti uitam habent indultam. Ibi Wascones sacramentis firmantes promittunt regi Dagoberto et filiis suis et regno Francorum omni tempore se esse fideles, sed solito more mentiti sunt. Permissu Dagoberti reuersi sunt ad suas sedes.

Dagobertus rex eodem anno Spinogello uilla super Sequanm fluuium, non procul a Parisius, adueniens, profluuio uentris inibi egrotare cœpit. Exinde ad basilicam Sancti Dionisii a suis defertur. Post paucos dies Dagobertus emisit spiritum, sepultusque est in ecclesia ipsius sancti martyris, quam ipse condigne edificauerat, atque auro et gemmis multisque preciosissimis speciebus ornauerat.[119] Tanteque opes ab eodem uille et possessiones multe per plurima loca ibidem collate sunt, ut mirarentur plurimi. Psallentium inibi instituere ad instar monasterii sanctorum Agaunensium iusserat,[120] quod studio et industria abbatis Aigulfi est adimpletum. Multas ecclesias spoliauit, ut hanc ditaret. Omni quippe deuotione sua circa obsequium specialis patroni intentus erat, et ideo post mortem spe sua frustratus non est. Qualiter uero per hunc martyrem auxiliantibus sanctis Mauricio atque Martino a potestate demonum anima eius erepta fuerit, cuidam solitario diuinitus monstratum est. Quandiu enim uixit basilicas horum sanctorum specialius honorauit, et quamuis fuerit cupiditati et amori mulierum intentus, in elemosinis tamen pauperum fuit largus.

Post Dagoberti discessum, filius suus Clodoueus adhuc sub tenera ętatę adscitur in regnum.[121] Omnes quippe leudi de Neustria et Burgundia eum Masollaco uilla sublimant in regem. Ęga uero quem Dagobertus custodem pueri et regni tutorem reliquerat, cum Nantildę regina condigne gubernabat palacium et regnum. Anno ii regni Clodouei apud Constantinopolim sublimatur in imperium Constantinus filius Constantini.[122] Eius tempore grauissime a Sarracenis uastatur imperium. Tempore enim Heraclii imperatoris Sarracenorum gens de finibus suis egressa, regna quę sub imperii regimine erant inruunt ad deuastandum, contra quos Heraclius exercitum ad resistendum dirext. Sarraceni milites superant eosque gladio grauiter trucidant. Fertur in eo prelio cl milia militum a Sarracenis fuisse interfecta. Iterum Heraclius congregat multitudinem exercitus, iterum uincitur. Ad ultimum infelix Euthichetis heresim sectans, Christi cultum reliquens crudeliter uitam finiuit. Cui successit in imperium Constantinus filius eius, cuius tempore respublica a Sarracenis nimium uastatur. Durauit hęc uastitas per annos xlvii usque ad tempora Constantini superius memorati. Tunc est Hierosolima capta, et ceterę euersę ciuitates. Ęgyptus superior et inferior peruaditur, Alexandria capitur et predatur, Africa

119 When Dagobert I died in 639, he was buried at St-Denis, establishing the basilica as the royal burial spot of choice.

120 The famous day and night service of St-Maurice of Agaune.

121 Clovis II (639–657) succeeded Dagobert I.

122 Constans II, son of Constantine III, became emperor in 641. It was during his reign that Byzantium fully felt the attacks of the Muslims under the caliphate. These attacks had first begun under Constantine III's father, Heraclius.

tota uastatur et a Sarracenis possidetur, Asia et Europa quatiuntur, omnia regna mari contigua peruagantur. Ad postremum ipse imperator Constantinus constrictus atque compulsus effectus est Sarracenorum tributarius, ut Constantinopolis cum paucis prouintiis et insulis et urbs Roma cum sua patria sui ditione reseruaretur. Tribus annis circiter et ferme adhuc amplius, per unumquemque diem mille solidos auri Sarracenorum erariis supplebat. Tandem resumptis uiribus Constans imperium aliquantisper recuperans, tributa Sarracenis implendum refutat.

Anno iii regni Clodouei, Ęga cui Dagobertus rex commiserat regni curam moritur, et in loco eius Erchinoaldus maior domus constituitur. Eo tempore Sentila rex Hispanie quem Sisenandus oppresserat moritur, et in loco eius Tolga ipsius filius patris precibus subrogatur. Gothorum principes et primates uidentes deperire statum regni, eo quod princeps esset inualidus et minus sciens, ut pote adolescentulus, tandem eligunt unum ex primatibus nomine Chintasindum. Collectis plurimis senatoribus Gothorum cum cetero populo Hispanie sublimatur in regnum, Tolgane degradato et ad clericatum tonsorato. Chintasindus omnem Hispaniam suę redegit ditioni, multos Gothorum interfecit, quos in degradatione regum priorum una secum nouerat conscios. Cumque esset plenus dierum, filium suum nomine Richisindum in omne regnum Hispanię sublimauit.

Pipinus defuncto Anchiso patre suo maior domus Sigiberti regis in regno Austrasiorum factus est.[123] Fuit namque Pipinus Deum timens, amator iusticię, consilio prouidus, fide plenus, cautus in omnibus sapientie studiis, intentus in armis, strenuus, audax animo. Gubernauit regnum quandiu uixit grandi moderatione, nec ullo munere potuit unquam a iusticia auerti.

Anno iiii regni Clodouei, Namtildis regina cum ipso filio suo rege Aurelianis ciuitatem in regnum Burgundię ueniens, ibi omnes seniores, pontifices scilicet, duces et primates totius regni ad se uenire precepit. Namtildis singillatim blanditiis cunctos adtrahens, Flaucatum ex genere Francorum maiorem domus in regno Burgundię electione pontificum et principum laude. In hoc gradu honoris stabiliuit, neptemque suam nomine Ragnebertam eidem desponsauit. Flaucatus regnum Burgundię peruagatur, atque cum Erchinoaldo maiorę domus se in amiticia obligans, Wilbadum patricium interficere disponebat. Eo anno Namtildis regina moritur.

Ipsoque anno Flaucatus cum Clodoueo rege et Erchinoaldo maiore domus et aliquibus primatibus Neustrasiis de Parisiaco promouens per Senonas et Autisiodorum Augustidunum[124] accesserunt. Ibique Clodoueus Wilbadum ad

123 Pippin II of Herstal (d. 714), mayor of the palace.

124 Sens, Auxerre, and Autun.

se uenire precepit. Wilbadus patricius considerans Flaucatum cum ceteris ducibus de suo interitu inesse consilium, colligens secum plurimam multitudinem exercitus, etiam pontifices seu nobiles et fortes quos congregare potuit, Augustidunum iter arripuit. Cui obuiam a Clodoueo rege et suis ducibus Ermenricus domesticus dirigitur, eo quod Wilbadus trepidabat proprius accedere. Sed accepta securitate ex parte regis Augustidunum peraccessit, legato regis condignis muneribus prius honorato. In crastinum Flaucatus et ceteri duces, qui de interitu eius conspirauerant, maturius ab urbe promouerunt cum exercitu. Erchinoaldus cum Neustrasiis quos secum habebat bellum adgreditur. E contra Wilbadus tela sumens, et quascumque potuit adunare Falanges, occurrit eis. Flaucatus, Amalgarius, Chramanlenus, et Walbertus duces contra Wilbadum confligunt. Ibique Wilbadus interficitur, plurimi cum ipso de suis gladio trucidantur. His ita gestis Flaucatus in crastino de Augustiduno promouens, Cabilono[125] perrexit. Ingressus in urbem in crastino ipsa ciuitas incendio concrematur. Flaucatus iudicio Dei percussus uexatus a febre conlocatur in scaua. Euectu nauale per Ararim fluuium cognomento Sagonna, Latona[126] properans, in itinere xi die post Wilbadi interitum emisit spiritum. Sepultusque est in basilica Sancti Benigni in suburbio Diuionense.[127]

Langobardorum per hec tempora per hec tempora fuerunt hii reges. Post Autharium regnauit Ago filius eius, hic misit legatos ad Clotarium offerens xxxv milia solidorum, ut tributa quę Langobardi Francorum regibus soluebant, xii milia solidos cassaret. Quod Clotharius concessit, et pacem perpetuam cum Langobardis sacramentis et pactis firmauit. Post hunc regnauit Adloaldus filius eius. Quo interfecto ueneni populo ob nimiam crudelitatem suam, Charoaldus dux Taurinensis,[128] qui Gundebergam ex genere Francorum habebat uxorem, sublimatur in regnum. Charoaldus credens dictis mendacibus Gundebergam reginam in Caumello[129] castro in unam turrim exilio trudit. Clotharius rex legatos ad Charoaldum dirigit, quare reginam parentem Francorum humiliasset. Charoaldus regis Francorum reuerentiam habens, Gundebergam reductam post tres annos de exilio sublimat in regno. Post hęc Caroaldus rex moritur. Gundeberga regina unum ex ducibus, Chrotarium nomine, de territorio Briscia, acceptis ab eo sacramentis ut nunquam ab eo degradaretur de regni culmine, sumens illum in coniugium stabiliuit in regnum. Postea Chrotarius aliquantis transactis annis, oblitus sacramenta quę fecerat, Gundebergam de solio regni

125 Chalon-sur-Saône.

126 St-Jean de Losne is on the Saône.

127 The basilica of St-Bénigne, on the outskirts of Dijon.

128 Turin.

129 Fredegar reads rather “Laumello,” the modern locale of Lomello.

deiectam in unum cubiculum apud Ticinum[130] in aula palacii retrudit, eamque priuato habitu uiuere fecit. Quinque anni sub ea trusione transierunt. Illa cum esset Christiana benedicebat Deum in hac tribulatione posita.

Tandem placuit Deo ut mitteretur Aubedo legatarius a Clodoueo rege ad Chrotharium Longobardorum regem. Qui ueniens Papiam ciuitatem, quę cognominatur Ticinis, cernensque reginam a qua benigne in legationem ueniens susceptus fuerat esse retrusam, inter cetera Chrothario regi suggessit, quod reginam parentem Francorum, per quam etiam regnum adeptus fuerat, non debuisset ita humiliare. Pro qua re Francorum reges et omnes Franci ei essent ingrati. Chrotharius de presenti ob Francorum reuerentiam Gundebergam de custodia iubet egredi, et per totam ciuitatem et foris regali ordine per loca sanctorum adoracionem procedere. De uillis et opibus fisci, omnia quę amiserat ei restaurari precepit, quod usque diem sui obitus regio cultu post feliciter tenuit. Aubedo uero a Gundeberga regina fortite remuneratus repedauit ad regem.

Defuncto Sigiberto Austrasiorum Francorum rege, filius eius Dagobertus succedit in regnum.[131] Pipinus ut diximus post regem totius regni curam gerebat cuius filius nomine Grimoaldus sub imperio patris palacio preerat. Hic considerans Dagobertum inertem et ad regni curam minus utilem, fecit eum tonderi ad clericatus ordinem. Clodoueus igitur rex, qui et Clotharius dictus est, xviii annis in regni administratione complens, defunctus est in primeuo flore iuuentutis, relictis tribus filiis, Clothario, Childerico, et Theoderico, una cum matre eorum Baltechilde regina. E quibus Clotharius natu maior regnum patris sui Clodouei Neustrię et Burgundię obtinuit. Childericus uero Austrię et Germanie sedem adeptus est.[132]

130 Pavia

131 When Sigibert III died in 656, his son Dagobert II should have succeeded, but Pippin I's son Grimoald, mayor of the palace, had him tonsured. The chronicle does not here discuss Grimoald's ultimately unsuccessful efforts to rule through an infant Merovingian, turning his attention instead to Sigibert III's brother Clovis II. For the attempted coup, see Bouchard, *Rewriting Saints and Ancestors*, pp. 108–109 and 282n9. Here the chronicle seems to have confused Pippin with his grandson Pippin II (of Herstal), both of whom had sons named Grimoald who became mayors of the palace.

132 King Clovis II (639–657), who was not in fact called Chlothar, and his wife Baltildis were the parents of Chlothar III (657–673), who took Neustria and Burgundy; of Theoderic III (675–690), who took Neustria and Burgundy after his older brother's death; and of Childeric II (662–675), who took Austrasia during their father's lifetime and briefly challenged his brother Theoderic for Neustria and Burgundy before his own death. The account here was derived from the *Liber Historiae Francorum* 44, MGH SSRM 2:316–317; and from the "continuations" of Fredegar, *Fourth Book with Its Continuations* 1–2, pp. 80–81. The confusion between Clovis and Chlothar is doubtless due to the chronicler wanting to fit Clovis into a story in which Chlothar was the principal royal benefactor of Bèze.

Carta de Birgiliis

Nunc[133] uero id uidetur huic nostrę narrationi inserendum, illud quod supra narrare promisimus, qualiter uidelicet locus Dornatiacus qui Birgillias dicitur[134] huic Besuensi loco cum appenditiis suis donatus sit atque coniunctus. Hisdem namque fere temporibus Donato, de quo supra meminimus, existente Bisonticensis sedis archiepiscopo, Adalsinda abbatissa que ei loco preerat, malorum hominum iniuriis et plurimis aduersitatibus affecta, cum amplius pati non posset, in manu Waldaleni abbatis fratris sui Deo et sanctis apostolis eius, Petro et Paulo, locum illum cum omnibus appenditiis suis donauit, conconcessu ipsius Donati Bisonticensis archiepiscopi,[135] sicut ipsius epistola subscripta docebit.

1

Bèze, February 658

Adalsinda and her brother Adalricus give Waldalenus a monastery her parents had established, St-Martin of Brégille. Various difficulties make it impossible to live there longer.

Cartulary, fol. 24r–v.
Bougaud-Garnier, pp. 240–241.
d'Achery, *Spicilegium*, 2:402.
Pardessus, *Diplomata, chartae, epistolae, leges*, 2:105–106, no. 328; dated 657.
Gallia christiana (GC) 15 (1860), instr. 3–4, no. 2; from Pardessus.
Summarized in Brequigny, *Table chronologique des diplômes, chartes, titres et actes*, 1:59; dated 652.

Domino sancto et in Christo amabili fratri Waldaleno,
Adalsinda abbatissa

Dum malorum hominum uexata iniuriis et uariis aduersitatibus uexata, ibidem stare non possem, inde ego et germanus meus Adalricus uobis et

---

133 At this point, on fol. 23v, the chronicler of Bèze took up his own monastery's account again. The preceding folios were taken from the chronicle of St-Bénigne, ending on p. 61 of the printed edition.

134 St-Martin of Brégille, 2 km east of Besançon, across the Doubs. See Prinz, *Frühes Mönchtum in Frankenreich*, p. 40. In 1049, when it was dependent on the archbishop of Besançon, it was referred to as "abbatia S. Martini de Berzeliis, quae alio nomine uocatur Dorcatonge coenobium." GC 15, instr. col. 13, no. 1.

135 Donatus, bishop of Besançon (627–658).

fratribus uestris petiuimus ut ad monasterium Sancti Petri habitare sub regula uel ordine in Dei nomine deberem, quod et uos pro caritatis studio concessistis. Ideo monasterium Dornatiacum in honore Sancti Martini situm[1] quod genitor meus Amalgarius et Aquilina mater mea construxerunt, et ei maximam partem de suis facultatibus delegauerunt, hoc recipere in Dei nomine debetis, cum uillis ad eundem locum pertinentibus, et omnibus uniuersaliter appenditiis suis, uillam scilicet Assonam,[2] uillam Parniacum, Potenciacum, et medietatem quam in Balatonna genitores uestri tenuerunt. Reliqua uero, que ad ipsum monasterium Dornatiacum genitores nostri[3] delegauerunt, a die presenti in Dei nomine recipite. Et de uilla Montaniaco[4] quod genitor uester[5] Amalgarius et Amolaldus de fisco pariter promeruerunt, portionem nostram a die presenti in uestra dominatione reuocate, ut nec ego nec quislibet de parte nostra uel ulla apposita persona aduersum uos de supradictis rebus calumpniam ad laborem generare presumat. Si quis uero fecerit, conferat una cum sacratissimo fisco auri libras xx, argenti pondo quinquaginta.

Actum publice Fonte Besua monasterio. In Dei nomine ego Adalsinda hanc traditionem nostram subscripsi. Hermena monacha iussu domne meę Adalsinde subscripsi. S. Daginus hanc donationem. S. Manaulfus presbyter. S. Victor. S. Proculus. S. Walibertus. S. Landebertus. S. Trasgarius. S. Rogitus. Ego Allo hanc traditionem scribsi [*sic*] et dictaui, anno ab incarnatione Domini DCLII, indictione x, epacta vi, Clothario rege regnante in Francia[6] primo anno regni eius, uenerabili uiro Donato Besonticam sedem tenente,[7] die Mercoris proximo ante medium mensis Febroarii.

The year of Chlothar's reign and the year of the incarnation do not match. Given that charters of the era were more likely to be dated by regnal years than the incarnation, 657 (old style, 658 new style) seems the most likely date – and, if the year was indeed given (and given correctly), a *V* might have disappeared in copying.

1 St-Martin of Brégille.
2 Auxonne, 32 km south-southeast of Bèze. The other places are not identified and were most likely near Besançon.
3 This "nostri," added interlinearly, contrasts with the "uestri" in the previous line.
4 Montigny, 17 km northeast of Bèze.
5 Pardessus reads "noster," although the cartulary quite clearly reads "uester." "Noster" is indeed the more likely reading, as "nostri" would be more appropriate two lines earlier.
6 King Chlothar III (657–673).
7 Donatus, bishop of Besançon (627–658).

This document has many signs of authenticity, as discussed further in the introduction, even though it was probably recopied and "improved" between the seventh century and the twelfth. Adalsinda is giving a monastery located some seventy kilometres away to Bèze, accompanied by property which was not part of the monastery's patrimony in future years. Nothing in it suggests that Adalsinda was the abbot's sister, except for the "uester."[8] Given the similar appearance of *noster* and *uester* when abbreviated, a mistake would have been easy for the copyist to make. The year of the incarnation in the dating formula is the only anachronistic detail. The bishop of Besançon is the correct person for the date. The fact that the charter does not even say that Amalgarius founded Bèze, which was of course the later narrative at the monastery, also adds to the likelihood of authenticity.[9]

Tempore igitur Clotharii regis cum locus iste copiosissime ditatus fuisset et religionis studio floreret, inimicus tocius boni diabolus omni conamine efficere uoluit, ut bona quę ibi fideles quique donauerant inde auferrentur, et si fieri potuisset in perpetuam obliuionem traderentur. Nam mortuo Amalgario duce, Francis inter se discordantibus et intestino furore inter se dimicantibus et terras sue potestatis bello plusquam ciuili uastantibus, contigit hoc monasterium rabiem talium perpeti, et dampna rerum omnium sustinere, in tantum ut etiam instrumenta cartarum et donationum quę prefatus Amalgarius aliique Deum timentes et honorantes eidem monasterio contulerant, tollerent, et in perditionem darent. Sed hanc iacturam predictus Waldelenus abbas releuare satagens, egit cum Sichelmo duce tunc in Burgundia ducatum agente ut relationem acciperet rerum ipsius monasterii, multorum bonorum hominum confirmatam consensu et subscriptionibus. Tali igitur auctoritate fretus, ad regem Clotharium se contulit, eique cuncta innotuit, et ut eius preceptum ad perpetuam tuitionem mereretur super hoc facto expetiuit. Cuius peticioni predictus rex assensum prebuit, et suam preceptionem clementer concessit. Quod ex ipsis conscriptionibus melius edocebimus.

8 Yaniv Fox mistakenly says that Abbot Waldalenus, whom he accepts as Adalsinda's brother, gave St-Martin of Brégille to his sister, rather than the other way around; *Power and Religion in Merovingian Gaul*, p. 101.

9 The late twelfth-century "Annales" of Bèze say that in 652 "Archbishop" Donatus of Besançon gave the monastery the church St-Martin of Brégille, doubtless on the basis of this charter. "Annales Besuenses" 652, MGH SS 2:248.

2

1 October 663

Sichelm asks three mayors of the palace to request from the king a grant of immunity for Bèze, founded by Duke Amalgarius. The monks' property records have been stolen at the same time as evil men devastated the house and took its goods.

Cartulary, fol. 25r–v.
Bougaud-Garnier, pp. 242–243.
Pardessus, *Diplomata*, 2:131, no. 348 (abbreviated).
Recueil des historiens des Gaules et de la France (RHGF) 4:647, note (a).
Summarized in Brequigny, *Table* 1:61; dated 657.

Epistola Sichelmi ducis transmissa maioribus palatii

Dominis nostris propriis Radeberto, Chrodeberto, Emerulfo maioribus domus sacri palacii, Sichelmus cum reliquis fidelibus et seruientibus uestris, quorum subscriptiones uel signacula in hanc subgestionem subter teneantur inserta. Credimus quod gloriosissimus domnus noster auditum habeat qualiter illustris uir Amalgarius tempore ducatus sui in loco Fonte Besua nuncupato, in pago Attoariense,[1] in honore sanctorum apostolorum Petri et Pauli monasterium construxit, ubi etiam monachorum congregationem ad habitandum coniunxit, et de facultate sua maximam partem supradicto monasterio delegauit. Credimus etiam ad uestram peruenisse noticiam, qualiter ipsum monasterium ante hos dies a malis hominibus irruptum fuerit, atque uastatum, et omnes res quas ipsi monachi habebant, cum ipsis cartis deportate, et omnis habitatio eorum in directionem et deuastationem missa. Vnde humiliter pietati uestrę suggerere presumimus, ut hoc gloriossimo domno nostro innotescere faciatis, ut per suam clementiam talem auctoritatem ipsi loco conscribi iubeat, ut supradictas res, quas boni homines ibidem delegauerunt, nullus inuadere, aut uiolare, uel inquietare presumat, sed quę in presenti habere uel possidere uidentur ipsi monachi, uestris et futuris temporibus sine inquietudine per uestrum preceptum habere et tenere possint. Et ut eos pro uita uestra et stabilitate celsitudinis uestrę et regni uestri, Dei misericordiam attentius delectet exorare.

1 Bèze was in the pagus of Attuyer, the region north of Dijon.

Dominicus audiuit subgestionem.[2] Farulfus subgessit. Abbo subgessit. Ermenbertus subgessit. Frodoaldus subgessit. Warato subgessit. Fugoaldus subgessit. Eurcharius subgessit. Data sub die kalendas Octobris, anno vii regnante domno nostro Clothario rege.[3]

Hanc subgestionem regi innotuerunt, et quid ipse de hoc decreuerit, eius preceptum declarabit.

It would be easy to label this document a forgery. The mayors of the palace listed do not all appear to be actual mayors of the palace, although they *were* all real people.[4] Amalgarius is called a duke and is said to have founded Bèze, which he was not in his daughter's charter for Bèze. The reference to evil people who have taken the records of the monastery, requiring a new confirmation of all its property, raises suspicions.

And yet this charter may be, at heart, authentic. The dating formula is in the right format. There was, after all, a seventh-century sample letter in the formulary of Marculf, in which a king confirms a church's possessions after its documents are lost or burned, so the possibility was not outlandish.[5] Having someone direct his request to the mayors of the palace, asking them to intercede with the king for him, was an appropriate Merovingian-era procedure that probably would not have occurred to a later forger, more likely to go straight for a royal charter – such as the following. Having the charter issued by Sichelm, rather than Amalgarius himself, complicates the story, making it less like the straightforward account a forger might create. Sichelm indeed appears as Syghichelmus, consenting to and signing an authentic royal charter of 654, in which Radobertus appears as mayor of the palace.[6] The following document (no. 3) appears to have been created in response to this one; later monks would have been worried that they did not have the royal charter in their archives that this document appeared to anticipate.

2 At this point the scribe inserted the mark which in Merovingian scribal practice stood for *subscripsi*, that is "sub" with the *s* going to the right as an arch, some lines across it, and the end of the arch becoming a *b*. The mark's presence certainly indicates that John had seen authentic Merovingian-era documents.

3 King Chlothar III (657–673).

4 Radobertus was mayor of the palace in an authentic document of 654, of which the original still survives; MGH DD regum francorum e stirpe Merovingica, 1:216–220, no. 85; *Chartae Latinae Antiquiores*, 13:36–41, no. 558. The names Chradobercthus and Ebrulfus appear among this document's signatories.

5 Marculf, "Formulae" 1.34, MGH Form., pp. 64–65.

6 MGH DD regum francorum e stirpe Merovingica, 1:220, no. 85.

3

Nîmes, August 664

King Chlothar III issues a charter to Duke Sichelm to confirm the possessions of Bèze. The king recalls that the couple Amalgarius and Aquilina founded the monastery and notes that Waldalenus is now abbot.

Cartulary, fols. 25v–26v.
Bougaud-Garnier, pp. 243–245
RHGF 4:647–648, no. 44.
Pardessus, *Diplomata*, 2:134–135, no. 351.
MGH DD imperii, pp. 39–40, no. 42; dated 664.
MGH DD regum francorum e stirpe Merovingica, 1:234–237, no. 91, from the cartulary; called false, dated 658.
Summarized in Brequigny, *Table* 1:61; dated 658.

Preceptum Clotharii regis

Clotharius rex Francorum[1] uiro illustri Sichelmo duci. Regem cęlorum qui super omnes reges termino inmenso nullo imperio regitur, et super omnes sedes angelicas sua pietate et potentia tenet principatum, erga solium regni nostri quod ipse nobis ad regendum commisit, credimus esse cultorem,[2] si oportuna beneficia ad loca sanctorum deuota mente prestamus uel nostris oraculis confirmamus. Igitur uenerabilis uir Waldelenus abbas ad presentiam nostram ueniens, glorię regni nostri subgessit quod genitor suus Amalgarius et genitrix sua Aquilina quondam pro Dei amore monasterium nuncupatum Fontem Besuam in pago Attoariorum[3] suo opera in honore Sancti Petri et Pauli edificassent, et monachos ibidem sub regula Beati Columbani seu Beati Benedicti adunassent, et maximam partem de facultate sua ipsi monasterio delegassent.

Sed postea insidiante parte aduersa ipsum monasterium a malis hominibus irruptum et expoliatum fuerit, et omnes carte quas de supradicto loco uel de reliquis locis memoratus Amalgarius uel coniunx sua ibi delegauerant cum multis aliis rebus ablate. Vnde memoratus Waldelenus relatione uestra pro firmitatis studio petiit celsitudinem nostram, ut quascumque res ipsius monasterii seu prescripti loci in Dei nomine per precepti nostri auctoritatem deberemus confirmare. Cuius peticione mercedem nobis in omnibus adquirere cupientes,

1 King Chlothar III (657–673).
2 The manuscript reads "cultotorem."
3 Bèze was in the pagus of Attuyer, the region north of Dijon.

nos id prestitisse et confirmasse cognoscite. Precipimus igitur ut quidquid constat a prefato Amalgario et eius matrona Aquilina uel ab aliis Deum timentibus hominibus ipsi monasterio collatum, ad integrum hoc habeat, teneat, et possideat, et nostris et futuris Deo auxiliante temporibus ipsam scilicet Besuam cum omnibus appenditiis suis, cum terris et edificiis, cum siluis et accessibus omnibus, cum mancipiis et colonis et seruientibus totum liberrime et integerrime, Vetus Vineas cum omnibus appenditiis suis et siluis, Tilerias, Beriam,[4] Tregias, Cypetum, Buxatellum,[5] Vendoueram, Auxiliacum, cum appenditiis suis et siluis et colonicis, Blaniacum,[6] Berlariam, Baymam, Viriacum,[7] Attiniacum, Nouiliacum, uillam Calatunnam,[8] Curtem Molinensem, Mercennacum[9] cum uineis xii et uinitoribus et colonicis, qui excoleri uidentur, apud Cocheiacum[10] uineas non minime quantitatis. In pago Belnensi uineas octo, cum uinitoribus et colonicis, in uillam que Vaona[11] dicitur, uineas et terras cum seruis et ancillis excolentibus eas, terras quas habebat in Diuione et in fine Domni Petri,[12] et Longouico, et in Canauis, et in Arzilias,[13] et Tremolde, et Prouiso, et Disto,[14] in Gibriaco[15] uinearum non modicam quantitatem cum uinitoribus et colonicis et siluis et pratis et omnibus adiacentiis suis, cum seruis et ancillis, omnia omnino liberrime, in uilla et in Chaciaco[16] quidquid habebat ipse Amalgarius, in uilla que Patriniacus[17] dicitur, mansum unum optimum cum omnibus appenditiis suis, uillam Maiescum cum adiacentiis suis, uillam Alteriacum, et

4 Viévigne, 4 km southwest of Bèze; Tilchâtel, 9 km northwest of Bèze; and Beire, 8 km southwest of Bèze.

5 Treige is now a farm 7 km southwest of Bèze. Spoy is 6 km southwest of Bèze. According to Roserot, *Dictionnaire topographique du département de la Côte-d'Or*, Buteau is a now-ruined village near Viévigne.

6 Véronnes, 7 km north-northwest of Bèze; Oisilly, 9 km southeast of Bèze; and Blagny, 8 km east-southeast of Bèze.

7 Garnier suggests that Berlaria may be Berthaut, which was a hamlet in the commune of Fontaine-Française. The next two places are unidentified.

8 Athée, 27 km east-southeast of Bèze; and Neuilly, 7 km southeast of Dijon. The following place is unknown.

9 Crimolois, 9 km southeast of Dijon; and Marsannay, 7 km southwest of Dijon.

10 Couchey, 8 km south-southwest of Dijon.

11 Vosne, 19 km south-southwest of Dijon, in the pagus of Beaune.

12 Dampierre, 7 km east-northeast of Bèze.

13 Longvic, 4 km southeast of Dijon; Chenôve, 5 km southwest of Dijon; and Aisery, 20 km southeast of Dijon.

14 Trimolois, the name of a former hamlet between Chenôve and Dijon; Prenois, just outside Dijon; and Daix, 5 km northwest of Dijon.

15 Gevrey, 12 km southwest of Dijon.

16 Cessey-sur-Tille, 21 km south-southwest of Bèze.

17 Perrigny, 7 km south-southwest of Dijon.

uillam Boensem,[18] similiter cum omnibus appenditiis suis, uillam Talamarum et uillam Ginceniacum,[19] omnia hec integerrime hac liberrime cum omnibus ad ea pertinentibus.

Vt autem hęc scriptio firma et stabilis in euum permaneat, et a nullo nostrorum successorum sit permutanda, nostro nomine insigniri et anuli impressione iussimus sigillari.

Signum Clotharii[20] regis. Datum mense Augusti, anno ab incarnatione Domini DC^mo^ LVIII, indictione i, anno viii regni Clotharii. Actum Nemauso feliciter. Non solum autem hęc confirmauit sed et defensorem et aduocatum Gengulfum uirum illustrissimum predicto monasterio constituit, quod eius littere indicabunt.

This charter is most likely a later forgery.[21] Much of the language seems, as Theo Kölzer noted in preparing the new edition for the MGH, to have been borrowed from Adalsinda's charter. Having the abbot ask the king directly for a confirmation would have made more sense in the ninth through twelfth centuries than it would have in the seventh, when a petitioner would have gone through friends of the monastery and mayors of the palace. I have assigned the date 664, which would have been the year based on the reign of Chlothar if it were authentic, rather than the year of the incarnation, because this was clearly intended to have been issued after document 2.

The list of property includes many of the places where the monastery later owned property; however, it also includes a number of places that either do not appear again in the monastery's lists of possessions, or else only much later – especially villas located south of Dijon. Longvic, Chenôve, Cessey-sur-Tille, and Athée may have been borrowed from the list of property which Bishop Gregory of Langres and the noble lady Goyla were supposed to have given St-Bénigne in the early sixth century, as recorded in that house's chronicle – which the Bèze chronicler partially copied.[22] And yet in another, more likely authentic document from 827, Abbot Seraphim of Bèze gave St-Bénigne, in

18 Maâtz, 30 km north-northeast of Bèze; Autrey, 17 km east-northeast of Bèze; and Bouhans, 2 km southeast of Autrey.

19 Talmay, 18 km southeast of Bèze; and Jancigny, 14 km southeast of Bèze.

20 The king's name is given in the form of a cross-shaped monogram, such as used by Charlemagne, never found in original Merovingian-era documents.

21 Kölzer, *Merowingerstudien II*, pp. 2–6.

22 *Chronique de l'abbaye de Saint-Bénigne*, pp. 15–16, 40–41. At the beginning of the tenth century Bèze did have some property at Longvic, even if not in the other locations, because some land given to St-Étienne of Dijon there was identified as bordering Bèze's property; *Chartes de l'abbaye de Saint-Étienne de Dijon (VIIIe, IXe, Xe et XIe siècles)*, 1:47, no. 28.

exchange for lands at Lux and Véronnes, property in villas that seem to match many of these villas.[23] This exchange is known only from St-Bénigne's copy of the document and is unrecorded in Bèze's surviving records, but if Bèze had had the property to give away, the monks must have acquired it earlier. Indeed, the current document (no. 3) may have been confected in part on the basis of Bèze's now-lost copy of the exchange agreement. Seraphim gave, according to St-Bénigne's charter, land at Dijon, Dampierre, Longvic, Chenôve, Aisery, Trimolois, Fontaine, Prenois, and Daix.

4

18 August 667

King Chlothar writes to Abbot Waldalenus, recalling that his parents had founded Bèze and urging him to make Gengulf the advocate of the monastery.

Cartulary, fol. 27r.
Bougaud-Garnier, p. 245.
Pardessus, *Diplomata*, 2:141, no. 356; dated 666.
RHGF 4:649, no. 46; dated 666.
MGH DD imperii, pp. 40–41, no. 43, dated 666.
MGH DD regum francorum e stirpe Merovingica, pp. 273–275, no. 106, from the cartulary; called false, dated 667.
Summarized in Brequigny, *Table* 1:64; dated 665.

Quo modo Clotharius constituit aduocatum Beatum Gengulfum huic loco

Venerabilis uir Waldelenus abbas de monasterio Sancti Petri Fontis Besue, quod suus genitor Amalgarius eiusque matrona Aquilina quondam suo opere uisi fuerunt edificasse, clementię regni nostri subgessit, eo quod ipsum monasterium a malis hominibus fuisset uastatum et instrumenta cartarum una cum reliquis rebus quamplurimis exinde fuissent deportate. Ob hoc petit a nobis, ut illuster uir Gengulfus omnes causas ipsius monasterii ad prosequendum et redintegrandum deberet recipere. Cui nos hoc beneficium prestitisse cognoscite. Quapropter per presens hoc preceptum iubemus, ut memoratas omnes causas ipsius monasterii ex nostro permissu licentiam habeat prosequi, et unumquodque ut iustum est restituat, sic tamen, quamdiu eorum pariter fuerit uoluntas.

23 *Chartes et documents de Saint-Bénigne de Dijon*, 1:76, no. 43. See also *Chronique de l'abbaye de Saint-Bénigne*, p. 92.

Data xv kalendas Septembri, anno x regni domni Clotharii regis[1]

Kölzer argues for the falsity of this document, dated by the regnal years of King Chlothar.[2] It appears to have been confected as an effort to tie a local saint to the monastery. According to his vita, Gengulf, who had property at Véronnes, was assassinated in 670 at his wife's instigation, because he reproached her for her adultery.[3]

His igitur auctoritatibus regiis et principum adiutoriis fultus predictus Waldalenus abbas res ad ipsum monasterium pertinentes legitime et quiete tenuit, et monasticum ordinem cum suis monachis sicut multis indiciis clarum est, regulariter et deuote custodiuit. Cuius exemplo multi ad monasticam religionem se contulerunt, sua secundum Domini preceptum quedam pauperibus quedam eidem loco sancto conferentes, quorum donationes ad huc retinemus cum instrumentis kartarum.

Clotharius igitur rex[4] postquam aliquot annis tenuit regnum, inmatura preuentus morte, reliquit illud sine herede. Cuius obitum dolentes Francorum principes, germanum eius Childericum regem[5] Austrasiorum quem audierant sapienter et prouide regnum disponere in omni sublimant Francorum regno. Adeptus uero principatum, quicquid aduersus leges regum priorum ac maiorum principum, quorum uita quondam laudabilis extiterat, ineptum atque contrarium repperit, ad pristinum statum prudentissime reuocauit.

Childericus[6] ergo rex paucis annis quibus regnum Francorum obtinuit, ęquo moderamine iustisque legibus disponens ipsum regnum defunctus est, et germanus eius Theodericus[7] in regno fratris loco sublimatus, quod tenuit annis xvi. In diebus eius Sanctus Leodegarius[8] est interfectus ab Ebroino maiore

1 King Chlothar III (657–673).

2 Kölzer, *Merowingerstudien II*, pp. 7–10. Although I would not argue for its authenticity myself, Kölzer is unconvincing in his argument that it derived from Marculf's "Formulae," for the wording is quite different.

3 AASS May 2:644–647. This vita doubtless dates from the late seventh century. It says that St Gengulf did not have miracles "yet," and although it mentions Pippin of Herstal as mayor of the palace, the author gives no suggestion that he knew Pippin's descendants would become kings.

4 King Chlothar III (657–673). This paragraph is taken from the chronicle of St-Bénigne (p. 64 in the printed edition). Although the information is the same as that given at the beginning of the continuations of Fredegar, the phrasing is very different.

5 King Childeric II (662–675).

6 After skipping a brief section on gifts to St-Bénigne, the chronicle of Bèze here returns to St-Bénigne's chronicle for this paragraph (p. 65 in the printed edition).

7 King Theoderic III (675–690).

8 Leodegarius, bishop of Autun (659–679). He was sainted as a martyr.

domus et Sanctus Lambertus Tungrorum episcopus a Dodone comite.[9] Hii uno tempore innocenter occisi, coronam martyrii sunt adepti.

Iste Theodericus rex munificentiam largitatis sue huic loco inpendere dignatus est, cuius exemplar precepti necessarium subiecere iudicamus.

5

4 September 679

King Theoderic III takes goods in Austrasia from Duke Adalricus, who has been unfaithful to him, and gives them instead to Bèze.

Cartulary, fols. 27v–28r.
Bougaud-Garnier, p. 247.
Pardessus, *Diplomata*, 2:177–178, no. 386; dated 677.
PL 87:1324–1325, no. 5; dated 677.
RHGF 4:657, no. 58; dated 676.
MGH DD imperii, p. 43, no. 46, dated 677.
MGH DD regum francorum e stirpe Merovingica, pp. 306–308, no. 120, from the cartulary; called false, dated 679.
Summarized in Brequigny, *Table* 1:67; dated 677.

Incipit preceptum regis Theoderici

Merito beneficia que possident amittere uidentur, qui non solum largitoribus ipsorum beneficiorum ingrati existunt, uerum etiam infideles eis esse comprobantur. Ad huiusmodi igitur exemplum postquam omnibus patefactum est, qualiter Adalricus dux Deo sibi contrario nobis infidelis apparuit, et se Austrasiis consociauit, ut aduersum nos et nostros fideles scelera sua si Dominus Deus permisisset exercuisset, nos propter ipsum facimus omnes res suas ad nostrum fiscum iussimus reuocari. Cognoscat itaque utilitatis uestrę magnitudo, quod res nominatas fiscafelinis una cum appenditiis suis et adiacentiis suis et cum colonica Treuario et quidquid supradictus Adalricus de quolibet adtracto ibidem tenuit uel possedit ei monasterio quod appellatur Fons Besue, quod est in honore Sancti Petri et Pauli ac ceterorum sanctorum constructum,

9 Lambert of Maastricht, bishop of Tongres (killed c. 700), was also sainted as a martyr. His killer Dodo was by the tenth century called the brother of Alpaidis, Pippin of Herstal's second wife, although this identification is not now widely accepted. It is argued for by Gerberding, *Rise of the Carolingians and the "Liber Historiae Francorum,"* pp. 116–119; and against by Joch, *Legitimität und Integration*, pp. 130–145.

ubi uenerabilis uir Waldalenus preesse dinoscitur, plena et integra gratia totum nos concessisse.

Quapropter per hoc nostrum preceptum decernimus ordinandum, et in perpetuum uolumus esse mansurum, ut memoratus abbas Waldalenus predicto monasterio Fontis Besue res iamdictas una cum edificiis, mancipiis, accolabus, terris, pratis, siluis, pascuis, aquis, aquarumque decursibus accessibusque omnibus uel reliquis quibuscumque beneficiis cum omni usufructuario ex nostre largitatis munere perpetualiter recipiat possidendas. Et ut hęc preceptio firmior habeatur, et futuris temporibus inconuulse teneatur, manus nostre subscriptionibus eam decreuimus roborare.

Signum Theoderici regis.[1]

Glybertus notharius subscripsit.[2]

Datum mense Septembri die iiii, anno quarto regnante Theoderico rege.

In spite of some anomalies in the signatures, most notably a Carolingian-style monogram, and the unlikelihood that the king would have granted all of a rebellious duke's property to the monastery, much of the phrasing of this document is similar to that found in genuine documents of seventh-century Frankish kings, making it likely that the monks indeed had a genuine charter of Theoderic III on which this one was based.[3] I have dated it by Theoderic's years as king.

John, the compiler of the cartulary-chronicle, clearly believed that the *Adalricus dux* of this charter was the same man as the Adalricus who was supposed to be the brother of Abbot Waldalenus in document 1.

Tempore igitur predicti Waldaleni monasticus ordo regulariter floruit, quem successores eius abbates ut boni filii mores paternos emulantes, in regulari institutione imitati sunt: Bercangus uidelicet qui illi in regimine successit, et Ferreolus qui post Bercangum regimen monasterii suscepit, sed et Sirannus uir religiosus pastoralem curam nobiliter tenuit. Talibus itaque fundatoribus,

1 King Theoderic III (675–690). His name is in the form of a cross-shaped monogram, a format not found in any original Merovingian-era documents.

2 In a surviving original charter from 679 for St-Denis, one Aghliberthus signed after King Theoderic, giving some likelihood that this charter was (at least in part) authentic. MGH DD regum francorum e stirpe Merovingica, p. 312, no. 122. The term *notharius*, however, would not have been used. The word "subscripsit" is given as an abbreviation such as really would have been found in a Merovingian-era document, a "sub" with the *s* going to the right as an arch, some lines across it, and the end of the arch becoming a *b*.

3 Kölzer, *Merowingerstudien II*, pp. 10–15.

plantatoribus, rigatoribus, Deo incrementum prebente in predicto cęnobio monastica institutio sollerter uiguit, permansitque usque ad tempora Pipini, Magni Karoli genitoris.[4]

In[5] illo tempore deficientibus iam a pristino uigore regibus, cura tocius regni administrabatur per duces et principes domus, inter quos omnes preminebat Pipinus quem supra retulimus, uir omni sapientia adornatus, eiusdemque regni maxima pars erat in manu eius. Hic deuicta Frisia atque ipsius regni fugato rege nomine Ratbodo, misit illuc ad predicandum seruos Dei uenientes ex Brittannia, Willebrordum[6] et socios eius, qui non paruam populi multitudinem ad Christum conuerterunt. Theoderico rege defuncto, Childebertus filius eius successit in regnum.[7]

Anno ab incarnatione Domini DCCVIIII Pipinus perrexit in Suuanos[8] contra Wilarium. Item anno sequenti commouit exercitum super predictum tyrannum. Anno tercio aquę uehementer inundauerunt, et Childebertus rex mortuus est, et exercitus Francorum erat in Suuanis. Anno iiii iterum exercitus Francorum in Suuanis contra Wilarium perrexit, et Eribertus rex Langobardorum mortuus est.

Anno DCCXIIII, Pipinus mortuus est in mense Decembrio, et Grimoaldus filius eius similiter mortuus est, et Karolus successit in locum patris.[9]

Anno DCCXV, Dagobertus rex mortuus est,[10] et Saxones deuastauerunt terram Bagoariorum.[11] Anno DCCXVII bellum fuit in Vinciaco inter Karolum et Ragamfredum maiorem domus.[12] Fugitque Ragamfredus, et exercitus eius cesus est plaga magna usque ad fluuium Wisera. Anno sequenti Karolus intrauit Saxoniam uastauitque eam. Anno DCCXXI expugnauit Eudo Sarracenos

4 Pippin II of Herstal (d. 714) was father of Charles Martel, not of Charlemagne.

5 Having paused to copy a royal charter and give a brief overview of his house's first abbots, the chronicle of Bèze here begins again, on fol. 28v, to copy the chronicle of St-Bénigne, picking up where he left off (p. 65 in the printed edition). Charles Martel did not in fact immediately succeed his father; it took him close to a decade to consolidate his position.

6 The missionary Willibrord (d. 739), originally from Britain, preached to the Frisians.

7 King Theoderic III was succeeded within a few years of his death by his son, King Childebert III (694–711).

8 The campaign in Swabia.

9 Here the chronicler of Bèze skips a paragraph in the chronicle of St-Bénigne (p. 66 in the printed edition) concerning gifts to that monastery. The account oversimplifies the succession to Pippin of Herstal.

10 Dagobert III (711–715/716).

11 Bavaria.

12 Charles Martel, fighting to succeed his father, defeated Ragamfred, mayor of the palace for Neustria, at the battle of Vinchy.

de terra sua.[13] Anno quarto post hunc expugnauit Karolus Andegauis, quia rebellabant aduersus eum. Theodericus filius Dagoberti iunioris regio tunc sublimatus erat in solio. Cui successit Clotharius, et Clothario Childebertus, Childeberto Childericus,[14] in quo defecit generatio Clodouei regis quę usque tunc regnauerat.

Anno DCCXXV Karolus subiecit sibi Bagoarios, et Sarraceni irruerunt Galliam. Anno ab hinc vi Karolus perrexit in Suuanis contra Lanfredum. Sequenti anno Karolus fuit in Wasconia contra Eudonem, et Ragamfredus tyrannus mortuus est. Anno sequenti Karolus pugnauit contra Sarracenos in mense Octobri, die sabbati, iuxta ciuitatem Pictauis.[15] Iterum anno DCCXXXVII innumera multitudo Sarracenorum coadunata, quę xii reges habebat super se, quorum primus et maximus erat Abdirama rex Cordubę ciuitatis, occupauerunt Gothiam, obsederuntque Narbonam ciuitatem.[16] Quod audiens Karolus congregauit exercitum copiosum, insuper et Liudbrandum Langobardorum regem conuocauit in auxilium. Consertoque cum Sarracenis prelio, ita eos contriuit, ut de tanta multitudine uix aliquis potuerit euadere, sed et usque hodie gens illa truculenta Francorum formidat arma. Anno DCCXXXVIIII, Karolus intrauit in Prouinciam usque Massiliam,[17] inuasit Wasconiam, uastauit Fresiam, expugnauit Saxoniam, contriuit Alamanniam atque Bagoariam. Anno DCCXLI Karolus Tudites mortuus est, qui propterea appellatus est Tudites, quod est malleus fabri, quia sicut malleo uniuersa tunduntur ferramenta, ita Karolus omnia regna sibi uicina adtriuit.

Defuncto Karolo filii eius Karlomannus et Pipinus susceperunt curam regni.[18] Anno DCCXLII Karolus[19] perrexit Vasconiam. Anno sequenti uastauit Alamanniam. Anno iiii Karlomannus et Pipinus inuaserunt Saxoniam. Anno vii Karlomannus relicta cura regni Pipino fratri Romam perrexit, atque in Monte Sarapti monachus habitationem instituit. Postea non ferens molestiam crebro se uisitantium eorum qui de Francia pergebant ad limina apostolorum, ad Sanctum Benedictum in Montem Cassini[20] commigrauit. Anno DCCLII

13 Eudo was duke of Aquitaine. According to Fredegar's continuators, he was responsible for inviting into Francia the Saracens Charles ultimately defeated at Poitiers.

14 The chronicle's chronology is here confused. In the order named, the kings are Theoderic IV (721–737), son of Dagobert III; Chlothar IV (717–719); Childebert III (694–711), the father of Dagobert III; and Childeric III (743–751).

15 The famous battle of Poitiers, usually dated 732.

16 Narbonne, located in the region of Gothia.

17 Marseilles, in Provence.

18 After Charles Martel's death in 741, his sons Carloman and Pippin the Short became mayors of the palace for Frankish realms.

19 Carloman is clearly meant; the slip was made in the chronicle of St-Bénigne.

20 Montecassino, St Benedict's monastery in Italy.

domnus Pipinus rex sacratus est per manus Stephani pape et duo filii eius Karlomannus et Karolus, qui Magnus dictus est.[21]

Pipinus[22] igitur rex habuit quendam fratrem, nomine Remigium,[23] cui in Burgundia plurima loca concessit. Inter quę etiam res ad episcopatum ecclesię Lingonensis pertinentes, quas sicut sibi uisum est suis asseclis dimisit. Sed, o nefas! monasterium hoc Angle uxori cuiusdam Theotardi,[24] quia eius stupro potitus fuerat, non custodiendum, sed diripiendum dedit. Quam presumptionem ut dignum erat indigne ferentes monachi monasterium reliquerunt, preter paucos etatę et debilitate confectos. Reliqui uero Luxouium cenobium[25] expetiuerunt, aliaque monasteria in quibus nouerant ordinem monasticum permanere.

Predicta autem Angla res monasterii ut talem decebat disponebat. Ab ingressu autem sacrosancte basilice apostolorum senibus illis qui remanserant prohibentibus, aliquamdiu temperauit, sed postquam cetera sacra loca inpune temerauit, etiam ipsum oratorium audacter ingredi presumpsit, statimque quia contra Deum uesaniret, experta est. Nam ut a uiris fide dignis, qui ab eis qui presentes fuerunt et uiderunt et audierunt, comperimus. Statim ut ingressa est predictum oratorium inuisibili igni ardere cepit. Magnisque clamoribus se exuri uociferans, ut in fluuium Besuę qui iuxta decurrit deportaretur postulabat. Quod ilico factum est. Sed non ualuit talis aqua talem extinguere ignem. Tunc ad fontem misericordię cucurrit, predictis senibus monentibus et docentibus, sicque saluari meruit. Prius tamen temeritate confessa, emendationem in reliquo talis presumptionis promisit. Honorauit etiam predictum locum donariis quibus potuit, quorum quedam ob testimonium tanti ausus apud nos seruantur. Postquam autem remoto Remigio episcopatus Lingonensis episcopis legitimis cessit, hoc monasterium ab episcopo receptum est.

Sed non fuit illi cura digna pastore ut oues dispersas ad proprium ouile reuocaret, magis gaudens quod res monachis delegate in suos suorumque usus cederent.

21 In 754, several years after Pippin the Short had become king of the Franks (751–768), Pope Stephen II came to Francia and blessed him, along with his wife and two young sons, Charlemagne and Carloman. On this event, see Bouchard, "Childeric III and the Emperors Drogo Magnus and Pippin the Pious."

22 At this point, the bottom of fol. 29v, the chronicler of Bèze stopped following the chronicle of St-Bénigne (at p. 68 in the printed edition).

23 Remigius, son of Charles Martel and half-brother of Pippin the Short. He was bishop first of Langres and then of Rouen (753–762). See *Chronique des abbés de Fontenelle (Saint-Wandrille)* 8.2, p. 100.

24 Angla and her husband Theotard are not otherwise known. It is striking that the male monastery of Bèze should be given to a woman.

25 The monastery of Luxeuil.

Sicque monasticus ordo ex hoc loco penitus est deletus, nullique succedentium episcoporum cure fuit, ut pristinam religionem in hoc loco repararet, sed alii abbates canonici ordinis constituerunt, alii sibi seruiendum decreuerunt, donec ad piissimi augustę recordationis Hludouici[26] imperium uentum est.

Anno[27] iiii Pipinus rex intrauit Longobardiam, et Stephanus papa reuersus est Romam. Eodem tempore Sanctus Bonifacius genti Fresonum predicans suscepit martyrium.[28] Anno vi iterum Pipinus rex perrexit Langobardiam, et Aistulfus rex mortuus est. Anno sequenti delata sunt organa de Grecia, missa ab imperatore cum ceteris muneribus domno Pipino regi. Anno DCCLX Pipinus rex perrexit Wasconiam contra Waifarium.[29] Iterum anno sequenti cum filiis Karolo et Karlomanno perrexit Aquitaniam et adquisiuit ciuitatem Bituricas.[30]

Anno DCCLXII iterum Pipinus rex cum exercitu perrexit Aquitaniam una cum Karlomanno, captoque omni pago Aluernico, ciuitatem Claromontem et Burbonis[31] castrum igne cremauit. Anno DCCLXIIII Pipinus rex placitum magnum habuit cum Francis apud uillam Carisiacum.[32] Eodem anno fuit hiemps grauissima, et tenuit gelu anono x kalendas Ianuarii, usque vi kalendas Aprilis. Anno DCCLXVII iterum Pipinus rex intrauit Aquitaniam, et conquisiuit Lemouigas ciuitatem,[33] et Berta regina uxor eius apud Biruricas hiemauit eodem anno. Sequenti anno, uidelicet DCCLXVIII, Pipinus rex obiit viii kalendas Octobris apud Parisius ciuitatem, morbo intercutis aque, et Waifarius fuit interfectus.

Eodem anno domnus rex Karolus et Karlomannus uncti fuerunt in reges vii idus Octobris.[34] Franci[35] siquidem facto solempniter generali conuentu, ambos

26 Emperor Louis the Pious (814–830).

27 At this point, fol. 30v, the chronicler of Bèze once again began following the chronicle of St-Bénigne, picking up where he had left off (p. 68 of the printed edition).

28 Boniface, originally from Anglo-Saxon England, was killed in 754 while attempting to convert the Frisians.

29 Waifar, duke of Aquitaine, was grandson of Eudo, who had given Charles Martel a great deal of trouble.

30 Bourges. Here the chronicler of Bèze skips a paragraph in the chronicle of St-Bénigne (pp. 68–69 in the printed edition) detailing gifts to that monastery.

31 Clermont and Bourbon are in the Auvergne.

32 Quierzy-sur-Oise.

33 Limoges.

34 Charlemagne and his younger brother Carloman were initially both kings of the Franks after the death of their father, Pippin the Short, in 768, although, as Einhard relates, Carloman soon died (*Vie de Charlemagne*).

35 At this point the chronicler of St-Bénigne, and the chronicler of Bèze who copied his account, began drawing from Einhard, *Vie de Charlemagne*, at chapter 1.3, p. 4 in the printed edition. The chronicler added dates to Einhard's account, to make it more like annals. As he had with Fredegar, he condensed as he went.

sibi reges constituunt, ea conditione premissa ut totum regni corpus ex equo partirentur, et Karolus eam partem [quam pater eorum Pipinus tenuerat, Karlomannus uero eam partem][36] cui patruus eorum Karlomannus prefuerat, regendi gratia susciperet. Suscepte sunt utrimque conditiones, et pars regni diuisi iuxta modum sibi propositum ab utroque recepta est, mansitque ista quamuis cum summa difficultate concordia, multis ex parte Karlomanni societatem separare molientibus, adeo ut quidam eorum bella committere sint meditati. Sed in hoc plus suspicionis quam periculi fuisse, ipse rerum exitus approbauit. Defuncto Karlomanno uxor eius cum filiis et quibusdam qui ex optimatum eius numero primores erant Italiam fuga peciit, et nullis existentibus causis spreto mariti fratre, sub Desiderii regis Langobardorum patrocinium secum suis liberis contulit. Et Karlomannus quidem post administratum communiter quadriennio regnum decessit. Karolus autem fratre defuncto constituitur rex solus omnium Francorum.

Anno igitur DCCLXVIIII, sui uero regni secundo, omnium bellorum quę gessit primo Aquitanicum, a patre inchoatum sed nondum finitum, quia cito peragi posse uidebatur, fratre adhuc uiuo etiam et aliud ferre rogato suscepit. Et licet eum frater promisso frustrasset auxilio, susceptam tamen expeditionem strenuissime exsequutus, non prius ab incepto desistere uoluit, quam hoc quod efficere moliebatur perfecto fine concluderet. Nam et Hunaldum, qui post Waifarii mortem Aquitaniam occupauerat, bellumque iam pene peractum reparare tempauerat, Aquitaniam relinquere et Wasconiam petere coegit. Quem tamen ibi consistere non sustinens, transmisso amne Garomna, Lupo Wasconum duci mandat ut perfugam reddat, quod nisi festinato faciat, bello se eum expugnaturum, Lupus saniori usus consilio, non solum fugitiuum reddidit, sed etiam se ipsum cum Prouincia cui preerat eius potestati commisit. Compositis igitur rebus in Aquitania eoque bello finito, regni quoque socio iam rebus humanis exempto, precibus Adriani Romane urbis episcopi[37] exoratus, bullum contra Langobardos suscepit.

Anno DCCLXXII Karolus rex intrauit Italiam et concitato bello quod prius quidem et a patre eius, Stephano papa supplicante, cum magna difficultate susceptum est, quia quidam e primoribus Francorum cum quibus consultare solebat adeo uoluntati eius renisi sunt, ut se regem deserturos domumque redituros libera uoce proclamarent. Ceptum tamen est tunc contra Haistulfum regem et celerrime completum. Sed licet sibi et patri belli suscipiendi similis ac potius eadem causa subesse uideretur, haut simili tamen laborare certatum

36 Here the chronicle of Bèze accidentally skipped a phrase; I have supplied it from the chronicle of St-Bénigne, from which he was working.

37 Pope Hadrian I (772–795).

et fine constat esse completum. Pipinus siquidem Haistulfum regem paucorum dierum obsidione apud Ticinum[38] compulit et obsides dare, et erepta Romanis restituere, atque ut reddita non repeterentur sacramento fidem facere. Karolus uero post inchoatum a se bellum non prius destitit, quam et Desiderium regem, quem longa obsidione fatigauerat, in deditionem susciperat. Filium eius Adalgisum, in quem spes omnium inclinata uidebatur, non solum regno sed etiam Italiam excedere cogeret, omnia Romanis erepta restitueret. Chrodgausum Foroiulii[39] ducatus prefectum res nouas molientem opprimeret, et Stabilinum socerum eius Tarnisa ciuitate obsessum caperet, totamque Italiam subiugaret, subacteque filium suum Pipinum regem preficeret. Finis huius belli fuit subacta Italia, et rex Desiderius perpetuo deputatus exilio in Francia, filius eius Adalgisus Italia pulsus, et res a Langobardorum regibus ereptę, Adriano Romanę ecclesię rectori restitutę. Italiam intranti quam difficilis Alpium transitus fuerit, quanto labore Francorum in uia montium iuga et eminentes in cœlum scopuli, atque aspere cautes superate longum est enarrare.

Anno DCCLXXVI, rex Karolus ut audiuit quod Saxones iterum rebellassent contra Francos, commouit exercitum aduersus eos, bellumque, quod quasi intermissum uidebatur repetitum est. Saxones siquidem sicut omnes fere gentes Germaniam incolentes, et natura feroces et cultui demonum dediti, nostręque religioni contrarii, neque diuina neque humana iura uerentur transgredi. Suberant et cause quę cotidie pacem turbare poterant, termini uidelicet utrorumque ubique in plano positi in quibus cedes et rapina et incendia uicissim fieri non cessabant. Ob quam rem edificauerunt Franci in finibus Saxonum ciuitatem quam uocauerunt Karoli urbem. Susceptum uero est aduersus eos bellum, quod magna utrimque animositate, maiore tamen Saxonum quam Francorum dampno per continuos xxxiii annos gerebatur. Videntes Saxones quia non poterant Francis resistere, uenerunt maiores natu ad domnum regem Karolum postulantes pacem, et baptizata est multitudo populi ipsorum.

Anno DCCLXXVII gloriosus rex Karolus uenit Saxoniam loco qui uocatur Patris Brunna,[40] et habuit ibi placitum magnum, et ibi conuenerunt Saxones ad baptismum Catholicum. Edificaueruntque ibi ecclesiam Franci, multaque milia populorum ibi baptizata sunt, ea condicione a rege proposita et ab illis suscepta, ut abiecto demonum cultu et relictis patriis ceremoniis, Christiane fidei sacramenta susciperent, et Francis adunati unus cum eis populus efficerentur. Hoc bellum licet per multum temporis spacium traheretur, ipse non amplius cum hoste quam bis in acie conflixit, semel iuxta montem qui Osneggi dicitur

38 Pavia.
39 Friuli.
40 Paderborn.

in loco Theothmelli nominato, et iterum apud Alsa fluuium, et hoc uno mense paucis quoque interpositis diebus. His duobus preliis hostes adeo profligauit ac deuicti sunt, ut ulterius regem neque prouocare neque uenienti resistere auderent. Plures tamen eo bello tam ex nobilitate Francorum quam Saxonum, et functi summis honoribus uiri consumpti sunt. Rex itaque omnium qui sua etatę gentibus dominabantur et prudentia maximus, et animi magnitudine prestantissimus, nichil in his que uel suscipienda erant uel exequenda, aut propter laborem detractauit aut propter periculum exhorruit.

Anno DCCLXXVIII Karolus rex assiduo ac pene continuo cum Saxonibus bello decertans, dispositis per congrua confiniorum loca presidiis, Hispaniam adgreditur quam maximo poterat belli apparatu, saltuque Pirinei[41] superato, omnibus quę adiit oppidis atque castellis in deditionem acceptis, scilicet Pampilona, Osca, Barcilona, atque Gerunda. Deinde acceptis obsidibus saluo et incolumi exercitu reuertitur, preter quod in ipso Pirinei iugo Wasconam perfidiam parumper in redeundo expertus est. Nam cum agmine longo ut loci et angustiarum situs permittebat, porrectus iret exercitus, Wascones in summis montis uertice positis insidiis, est enim locus ex opacitate siluarum quarum ibi maxima est copia insidiis ponendis oportunus, extremam impedimentorum partem, et eos qui nouissimi agminis incedentes subsidio precedentes tuebantur, desuper incursantes in subiectam uallem deiciunt. Consertoque cum eis prelio usque ad unum omnes interficiunt, ac direptis inpedimentis, noctis beneficio que iam instabat, protecti, summa cum celeritate in diuersa disperguntur. In quo prelio Egichardus regię mensę prepositus, Anselmus comes palacii, et Ruodlandus Brittanici limitis prefectus, cum aliis compluribus interficiuntur. Domuit et Brittones qui ad occidentem in extrema quadam parte Gallie super litus Oceani residentes dicto audientes non erant, missa in eos expeditione qua et obsides dare et que inumgebantur se facturos polliceri coacti sunt.

Iterum Karolus rex Italiam ingressus cum exercitu ac per Romam iter agens, Capuam Campanie urbem accessit, atque ibi positis castris bellum Beneuentanis ni dederentur comminatus est. Preuenit hoc dux gentis Aragisus, filios suos Rumoldum et Grimoldum, cum magna pecunia obuiam regi mittens, rogat ut filios obsides suscipiat, seque cum gente imperata facturum pollicetur, preter hoc solum si ipse ad conspectum regis uenire non cogeretur. Rex utilitate gentis considerata et oblatos sibi obsides recepit, et que petebatur concessit, unoque ex filiis eius obsidatus gratia retento, legatos ob sacramenta a Beneuentanis exigenda atque suscipienda cum Aragiso dimissis Romam rediit, indeque Galliam reuertitur.

Anno DCCLXXXVII Baioaricum bellum et repente ortum, et celeri sine completum est, quod superbia Tassilonis ducis excitauit. Qui iuncto federę

41 The Pyrenees. The castles listed below are not in Einhard.

cum Hunis, qui Baioariis sunt ab oriente contermini, non solum imperata non facere, sed etiam bello regem prouocare temptabat. Cuius contumatiam animositas regis ferre nequiuit, ac proinde contractis undique copiis Baioariam petiturus, ad Lechum amnem cum maximo uenit exercitu. Is fluuius Baioarios ab Alamannis diuidit, cuius in ripa castris collocatis, animum ducis per legatos statuit experiri. Ille non pertinaciter agere uel sibi uel genti utile ratus, supplex se regi permisit, obsides dedit, inter quos et Theudonem filium suum. Data insuper fide cum iuramento, quod ab illius potestate ad defectionem nemini suadenti assentiri deberet. Sicque bello quod quasi maximum futurum uidebatur, celerrimus est finis impositus. Anno sequenti Tasilo dux ad regem euocatus, eo quod pactum uiolare conatus sit, non est redire permissus, neque regnum illud ulterius duci sed comitibus ad regendum est commissum. Anno xv regni Karoli regis obiit Hildegardis regina, coniux predicti principis, et Berticada mater ipsius eodem anno est defuncta.

Anno DCCLXXXVIIII bellum illatum est Sclauis, qui nostra consuetudine Wilei uel Winidi sua uero locutione Weletabi dicuntur. Causa belli erat quod Abotritos, qui cum Francis olim foederati erant, assidua incursione lacessebant, nec iussionibus coerceri poterant. Sinus quidam ab occidentali Oceano orientem uersus porrigitur, longitudinis quidem incomperte, latitudinis uero quę nusquam centum milia passuum excedat, cum in multis locis contractior inueniatur. Hunc multe circumsedent nationes, Dani sequidem ac Sueui, quos Nordmannos uocamus, et septemtrionale litus, et omnes in eo insulas tenent, at litus australe Sclaui et Agisti et alie diuerse incolunt nationes. Inter quos uel precipui sunt quibus tunc a rege bellum inferebatur Weletabi, quos ille una tantum et quam per se gesserat expeditione, ita contulit ac domuit, ut ulterius imperata facere minime rennuerent.

Anno DCCXCI, rex Karolus commoto magno exercitu bellum Hunis intulit. Quod maximum omnium quę ab illo gesta sunt bellorum preter Saxonicum fuit, quod ille et animosius quam cetera et longe maiori apparatu administrauit. Vnam tamen per se expeditionem in Pannoniam, quam prouinciam ea gens incolebat, tunc fecit, cetera filio suo Pipino ac prefectis prouinciarum, comitibus etiam perficienda atque legatis commisit. Quod cum ab his strenuissime fuisset administratum, octauo tandem anno completus est. Tota in hoc bello Hunorum nobilitas periit, tota gloria decidit, omne ecsprecium,[42] et congesti ex longo thesauri direpti sunt. Neque ullum bellum contra Francos exhortum humana potest memoria recordari, quo illi magis ditati et opibus aucti sunt. Tantum auri et argenti in regia repertum, tot spolia preciosa in preliis sublata,

42 The phrase "omne ecsprecium" is doubtless an error. The scribe half erased and rewrote it. In the chronicle of St-Bénigne it reads "pecunia," and "omnes pecunia" in Einhard.

ut merito credi possit hoc Francos Hunnis iuste eripuisse, quod illi ceteris gentibus iniuste abstulerant. Duo tantum ex proceribus Francorum eo bello interierunt, Hericus dux Foro Iulii et Hierulus[43] Baioarie prefectus. Ceterum incruentum pene Francis hoc bellum fuit, et prosperum exitum habuit, tam etsi diutius sui magnitudine traheretur. Post quod et Saxonicum sue prolixitati conuenientem finem accepit. Boemanicum quoque et Linonicum que postea exorta sunt diu durare non potuerunt. Quorum utrumque ductu Karoli filii sui, quem Burgundię regno prefecerat, celeri fine completum est.[44]

Rex autem Karolus ultimum bellum egit contra Nordmannos quidam uocantur. Qui primo quidem piraticam exercentes, deinde maiori classe adgregata littora Gallie atque Germanię uastabant. Quorum rex Gotefridus adeo uana spe inflatus erat, ut sibi totius Germanię potestatem promitteret, Frisiam quoque atque Saxoniam haut aliter quam suas prouincias estimabat. Iam autem Abodritos uicinos suos in suam ditionem redegerat. Iactabat etiam se breui Aquisgrani,[45] ubi regis comitatus erat, cum maximis copiis aduenturum. Nec dictis eius fides abnuebatur, quin potius uerba sequeretur effectus operis, nisi festinata fuisset morte preuentus. Nam a suo satellite interfectus, belli a se inchoati celerem finem imposuit.

Hęc sunt bella quę rex potentissimus per annos quadraginta et septem tot enim annis regnauit, in diuersis terrarum partibus summa prudentia atque felicitate gessit, quibus regnum Francorum quod post patrem Pipinum magnum quidem et forte susceperat ita nobiliter ampliauit, ut pene duplum illi adiecerit.

Nam cum prius non amplius quam ea pars Gallie quę inter Rhenum et Ligerim Oceanumque ac mare Balearicum iacet, et pars Germanie que inter Saxoniam et Danubium Hrenumque ac Salam fluuium[46] qui Thuringos et Sorabos diuidit posita, a Francis qui orientales dicuntur incolitur, et preter hęc Alamanni atque Baioarii ad regnum Francorum pertinerent. Ipse per bella memorata primo Aquitaniam et Wasconiam, totumque Pirinei montis iugum, et usque ad Hiberum amnem qui apud Nauarro ortus et fertilissimos Hispanie agros secans, sub Dertose[47] ciuitatis męnia Balearico mari miscetur. Deinde Italiam totamque ab Augusta Pretoria[48] usque in Calabriam inferiorem, in qua Grecorum ac Beneuentanorum constat esse confinia, decies centum et eo amplius passuum

43 Einhard reads "Geraldus."

44 Here the chronicler of Bèze skips a section of the chronicle of St-Bénigne (pp. 78–82 in the printed edition) which concerns the history of that house.

45 Aachen.

46 The Danube, Rhine, and Saale rivers.

47 Tortosa.

48 Aosta.

milibus longitudine porrigitur. Tum Saxoniam que quidem Germanię pars non modica est, et eiusque a Francis incolitur duplum in lato habere putatur, cum ei longitudine possit esse consimilis. Postquam utramque Pannoniam et adpositam ex altera parte Danubii Daciam, Histriam quoque et Liburniam[49] atque Dalmatiam, exceptis maritimis ciuitatibus quas ob amicitiam et iunctum cum eo foedus Constantinopolitanum imperatorem habere permisit.

Deinde omnes barbaras ac feras nationes que inter Renum ac Visulam fluuios,[50] Oceanumque ac Danubium posite, lingua quidem pene similes, moribus uero atque habitu ualde dissimiles, Germaniam incolunt, ita perdomuit ut eas tributarias efficeret, inter quas fere precipue sunt Weletabi, Sorabi, Abodriti, Boemani, cum his namque bello conflixit. Ceteras quarum multo maior est numerus in dedicionem accepit.

Auxit etiam gloriam regni sui quibusdam regibus ac gentibus per amicitiam sibi conciliatis. Adeo namque Adefonsum Gallicie atque Asturice regem[51] sibi societate deiunxit, ut is cum ad eum litteras uel legatos mitteret, non aliter illum quam proprium dominum suum appellari iuberet. Scottorum quoque reges sic habuit ad suam uoluntatem per munificentiam inclinatos, ut eum numquam aliter nisi Dominum seque subditos, et seruos eius pronuntiarent. Cum Aaron rege Persarum,[52] qui excepta India totum pene tenebat Orientem, talem habuit in amicitia concordiam, ut is gratiam eius omnium qui in toto orbe terrarum erant regum ac principum amicitię preponeret, solum que illum honore ac munificentia sibi colendum iudicaret. Imperatores etiam Constantinopolitani, Nicoforus, Michael, et Leo,[53] ultro amicitiam et societatem eius expetentes, complures ad eum misere legatos. Cum quibus tamen propter susceptum a se imperatoris nomen et ob hoc quasi imperium eis eripere uellet, ualde suspectus, foedus firmissimum statuit, ut nulla inter partes cuiuslibet scandali remaneret occasio. Erat enim semper Romanis et Grecis Francorum suspecta potentia.

Habuit uxorem nomine Hildegardam de gente Sueuorum, precipue nobilitatis feminam, de qua tres filios, Karolum scilicet, Pipinum, et Ludoicum, totidemque filias Hruodtridem, et Berethtam et Gislam genuit. Defuncta Hildegarda Fasteradam duxit uxorem, de qua habuit duas filias, Theoderadam et Hildrudem, que de orientalium Francorum Germanorum uidelicet gente erat. Qua obeunte, Leudgardam Alemannam duxit. Post cuius mortem, tres habuit

49 The manuscript reads "Liburnia."

50 The Vistula river.

51 Alfonso, king of Galicia and Asturia.

52 The caliph Haroun-al-Raschid.

53 Emperors Nicoforus I, Michael I, and Leo V.

concubinas, Gersuindam, Adalindam, et Reginam, que ei Drogonem et Hugum genuit.[54]

Ex his omnibus duos tantum filios et unam filiam priusquam moreretur amisit, Karolum et Pipinum quem Italie regem prefecerat, et Ruodtrudem que filiarum eius primogenita, et a Constantino Grecorum imperatore desponsata erat. Erat ei filius nomine Pipinus ex concubina editus, facie quidem pulcher, sed gibbo deformis. Is cum pater bello contra Hunos suscepto in Bauuaria hiemaret, egritudine simulata cum quibusdam e primoribus Francorum qui eum uana regni promissione illexerant aduersus patrem coniurauit. Quem post fraudem detectam et coniuratorum dampnationem, detonsum in cœnobio Prumia[55] religiose iamque uolentem uacare permisit.

Facta est et alia prius contra eum in Germania ualida coniuratio, cuius auctores partim luminibus orbati, partim membris incolumes, omnes tamen exilio deportati sunt. Neque ullus ex eis est interfectus nisi tres tantum, qui cum se ne comprehenderentur strictis gladiis defenderent, aliquos etiam occidissent, quia aliter coherceri non poterant interempti sunt. Harum tamen coniurationum Fastrade regine crudelitas causa et origo extitisse creditur, et idcirco in ambabus contra regem conspiratum est, quia uxoris crudelitati consentiens, a naturę suę benignitate ac solita mansuetudine immaniter exorbitasse uidebatur.[56]

Colebat preceteris sacris et uenerabilibus locis apud urbem Romam Beati Petri apostoli ęcclesiam, in cuius donaria magna uis pecunie tam in auro quam in argento, necnon et gemmis, ab illo congesta est, multa et innumera pontificibus munera missa. Neque ille toto regni sui tempore quicquam duxit antiquius, quam ut urbs Roma suo labore ueteri polleret auctoritate, et ecclesia Sancti Petri per illum non solum tuta ac defensa, sed etiam suis opibus pre omnibus ecclesiis esset ornata atque ditata. Quam cum tanti penderet, tamen intra quadraginta septem annorum spacium quibus regnauit, quater tantum illo uotorum soluendorum ac supplicandi causa profectus est. Vltimi aduentus sui non solum he fuere cause, uerum etiam quod Romani Leonem pontificem[57] multis affectum iniuriis, erutis scilicet oculis linguaque amputata, fidem regis implorare compulerunt. Idcirco Romam ueniens propter reparandum qui nimis conturbatus erat, ecclesię statum, ibi totum hiemis tempus extraxit, quo tempore imperatoris et augusti nomen accepit.[58]

54 Following Einhard, the chronicler leaves out Charlemagne's first wife, mother of Pippin the Hunchback, as well as his brief second marriage to the daughter of the king of the Lombards. Einhard appears to have been the first to label Pippin a hunchback.

55 Prüm.

56 Here the chronicler skips the personal information on Charlemagne in Einhard's chapters 21–26.

57 Pope Leo III (795–816).

58 The chronicle is here rather laconic on Charlemagne's coronation as emperor on Christmas Day 800.

Extremo uite tempore cum iam et morbo et senectute premeretur, euocatum ad se Hlugdouicum filium Aquitanię regem, qui solus filiorum Hildegarde supererat, congregatis sollempniter de toto regno Francorum primoribus, cunctorum consilio consortem sibi tocius regni et imperialis nominis heredem constituit. Impositoque capiti eius diademate imperatorem et augustum iussit appellari. Susceptum est hoc eius consilium ab omnibus qui aderant, magno cum fauore. Nam diuinitus ei propter regni utilitatem uidebatur inspiratum, auxitque maiestatem eius hoc factum, et exteris nationibus non minimum terroris incussit.

Decessit anno ab incarnatione Domini octingentesimo quintodecimo, etatis uero sue septuagesimo secundo, et ex quo regnare cęperat quadragesimo septimo, v kalendas Februarii. Appropinquantis finis complura fuere prodigia, ut non solum alii sed etiam ipse hoc minitari sentiret. Per tres namque continuos uiteque termino proximos annos, et solis et lune creberrima defectio, et in sole macula quedam atri coloris septem dierum spacio uisa est. Ipse quoque cum ultimam in Saxonia expeditionem contra Gotefridum regem Danorum ageret, quadam die cum ante solis ortum castris egressus iter agere cepisset, uidit repente delapsam celitus facem cum ingenti lumine, a dextra in sinistram per serenum aerem transcurrere. Cunctisque hoc signum quod portenderet ammirantibus, subito equus quem sedebat capite deorsum merso cecidit, eumque tam grauiter ad terram elisit, ut fibula sagi rupta, balteoque gladii dissipato, a festinantibus qui aderant ministris exarmatus, et sine amminiculo leuaretur. Iaculum etiam quod tunc forte manu tenebat ita elapsum est, ut uiginti uel eo amplius pedum spacio longe iaceret.

Sepultus est in basilica quam ipse Aquisgrani palacii edificauerat, propter amorem Dei et Domini nostri Ihesu Christi, et ob honorem Sanctę et perpetue uirginis genitricis eius Marię. In hac sepultus est eadem qua defunctus est die. Arcusque supra tumulum deauratus extructus est, cum imagine et titulo hoc modo descripto, "Sub hoc conditorio situm est corpus Karoli Magni atque orthodoxi imperatoris, qui regnum Francorum nobiliter ampliauit, et per annos quadraginta septem feliciter rexit."

Post[59] cuius excessum, Ludouicus cognomento Pius adeptus sedem imperii, magno moderamine per annos uiginti quinque Francorum regnum disposuit. Et fines regni quos pater eius pugnando longe lateque dilatauit, hic sapienter preuidendo undique ab hostibus custodiuit. Nam et Grecorum calliditates et cauillationes prudenti consilio deuitauit, et Sarracenorum perfidiam, qui ab Hispanię partibus erumpere cupiebant, fortiter compescuit, et Danorum audaciam potenti uirtute terruit. Habuit filios tres, Lotharium, Ludouicum, atque Pipinum. Defuncta coniuge priori duxit aliam Iudit nomine, ex qua suscepit

59 At this point the chronicle stops following Einhard.

Karolum.[60] Diuisiones uero regni inter liberos ita fecit, ut Lotharius qui maior natu erat cui et imperii concessit, insignia post se regnum Italie obtineret, et partem Francie quam Mosa et Renus flumina inter se includunt, partemque Burgundie. Ludouicus uero Germaniam, hoc est Bauuariam et Saxoniam, et reliqua regna quę Karolus Magnus pater suus bellando subegerat, id est Pannoniam, Daciam, Histriam, Liburniam, atque Dalmaciam, barbaras quoque gentes quas tributarias fecerat, Weletabos, Sorabos, Abodritos, Boemanos, et reliquos quos longum est enumerare. Has omnes gentes memoratus Augustus Ludouicus omni tempore uite sue habuit subiectas. Pipino etiam concessit regnum Aquitanie cum Wasconia, et omnem terram usque Hispaniam quam Karolus subiugauerat.

Karolus qui minimus erat natu adeptus est Franciam et Burgundiam atque Neustriam, de qua re indignati sunt fratres sui, uel quia ex alia matre natum nolebant eum sibi equari, uel quod principalis et melior pars regni ei conlata fuisset a patre. Vnde post mortem Augusti graue exortum est bellum inter eos, sed quamuis in hac pugna uires exercituum Francorum contriuerint, et exteris nationibus occasionem rebellandi contulerint, tamen quod a patre eorum factum fuerat immutare non ualuerunt. Ad extremum Karolus regnum etiam Aquitanię obtinuit. Pipino siquidem ante patrem defuncto, remansit filius Pipinus et ipse uocatus. Quem minus utilem ad regnum gubernandum uidentes primates sui et principes, ad Karolum se contulerunt.

In[61] diebus Hlucdouuici imperatoris episcopus Lingonensis, Betto nomine, fecit quasdam diuisiones de terra Sancti Petri, sicut hic demonstrabimus.

6

Montigny, May 816

Count Hildegarn, at the request of Bishop Betto of Langres, defines the boundaries and property of Bèze in a public court. Nine witnesses swear to the details. They declare that all of this belonged to Bèze under Pippin the Short and Charlemagne and that Aldo and his heirs have no right to it.

---

60 As the chronicler goes on to relate, Louis the Pious (814–840) divided his realm between his four sons, Lothar receiving the imperial crown along with Italy and the part of Francia between the Rhine and Moselle, while Louis was assigned Germany and eastern regions, Pippin Aquitaine and Gascony, and Charles (born to the emperor's second wife) Francia, Burgundy, and Neustria.

61 The chronicler of Bèze had been copying the chronicle of St-Bénigne for some time, but here, on fol. 38v, he left that chronicle (p. 90 in the printed version) for information on his own monastery.

Cartulary, fols. 38v–39v.
Bougaud-Garnier, pp. 250–251.
Summarized in Brequigny, *Table* 1:150; dated 2 May 815.

Notum fiat posteris et memorie commendetur quod ante illustrem uirum Hildegarnum comitem, seu iudices quos scabineos uocant, et quamplures personas qui cum eo aderant in Montaniaco uilla[1] in mallo publico ad multorum causas audiendas, et rectas iusticias terminandas, ibi ueniens Betto episcopus[2] et aduocatus suus Burgoardus, nouem legitimos testes ibi presentauit, quorum nomina hec sunt, Symeon, Agano, Betrannus, Gono, Marchirius, Adalardus, Geruio, Gerento, Syrannus. Isti testificauerunt et iurauerunt de finibus Besuensis monasterii, quod a fine Pontense[3] et a fine Vendobrinse seu Vilense, et Vetus Vendobrinse et Vaurinse,[4] et Tillense et Vetus Viniense et Bustellense et Bustense et Lucense, et Burbureninse et Berechelpo Vilare,[5] per istas marcas inter ipsos fines immunitas Sancti Petri est ad integrum. Et in loco qui dicitur Boscus Monachorum, similiter et in alio loco qui dicitur Longo Bosco[6] immunitas Sancti Petri ad integrum. Et in alio Longo Bosco communitas. Et in ipso fine Bustellense immunitas ad integrum, et ab ipso fine Bustellense usque ad uiam petrosam, et deinde usque ad stratam fractam[7] et deinde usque ad finem Burburenensem atque Vilarum, immunitas Sancti Petri est ad integrum. Per istas marcas euntes ipsi nouem testes, quos supra nominauimus, misso secum Balacterio illustri uiro ab Hildegarno comite et a suis scabineis, dixerunt et per iudicium testificauerunt quod a tempore Pipini regis et deinceps per tempus

1 Montigny, 17 km northeast of Bèze.

2 Betto, bishop of Langres (791–820).

3 The places indicated as marking the bounds of Bèze's immunity are not listed in a line, but those that can be identified do form a rough circle around the monastery. A number of the names refer to places that are not found again in the monks' records, which is probably an indication of the authenticity of this document. "Pontensis" is one of the unidentified places; it may refer to a bridge over the Venelle, whose source is 5 km northwest of Bèze.

4 The village now known as Véronnes, 7 km north-northwest of Bèze, is composed of two sections, less than a kilometre apart, of which one was considered "old" and one "new" in the ninth century. The newer portion is here called "Vilensis," the older portion "Vaurinsis."

5 Tilchâtel, 9 km northwest of Bèze; Viévigne, 4 km southwest of Bèze; the nearby ruined village of Buteau (its name given in two forms); Lux, 5 km northwest of Bèze; and Bourberain, 4 km north-northeast of Bèze. The last place named is unidentified.

6 The "woods of the monks" would have been that adjacent to Bèze. The "long woods" is generally identified with the woods of Velours, which runs north-south for some distance, west of the monastery.

7 The "stony way" and the "broken street" were most likely old Roman roads; two ran from Mirebeau, near Bèze.

domni Karoli Magni imperatoris[8] uidissent inde legitimas uestituras ad partem Sancti Petri haberi, ita ut nec Aldo, nec heredes sui ullam legitimam uestituram exinde umquam habuissent, sed per legem et per iusticiam uestitura Sancti Petri Fontis Besuensis erat. Tunc ipsi scabinei unanimiter iudicauerunt, quod omni tempore ipse res per illas marchas ad partem Sancti Petri essent uendicate atque legibus conquisite.

His praesentibus testibus: Balacterio,[9] Madalberto, Beato, Eppleno, Baldrico, Aysono, Vormerio, Milone, Albrico notario, Ferlagio, Leuduino, Arberto, Seruio. Walterius presens fuit et subscripsit. Data noticia die Mercoris proxima in mense Maio, anno ii regnante domno nostro Hlucdouuico rege atque imperatore.[10]

This document is dated by Louis the Pious.

7

819

Betto, bishop of Langres, and Viscount Balactarius attest that thirteen witnesses have spelled out what Bèze has near Autrey. The viscount acts on behalf of Count Hildegarn.

Cartulary, fols. 39v–40r.
Bougaud-Garnier, p. 252.

Noticia qualiter ante Bettonem episcopum[1] et Balactarium uicecomitem ad uicem Hildegarni comitis seu scauineorum qui ibidem aderant, ueniens Bornardus aduocatus[2] monasterii Sancti Petri Fonti Besuae et Betto episcopus in fines Bodingis uillę et Alteriaci uillę,[3] ibi dedit tredecim testes appellatos his nominibus, Vrsnaldum, Aglardum, Gairindum, Marcherium, Aggonem, Symeonem, Garinum, Adalardum, Sirannum, Winierium, Vlgerium, Amalerium, Flauminum. Isti testificauerunt quod inter illas ueteres uias, quarum una pergit de Alteriaco uilla ad Colonias uillam, et altera pergit de Furto uilla ad

8 Pippin the Short (751–768) and his son, Charlemagne (768–814).
9 He was Count Hildegarn's viscount; see the following document.
10 Emperor Louis the Pious (814–830).
1 Betto, bishop of Langres (791–820).
2 It seems most likely that he is the same person as the advocate Burgoardus of the previous document.
3 Autrey is 17 km east-northeast of Bèze, and Bouhans is 2 km southeast of there.

Willarum,[4] inter istas duas uias usque ad locum qui dicitur Vaccaria, et illum fontem qui dicitur Springus,[5] terra Sancti Petri est, tam in campis, quam in siluis, et semper exinde uestita fuerit ipsa casa Dei, monasterium scilicet Sancti Petri Besuensis, per legem et per rectum.

Actum his presentibus, Madalberto, Adalelmo, Balacterio uicecomite, Vrsnado, Gunduino, Flaumiro, Siranno, Aglardo, Marcherio, Aggone, Giruio, Adalardo, Winierio, Vlgerio, Bettone uicario et misso ab Hyldegarno comite, Zizone, Vnibaldo, Hugberto, Aribasto, Vcbalto, Angalberto, Laifino. Ego Aldoerius lector hanc noticiam scripsi, anno iiii imperii domni nostri Hlucdouuici regis atque imperatoris.[6]

In the two preceding documents the bishop of Langres sought to determine the property of Bèze, which appears to have lost its regular life during the preceding century, as there were no surviving records for the house from the eighth century, and there were no monks there when the bishop acted. In fact, regular life was not re-established until 830, under Bishop Betto's successor. The Aldo who claimed the house's property as his has not been further identified.

Because much of the property listed here was not later claimed by the monks, there is no reason to doubt these charters' authenticity. There is a fair amount of overlap between the people who appear in them.

Cum uero inimicus totius boni diabolus conspexisset hoc Besuense monasterium religione florere, indoluit terrigenas illuc humilitate et obędientia conscendere, unde ipse superbia et inobedientia corruerat. Egit itaque ut monasticus ordo ex hoc loco penitus deletus esset. Nec hoc parui temporis interuallo, sed a tempore Pipini regis et tempore Karoli usque ad tempus domni Hlucdouuici imperatoris durauit. Hic enim Bettone episcopo defuncto, Albericum uirum dignum episcopatu ecclesię Lingonensi constituit,[7] qui hunc locum tali ex causa noscitur restaurasse.

Erat predictus episcopus in Besua sanus et hilaris, cum subito grauissimo dolore intestinorum corripitur, nullumque remedium tanti cruciatus consequi

4 The road from Autrey to Colonge, which is 13 km southeast of Bèze and 8 km southwest of Autrey; and the road from Feurg, which is 18 km east of Bèze, to Velet, which is 23 km east-southeast of Bèze and 6 km southeast of Feurg.

5 These places are not identified, although there are several streams, ponds, and fountains in the vicinity.

6 Emperor Louis the Pious (814–830).

7 Alberic, bishop of Langres (821–838).

poterat. Medicis autem multum laborantibus et nichil proficientibus, desperare cępit et de sola morte cogitare. Omnibus autem suis gementibus et flentibus et mortem eius expectantibus, ipse in somnum deductus est. Viditque in somnis uenire ad se ueneranda canitię reuerendum uirum, a quo cum interrogaretur quomodo se haberet, respondit ut erat, nimiis doloribus urgueri ad mortem. Tum ille requisiuit quam mercedem retribueret illi, qui ei a Domino, non solum uitam impetraret, sed et salutem et diuturnitatem. Respondit, quamuis nulla recompensatio digna esset talibus promissis, tantum quantum posset et ab illo imperaretur, rependeret. Tum ille senex, "Monasterium hoc," inquid, "sub meo et fratris mei Pauli nomine Domino consecratum fuit, et bonis fratribus ac Deum timentibus monachis habitatum. Nunc uero ut ipse cernis desolatum est. Promitte ergo mihi ut hunc locum restaures, et monasticum ordinem in eo repares, et tibi a Domino salutem impetrabo." Promisit sub iure iurando, et a somno excitatus est. Statimque eum omnis dolor deseruit, ac si illis diebus nullum esset expertus cruciatum, surrexit sanus, luctusque omnium in gaudium conuersus est. Retulit quid uiderat, quid etiam ipse promiserat, et sub qua conditione salutem meruerit.

Precatur omnes ut adiutores existerent ad implendam promissionem. Quanto autem studio, quantaque cura memor iuramenti et promissionis, hoc monasterium reparauerit, melius ipsa opera quam uerba testantur. Monachos ex monasteriis sumptos adunauit, abbatem prefecit, et non solum res ad ipsum monasterium pertinentes restituit, sed et alias res de episcopatu ecclesię suę, cum consilio synodi prouincialis, et consensu ecclesię sue subiecit. Hic itaque Albericus episcopus timens quod experimento didicerat de eodem Besuensi monasterio, ne de rebus quas ei donauerat per successorum prauam peruasionem iterum spoliaretur, studuit non tantum sua, sed etiam regali auctoritate confirmare, quecumque ad presens sua uel in posterum aliorum fidelium munificentia possideret. Adiit itaque Hlucdouuicum imperatorem, et super hac re regale preceptum quesiuit. Annuit imperator, et sicut scriptum est infra, sua auctoritate confirmauit.

8

830

Emperors Louis the Pious and Lothar confirm, at the request of Bishop Alberic of Langres, that the bishop has restored Bèze, which had lost its regularity and fallen into ruin. He has reconstructed the house, brought in monks, made Seraphim the abbot, and made them gifts. Alberic also confirms gifts from others, including churches, all of which the emperors enumerate.

Cartulary, fols. 41r–42v.
Bougaud-Garnier, pp. 254–257.
Louis the Pious, *Diplomata*, RHGF 6:565–666, no. 157.
Louis the Pious, *Diplomata ecclesiastica*, PL 104:1186–1187, no. 152, from RHGF.
Mansi, *Sacrorum conciliorum collectio*, vol. 14, cols. 627–628.
Labbe and Cossart, *Sacrosancta concilia*, vol. 7, cols. 1670–1672.
Summarized in Böhmer, *Regesta imperii*, vol. 1, p. 349, no. 878 (849).
Summarized in Brequigny, *Table* 1:179.

Preceptum Hlucdouuici imperatoris

In nomine Domini Dei et Saluatoris nostri Ihesu Christi, Hlucdouuicus et Hlotharius diuina ordinante prouidentia imperatores augusti.[1] Si peticionibus seruorum Dei iustis et rationabilibus diuini cultus amore fauemus, superna nos gratia muniri non diffidimus. Proinde comperiat omnium fidelium nostrorum, presentium scilicet ac futurorum sollertia, quia suggessit mansuetudini nostre uir uenerabilis Albericus Lingonensis ecclesię presul,[2] qualiter quandam abbatiam cuius uocabulum est Fons Besuus ex rebus uidelicet episcopatus sui, ubi condam monachi regulariter uiuentes fuerant, sed moderno tempore penitus erat destructa, a fundamentis reedificauit, edificia congrua construxit, monachos adunauit, abbatem etiam eis nomine Seraphin prefecit. Et ut monachi in eodem loco Domino adiuuante congregati melius et liberius sub norma sanctę regulę Deo militarent, non solum res que ad predictam abbatiam legaliter pertinebant ibi reddidit, sed etiam alias res de prefato episcopatu ibidem subiecit.

Sed et constitutionis cartulam, quam ipse una per consensum metropolitani sui Agobardi archiepiscopi[3] et suffraganeorum suorum, necnon et cleri sibi subiecti, et quorumdam laicorum nobilium confirmauerat nobis ostendit, in qua plenius conscriptum erat, non solum res ad iam dictam abbatiam legaliter pertinentes ibi reddidisse, uerum etiam ei quasdam res de memorato episcopatu suo ibidem subiecisse quarum hęc sunt nomina: Pauliacum cum appenditiis suis, Bellenauum uicum cum suis appenditiis, Arcionem[4] cum appenditiis suis. Istas uillas cum omnibus adiacentiis, seu et omni re superposita, campis, pratis,

1 Emperors Louis the Pious (814–840) and his son Lothar I (840–855). Lothar had become co-emperor in 817.
2 Alberic, bishop of Langres (821–838).
3 Agobard, archbishop of Lyon (816–840).
4 Pouilly, 15 km northeast of Bèze; Belleneuve, 12 km south of Bèze; and Arçon, 1 km east of there.

siluis, pomiferis, pascuis, accessibus aquis, aquarumque decursibus, et omnes redditus totum ad integrum, una cum mancipiis, libertis, cum omni peculio ipsorum una cum acolabus dedit ad seruitium monachorum iure perpetuo ad possidendum.

Ecclesiam etiam que est in ipsa Belenauo uilla, in honore Sancti Stephani, prorsus ab omni consuetudinali exactione liberrimam. Ecclesiam quoque de uilla que dicitur Danbrum cum appenditiis suis, et uillam Danblin[5] cum ecclesia et omnibus appenditiis suis. Et uillam Trescasas[6] cum ecclesia et omnibus appenditiis suis. Item ecclesiam de uilla que dicitur Sancti Sequani[7] cum appenditiis suis. Et ecclesiam de uilla Morniaco cum omnibus ad eam pertinentibus. Necnon etiam ecclesiam que est in ualle Verona in honore Sancti Mauricii. Ecclesiam de uilla Beria in honore Sancti Laurentii, cum omnibus appenditiis suis.[8] Preterea in territorio Diuionensi[9] decimas illarum uinearum quas donauerat huic ecclesię domnus Amalgarius dux et fundator huius sacri cęnobii. Apud uillam quę dicitur Fiscinis[10] uinearum non modicam quantitatem, cum pratis et campis et seruis et ancillis ad ea excolenda. Et in uilla Fisciaco uineas similiter, et in Marcennaco[11] similiter.

Horum omnium facta donatione precibus quibus ualuit exorans nostram clementiam, ut super eandem constitutionem nostram auctoritatem firmitatis gratia mereretur habere, qualiter predictus locus, quem pro diuino amore et nostra elemosina restaurauit, et monachos ibi congregauit, qui pro nobis et cuncto populo nobis subiecto perpetim Domini misericordiam exorent, nostra auctoritate confirmatus esset, uidelicet ut si cuilibet successorum eius animo sederit, ut alias res ibi superaddere uelit in suo iure et potestate, salua discretionis ratione id faciendi permaneret, sin autem sua deuotio quę per consilium tantorum bonorum uirorum facta et confirmata est, nostro liberalitatis precepto firma et stabilis permaneret.

Cuius peticionem dignam ac rationabilem iudicantes, hos nostros imperiales apices fieri iussimus, per quos decernimus atque iubemus ut memoratus ordinationis modus quem predictus uenerabilis Albericus episcopus in prefato loco constituit, inuiolabilis permaneat. Et nullus rector qui in eodem loco

5 Drambon, 17 km south-southeast of Bèze. The two twelfth-century places have been united in one modern village.

6 Trochères, 14 km south-southeast of Bèze.

7 St-Seine-sur-Vingeanne, 13 km northeast of Bèze.

8 Mornay, 16 km northeast of Bèze; Véronnes, 7 km north-northwest of Bèze; and Beire, 8 km southwest of Bèze.

9 Dijon is 24 km southwest of Bèze.

10 Fixin, 10 km southwest of Dijon.

11 Fixey, 9.5 km southwest of Dijon; and Marsannay, 7 km southwest of Dijon.

successerit, licentiam habeat prescriptum ordinem permutare aut res quas ibi reddidit siue subiecit ullo modo auferre, sed eius constitutio per hanc nostram confirmationem firma et stabilis permaneat. Et ut hęc auctoritas confirmationis nostre per futura tempora inuiolabilem atque inconuulsam obtineat firmitatem, de anulo nostro subter illam iussimus assignari.

Signum Ludouici[12] imperatoris.
Signum Lotharii filii eius.
Actum anno ab incarnatione Domini octingentesimo XXX, indictione viii, epacta xv.

Suscepta deinde regali auctoritate Albericus episcopus confirmatisque ut prediximus rebus rediens domum, ut presentibus notum atque futuris fieret, propriam inde conscriptionem fecit, in qua omnia quę huic cenobio donauerat, queque in posterum futurorum fidelium largitate donanda sperabat inserens, sic ait.

9

Langres, 20 November 830

Bishop Alberic of Langres issues his own charter for Bèze. In it he recalls its foundation by Duke Amalgarius and confirms everything spelled out in the imperial charter attesting to the house's refoundation, with the assent of regional bishops.

Cartulary, fols. 42v–44r.
Bougaud-Garnier, pp. 257–260.
Mansi, *Sacrorum conciliorum collectio*, vol. 14, cols. 628–630.
Labbe and Cossart, *Sacrosancta concilia*, vol. 7, cols. 1672–1673.
Summarized in Brequigny, *Table* 1:178.

Carta domni Alberici episcopi

In nomine Domini nostri Ihesu Christi. Notum sit omnibus fidelibus sancte Dei ecclesie quod ego Albericus, dono Dei episcopus Lingonensium,[1] rępperi locum iam dirutum quod dicitur Fons Besuus, in honore constructum sanctorum apostolorum Petri et Pauli, necnon et aliorum plurimorum, ubi iam olim monachi regulariter Deo famulati fuerant sub Amalgario duce, permittente

12 Done as a monogram.
1 Alberic, bishop of Langres (821–838). The priests signing at the end of the document are most likely members of the Langres cathedral chapter.

Chlotario rege.[2] Ideoque ob amorem Dei et ueniam delictorum meorum, Deo inspirante, cogitaui reędificare supradictum locum, permittente gloriosissimo augusto Hlucdouico et consentiente piissimo filio eius Hlothario imperatore.[3] Congregaui ibi monachos sub abbate nomine Seraphin, qui ibi regulariter degerent et Deo in perpetuum fideliter deseruirent. Concessi enim eis quicquid supradictus locus per cartarum donationem assecutus est, et quicquid nostri predecessores de hoc loco abstraxerant, propter elemosinam supradicti principis eiusque filiorum libenter restauraui. Ideoque per consilium archiepiscopi nostri Agobardi[4] et consentientibus coepiscopis nostris necnon et piissimis nostris principibus, seu omni clero nostro, necnon et omnibus fidelibus ecclesię nostrę, addidimus supradicto loco de episcopatu nostro uillas his nominibus, Pauliacum cum appenditiis suis, Bellenauum uicum cum suis appenditiis, Arcionem[5] cum appenditiis suis. Istas uillas cum omnibus adiacentiis, seu et omni re superposita, campis, pratis, siluis, pomiferis, pascuis, accessibus aquis, aquarumque decursibus, et omnes redditus totum ad integrum, una cum mancipiis, libertis, cum omni peculio ipsorum, una cum accolabus dedit ad seruitium monachorum iure perpetuo ad possidendum.

Ecclesiam etiam que est in ipsa Belenauo uilla, in honore Sancti Stephani, prorsus ab omni consuetudinali exactione liberrimam. Ecclesiam quoque de uilla que dicitur Danbrum,[6] cum appenditiis suis, et uillam Trescasas[7] cum ecclesia et omnibus appenditiis suis. Item ecclesiam de uilla que dicitur Sancti Sequani[8] cum appenditiis suis; et ecclesiam de uilla Morniaco cum omnibus ad eam pertinentibs, necnon etiam ecclesiam quę est in ualle Verona in honore S. Mauritii, ecclesiam de uilla Beria[9] in honore S. Laurentii, cum omnibus appenditiis suis. Preterea in territorio Diuionensi[10] decimas illarum uinearum quas donauerat huic ecclesię domnus Amalgarius dux et fundator huius sacri cenobii. Apud uillam que dicitur Fiscinis,[11] uinearum non modicam quantitatem, cum pratis et campis, et seruis et ancillis ad ea excolenda. Et in

2 King Chlothar III (657–673). This may be a reference to document 3.

3 Emperors Louis the Pious (814–840) and his son Lothar I (840–855). This is a reference to the previous charter.

4 Agobard, archbishop of Lyon (816–840).

5 Pouilly, 15 km northeast of Bèze; Belleneuve, 12 km south of Bèze; and Arçon 1 km east of there.

6 Drambon, 17 km south-southeast of Bèze.

7 Trochères, 14 km south-southeast of Bèze.

8 St-Seine-sur-Vingeanne, 13 km northeast of Bèze.

9 Mornay, 16 km northeast of Bèze; Véronnes, 7 km north-northwest of Bèze; and Beire, 8 km southwest of Bèze.

10 Dijon is 24 km southwest of Bèze.

11 Fixin, 10 km southwest of Dijon.

uilla Fisciaco[12] uineas similiter, et in Marcennaco[13] similiter, in substantiam monachorum et alimoniam pauperum, et ut ibidem delectetur seruis Dei Domino seruire, et pro rege eiusque coniuge necnon et liberis ipsius et totius imperii eius stabilitate iugiter Domini misericordiam implorare. Ea uidelicet ratione hoc constituimus, ut semper subiectus sit iamdictus locus ecclesię Sancti Mammetis,[14] et ut nec ego ipse, nec ullus de successoribus meis hanc conscriptionem uiolare presumat, domni imperatoris confirmationem in ea fieri postulaui.

Auctum Lingonis ciuitate publica. In Christi nomine Agobardus Lugdunensis ecclesię archiepiscopus subscripsi. Angericus episcopus subscripsi.[15] Albericus episcopus a me facta subscripsi. In Christi nomine Faoua Cabilonensis subscripsi. Modoinus Augustudunensis subscripsi. Winitharius indignus abbas Calticensis subscripsi.[16] Audinus indignus corepiscopus subscripsi. Motuinus indignus presbyter subscripsi. Hiltibaldus Matiscensis episcopus subscripsi.[17] Ragenardus presbyter subscripsi. Ego in Dei nomine Iacob licet indignus corepiscopus subscripsi. Sigoaldus presbyter subscripsi. Wanilo presbyter subscripsi. Adalbertus presbyter subscripsi. Symeon presbyter subscripsi. Vnricus diaconus subscripsi. Baius diaconus subscripsi. Beatus diaconus subscripsi. Fridericus subscripsi. Theutmarus subscripsi. Ragenaldus subscripsi. Signum Humberti. Signum Hiltanni. Signum Bertardi. Signum Fulcuini. Signum Eruic. Signum Radaldi. Betto subscripsi. Bernorogitus subscripsi. Ragnoardus subscripsi. Bavo subscripsi. Ragenardus subscripsi. Hilpericus subscripsi. Hildigisus presbyter subscripsi. In Christi nomine Bernardus archiepiscopus[18] subscripsi. Godelsadus abbas subscripsi. Birico ac si indignus leuita subscripsi. Actum anno ab incarnatione Domini octingentesimo XXX, indictione viii, epacta xv, xii kalendas Decembris, anno Christo propitio xiiii imperii domni Hlucdouici imperatoris et Hlotharii augusti filii eius vi.

Although Bishop Betto had started the process of re-establishing Bèze after the disasters of the eighth century, when the monastery had ended up in the

12 Fixey, 9.5 km southwest of Dijon.

13 Marsannay, 7 km southwest of Dijon.

14 The cathedral of Langres.

15 Angericus, archbishop of Embrun.

16 Bishops Faova of Chalon (c. 813–c. 838) and Modoinus of Autun (815–c. 840), and Winither, abbot of Couches, a monastery dependent on Flavigny for most of its history.

17 Hildebald, bishop of Mâcon.

18 Bernard, archbishop of Vienne.

hands of a laywoman, the process was not completed for at least a dozen years. Abbot Seraphim first appears in a charter in 827, three years before these two documents were issued in 830. Presumably the bishops of Langres had kept the monastery and its goods in their hands in the intervening dozen years. Although the documents do not mention Bishop Alberic's vision of St Peter, which led him to re-establish regular monasticism there according to the chronicler, the bishop certainly wanted to make the house's position stable and permanent, as he had it confirmed both by the emperors and by all the regional bishops.

Tempore uero domni Alberici episcopi,[19] facte sunt plurime commutationes uel coemptiones terrarum, tam ab ipso pontifice quam a rectoribus loci istius. Inter quas facta est commutatio a Seraphin abbate nostro et Herleberto abbate Diuionensi.[20] Dedit Herlebertus in uillis Luco et Verona[21] quicquid erat iuris Sancti Benigni, et Seraphin e contra tradidit terras Sancti Petri que erant in Diuione et in fine Domni Petri, et Longouico, et in Canauis, et in Arzilerias, et Tremoldo, et Fontanis, et Prouiso, et Disto.[22] Nec suffecit huic loci istius amatori Alberico episcopo, suo tempore munificentissime locum istum ampliare, sed audiens qualiter Betto episcopus predecessor suus[23] fines Besuensis territorii legaliter nouem legalibus testibus terminauerat, sua auctoritate id ipsum confirmauit. Ipso tempore quidam Hligarius nomine dedit ad hunc locum in Aquato uilla[24] terram hereditatis sue, pro peccatis suis minuendis, hoc est mansum indominicatum una cum domo et horreo. Habet uero ipsa terra perticas arpennales in longo xliii et pedales decem, et in lato de uno capite superiore perticas viiii, et pedes iiii, totum ad integram, tam terris, curtiferis, quam edificiis desuper positis, campis, pratis, siluis, pascuis, aquis, aquarumque decursibus, totum ad integrum dedit.

---

19 Alberic, bishop of Langres (821–838).

20 Herlebert governed St-Bénigne of Dijon at this time on behalf of the bishop.

21 Lux, 5 km northwest of Bèze; and Véronnes, 7 km north-northwest of Bèze.

22 Dampierre, 7 km east-northeast of Bèze; Longvic, 4 km southeast of Dijon; Chenôve, 5 km southwest of Dijon; Aisery, 20 km southeast of Dijon; Trimolois, which used to be between Chenôve and Dijon; Fontaine, 4 km northwest of Dijon; Prenois, near Dijon; and Daix, 5 km northwest of Dijon. Abbot Seraphim of Bèze gave St-Bénigne land at these villas, in exchange for lands at Lux and Véronnes, in 827, according to a charter in St-Bénigne's cartulary; *Chartes et documents de Saint-Bénigne de Dijon*, 1:76, no. 43. The chronicler appears to be paraphrasing his monastery's copy of the exchange agreement. See above, the discussion after document 3.

23 Betto, bishop of Langres (791–820). This is a reference to document 7 above.

24 Ahuy, 22 km west-southwest of Bèze.

10

c. 830

A certain Widaldus sells land at Chazeuil to Bishop Alberic, which he gives to Bèze.

Cartulary, fol. 44v.
Bougaud-Garnier, p. 261.

Carta de Casoto

Similiter quidam Widaldus nomine uendidit domno Alberico episcopo[1] terram in uilla Casoto nomine[2] mansum unum, et de terra iornales septem. Domnus uero Albericus dedit eam Sancto Petro.

11

21 January 830

Aylard sells all he or his mother had at Buteau to Bishop Alberic.

Cartulary, fol. 44v.
Bougaud-Garnier, p. 261.

Carta de Bustello

Item alius quidam Aylardus nomine res iuris sui sitas in pago Atoariense, in loco qui dicitur Bustellus,[1] et in ipsa fine Bustellense seu et ibidem aspiciente, quicquid ibidem genitrix sua uisa fuit habere, tam in mansis quam campis, pratis, siluis, pomiferis, pascuis, accessibusque, omnibus uendidit domno Alberico episcopo, per manus abbatis Seraphin, Radulfo et Amalarico testibus, xii kalendas Februarii, anno xvi imperii Lucdouici.[2]

The two preceding documents are given rubrics in the cartulary as though they were transcriptions of complete documents, even though they were just summaries. Document 11 does not specify that the bishop passed Buteau on to the monks, but he presumably did so. The documents copied or paraphrased

1 Alberic, bishop of Langres (821–838).
2 Chazeuil, 10 km north of Bèze.
1 Buteau, a now-ruined village near Viévigne. It is in the pagus of Attuyer, the region north of Dijon.
2 Emperor Louis the Pious (814–840).

in this section indicate where the property came from that the emperors confirmed in 830.

12

Bèze, 30 March 827

An exchange between Seraphim, abbot of Bèze, and Abbot Theuto of St-Léger, done in the presence of Bishop Alberic. Theuto gives some land at Bèze, bordering land the monks there already had, in exchange for land at Baissey.

Cartulary, fols. 44v–45r.
Bougaud-Garnier, pp. 261–262.

Carta Teutonis abbatis

Similiter etiam facta est commutatio inter abbatem Besuensem nomine Seraphin et abbatem Theuthonem monasterii Sancti Leodegarii, quod Campellense nominatur, cuius series ita se habet.

Auxiliante domino nostro Ihesu Christo placuit atque conuenit coram domno Alberico Lingonensi episcopo,[1] inter abbatem Seraphin et Theuthonem abbatem de monasterio Sancti Leodegarii,[2] ut aliquid de terris Sancti Petri Besuensis et Sancti Leodegarii pro communi oportunitate mutare deberent, quod ita fecerunt. Dedit Theutho abbas de parte sua ad partem Seraphin coram Alberico episcopo, in cenobio Sancti Petri Besuensis, curtile unum situm in uilla Besua. Habet idem curtile in longo perticas arpennales xlviii, et in transuerso perticas arpennales tres, et pedales septem. De utroque latere terra Sancti Petri est. Dedit autem Albericus episcopus et Seraphin abbas de terra Sancti Petri Besuensis ad partem Theotonis abbatis Sancti Leodegarii curtile unum situm in uilla Baciaco.[3] Terminatur autem ab uno latere terra Flauiniacensis monasterii,[4] et habet perticas arpennales xvi, et in transuerso perticas arpennales v. Similiter in alio loco in ipsa fine Basciacense peciolam unam de terra quę habet in longum perticas arpennales viii, et in transuerso perticas arpennales iiii. Si quis uero quod nec fieri credimus de heredibus nostris aut qualibet persona contra hanc commutationem uenire conatus fuerit, inferat ei cui litem intulerit duas untias de auro.

1 Alberic, bishop of Langres (821–838).

2 Seraphim, abbot of Bèze, and Theuto, abbot of St-Léger-de-Champeaux. This small monastery was 19 km south-southeast of Bèze. It later became a priory of St-Germain of Auxerre, given to that house by Duke Henry of Burgundy (d. 1002). See Deflou-Leca, *Saint-Germain d'Auxerre et ses dépendances*, pp. 273–274.

3 Baissey, 31 km north of Bèze.

4 The monastery of Flavigny.

Actum Fonte Besua monasterio publico, iii kalendas Aprilis, anno xiii imperii domni Hlucdouici imperatoris.[5]

13

829

Bishop Alberic buys land at Buteau and Viévigne from the woman Adda for fifty solidi.

Cartulary, fol. 45r.
Bougaud-Garnier, p. 262.

Carta de Bustello

Anno quinto decimo imperii Hlucdouici, domnus Albericus Lingonensis episcopus[1] emit terram de quadam femina nomine Adda, et Laburdo et Albuino et Laibulfo, quę sita est in loco qui dicitur Bustellus, qui est in fine Vetusuineis,[2] omnia que habere uidebantur in ipso Bustello et in Blaniaco,[3] tam terris curtiferis, quam ędificiis desuper positis, campisque, pratis, siluis, exaratis, pomiferis, pascuis, aquis, aquarumque decursibus, accessibusque omnibus. Omnia ex integro uendiderunt, et acceperunt precium solidos L.

Again, although the document does not specify that Bishop Alberic subsequently gave the land to Bèze, he must have done so. The monks later had quite a bit of property in this region. The following document similarly records an episcopal purchase which presumably benefited the monks.

14

832

Bishop Alberic buys five male and female serfs from a certain Narduin for fifteen solidi.

Cartulary, fol. 45r.
Bougaud-Garnier, p. 263.

---

5 Emperor Louis the Pious (814–840).

1 Alberic, bishop of Langres (821–838).

2 Viévigne, 4 km southwest of Bèze. The now-ruined village of Buteau was nearby.

3 Blagny, 8 km east-southeast of Bèze.

Item alia

Anno viii x imperii Hlucdouici iterum emit domnus Albericus Lingonensis episcopus[1] seruos, Arlebaldum atque Hayconem, cum ancilla nomine Humeldi et filiabus suis, Adalberga et Eldeardi, de quodam Nerduino nomine qui accepit precium solidos xv.

Lucdouico[2] Pio terreni insignia regni anno Dominice incarnationis DCCCXL perpetua felicitate commutanti, filii eius graui pernicie in semet dissidentes, unitum prius pulcherrima de diuersis nationibus compage Francorum regnum feda sectione sciderunt. Qua de re contigit, ut dum optimates aule uniuscuiusque filiorum regis aduersus alter utrum affectare se simulant gratiam, quicquid utile sibi fore estimauissent expetere non dubitarent. At regii adolescentes, dum sibi quisque consulit, et ne alter ei preferatur, cauet iniustis aliquando peticionibus, inuito nichilominus aliquotiens animo fauere cogebantur.[3]

Exorta ut diximus discordia inter fratres, tunc demum inter regni primores, conglobantur horribilia bella ueluti intestina. Deseritur custodia littorum maris Oceani, augescit numerus hostium, crescit innumerabilis multitudo Nortmannorum, Danorum, atque Brittonum. Fiunt passim Christianorum strages, depredationes, uastationes, incensiones. Capiuntur quascumque adeunt ciuitates, nemine resistente. Capitur Burdegala, Petragorium, Sanctonum, Lemouigas, Engolisma, atque Tolosa, Andegauorum, Turonensium, perinde et Aurelianensium ciuitates[4] pessum dantur. Ad ultimum uidentes reges sua discordia addi uires extraneis, et dampna ciuium esse lucra hostium, pacificantur inter se primum. Tum deinde cum hostibus, quia regno eos expellere non potuerunt, pactum cum eis ineunt, et quod armis tueri debuissent, pecuniis redimunt.

Lotharius igitur obtinens imperii sceptra, contentus fuit parte regni cum Italia atque urbe Roma. Eo tempore Sarraceni inuadentes urbem Romanam, spoliauerunt sepulem apostolorum et cetera sanctorum loca. Anno qui fuit ab incarnatione Domini DCCCXLIIII Lotharius habuit filium nomine Hlucdouicum, quem cupiens sibi successorem fieri, ut coronam imperii sumeret, misit Romam, et cum eo Drogonem Mettensem archiepiscopum, suum scilicet

1 Emperor Louis the Pious (814–840) and Alberic, bishop of Langres (821–838).

2 Here, on fol. 45v, the chronicle of Bèze starts once again copying the chronicle of St-Bénigne (from pp. 93–94 of the printed edition), having skipped over a long section specifically concerning that house.

3 Here the chronicler of Bèze skipped a short section in which the chronicler of St-Bénigne detailed acquisitons by his house (p. 93 of the printed edition).

4 Bordeaux, Perigueux, Saintes, Limoges, Angoulême, Toulouse, Angers, Tours, and Orléans.

auunculum, et reliquos principes regni sui. Qui uenientes Romam nimis austere egerunt cum Romanis, unde animos eorum ad rancorem concitauerunt. Accepto imperio domum reuersus, non longe post decessit. Scriptum in gestis pontificum Romanorum.[5]

De obitu Alberici episcopi

Non[6] est nostrę possibilitatis uerbis ostendere quante deuotionis erga hunc locum domnus Albericus episcopus[7] extiterit, quantumque eum dilexerit. Verumptamen si uerba nostra ad hoc non sufficiunt, opera ipsius et beneficia clamant et ostendunt. In hoc enim apparet illum monasterium istud super omnia dilexisse, quod quecumque potuit et undecumque huic loco attrahere, non omisit. Adnotauimus quedam de donariis ipsius prout tenuitas memorie nostre recordari potuit. Quorum quedam adhuc retinemus et possidemus, quedam partim debilitate nostra, partim infidelitate peruasorum perdidimus.

Est apud nos pallium satis pulchrum[8] uisu, columbis in eo seriatim et pulcherrime contextis, unde ipse multis diebus infulam habuit. Sunt apud nos de libris quos ipse sanctis apostolis Petro et Paulo obtulit. Textus euangeliorum unus. Augustinus ad Litteram. Liber Regum cum Actibus Apostolorum in eodem uolumine. Beda super Lucam. Quippe non inmerito sperabat salutem et uitam anime per eos a Domino Ihesu Christo consequi, per quos sanitatem corporis et ualitudinem receperat. Huius itaque spei atque fidei constantia fisus postquam plurima huic loco ante se premisit, ad extrema uite propinquans, in hoc monasterio se sepeliri uoluit, quod et factum est. Iacet namque benedictum corpus ipsius ad dexteram partem altaris Sanctę Marię, anima uero ipsius cum electis et sanctis Dei requiescat in pace. Amen.

15

c. 840

For the good of his soul and at the urging of Bishop Theobald, one Eurulf gives two fields and a meadow at Oisilly to Bèze.

---

5 Young King Louis's trip to Rome with his great-uncle Drogo, bishop of Metz, and his coronation by Pope Sergius II is recounted more positively in *Le liber pontificalis* 104, pp. 87–90.

6 Here, on fol. 46r, the chronicler of Bèze returns to the history of his own house.

7 Alberic, bishop of Langres (821–838).

8 The cartulary reads "pulcrhum."

Cartulary, fols. 46v–47r.
Bougaud-Garnier, p. 264.

Carta de Auxiliaco

Per idem tempus defuncto Seraphin abbate qui uices pastoris in hoc loco tenuerat, successit ad regimen animarum Walcaudus abbas, eundem in ęcclesiasticis gerens officium. Obeunte itidem Alberico episcopo Lingonum, Teutbaldus episcopus adeptus est kathedram.[1] Hic sicut predecessor suus studiosus huius loci cultor, fecit commutationes terrarum in aliquibus locis cum quibusdam hominibus.

Quidam namque, Eurulfus nomine, pro remedio anime sue per consilium Teutbaldi episcopi dedit Sancto Petro Besuensis cęnobii unum campum situm in uilla que dicitur Auxiliacus,[2] qui terminatur de uno latere terra Sancti Leodegarii,[3] de alio uero ipsi heredes tenent, de una fronte fluuio procurrente, de alia uero fronte strata publica. Infra uero istas terminationes totum ad integrum contulit Sancto Petro. In alio etiam loco campum unum in eadem uilla, qui habet terminationes, ex uno latere siluam communem, de alio uero latere uiam publicam, ex una fronte terram Godefredi, de alia itidem fronte ipsi heredes tenent. Similiter in alio loco pratum unum qui habet terminationes, ex una fronte fluuium procurrentem, ex alia uero fronte et ex uno latere ipsi heredes tenent.

Signum Adalmari. Signum Odolgarii.

This document appears to have been given not long after the death of Bishop Alberic in 838.

16

c. 840

Bishop Theobald and Abbot Walcaud make an exchange of fields located at Maâtz with one Vulfric.

Cartulary, fol. 47r.
Bougaud-Garnier, p. 265.

1 After the death of Bishop Alberic of Langres (821–838), Bishop Theobald succeeded (838–856).
2 Oisilly, 9 km southeast of Bèze.
3 St-Léger, 19 km south-southeast of Bèze. It was a small monastery at the time; see document 12 above.

Carta de Maiasco

Domnus itaque Teutbaldus episcopus et Walcaudus abbas[4] fecerunt commutationem cum quodam Vulfrico nomine, de terris eorum. Dedit ergo Vulfericus de parte sua ad partem Sancti Petri campum unum situm in pago Atoariense, in uilla que dicitur Maiascus[5] seu in ipse fine, qui habet terminationes, ex uno latere terram Sancti Petri, ex alio uero terram ipsius donatoris, et ex una fronte terram Sancti Mammetis,[6] ex alia uero fronte stratam publicam, et habet perticationes, in longo perticas xxv, pedum x, et in lato perticas xi, et ex ambabus frontibus perticas xi, pedum iiii. E contra dedit Waulcaudus abbas de parte Sancti Petri ad partem Vulfrici campum unum situm in pago Atoariense, in uilla que dicitur Maiascus.

This document was doubtless given at about the same time as the previous one.

Vbicumque ergo potuit Teutbaldus episcopus hunc locum nostrum inmeliorari curauit. Post cuius obitum, domnus Isaac suscepit presulatum.[7] Hic predecessorum bonum sequens exemplum, multa bona huic monasterio contulit.

Karolus[8] igitur, qui cognominatus est Caluus,[9] imperium adeptus, ecclesiarum Dei cultor deuotus, omni nisu quo potuit studebat in cultu religionis deprauata corrigere, destructa reędificare, collapsa erigere. Anno Dominice incarnationis DCCCLXXI, regens Francorum regnum, erga cultum ecclesię Dei fuit studiosissimus, quapropter multa euicit pericula, et regni eius semper augmentabatur gloria. Defuncto siquidem ut iam dictum est Pipino fratre suo rege Aquitanię, filioque eius in regno subrogato, moderationem regni non strenue agens, a suis derelictus ac deiectus est, et monachus in monasterio Sancti Medardi factus.[10] Karolus uero a cunctis principibus expetitus, Aquitanie regnum est adeptus. Post non multos etiam annos mortuo Lothario imperatore

---

4 Bishop Theobald of Langres (838–856) and Walcaud, the first abbot after Seraphim, the reforming abbot of the 820s and 830s.

5 Maâtz, 30 km north-northeast of Bèze. It is in Attuyer, the pagus that stretches north of Dijon.

6 The cathedral of Langres.

7 Isaac, bishop of Langres (858–880).

8 From here to the end of the paragraph (fol. 47r–v), the chronicler of Bèze follows the chronicle of St-Bénigne (pp. 98–99 in the printed edition). Interestingly, the Bèze chronicler's first sentence comes *after* the rest of the paragraph in the chronicle of St-Bénigne.

9 King Charles the Bald (840–877).

10 St-Medard of Soissons.

fratre eius, Karolus suscepit imperium. Sed Lucdouuicus alter frater cupiens inuadere monarchiam regni, iterum contra Karolum bellum concitat, Nortmannos ceterasque gentes in regnum Karoli euocat. Auxiliante autem Domino, Karolus fratrem de finibus suis expulit, et Nortmannos intra Neustriam compressit.[11] Hęc fuit secunda eruptio Nortmannorm in Francia. Aliquantis transactis annis Lucdouuicus defunctus est, reliquens tres filios, Lucdouuicum scilicet, Karlomannum, et Karolum.

17

c. 860

Baldric, son of Roman, gives a manse at Lux for the good of his and his father's and ancestors' souls. The gift includes a mill, which one Utlaius later claims as in part his, before Lady Eva. The monks, however, have many witnesses to the original gift from Baldric and his clerical brother Josmund, so Utlaius is forced to give up his claim. Later, however, Abbot Teutbert grants the mill to Utlaius.

Cartulary, fols. 47v–48r.
Bougaud-Garnier, pp. 266–267.

Carta de Luco

Defuncto igitur Walcaudo abbate, Warinus successit.[1] Huius itaque diebus quidam homo, Baldricus nomine, pro remedio anime sue et genitoris sui, nomine Romani, reliquorumque antecessorum suorum, dedit Sancto Petro unum mansum qui est in Luco[2] superiori, uel in ipsa uilla Lucensi, cum omnibus appenditiis suis, et habet terminationes ex uno latere et de una fronte terram Sancti Marcellini, et ex alio latere et de una fronte fiscum similiter. De rebus autem suis que sunt site in ipso pago et in fine Lucensi seu in ipsa uilla Luco, mansum cum suprapositis campis, pratis, curtiferis, siluis, pascuis, pomiferis, et uno molendino in Busceria, aquis, aquarumque decursius, exitibus et regressibus, accessibusque omnibus, quicquid de parte genitorum

11 Louis the German did not in fact invite the Norsemen into Francia. The chronicler seems to have confused two kings named Charles; the Norse settlement in Normandy took place not under Charles the Bald but rather under Charles the Simple, his grandson.

1 Possibly the same Warin who was rector of Flavigny in the 850s; *Cartulary of Flavigny*, ed. Bouchard, p. 146.

2 Lux, 5 km northwest of Bèze.

suorum uel quicquid per instrumenta kartarum conquisiuit, totum iure perpetuo eidem cenobio tradidit.

Post aliquantos autem annos ueniens quidam Vtlaius nomine ante Euam dominam suam in campo limito, proclamabat quod partem habere deberet in molendino quem Iosmundus clericus et frater suus Baldricus dederant Sancto Petro in Luco, absque ullius contradicto. Iussit itaque Eua fidelibus suis ut irent com [*sic*] predicto Vtlaio ad monsterium Besue pro tali causa inquirenda. Venit ergo Aldricus a partibus ut Vtlaii cum ceteris quamplurimis, mouens rationem de predicto molendino contra abbatem uel monachos. Itaque monachi testes habuerunt quamplurimos, e contra Vtlaius nullum inde habuit testem, quia omnes eum sciebant esse mendacem. Sicque spe sua fraudatus, quicquid calumpniabatur, totum monachis dimisit ac uuirpiuit.

Postea uero Teutbertus abbas qui supramemorato Warino successerat ipsum molendinum Vtlaio ea ratione recondonauit, ut si in deterius deuenisset, xxx solidos persolueret. Habet autem idem molendinum terminationes de ambabus partibus Tilam,[3] et ex una fronte Isaccus et uxor eius tenent, et de alia fronte est exitus et regressus et semita quę ad ipsum farinarium pergit.

I have dated the original donation to roughly 860, but it is impossible to give a more exact date than the middle of the ninth century. The Lady Eva may be related to the dukes of Aquitaine.

18

c. 875

The knight Epplenus of Dijon gives arable land at Viévigne, for his soul and his relatives. The donated land is large enough to plant one hundred measures of grain.

Cartulary, fol. 48r–v.
Bougaud-Garnier, p. 267.

Karta de Vetusuineis

Quidam etiam miles Diuionis castri, Epplenus nomine, pro remedio sui atque parentum suorm, dedit huic Besuensi ęcclesię in uilla quam Veteres Vineas[1]

3 The river Tille, which runs through Lux.

1 Viévigne, 4 km southwest of Bèze.

uocant, uel in finibus eiusdem uille, tantum spacium de terra arabili ubi possunt[2] seminari annone modii centum.

This is most likely the same Eppelenus who made generous gifts to St-Bénigne in 878.[3] Calling him a knight of the castle of Dijon is likely to be a twelfth-century characterization in what is clearly a brief paraphrase of a charter.

19

c. 870

Roger gives Bèze a field at Oisilly.

Cartulary, fol. 48v.
Bougaud-Garnier, pp. 267–268.

Carta de Auxiliaco

Alius quidam homo nomine Rogerius donauit eidem ecclesię campum unum qui est situs in pago Atoariorum, in uilla Auxiliaco,[1] et habet terminationes de uno latere terram Sancti Petri, de alio terram fiscalem, de una fronte stratam publicam, de alia Vincennam fluuium procurrentem.[2]

20

Baissey, 870

A quarrel is settled over the tithes of the churches at Lux, the agreement taking place at a synod at Baissey.

Cartulary, fols. 48v–49r.
Bougaud-Garnier, p. 268.

Carta de Luco

Cum resideret uenerabilis episcopus Isaac in kathedra episcopali,[1] uilla Basiaco[2] omnisque clerus ipsius proptus undique ad eum congregaretur, ceterua

---

2 The manuscript reads “posunt.”

3 *Chartes et documents de Saint-Bénigne de Dijon*, 1:142–144, no. 109.

1 Oisilly, 9 km southeast of Bèze, in the pagus of Attuyer.

2 The river Vingeanne, which runs by Oisilly.

1 Isaac, bishop of Langres (858–880).

2 Baissey, 31 km north of Bèze.

quoque admodum nobilium abbatum cum archidiaconibus et presbyteris, cętuque uniuerso in synodo generali, quiddam de causis ęcclesiasticis ordinatura. Inter cetera sancta colloquia quę pariter habuerunt, altercatio quedam exhorta est inter Ansuinum Sancti Martini Luensis[3] presbyterum et Adalardum eiusdem uillule Sancti Marcellini presbyterum, de decimis ipsarum ęcclesiarum, loquente Ansuino quod omnis decima cum integritate ab antiquo sue foret ecclesię, quę e contrario profitente et toto annisu Adalardo reluctante, sue ecclesię prorsus magis esse debere. Continuo itaque in ipsa synodo exurgentes testes ualde preclari et idonei, superius memorati Ansuini presbyteri qui ueris indiciis Adalardum refutantes, approbauerunt et definierunt secundum quod antiquitus fuit stare debere, scilicet Magenardus abbas et archidiaconus Otbertus, qui eodem archidiaconatus fungebatur officio, Arnoldus eodem florens honore, Isaac, Fredradus, Adalmannus, Euorinus, et omnis fere synodus. Horum ueridicorum testium testimoniis satis confirmatus et roboratus est presbyter Ansuinus, et taliter uterque eorum querele huius finem accepit.

Aucta sunt hęc anno Dominice Incarnationis DCCCLXX, indictione iii, regnante Karolo rege,[4] ecclesiam autem Lingonensem regente uenerabili Isaac pontifice.

Although Bèze is not specifically mentioned, the monks did own property at Lux and presumably benefited from the tithes. The church dedicated to St Marcellinus depended on the bishop of Langres, as document 21 indicates. The preceding group of donation charters were probably all issued within ten or fifteen years of each other.

Obitus domni Isaac episcopi

Isaac[5] deinde huius uite diem obeunte, eius loco Geylo substituitur episcopus,[6] huic Besuensi monasterio amicissimus, et nobis fere omnibus melioribus optimus. Cum enim alii nobis prouiderint terrena subsidia, iste apud Deum nobis procurauit animarum patrocinia. Rediens enim ex Aquitania, beatissimi Prudentii martyris corpus huic loco intulit, et cum aliis multis sanctorum pignoribus ad exorandum Deum pro se et pro nobis ut decuit collocauit. Ad quorum honorem et reuerentiam quedam de episcopio suo ad luminaria obtulit

3 Lux, 5 km northwest of Bèze.

4 King Charles the Bald (840–877).

5 Isaac, bishop of Langres (858–880).

6 Geilo, bishop of Langres (880–889). He had earlier been abbot both of Flavigny and of St-Philibert of Tournus. His election was contested, but he had the support of King Boso (879–887). See Bautier, *Chartes, sceaux, et chancelleries*, 1:217–229.

exibenda, et eorum que obtulit facta legaliter et publice donatione scriptum edidit hoc modo.

21

8 October 883

Bishop Geilo of Langres gives the monastery of Bèze the relics of the martyr St Prudentius. He also gives money for lights, to be taken from episcopal revenues from a chapel at Lux. He gives the monks two churches as well.

Cartulary, fols. 49r–50r.
Bougaud-Garnier, pp. 269–270.
Summarized in Brequigny, *Table* 1:332.

De collatis huic loco a Geilone episcopo

Omnibus dignitatibus, sublimibus, ac mediocribus utriusque sexus et ordinis, notum esse uolumus qualiter ego Geylo Lingonensis ecclesię humilis episcopus,[1] Dei omnipotentis inspiratione commotus, beatissimum Prudentium Christi martyrem Besuensi monasterio in honore sanctorum apostolorum Petri et Pauli constructo digno honore collacauerim. Qui beatus martyr ante introitum atrii et in ingressu templi ac deinceps miraculis ut omnibus Christi circumquaque fidelibus patefactum est claruit. Nutu ergo diuine maiestatis pulsatus contuli illi aliquid ad luminaria prebenda ex reditibus Sancti Mammetis in Luco[2] superiori, capellam uidelicet Sancti Marcellini, cum appenditiis suis et mancipiis utriusque sexus, quę ab episcopo Virdunensi[3] ante paucos dies digna commutatione euindicaui.

Pontiliacum[4] etiam cum adiacentiis suis, et eccleiam in honore Sancti Yppolyti in eodem loco consecratam, eidem sanctissimo martyri Prudentio contuli. Ecclesiam quoque de Chasuit[5] ad integrum cum omnibus appenditiis suis eidem sancto delagaui, ita ut ab hac die has donationes habeat, teneat, atque possideat in perpetuum, nullo contradicente. Hoc solum a successoribus meis in Deum et propter Deum obnixis precibus exorando deposco, ut si addicere aliquid placuerit, faciant; et si non, hęc parua a nobis tradita non demant nec subtrahant. Quod et si qui temptati a diabolo inuadere hęc dona conati fuerint,

1 Geilo, bishop of Langres (880–889).
2 Lux, 5 km northwest of Bèze.
3 Verdun.
4 Pontailler-sur-Saône, 21 km southeast of Bèze.
5 Chazeuil, 10 km north of Bèze.

non permittatur eis locus in ecclesia cum ceteris Christianis. Et nisi cito resipiscant, maledictionibus cum Datan et Abiron et cum Iuda traditore Domini, penis gehennalibus subiciantur, insuper et auri libras quinque in ultione rectoribus ecclesię Besuensis persoluant.

Ego Geylo humilis episcopus hanc traditionem in synodali conuentu peregi et confirmari rogaui, anno ab incarnatione Domini octingentesimo octogesimo tercio, indictione prima, epacta nona, regnante Karolo Magno.[6] Signum domni Geylonis episcopi, harum rerum donatoris. S. Helie. S. Oberti. S. Galcaudi. S. Helgaudi. S. Arnaldi. S. Guntardi. S. Odonis et reliquorum omnium qui illi synodo affuerunt, die Dominico, mensis Octobris, viii idus eiusdem mensis.

Bishop Geilo had taken the relics of St Prudent, a martyr saint from third-century Narbonne in Aquitaine, in what could be considered a "pious theft," according to a twelfth-century account, written at roughly the same time as the cartulary was compiled and using this charter.[7] The account of Geilo's theft of the relics said that Prudent was not being properly revered because of the wars and disasters of the time. See also document 39, where this gift is confirmed.

22

St-Marcel-lès-Chalon, 18 May 887

A council of bishops, at the urging of Bishop Geilo of Langres, confirms the settlement of quarrels over tithes at Lux which Bishop Isaac of Langres had earlier reached.

Cartulary, fol. 50r–v.
Bougaud-Garnier, pp. 270–272.
Summarized in Brequigny, *Table* 1:338; dated 887.

Carta de ecclesia Sancti Martini de Luco

Anno incarnationis Dominice DCCCLXXXVI, anno quoque domni et serenissimi Karoli imperatoris Augusti[1] in Gallia imperantis secundo, indictione v, xv kalendas Iunii, sacer episcoporum conuentus ob pacem et tranquilitatem sancte Dei ecclesię statuendam, et ęcclesiastica negotia decernenda, apud ecclesiam

6 King Charles the Bald (840–877).

7 Teobaudus, "Acta, translationes, et miracula S. Prudentii martyris" 2, AASS October 3: 352–354. Geary, *Furta Sacra*, pp. xi, 116–117.

1 Emperor Charles the Fat, who became king of West Francia in 884 (depossed 887).

Sancti Marcelli martyris, in suburbio Cabilonensi,[2] in Christi nomine coadunatus est. Vbi fuerunt domni et sanctissimi archiepiscopi, Aurelianus, Bernuinus,[3] necnon et reuerendissimi episcopi, Adalgarius, Geylo, Stephanus, Gyraldus, Atalbaldus, Isaac, et Leboinus,[4] Geylo denique supramemoratus Lingonensis ecclesię reuerendus antistes, una cum suprascriptis patribus, in hoc sacrosancto residens conuentu eorum auribus intimauit de suprascripta noticia, qualiter domnus Isaac antecessor suus res ecclesię in Luco, in honore Sancti Martini, in sua sancto synodo a partibus Sancti Martini de Luco superiori capelle, uidelicet Sancti Marcellini, contra Adalardum eiusdem capelle presbyterum iuste et legaliter euindicauit de rebus et decimis.[5] Tunc omnes episcopi prefati hęc audientes in commune relationem Geylonis uenerabilis episcopi et noticiam euindicationis domni Isaac simul consenserunt, et consentiendo roborauerunt, ut si quis temeraria sacrilegaque presumptione conuictus, atque ceca cupiditate cecatus, hoc quod Dei et domni Isaac et nostra confirmamus auctoritate in aliquo infringere presumpserit, ęterna se sciens dampnatione multandum, et cum diabolo et angelis eius sempiterno incendio concremandum, atque cum Iuda traditore Domini et cum Datan et Abiron perpetuali pęna cruciandum, et insuper a liminibus sanctę Dei ecclesię, et cetu omnium fidelium Christianorum tamdiu habeatur extorris, donec inlicita presumptione resipiscens, condigna penitentia subleuetur.

This episcopal synod, held at St-Marcel, also confirmed the rights of the bishops of Langres[6] and of the monastery of Charlieu.[7] It is also mentioned in the records of St-Étienne of Dijon, where the same bishops, led by Bishop Geilo of Langres, swore not to let the canons of that church suffer through losing what little property they had.[8] In the records of the bishops of Langres and in the cartulary of St-Étienne, the synod is dated 887 rather than 886. The year 887 is probably more accurate, given the indiction, which all sources give as *v*.

2 The monastery of St-Marcel-les-Chalon. In the ninth century the monastery was in secular hands, governed by provosts.

3 Archbishops Aurelian of Lyon (875–895) and Bernoin of Vienne (886–899).

4 Bishops Adalgar of Autun (875–894), Geilo of Langres (880–889), Stephen of Chalon (886–889), Gerald of Mâcon (886–926), Adalbald of Belley (c. 885–c. 900), Isaac of Valence (c. 880–c. 900), and Leboin, *chorévêque* of Lyon.

5 This reference to Isaac, bishop of Langres (858–880), and to Lux, 5 km northwest of Bèze, refers to the agreement worked out in 870; see document 20 above.

6 Martène and Durand, *Thesaurus novus anecdotorum,* vol. 4, cols. 67–70.

7 RHGF 9:313.

8 *Chartes de l'abbaye de Saint-Étienne de Dijon (VIIIe, IXe, Xe et XIe siècles)*, pp. 21–24, no. 10.

23

c. 850

Isaac gives Bèze a manse at Lux and some additional fields. This is done under Abbot Walcaud.

Cartulary, fols. 50v–51r.
Bougaud-Garnier, p. 272.

Carta de Luco mediano

His diebus homo quidam cuius nomen erat Isaac dedit monasterio Besuensi mansum unum qui est situs in pago Atoariensi, in uilla quę dicitur Lucus Medianus,[1] et habet terminationes de una fronte Thilam fluuium[2] procurrentem, de alia fronte stratam publicam. Donauit quoque supradictus Isaac eidem loco in fine quę dicitur Mons Mainberti, in loco qui dicitur Spinido, terre iornales duos. In alio uero loco qui dicitur Cabrario iornales duos, et in alio qui dicitur Fontinella[3] iornales tres. Ipsamque donationem Walcaudo, tunc temporis ipsius loci abbati, et successoribus eius perpetuo contradidit.

This document can be dated to the mid-ninth century by the mention of Abbot Walcaud. The donor Isaac is unlikely to be the same as the bishop of Langres of that name. He is most likely the Isaac, father of Otger and Waldric, found in document 25.

24

c. 850

Ingelgerius and his wife Amalildis sell the monks of Bèze some property at Viévigne, for two solidi and eight denarii.

Cartulary, fol. 51r.
Bougaud-Garnier, pp. 272–273.

---

1 Lux, 5 km northwest of Bèze, is in the pagus of Attuyer.

2 The river Tille, which runs through Lux.

3 Fontenelle, 9 km northeast of Bèze. The other places mentioned are unidentified but were presumably nearby. It is possible that "Cabrarius" is identical with la Craie, now the name of a farm 1 km northeast of Fontenelle. Garnier identifies Mons Mainberti as Montrementier, which he calls a *climat*.

Carta de Vetus Vineis

Alius quidam homo nomine Ingelgerius et uxor eius Amalildis uendiderunt fratribus Besuensis cęnobii in uilla quam Veteres Vineas[4] appellant unum ortum, qui terminatur de uno latere terra ipsius hereditatis, de alio latere terra Sancti Leodegarii, de una fronte terra Sancti Petri, de alia uero strata publica. Habet etiam idem ortus perticationes agripennales, de una fronte a parte uineę Sancti Petri perticas duas, pedum sex, de alia fronte perticam unam. Habet et in longo perticas undecim, pedum nouem. Infra istas perticationes uel terminationes totum ad integrum uendidit predictus Ingelgerius monachis Besuensibus, acceptoque ab eis precio solidis duobus et denariis octo, concessit perpetualiter possidendum.

25

c. 860

Otger gives a serf for the souls of his father Isaac and brother Waldric because Waldric blinded a different serf of Bèze.

Cartulary, fol. 51r.
Bougaud-Garnier, p. 273.

Item alia

Vir quidam Otgerius nomine, pro remedio anime patris sui Isaac et fratris sui Waldrici, dedit Sancto Petro Besuensis cenobii seruum quendam Amalerium nomine, eo quod ipse Waldricus frater datoris cuidam seruo Sancti Petri, qui Lanfredus dicebatur, oculos eruisset.

Otger's father is probably the same Isaac as in document 23. The dating in this section must be very approximate but is doubtless somewhere in the middle years of the ninth century.

26

c. 870

Bernard and his wife Imiltrudis give Bèze, where Theodebert is abbot, part of a vineyard at Neuvelle.

Cartulary, fol. 51r.
Bougaud-Garnier, p. 273.

---

4 Viévigne, 4 km southwest of Bèze.

Carta de Nououico

Item alius quidam Bernardus et uxor eius Imiltrudis dederunt Theutberto Besuensi abbati[1] et monachis sub eo uiuentibus partem de uinea quadam sita in pago Atoariorum, in uilla Nououico,[2] ut haberent potestatem faciendi de ea, quicquid pocius elegissent.

27

c. 870

Aigard, a soldier, and his wife Rotlindis make gifts to the monks of Bèze, located at Villers in the Portois. The monks in return give them four pounds.

Cartulary, fol. 51r–v.
Bougaud-Garnier, pp. 273–274.

Carta de Villare

Miles quidam Portuensis pagi,[1] Aigardus nomine, et coniux eius Rotlindis uocata concesserunt beatissimo Petro in Besuensi cenobio famulantibus cunctas res iuris sui sitas in pago Portuensi, in uilla nuncupata Villare,[2] et totum quicquid in ipsa uilla uel in finibus eius possederant, campos scilicet, prata, pascua, decimas, riuos, fontes, aquas, aquarumque decursus cum adiacentiis suis, et quodcumque dici aut nominari potest, et quod per nomen eorum ibidem euendicare monachi possent. Acceptoque ob hoc ab ipsis monachis precio quod conualuit ad quattuor libras argenti, hanc tantam donationem testamento confirmauerunt, et possidendam eidem cęnobio perhenniter decreuerunt.

Several documents in this section are said to be donations from a *miles*. In the twelfth century in which the cartulary-chronicle was composed, that would have meant a knight. It is unclear whether the chronicler John, who was paraphrasing and condensing as he went, labelled these donors *milites* because their status seemed to deserve such a title or whether they were actually called this in the original documents. In my own summaries I call them soldiers, the earlier meaning of the word.

---

1 Theodebert, abbot of Bèze.
2 Neuvelle, 24 km northeast of Bèze, in the pagus of Attuyer.
1 The pagus of Portois.
2 Villers, 4 km north-northeast of Port-sur-Saône, the capital of the Portois. Villers is 66 km east-northeast of Bèze.

28

c. 870

Guttinus gives a manse in the pagus of Attuyer, including its serfs.

Cartulary, fol. 51v.
Bougaud-Garnier, p. 274.

Item alia carta

Quidam Guttinus nomine dedit eidem Besuensi cenobio mansum unum in pago Atoariensi et quicquid ad ipsum mansum pertinebat, in campis, pratis, siluis, aquis, et mancipiis utriusque sexus in eodem manentibus.

29

c. 870

Aurail and his wife Ermengard sell the monks of Bèze a manse located at Pont, in the pagus of Attuyer. They also sell other property at Véronnes and Lux for sixty solidi.

Cartulary, fols. 51v–52r.
Bougaud-Garnier, p. 274.

Carta de Ponto

Aurailus quidam et uxor eius Ermengardis uendiderunt monachis Besuensibus mansum unum cum appendiciis suis, campis scilicet, pratis, siluis, pascuis, arboribus pomiferis, aquis, aquarumque decursibus, quod situm est in pago Atoariorum in uilla quę dicitur Pontus,[1] et habet terminationes de uno latere terram Sancti Leudegarii, de alio terram fiscalem, de una fronte stratam publicam, de alia uero prata. Vendiderunt etiam et alias res suas sitas in fine Vendourensi, et in fine Pontensi, et in fine Iulensi.[2] Acceptisque a monachis pro hac largitione lx solidis, potestati eorum eam perhenniter possidendam tradiderunt.

1 "Pont" was probably the name of a hamlet at a bridge near Bèze. The pagus is Attuyer.
2 Véronnes, 7 km north-northwest of Bèze; and Lux, 5 km northwest of Bèze.

30

c. 870

Waldrannus, a soldier, gives Bèze a female serf and her descendants, for the good of his soul and his relatives'. She will pay the monks two denarii a year as well as performing service.

Cartulary, fol. 52r.
Bougaud-Garnier, pp. 274–275.

Item alia

Quidam miles nomine Waldrannus pro requie animę suę et parentum suorum dedit prefato cęnobio ancillam unam nomine Lampacem, ut ibidem deseruiret, cum omni semine suo ex ea progenito, et annis singulis in festiuitate sanctorum apostolorum Petri et Pauli denarios duos persolueret, et ut ceterę colone seruitium omne faceret.

31

c. 870

A woman named Landrada gives Bèze a manse located at Lux.

Cartulary, fol. 52r.
Bougaud-Garnier, p. 275.

Carta de Luiat

Landrada quoque quedam femina mansum iuris sui in uilla quę dicitur Luiat[1] situm dedit eidem cęnobio Besuensi. Quod mansum terminatur de uno latere terra Flammeria, de alio terra Sancti Leudgarii, de una fronte strata publica, de alio uero Thila fluuio procurrente.[2]

1 Lux, 5 km northwest of Bèze.
2 The river Tille, which runs through Lux.

32

c. 870

A *colonus* of the monastery named Gautsomus and his wife give a serf, who shall be a *colonus* as Gautsomus is.

Cartulary, fol. 52r.
Bougaud-Garnier, p. 275.

Item alia carta

Quidam etiam colonus Sancti Petri qui Gautsomus uocabatur et uxor eius Manuheldis seruum iuris sui nomine Gunduinum dederunt eidem sepe nominato loco, ea tamen ratione ut colonus permaneret, sicut et ipse Gautsomus.

It is interesting to note that one of the servile dependents (*colonus*) of Bèze has a serf (*seruus*) of his own, who is also characterized as a *colonus*. In this section I have dated the documents to roughly 870 because they appear to have all been given around the same time, in the second half of the ninth century, before the monastery was sacked by the Vikings.

33

c. 870

A soldier named Hugh gives Bèze a serf with his family, for the good of his soul and his ancestors'.

Cartulary, fol. 52r.
Bougaud-Garnier, p. 275.

Item alia

Miles quidam Hugo nomine, pro requie animę suę et antecessorum suorum, dedit ad ipsum locum Besuensem seruum quendam nomine Vulfingum, necnon et uxorem illius nomine Aymam, et infantes illorum, Ermenasiam, Suffuciam, Susannam, Adalsinnam, Suppliciam, et Godolbergam.

34

c. 960

The noblewoman Wandelmodis gives Bèze a serf with his sons, for the soul of her husband Humbert and for her ancestors. The serf has half a manse at

Framont. He shall pay annual dues in wheat and oats as well as two denarii for wax. In addition, Wandelmodis gives another serf with a manse at Pichanges, along with his mother, as well as some vineyards at Marsannay.

Cartulary, fol. 52r–v.
Bougaud-Garnier, pp. 275–276.

Carta de Picangiis et Mercennaco

Mulier quedam nobilis nomine Wandalmodis, pro requie anime mariti sui Humberti et reliquorum antecessorum suorum, donauit ad locum sanctorum apostolorum Petri et Pauli, necnon et Sancti Prudentii martyris, in uilla Fracto Monte[1] seruum nomine Gundulfum, cum filiis suis Vulferio, Waringaudo, Rainbaldo, et dimidium mansum quem ipsi tenebant, tali seruitio, ut omnibus annis in coruata monachorum iornalem unum de tritico et alium de auena persoluerent, et eulogias, et in cera duos denarios. Dedit etiam eadem Wandalmodis supradicto loco in uilla Pichanias[2] seruum nomine Humbertum cum matre Plectrude, et mansum unum ibidem, et quicquid ad ipsum mansum pertinebat. Similiter etiam dedit eidem loco in pago Diuionensi in uilla Mercennaco[3] iornalem unum de uinea.

It is most likely that Wandelmodis's late husband was Humbert I of Salins, brother of Count Leotold I of Mâcon. Humbert's daughter was the mother of another Wandelmodis.[4] I have assigned this and the following document an approximate date that would correspond to the death of Humbert I's brother Leotold. Here the cartulary has left the ninth century for the tenth, after the monastery's sacking by the Vikings.

35

c. 960

The noblewoman Eva gives a village with all its appurtenances, located in the pagus of Attuyer. She invests the monks with it by giving them a serf.

Cartulary, fol. 52v.
Bougaud-Garnier, p. 276.

1 Framont, 25 km northeast of Bèze.
2 Pichanges, 9 km west of Bèze.
3 Marsannay, 7 km southwest of Dijon.
4 Bouchard, *Sword, Miter, and Cloister*, pp. 262–264. Mathieu, "A propos d'une généalogie mâconnaise du XIe siècle."

Carta de Viuers

Nobilis quedam femina nomine Eua dedit eidem ecclesię Besuensi res proprii iuris sitas in pago Atoariorum, in loco qui dicitur Viuarius,[5] ipsam uidelicet uillam Viuers appellatam et quicquid ibi adiacet, totum ex integro predicto loco concessit, mansa, seruos, ancillas, curtiferas terras, siluas, aquas, aquarumque decursus, cum mancipiis utriusque sexus, et per seruum nomine Aiembaldum uestiuit ex his rebus predictam ęcclesiam Besuensem.

The noblewoman Eva is not identified. One possibility is that she was the sister of William the Pious of Aquitaine by that name, but in that case the charter would have to be redated at least half a century earlier.

36

c. 900

Helias, a leuita, gives a vineyard at Bressey-sur-Tille to pay for lighting the church of Bèze.

Cartulary, fol. 52v.
Bougaud-Garnier, p. 277.

Carta de Brescono

Leuita quidam nomine Helias dedit in pago Diuionensi in uilla Breschone,[1] ad luminaria eiusdem Besuensis ecclesię, uineam unam bene cultam, ut in perpetuum eam possideret sine aliqua contadictione.

37

c. 900

Adoerius, converting to the monastic life at Bèze, gives a vineyard at Fixey.

Cartulary, fols. 52v–53r.
Bougaud-Garnier, p. 277.

5 This place remains unidentified, though Garnier calls it Vivers.

1 Bressey-sur-Tille, 19 km south-southwest of Bèze. An early tenth-century document of St-Étienne of Dijon mentions vineyards belonging to St-Pierre, located at Bressey; *Chartes de l'abbaye de Saint-Étienne de Dijon (VIIIe, IXe, Xe et XIe siècles)*, p. 51, no. 32.

Carta de Fissins

Adoerius quidam in eodem cęnobio ex laico conuersus, in uilla Diuionensis pagi quę Fissciacus[1] appellatur, dedit uineam unam quę terminatur de uno latere terra Sancti Benigni de Longouico, de alio uia publica, de una fronte uinea Sancte Marie de Balma, de alia terra Sancti Eusebii de Escubilibus.[2] Habet ipsa uinea ex uno latere in longum perticas agripennales xxiiii, de alio perticas xx, pedum ii, de una fronte perticas xx, de alia uero perticas xv, pedum vii.

The two preceding documents are dated c. 900 because of where they are placed in the cartulary-chronicle and because they seem to correspond to material mentioned by documents from St-Étienne of Dijon from around that time.

Karolus[3] autem imperator secundo[4] Romam ire disponens, Italiam ingreditur. E contra Karlomannus Lucdouuici regis fratris eius filius[5] per aliam uiam eandem terram ingressus, cum inmenso exercitu fit ei obuius. Karolus uero Galliam reuersus, atque fines Lugdunensium pertingens, ibi de uita functus est. Atque in monasterio apostolorum Petri et Pauli conditus, loco qui dicitur Nantoade,[6] a multitudine aquarum in ibi confluentium. Postmodum per admonitionem angelicam inde translatus, Parisius in ecclesia Sancti Dionisii regali sepultura est tumulatus[7]. Successit patris in solio Lucdouuicus,[8] biennio uix regio nomine functus. Huius in diebus Iohannes papa Romanus Franciam uenit, et apud Trecas ciuitatem[9] cum eodem rege collocutus, paruo tempore ibidem moratus, sicque Romam est reuersus.

Is[10] diebus effera Danorum natio tertiam Neustrasiis inflictura cladem aduenit. Intulissetque maiorem superioribus, ni Hugo[11] per Gallias abbatis honore

1 Fixey, 10 km southwest of Dijon. A vineyard at Fixey was said to border the land of St-Pierre of Bèze in a 923 document from St-Étienne of Dijon; *Chartes de l'abbaye de Saint-Étienne de Dijon (VIIIe, IXe, Xe et XIe siècles)*, 1:52, no. 33.

2 The vineyard is surrounded by property belonging to other churches, those of Longvic (4 km southeast of Dijon), Beaune, and an unidentified St-Eusèbe.

3 At this point, on fol. 53r, the chronicler of Bèze again begins following the chronicle of St-Bénigne (picking up on p. 108 of the printed edition).

4 King Charles the Bald (840–877).

5 King Carloman (876–880), son of Louis the German (840–876).

6 Nantua.

7 Charles was buried at St-Denis, on the outskirts of Paris.

8 King Louis II (877–879).

9 Troyes.

10 At this point the chronicler of St-Bénigne began following the *Miracula* of St-Benoît, on p. 93 of *Les miracles de saint Benoît*, E. de Certain's printed edition. The Burgundian chronicler, however, attributed Hugh's success to God (as given here), not to St Benedict.

11 Hugh the Abbot of the Welf dynasty (d. 886).

preditus eorum temerarios compescuisset ausus. Auxiliante namque Deo parua manu tantas hostium phalanges fudit, ut uix superesset qui nuntiare potuisset. Qua plaga humilitati Dani, Gallias per aliquod spacium temporis quietas reliquerunt. Huic bello prefuit Lucdouuicus rex. At Hugone ultimos uite sue claudente soles, Lucdouuicoque principe post amministratum, ut diximus, biennio regnum, diem obeunte, Karolus qui Simplex postea est dictus[12] in cunis euum agens patre orbatus remansit.

Supererant duo filii Rotberti Andegauorum comitis, fratres Hugonis abbatis.[13] Senior Oddo diccebatur, Robertus alter patrem nomine referens. Ex his maiorem natu Oddonem Franci tutorem pueri, regnique elegere gubernatorem, quia recidiui Nortmannorum excursus imminebant.[14] In partibus uero regni quę Lotharius et Lucdouuicus tenuerant, filii eiusdem Lucdouuici regnabant. Nam Lotharius sine filiis obierat. Ex his tribus fratribus unus patris nomine uocatus, alter Karlomannus, tercius Karolus est dictus. Sed duobus intra quinquennium defunctis ad iuniorem Karolum rerum summa peruenit.[15] Postque imperii monarchiam est adeptus.[16]

Refert quidam scriptor in eo opere quod metrico stilo composuit de excidio Parisiace urbis,[17] quo per vii annos a Nortmannis obsessa atque uastata est. Hunc Karolum congregato inmenso exercitu expugnare Nortmannos uoluisse. Quod illi audientes, legatos mittunt ad Karolum, promittunt se ei subici, cuncta ab eo imperata facere, ad quod uoluisset paratos fore, tantum si permittantur intra regnum consistere, et pacifice Francis cohabitare. Quibus promissionibus delusus, rex credens uera esse quę dicebantur, intermisit bellum. Nec multo post Karolus moritur. Nortmanni uero resumpta audacia, inuadunt ciuitates Beluacensium atque Meldorum, necnon et Milidunum deuastant castellum. Capitur Carnotis[18] ac relique secus undique ciuitates, nam in primo suo aduentu Rotomagum, Ebroas, Baiocas[19] et ceteras Neustrie ciuitates depopulati fuerant.

---

12 King Charles the Simple (d. 929).

13 Robert the Strong (d. 866) left two sons, both of whom became kings, Odo (888–898) and Robert I (923–924). Hugh the Abbot was not their brother; this identification, which originated with the eleventh-century chronicler of St-Bénigne, seems to have been that chronicler's effort to explain why Hugh the Abbot ended up with some of Robert the Strong's holdings. See Bouchard, *"Those of My Blood,"* p. 20.

14 The chronicler of St-Bénigne stopped following the *Miracula* of St-Benoît at this point.

15 Charles, called the Simple, outlived his brothers to become king.

16 Here, on fol. 53v, the chronicler of Bèze skips a paragraph in the chronicle of St-Bénigne concerning Bishop Geilo's generosity to that house (pp. 109–110 in the printed edition).

17 Abbo, *Bella Parisiae urbis.* The account is written as a poem.

18 Chartres.

19 The Neustrian cities of Rouen, Évreux, and Bayeux, which would become the principal Norman cities.

Gallias insuper peruagantur, Hispanias adeunt, Rodanum intrant fluuium, Italiam populantur et totum Christianorum pessumdatur regnum.[20] Interea congregati Francię principes consilium de magnis ineunt rebus, Oddonem licet reluctantem constituunt regem. Qui mente benignus et reipublicę hostes arcendo strenue prefuit, et Karolo postquam adoleuit sua repetenti pacienter regna refudit. A quo parte regni redonatus, quoad uixit tempore hostibus terribilis extitit. His temporibus incarnationis Christi DCCCXCI uoluebatur annus.

De[21] destructione[22] huius loci

Veniens ad obitum prefatus ac uenerabilis Geylo episcopus,[23] cognoscens et ipse multa ad dimittendum seu purgandum in seipso, antequam occurreret cum omnibus nobis in generali resurrectione, ei in cuius conspectu non sunt mundi etiam ipsi cęli, quibus in uita deseruierat, in morte non solum animam sed etiam corpus commendauit. Precepit itaque corpus suum ad hoc Besuense monasterium deferri, et se totum Deo et sanctis eius apostolis quibus datum est claudere cęlum uel aperire quibus uoluerint, committens necnon et gloriosissimo aliorum sanctorum quorum hic reliquie habentur, patrocincio cum predecessore suo Alberico Lingonensi itidem episcopo[24] sepultus est.

Circa idem fere tempus secundum quod scriptum est, risui nostro dolor admixtus est, et extrema gaudii nostri luctus occupauit. Nam uenientibus per Franciam in Burgundia Normannis, monasterium istud Besuense penitus contigit desolatum iri. Et cum septies inueniamus locum istum a perfidis Christianis seu a paganis uiolatum atque destructum, hęc ultima destructio non inmerito enphatice a nobis dicitur, "Desolatio desolationum."

Dicamus igitur sicut in antiquis menbranulis nostris uix recolligere potuimus quomodo et a quibus sexies deuastatum sit, ut tandem ad hanc ultimam et atrocissimam desolationem paulo latius disserendam accedamus. Prima uice a Christianis per intestina bella, qui hunc locum inuadentes abstulerunt inde cum aliis rebus etiam omnes cartarum auctoritates. Vnde iam in precedentibus aliquantulum mentionem fecimus. Alia uice a Vuandalis, perfidis paganis. Tertia uice a Sarracenis, quando Augustidunum ciuitatem[25] destruxerunt, anno ab incarnatione Domini DCCXXXI. Fertur etiam una uice a monachis hunc

20 The author has overstated in having the Norsemen invade Spain after overrunning Gaul, crossing the Rhône to take over Italy and all Christian realms.

21 Here, on fol. 54r, the chronicler of Bèze stops following the chronicle of St-Bénigne (p. 111 in the printed edition).

22 The cartulary reads "destrutione."

23 Geilo, bishop of Langres (880–889).

24 Alberic, bishop of Langres (821–838).

25 Autun.

relictum fuisse locum, ob merum cuiusdam morbi qui hanc uastabat regionem. Quarta uice tempore Remigii, fratris Pipini regis, Magni Karoli patris,[26] pro quadam femina nomine Angla, cui predictus Remigius hunc locum donauerat, unde et nos in superioribus mentionem fecimus. Cuius rei ordinem qui plenius nosse desiderat, ad eam descriptionis narratiunculam recurrat. Sed et hoc sciendum quod ex hoc tempore usque ad domnum Albericum, qui hunc locum reparauit, ab ordine monastico penitus cessauit.

Iam uero dicendum est de illa ultima desolatione, quę non solum huic loco obfuit, uerum etiam totam Franciam ipsis Normannis uastantibus, neque uspiam Francis totam[27] resistendi firmitatem repperientibus, multa sanctorum corpora Diuioni castro inuecta sunt, eo quod firmissimum et inexpugnabile uideretur, quorum quędam postea sunt relata, quibusdam ibi remanentibus, alia sunt ad alia loca translata. Delatum est a Suessonicis corpus Beati Medardi episcopi. Delatum est a Taruuanensibus corpus Beatissimi Siluini eorum episcopi.[28] Nostri quoque patroni, Beatissimi Prudentii, corpus eodem delatum et in basilica Beati Stephani[29] collocatum, multis annis permansit. Tandem Deo nobis propitio, paceque reddita, Beati Prudentii corpus inde est relatum, et Beati Siluini corpus cum Beata Anglia,[30] eius familiarissima, nobis a Deo donatum. Sicque factum est ut cum huius loci protectionem principaliter habeat cum Paulo princeps apostolorum Petrus, unum ipsius exornet latus beatissimus martyr Prudentius, alterum cum uenerabili Anglia, beatus Siluinus episcopus. Aliquantisper protelauimus desolationis nostrę narrationem, nolentes silentio contegi qualiter nobis qui putabamur nostro patrono desolati, postmodum a Deo sint pro uno duo procurati. Nunc ad ea quę omiseramus redeamus.

Audientes hi qui hic erant monachi Normannorum aduentum, quidam timore pene ac mortis se occultauerunt, quidam ad alia monasteria demigrauerunt. Nec mirum, quoniam qui hic remanserunt, gladio interfecti sunt, quorum nomina hęc sunt. Ayrmannus monachus, Genesius monachus, Beraldus monachus, Sifardus monachus, Rodco monachus, Ansuinus presbyter, Adalricus puerulus. Hi omnes pro Christo pie iugulati talionem ei reddentes, sacrificium Deo effecti sunt, anno ab incarnatione Domini DCCCLXXXVIII.

---

26 Remigius, brother of King Pippin the Short (751–768).

27 The cartulary reads "tutam."

28 Many relics were taken to Dijon for hoped-for protection from the Vikings. As well as Bèze's relics, these included those of St Medard of Soissons and St Sivin of Thérouanne. The manuscript reads "Assuessonicis."

29 The basilica of St-Étienne of Dijon.

30 The words "Beata Anglia eius familiarissima" here, as well as "uenerabili Anglia" below, are written in a different although contemporary hand, in a spot that was apparently left blank originally.

Verumtamen cum nemo repertus sit qui eis posset uel auderet resistere, fuit isdem temporibus quidam dux nostrarum partium, Richardus nomine, qui a iusticie studio dictus est et ipse "Iustificator."[31] Hic pro libertate patrie partim zelo succensus, plurimum uero pro ecclesiis Dei defendendis, Deum habens adiutorem, expugnare illos aggressus est. Et licet usque ad hanc Besuam hostilis impetus procurrerit, et hic rabies insanie eorum adeo efferbuerit, ut et monachos nostros ut prediximus gladiis interemerit, et omnia uastauerit, in tantum ut et fontem ipsum de se gurgitem magni fluuii euomentem, potatione quadrupedum innumerabilium per totum quatriduum exsiccauerit, ad Diuionem tantum eos aspirare, nec loci firmitas nec ducis nominatissimi permisit metuenda bellicositas. Quin immo occurrens eis prefatus dux Richardus in loco uocato Argentoilo[32] cummisso cum eis prelio cęsa est, eorum quamplurima multitudo. Sicque Dani cum Normannis retro redire sunt coacti.

Anno[33] incarnati Verbi DCCCXCIII, Odone regnante[34] in Francia, Arnulfo in Italia atque Saxonia, Karolus iam iuuenis regni repetit sceptra, atque memoratus Arnulfus imperii inuasit monarchiam. Tunc primum a Francorum regibus ad extraneos translatum est imperium, principibus regni uilipendentibus Karolum ob mentis tardum ingenium, Odone rege xii anno regni sui defuncto, qui quoad uixit hostes fortiter compressit. Reciproci Normannorum et Danorum insurgunt fluctus, Hungri ab Aquilone, Sarraceni a Meridię ac finibus Hispanię prorumpentes, in interitum confluunt Gallię. Per omnia seuit gladius, cuncta dantur incendio, sanctorum loca traduntur exterminio.

Anno DCCCCXI incarnati Verbi, xiii kalendas Augusti in sabbato, cum obsiderent Normanni Carnotinam urbem[35] et iam essent penitus capienda, superuenientes Richardus et Robertus[36] cum suis, Dei auxilio, et Beatę Marię patrocinio roborati, fecerunt stragem maximam paganorum, a paucis qui remanserunt obsides capientes. Habuit[37] isdem Richardus filium nomine

---

31 Richard le Justicier (d. 921), duke of Burgundy and brother of King Boso. For his family, see Bouchard, *"Those of My Blood,"* pp. 74–97.

32 Argenteuil.

33 At this point, on fol. 56r, the chronicler of Bèze once again begins following the chronicle of St-Bénigne (pp. 113–114 of the printed edition), although only for one paragraph.

34 King Odo (888–898), first king from the family that became the Capetians. Contrary to what the chronicler says below, he was king for ten years, not twelve.

35 For the semi-legendary 911 battle of Chartres, in which the chemise of the Virgin was later considered to have played a role, see Fassler, *Virgin of Chartres*, pp. 16–23.

36 King Robert I (923–924), brother of King Odo and grandfather of Hugh Capet.

37 After skipping a short section concerning the abbots of St-Bénigne, the chronicler of Bèze here, on fol. 56r, once again begins following St-Bénigne's chronicle, through the end of the paragraph (p. 115 of that chronicle's printed edition).

Rodulfum, qui fuit rex Francorum.[38] Alter filius uocatus est Boso, qui Burgundię superioris, quę Gallia Comata dicitur, accepit regnum.[39] Tercius filius dictus est Hugo, cognomento Capito, qui fuit dux inferioris Burgundię.[40] Exorta discordia inter Karolum et regni principes, lites ac bella, rapine et incendia, innumera undique seuiunt mala, tandem rex facti penitens, principes ad concordiam commouet, pacem exoptatam cum eis firmat.

38

c. 890

An exchange of fields at Pouilly between Abbot Walcaud and Teuthard.

Cartulary, fol. 56v.
Bougaud-Garnier p. 281.

De commutatione facta inter Walcaudum abbatem et Teutardum
Eo tempore facta est commutatio inter quendam Teuthardum et Walcaudum abbatem, de terris quę sub iure eorum uidebantur esse. Dedit itaque Teuthardus de parte sua ad partem Walcaudi abbatis campum unum, situm in pago Atoariense in fine Pauliacinse,[1] et contra Walcaudus abbas de parte sua dedit Theuthardo campum unum situm in ipso fine Pauliacinse.

This document probably was given at about the same time as the following one.

Obitus Geylonis

Defuncto uero Geylone episcopo Teutbaudus successit. Sed et isto defuncto, Agrimus episcopus successit,[2] in cura postorali ualde sollicitus. Hic Pontiliacum et ecclesiam Sancti Yppolyti a quodam Waltario nobis iniuste ablatam restituit, sicut hic demonstrabimus.

---

38 Raoul, son of Richard le Justicier, succeeded his father-in-law Robert I as king of the Franks (924–936).

39 Richard le Justicier did indeed have a son named Boso, but the chronicler has here confused Richard's son Boso with Richard's brother King Boso (879–887).

40 The chronicler has here confused Hugh the Black, Richard's son, with Hugh Capet, his first cousin though a generation younger.

1 Pouilly, 14 km northeast of Bèze, in the pagus of Attuyer.

2 After the death of Bishop Geilo in 889, there was a contested election between Theobold and Agrin. Theobold was blinded in 895, and Agrin took the see, supported by Richard le Justicier and the archbishop of Lyon. See Bautier, *Chartes, sceaux, et chancelleries*, pp. 229–231.

39

12 April 890

Bishop Agrin confirms that his predecessor Geilo brought the relics of St Prudentius from Aquitaine and established the saint at Bèze, as well as giving the monks property at Pontailler and the church of St-Hippolyte. The property was taken unjustly by one Walter, but Agrin now restores it at Abbot Walcaud's request.

Cartulary, fols. 56v–57v.
Bougaud-Garnier, pp. 282–283.
Summarized in Brequigny, *Table* 1:343; dated 889.

Carta et confirmatio Agrimi episcopi de collatis huic loco a Geylone episcopo

Agrimus diuina dispensante clementia humilis episcopus,[1] omnibus ęcclesię Dei fidelibus utriusque sexus et ordinis, usquam locorum degentibus. Ad multorum constat peruenisse noticiam qualiter Geylo pie recordationis episcopus predecessor meus[2] Sanctum Prudentium de Aquitania transferens, in nostrum episcopium Lingonense detulit, et in Besua monasterio ad laudem et gloriam nominis Dei sollempniter collocauit. Vbi ob amorem Dei et reuerentiam eiusdem Sancti Prudentii quasdam res ecclesię suę, uidelicet Pontiliacum[3] cum adiacentiis suis, et ęcclesiam in honore Sancti Yppolyti consecratam eidem monasterio contulit, quatinus monachis et Dei seruis ibidem Domino famulantibus, futuris temporibus proficiant in aucmentum.

Quo quidem de hac uita sublato, sicut reliquę res ecclesię nostrę inrationabiliter ad uotum diripientium distracte sunt, ita quoque et Pontiliacus a loco ubi fuerat a prefato presule collatus est a Waltario, sicut certissimum est, sacrilege inuasus et indebite alienatus. Vnde Gaulcaudus abbas prefati Besue monasterii, cum confratribus suis monachis, nostram humilitatem adiens, preiudicium iniuste loco illatum lacrimosis questibus innotuit, et ut nostra munificentia sublata indebite redderentur, pro amore Dei, et reuerentia Petri

1 Agrin became undisputed bishop of Langres (895–912) after the blinding of Bishop Theobold (889–895). He had claimed the see since 889 and acts as bishop in this charter.

2 Geilo, bishop of Langres (880–889).

3 Pontailler-sur-Saône, 21 km southeast of Bèze.

et Pauli apostolorum principum Sanctique Prudentii humiliter deprecatus est. Nos igitur deprecationem illius paternę suscipientes, eamque cum fidelibus ecclesię nostrę clericis ac laicis pertractantes, et iustam racionabilemque et rectam perspicientes, consilio et consensu tocius ecclesię nostrę sicut prefate res ab antecessore nostro sepedicto loco concesse sunt, et nos quoque presentialiter concedimus, et hac nostra auctoritate regnante Domino nostro in perpetuum consecramus.

Vt autem presens nostra restitutio futuris temporibus uigorem inuiolabilem optineat, et de cetero indebitam, iniustamque nesciat pati iacturam, manu propria roborauimus, fideliumque nostrorum subscriptionibus confirmare iussimus, successoribus nostris per sanctam et inextricabilem Trinitatem humiliter obnixeque suggerentes, ut quę a nobis pie statuta sunt, ab illis inuiolabiliter conseruentur.

Agrimus sanctę Lingonensis ecclesię humilis episcopus in Christi nomine roboraui et signaui. Otbertus prepositus et archidiaconus signaui. Bernardus archiclauerius signaui. Madalgaudus diaconus signaui. Isaac archidiaconus signaui. Emmarricus archidiaconus signaui. Euuardus diaconus signaui. Helgaudus presbyter signaui. Vrsinus presbiter signaui. Arnaldus archidiaconus signaui. Fulculfus diaconus signaui. Albericus diaconus signaui. Acleuertus subdiaconus signaui. Vulleus subdiaconus signaui. Sequinus subdiaconus signaui. Iosselmus acolitus signaui. Gislerius acolitus signaui. Ego Brantio indignus presbyter hanc restitutionem scripsi et dictaui, ii idus Aprilis, indictione viii, anno ii regnante Oddone rege.[4]

See document 21 for Bishop Geilo's gift of St Prudentius's relics to Bèze. The signatories are presumably the cathedral chapter of Langres.

40

Late ninth century

Alard gives Bèze a *curtilis* located at Taniot, with all its appurtenances.

Cartulary, fol. 57v.
Bougaud-Garnier, p. 284.

4 Odo, king of France (888–898).

Karta de Tanaxtello

Quidam homo nomine Alardus dedit res suas proprias in uilla quę dicitur Taxnatello,[1] uel in ipsa fine, id est curtile unum quod terminatur de uno latere terra Sancti Leodegarii,[2] de alio latere terra Willerii, de una fronte strata publica, de alia fronte fisco. Infra ipsas terminationes et quicqud ad ipsum mansum aspicit tam terris quam etiam pratis, siluis, pascuis, aquis, aquarumque decursibus, exitibus et regressibus, omnia ad integrum dedit Deo et ecclesię Besuensi.

41

888–898

The couple Karl and Rotrudis give Bèze and Abbot Walcaudus some property at Lux and other nearby places.

Cartulary, fol. 56v.
Bougaud-Garnier, p. 284.

Carta de Luco

Eodem tempore quidam homo nomine Karlus et uxor sua Retrudis dederunt Besuensi ecclesię et abbati Walcaudo res proprias sitas in uilla quę dicitur Lucus,[1] habentes terminationes de uno latere terram Sancti Vincentii, de alio stratam publicam, de una fronte fiscum, de alia fronte conturnum uicinorum. Similiter dedit in ipsa fine iornalem unum et peciolam de terra, et in alia fine quę dicitur Campania[2] dedit iornales duos. In alia autem fine quę dicitur Mons Mainberti,[3] iornalem unum et peciolam de terra. In alio uero loco dedit ubi possunt seminari de tritico modii octo et ancillam nomine Mainbergam, tempore regis Oddonis.[4]

This document is dated by King Odo.

1 Taniot, 7 km south of Bèze.
2 St-Léger, 19 km south-southeast of Bèze. The monks of this house presumably had property at Taniot.
1 Lux, 5 km northwest of Bèze.
2 Champagne, 10 km southeast of Bèze.
3 Garnier identifies this as Montrementier, a *climat*. It is also mentioned in document 23.
4 Odo, king of France (888–898).

Defuncto uero Agrimo episcopo, successit Warnerius episcopus.[5] Hic petentibus monachis cęnobii huius Beatum Prudentium martyrem retulit de Diuioni, cum innumerabilibus clericis diuersi ordinis, et a plebe innumerabili utriusque sexus cum honoris tripudio susceptus est. Denique monachis predicti cęnobii cum infinito populo eminus a monasterio ei obuiam occurrentibus, cum inmensis laudibus receptus est, anno Verbi Incarnati diuini DCCCCXXI, nono kalendarum Octobrium die.

Defuncto autem Walcaudo abbate, Walcadus successit, sed et isto obeunte Galcaudus successor efficitur.[6] Sed et isto defuncto successit abbas nomine Milo, postmodum Matisconensis episcopus,[7] qui nichil boni in hac domo gessit. Obeunte autem Warnerio Lingonensi episcopo, successit Gotselmus in episcopatus honore, anno primi regni Rotberti.[8] De quo quia mentio facta est, oportet dicere quomodo regnum acceperit.

Oddone[9] rege defuncto, Rotbertus frater ipsius[10] sperans et cupiens eam regni partem quam ipse tenuerat adipisci, quia ei a Karolo qui totius regni erat dominus[11] non reddebatur, palam tyrannidem inuasit. Et hoc post mortem Richardi ducis, qui ab executione iustitię cognomen accepit.[12] Ipse namque quamdiu uixit, Karolo regi semper fidelis extitit. Rotbertus[13] igitur affectatę tyrannidis potentiam palam exercere cupiens, a quibusdam episcopis diademate se regio coronari, ac sceptro regni insigniri, partim blandiciis partim minis extorsit.

Sed nequaquam huius presumptio letos habuit exitus. Denique postquam uno regnauit anno, Suessonicis in campis bello a ducibus Karoli exceptus, uitaque spoliatus, licet exercitus eius uictoriam obtinuerit, ipse tamen nefarię temeritatis precium luit. Nec tamen socii defectionis interitu eius territi, perfidie

5 Warner, bishop of Langres (912–923).

6 These three may or may not all be the same person, most likely related to the Walcaud who had been abbot in the early ninth century. A single Abbot Walcaud may not account for the time between when the monks returned from Dijon and when Milo took office, but it is also possible that there was a period without an abbot at all.

7 Milo, bishop of Mâcon (981–993).

8 Jocelin became bishop of Langres (923–931).

9 Here, on fol. 58r, the chronicler of Bèze once again begins to copy the chronicle of St-Bénigne (pp. 122–123 of the printed edition).

10 Robert I (922–923) became king of the Franks only long after the death of his brother Odo (888–898). As noted below, Robert's reign was only a year long, being cut short at the battle of Soissons.

11 King Charles the Simple (898–922).

12 Richard le Justicier (d. 921) was indeed, as the chronicler says, always loyal to the Carolingians, even fighting for them against his own brother in the 880s.

13 At this point the chronicler of St-Bénigne again began drawing on the *Miracula* of St-Benoît, chapter 2.3, pp. 98–99 in the printed edition.

deseruere contumaciam. Quin potius Herbertus comes Virmandensis[14] infando scelere domnum suum regemque tocius Francie Karolum dolo captum, uinculisque irretitum Paronne direxit tenebroso domicilio recludendum. Et quia regni status sine principe agebatur in incertum, maxime cum Hugoni, Rotberti filio, qui post probis actibus Magni nomen promeruit,[15] puerilis obsisteret ętas quominus regias assumeret infulas, et Herberti cunctos haberet odium, maxime eos quos humanitatis respectu ad misericordiam erumna principis permouebat. Tandem Rodulfus Burgundia oriundus, Richardi ducis filius, regende preficitur Francorum patrie.[16] Qui adeptus regni solium, et in malefactoribus fuit ultor seuerus, et in coercendis hostibus ac tuendo regno sagacissimus. Eius in diebus Danorum atque Nortmannorum iterum adueniunt phalanges, et non solum Franciam sed etiam totam percurrunt Burgundiam. Contra quos Rodulfus sumptis armis, ita proteruos eorum compescuit incursus, ut usque nunc Gallias ab eorum inuasione faciat manere quietas.

Defuncto[17] autem Gotselmo episcopo, successit ei in episcopatus honore Letericus episcopus, post hunc Ęricus, deinde Achardus, atque post Widricus.[18] Transierunt sub his pontificibus anni ferme xl et amplius, in quibus semper in deterius processit huius loci status, episcopis et abbatibus alia magis quam id curantibus.

Rodulfo[19] rege defuncto absque liberis, nam filius eius Lucdouuicus nomine, quem habuit ex Emma regina coniuge sua, defunctus est ante obitum patris. Et Karolus ergastulo clausus, animam non corpus custodia exemit, qui dum uiueret Simplex dictus est ob benignitatem animi,[20] sanctus nunc recte potest uocari, quoniam iniuste ab infidelibus suis et periuris longa custodia carceris afflictus, uitę supernę est transmissus. Hic reliquit filium Lucdouuicum ex Headgiua Anglorum regis filia susceptum.[21] Qui calamitatis paternę procellis semet inuolui metuens, ad Anglos Saxones maternę affinitatis inuitatus gratia se contulit. Post excessum uero Rodulfi regis ab Hugone Magno

14 Herbert, count of Vermandois, was connected to Robert I by marriage; see Bouchard, *"Those of My Blood,"* pp. 52–53.

15 Hugh the Great, son of Robert I and father of Hugh Capet.

16 Raoul (923–936) succeeded his father-in-law Robert I as king. At this point the Burgundian chroniclers ceased following the *Miracula* of St-Benoît.

17 Here, on fol. 58v, the chronicler of Bèze briefly returns to concerns of his own house.

18 Bishops of Langres Leotheric (931–933), Heric (933–945), Achard (948–970), and Widric (970–980).

19 Here, on fol. 59r, the chronicle of Bèze once again copies a section from the chronicle of St-Bénigne (pp. 126–127 in the printed edition).

20 Charles the Simple (898–922).

21 Louis IV (936–954).

reuocatus, specie tenus regno redditus est patrio, anno incarnationis Dominice DCCCCXXXVIII, indictione xi. Cuius regni amministratio ius dominationis exercere cupuenti, laboriosa illi fuit, tamen sui a Thebaldo Carnotensium comite[22] captione, quam post regni recuperatione, uaria instabilis fortune prouentu.[23]

Lucdouuicus rex moriens, duos superstites dimisit liberos, Lotharium atque Karolum, quos genuerat ei Gerberga soror Ottonis Romanorum postea imperatoris.[24] Karolus euo iunior priuatis in edibus senuit, in hereditatem omnem Lotharius successit.[25] Qui potestate regia functus est per xxx et eo amplius annos.

De Brunone episcopo

Anno[26] ab incarnatione Domini DCCCCLXXX, indictione viii, regni Lotharii regis xxv anno, dedit idem rex Brunoni Remensis ecclesię clerico,[27] suo uero parenti propinquitate consanguinitatis existenti, episcopatum Lingonicę ciuitatis. Ordinatus est autem idem Bruno episcopus per manus Burchardi Lugdunensis archiepiscopi,[28] in ecclesia Sancti Stephani, xxiiii gerens anno etatis. Et eodem anno susceptus est a clero Lingonicę urbis, ab incarnatione uidelicet Christi DCCCCLXXXI. His assecutus episcopatum, omni quo potuit nisu sequi studuit exemplum boni pastoris. Monasteria igitur ipsius ad diocesim pertinentia in spiritalibus religione, in temporalibus necessaria pene adnullata gubernatione considerans, cepit querere quatenus Dei dispensante nutu, suum in statum ea quiuisset reparare.

Cum[29] uero de huius Besuensis monasterii multimodis desolationibus dissereremus, diximus prout memorię occurrere potuit, secundum quod in scedulis ueteribus inuenimus, sexies desertum et fere adnullatum fuisse. Verum tamen postea diligentius cetera perscrutantes, inuenimus hunc eundem locum

22 Theobold, count of Chartres.

23 Here the chronicler of Bèze skips two sentences specifically concerning St-Bénigne.

24 Louis IV married Gerberge, sister of Otto I (936–973).

25 King Lothair of France (954–986).

26 Having skipped a section concerning the monastery of St-Bénigne, the chronicler of Bèze continues to follow that house's chronicle for this paragraph (pp. 128–129 in the printed edition).

27 Bruno, bishop of Langres (980–1016). He was a great-grandson of Henry the Fowler, via his mother, and a nephew of King Lothair. He had been a cleric at Reims before becoming bishop. His ordination at age twenty-four was six years short of the canonical minimum, yet he still proved himself an excellent bishop. See Bouchard, *Sword, Miter, and Cloister*, pp. 393–394.

28 Burchard, archbishop of Lyon (979–1031).

29 Here, on fol. 59v, the chronicler of Bèze returns once again to the concerns of his own house.

ab Hungris[30] combustum quinquies, quippe cui nullum erat a terreno principe defensaculum, nec loci ad resistendum inimicis munimentum. Harum combustionum due quo tempore euenerint, notum nobis est. Anno namque DCCCCXXXVI incarnati Verbi uenerunt Hungri in Burgundiam mense Iulio. Iterum anno DCCCCXXXVII incarnati Verbi Lucdouuico filio Karoli uncto in regem, et nondum eodem anno euoluto, Hungri uenientes per Franciam et per Burgundiam atque Aquitaniam, deuastauerunt omnia. Que uastatio in tantum huic loco obfuit, ut per l et unum annos, usque ad annum scilicet incarnati Verbi DCCCCLXXXI quo domnus Bruno Lingonensi ecclesię preficitur episcopus respirare ad priorem statum nequiuerit.

Videns[31] igitur domnus Bruno episcopus statum huius loci et abbatiam Sancti Benigni Diuionensis in ambiguo positum, supplex adiit domnum Maiolum Cluniacensis monasterii abbatem,[32] multaque prece poposcit quatinus eius auxilio quiuisset eas reparare in melius, et interius religionem et exterius possessiones. Cuius precibus flexus reuerendus abbas Maiolus dedit ei[33] quendam fratrem feruentissimum sui ordinis executorem, et totius nobilitatis lampade prefulgidum atque in uera humilitate et fraternę dilectionis caritate, nec ne summe discretionis quę uirtutum omnium mater esse dinoscitur honestate, laudabiliter radicatum et fundatum, nomine Willelmum,[34] qui prefecit eum monasterio Sancti Benigni Diuionensis spiritalem patrem. Hic Italia extitit oriundus, alto satis germine et nobili prosapia editus. Quem supradictus domnus Maiolus Roma ueniens, inuenit in monasterio Lauceio dicto[35] ubi a puero educatus fuerat. Assumensque eum ipso deprecante, secum adduxit Cluniacum, etatę iuuenili florentem.

30 The Magyars who swept through parts of Europe in the tenth century were always called Huns by contemporary chroniclers.

31 Here, on fol. 60r, the chronicler of Bèze begins copying a section from the chronicle of St-Bénigne (pp. 130–133 in the printed edition).

32 Maiolus, abbot of Cluny (948–994). For his achievements, see Rosenwein, *Rhinoceros Bound.*

33 The chronicler of Bèze here (fol. 60r) skips over details from the chronicle of St-Bénigne on the twelve monks who came to that house from Cluny (pp. 130–131 in the printed edition).

34 William, abbot of St-Bénigne (990–1031), originally from Italy, was a monk at Cluny before being set over several Burgundian monasteries, including Bèze. The chronicler of St-Bénigne drew many details from the vita written by Raoul Glaber, who had been a monk under William; "Vita Domni Willelmi abbatis," ed. Neithard Bulst, in Raoul Glaber, *Five Books of the Histories*, pp. 254–298. See also Bulst, *Untersuchungen zu den Klosterreform Wilhelms von Dijon.*

35 Locedia, in the diocese of Vercelli.

Ordinatus est igitur abbas a domno Brunone episcopo, anno ab incarnatione Domini DCCCCXC, indictione iii. Officio uero abbatis accepto, diuinis seipsum cepit exercere uirtutibus. Erat enim corpore castus, mente deuotus, affabilis alloquio, prudentia preditus, temperancia clarus, interna fortitudine firmus, censura iustitie stabilis, longanimitate assiduus, pacientia robustus, humilitate mansuetus, bonorum operum gratia plenus, karitatis equidem affluens uisceribus.[36] Pro pauperibus semper erat sollicitus, Christum uero totis diligens uisceribus, dum sicut Martha corporaliter non ualebat, in egenis illum cotidie spiritaliter reficiebat. Omnibus hospicii perlargum prebuit usum, nemo est exceptus, perpessus nemo repulsam. Diuinorum preceptorum delectabatur eloquiis, quia ex his et suos mores componere, et sibi commisso instruebatur docere et corrigere. Cunctis seipsum bene uiuendi prebeat exemplum. Et sicut in ordine ita primus studebat ut esset in opere, iuxta illud euangelistę, "Cœpit Ihesus facere et docere" [Acts 1:1]. Peccantes uero zelo pii amoris coram omnibus arguebat, ut ceteri timorem haberent. Sed et uerba quę sub increpatione proferebat, ut reprehendenda reprehenderet, quasi stimuli dura uidebantur et aspera, ut pœne timerentur plusquam uerbera, iuxta illud, "Verba sapientis, quasi stimuli, et quasi claui in altum defixi" [Ecc. 12:11]. Alios quidem blandimentis, alios ammonitionibus, alios terroribus, et ita iuxta apostolum predicans uerbum, instabat oportune, inportune arguens, obsecrans, increpans, in omni pacientia et doctrina. Miserorum uero haut secus, ac si ipse pateretur, affitiebatur calamitatibus. Os eius ita replebatur ex cordis abundantia, ut in eodem ore pene nichil aliud nisi lex resonaret diuina, et quia scriptura dicit, "Qui audit, dicat ueni" [Rev. 22:17]. Ideo quoscumque poterat, a seculi nequitia suadendo subtrahebat. Et sicut celestę per desiderium totis ipse uiribus ad supernum regnum anelabat, ita secum pergere omnes homines si fieri posset exoptabat. Sed nullatenus est fraudatus a desiderio, quod in se conceperat uera dilectio. Ille enim qui caritas est, qui se timentium complet uoluntatem, uiri Dei feruentem affectum perduxit ad effectum. Ad eius quippe monita multi quę possederant relinquentes, regulari se disciplinę subdiderunt, et Beati Benedicti sequentes uestigia, semetipsos abnegantes, uero regi totis uiribus militauerunt. Partibus namque ex diuersis ad eius cœnobium multitudo confluxit innumerabilis. Sed nationibus licet diuersi mente tamen erant uniti, ut illud ad litteram in eis impletum uideretur, quod de inicio nascentis ecclesię in apostolorum actibus legitur, "Erat illis cor unum, et anima una" [Acts 4:32].

36 According to the editors of the chronicle of St-Bénigne, two lines were scratched out at this point. The scratching out must have happened before the chronicler of Bèze used the manuscript, because he continued the text without a break. Presumably the original scribe of St-Bénigne realized he had repeated a sentence, easy enough to do as two consecutive phrases end in the same word.

Tempore[37] quo hęc gerebantur, Hugo rex, Hugonis Magni filius, cum Rotberto filio Francorum pociebatur regno.[38] Lothario namque regi celestę ut credimus pro terreno commutanti, Lucdouuicus filius successit.[39] Qui inmatura adolescens preuentus morte, destitutum proprio herede Francorum deriliquid regnum. Sane patruus eius Karolus conabatur si posset a sui generis auctoribus diu possessum sibi uendicare regnum, sed eius uoluntas nullum sortitur effectum.[40] Nam Franci primates eo relicto, ad Hugonem qui ducatum Francię strenuę tunc gubernabat, Magni illius Hugonis filium cuius iam mentio facta est, se conferentes, eum Nouiomo ciuitate[41] solio sublimant regio. Is eodem anno Rotbertum filium sibi consortem regni elegit. Cepit regnare anno DCCCCXCI ab incarnatione Christi, et regnaui x annis. Post cuius mortem Rotbertus solus obtinuit regnum. Hugonis regis fuerunt fratres duo, Otto et Heinricus, filii Hugonis Magni ducis Francorum. Post mortem patris accepit Hugo ducatum Francie, et Otto Burgundie. Habuit uxorem filiam Gysleberti, qui post Hugonem, fratrem Rodulfi regis, ducatum Burgundię tenuit. Sed eo in adolescentia absque liberis defuncto, Heinricus successit frater suus.[42] Hic fuit comptus bonis moribus, precipue mansuetudine, uir ecclesiasticus. Ipse denique Heinricus dux, audita fama religionis eximii patris Willelmi, commisit ei abbatiam Verziacensem,[43] pene ad nichilum redactam, ut ab ipso restrueretur in pristinum statum, quod et fecit, auxiliante Deo.

Domnus autem episcopus Bruno considerans patrem Willelmum ita feruentem in religione ac monastica institucione, et loca ei commissa de die in diem in melius proficere, omnia in suo episcopio monasteria ipsius delegauit prouidentię. Videns uero abbatiam istam Besuensem, in honore et nomine beatorum apostolorum Petri et Pauli dicatam, pene ad nichilum redactam, monuit instanti prece, ut eam secundum regularem emendare curaret institutionem. Cuius annuens precibus istud cœnobium in paucis annis ad regularem commutauit statum, monasterium etiam Sancti Iohannis quod Reomaus dicitur, locum sancti Michaelis archangeli iuxta castrum Tharnodorum, abbatiam

37 Having skipped a page in the chronicle of St-Bénigne concerned with the affairs of that house, the chronicler of Bèze, on fol. 61r, continues to follow the earlier chronicle (pp. 134–137 in the printed edition).

38 Hugh Capet, king of France (987–996), and his son, King Robert II (996–1031), who acted as co-king for several years with his father.

39 King Louis V (986–987).

40 Charles of Lorraine tried unsuccessfully to succeed his nephew Louis V.

41 Noyon.

42 Hugh Capet's brother Otto became count of Autun and Dijon through his marriage with the daughter of Count Giselbert (d. 956). When Otto died in 965, his brother Henry took the duchy of Burgundy. See Bouchard, *"Those of My Blood,"* pp. 146–147.

43 The monastery St-Vivant of Vergy.

Melundensem ubi Sanctus Walerius archidiaconus et martyr quiescit.[44] Quas omnes ita strenuę gubernauit, ut post eum singulę singulis abbatibus distributę statui illius temporis quo ab eo regebantur non quierint equari.

Anno sexto sue ordinationis Willelmus abbas Romam perrexit ad apostolorum limina, eorum patrocinia exposcens prece deuota, indeque ad sanctum angelum montem petiuit Garganum. Sed Beneuentum ueniens, grauissime infirmitatis adstrictus est compede. Cuius infirmitatis diuturno afflictus langore, cum iam a suis desperaretur posse euadere, quadam noce raptus in spiritu tribunali metuendi iudicis sistitur, ubi cum pro aliquibus increparetur excessibus, et maxime pro indiscreta seueritate, proque his culpis metueret, dampnari ęternis gehennę suppliciis, ut sibi uisum est, sanctus papa Gregorius[45] in sua eum suscepit fide, diligentiori deinceps uicturum sollicitudine, et priora errata pietatis ac misericordie operibus expianda correcturum fore. Post uisionem in semet reuersus, et ab infirmitate cepit eadem conualescere die, et priorem austeritatem permutauit in maximam pietatem. Sic quę postea omni uitę suę tempore Sanctum Gregorium speciali coluit dilectione.

Cœperunt denique ex sua patria, hoc est Italia, multi ad eum conuenire, aliqui litteris bene eruditi, alii diuersorum operum magisterio docti, alii agriculturę scientia prediti, quorum ars et ingenium huic loco profuit plurimum. Cum[46] uero Willelmus abbas augustorum seu regum palacia adiit, in eis non que sua sunt sed quę Ihesu Christi quesiuit, ut ex eorum scilicet familiari collucutione subuenire oppressis sua interuentione, aut certe ex seculari uel clericali habitu Deo lucri faceret, ut iuxta Domini preceptum propria relinquerent, et secularibus curis semotis, Deo in tranquillitate seruire studerent.

Conueniębant igitur ad eum plurimi ut diximus, et licet diuersi nationibus mente tamen erant uniti. Letabatur pastor in sui gregis aucmento, magisque gaudebat quod omnes instabant operi proposito. Verum quia super gregem sibi commissum sollerti uigilauit cura, diuina promeruit gratia de fructu laborum suorum in hac gaudere uita. Nam regularis uitę disciplinam, quę iam pene deciderat per ueterum neglegentiam, prout Beatus Benedictus eam composuit, in pristinum statum corrigendo restaurauit, ac per diuersas mundi partes per plura monasteria a regulari tramite deuia, tam per se quam per suos quos abbates ordinauerat, monastico ordini subdidit. In hoc uero gaudens

44 The monasteries of Moûtier-St-Jean, St-Michel of Tonnerre, and Molosmes.

45 Pope Gregory I (590–604).

46 At this point, on fol. 62v, the chronicler of Bèze skips a long section in the chronicle of St-Bénigne concerning the foundation and rebuilding of their church (pp. 137–148 in the printed edition), then begins following it once again (pp. 148–149).

gratulabatur Deo, quod eorum quos sua sub cura educauerat, ad monasticum regendum ordinem fore multos idoneos uidebat.[47]

Cum primum abbatis suscepit officium uenerabilis Willelmus, quidam[48] castri Diuionensis ciuis nobili ortus genere, Rodulfus Albus uocatus nomine,[49] uenit ad conuersionem inter ipsa primordia eius noue ordinationis, cuius pecuniis releuata est paupertas predicti patris et consilio atque adiutorio subleuata sollicitudo regiminis huius loci Besuensis monasterii. Adhuc quippe erat ei paucitas monachorum, quem predictus frater ita iuuabat in exterioribus curis, ut solus supplere uideretur solamem plurium. Sed preter eius uotum, hoc solatium tulit illi paucitas dierum.

Si[50] huius uiri mentionem facientes, paululum excesserimus ordinem rationis, ne cuiquam ueniat in fastidium. Cure enim nobis fuit, eos precipue annotare, qui erga hunc locum deuotiores seu munificentiores extitere. Hic uero Rodulfus, quoniam hęc ęcclesia secundum quantitatem quia parua erat tantis patronis, Petro dico et Paulo, non uidebatur condigna a fundamentis incipiens et ad perfectum usque perducens, in eo statu quomodo est consummauit. Rexit autem hunc locum sub abbate Willelmo, prior magnus tam in exterioribus quam in interioribus prouidendis et amministrandis strenuissimus, quippe qui hoc ipsum iugi cura et exercitio didicerat. Fuerat namque antequam ueniret ad conuersionem uicecomes Diuionensis. Conuertens itaque studium seculare in ecclesiasticum, ex bonis initiis meliores fines obtinuit. Obiit uero huius uite diem idibus Nouembris, cuius anima requiescat in pace. Amen.

Alter[51] quidam monachus uocatus Hunaldus quem predictus pater uidens sollertis ingenii, retinuit sibi ceteris abeuntibus. Ad ultimum post obitum predicti patris abbatiam Tharnodorensem[52] assecutus, ibidem quieuit. Alter[53] quoque subiunctus est memorato patri Theodericus dictus, quem post diutinam

47 At this point, fol. 63r, the chronicler of Bèze skips a short section of the chronicle of St-Bénigne (on p. 149 in the printed edition), then briefly picks it up again (from pp. 149–150).

48 After this word there is a blank in the manuscript where a word was erased, doubtless due to a copying error.

49 Rudolph was viscount of Dijon and brother of Lambert, first hereditary count of Chalon. See Bouchard, *Sword, Miter, and Cloister*, p. 307.

50 Now the chronicler of Bèze, on fol. 63r, has turned again to the affairs of his own house.

51 The chronicler of Bèze here, on fol. 63v, turns to a slightly earlier section of the chronicle of St-Bénigne (p. 149 of the printed edition), editing it severely down.

52 St-Michel of Tonnerre. For Hunald's election there, see GC 4, instr. col. 143, no. 19.

53 Here, still on fol. 63v, the chronicler of Bèze jumps ahead to once again follow the chronicle of St-Bénigne (pp. 150–159 of the printed edition), although he edits down as he goes.

erudicionem Fiscamnensi cęnobio constituit priorem, ad ultimum Gemmeticensium prefecit abbatem.[54]

Quidam etiam Mettensis ęcclesię clericus generosis ortus natalibus nomine Benedictus, eius discipulatui est adgregatus, breuique in tempore studendo eum imitari, doctrina et conuersatione perfectionem adtigit monasticę uitę. Per eius igitur relationem conperit domnus Adalbero Mettensis pontifex patris Willelmi religiosam conuersationem. A quo suppliciter euocatus atque Sancti Arnulfi abbatia donatus, eundem Benedictum ibidem constituit patrem.[55] Vbi pro multos annos sacris intentus actibus uita functus, claruit, multis uirtutibus.[56] Domnus igitur Bertoldus Leucorum episcopus[57] confabulationem quesiuit sepefati abbatis Willelmi. In cuius uerbis considerans inconcussam inadulatamque constantiam mentis, cęteraque insignia uirtutum in eius actis et moribis resplendentia admiratus, monuit ut abbatiam sancti Apri[58] suscipiens, emendare curaret, quod et fecit.[59]

Plures uero sacerdotum uel abbatum sibi commissorum locorum uel ecclesiarum relinquentes curam, ad patris Willelmi confluebant doctrinam. Quidam episcopus ciuitatis Albingate, que est iuxta Ienuam ciuitatem[60] super mare sita in Italia, relicto episcopio, predicti patris se subdidit imperio. Alter quoque episcopus Barnabas uocatus, genere Grecus, sub eius magisterio plurimis annis est conuersatus. Alius uero Benignus dictus episcopus a Roma adueniens per aliquot annos uero ipso commoratus fuit subiectus et obędiens. Abbates etiam perplures ex diuersis partibus uenientes, sponte se ipsi subiciebant obędire parati, inter quos fuerunt abbas Iohannes dictus Capuanus, alter quoque Iohannes abbas monasterii Sancti Apollinaris in urbe Rauenna, Benedictus quoque abbas monasterii Sancti Seueri urbis Classis, Anastasius etiam et Marcus abbates et alii plures, quos longum est enumerare. Monachorum uero non est numerus qui ab illis uenerunt partibus.[61]

---

54 The monasteries of Fécamp and Jumièges, both in Normandy.

55 The monastery of St-Arnould of Metz.

56 Here, on fol. 63v, in the interests of the brevity that he had mentioned above, the chronicler of Bèze skips two pages in the chronicle of St-Bénigne (pp. 150–151 in the printed edition).

57 Bertold, bishop of Toul.

58 The monastery of St-Evre of Toul.

59 Here again, on fol. 64r, the chronicler of Bèze skips a short section from the chronicle of St-Bénigne (pp. 151–152 in the printed edition).

60 Albenga, near Genoa.

61 Here, on fol. 64r, the chronicler of Bèze skips over a section from the chronicle of St-Bénigne (pp. 152–153 in the printed edition).

Ipsi denique sancti uiri patres et doctores heremitarum existentes, fama sanctitatis longe lateque notificati, Romaldus scilicet, Willelmus ac Martinus,[62] quos in magna ueneratione habebat urbs Rauenna, ceterique quos intra se concludit Italia, patris Willelmi expetebant societatem. Quia sanctorum coniunctio grata et iocunda, ecclesięque pernecessaria et econtra societas malorum impedimentum bonorum.

Ipsi uero cultores heremi relicta quiete solitudinis, gaudebant sub eius magisterio associari cenobitis. Ex eorum ergo numero adiuncti fuerunt ei duo, Iohannes et Paulus, litteris eruditi. Quorum sapientia ad salutem multarum profecit animarum. Horum uterque monasticę religionis feruentissimus, et in cęnobiali conuersatione ceteris erant imitandi, et in contemplatiua uita lectioni et orationi assidue studentes, uidentibus exemplo fuerunt pariter et amiracioni. Reuerende memorię Paulus apud nos in pace quieuit. Iohannes uero homo Dei ob sanctam conuersationem uocatus a domno patre Willelmo, Fructuariensi[63] cęnobio abbas est institutus. De quo loco, quia occasio se prebuit, intimandum paucis uidetur qualiter fundatus fuerit. Duo germani fratres fuerunt sepędicti abbatis Willelmi, unus uocatus est Nitardus, alter Godefredus.

Primus eorum honore comitatus enituit, alius milicię stipendiis contentus fuit. Quos predictus pater sepę amonendo, a mundi illecebris abduxit, et ad Christum conuertit. Venientes ergo uterque ad conuersionem, exceptis aliis rebus, dederunt Deo[64] quoddam iuris sui predium, Vulpianum uocatum, quodam presagio futurorum. In quo loco domnus Willelmus fundauit ecclesiam,[65] ut in hereditate parentum suorum aliquid acceptum Deo edificaret, atque ut fructus bonorum operum quę ibi geruntur sibi et illis esset abolicio peccatorum, et eternę uitę digna reconpensatio premiorum. Vnde et Fructuariensis ille locus est uocatus. In breui ergo tempore factum est nobile cęnobium, ubi de hoc loco[66] et de Diuionensi spiritalia et temporalia subsidia sunt delata, reliquie scilicet multe

62 Romuald, founder of the order of Camaldoli in Tuscany, was active in both northern Italy and southern France at the end of the tenth century and the first decades of the eleventh (d. c. 1027); Marinus was his companion and William among his disciples. Peter Damian wrote the *Vita Beati Romualdi*.

63 Fruttuaria, in Italy.

64 The chronicler of St-Bénigne says rather that they gave Volpiano to the monastery of St-Bénigne (p. 155).

65 The chronicler of St-Bénigne, although not the chronicler of Bèze, notes that this church was dedicated to St Benignus (p. 155).

66 The chronicle of St-Bénigne does not have the next three words (p. 155); for him "hoc loco" was naturally his own monastery.

sanctorum, uolumina librorum, omniaque ecclesiastica ornamenta, et monachi plurimi pariter illuc abierunt. Sed et de aliis sue ditioni subiectis locis, ac undecumque allatis supplementis, magnificatus est locus possessionibus et diuitiis. Ita ut in uita eius congregatio ipsius loci centum numero constaret monachis, exceptis locis cellarum ei loco subditis, quę fere xxx existunt.

Conuocatis ergo episcopis patrię, rege quoque Arduino, qui ibi postmodum quieuit, sua cum coniuge ac multis nobilibus ipsius regni, in honore Sancte Dei genitricis Marię, Sanctique Benigni, et omnium sanctorum, fecit locum illum sacrari. Constituit et alia monasteria in eadem patria, ubi deputatis monachis et abbatibus ordinatis adhuc ordo iuget monasticus. Sanctimonialium etiam instituit monasterium.

Audita uiri Dei fama nobilissimus Normannorum comes Richardus,[67] misit ad eum reuerenter supplicans ut ad se ueniret. Qui tandem libenter ut rogatus fuerat pergens, uenit ad eum, a quo sicuti decebat utrumque honorifice susceptus est. Multisque eius precibus exoratus est, ut ecclesiam sanctę et indiuiduę trinitatis nomine et honore dicatam, in loco qui Fiscannus dicitur,[68] olim constructam et a se in ampliorem statum decenter reformatam susciperet, atque monachorum collegio decoraret. Cuius precibus annuens, ita prefatum locum omnibus religiosis studiis, ceterisque bonorum copiis adornauit, ut pre cunctis illius prouincię locis, felicibus semper floreat incrementis. In quo loco multi conuenerunt nobiles uiri tam clerici quam laici, eius doctrinis cupientes institui. Inter quos Osmundus episcopus sancte et religiose uite extitit monachus.

Duo quoque clerici liberalibus artibus adprime eruditi, aula regis postposita, Willelmum patrem expecierunt mente deuota. Vnus eorum uocabatur Lecelinus, alter Beringerius. E quibus prior postmodum abbas extitit, sequens in eodem loco uite finem accepit. De transmarinis etiam partibus, hoc est Anglorum terra, uir quidam nobilis regali prosapia clarus, Clemens nomine, relictis seculi pompis ad idem monasterium uenit, Deo inibi cupiens militare. Sed cum ab hominibus ex sua patria aduentantibus crebro inuiseretur, magis diligens Deo seruire cum quiete, quam uanitates mundi frequenter audire, Diuionense expetiuit cęnobium, ubi laudabilis uite compleuit cursum. Fuit itaque secundum ethimologiam sui nominis clemens animo, omnibus uirtutibus adornatus, precipue humilitate, qua in tantum se abiectum et uilem asserebat, ut cum sacerdocii gradu fungeretur, nunquam in omni uita sua nisi semel ad hoc ministerium accedere presumpserit.

67 Richard II, duke of Normandy (996–1026).

68 Fécamp in Normandy. William reformed the house in 1001.

Postquam igitur per annos fere xxx Willelmus abbas Fiscannense rexit cęnobium, cum iam senectute simul et egritudine grauaretur, et elegisset sibi Fructuariensem locum ad habitandum, desiderans in patrio solo quiescere. Considerans princeps regni Robertus, qui post patrem et fratrem defunctos primatum tenebat Normannorum,[69] peciit per legatos eundem patrem ut abbatem sibi substitueret, quia loci status aliter sine detrimento manere non posset. Ad cuius peticionem, quendam sibi ualde dilectum monachum, eiusdem loci priorem, nomine Iohannem, constituit abbatem, licet eum alibi magis obtasset preficere. Hic Italia partibus Rauenne ortus, litteris eruditus, ac medicinali arte per ipsius patris iussionem edoctus, religiose conuersationis eius, doctrine quoque ac omnium uirtutum ipsius pre cunctis aliis extitit imitator studiosus. Qui ab exilitate corporis Iohannilinus diminutiuo nomine est dictus, sed humilitatis, sapientie, discretionis, ac ceterarum uirtutum tanta in eo refulsit gratia, ut sicut sanctus refert Gregorius in libro dialogorum[70] de Constancio presbitero, ita et in hoc mirum esset intuentibus, in tam paruo corpore gratię Dei tanta dona exuberare.

Commisit et alia loca memoratus comes Richardus sepefato abbati Willelmo, scilicet Gemmeticum, ut iam diximus, monasterium Sancti Audoneni,[71] Montem Sancti Michaelis archangeli,[72] in quo loco post mortem predicti patris supradictus Iohannes abbas constituit patrem quendam monachum prenominati patris Willelmi. Vocatus est autem isdem frater Subpo, Romanorum patria exortus, et iamdicti magistri institutione in omni sanctitate educatus. Qui postmodum quibusdam contrarietatibus exortis, relicto ipso loco, Fructuariensem abbatiam annis pluribus rexit. Robertus etiam rex abbatiam Sancti Germani apud Parisius[73] precatus est predictum patrem ut susciperet, et secundum regularem institutionem ordinaret, quod et fecit. Necnon et Odo comes pari deuotione locum Sancto Faronis in urbe Meldorum[74] eidem commisit uenerabili patri. Sed et honorabilis presul Mettensis ecclesię Theodericus Gorziensem abbatiam[75] eodem zelo Dei commendauit illi, defuncto ipsius loci abbate.[76]

69 Robert, duke of Normandy (1027–1035).

70 Gregory the Great, *Dialogues* 1.5, pp. 59–68.

71 St-Ouen of Rouen.

72 Mont-St-Michel.

73 St-Germain-des-Prés.

74 Count Odo II of Blois (996–1037) gave the church of Meaux.

75 Theoderic, bishop of Metz, gave Gorze to Abbot William's direction.

76 At this point, on fol. 66v, the chronicler of Bèze returns to the history of his own house.

Longum est enumerare singula quę domnus Bruno episcopus in hoc loco egit bona, sed tamen quę in kartis nostris repperire potuimus, demonstrabimus.

42

c. 1008

Bishop Bruno confirms St-Bénigne's property at Bressey, at the request of Abbot William.

Cartulary, fols. 66v–67v.
Bougaud-Garnier, pp. 289–290.
Chartes et documents de Saint-Bénigne de Dijon, 2:12–13, no. 206; from the cartulary, dated 995–1008.
Duchesne, *Preuves de l'histoire de la maison de Vergy*, pr. pp. 55–56; from the cartulary.
Summarized in Brequigny, *Table* 1:519; dated 1008.

In nomine Domini Dei et Saluatoris Iheus Christi, Bruno diuina disponente clementia sanctę Lingonensis ecclesię humilis episcopus.[1] Si locis omnibus et precipue sacris eorumque rectoribus nostrę indignitati diuinitus commissis in sibi necessariis prout ualemus pie et oportune consulimus, eorumque anxietatibus sollicita cura subuenimus, non solum in hoc uenerabilium et Deo deuotorum pontificum, piorumque pastorum usum et consuetudinem exequimur, sed etiam saluti animę nostrę prouidemus.

Idcirco nouerit omnium ecclesię nostrę et nostri scollercia quod ueniens domnus abbas Willelmus,[2] quem ob sanctitatem et uenerabilem religionem locis in nostro diocesi manentibus, Diuionensi atque Besuensi, amanter prefecimus, insinuauerit nobis quasdam res de ipsis abbatiis inter se necesse esse, reddendi census gratia transferri, nosque id laudare et omnimodo consentire debere. Cuius prouidentiam et laudabilem discretionem non solum laudauimus, sed etiam ut secundum suum uelle locorumque necessitate id accelerare deberet attente monuimus. Sumptum est itaque de abbatia Sancti Petri

1 Bruno, bishop of Langres (980–1016).
2 William, abbot of St-Bénigne (990–1031), also became abbot of Bèze and several other Burgundian houses.

Besuensis et coniunctum abbatię Beati Benigni Diuionensis, quicquid habere dignoscebatur in Bruciaco uilla,[3] eo tenore ut omni anno octo modios uini ante festiuitatem Sancti Prudentii[4] in censum reddant. Et quicquid supradiximus perpetualiter monachi Beati Benigni possideant. Quod si neglegentia uel obliuione hoc termino redditum non fuerit, censum duplo restituant et conuentum inconuulsum permaneat.

Quod si quisque post decessum nostrum hoc decretum multorum nobilium ore laudatum infringere temptauerit, nisi cito resipuerit, et pęnitentiam condignam habuerit, anathematis iugulum caueat, quo ferire decreuimus quoscumque qui nostrorum decretorum cupiunt statuta euellere. Et ut hoc per secula inconuulsum permaneat, manu nostra subterfirmauimus, et ut a pluribus firmaretur rogauimus.

Signum Brunonis episcopi. Signum Lamberti prepositi.[5] Signum Teudrici archidiaconi. Signum Beraldi archidiaconi. Signum Widonis presbiteri. Signum Teudonis archiclaui. Signum Widonis archidiaconi. Signum Beraldi ypodiaconi. Signum Oddonis. Signum Amelii. Signum Brunonis pueri.[6] Signum Humberti pueri. Signum Niuardi. Signum Gozelmi.

It is interesting to note that this document, although detailing property belonging to St-Bénigne, ended up in Bèze's cartulary-chronicle. The list of witnesses, doubtless the cathedral chapter of Langres, is extremely similar to the following document's, which is why I have dated it c. 1008. The present document must have been given first, however, because young Bruno was not yet archdeacon.

De conlatis huic loco a Brunone episcopo

Crescente autem in hoc religionis studio, domnus Bruno episcopus nimium exilaratus de bona eorum conuersatione, de suo iure quodcumque necessarium et utile eis foret, libenti animo tribuebat. Inter cetera igitur quę huic loco contulit, statuit ut de ecclesiis a sex leugis uel infra a Besua tempore rogationum omnes tam uiri quam mulieres cum oblationibus ad sanctorum apostolorum Petri et Pauli limina conuenirent.

---

3 Bressey-sur-Tille, 19 km south-southwest of Bèze, east of Dijon.

4 The saint's feast day is 6 October, which is significant because Bèze had his relics, as well as being an appropriate day to deliver new wine.

5 Lambert succeeded Bruno as bishop of Langres (1016–1031).

6 This was most likely Bishop Bruno's nephew Bruno, who eventually became treasurer of Langres. See Bouchard, *Sword, Miter, and Cloister*, p. 394.

43

1008

Bishop Bruno of Langres seeks to increase the revenues for lighting at Bèze, where William is abbot. All men and women who makes offerings to churches within six leagues of the monastery shall bring them there instead of to Langres during rogation days.

Cartulary, fols. 67v–68v.
Bougaud-Garnier, pp. 291–292.
GC 4, instr. col. 138, no. 14.
Duchesne, *Preuves de l'histoire de la maison de Vergy*, pr. pp. 56–57; from the cartulary.
Summarized in Brequigny, *Table* 1:519.

In nomine Patris et filii et spiritus sancti.

Considerans ego Lingonensium Bruno episcopus[1] oficii mei negligentiam in dampnationem animę męe cedere, iuxta sensus mei modum elaboraui ecclesiis Dei prouisores efficere, qui in eis talentum uerbi Dei disseminantes, mecum pariter de eo ipsi Domino Ihesu Christo lucrum reportantes, eternę vitę remuneratione ditarentur.

Volui igitur ecclesię Besuensi domnum Guillelmum[2] uirum religiosissimum abbatem preesse, qui dum in ea cuncta regulariter ac religiose disponeret, intelligens propria in quibusdam non satis sufficere, quesiuit ab ecclesia Lingonensi ecclesię Besuensi aliquid ad luminarii opus conferri. Cognoscens itaque peticioni uiri Dei non esse contradicendum, cum consilio tocius capituli Lingonensis statui, ut de ęcclesiis a sex leugis uel infra a Besua, tempore rogationum, omnes tam uiri quam mulieres cum oblationibus ad sanctorum apostolorum Petri et Pauli limina conueniant. Illud quoque non ociose mecum reputans, quia cum tempore eodem Lingonas uenire deberent, alii longitudine uie, alii inbecillitate corporis, seu aliquibus aliis occasionibus retardati, pabulo diuini uerbi, et peccatorum remissione, quam ibi deberent accipere frustrabantur. Veniant igitur illo tempore statuto, et de peccatis suis ueniam postulantes ab eis, quorum lingue claues cęli facte sunt, a monachis illic Deo seruientibus de salute animarum suarum ammoniti, facta absolutione, et data benedictione,

1 Bruno, bishop of Langres (980–1016).
2 William, abbot of St-Bénigne (990–1031), also became abbot of Bèze and several other Burgundian monasteries.

leti reuertantur in pace. Quicumque uero huic nostrę institutioni contraire presumpserit, Dei omnipotentis auctoritate, et eorum quique ligauerint in terra erunt ligata et in cęlo [Matt. 16:19], atque omnium sanctorum anatematizentur et excommunicentur. Amen.

Et ut hoc per secula inconuulsum permaneat, manu nostra subter firmauimus, et ut a pluribus firmaretur rogauimus. Signum Brunonis episcopi. Signum Guillelmi abbatis. Signum Lamberti prepositi. Signum Beraldi archiaconi. Signum Teudrici archidiaconi. Signum Brunonis archidiaconi. Signum Teudonis archiclaui. Signum Widonis archidiaconi. Signum Amelii. Signum Widonis presbiteri. Signum Beraldi ypodiaconi. Signum Niuardi. Signum Gocelmi et aliorum multorum. Ego Airardus cancellarius scripsi, et cum ceteris laudator et roborator extiti. Acta sunt hęc anno ab incarnatione Domini MVIII, indictione vi, epacta xi, concurrente iiii, regnante Roberto rege[3] et Domno Brunone sedem Lingonicam tenente.

Beniuolentiam domni Brunonis episcopi atque deuotionem erga hunc locum noticię futurorum commendare uolumus, nobis hodieque et posteris nostris quamdiu seculum durabit profuturam. Est ęcclesia non multum distans ab hoc Besuensi loco in honore Sancti Leodegarii dedicata,[4] largissimis prediis et latifundiis a regibus et ducibus et comitibus dotata. Cuius loci monachi non minimas iniurias et importunitates huic loco inferebant, terras nostras occupantes, iniustas consuetudines in ipsis terris imponentes. Et quoniam possessiones nostrę intra possessiones eorum contigue erant, iusto latius manus extendentes, ut pote terrenorum principum quamuis iniusto auxilio confisi, quacumque poterant de nostris rebus locum suum ampliabant.

Est uilla quę dicitur Cusiriacus in parręchia nostra, eius uillę quę dicitur Belenaua,[5] ubi cum monachi Sancti Leodegarii ecclesiam et nouam parrechiam construere uoluissent. Audiens hoc domnus Bruno episcopus, excommunicauit et anathematizauit eos qui ibi ecclesiam construerent et qui diuinum officium ibi cęlebrarent. Considerans tamen quoniam parrechialis ecclesia, Belenaua scilicet, nimis longe aberat, ut bonus pastor animarum cure prospiciens, ne ue longinquitate uie, aut negligentia sacerdotis, aut ignorantia plebi animę diuini uerbi pabulo fraudarentur, statuit ut ad uillam, Besuimculam nomine,[6] quia prope erat, ad missas et Christianitatis officium conuenirent, eo uero tenore ut

3 Robert II, king of France (996–1031).

4 St-Léger-de-Champeaux. This small monastery, 19 km south-southeast of Bèze, had recently been made a priory of St-Germain of Auxerre.

5 Cuiserey, 11 km southeast of Bèze; and Belleneuve, 12 km south of Bèze.

6 Bézouotte, 10 km southeast of Bèze.

quia dignus est operarius mercede sua, medietatem eorum quę ad presbiteratum pertinerent, illi ecclesię condonarent. Item in uilla quę dicitur Anblins,[7] quoniam ipsi in aqua partem nobiscum habebant, ceperunt calumpniari, et siquid uellemus edificare ipsi quantum poterant impediebant. Accessit Pater Bruno episcopus, et ipse in medio aquę sudem acutam infixit, quę hodieque ibi manet, ut monachi Sancti Leodegarii medietatem aque usque ad palum haberent, et alia medietas usque ad palum nobis in pace remaneret.

In uilla nostra quę Trecasas dicitur[8] uoluerunt aliquando coruatam consuetudinaliter facere. Cum uero non fuisset alius qui resisteret, quidam rusticus zelo iusticie et fidei accensus, accessit ubi boues iuncti fuerant, et iuncturas super capita eorum, quas rustici conuinculas appellant, omnes truncauit. Tamen timens ne pro hoc facto quamuis iniuste ei malum inferretur, aufugit. Iterum Bruno episcopus noster, et nomine et re, cum hoc audisset non piguit ad locum accedere, et prius quam de hac re incepisset disserere, rusticum illum qui timore delituerat, nec audebat redire, demandans, "Vbi est," inquit, "filius meus qui hoc fecit et ita uiriliter loco mei egit?" Qui cum uenisset ante eum, "Tu es," inqit, "filius Sancti Petri et meus. Ne paueas pro certo habens quia qui te odit, me odit. Securus esto, nam qui te ledet, mecum quoque diuidet illud." His dictis, cum per indigenas loci et antiquos quibus noticia et memoria preteritorum fuerat, comprobatum fuisset, nullo modo monachos illos consuetudinem quam reclamabant in nostram uillam habere, domnus Bruno episcopus remeauit ad sua.

44

Fouvent, 26 March, c. 1008–1016

Girard of Fouvent recognizes that he had been receiving tithes unjustly from the church of St-Prudent of Neuvelle, and he turns them over to Abbot William. His wife Gertrude and son Humbert agree.

Cartulary, fols. 69v–70r.
Bougaud-Garnier, pp. 294–295.

Karta de decimis Noueuille

Per idem tempus quo domnus Guillelmus abbas Besuense regebat monasterium, miles quidam nomine Gyrardus cognouit se non recta consuetudine accipere decimas cuiusdam ecclesię ad ipsum monasterium pertinentis, quę in comitatu Adtoriense, loco nuncupato Nouauilla,[1] in honore Sancti Prudentii est

7 Drambon, 17 km south-southeast of Bèze.
8 Trochères, 14 km south-southeast of Bèze.
1 Neuvelle, 24 km northeast of Bèze, in the pagus of Attuyer.

consecrata, eo quod decime illius ecclesię ad alteram quasi matrem transportabantur ecclesiam, constitutam in uilla quę dicitur Frasnetum.[2] Cum igitur apud castellum suum, cui nomen est Fonsuenti,[3] vii kalendas Aprili resideret, reddidit pro remedio animę suę et uxoris filiique sui, nomine Humberti, ipsas decimas ad iamdictm monasterium, cui ipsa iure hereditario subiacebat capella. Hoc autem factum est sub presentia et consensu uxoris sue nomine Gertrudis, et predicti filii sui Humberti, atque ut nemo de heredibus uel successoribus eorum iam amplius ipsas decimas repetendi haberet licentiam, hanc fieri noticiam iusserunt quam si quis calumpniatus fuerit, perpetue excommunicationis feriatur anathemathe.

Nomina testium qui hanc noticiam firmauerunt hęc sunt, Theodericus, Humbertus, Aymo, Ioffredus, item Humbertus, Arembertus, Gybuinus, Mainfredus, item Aymo, Wido presbiter, Deodatus, et alii quamplures illustres uiri, qui omnes testimonium firma ratione prebuerunt, melius et rectius iam dictam ecclesiam per se debere stare cum decimis suis in parte et possessione Besuensis monasterii, quam alteri cuilibet subiacere ecclesię.

See also the following document, where Girard of Fouvent's yielding of the tithes is confirmed. Although the year is not given for this document, it must date to very close in time to the following one.

45

Langres, 1008–1016

Bishop Bruno of Langres attests at a synod that the knight Girard of Fouvent has given up the tithes he had been collecting at Neuvelle. A monk of Bèze named Benedict showed the synod the charter that Girard issued to this effect.

Cartulary, fol. 70r–v.
Bougaud-Garnier, p. 295.

Item alia

Cum apud Lingonicam sedem nostram ego in Dei nomine Bruno episcopus[1] nostrique archidiaconi collecta diocesis nostrę filiorum multitudine, generalem ageremus synodum, adiit presentiam nostram quidam monachus Besuensis monasterii nomine Benedictus, premonstrans cartulam quam ante fecerat miles

2 Frânois, 2 km southeast of Neuvelle.
3 Fouvent, 35 km northeast of Bèze.
1 Bruno, bishop of Langres (980–1016).

quidam nomine Gyrardus,[2] ex consensu uxoris sue nomine Gertrudis et filii sui Humberti, reddens ad iam dictum locum decimas cuiusdam ecclesię in comitatu Adtoariensi, Noua scilicet uilla,[3] sub honore Sancti Prudentii consecrate. Quam uidelicet cartulam omnes pariter audientes firmauimus atque laudauimus. Et quia eadem ecclesia in predio prescripti monasterii erat constructa, decreuimus atque statuimus ut decimę ipsius omni tempore iure hereditario ad idem deuenirent monasterium, nullo de nostris successoribus neque de heredibus predicti Gyrardi contradicente, neque calumpniam faciente. Si quis hoc testamentum calumpniatus fuerit, repetantur ab eo cuncta delicta usque ad nouissimum quadrantem.

Actum publice Lingonis. Nomina testium qui hoc firmauerunt testamentum, Lambertus prepositus.,Teudo abbas et archidiaconus,[4] Beraldus archidiaconus, item Beraldus archidiaconus, Bruno archidiaconus nepos domni Brunonis episcopi.

This is a confirmation of the previous document. It is dated by Bishop Bruno and by his nephew Bruno's first appearance as archdeacon.

46

c. 1016

The brothers Fulbert and Berengar give Bèze an allod at Buteau, which they are leaving beause of their neighbours' enmity. They and their posterity will give a measure of wax each year. If any of the family come back, they shall hold their former hereditary property from the abbot and monks. They are leaving the diocese of Langres for that of Besançon. The monks ask the bishops to confirm this agreement.

Cartulary, fols. 70v–71r.
Bougaud-Garnier pp. 296–297.

Karta de Bustello

Notum esse uolumus presentibus et futuris quod Fulbertus et Berengerius fratres recedentes de Bustello,[1] pro inimicitiis quas uicini eorum contra eos exercebant, dederunt alodum ipsius uici Bustelli Sancto Petro, et se ipsos et

2 Girard of Fouvent, 35 km northeast of Bèze. This is a reference to the previous document.

3 Neuvelle, 24 km northeast of Bèze, in the pagus of Attuyer.

4 As well as being archdeacon of Langres, Teudo was abbot of St-Étienne of Dijon, a house of secular canons; see *Chartes de l'abbaye de Saint-Étienne de Dijon (VIIIe, IXe, Xe et XIe siècles)*, pp. 78–79, no. 55; a document from 1006.

1 Garnier identifies this as a ruined village called Buteau, near Viévigne.

omnem posteritatem suam commendauerunt perpetualiter eidem Sancto Petro, una denerata cerę omni anno tam uirum quam mulierem, ea conuentione ut si ipsi aut aliqui ex eorum progenie reuerterentur in regionem, hereditatem suam quam sancto dederant ab abbate loci et monachis tenerent. Discedentes itaque de episcopatu Lingonico tempore Brunonis episcopi et ducis Heinrici,[2] uenerunt in diocesim archiepiscopatus Vesuncionensis tempore Hectoris archiepiscopi et comitis Willelmi,[3] peruenerunt in locum qui dicitur Rollens,[4] et remanserunt ibi super terram Teduini et Beroardi fratris eius, qui scilicet Teduinus pater fuit Bernardi. Ea uero conuentione in terra illorum remanserunt, ut ipsis reditus et consuetudines terrę persoluerent, Sancto uero Petro Besuę censum quem debebant annuatim deportarent.

Timentes autem monachi ne per succedentia tempora heredes Teduini et Beroardi fratris eius ipsis hominibus aliquam uiolentiam irrogarent, uel in seruitutem eos redigere uellent, cum abbate suo Willelmo[5] adeuntes concilium in quo archiepiscopus Hector et episcopus Bruno cum aliis episcopis residebant, deprecati sunt ut hanc kartam pariter et libertatem istorum hominum ęcclesiastica auctoritate roborarent. Quod ipsi libenter concedentes cum consensu aliorum episcoporum et totius sancti concilii eosdem homines liberos Sancti Petri esse statuerunt, et perpetuo anathemate excommunicauerunt, qui illis seruitutis iugum imponere ullo modo ausi fuissent.

Signum Hectoris archiepiscopi. Signum Brunonis episcopi. Signum Walterii episcopi. Signum Burchardi episcopi. Signum Gosleni episcopi.[6]

This charter is dated by Bishops Bruno, Hector, and Jocelin.

47

c. 1008–1016

Gibuin gave Bèze a serf along with his wife and children, and also a manse, which is in two parts, located in two separate villages. Later, on the day of his burial, his relatives give Bèze a female serf in addition.

Cartulary, fol. 71r.
Bougaud-Garnier, p. 297.

---

2 Bishop Bruno of Langres (980–1016) and Duke Henry I of Burgundy (d. 1002).

3 Hector, archbishop of Besançon (1002–1016), and Count Otto-William of Burgundy (981–1026).

4 Garnier identifies this as Roulans, a canton of Doubs.

5 William, abbot of Bèze (995–1031); he was also abbot of St-Bénigne of Dijon.

6 Walter, bishop of Autun (978–1018); Burchard, archbishop of Lyon (979–1031); and Jocelin, bishop of Mâcon (1016–1031).

Karta de Buxiaco et Delama

Quidam homo, Gybuinus nomine,[1] dedit Deo et Besuensi ecclesię unum seruum nomine Walcaudum cum sua coniuge atque omnibus qui ex his fuerint propagati, et unum mansum qui diuisus est in duas partes. Vna pars est in uilla cuius uocabulum est Buxiacus,[2] quę de duobus lateribus diuiditur a terra Gyrardi militis,[3] et de tercio a terra Sancti Petri Besuensis, et de quarto ab aqua quę uocatur Tyla, in qua xxx et ii iornales appendunt. Et alia pars est in uilla quę dicitur de Lama,[4] quę partitur undique a terra Sancti Petri, in qua appendunt xx et viii iornales.

Postmodum uero in die depositionis sue cum fuisset delatum corpus eius ad sepulturam omnis affinitas eius dederunt unam ancillam nomine Abdiardam et confirmauerunt hanc iterum kartam. Quicumque uero dempserit quippiam ex his supradictis rebus, sit anima eius abstracta a consortio Dei.

There is enough overlap with the people in document 44 to suggest that this was given around the same time.

48

Early eleventh century

Ogger claimed two female serfs and their children from Bèze. There was going to be a trial by combat before Bishop Bruno to settle the case, but it is avoided when the monks give Ogger fifty solidi and he abandons his claim.

Cartulary, fol. 71r–v.
Bougaud-Garnier, p. 298.

Item alia

Hisdem etiam diebus, Oggerius calumpniam inferens ancillis cum propriis filiis, uni Susanne et nomen alteri Hildegarde, a monachis Sancti Petri per multorum curricula temporum, iure possessis conabatur in suam pertinaciter transducere seruitutem. Quapropter iubente Brunone episcoporum[1] precellentissimo

1 Most likely Gibuin, brother of Hugh III of Beaumont. He is probably identical with the Gibuin who witnessed document 44.

2 Bussières was the name of a now-ruined village near Lux.

3 Probably Girard of Fouvent.

4 Damalix is now the name of a farm near Lux.

1 Bruno, bishop of Langres (980–1016).

fidelium suorum factus est conuentus, insuper etiam campiendi est dies statutus. Sed ne homicidii uel periurii noxam incurreret ipse Oggerius,[2] oblati sunt ei a monachis ibidem manentibus quinquaginta solidi, quibus acceptis, sic tandem ab hac querela sponte reticuit.[3] Et quamuis iniuste temptasset eas ad suum inflectere seruicium, accepto in redemptionem ut ita dicam precio, Sancto Petro, cui uerius pertinebant, reddidit coram testibus, ita ut nec ipse nec sui coheredes uel aliqua suspecta persona audeat de his aut eorum progenie aliquando aliquam calumpniam inferre.

Hi sunt testes, Gyrardus comes, Walterius, Nerduinus, Aldo, Oddo, Hugo comes,[4] Odilo.

I have dated this document to the early eleventh century by its placement in the cartulary and the comment that the events happened around the same time as the preceding. It took place in any event before Bishop Bruno's death in 1016.

49

Early eleventh century

Jotsald gives Bèze a vineyard at Gevrey, for the good of his soul and those of his friends and sons.

Cartulary, fols. 71v–72r.
Bougaud-Garnier, pp. 298–299.

Karta de Gibriaco

Per idem tempus quidam homo, Iozaldus nomine, pro remedio animę suę, per consilium filiorum et amicorum suorum, dono tradidit ad locum Sancti Petri Besuensis quandam uineam in uilla Gibriaco,[1] in loco nuncupato Casaullo cum iacentem, quę habet in longo xxvi perticas, in lato perticas x et vii, et terminatur de uno latere terra Sanctę Marię, ex alio latere de ipsa hereditate, de una fronte strata publica, de alia terra fiscali. Hanc autem hereditatem duo antecessores sui, Wicherannus scilicet et Archirannus, donauerant ei et uxori sue Tetsane et duobus infantibus suis, Ostrado et Vucheranno. Sicut ergo ab

2 The cartulary here abbreviates his name to a simple *O*.
3 Trials by ordeal were theatened more than actually carried out; see White, "Proposing the Ordeal and Avoiding It."
4 The counts are Girard of Fouvent and Hugh of Beaumont.
1 Gevrey, 12 km southwest of Dijon.

ipsis duobus antecessoribus suis donata sunt, ita ipse Deo et Sancto Petro et Besuensi monasterio tradidit perpetualiter habendam atque possidendam.

Again, this appears to have taken place early in the eleventh century.

50

1026–1031

Lambert gives himself to the monks of Bèze to serve them. He shall take charge of the alms that Count Raynald gives to the monastery, using the money to clothe the monks. To symbolize this agreement, Lambert gives the monks two donkeys, and his wife gives ten solidi. They also give the monks a boat. The monks name him their advocate and promise to provide him with clothing, shoes, and food.

Cartulary, fol. 72r–v.
Bougaud-Garnier, pp. 299–300.

Karta de Setis

Nouerint fideles per succedentia tempora quod quidam homo, Lambertus nomine, cum esset ingenuus et maneret apud Setas[1] cum uxore sua nomine Eremburgi, ac liberis Framiero et Dominico, eiusdem conditionis gratis se tradidit Sancto Petro ad seruiendum in loco qui dictir Fons Besua ac monachis ibi degentibus famulantibus Deo, quatinus libertas eterna proueniret animabus eorum. Sed hoc fecit eo tenore, ea conditione, eo tenore ut ipse et successores eius fideliter custodirent elemosinam quam comes regionis Rainaldus[2] una cum sua coniuge tribuit supradicto Sancto Petro. Nam quicquid in lucro aut negotio aliquid exinde potuerint lucrari, reddant ad uestitum fratrum in camera supradicti loci.

Et ut hęc scriptio firma maneret, in presenti dederunt in recordatione huic conuentui uir duos asinos et eiusdem uiri uxor x solidos ad restaurandam caldariam. Similiter et unam nauim dederunt. Nam nouerint monachi ipsius loci non eum habere alium aduocatum nisi ipsos, et ideo omni tempore eum in uestitu, in calciatu, ac cibo semper gubernari. Et ut insuspecti manerent, anathematizauerunt seniores loci quicumque, in aliquo aut quippiam ei moleste

1 Garnier identifies this as Les Brosses, near Bèze.
2 Raynald, count of Burgundy (1026–1057). His wife Judith was daughter of the duke of Normandy.

fecerit, aut eius liberis, perpetua anathematizatione, ex auctoritate Dei, Sanctique Petri, ob cuius amorem se tradidit ipse Lambertus ad seruiendum, nisi satisfactio facta promeruerit ueniam.

Testes huic subscriptioni omnes habitatores sancti loci ipsi sunt, Aldo prepositus, Humbertus, Wido decanus, Otbertus, Necteus, Rainerius. Hęc enim acta sunt tempore Willelmi abbatis[3] ac prepositi loci Benedicti nomine.

This document is dated by Count Raynald and Abbot William.

51

995–1031

An agreement is reached with the parishioners of Talmay, who wish to build houses adjoining the church of St-Valerius.

Cartulary, fol. 72v.
Bougaud-Garnier, p. 300.

Carta de Talamaro

Peruersorum calliditas dolos corde machinantium exigit ut res decretę litterari tradantur scedulae, ob cautele studium et munimen sequentium. Quos ita sape leuis circumuoluit inconstantia, ut etiam testimoniali manu roborata, sinistrorsum subdola certent refragari sollertia. Talium precauentes uersutias fratres loci Besuensis, sub domni abbatis Guillelmi[1] excubantes regimine, descripsimus conuentionem quam fecimus cum parrechianis uillę Talannaci,[2] de atrio ecclesię Sancti Valerii. Timentes enim hostiles impetus, ad nos uenere unanimes poscentes ipsum atrium sibi dari in auxilium, ad construenda domicilia et condendi propria. Horum itaque euicti inportunitate, atrium in commune census sub raciocinio indulsimus, eo uidelicet condicionis ordine, ut qui senum pedum uel septem mensuram usurparet in dominio, duorum qui uero aut duodecim aut trecdecim quattuor denariorum censum die festiuitatis sancti Benigni solueret. Qui uero statutum transiret terminum, iam sciret cum usura secundum legem reddendum.

3 William, abbot of Bèze (995–1031); he was also abbot of St-Bénigne of Dijon.
1 William, abbot of Bèze (995–1031); he was also abbot of St-Bénigne of Dijon.
2 Talmay, 18 km southeast of Bèze.

This charter is dated by Abbot William, but it most likely occurred late in his abbacy.

52

996–1031

Hildegard makes gifts of hereditary property at Lux for her soul and those of her husband and sons, Norjod and Hildebert. The gift consists of a number of *curtiles* in that area.

Cartulary, fols. 72v–73v.
Bougaud-Garnier, pp. 301–302.

Karta de Luco et Buxiaco

Quedam femina, Heldegardis nomine, pro remedio animę suę et uiri sui filiorumque, scilicet Norgaudi et Heldeberti, tradidit hanc terram cum appenditiis suis quam iure hereditario possidere uidebatur monasterio sanctorum apostolorum Petri et Pauli, quod est situm in loco qui dicitur Fons Besue. Et ut hoc profuturum posteris foret et firmius crederetur, litteris adsignare rogauit.

Igitur in Bussiaco uilla[1] quattuor sunt curtilia, duo ex una parte fluuii qui dicitur Tila, et alia duo ex alia parte eiusdem fluuii. Ex uno latere est terra Sancti Saluatoris, ex alio terra Gybuini, ex uno capite currit predictus fluuius, id est Tila, ex alio est uia publica. Iuxta autem alia duo curtilia quę sunt ex alia parte eiusdem fluuii, ex una parte est terra Gyrardi, ex alia terra Gybuini, ex una fronte terra predicti Gyrardi,[2] ex alia sepedictus currit fluuius. In Luco autem uilla[3] secus pontem curtile unum. Ex omni parte est terra eiusdem predicti monasterii. In eadem uero uilla est et aliud curtile, ex una parte terra Sancti Petri, ex alia terra Willerii, ex una fronte uia publica, ex alia sepedictus fluuius.

Item in alia uilla, Luco dicta, ad Sanctum Martinum duo curtilia, ex una parte est quidam exitus ad aquam pergendi, ex alia est terra Sancti Leodegarii, ex una fronte currit Tila, ex alia predicta uia. Item in iamdicta uilla Luco ad pontem sunt tria curtilia modica, ex omni parte eiusdem monasterii terra

1 Bussières was the name of a now-ruined village near Lux.

2 It seems likely that these adjacent landowners were Gibuin of Beaumont and Girard of Fouvent, often found in Bèze's charters at this time.

3 Lux, 5 km northwest of Bèze. It is also on the river Tille.

consistit. Item in eadem uilla unum curtile, ex una parte est terra Gyraldi, ex alia terra Sancti Saluatoris, ex una fronte tenet ipsum monasterium, ex alia fluuius iam iamque uocatus. Item in eadem uilla unum curtile, ex duabus partibus terra Sancti Leodegarii, ex una fronte terra Gybuini, ex alia sepedictus fluuius.

Hęc ergo supradicta Heldegarda cum predictis filiis iamdicto contulit monasterio, et fideli subscriptione legitimis testibus corroborauit, regnante Roberto Francorum rege.[4] Contulit nichilhominus cum omnibus his predictis curtilibus, omnia quę ad ipsa pertinent, id est prata quattuor, terras arabiles et pascua, et cuncta quę hereditario iure possidebat in his predictis tribus uillis.

This charter is dated by King Robert, but it probably happened later in his reign.

53

1 January 997–1016

Aremburg makes gifts at Lux and Framont of property and serfs, for the souls of her husbands and sons. She shall retain the income from them for her lifetime.

Cartulary, fols. 73v–74r.
Bougaud-Garnier, pp. 302–303.

Karta de Lu et Fracto Monte

Item alia quedam femina, Heremburgis dicta, pro anima sua animabusque seniorum suum seu filiorum, dedit Deo necnon sacrosancte ecclesie in loco qui Besua dicitur, in Beati Petri apostoli honore dicate, quasdam res iuris sui, scilicet colonicas quattuor sitas in pago Lingonico, quarum in uilla quę dicitur Lu[1] ad Sanctum Martinum, tres sunt. Has igitur tres cum seruis supermanentibus iamdictę dedit ecclesię, eo pacto ut in uita sua iure usuario eas possideret, post obitum uero suum ad illius ecclesię rectores perueniant. Alia autem colonica sita est in eodem pago, in uilla quę dicitur Fractus Mons.[2] Hanc iamdicte ecclesię in uestitura tradidit, ut rectores eiusdem loci teneant et possideant.

4 Robert II, king of France (996–1031).

1 Lux, 5 km northwest of Bèze, in the Langres region. It was, strictly speaking, in the pagus of Attuyer, but the use of the Carolingian-era pagus terminology was rapidly falling out of use in the eleventh century.

2 Framont, 25 km northeast of Bèze.

Nomina uero seruorum et ancillarum his in terris degentium hęc sunt, Stephanus et uxor eius Deodata et filii eorum, Mainardus, Leotasius, Danucia, Ermengarius, Rainardus, Ernuicia, Mainardus, Bernardus, Fulgerius, Rotrudis, Olosma. Has igitur cum seruis et omnibus appenditiis sancte ęcclesię predicte, cui domnus Guillelmus abbas[3] preerat, iamdicto conuentu concessit, pro his quorum superius memoriam feci, necnon pro anima Leudonis, qui ei has contulit.

Signum Heremburgis quę fieri et firmare precepit. Signum Lebaldi presulis.[4] Signum Adalardi presbiteri. Signum Iohannis leuite. Signum Haymonis leuite. Signum Constantini. Data per manum Rannulfi leuite, vi feria, primo die mensis Ianuarii, regnante Roberto rege.[5]

The lady Aremburg of Brancion was the mother of Bishop Letbald of Mâcon, which is why he appears in this charter. At about the same time she gave St-Bénigne seven *mansi*, also located in Lux, along with the serfs living there.[6] Although the year of this charter is not specified, the earliest the document could have been given is 997, the first 1 January when Robert II was sole king, and the latest is 1016, while Bishop Letbald was still alive.

54

Early eleventh century

The knight Hirmuin gives Bèze a serf with wife and children for the soul of his late son, also named Hirmuin. Hirmuin's wife agrees.

Cartulary, fol. 74r.
Bougaud-Garnier, p. 303.

Item alia

Quidam miles uocabulo Hyrmuinus Besuense adiens monasterium, ex consensu uxoris sue nomine Beztile, dedit ad ipsum locum pro amore Sancti Petri ac Sancti Prudentii, necnon et pro remedio anime cuiusdam filii sui nomine Hyrmuini, nuper defuncti, quendam seruum uocabulo Euuardum, cum uxore sua nomine Stephana et infantibus illorum, ea ratione ut tam ipsi quam omnis

3 William, abbot of Bèze (995–1031); he was also abbot of St-Bénigne of Dijon.

4 Letbald, bishop of Mâcon (993–1016).

5 Robert II, king of France (996–1031).

6 *Chronique de l'abbaye de Saint-Bénigne*, p. 175. For Aremburg, see also Bouchard, *Sword, Miter, and Cloister*, p. 297.

posteritas illorum ab ipsa die in seruitio et dominatione monachorum iamdicti monasterii iure hereditario permaneant, nullo contradicente, neque calumpniam faciente.

Like other charters in this part of the cartulary, this should doubtless be dated to the early years of the eleventh century.

55

Early eleventh century

The knight Hugo makes a gift of a manse at Flacey, for the burial of his wife Wandelmodis.

Cartulary, fol. 74r–v.
Bougaud-Garnier, pp. 303–304.

Carta de Flaciaco

Alius miles Hugo nomine tradidit Sancto Petro, pro sepultura uxoris sue Wandelmodis et pro remedio anime eius, mansum i in uico qui Flaciacus dicitur,[1] cum omnibus appenditiis suis, terris scilicet arabilibus, siluis atque pratis. Et ut hęc donatio nulli umquam calumpnie pateat, sed iugiter inconuulsa permaneat, hanc kartulam altari eius superposuit, et eam manu sua firmauit, roborandamque testibus fidelibus tradidit.

All the charters in this section appear to date from the time of Abbot William (d. 1031), if not indeed from the time of Bishop Bruno (d. 1016).

56

995–1031

The knight Milo of Beire makes a post-obitum gift to Bèze and Abbot William. The gift consists of one-third of the church of Beire. He keeps a third himself, and the final third is held by the priest. He also adds some land to the gift.

Cartulary, fols. 74v–75r.
Bougaud-Garnier, pp. 304–305.

1 Flacey, 10 km west-southwest of Bèze.

Karta de Beria

Notum esse uolumus omnibus fidelibus tam futuris quam presentibus quod quidam miles Milo nomine, de uilla quę dicitur Beria,[1] domni Willelmi abbatis[2] qui huic monasterio Besuensi preesse dinoscebatur, ac domni Benedicti, qui post ipsum prioratus officio fungebatur, clementiam adierit poscens sibi de rebus eiusdem monasterii in beneficio donari, promittens se in omnibus iamdicti monasterii seruiciis subditurum, eiusque utilitatibus pro posse omnimodis profuturum. Qui cum in precibus suis, tam per se quam per suos internuntios assiduus perstaret, eius coactus postulationibus iam dictus prior domnus Benedictus, ex consensu supradicti domni abbatis Willelmi, dedit ei terciam partem ecclesię prescriptę uillę, Berie scilicet, parte altera retenta, nam terciam presbiter pro seruitio tenebat. Dedit etiam ei mansum unum in uico quod dicitur Altauilla et unum quartarium in uilla quę dicitur Iuuenalis,[3] et unum iugerum de uinea in uilla quę dicitur Curtis Adonis. Ea tamen conuenientia, ut hoc ipsum beneficium diebus uitę sue teneret, post obitum uero suum nec filius eius nec filia aut aliquis ex eius parentela se de eo intermittere, aut presumere auderet, nisi eis bona uoluntate aut gratanti donatione abbatis aut monachorum eius concederetur.

Quam conuenientiam in persona sua ac filii sui Aduini sub iure iurando firmauit, presente ipso filio suo ac gratanter consentiente. Cui rei etiam fideles testes adhibuit, quorum hęc sunt nomina, Oddo, Rotbertus, Wido decanus, Luitprannus, Aldo prepositus, Albertus monachus, Rotbertus monachus.

De obitu Brunonis episcopi

Quia longum est enarrare cuncta, quę huic loco conlata sunt tempore Brunonis episcopi,[4] ad ipsius uite finem ueniamus. Sed[5] ante paucis describere curabimus quis fuerit modus uite eius. Fuit itaque in elemosinis largus, in uigiliis sedulus, in oratione deuotus, in karitate perfectus, in humanitate profusus, in sermone paratus, in conuersatione sanctissimus. Erat inreuerentibus terribilis aspectu, reuerendus incessu, metuendus seueritate, uenerandus benignitate.

1 Beire, 8 km southwest of Bèze.

2 William, abbot of Bèze (995–1031); he was also abbot of St-Bénigne of Dijon.

3 Garnier suggests Auvillars, near Fouvent, and Genevrières, near Faye-Billot (in the modern département of Haute-Marne). I have not identified Curtis Adonis.

4 Bruno, bishop of Langres (980–1016).

5 Here, beginning on fol. 75r, the chronicler of Bèze takes the description of Bishop Bruno's merits from the chronicle of St-Bénigne (pp. 172–173 in the printed edition), although the two chronicles have overall gone in separate directions, describing gifts to their own houses.

Censuram auctoritatis temperabat mansuetudo humilitatis. Non persone potentiam, sed morum elegantiam adtendebat in singulis. Et tanto unumquemque eminentius honorabat, quanto sanctius uiuere didicisset. Clericorum ac monachorum, sanctimonialium quoque necnon uiduarum et pupillorum pater erat, atque inter diuites et pauperes ita medius, ut pauperes illum quasi patrem aspicerent, diuites uero quasi superiorem sibi diuitem timerent. Quamdiu uixit, ita Burgundiam patrocinando protexit atque defendit, non clippeo et lancea, sed consilii prudentia, quo sibi principes patrię omnes deuinxerat, ut cum rex Francorum Rotbertus,[6] cum exercitu maximo hanc patriam sepe intrans, incendiis et rapinis plurima loca uastauerit, nichil in ea retinere potuit, quamdiu Bruno episcopus uixit.[7]

Anno ab incarnatione Domini MXVI domnus episcopus Bruno obiit, ii kalendas Februarii, peractis in episcopatu annis xxxv. Cui successit Lambertus episcopus[8] et ipse aucmentator bonorum huius loci deuotus.

57

c. 1010–1016

Henry is to be buried at Bèze with his wife and son because they had returned Neuvelle to the monks; his father had reeeived it in beneficium. When they gave the monks Neuvelle, Prior Benedict had given them a manse for their lifetimes. Their anniversaries shall be celebrated in the same manner as those of dead monks.

Cartulary, fol. 75v.
Bougaud-Garnier, pp. 305–306.

Karta de Nouauilla

In cuius diebus quidam Heinricus et filius eius Vlgerius et uxor sua nomine Aldrudis sepulturam sunt adepti in monasterio Sancti Petri Besuensis. Ex hac uidelicet causa, quo uillam Noueuille[1] quam tenuit pater eius in beneficium, rediderint Sancto Petro pro remedio animarum suarum. Ne autem hęc redditio frustraretur, dedit ei domnus Benedictus prior mansum unum in uilla quę Corcellis uocatur[2] tempore uitę suę, et post obitum eius rediret ad Sanctum

6 Robert II, king of France (996–1031).
7 Here, on fol. 75v, the chronicler of Bèze once again turns to the affairs of his own house.
8 Lambert, bishop of Langres (1016–1031).
1 Neuvelle, 24 km northeast of Bèze.
2 Courcelles, 68 km west-northwest of Bèze.

Petrum. Hoc autem ne oblitteraretur, monachis sibi tunc cognitis decidentibus, his litteris sub testificatione priorum manifestandum rogauit posteris adnectendum. Et hoc ut sicuti fratrum defunctorum anniuersaria dies cęlebratur, ita et ipsius celebretur.

Humbertus clericus Tilecastri[3] testis. Wido decanus testis, et alii multi.

This document was given after the abbey's 995 restoration under Abbot William and, according to the following document, before the death of Bishop Bruno. It most likely took place close to the end of this period.

58

Tilchâtel, February 1018

Henry tries to reclaim Neuvelle, which he had given to Bèze after long holding it in beneficium. But Bishop Lambert forces him to return it, and he then works out agreements with the monks over their relative rights there.

Cartulary, fols. 75v–76v.
Bougaud-Garnier, pp. 306–308.
Summarized in Brequigny, *Table* 1:532; dated 1017.

Item alia

In nomine summe et indiuiduę Trinitatis, Patris et Filii et Spiritus Sancti. Notum esse omnibus uolo quod ego Heinricus quicquid Sanctus Petrus in Nouauilla[1] uidetur habere quondam in beneficio tenueram, sed a Brunone episcopo[2] sublatum monachis est restitutum. Sed ego post mortem Brunonis resancciui, unde Abbas Willelmus indignatus cum monachis uersis ad Lambertum episcopum[3] clamoribus, compulsus sum Nouamuillam intermittere. Postea uero presumptione in humilitate mutata, ipsum Lambertum episcopum promerui adiutorem, quo intercedente ipsam terram quę tribus mansis et dimidio diuiditur, hac conditione monachi mihi reddiderunt, ut retenta coruata suis usibus, et Dauid et filio et Rainaldo cum terra quam tenent, alios iornales haberem et carroperam et censum cum eulogiis. Monachi uero de hominibus receptum et placitum reciperent, cum quo etiam

3 Tilchâtel, 9 km northwest of Bèze.
1 Neuvelle, 24 km northeast of Bèze.
2 Bruno, bishop of Langres (980–1016).
3 Lambert, bishop of Langres (1016–1031).

quicquid super tria mansa et dimidium in ipsa uilla inuentum est. Quicquid etiam assum est et in curtilis et terra arabili pratum quoque indominicatum et siluam et molendina. Hoc etiam mea promissione firmatum est, ut ab hominibus preter legalem censum terrę nec occasione hospitii, nec noua necessitate aliquid exigerem. Quod si presumerem iterum terram perderem, nisi monachos satisfactione placarem. Huius igitur terrę indulto seruitio militari, nichil aliud a me exigitur, nisi continua defensio contra predatores et fraudatores eiusdem ecclesię. Sed ne in hoc uiderer grauari, non contra potentiores sed contra ęquales michi genere et potestate et contra inferiores michi in utroque, in qua defensione si negligens comprobabor, iterum perdendi terram conditione constringor.

Hanc ergo terram Nouęuillę hac conditione receptam cum omni alia quam ex parte Sancti Petri habebam, id est monasteriolum cum ecclesia in ipso alodo sita, et in Fracto Monte[4] mansum unum, et in Waynart dimidium mansum. In Manneio quoque[5] quartarium unum pro remedio animę meę in ius ac proprietatem prebende monachorum retrado, et omnes posteros meos alieno et in omnibus bonis quę ex parte Sancti Petri pro beneficio tenui, ne ius hereditarium requirant ex heredo, et ad excludendam requirende hereditatis occasionem, omnem quod habui per hanc carte noticiam coram positis testibus reddo.

Ego quoque Lambertus Lingonice sedis episcopus huius redditionis testis adsisto. Et quia mea dispositione id actum ut ad prebendam monachorum redeat Nouauilla et omnis alia terra quam Heinricus tenuit in beneficio gratanter confirmo. Et ne ulterius beneficiali more post obitum Heinrici ab usibus monachorum subtrahatur interdico, et auctoritate Patris et Filii et Spiritus Sancti cum inuocatione Sancti Petri apostolorum principis consentientes et subtrahentes excommunico.

Signum Lamberti episcopi. Signum Beraldi. Signum Rotgerii. Signum Widonis. Ego Heinricus propria manu firmo, testesque adhibeo. Signum Gyrardi comitis.[6] Signum Milonis. Signum Oldebranni. Acta sunt hęc Tilecastro[7] publice, presente domno Lamberto episcopo, anno ab incarnatione Domini nostri Ihesu Christi MXVII, indictione xv, regnante Rotberto rege Francorum,[8] mense Febroario.

---

4 Framont, 25 km northeast of Bèze.

5 These last two places are unidentified; presumably they were near Neuvelle and Framont.

6 Girard of Fouvent, 35 km northeast of Bèze. The Milo who signs after him may be the knight Milo of Beire, found in document 56.

7 Tilchâtel, 9 km northwest of Bèze.

8 Robert II, king of France (996–1031).

Because the new year began at Easter in Burgundy, this document should be dated 1018 "new style." See also the preceding document.

59

Langres, May 1019

Bishop Lambert of Langres attests that Girard of Fouvent wants to build a monastery at Fouvent, to be under the abbot of Bèze. Girard holds the land on which he wants to build from the bishop, so he gives him in exchange some hereditary land of his wife, Gertrude. The bishop will consecrate a cemetery to which those buried at Fouvent may be moved.

Cartulary, fols. 76v–78r.
Duchesne, *Preuves de l'histoire de la maison de Vergy*, pr. pp. 62–63; from the cartulary, abbreviated, starting with Ego Lambertus.
GC 4, instr. col. 141, no. 17.
Bougaud-Garnier, pp. 308–310.
Summarized in Brequigny, *Table* 1:535.

Karta Fontis Venne

In nomine sanctę et indiuidue Trinitatis. Omnibus ortodoxę fidei cultoribus. Luce clarius patet humanum genus tam diabolica seductione, quam proprię nature fragilitate, creatorem suum cotidie offendere, eiusque iram incessanter irritare, iuxta illud apostolicum, "In multis offendimus omnes" [James 3:2]. Et si omnes quod uerum est offendere dicit, neque cautos ac perfectos a generalitate offendentium excludit, quanto magis nos omnino seculares qui dominicorum uix preceptorum meminimus, in quorumque actibus, nichil pene nisi peccatum cognosci potest offendere credere debemus? Multa et enim mala scienter perpetramus, et in multa ignoranter incurrimus, de quibus necessitas magna instat, ut antequam ad districti iudicii tribunal duci cogamur, quomodo cumque absolui laboremus. Et quia dominicis et euuangelicis uerbis, receptorem prophete et iusti, mercedem prophete et iusti accipere instruimur [Matt. 10:41], si quem Dei seruitorem quod nomine iusti sonari uidetur, receperimus aliquantulam offensarum nostrarum sarcinam leuiare existimamus. Sed ne diutius in loquendo moremur, iam ceptorum intentionem ad medium deducamus.

Ego Lambertus Dei gratia Lingonensis ecclesię presul[1] notum iri uolo cunctis sanctę Christianitatis filiis presentibus et futuris quod Gyrardus Fontisuennę

1 Lambert, bishop of Langres (1016–1031).

castri[2] dominus ante prędictum castrum monasterium in honore et memoria Sancti Sepulchri ac Sanctę Marię semper uirginis ędificare uolens, ibi monachos qui semper Deo seruiant locare disponit. Ad claustrum quoque et officinas, ad hortum et horrea et ad cuncta necessaria ipsius loci componenda dat eis terram ab ulteriori rippa Vennę aquę,[3] quę est Lingonis uenientibus ad castrum sinistra, usque ad siluam que est eisdem dextera, de altera uero parte a cruce quę fixa est in media calme usque ad ipsum castrum per uiam quę ducit ad siluam. Et quia ipsum castrum cum adiacenti terra de casamento nostrę dioceseos noscitur esse, per laudamentum nostrum concedit Sancto Mammeti[4] commutationem predicte terrę apud Artionis Curtem uillam,[5] quam de hereditate Geretrudis uxoris suę contigit habere. Quam etiam terrę commutacionem pro remedio animę meę predicte laudo ecclesię, ut et ipse particeps fiam elemosinę.

Vult autem predictus Gyrardus hunc locum tali conuentione construere, ut in subiectione et in disciplina Sancti Petri Besuensis atque abbatis ipsius ecclesię permaneat omni tempore. Similiter quicquid ipsi loco ad presens dat, et quicquid in futurum dederit uita comite, et ceteri quique fideles pro remedio animarum suarum uoluerint inpertire, in predictę abbatie Besuensis semper subsistat ditione.

Rogat etiam me obnixe episcopali auctoritate confirmare, ut omnium militum defunctorum corpora, quę ab hoc Fontisuenne castro ab Besuam, ut consuetudo eius est, non potuerint portari, in cymiterio istius loci a me consecrato, consuetudinaliter tumulentur. Cuncti etiam qui intra castellatum uel in ipso ambitu et receptu castellati mortui fuerunt in predicto Sanctę Marię cymiterio perpetua obseruatione sepeliantur. Cuius peticionis intencionem fidelem et deuotam intelligens, libenter cum consensu omnium archidiaconorum et aliorum fidelium, quod poscit annuo et confirmo et Sancto Petro Besuensi illum locum laudo, et insuper hanc litterarum noticiam fieri iubeo, quam etiam propria manu firmo. Quam peticionis firmationem siue conuentionem ac scriptionem, si quis peruersa mente deceptus aliter mutare aut penitus euertere exorsus fuerit, anathematis ęterni et perpetuę maledictionis uinculo uulneratus, ac legis rectitudine conuictus, centum auri libras persoluat et quę in ista carta continentur inuiolata permaneant.

Ego Lambertus Lingonicę sedis episcopus ut sit memorabile seculis hanc cartam fieri iussi et signaui. Beraldus Suessionis ciuitatis episcopus signauit.[6]

---

2 Fouvent, 35 km northeast of Bèze.

3 Fouvent is at the source of the river Vannon.

4 The cathedral of Langres.

5 Arçon, 12 km south of Bèze.

6 Berald, bishop of Soissons.

Beraldus ueteranus archidiaconus et abbas signauit. Gyrardus comes Fontisuennę signauit. Bruno archidiaconus signauit. Gyrardus diaconus signauit. Gyrardus signauit. Hugo comes[7] signauit. Oddo archidiaconus et abbas signauit. Wido signauit. Rotgerius signauit. Hugo capellanus signauit. Item Hugo signauit. Raynoldus signauit. Acta publice Lingonas, anno ab incarnatione Domini MXVIIII, indictione ii, epacta xii, concurrente iii, mense Maio, regnante Rotberto Francorum rege.[8] Ego Odolricus dictaui ad uicem Beraldi cancellarii, die Iouis scripsi et subscripsi.

This establishment of a priory at Fouvent is also mentioned in the Annales of Bèze.[9] See the following document, which preceded this one.

60

Langres, 16 April 1018

Count Girard, along with his wife Gertrude, attests that he wishes to found a monastery at Fouvent, on land he obtains from the bishop of Langres in exchange for other property. Girard's and Gertrude's sons sign, Humbert and Girard, a cleric.

Cartulary, fols. 78r–79r.
Bougaud-Garnier, pp. 310–311.

Item alia

In nominae sancte et indiuidue Trinitatis. Ego Gyrardus[1] notum uolo esse omnibus fidelibus adhuc in carne degentibus et in futurum uenientibus me cum Gertrude uxore mea quandam partem hereditatis meę Lamberto episcopo[2] in excambio per unum conuentum dedisse.

Erat quedam campestris terra subtus meum castrum quod Fonsuenti uocatur, in qua monasterium construere uolebam. Videns ergo hoc me non posse adimplere sine episcopi licentia, tantundem terre dedi ipsi domino meo pro eodem loco in uilla quę dicitur Arcuncurtis.[3] Terminatur autem ipsa terra in fronte terra Sancti Petri Genouensis ecclesię, et circumquaque hereditas mea noscitur

7 Hugh III, count of Attuyer and lord of Beaumont, 7 km east of Bèze.
8 Robert II, king of France (996–1031).
9 MGH SS 2:249.
1 Girard, lord of Fouvent, 35 km northeast of Bèze.
2 Lambert, bishop of Langres (1016–1031).
3 Arçon, 12 km south of Bèze.

cumiacere. Tali uero tenore tradidi ut locus ille in quo sedes constructa est monasterii in honore Sancti Sepulchri et Sanctę Marię semper uirginis abbatię Besuensi Sancti Petri semper subiaceat, et sub abbatis potestate permaneat.

Si quis ergo contra hoc factum, quod non spero per Dei gratiam futurum, ex heredibus nostris aliquam calumniam inferre temptauerit, coactus legibus in fiscum regis persoluat unam libram auri. Hęc autem traditio omni tempore permaneat firma et stabilis, quam propria manu firmaui et firmandam tradidi, testibus subscriptis. Signum Gyrardi. Signum Gertrudis. Signum Gyrardi clerici. Signum Humberti filiorum eorum. Signum Haymonis. Signum Otberti. Signum Nocheri. Signum Aymonis. Signum Arluini. Signum Nerduini. Signum Willelmi. Signum Lentilli. Signum Arnulfi. Signum Otberti Normanni. Signum Teubaldi. Acta sunt hęc Lingonis xvi kalendas Maii, indictione ii, regnante rege Rotberto tricesimo secundo anno, et Hugone filio eius iii. Ego Odolricus dictaui ad uicem Beraldi cancellarii, die Iouis scripsi et subscripsi.

See also the preceding document, given after this one.

61

c. 1019

Bishop Lambert gives Arçon to the monastery at Fouvent, which is dependent on Bèze. The bishop had received the property from Girard of Fouvent when he founded the monastery near his castle.

Cartulary, fol. 79r–v.
Bougaud-Garnier, pp. 311–312.

Karta de Arcionis curte

In nomine sanctę et indiuidue Trinitatis. Manifestum iri cupimus tam presentibus quam futuris quod ego Lambertus gratia Dei Linguonensis ęcclesię episcopus[1] dedi Deo et monasterio Sancti Sepulchri et Sanctę Marię, quod est constructum ante castellum Fontisuenne a Gyrardo[2] et Gertrude uxore eius in terra casamenti nostri, me laudante, terram Arcionis curtis,[3] quam mihi ipse

1 Lambert, bishop of Langres (1016–1031).
2 Girard, lord of Fouvent, 35 km northeast of Bèze.
3 Arçon, 12 km south of Bèze.

Girardus et uxor eius pro commutatione terrę casamenti nostri in qua monasterium edificauerant reddiderunt. Ergo illis rogantibus tradidi eam liberam Deo et Sancto Sepulchro et Sanctę Marię et Sancto Petro ad monasterium Fontisuenne, eo tenore ut ipse particeps fiam eorum elemosine. Et quia ipsa terra de potestate Louuncurtis[4] erat, separauerunt eam ab ipsa potestate, et ex toto liberam fecerunt ut nullus ministerialium ipsius potestatis in ipsa terra amplius presumat accipere aut tollere, et homines qui in illa terra habitauerint siluam ipsius potestatis ad edificandas domos et faciendum sibi focum sicut ante utantur, et pastionem ad suos porcos et alias bestias quas habuerint, consuetudinaliter similiter utantur. Et quicumque pro ipsa silua aut pro ipsa pastione aliquid demandare presumpserit, perpetua maledictione et excommunicatione feriatur.

Signum Lambertis episcopi. Signum Girardi. Signum Gertrudis. Signum Humberti patris Theoderici. Signum Haymonis patris Widonis Burgundionis uille.[5] Signum Haymonis patris Manasse.

This document must have been given within a short time of the previous two.

62

Langres, 8 January 1023

Lambert, bishop of Langres, gives Bèze an altar at St-Seine-sur-Vingeanne, at the monks' request. Agreeing are both canons of Langres and the knight Humbert, all of whom had previously controlled said altar.

Cartulary, fols. 79v–80r.

Duchesne, *Preuves de l'histoire de la maison de Vergy*, pr. pp. 63–64; dated 1022.

Bougaud-Garnier, pp. 312–314.

Summarized in Brequigny, *Table* 1:544; dated 1022.

Karta Helprici curtis

In nomine summe et indiuidue Trinitatis, uidelicet Patris et Filii et Spiritus Sancti. Ego Lambertus gratia Dei Lingonensis presul[1] notum cupio fore

4 Lavoncourt, 42 km northeast of Bèze.

5 Bourguignon, 40 km northeast of Bèze.

1 Lambert, bishop of Langres (1016–1031).

omnibus Christum Deum uere credentibus quia cum quadam die essem apud Lingonas, et pro modulo cum meis tractarem clericis simul et catholicis laicis de statu Sanctę Matris ecclesię confirmando, et de religionis deprauatę uigore recuperando, ecce quidam Besuensis cęnobii fratres meis sese presentauere optutibus, supplicibus efflagitantes precibus quo eorum necessitudini caritate fraternitatis compatiens, altare ecclesię Helprici curtis[2] concederem ad supplementum presentium ac futurorum fratrum. Cuius peticionis implorationem auditam incunctanter studui rebus adimplere, quoniam subsidio fulciebatur mercedis futurę.

Consentientibus itaque Lingonensium ecclesię clericis pariter ac fidelibus laicis, B. uidelicet prepositus, necnon et L. archidiaconus, in cuius supradictum est altare ministerio, Besuensi ecclesię prelibatum altare eternę retributionis gratia ad fratrum releuandam necessitudinem tradidi, ea conditione ut obsequia nostre sedi debita temporibus congruis persoluantur. Inter ceteros presens aderat miles quidam Humbertus nomine, in cuius beneficio altare predictum uidebatur situm. Hic Dei gratiam consequi desiderans beneficium illud fratribus eiusdem loci concessit, dicens, "Ego Humbertus ob omnipotentis Dei amorem et animę meę saluationem dono Sancto Petro et fratribus Besuensis cęnobii beneficium ecclesię Helprici curtis, consentiente mea coniuge, Histiburge scilicet nomine, et Siguino filio meo, perpetuo iure possidendum, ita ut ab hac die suis usibus illud adtribuant et inde subministrent, et licentiam faciendi quicquid inde sibi placuerit habeant. Si quis uero heredum meorum, quod absit, huic donationi calumpniam infferre temptauerit, legibus coactus auri libras decem persoluat, et hęc donatio firmitatis et stabilitatis uigorem perpetuo obtineat."

Actum Lingonis publice vi Idus Ianuarii, indictione v, anno Incarnati Verbi MXXII, regnante Rotberto.[3] Signum Lamberti episcopi. Signum Brunonis archiclaui. Signum Gyrardi archidiaconi. Signum Humberti archidiaconi. Signum Oddonis decani. Signum Ansculfi presbiteri. Signum Hugonis presbiteri. Signum Constantii presbiteri. Signum Mauricii presbiteri. Signum Widonis laici. Signum Gotzelmi laici. Signum Odolrici laici. Signum Widonis laici. Signum Rotgerii laici. Signum alterius Rotgerii. Signum Humberti laici. Signum Siguini filii eius.

This document should be dated 1023 "new style."

2 St-Seine-sur-Vingeanne, 13 km northeast of Bèze.
3 Robert II, king of France (996–1031).

63

Dijon, 17 February 1024

The history of Viévigne is recounted, starting with the supposed original gift by the founder Amalgarius. At a certain point one Hugh took it over, and his descendants seized it again even though the monks had briefly reclaimed it under Bishop Bruno. Now the brothers Girard and Lambert restore the property to Bèze for the good of their souls.

Cartulary, fols. 80r–81r.
Bougaud-Garnier, pp. 314–315.
Summarized in Brequigny, *Table* 1:546; dated 1023.

Karta de Vetus Vineis

Notum sit fidelibus Christianis presentibus et futuris, post constructionem Besuensis cęnobii ab Amalgario duce in honore beatorum apostolorum Petri et Pauli, non parue amplitudinis predia inibi ab eo collata, cum quibus et alodum quod dicitur ad Vetusuineas[1] concessit. In quo loco seruorum Dei aggregans multitudinem sub regulari disciplina uiuere paratos, filium suum eis prefecit nomine Wandalenum. Post multorum uero temporum curricula, partim inuasione hostium, partim irruptione Hunorum, a quibus idem locus quinquies traditur concrematus, nec minus incuria pontificum ut prius augmentum perpeti cepit detrimentum, donec Betto Lingonensem adipisci promeruit sedem. Qui quandiu rebus humanis interfuit, ut idoneus pastor prefuit. Quo decedente, Albericus successor eligitur. Quique per uisitationem apostolicam, diuina sibi opitulante misericordia, ipsum locum in pristinum reparauit statum, necnon suis ampliauit donis, diuque in honoris perseuerauit stabilitate et religionis.

Postea autem utrum gratia beneficii an presumptionis, Vetusuineas quidam Hugo tenuit, quo defuncto iterum locus resumpsit, et quietam ac solidam tempore Brunonis Lingonensis episcopi[2] possedit. Post cuius decessum, sicut cetera loca sanctorum, locus Besuensis in direptionem cecidit. Tunc qui uidebantur pacifici, predones sunt effecti. Inter quos quidam Gerardus et frater eius Lambertus, de progenie suprascripti Hugonis progeniti, quasi iure hereditario Vetusuineas inuaserunt. Sed cum tali inuasione nichil proficerent, tandem conuicti iustitia loco sponte restituerunt. In qua restitutione, si qua sibi ab antecessoribus rectitudo uideretur, sponte indulserunt, tam pro remedio

1 Viévigne, 4 km southwest of Bèze. It is mentioned in document 3.
2 Bruno, bishop of Langres (980–1016).

animarum suarum, quam parentum suorum, et pro promerenda indulgentia predę porcorum et arsurę Fielinx uille[3] quam iniuste fecerunt, adhibitis testibus qui restitucionem uiderunt et satisfactionem. Et ut hęc restitucio et satisfatio memoraliter permaneat, hanc noticiam fieri petierunt, manu sua et horum testium corroboratam.

Signum Gyrardi. Signum Lamberti qui hanc kartam fieri petierunt. Signum Heluidis matris eorum. Signum Widonis et uxoris eius. Signum Walterii clerici. Signum Widonis decani. Signum Oddonis. Signum Rotberti. Signum Erlebaldi. Signum Aldonis. Acta publice apud Diuionem castrum, xiii kalendas Marcii, anno ab incarnatione Domini MXXIII, regnante Rotberto rege.[4]

This document should be dated 1024 "new style."

64

Bèze, October 1027

Ezelina, wife of the knight Narduin, gives a manse at Viévigne for her husband's soul. She adds another manse at Theuley.

Cartulary, fol. 81r.
Bougaud-Garnier, pp. 315–316.

Item alia et de Tusleio

Quedam mulier nomine Ezelina, uxor Nerduini militis,[1] tradidit unum mansum pro redemptione animę prescripti mariti Sancto Petro Besuensi, in uilla cui uocabulum est Vetusuineis,[2] cum uno seruo et cum omnibus quę ad ipsum mansum pertinent. Dedit etiam ad Tusleium[3] unum mansum in quo sunt quattuor iugera, et de terra arabili xxviiii, et pratum ad unam carratam.

Et ut hęc donatio in perpetuum firma sit et stabilis, his subscriptis testibus firmauit et firmare rogauit. Hii sunt Gybuinus frater supradicti militis,

3 Fiélin, 3 km south-southwest of Bèze.
4 Robert II, king of France (996–1031).
1 Narduin was of the family of the lords of Beaumont; see Bouchard, *Sword, Miter, and Cloister*, pp. 321–322.
2 Viévigne, 4 km southwest of Bèze.
3 Theuley, 20 km northeast of Bèze. When a Cistercian house was established there in 1130, the foundation charter said that the property had been held from Lord Hugh of Beaumont, who gave his permission; GC 4, instr. cols. 163–164, no. 40.

Bernardus, Aldo. Reddidit etiam saluamentum de uilla quę uocatur ad Septem Fontes,[4] quę iam Sancto Petro fuerat. Data[5] publice Besua anno ab incarnatione Domini MXXVII, indictione x, epacta xi, concurrente vi, mense Octobris, regnante Rotberto Francorum rege.[6]

65

1027

Haymo gives Bèze a manse at Flacey.

Cartulary, fol. 81r–v.
Bougaud-Garnier, p. 316.

Karta de Flaciaco

Quidam etiam homo nomine Haymo unum mansum cum omnibus appendiciis suis, terris scilicet arabilibus, siluis atque pratis, in uico qui Flaciacus[1] dicitur monasterio sanctorum apostolorum Petri et Pauli, Sanctique Prudentii martyris, dedit, quod est situm in loco qui dicitur Fons Besue.

Et ut hoc profuturum posteris foret et firmius crederetur, litteris adsignare rogauit sub legitimis testibus, anno ab incarnatione Domini supradicto. Hii sunt testes, Signum Bernardi, Signum Oddonis, Signum Rotberti, Signum Aldonis, Signum Hugonis.

The wording of this paraphrased charter suggests it, like the previous one, was given in 1027.

De obitu Abbatis Willelmi

Sunt adhuc plurima quę describi possent, sed his[2] omissis obitum patris Willelmi[3] intimare curamus. Postquam per annos xlii uineę Dominice sedulus cultor ea excolendo iugiter propagare, amplificareque curauit, cum iam senio

---

4 Sept-Fontaines, 46 km east-northeast of Bèze.

5 This word originally read "Acta"; it is corrected in the margin.

6 Robert II, king of France (996–1031).

1 Flacey, 10 km west-southwest of Bèze.

2 Although the chronicles of Bèze and St-Bénigne had each been detailing gifts to their own monasteries for some pages, at this point, on fol. 81v, the chronicler of Bèze again begins to copy the latter chronicle (pp. 177–178 in the printed edition).

3 William, abbot of Bèze (995–1031); he was also abbot of St-Bénigne of Dijon.

infirmitatibusque multis pregrauatus obtaret dissolui et cum Christo esse, bonam consummationem laborum suorum adimplere cupiens, per omnia monasteria quę sub eius fuerunt magisterio, incipiens ab Italia, circuiendo, et fratres exhortando ut ea que ab ipso didicerant, mente retinerent, et opere adimplere satagerent. Siquidem doctrine fuit, ut iuxta quod precipit Sancti Benedicti Regula, in uerbo, in omni actione, in uestitus qualitate, humilitatem uidentibus se semper ostenderent. Et ut honore inuicem se preuenientes, dilectionem sine simulatione exiberent. His et aliis uirtutum operibus intentos, etiam distincte legendi et psallendi magisterio erudiuit. Hęc docendo ceteris monasteriis peragratis, peruenit ad cęnobium nomine Fiscannum,[4] ubi plus solito infirmitate pregrauatus, sentiens sibi imminere ultimum uocationis suę diem, conuocatis fratribus, per octo dies exhortans eos atque absolutione et oratione Deo commendans, octauo die Natalis Domini sumpto Christi corporis et sanguinis sacramento, reddidit Deo spiritum. Cuius corpus a medicis qui ibi aderant conditum aromatibus, honorifice traditus est sepulture in ipso monasterio, ante altare Sancti Taurini confessoris.

Ipso[5] eodem tempore quo rex Rotbertus monarchiam regni tenebat,[6] cum audisset in partibus istis quosdam existere, qui circumquaque res alienas uiolenter diripientes, ut liberius inpuneque retinerent, firmitates et castella noua sibi construxerant, cum copioso ut regem decebat exercitu, Miribellum[7] ad expugnandum et diruendum aduenit. Erat enim illud una ex mansionibus raptorum, quod et Deo fauente in breui effecit. Sed dum ibi obsideret, nuncius aduenit, dicens patrem nostrum Willelmum abbatem[8] ab hac uita decessisse.

De Olgerio abbate

Nolens itaque Rotbertus rex locum istum diu sine pastore manere, ne lupi rapaces gregem inuaderent, domnum Vlgerium, qui tunc uicem prioris sub abbate Willelmo tenebat, hunc loco abbatem substituit.[9] Obiit[10] uero predictus pater noster Willelmus anno ab incarnatione Domini MXXXI. Et in ipso anno

4 Fécamp.

5 Here, on fol. 82r, the chronicler of Bèze returns briefly to issues not found in the chronicle of St-Bénigne.

6 Robert II, king of France (996–1031).

7 Mirebeau, 9 km south-southeast of Bèze.

8 William, abbot of Bèze (995–1031); he was also abbot of St-Bénigne of Dijon.

9 Ulger, abbot of Bèze (1031–c. 1055).

10 Here, on fol. 82r, the chronicler of Bèze once again begins following the chronicle of St-Bénigne, picking up where he had left off two paragraphs earlier, skipping only one sentence on William's successor as abbot of St-Bénigne (pp. 178–179 in the printed edition).

defunctus est domnus Lambertus Lingonum episcopus, x kalendas Septembris, antequam ipse pater finiretur. In cuius locum substituit Rotbertus rex episcopum Richardum uocatum,[11] clericum litteris optime eruditum et bonis moribus ornatum, tamen contra uolumptatem cleri et plebis tocius. Quapropter post menses v adepti episcopatus, captus ac pulsus ciuitate, non multis post diebus ueneno uitam finiuit. Rex autem consiliis regine Constantie ad iram animo prouocatus, iterum dedit episcopatum cuidam clerico Carnotensis ecclesię. Hugo hic erat dictus, fuissetque utile uas in domo Dei, si iuuenilia desideria euitare et superbiam calcare curasset. Sed his adiecta crudelitate eundo per fas et nefas, ad ultimum postquam per annos xviii Lingonicum tribulauit clerum et populum, pulsus a sede iudicio domni Leonis Noni papę,[12] et archiepiscoporum, Halinardi scilicet Lugdunensis, Hugonis Besonticensis, Widonis Remorum, Euuardi Treuerorum,[13] aliorumque multorum qui presentes fuerunt in concilio habito Remis ciuitate, in presentia memorati Pape Leonis, ubi adfuerant pene tocius Gallię tam archiepiscopi quam episcopi, cum innumerabili multitudine cleri et populi.

Huius itaque Hugonis[14] ordinatione instante,[15] cum esset deductus ab Heinrico rege[16] iuuene ad ciuitatem Linguonas cum magna ambitione, nunciata est predicto regi mors patris sui Rotberti regis,[17] qui regnauit annis xli, et ipse Heinricus regni sextum iam annum agebat. Supradictus[18] uero Hugo episcopus cum suscepisset episcopatum non fuit ut decuisset circa Dei ecclesias sollicitus augmentator, sed e contrario negligens et distractor. Quapropter cum huic loco multas inportunitates inferret et exactiones insolitas, et domnus Vlgerius abbas nullomodo ei uellet adsentire, ipse Halinardum Diuionensem abbatem huic loco constituit abbatem.[19] Qui ueniens cum suis monachis, per uiolentiam

11 Richard, bishop of Langres (1031).

12 Pope Leo IX (1049–1054), who forced many bishops out of office at the 1049 Council of Reims, if they had come to their sees uncanonically.

13 Archbishops Halinard of Lyon (1046–1052), Hugo I of Besançon (1031–1067), Gui of Reims (1033–1055), and Eberhard of Trier (1047–1066).

14 Starting here and continuing to "Diuionem duxit," this section is also printed in RHGF 11:203, from *Spicilegium*.

15 Hugh, bishop of Langres (1031–1049).

16 Henry I, king of France (1031–1060).

17 Robert II, king of France (996–1031).

18 Here, on fol. 82v, the chronicler of Bèze returns to the affairs of his own house.

19 After Abbot William died in 1031, having headed both St-Bénigne and Bèze, the two houses each elected their own abbots, respectively Halinard (1031–1052 – he also became archbishop of Lyon in 1046 while continuing as abbot) and Ulger (1031–c. 1055). The chronicler, who has nothing good to say about Bishop Hugh, is writing with the knowledge that he was deposed at the Council of Reims.

Hugonis episcopi domnum Vlgerium abbatem nostrum cum quibusdam ex nostris monachis captos Diuionem duxit. Suos autem monachos hic dimettens, non ad conseruandum et ędificandum, sed ad destruendum et diripiendum quę intus erant, locum istum eis contradidit. Quod postea claruit, nam quadam uice simulantes se ituros ut uinum deferrent, uas uinarium, quod tunnam uocant, plaustro superponentes, ornamenta cum libris et thesauri maxima parte in uase illo reposuernt. Sed huius uille homines hoc intelligentes, maxime ex eo, quia tunna nimis erat ponderosa, eam aperuerunt, et res nostras intus inuenientes, retinuerunt. Ferunt quidam ex nostris tunc temporis excepta aliorum ornamentorum non minima quantitate, x et vii cappas, cum textu Euuangeliorum et cruce preciossima, Diuionem a monachis illis deportatas.

Factum est autem dum domnus Vlgerius abbas ita Diuioni haberetur, monachi illius qui ex hoc loco dispersi fuerant, notificauerunt ei quatinus ad exeundum de monasterio se prepararet. Illi uero mittentes ei equos cum quibus aufugeret, competenti loco collocauerunt. Quo comperto ipse de monasterio exiens, equos ascendit, cursuque perpete castrum illud quod iuxta nos est, Bellimontem dictum,[20] expetiit. Vnde ipse cum suis monachis Diuionenses, qui male locum istum inuaserant, expugnans, uellent nollent ad propria redire coegit. Ipse autem ecclesię suę redditus, locum istum postea diu bene ac regulariter gubernauit.

66

Bèze, 21 March 1032

Three brothers – Gui, Odilo, and Anseric – give Bèze land at Mornay. They had claimed it as hereditary property, though the monks had felt it was rightly theirs since the time of Bishop Bruno. The brothers add an additional gift at Oisilly and will be buried at the monastery.

Cartulary, fols. 83v–83^{bis}v.
Bougaud-Garnier, pp. 318–320.
RHGF 11:638 (fragment).

Karta de Mornado

Culpa primi parentis faciente, accidit eius generi post ipsum, ut qualis ipse exstitit tales post se natos relinqueret. Qua de re sicut ipse miseria non caruit,

20 Beaumont, 7 km east of Bèze.

ita omnes miseros genuit, et sicut ipse oblitus est beatitudinis a Deo sibi conlate, sic omnes homines obliuiosos reddidit. Quia ergo homo obliuiosum est animal, et sepe labefactari possunt cause rerum gestarum a mente humana, nisi atramento scribantur et cartarum apicibus inserantur, quibus futuri ea quę uel uisu, uel auditu non didicerunt, harum exemplis erudiantur. Idcirco nos quę temporibus nostris acta sunt et priscorum senectus meminit notificanda intimamus.

Omnibus itaque notum esse uolumus presentibus et futuris qualiter quandam terram in uilla Mornado[1] sitam, quę iure Sancto Petro debebatur, tres fratres his nominibus, Wido, Odilo, Ansericus, sancciuerint. Nam tempore Brunonis episcopi[2] extitit quidam miles Lezelinus nomine, qui ipsam terram contra ius ipsius episcopi et seniorum loci suprascripti tenere uoluit, quod uidelicet nequiuit. Post hunc extitit aliis Humbertus cognomine qui ipsam terram similiter inuasit. Qui ad obitum ueniens, reddidit ad limina Sanctorum Petri et Pauli loco iam dicto, quęcumque in ipsa terra tenere uidebatur, siue iuris sui, siue iniustę ablata, omnia reddidit per caligulam suam, quę uulgo osa dicitur, quam impleuit de ipsa terra et uirgulam de uiridario sumpsit ad testimonium, quę uideliciet transmisit per nuntios suos, sed per incuriam non admissa fuerunt sancto loco.

Hinc ergo fratres suprascripti hereditari cupientes terram inuadunt, quasi a proauis sibi dimissam, et ut eis libitum fuit agentes multaquę ui insistentes, contra uoluntatem seniorum loco Sancti Petri degentium conati sunt agere, quod et fecerunt. Attamen illi non destiterunt a proposito uoluntatis sue, tam per semetipsos quam et per principes regni semper clamantes, et iniustam eorum calumpniam patefacientes. Tandem Deo uolente et ipsis resipiscentibus, cum consilio suorum seniorum, adierunt simul limina Sanctorum apostolorum Petri et Pauli, penitentiam agentes, ibique quicquid in supradicta terra tenere uidebantur, siue iuste siue iniuste, omnia contulerunt ad ipsum locum, eo scilicet tenore ut post obitum eorum ipsa terra in testimonium sit sepulturę et societatis eorum, quam et pro hoc reddiderunt. Insuper etiam aliam terram sitam in uilla Osiliaco dicta,[3] quę in conuadio contra ipsos erat, illis reddiderunt seniores loci suprascripti.

Actum est publice Besua monasterio, die festo Sancti Benedicti abbatis, uidelicet xii kalendas Aprilis, anno primo ordinationis domni Otgerii abbatis.[4]

1 Mornay, 16 km northeast of Bèze.
2 Bruno, bishop of Langres (980–1016).
3 Oisilly, 9 km southeast of Bèze.
4 Ulger, abbot of Bèze (1031–c. 1055).

Signum Hugonis comitis Belmontis[5] qui hanc redditionem fieri iussit. Signum Oddonis nepotis eius.[6] Widonis decani. Willerii. Odonis militis. Leutpranni. Aldonis prepositi. Et hęc nomina fratrum. Signum Widonis, Odilonis, Anserici.

67

July 1026

Milo of Tilchâtel gives a manse at Framont, for the good of his soul.

Cartulary, fol. 83bisv.
Bougaud-Garnier, p. 320.
RHGF 11:639 (fragment).
Summarized in Brequigny, *Table* 1:554.

Karta de Fracto Monte

Presentium ac futurorum pro certo karitas agnoscat quia Milo quidam de Tilecastro[1] dedit Sancto Petro Sanctoque Prudentio, pro remedio animę suę, apud Fractum Montem[2] unum mansum, ad quem appendunt nouem iugera de terra aratoria et una sectura prati. Et ut hoc profuturum posteris foret et firmius crederetur, litteris adsignare rogauit sub legitimis testibus.

Anno ab incarnatione MXXVI, indictione viiii, epacta nulla, concurrente iiii, mense Iulio. Regnante Rotberto Francorum rege.[3] Hii sunt testes. Signum Widonis. Signum Oddonis et fratris eius Rotberti. Signum Aldonis et filii eius Milonis. Signum Otberti.

Lord Aldo I of Tilchâtel was the father of a man named Otbert. The Milo of this charter was also undoubtedly a son of Aldo I.[4]

---

5 Count Hugh III of Attuyer, lord of Beaumont, 7 km east of Bèze.

6 Odo was the son of Count Hugh's younger brother Narduin; see Bouchard, *Sword, Miter, and Cloister*, pp. 321–322.

1 Tilchâtel, 9 km northwest of Bèze

2 Framont, 25 km northeast of Bèze.

3 Robert II, king of France (996–1031).

4 Bouchard, *Sword, Miter, and Cloister*, pp. 366–367.

68

1026

Milo of Beire gives Bèze a manse in that village, along with a serf and his wife and children, for the good of his soul.

Cartulary, fol. 83bisv.
Bougaud-Garnier, pp. 320–321.

Karta de Beria

Hoc etiam anno Milo de Beria[1] dedit Sancto Petro in monasterio qui dicitur Fons Besue, pro remedio animę suę, in ipsa uilla unum mansum, ad quem adiacent viiii iugera de terra aratoria et una sectura prati, cum seruo nomine Lamberto, uxore et infantibus. Testes Wido, Bernardus, Aldo, Lambertus, Grimeius, Romarus, Hugo filius Aldonis.

69

c. 1026

Elinard gives Bèze a manse at Is-sur-Tille, along with a serf and his wife and children, for the good of his soul.

Cartulary, fol. 83bisv.
Bougaud-Garnier, p. 321.

Karta de Icio

Elinandus etiam dedit unum mansum Sancto Petro Besuensis cęnobii apud Icium,[1] pro animę suę remedio, cum seruo nomine Teduino, uxore et infantibus, ad quem appendunt viiii iugera de terra aratoria et una sectura prati. Testes Wido, Hugo, Aldo, Stephanus.

The similar list of witnesses suggests this document was given at the same time as the previous and succeeding ones.

---

1 Beire, 8 km southwest of Bèze.

1 Is-sur-Tille, 14 km northwest of Bèze.

70

c. 1026

Odilo gives a manse at Is-sur-Tille, along with a serf, his wife, and children.

Cartulary, fols. 83bisv–84r.
Bougaud-Garnier, p. 321.

Item alia

Odilo dedit similiter in eadem uilla Sancto Petro Besuensis cęnobii unum mansum, cum seruo nomine Ansaldo, cum uxore et infantibus. Testes Wido, Aldo, Bernardus, Armannus, Robertus.

This was most likely given at the same time as the previous documents.

71

Bèze, November 1034

Odo of Beaumont and his son Narduin have been killed, and their relatives make a gift, that is, Odo's uncle, brother, and wife. The gift consists of three serfs with their children, along with some property in the village of Bèze and nearby, with its income.

Cartulary, fol. 84r–v.
Bougaud-Garnier, pp. 321–223.
RHGF 11:639 (fragment).
Summarized in Brequigny, *Table* 2:7.

Karta de Besueta

In Dei omnipotentis nomine. Notum fore uolumus quibusque scire cupientibus qualiter pro remedio animę Odonis optimi militis atque elegantissime iuuentutis filii uidelicet Nerduini,[1] ictu repentino interfęcti, dederunt ad memoriam Sanctorum apostolorum Petri et Pauli Sanctique Prudentii martyris in loco

1 Odo of Beaumont was the son of Narduin, the younger brother of Hugh III. Odo named his son Narduin after his own father. For the family of the counts of Attuyer and lords of Beaumont, which is 7 km east of Bèze, see Bouchard, *Sword, Miter, and Cloister*, pp. 319–322.

Besuensis monasterii auunculus eius, Hugo uidelicet comes Belmontensis, et ipsius Odonis uxor Gertrudis fraterque eiusdem Hugo[2] seruum nomine Teodericum, itemque alium nomine Stephanum, atque ancillam unam nomine Leutgardam, cum omni successione generis filiorum et filiarum eorundem.

Item dederunt mansum unum liberrimi alodi permaximum seu coloniam pergrandem in uilla Besueta, cum omnibus appenditiis quę ad ipsum mansum pertinent, id est terris cultis et incultis, et pratis, et decursus et usus aquarum, et usus siluarum in giro circumiacentium, tam circa Besuam quam circa Vinzennam fluuios,[3] que admodum predictus Oddo uel pater eius seu auus in uita tenuerunt, absque ullo contradicente, illorum generis seu extranei. Debet enim predicta terra per annos singulos frumenti modios quattuor et de tremisse modios tres et dimidium, et mense Maio denario vi. Deinde multonem et porcum et per uindemias carroperum et uini sextarium, et in Natiuitate Domini uini sextarios duos. Et ut ab hodierna die et deinceps sit in dominium predictorum sanctorum Besuensis cęnobii, ut faciant monachi inibi Deo deseruientes quicquid illis utilitatis melius uidebitur et placuerit.

Et ut hęc firma in omni tempore et stabilis ęlemosinę donatio maneat, cum uoluntate parentum et consensu omnium fidelium nostrorum publice tangentes manibus propriis roboramus, et nomina nostra et precipuorum nostrorum conscribi facimus. Si quis uero, quod absit, huic nostre factioni quam pro Dei amore et anime cari parentis nostri redemptione fecimus in aliquo contrarius calumpniator extiterit, iram ęterni iudicis eiusque clauigeri Petri sentiet, si non cum satisfactione emendauerit.

Nomina firmatorum qui hanc cartam firmauerunt. Signum Hugonis comitis. Signum Letgardis comitisse. Signum Gertrudis uxoris Odonis militis. Signum Gybuini.[4] Signum Richardi. Signum Nerduini filii eius. Signum Widonis archidiaconi. Signum Hugonis. Signum Widonis. Signum Odilonis. Signum Ioffredi. Signum Bernardi. Signum Bernardi alterius. Signum Willerii. Signum Richardi. Signum Vlrici. Signum Olgerii. Signum Wilenci. Signum Humberti. Actum Besua publice, anno ab incarnatione Domini MXXXIIII, indictione ii, epacta xxviii. Regnante Heinrico rege viii anno regni eius,[5] mense Nouembri. Ego Heldemannus monachus scripsi et subscripsi.

---

2 Hugh III of Beaumont, count of Attuyer, married Letgardis, who signed below. The late Odo, his nephew, had had a wife named Gertrude and a brother named Hugh.

3 The rivers Bèze and Vingeanne, which flow roughly south by, respectively, the monastery of Bèze and Beaumont.

4 Gibuin, a cleric, was younger brother of Hugh III.

5 Henry I, king of France (1031–1060). The dating formula counts his regnal years from his original coronation.

72

Bèze, 30 June 1036

The knight Richard gives Bèze a manse at Fontenelle, for the good of his soul. His wife and son agree.

Cartulary, fols. 84v–85r.
Bougaud-Garnier, pp. 323–324.
RHGF 11:639 (fragment).
Summarized in Brequigny, *Table* 2:12.

Karta de Fontanellis

Quidam miles Richardus nomine, mente non inconuenienter pertractans et admodum timens sacri eloquii consilio fretus, confidenter aggrediens illud, "Facite ęlemosinam et ipsa orabit pro uobis, et omnia munda sunt uobis" [Luke 11:41], et "Date et dabitur uobis" [Luke 6:38] atque similia, unde pro remedio anime sue celesti ianitori atque apostolorum principi Sancto Petro Besuę Fontis donauit mansum unum, in loco qui uocatur Fontanellas.[1] Quod quidem coniux sua, Radmodis nomine, et filius eius Hugo fautores libenter concesserunt, immo amplius etiam se daturos sancto loco promiserunt.

Actum uero hoc publice in prefati sancti cęnobio et super eiusdem altare. Regnante Domino nostro Ihesu Christo cum Spiritu Sancto in paternę maiestatis dextera, anno incarnationis ipsius MXXXVI, indictione iiii, epacta xx, pridie kalendas Iulii, iiii feria, iii lune, in qua Beati Pauli passio celebrę recolitur, pridie coapostoli eius Petri festo,[2] debito honore peracto. Rege Heinrico in sceptris Francorum agente, Hugone uero in pontificatus honore ęcclesiam regente sanctę sedis Lingonice.[3]

73

c. 1034

The cleric Gibuin makes gifts for his brother Narduin and the latter's sons. The gifts consist of property with serfs, located near Bèze.

Cartulary, fol. 85r–v.
Bougaud-Garnier, p. 324.

---

1 Fontenelle, 9 km northeast of Bèze.

2 The feast of Saints Peter and Paul is normally celebrated on 29 June. The monks of Bèze appear to have separated the two saints and slightly changed the dates.

3 Henry I, king of France (1031–1060), and Hugh of Verdun, bishop of Langres (1031–1049).

Karta de Cauiniaco et Priniaco atque Blaniaco

Quidam Gybuinus clericus, tactus timore diuino, ob peccaminum suorum remissionem seu fratris sui Narduini, filiorumque eius nepotum suorum, Oddonis uidelicet et Hugonis,[1] donauit dimidium mansum unum in uilla quę Priniacus dicitur,[2] et unum curtile cum seruo qui in eadem terra stabat nomine Humbertus, cum filiis duobus Dodone et Humberto. Reddidit etiam terram quandam sitam in Cauiniaco uilla[3] quam frater suus supranominatus Nerduinus tenere uisus est aliquando iniuste. Reddidit saluamentum de uillis Auxiliaci atque Blaniaci.[4] Reddidit etiam Oldierium cum fratre eius nomine Hugone et sorore nomine Fratburga, quos tenebant in saluamentum supradictus frater suus et nepotes sui. Donauit etiam seruum Guntarium et Ingerranum cum filio Stephano. Nam Ingerrannus pro Oddone ante fuerat datus, filius uero ius pro Hugone. Ipse Gybuinus qui donationem fecit firmauit carta.

This document was probably given about the same time as document 71.

74

Bèze, 27 March 1036

Otbert gives up his claims to property at Viévigne, as he is leaving on pilgrimage to Rome.

Cartulary, fol. 85v.
Bougaud-Garnier, pp. 324–325.
Summarized in Brequigny, *Table* 2:12.

Karta de Vetus Vineis

Quidam homo Otbertus nomine reddidit Sancto Petro Besue Fontis quicquid reclamabat in uilla quę Vetusuineas dicitur,[1] die scilicet qui Dominicus habetur, cum in media Quadragesima "Letare Hierusalem" in uoce exultationis sacris concentibus ad missas extollitur,[2] ubi a domno Olgerio eiusdem loci

1 Gibuin, a cleric, and his brother Narduin were brothers of Hugh III of Beaumont. See above, document 71. Narduin was father of Odo and Hugh.

2 Garnier identifies this as Preigney, a now-abandoned hamlet near Is-sur-Tille, 14 km northwest of Bèze.

3 Chevigny, 3 km southeast of Bèze.

4 Oisilly, 9 km southeast of Bèze; and Blagny, 8 km east-southeast of Bèze.

1 Viévigne, 4 km southwest of Bèze.

2 The fourth Sunday in Lent.

abbate[3] et monachis peram peregrinationis simul et absolutionem Romam profecturus suscepit.

Actum uero hoc publice super altare memorati sancti apostolorum principis, v kalendas Aprilium, xxvi lune, rege Francorum Heinrico strenue in sceptris agente, Hugone uero pontificali in cathedra feliciter presidente, ecclesiamque Lingonice sedis pie regente,[4] anno ab incarnatione Domini MXXXVI, indictione iiii, epacta xx.

75

Bèze, 11 June 1044

The cleric Gibuin of Beaumont, while dying, gives Bèze all his hereditary property at Blagny. To this he adds a number of serfs with their families.

Cartulary, fols. 85v–86v.
Bougaud-Garnier, pp. 325–326.
Summarized in Brequigny, *Table* 2:32.

Karta de Blaniaco

Luce clarius constat quemque cupientem uafri hostis proterere molimina, indefesso nisu sectatorum Christi sequi debere uestigia. Rectorum quippe operum casta gestans precordia, cęlorum gliscit gaudia capescere felicia. Quę procul dubio consequitur ad cœlestes thesauros terrena transferens patrimonia [cf. Matt. 6:20], et inopum solans miserias liberalitatis munificentia. Admonet hoc nos diuina scriptura, redemptionem animę uiri contestans proprias diuitias, "Redimuntur namque misericordiis pauperum peccata, et ut ignis aqua, sic elemosinis ęterni rogi restiguitur flamma" [Ecc. 3:33].

Ob quam rem ego Gybuinus clericus, frater Hugonis castri Bellimontis,[1] diuina respectus misericordia et ad dierum meorum perductus extrema, concedo et do Deo omnipotenti et Sancto Petro omnem hereditatem meam in uilla Blaniaco[2] nuncupata. Omnem scilicet terram arabilem cum campis, pratis, siluis, pascuis, siue piscatoria, ex quibus eiusdem uille constat pars maxima. Preterea addo seruos Rotgerium et Alcherium, Vtbaldum, Warnerium, Sendradum, Archimbaldum, cum uxoribus eorum et filiis, omnique familia, et

3 Ulger, abbot of Bèze (1031–c. 1055).
4 Henry I, king of France (1031–1060); and Hugh of Verdun, bishop of Langres (1031–1049).
1 The cleric Gibuin, brother of Hugh III of Beaumont. Beaumont is 7 km east of Bèze.
2 Blagny, 8 km east-southeast of Bèze.

omnes seruos et ancillas ad eandem hereditatem meam pertinentes, quibuslibet locis habitent, ut ab hinc sancto et monachis ei seruientibus sicut actenus mihi seruiant, et consuetudines persoluant mente deuota. Ne uero post decessum meum huius elemosinę aliquis uiolator uel falsator accedat presumptione iniusta, Vlrico nepoti meo commendo coram omni populo ad altare Sancti Petri sua ratione eam demonstrare, et uice mea sancto et monachis tradere, et testem ueritatis cartam fieri, subnixa stipulatione, adhibitisque testibus et signantibus roborare. Signatorum nomina subsequenter exprimit scęda.

Signum Vlrici nepotis eius.[3] Signum Anserici militis. Signum Wilenci militis. Signum Walterii militis. Signum omnium monachorum qui adfuerunt. Signum Widonis archipresbiteri. Signum Constantii presbiteri. Signum Rotberti presbiteri. Signum Haymonis clerici. Signum Hugonis prepositi et totius familie. Actum publice monasterio Besuensi, anno ab incarnatione Domini Millesimo quadragesimo IV, indictione xii, epacta existente viii x, iii idus Iunii, die festiuitatis Sancti Barnabe apostoli, Heinrico regnum Francię tenente, Rotberto fratre eius Burgundie imperante,[4] et Hugone, qui postea repulsam meruit, in presulatu sanctę Lingonensis matris ecclesię nunc uero pastoris nomine presidente.[5]

For Gibuin, see also documents 71 and 73 above, as well as the following document.

76

c. 1045

After Gibuin died, his niece's husband Fulk claimed his gifts and granted them to two of his knights. Now he restores what he had taken.

Cartulary, fol. 86v.
Bougaud-Garnier, pp 326–327.

Item alia

Sane post defunctionem antefati Gybuini[1] in illa terra et seruis qui eam incolebant, quos ipse Sancto Petro et monachis reliquerat, Fulco qui neptem eius

3 Ulric, son of Hugh III of Beaumont.

4 Henry I, king of France (1031–1060), and his brother Robert I, duke of Burgundy (1031–1075).

5 Hugh of Verdun, bishop of Langres (1031–1049); the chronicler has added the comment about his ultimate removal from the see, which took place at the Council of Reims.

1 The cleric Gibuin, brother of Hugh III of Beaumont; see the preceding document.

in matrimonio habebat[2] consuetudines cepit requirere, et quidam duo milites, Hugo frater Oddonis Montis Saligonis et Wilencus de uilla Sancti Sequani,[3] quibus in beneficium ipsas tradiderat. Sed sepe ammonitus et iusticię ratione cumpulsus, ad monasterium ueniens, coram altare Deo et sanctis monachisque ipsis, seruis et ancillis, easdem consuetudines perdonauit et eisdem qui a se in beneficio tenebant hoc ipsum facere coegit, et a se et ab omnibus hominibus liberos eosdem seruos et ancillas constituit. Signum Fulconis. Signum Vlrici.[4] Signum Walterii. Signum Vuidonis.

This most likely happened shortly after Gibuin's death; see the preceding document.

77

Bèze, 1043

The knight Erembert restores a benefice that he had received from Abbot William. He had lost almost everything in civil wars and had intended to sell it, but the monks give him the price he would have received from selling, one hundred solidi, not wishing St Peter to lose his property.

Cartulary, fols. 86v–87v.
Bougaud-Garnier, pp. 327–328.
Summarized in Brequigny, *Table* 2:30.

Karta de Luco, Genciniaco, Cinciaco

In nomine ei omnipotentis, Patris et Filii et Spiritus Sancti. Quia mens humana labilis est et cito excidunt memorię res geste nisi cartarum apicibus inserantur, dignum ducimus nos minimi ea que nostris modo temporibus geruntur mandare posteris, ne sicut premisimus obliuione depereant.

Notum esse uolumus omnibus tam presentibus quam futuris qualiter Ærembertus quondam miles beneficium quod temporibus pristinis, uidelicet domni Willelmi[1] abbatis seu Rodulfi prepositi tempore, uisus est tenuisse reddiderit. Hic enim Ærembertus nobili ortus erat prosapia, secundum seculi dignitatem, sed propter intestina bella quę inter falsos Christianos geruntur, pene

2 Fulk, most likely of Mailly, married Ermengard, daughter and heiress of Hugh III.
3 Montsaugeon, 22 km north of Bèze; and St-Seine-sur-Vingeanne, 13 km northeast of Bèze.
4 Ulric was doubtless Ermengard's brother. For the family, see Bouchard, *Sword, Miter, and Cloister*, pp. 319–322.
1 William, abbot of Bèze (995–1031); he was also abbot of St-Bénigne of Dijon.

ad nichilum redactus erat, ita ut beneficium unde agimus uendere uellet et manibus alienis tradere. Quod nos agnoscentes, fratres uidelicet Sancti Petri Besuensis, dampnum esse arbitrantes si alienis manibus terram sancti uenundaret, ipsum aduocantes in nostro consilio, ammonuimus eum non recte agentem erga fidelitatem Sancti Petri, uerum ipsud precium quod ab aliis cupiebat sibi tribui, nosmet persolueremus. Quod et factum est.

Nam ipse miles adiens cęnobium Sancti Petri Besuensis, domno Olgerio abbate[2] presente, et ceteris fratribus eiusdem congregationis adsumptis, sed et aliis quamplurimis Deum timentibus clericis siue laicis adunatis in conuentu ipsorum, ante altare principis apostolorum Petri apostoli, reddidit ipse et filius eius Wido nomine, accepto precio centum solidorum pro commutatione terrę. Non habens omnino neque ipse neque ullus heredum eius aliquam occasionem repetendi, quod si repetere presumpserit, anathematis uinculo, agnoscat se arceri, auctoritate Petri apostoli. Beneficium uero, unde res agitur, diuersis in locis continetur. Nam in uilla Luco nomine ibi terminatur dimidium mansum, nichilhominus aliud dimidium Vendouera uilla,[3] Tasnato unum mansum, Genciniaco unum mansum, Cinciaco unum mansum.[4]

Testes sunt hii quod adnotamus. Signum Widonis decani. Signum Hugonis prepositi. Signum Odolrici Belmontis, filii Hugonis comitis.[5] Signum Walterii. Signum Odilonis. Signum Haymonis. Signum Alerici. Signum Brunonis camboni. Signum Rainaldi. Signum Rotmari. Signum Heruei. Signum Rainerii. Signum Otberti. Signum Humberti. Actum publice Besua monasterio, anno ab incarnatione Domini nostri Ihesu Christi MXLIII, regnante Heinrico rege in Francia, Rotberto fratre eius Burgundie imperante.[6]

---

2 Ulger, abbot of Bèze (1031–c. 1055).

3 Lux, 5 km northwest of Bèze; and Véronnes, 7 km north-northwest of Bèze. The monastery had had property at these two villae since 827, when Abbot Seraphim of Bèze acquired everything St-Bénigne had had there in exchange for other property around Dijon; *Chartes et documents de Saint-Bénigne de Dijon*, 1:75–76, no. 43. Although a forged charter of King Chlothar III asserted that the monks had had property at Lux from the beginning, this seems unlikely. Land at Lux, as well as Viévigne, Vonges, and Sacquenay, was among what Wideradus, founder of Flavigny, gave to his heirs when he made his testament in 717; *Cartulary of Flavigny*, ed. Bouchard, p. 24, no. 1.

4 Tanay, 7 km south of Bèze; Jancigny, 14 km southeast of Bèze; and Cecey, 18 km east-southeast of Bèze.

5 Ulric, son of Hugh III of Beaumont.

6 Henry I, king of France (1031–1060), and his brother Robert I, duke of Burgundy (1031–1075).

78

Gevrey, 1031–c. 1055

Higmar gives Bèze some serfs with their families in order to settle a quarrel. His brother and sister agree.

Cartulary, fols. 87v–88r.
Bougaud-Garnier, pp. 329–330.
Summarized in Brequigny, *Table* 2:31.[1]

Karta de Gibriaco

Ego in Dei nomine uocatus Higmarus. Notum esse uolo cunctis sanctę Dei ecclesię fidelibus et cunctis meis parentibus ac propinquis, presentibus atque futuris, quoniam sanctę religionis cultor eximius et monasterii, quod Besuense uocatur, Almiclauigeri Petri sub nomine et honore dicatum, abbas nomine Olgerius[2] cum pluribus sue dicionis monachis adiit fundum nomine Gibriacum, situm in comitatu Oscarensi,[3] mecum placitandi gratia pro quibusdam querimoniis quas inibi contra eum eram habiturus.

Considerans igitur predicti abbatis et eius cęnobitarum in Dei seruitio innocentię puritatem, et per eos placare Deum mihi posse considerans, consultu bonorum hominum qui aderant et premaxime Rotberti monachi atque Otberti militis necnon Heynrici sororii mei, pro Deo et animę meę et patris et matris atque omnium parentum meorum requię beata, perdono omnem querelam quam contra prefatum abbatem eiusque monachos habebam. Seruos uero meos Fulcherium et Albertum pro quibus calumpnia creuerat, absque ullo contradictore mea ex parte dono Deo et Sancto Petro ad monasterium Besuense monachis ibi degentibus, quoad uixerint seruituros et filios eorum quos habent et habituri sunt, omnesquę qui ex eis processuri sunt usque in ęternum.

Hanc autem donationis cartam fratri meo Bernardo et sorori meę Euę confirmare faciam et filio eius Odiloni. Si quis uero hanc donationem calumpniare conatus fuerit, non euindicet, sed insuper iram superni iudicis incurrens, predicto loco x libras auri coactus soluat. Actum Gibriaco publice. Signum Higmari qui

1 Brequigny gives an extremely brief summary of the group of fifteen charters that begins here and runs through document 92, suggesting that they were all given between 1043 and 1052.

2 Ulger, abbot of Bèze (1031–c. 1055).

3 Gevrey, 12 km southwest of Dijon, was in the county of Attuyer, near the Ouche river.

fieri et firmare rogauit. Signum Bernardi fratris eius. Signum Heinrici sororii eorum. Signum Euę uxoris eius. Signum Oydilonis filii eorum. Signum Otberti. Signum Gysleberti. Signum item Gysleberti. Signum Waldrici. Signum Humberti. Signum Arnulfi. Signum Widonis. Signum Walterii. Signum Otranni.

79

4 June, c. 1031–c.1055

Helgerius and his brother Guntard make an exchange with Bèze. They receive a benefice at Colonge in return for allodial property at Renève. They shall keep the property at Renève for their lifetimes but pay two solidi a year for it.

Cartulary, fol. 88r–v.
Bougaud-Garnier, pp. 330–331.

Karta de Renauis

Ego Helgerius cum fratre meo Guntardo beneficiis domni Benedicti, prioris Besuensis monasterii, et monachorum eiusdem loci prouocati, pro beneficio quod dederunt nobis in uilla quę Colonica[1] dicitur, dedimus Sancto Petro in uilla que Renauis[2] dicitur de alodo nostro mansum unum, habentem appendentia x et viii iugera, et pratum ad tria carra feni et usuarium silue quę ad eandem uillam pertinet. Ipsa autem terra ex una parte uillam ingreditur, ex altera strata publica quę ad Campanias[3] uadit terminatur, tercia quoque nostro alodo concluditur. Dedimus etiam et alium mansum in iamdicta uila Colonica, habentem appendentia vi iugera, et pratum ad unam carradam feni et usuarium silue quę ad eandem uillam pertinet. Ipsa autem terra ex una parte uillam ingreditur, ex altera terra Sancti Petri diuiditur, tercia terra Aremberti determinatur, quarta autem proximo riuo concluditur.

Hanc autem donationem eo tenore fecimus ut tempore uitę nostrę cum predicto beneficio ipsam terram teneremus, soluentes pro ea censum duorum solidorum annuatim in festiuitate Sancti Petri. Si autem unus ex nobis prior mortuus fuerit, eius pars statim ad eos reuertetur, nisi forte eorum spontanea uoluntate iterum

1 Colonge, 13 km southeast of Bèze.

2 Renève, 13 km south-southeast of Bèze.

3 Champagne, 10 km southeast of Bèze.

alteri concedatur. Et ut hęc donatio firmior permaneret, hanc cartam manu nostra firmauimus, atque altari Sancti Petri superposuimus. Testesque fideles adhibuimus. Signum Guntardi. Signum Helgerii. Signum Oddonis. Signum Raynardi. Signum Saleconis. Signum Bernardi. Data ii nonas Iunii.

This, along with most documents in this section, was doubtless given during the time of Abbot Ulger. These brothers appear again in document 106.

80

c. 1031–c.1055

Hildeberga makes a gift of a manse at Fontenelle, for the soul of her dead son Odilo, who is buried at Bèze. She will keep the usufruct for her lifetime but pay twelve pennies a year for it. Her living sons agree.

Cartulary, fols. 88v–89r.
Bougaud-Garnier, p. 331.

Carta de Fontinellis

In nomine sancte et indiuidue Trinitatis. Ego Hildeberga presentibus et futuris manifesto quia filius meus Odilo immatura etatę preuentus diem clausit ultimum, qui et sepultus est in cimiterio Sancti Petri Besuensis cęnobii. Pro cuius anima simul et mea dedi ad ipsum locum unum mansum apud Fontenellas,[1] quem tenebam lege dotalicii, in quo manebat quidam seruus Hamedeus nomine, ea ratione ut quamdiu uiuam usufructuario teneam, et uno quoque anno festiuitate Sancti Petri in uestitura duodecim denarios persoluam, atque post meum decessum ad dominatum Sancti Petri eiusdem loci sine omni contradictione pertineat.

Et ut hęc donatio firma permaneat, hanc kartam ob noticiam posterorum fieri iussi, et manu mea cum filio meo Ioffredo coram testibus firmaui, quorum ista sunt nomina. Signum Landrici filii mei. Signum Hagani Longi. Signum Gyrardi de Wisstrui. Signum Humberti de Campaniis.[2] Signum Rotberti de Baleneua.[3] Signum Oddonis. Signum Aldonis prepositi.

1 Fontenelle, 9 km northeast of Bèze.
2 Champagne, 10 km southeast of Bèze.
3 Belleneuve, 12 km south of Bèze.

81

Bèze, c. 1043

The knight Arembert of Longchamp returns the benefice he holds from the monks at Jancigny.

Cartulary, fol. 89r.
Bougaud-Garnier, p. 332.

Karta de Gentiniaco

Quidam miles, Arembertus nomine de Longocampo,[1] tenens beneficium Sancti Petri Besuensis in diuersis locis, adiens locum supranominatum, reddidit illi quandam partem, hoc est beneficium, quod situm est in uilla quę Ginciniacus uocatur,[2] ad integram, ita ut neque ipse neque alius heredum suorum repetere ualeant. Istam redditionem fecit presente domno abbate Olgerio[3] et aliis ex monachis eius adstantibus ante altare Sancti Petri.

Arembert is probably the same person as the knight Erembert of document 77. He returned other property he held in benefice in that document.

82

1031–c. 1055

The lady Alburgis makes a gift of property at Chevigny; she is married to the knight Ponce. Her ancestor Gibuin had originally given it, but family members had retained it.

Cartulary, fol. 89r.
Bougaud-Garnier, p. 332.

Karta de Cauiniaco

Quedam mulier Alburga nomine, in coniugo iuncta cuidam militi nomine Poncio, dedit siue ut quidam putant reddidit terram quę est sita in uilla uocitata Cauiniaco,[1] quam et antecessor quidam non mediocre nobilitatis progenitus,

1 Longchamp, 23 km south of Bèze.
2 Jancigny, 14 km southeast of Bèze.
3 Ulger, abbot of Bèze (1031–c. 1055).
1 Chevigny, 3 km southeast of Bèze.

nomine Gybuinus,[1] Sancto Petro concesserat, sed ab ea iure hereditario, sicuti uidebatur, taxata atque retenta fuerat. Signum Olgerii abbatis.[2] Signum Moroni prepositi. Signum Iohannis prioris et aliorum multorum.

Gibuin, Alburgis's great-great-grandfather, was son of the famous Richard le Justicier. Any donation charter he might have issued was long lost. See also document 84.

83

Bèze, 1031–c. 1040

Moronus becomes a monk at Bèze and gives the house half of his hereditary property. Serfs are included in the gift.

Cartulary, fol. 89v.
Bougaud-Garnier, pp. 332–333.

Carta de Calmontis uilla

In nomine summe et indiuidue Trinitatis. Notum esse uolumus tam presentibus quam futuris quod ego Moronus cognomine, timore Dei et timore peccaminum meorum tactus, adii Besuense cenobium ubi multorum sanctorum patrocinia continentur, precipue Sancti Petri apostolorum principis, cum collega suo Paulo apostolo, ubi preesse dinoscebatur domnus abbas Olgerius.[1] Ibi ergo adstantibus quibusdam eiusdem cęnobii monachis et fidelibus Christianis Deum timentibus, quorum nomine subtus adnectentur, feci me tonsorari et monachum deuoui sub norma Regule Sancti Benedicti confessoris permansurum.

Dedi ergo ad predictum cenobium medietatem quicquid iure hereditatis possidere uidebar Calmontis uilla,[2] uel ceteris circumiacentiis possessionibus, in pratis, in aquarum decursibus, in siluis, molendinis, sicut prefatus sum omnem medietatem per seruum nomine Arnaldum, quem dedi Sancto Petro, et per ipsum omnes seruos et ancillas tradidi sancto loco, astipulatione subnixa.

1 Alburgis was a niece of Hugh III of Beaumont, a family which remembered its descent from Count Gibuin in the tenth century. See Bouchard, *Sword, Miter, and Cloister*, pp. 321–322.
2 Ulger, abbot of Bèze (1031–c. 1055).
1 Ulger, abbot of Bèze (1031–c. 1055).
2 Unidentified. Garnier refers to it as Chaumontdel.

Actum publice Besua monasterio, Benedicto preposito adstante, Heldemanno monacho, Adelmo monacho, Oddone monacho, Gyrberga comitissa Fontisuenne,[3] et aliis multis.

Moronus is likely to be the same person who became provost, found for example in the preceding document, in which case this document would date to fairly early in Ulger's years as abbot.

84

c. 1040

Gibuin and his niece Ermengard give Bèze several serfs for the soul of his brother, Hugh III of Beaumont. Gibuin recalls his ancestry back three generations. He also gives up some customary dues he had been requiring.

Cartulary, fols. 89v–90v.
Bougaud-Garnier, pp. 333–335.

Karta de Altrisiaco et Maxiaco et Bodens et Lentiliaco

In nomine summe et indiuidue Trinitatis, Patris et Filii et Spiritus Sancti. Notum sit omnibus fidelibus tam uiuis quam et futuris qod ego Gybuinus et neptis mea Ermingardis tradimus Sancto Petro quattuor colonias in uico qui Altrisiacus[1] dicitur, pro remedio animę fratris mei Hugonis,[2] qui iam dictas colonias adhuc uiuens Beato Petro destinauerat, cum seruis et ancillis quorum hęc sunt nomina: Rodulfum cum uxore et infantibus suis, Abraham et Danninum fratres cum uxoribus et natis eorum, Orrannum et Laibonem cum uxoribus et infantibus eorum, Lambertum cum uxore et infantibus suis, Erbertum qui adhuc erat puer. Concedimus hęc Beato Pero libere cum omnibus appendiciis suis, ut sicut a diebus Gybuini proaui mei et filii eius Hugonis, necnon et Hugonis patris mei[3] stetis in nostra potestate, sic permaneat in potestate

3 Fouvent, 35 km northeast of Bèze. The lords of Fouvent were also counts of Auxois in the eleventh century.

1 Autrey, 17 km east-northeast of Bèze.

2 The cleric Gibuin was brother of Hugh III of Beaumont, father of Gibuin's niece Ermengard. Gui, mentioned below, was another brother. Ermengard, wife of Fulk, mentioned below, became the heiress to Beaumont. For the family, see Bouchard, *Sword, Miter, and Cloister*, pp. 319–322. Beaumont is 7 km east of Bèze.

3 The cleric Gibuin and his brother Hugh III of Beaumont were sons of Hugh II, son of Count Hugh I of Dijon (d. c. 950), son of a Gibuin who was most likely a brother of Hugh the Black.

Sancti Petri, ab ista die et deinceps, pro remedio animę fratris mei Hugonis, ut ipsi habeant consuetudinem quam ante habebant, tam in siluis, quam in pratis, aquis, campis, et cunctis confiniis. Et ut nullus deinceps maior, siue foristarius uel decanus, de potestate Altriaci hominibus iamdictis uel natis eorum qui de progenie eorum per succedentia tempora exierint aliquam molestiam inferre presumat. Et si per neglegentiam acciderit ut bestię istorum hominum sine custode in prato indominicato uel coruata incurrerit, non cogantur per legem emendationem soluere, sed tantummodo estimationem damni reddant. Hanc eandem cumsuetudinem cuncedimus[4] Sancto Petro de duobus curtilibus quos ante habeat in eadem uilla. Item damus Sancto Petro mansum unum in uilla quę Maxiacus dicitur[5] cum appendiciis suis.

Preterea dimittimus et abnegamus omnes consuetudines quas pater meus et fratres mei Hugo et Wido accipiebant in uilla quę Bodens dicitur, et in Lentiliaco,[6] pro remedio animarum illorum et nostrarum, excepto coruatam quam pro silua faciunt. Et si quis heredum meorum, quod minime futurum esse credo, hęc calumpniari tempauerit, repetere non ualeat et in dextera Dei omnipotentis et auctoritate Petri apostolorum principis anathema maranatha fiat. Et ut hęc karta firma et stabilis permaneat, manu propria firmaui, nepti et sponso eius Fulconi ceterisque fidelibus firmare precepi.

Signum Gybuini. Signum Fulconis. Signum Ermingardis. Signum Bernardi. Signum Widonis archidiaconi. Signum Richardi. Signum Goffredi. Signum Widonis. Signum Odilonis. Signum Odolrici. Signum Wilenci. Signum Leubranni. Signum Milonis. Signum Gosberti. Signum Humberti. Signum Lamberti. Signum Vlgerii.

Although the death of Hugh III of Beaumont cannot be precisely dated, his son-in-law Fulk first appears as count of Beaumont in 1043, so this charter was issued presumably not long before. See also document 82.

85

c. 1031–c. 1055

The lady Adelina and her sons give a manse at Lux, including its income, a house, and a serf.

---

4 Although this is clearly what the scribe wrote, it should be corrected to "consuetudinem concedimus."

5 Maâtz, 30 km north-northeast of Bèze.

6 Bouhans, 2 km southeast of Autrey; and Nantilly, 3 km southeast of there.

Cartulary, fol. 90v.
Bougaud-Garnier, p. 335.

Karta de Luco

Eodem tempore quedam mulier Adilina nomine, cum filiis suis Nocherio et Poncio, dedit unum mansum in uilla cui cognomen est Luco,[1] cum omnibus appenditiis suis, et censualibus pensionibus, domumque in eo consistentem, et seruum nomine Albericum.

86

c. 1031–c. 1055

The lady Ezilina gives allodial property at Bussières, including all appurtenances, with serfs, fields, woods, and waters. Her son Calo agrees.

Cartulary, fol. 90v.
Bougaud-Garnier, p. 335.

Karta de Buxiaco

Similiter Ezilina dedit alodum in uico cui nomen est Buxiaco,[1] cum omni integritate sua, appenditiis, colonicis, campis, siluis, aquis, laudante Kalone filio suo.

87

1031–c. 1055

Bernard gives Bèze all that he has at Viévigne.

Cartulary, fol. 90v.
Bougaud-Garnier, p. 335.

Item alia

Alius quidam homo, Bernardus nomine, dedit quicquid iuris sui uidebatur esse in finibus Vetus Vineis.[1]

1 Lux, 5 km northwest of Bèze.

1 Bussières was the name of a now-ruined village near Lux. Calo may be identical with the knight Calo of Grancey.

1 Viévigne, 4 km southwest of Bèze.

This Bernard was also known as Bernard Francus; see the following document.

88

c. 1031–c. 1055

Bernard Francus gives Bèze some land.

Cartulary, fol. 90v.
Bougaud-Garnier, p. 335.

Karta de Longa Boella

Item Bernardus qui uocatur Francus dedit Sancto Petro duos iornales de terra in fine que uocatur Longa Boella.[1]

89

c. 1031–c. 1055

Evard of Pont gives Bèze meadows and fields.

Cartulary, fol. 91r.
Bougaud-Garnier, p. 336.

Alia

Euuardus etiam de Ponto[1] dedit duas petiunculas de prato in loco qui uocatur Molonga prata, et duos campos ad Montannos[2] unum, et alium ad Pontem uillam.

90

c. 1031–c. 1055

Anna gives Bèze property at Pont for her burial.

Cartulary, fol. 91r.
Bougaud-Garnier, p. 336.

1 This place is unidentified.
1 Pont, no longer a community, was located between Bèze and Véronnes.
2 These places were presumably near Pont.

Item alia

Anna quedam femina, pro sepultura sua, dedit Sancto Petro unum curtile ad Pontem, id est in caustro.[1]

91

c. 1031–c. 1055

Milo, twin brother of Maiolus, gives Bèze a manse at Marey, including a serf and his family.

Cartulary, fol. 91r.
Bougaud-Garnier, p. 336.

Karta de Mariaco

Benigna mente futuris consulentes sepia menbranis imprimere cupimus quod Milo, qui dicebatur Bicellus id est Geminus,[1] frater Maioli cuius cognomen Mazilinus, dederit Sancto Petro in Mariaco uilla[2] unum mansum cum appendiciis suis et seruum nomine Gyrardum, cum uxore et infantibus suis.

92

c. 1031–c. 1055

Teto Tezilinus, a knight of Montsaugeon, gives Bèze a manse and a serf for his brother.

Cartulary, fol. 91r.
Bougaud-Garnier, p. 336.

Karta de Vachiriaco

Adnotandum credimus futuris quod Teto cuius cognomen Tezilinus[1] Montis Salionis[2] miles tradiderit Sancto Petro unum mansum in Vachiriaco quondam uico,[3] sed nunc deserto, simulque seruum nomine pro Euuruino fratre suo.

---

1 These last four words are added interlinearly.

1 These last three words are added interlinearly.

2 Marey-sur-Tille, 21 km northwest of Bèze.

1 These last three words are added interlinearly.

2 Montsaugeon, 22 km north of Bèze.

3 This place is unidentified.

93

c. 1031–c. 1055

Hugh, a cleric of Losne, gives Bèze a manse at Lux, which his father Gibuin had given him.

Cartulary, fol. 91r.
Bougaud-Garnier, pp. 336–337.

Karta de Luco

Iustum arbitramur memorie tradere quod Hugo clericus de Launna[1] delegauerit Sancto Petro unum mansum die festiuitatis eiusdem generalem missam celebrantibus senioribus. Publice itaque accedens ad altare, tradidit donationem circumspiciente populo, affirmans patrem suum Gybuinum ipsum mansum sibi dedisse, die quo benedicta est ei capitis corona. Est autem ipse mansus in Luco uilla, terra autem ad eum pertinens coniacet in ualle quę pro fluuiolo Vernela,[2] qui per eam fluit, Verne uallis dicitur.

Signum Olgerii abbatis.[3] Signum Maroni. Signum Hugonis. Signum Iohannis. Signum Widonis decani. Signum Rotberti presbiteri. Signum Gyraldi clerici.

Hugh later founded the small monastery of Notre-Dame of Losne; see document 120.

Eodem tempore Henricus[4] tercius imperator Burgundie regnum gubernabat. Rodulfus enim Burgundię rex sine liberis existens, Henricum secundum Cesarem heredem regni fecit, post quem ad Chonradum peruenit imperium.[5] Hic sororem predicti regis, nomine Gislam, habuit coniugem, de qua genuit tercium Henricum, cui ex successione paterna iure prouenit regnum Burgundię. In cuius regni termino sita est Lugdunum ciuitas, quam Lotharius Francorum

1 Losne, 31 km southeast of Dijon. Hugh was the son of Gibuin, also a cleric, of the family of the lords of Beaumont; see Bouchard, *Sword, Miter, and Cloister*, pp. 321–322.

2 Lux, 5 km northwest of Bèze, is just south of the source of the Venelle river.

3 Ulger, abbot of Bèze (1031–c. 1055).

4 At this point, on fol. 91r, the chronicler of Bèze once again begins following the chronicle of St-Bénigne (pp. 188–191 in the printed edition), although with some large omissions, as indicated below. The emperor is Henry III (1039–1056).

5 After the death of Rudolph III in 1032, the kingdom of Burgundy was attached to the empire, then under Conrad II (1024–1039).

rex dedit in dotem sorori suę Mathildę regine, quam despondit Chonrado Burgundie regi, patri supradicti regis Rodulfi.[6]

Erat[7] enim isdem rex Heinricus ualde religiosus, et circa diuinum cultum deuotissimus. Anno autem ab incarnatione Domini MXLVI perrexit memoratus princeps Romam, ibique tunc suscepit coronam imperii, die natalis Domini, per manus Clementis pape,[8] quem ipse imperator ordinari iussit, et deponi fecit Iohannem, qui tunc katedre presidebat, et Benedictum atque Siluestrum, qui in concilio tunc habito examinata eorum culpa inuenti sunt non solum symoniaci, sed etiam peruasores ecclesię Christi.[9] Huic concilio interfuit Halinardus Lugdunensium archipresul atque Hugo Chrisopolitanus archiepiscopus, aliique plures ex diuersis partibus coadunati episcopi.[10] Defuncto uero memorato papa Clemente, Romani pecierunt ab imperatore domnum Brunonem Leuchorum episcopum.[11] Hoc namque a Romanis imperator data pecunia non parua exegerat, ut sine eius permissu papa non eligeretur.[12]

Domno igitur Brunone, qui appellatus est Leo papa, ordinato, euocatus est ab ipso Rome ad concilium omnes episcopi Gallie,[13] ad pertractandum inibi de statu et correctione sanctę ecclesię. In ipso anno ipse domnus papa perrexit Franciam, et Remis habuit concilium episcoporum, sicut iam diximus, ibique deposuit Hugonem Lingonensem episcopum.[14] Tuncque fuit translatum corpus Sancti Remigii ab ipso domno apostolico et episcopis qui adfuerunt,

---

6 Lyon, according to the chronicler, became part of the kingdom of Burgundy via Mathilda, a French Carolingian princess who became Rudolph III's mother. Rudolph's half-sister, Gisela, married Conrad II.

7 Here on fol. 91v, the chronicler of Bèze has skipped a long section of the chronicle of St-Bénigne (pp. 188–190 in the printed edition) dealing with the election of Abbot Halinard of that monastery to the see of Lyon.

8 Clement II (1046–1047), put in by the emperor.

9 The Council of Sutri of 1046 formally deposed the three claimants to the papal see, so that Clement II might become pope: Gregory VI (originally named John), Benedict IX, and Sylvester III.

10 Here, on fol. 91v, the chronicler of Bèze skips three sentences on the emperor.

11 Bruno, bishop of Toul, became Pope Leo IX (1049–1054). The chronicler of St-Bénigne, and Bèze's chronicler with him, skips over the brief reigns of Benedict IX (again) and Damasus II.

12 Here, on fol. 91v, the chronicler of Bèze skips three sentences on the pope's character and education.

13 Here the chronicler of St-Bénigne makes special mention of Archbishop Halinard, in a phrase the chronicler of Bèze skips.

14 This short phrase about the deposition of Bishop Hugh of Langres (1031–1049) is not in the chronicle of St-Bénigne, which mentions instead that Halinard was with the pope.

et ecclesia ipsa sacrata.[15] Veniens uero idem papa ad ciuitatem Lingonas ordinauit ibi domnum Arduinum episcopum,[16] pro illo qui fuerat eiectus.[17]

Dumque ibi demoraretur, proferrenturque in medium diuerse diuersarum ecclesiarum disceptationes, ac inter se calumpnię ut pote ante patrem uniuersalem et apostolicum recte, et canonice terminande. Contigit etiam de nobis et de canonicis Lingonensibus rationem haberi. Ipsi namque uolebant de uinea nostra quę est sub Gibriaco[18] decimam habere. Vnde cum rationem intellexisset domnus papa Leo, erupit in uoce, et quid in archiuis sanctę Romanę ecclesię inde uiderat ostendit, dicens, "Sanctorum patrum, qui ante me sanctę Romane sedi prefuerunt, auctoritate sanctitum est, ut nulla ecclesia quę in honore Beati Petri apostolorum principis sit fundata, alteri ecclesię censum uel decimas persolut." Cuius rationis et auctoritatis pondere repressi ipsi canonici conticuerunt.

Isdem uero uenerabilis Arduinus episcopus inter cetera beneficia quę huic loco contulit, petente abbate Olgerio,[19] a summo pontifice Romanę ecclesię peciit fieri decretum, in quo continetur ut nullus presumat huic monasterio uim inferre, uel eum in subiectionem cuiuscumque monasterii redigere, et ut nullus audeat infra unam leuuuam a monasterio uim aliquam inferre. Cuius exemplar decreti placuit huic libro inserere, ut audientes discant quantum inmineat illis periculum qui non timent obligari anathematis uinculo per Petri apostoli uicarium. Anno incarnationis Dominice MLII, presidebat sanctę Romanę ecclesię domnus Leo papa. Cuius hęc sunt uerba.

94

2 October 1051

Pope Leo IX issues a privilege for Bèze. No one shall have authority over the house except the bishop of Langres.

Cartulary, fols. 92v–93r.

Bougaud-Garnier, pp. 338–339.

Leo IX, "Epistolae et diplomata pontificia," PL 143:788, no. 110; dated 1052.

15 Here the chronicler skips a sentence about a later council Leo held in Rome.

16 Harduin of Tonnerre, bishop of Langres (1049–1065).

17 Here, on fol. 92r, the chronicler of Bèze leaves the chronicle of St-Bénigne.

18 Gevrey, 12 km southwest of Dijon.

19 Ulger, abbot of Bèze (1031–c. 1055).

Summarized in Brequigny, *Table* 2:55; dated 1052.
Summarized in Jaffe, *Regesta pontificum Romanorum*, 1:541, no. 4261.

Priuilegium domni Leonis pape

Leo episcopus, seruus seruorum Dei, Olgerio abbati Besuensis monasterii,[1] tuis et successoribus, perpetuam in Domino salutem.[2]

Conuenit apostolico moderamini pia religione pollentibus beniuola compassione succurrere et petentium desideriis congruum impertiri suffragium. Quapropter inclinati precibus tuis, fili carissime, decreuimus more antecessorm nostrorum hoc nostro priuilegio apostolice tuicionis, uestro Besuensi monasterio propter inminentes persecutiones et propter innumeros casus qui superueniunt, dignam concedere libertatem. Videlicet ut nulla persona aut ulla potestas siue ecclesiastica seu secularis super eum audeat dominationem aut potestatem usurpare preter Lingonensem episcopum, qui ei patrocinetur iuste et canonice.

Sic tamen ut ei non lict neque ministris eius terras aut beneficia monasterii commutare uel dare nec uasa nec ornamenta seu uolumina subtrahere aut qualicumque occasione diripere. Omnia uero quecumque habet uel tenet uel adquiesierit supradictus locus habeat et teneat nostra apostolica confirmatione iure perpetuo, in cuiuscumque diocesi sit.

Interdicimus etiam nostra auctoritate ut nullus audeat supradicto monasterio uim inferre uel eum in subiectionem cuiuscumque monasterii redigere. Raptores cuiuscumque ordinis uel dignitatis sint qui res quę ad supranominatum cęnobium pertinent siue de hominibus seu de terris uel de qualibuscumque rebus unde sustentari et uiuere debent inibi Deo seruientes, rapuerint uel substraxerint, ligamus eos ligamine Sancti Petri usque quo congrue satisfaciant.

Prohibemus etiam ne infra unam leuuuam a monasterio liceat alicui aliquem inuadere uel eius res auferre. Statuentes apostolica censura ne ulla hominum persona magna uel parua contra hoc nostrum priuilegium uenire pertemptet. Quod qui fecerit, apostolico anathemati subiacebit, usque ad dignam satisfactionem. Qui uero se seruauerit, benedictionis nostrę gratia cumuletur et ęternę uitę particeps efficiatur.

Datum iiii nonas Octobris per manus Petri diaconi, bibliothecarii et cancellarii sancte apostolicę sedis. Indictione v, incarnationis Dominice anno MLII, pontificatus autem domni Leonis noni Papę iii.

1 Pope Leo IX (1049–1054) and Ulger, abbot of Bèze (1031–c. 1055).
2 This invocation is written in elongated capitals, such as would have been on the first line of an eleventh-century papal bull.

The date of 1052 is in error. October of the third year of Leo's papacy would be 1051. Theo Kölzer calls this privilege spurious, probably on the basis of the difficulties with the dating formula, even though he does not give an explicit reason.[3] And yet its emphasis on the monastery's dependence on the bishop would argue for authenticity.

De obitu Olgerii abbatis

Defuncto igitur abbate Olgerio, successit in regimine pastoralis officii abbas Oddo.[4] Quę autem in diebus eius data uel empta sunt in possessione agrorum, non est silendum.

95

c. 1055–c. 1065

The noble knight Ulger died while returning from pilgrimage to Jerusalem. He designated a manse at Viévigne with a serf and his family as a gift to Bèze. Ulger's wife Tetburgis, children, and men all agree.

Cartulary, fol. 93r–v.
Bougaud-Garnier, p. 340.

Karta de Vetus Vineis

Quidam igitur miles huius nostrę regionis, nobili prosapia ortus, Olgerius nomine, cum multis aliis loca Hierosolimitana expeciit, sed in reuertendo post multa pericula pro Christo tolerata, felici ut credimus obitu lucem presentis uitę reliquid.

Presentibus autem conuiatoribus et audientibus, Sancto Petro Besuę et eius monachis apud Vetusuineas[1] unum mansum uestitum cum seruo in eo habitante, nomine Arnaldo, delegauit, ita sicut pater ipsius Arnaldi uocabulo Ademarus usque in diem mortis suę tenuit, et eidem filio suo Arnaldo dimisit. Vxorem etiam eius nomine Tedindem cum filiis et filabus simul cum eo dari iussit. Pariterque palmas quas testes peregrinationis suę a Iericho tulerat altari superponi rogauit. Quam donationem coniunx eius, Tetburgis appellata, et filii eius libenti animo laudauerunt, et suos homines laudare compulerunt. Debet

3 Kölzer, *Merowingerstudien II*, p. 16.

4 Odo, abbot of Bèze (c. 1055–c. 1065), successor to Abbot Ulger (1031–c. 1055).

1 Viévigne, 4 km southwest of Bèze.

uero iste mansus porcum et arietem, sex panes, et tres sextarios uini, carroperam et omnes consuetudines, quas dominis persoluere debent serui.

Quos suos protulerunt testes, signamus calamo omnes. Signum Tetburgis coniugis eius. Signum Heinrici et Vlrici filiorum eius. Signum Tetbaldi. Signum Aldonis Claudi. Signum Formaldi. Signum Nerduini. Signum Humberti. Signum Nerduini iuuenis. Signum Widonis decani. Signum Hugonis prepositi. Signum Rotberti presbiteri. Signum Iohannis. Signum Arengerii et omnium seruorum ipsius apud mansiones conmorantium.

It seems most likely that this charter was given during the reign of Abbot Odo, since the cartulary scribe had just mentioned him. The offices that some of the signatory monks held were added interlinearly, presumably not in the original but added by the cartulary scribe.

96

1057–c. 1065

The knight Humbert, childless, gives all his hereditary allod in the counties of Attuyer and Auxois. His portion is separated from that of his brothers, Hugh and Ulric. He confirms while dying.

Cartulary, fols. 93v–94v.
Bougaud-Garnier, pp. 340–342.

Karta de Altrisiaco et Villare et Cinciaco

Alius quidam miles nomine Humbertus, omni prolis fiducia destitutus, tradidit Deo et Sancto Petro ad locum Besuensem, sanus et incolumis existens, omnem hereditatem alodi sui quę ei iure paterno cesserat, absque contradictione hominis ullius. Diuisus enim erat iam a fratribus suis, Hugone et Vlrico, et unusquisque partem suam singillatim separauerat a fratre suo. Quam donationem ad mortem perductus iterato confirmauit, et calumpniatores eternę maledictioni in ipsa mortis hora obligauit.

Omnem partem alodi in Altrisiacensi uilla,[1] cum omnibus consuetudinibus in omni potestate Altreiaca, in siluis, in campis, in pratis. Apud Villare[2] etiam omnem partem suę hereditatis, sicut ipse in uita sua tenuit. Noua casa, cunctum suum alodum, sicut ipse possederat. In Cincicaco[3] uero similiter alodum suum,

1 Autrey, 17 km east-northeast of Bèze.
2 Villers, 66 km east-northeast of Bèze.
3 Cecey, 18 km east-southeast of Bèze.

cum omni consuetudine, in aquis, in campis, in pratis, in siluis. Calmetis[4] necnon totum suum alodum sicut ipse in uita sua possedit. Romaniaca etiam et Ponto,[5] cunctum alodum cum omni consuetudine in aquis, in pratis, in campis, in siluis. Est etiam ibi molendinum unum, cuius terciam partem Sancto Petro tradidit. Berię[6] etiam omnem partem alodi sui, in aquis, in campis, in pratis, in siluis.

In comitatu Alsensi, in uilla quę dicitur Velinniaco, et in Villari Corcellis, Bretoneria[7] omnem alodum suum, cum omnibus appendiciis in campis, in pratis, in aquis, in siluis.

Signum domni Oddonis abbatis.[8] Signum Moroni monachi. Signum Hugonis monachi. Signum Theoderici monachi. Signum Willelmi comitis.[9] Signum Fulconis senioris Bellimontis.[10] Signum Gisleberti senioris Reseie.[11] Signum Walonis senioris Berię. Signum Odilonis. Signum Wilenci. Signum Landrici. Signum Widrici. Signum Rodulfi et Olgerii fratris eius. Signum Widonis. Signum Tetzilini. Signum Rotberti. Signum Bernonis. Signum Herialdi. Signum Gyrardi. Signum Isemberti. Signum Hugonis. Hanc donationem frater ipsius Humberti Hugo coram omni populo laudauit et omnem partem suam ex ipso alodo, quia tantumdem habet post mortem suam Sancto Petro concessit.

This document is dated by Abbot Odo and Count William.

97

Bèze, 8 February c. 1055–c. 1065

The knight Robert gives Bèze a manse at Mornay. Ermengard and her son Ulric, a cleric, had earlier given it. Robert receives a horse as a counter-gift from the monks.

Cartulary, fol. 94v.
Bougaud-Garnier, pp. 342–343.

---

4 Chaume, 13 km north-northeast of Bèze.

5 La Romagne, 16 km northeast of Bèze; and Pont, between Bèze and Véronnes.

6 Beire, 8 km southwest of Bèze.

7 The pagus of Auxois is to the west of that of Attuyer, where Bèze and most of its possessions were located. The places are Velogny, 60 km west-southwest of Bèze; Courcelles, 68 km west-northwest of Bèze; and Bretonnière, which according to Garnier was the name of a farm near Bussy-le-Grand, north of Alise.

8 Odo, abbot of Bèze (c. 1055–c. 1065).

9 Count William Tête-Hardi of Burgundy (1057–1087).

10 Fulk, son-in-law of Hugh III of Beaumont and his successor; Beaumont is 7 km east of Bèze.

11 Garnier identifies this place as La Rochette, near Oisilly.

Karta de Mornado

Nouerint omnes presentes et futuri quia quidam miles Rotbertus nomine, pro timore et amore Dei, delegauit ad locum Sancti Petri Besuensis monasterii quoddam mansum quo quędam matrona nomine Ermengardis et filius eius Odricus clericus destinauerant. Cuniacet autem mansum illud in Mornado uilla,[1] et habet ad se terras pertinentes, cultas et incultas, seruos et liberos in eis manentes, prata, pomiferas arbores, et aquarum cursus et recursus, quę omnia ad iamdictum locum Sancti Petri destinauit atque restituit. Et ut ex meliori uoluntate hoc factum esset, accepit a monachis ipsius loci caballum unum et societatem in omnibus benefactis eorum, et ex inde hanc cartam fieri curauit quam propria manu firmauit, et amicis atque parentibus suis tradidit firmandam atque laudandam.

Actum Besuensi monasterio publice vi idus Februarii. Signum Rotberti qui hanc kartam fieri mandait. Signum Oddonis. Signum Gozfredi. Signum Achardi et aliorum multorum.

This most likely dates from when Odo was abbot, as do other documents in this section. Ermengard may be the heiress of Beaumont by that name.

98

c. 1055–c. 1065

The woman Sufisia makes a gift to Bèze for her son Wido, born to Gislebert. The gift includes mansi at Belfond and Genevrières, with the serfs living there.

Cartulary, fols. 94v–95r.
Bougaud-Garnier, p. 343.

Karta de Geneurerias

Quedam mulier Sufisia nomine pro remedio animę filii sui Widonis, quem ex Gisleberto suscepit, dedit unum mansum Sancto Petro in uilla Bellifontis[1] cum omnibus appendiciis suis, et habet omnem consuetudinem in campo, in aqua, in silua. Seruum etiam in eo habitantem, nomine Martinum. Alterum mansum apud Geneurerias[2] cum omnibus appenditiis suis,

1 Mornay, 16 km northeast of Bèze.
1 Belfond, 39 km north-northeast of Bèze.
2 Genevrières, 38 km north-northeast of Bèze.

habentem consuetudinem in campo, in aqua, in silua, ea conuentione ut quindecim iornales arabiles de alodo suo in fine eiusdem uillę eidem manso ad perficiendum quod minus habebat adderet. Seruum quoque in eodem commorantem nomine Albericum, cum uxore Fratburge appellata cum infantibus suis.

Et ut perpetuali fulcimento perduraret elemosina, horum testium subtus inscribi rogauit nomina. Signum Sufisie. Signum Æduini patrasti eius. Signum Warnerii mariti sororis eius.[1] Signum domni Oddonis abbatis.[2] Signum Moronis monachi et aliorum multorum.

Gislebert, Sufisia's husband, may be the same as the Gislebert of document 96.

99

c. 1055–c. 1065

The knight Sewald of Montsaugeon gives Bèze a manse and a serf at Marey, for the soul of his brother.

Cartulary, fol. 95r.
Bougaud-Garnier, pp. 343–344.

Karta de Mariaco

Manifestum etiam esse uolumus modernis et successuris quod quidam miles nomine Seuualdus ex Monte Saligone[1] dederit Sancto Petro pro redempione animę fratris sui Eliranni unum mansum apud Mariacum uillam prope Tilecastrum,[2] cum omnibus appendiciis suis, simulque unum seruum nomine Odilardum.

Signum Seuualdi. Signum domni Oddonis abbatis.[3] Signum Moroni. Signum Petri. Signum Pontii militis.

1 The identifications of two of the witnesses as her father-in-law and brother-in-law are added interlinearly.
2 Odo, abbot of Bèze (c. 1055–c. 1065).
1 Montsaugeon, 22 km north of Bèze.
2 Marey-sur-Tille, 21 km northwest of Bèze. It is a dozen km from Tilchâtel.
3 Odo, abbot of Bèze (c. 1055–c. 1065).

100

c. 1055–c. 1065

The knight Sigfried, dying, gave Bèze two mansi at Flacey, along with a serf. His sister-in-law places the gift on the altar for him.

Cartulary, fol. 95r–v.
Bougaud-Garnier, p. 344.

Karta de Flaciaco

Notum esse uolumus omnibus post nos futuris quod miles quidam, nomine Sigefridus, dederit Sancto Petro ad extrema perductus duos mansos apud Flaciacum uillam.[1] In uno quidem Ærbertus manebat eius seruus, et debet festiuitate omnium sanctorum dimidium sextarium uini, natiuitate autem Domini unum sextarium uini, duos panes, et duas gallinas. Alius uero in eadem uilla coniacet desertus. Tradidit etiam decem diurnales terrę in finibus eiusdem uillę ad eosdem mansos pertinentes, cum pratis, siluis, et omnibus suis appendiciis.

Signum Ruzuidis uxoris Rotberti, fratris eiusdem Sigifredi, quę hanc donationem loco ipsius Sigifredi super altare posuit. Signum Oddonis fratris Mazilini. Signum Willerii. Signum Amalrici. Signum Petri clerici.

I have dated this document in the assumption that it was given when Odo was abbot.

101

Early eleventh century

The noblewoman Ermengard of Beaumont makes gifts to Bèze at Bouhans and Nantilly. She does so for the souls of her late husband Hugh and late son Gui. Her surviving sons – Hugh, Narduin, and Gibuin – agree.

Cartulary, fol. 95v.
Bougaud-Garnier, pp. 344–345.

Karta de Bodens et de Lentileio

Diuina auctoritate inspirata nobilis matrona, Ermengardis nomine,[1] Sanctum Petrum sibi fecit heredem, omnesque fratres Besuensis monasterii Deo ac ipsi

---

1 Flacey, 10 km west-southwest of Bèze.

1 Ermengard, widow of Hugh II of Beaumont and mother of Hugh III, the cleric Gibuin, Narduin, and the late Gui, all mentioned below.

summo apostolorum principi seruientibus suis usibus admisit, reddens illis saluamentum de Bodens et de Lentileio,[2] atque de cunctis quę ad ipsum saluamentum pertinent, pro remedio animę suę ac senioris sui Hugonis, filiique sui Widonis qui tunc fuerat defunctus, quique ipsum saluamentum post mortem patris iure hereditario possidebat. Cuius rei cooperatores fuerunt filii ipsius, Hugo uidelicet et Nerduinus, simul Gybuinus, qui adhuc uita perfruebantur.

Et ut hęc traditio nota fiat futuris sicut est presentibus, scripto mandare fecit, ut quod post mortem testare non poterat, testetur karta seruata, in ipsius monasterii archario. Hanc ergo ut inconuulsa permaneat, testibus adhibitis subscripsit manu propria. Ermengardis subscripsit, Hugo, Nerduinus, Gybuinus, hii sunt testes.

In spite of its placement in the cartulary, this document should be dated two generations earlier than some of the documents that come before it. See also document 84.

102

Early eleventh century

Gertrude of Fouvent gives a manse at Bussières, along with her sons Girard and Humbert, for the soul of her late husband, Girard. In addition, she gives a manse at Perrigny in return for a helmet and a hauberk.

Cartulary, fols. 95v–96r.
Bougaud-Garnier, p. 345.

Karta de Buxiaco

Notum sit omnibus tam presentibus quam futuris quod Gertrudis uxor Gyrardi militis de castro Fontisuennę,[1] cum filiis suis Gyrardo et Humberto, tradidit unum mansum pro redemptione animę prescripti mariti sui et filiorum suorum, ab ipso iam donatione facta Sancto Petro Besuensi in uilla cui uocabulum est Buxiacus,[2] ad integrum sicut uidebatur tenere Rotbertus maior, cum ipso uidelicet Rotberto et uxore et filiis, cum omnibus quę ad ipsum mansum pertinent, tam in terris quam in siluis et in pratis, uel in pascuis siue in aquis.

Et ut hęc donatio in perpetuum firma sit et stabilis, his subscriptis testibus firmauit et firmare rogauit. Hii sunt Aymo, Olgerius, Ioffredus, Librandus, Oddo, Arlebaldus, Wido, Aldo.

---

2 Bouhans, 18 km east-northeast of Bèze; and Nantilly, 3 km southeast of there.

1 Fouvent, 35 km northeast of Bèze. For Gertrude and her sons – Girard became a cleric – see Bouchard, *Sword, Miter, and Cloister*, pp. 284–286.

2 Bussières was the name of a now-ruined village near Lux.

Reddidit etiam unum mansum quod dudum Sancti Petri alodus fuerat in uilla Patriniaco,[3] acceptis pro precio duobus militantium instrumentis quę uulgo dicuntur helmum et osbergum.

This document must date from the early decades of the eleventh century, certainly before 1030, when Gertrude's son Girard was killed.[4] See also documents 59–61.

103

Mid-eleventh century

Richard of Beaumont gives land near Mornay, which his wife Wandelmodis had claimed, without admitting the claim was unjust.

Cartulary, fol. 96r.
Bougaud-Garnier, p. 346.

Karta de Moringas et Mornado

Notum sit presentibus et futuris Richardum de Belmonte[1] quandam terram sitam inter Moringas et Mornadam uillas,[2] ad abbatiam sancti Petri Besuensis monasterii pertinentem, diu calumpniasse mulieris suę ex parte et multa preiudicio abstulisse. Quam calumpniam monachi Sancti Petri satisfactionis causa sepe uoluerunt iuramento uel qualibet lege determinare, cum prefatus Richardus Dei nutu aspiratus, eandem calumpniam, siue iusta siue iniusta esset, Sancto Petro donauit, presentibus senioribus loci sub stipulatione super altare posita.

Ego Richardus cum uxore mea Wandelmode firmauimus et testibus roborandam tradidimus. Signum Widonis decani. Signum Aldonis. Signum Benedicti monachi. Signum Heldemanni. Signum Alberti.

It is impossible to date the documents in this section with any precision, though the time of Abbot Odo seems most likely.

3 Perrigny, 7 km south-southwest of Dijon.

4 *Chartes et documents de Saint-Bénigne de Dijon*, 2:77–78, no. 294.

1 Beaumont, 7 km east of Bèze. Richard does not appear to be a member of the family of the lords of Beaumont.

2 Mornay is 16 km northeast of Bèze. "Moringae" was presumably nearby; Garnier suggests la Villeneuve, 2 km to the west.

104

Mid-eleventh century

The knight Erembert, dying, asked to be buried at Bèze. For the good of his soul, his father, Oddo, gives half a manse at St-Maurice. Oddo himself died shortly thereafter, first taking the monastic habit.

Cartulary, fol. 96r–v.
Bougaud-Garnier, pp. 346–347.

Karta de Sancto Mauricio

Notum facimus karitati fidelium quia miles quidam nomine Herembertus, diu languoris molestiis pressus, tandem cum sibi finem uitę imminere sentiret ad memoriam beatorum apostolorum Petri et Pauli in Besuensi loco se sepeliri rogauit, quod et factum est. Pro cuius animę absolutione pater eius, nomine Oddo, eidem loco dimidium mansum cum dimidia mansione, quia partem alteram frater eius cum manso tenebat in uilla quę dicitur ad Sanctum Mauricium[1] cum terris adiacentibus, pratis et silua. In ipsa et in altera uilla Romania nominata[2] cum legali traditione dedit, and manu fidelium testium corroborari fecit, quorum ista sunt nomina, Hugo, Theodericus, Alelmus, Iohannes, alter Hugo, Teudinus, Hemma.

Quem ipse in breui tempore subsecutus, non solum apud eundem locum est sepultus, sed etiam sicut petierat monachili habitu indutus, huius uite in bono fine diem clausit. Post cuius obitum, nos unum fediolum quem tenebamus filio eius dedimus et tria iugera in commutatione accepimus, et nostris terris iunximus et duobus hominibus sub seruitio ad manendum dedimus, ex quibus unus seruus eius et loco dedit.

105

Mid-eleventh century

The knight Walo gives a manse at Tanay and another at Germigney for the soul of his wife Addila. He also gives two serfs with their families and spells out the rents the mansi owe.

Cartulary, fols. 96v–97r.
Bougaud-Garnier, p. 347.

1 St-Maurice, 16 km northeast of Bèze.
2 La Romagne, 2 km northwest of St-Maurice.

Karta de Tasnato et Germanico

Manifestum esse uolumus tam presentibus quam futuris quod quidam miles nomine Walo pro redemptione animę coniugis suę, uocabulo Addile, dedit Sancto Petro unum mansum alodi apud Tasnatum et alium apud Germaniacum,[1] qui persolut in debito census dimidiam eminam frumenti, dimidiam eminam auenę, unum sextarium uini, unum porcum precii vi denariorum, quinque denarios pro censu prati, unam rotam et unum bouem tempore uindemię. Dedit etiam seruos Hunaldum cum uxore et infantibus suis et Mainardum et medietatem infantum eius, absque ulla calumpnia.

Et ut hęc donatio perpetuum obtineret uigorem, litteris peciit notum fieri et testibus corroborari. Signum Walonis. Signum Fulconis. Signum Odilonis. Signum Milonis. Signum Warnerii. Signum Widonis. Signum Heinrici. Signum Widrici. Signum Warnerii.

106

4 June, mid-eleventh century

The knight Gontard and his brother Helger receive some property at Colonge from Bèze in benefice. Their brother Henry had earlier had it, along with the church there.

Cartulary, fol. 97r.
Bougaud-Garnier, p. 348.

Karta de Colonica uilla

Notum esse uolumus omnibus fidelibus tam futuris quam presentibus quod quidam miles, Gontardus nomine, cum fratre suo Helgerio nos adierit, deprecans ut eis aliquid daremus de terra Sancti Petri in beneficio, promittentes se omnimodis in seruitio Sancti Petri et nostro fideliter permansuros. Quod cum diu peterent, uicti eorum precibus dedimus eis quicquid Sanctus Petrus in uilla quę Colonica[1] dicitur habebat, quam dudum tenuerat frater eorum Heinricus cum ecclesia in ipsa uilla posita, indicentes eis annuatim in festiuitate Sancti Petri censum duorum solidorum, eo scilicet tenore ut tempore uitę suę idipsum, quod dedimus, tenerent, post decessum uero eorum ad ius Sancti Petri et monachorum eius rediret, ita ut nullus posterum eorum ullo modo ex eo se intermitteret, ni spontanea uoluntate uel amicabili abbatis aut monachorum eiusdem loci concessione.

---

1 Tanay, 7 km south of Bèze; and Germigney, 23 km southeast of Bèze.

1 Colonge, 13 km southeast of Bèze.

Si autem unus ex eis prior mortuus fuerit, eius pars statim ad nos reuertatur, nisi forte nostra spontanea uoluntate iterum ei concessum fuerit.

Vt autem hę conuenientię firmiores permanerent, hanc kartam manu sua firmauerunt, testesque fideles adhibuerunt. Signum Gontardi. Signum Helgerii. Signum Oddonis. Signum Raynardi. Signum Saleconis. Signum Bernardi. Data ii nonas Iunii.

These brothers also appear in document 79. There is a fair amount of overlap in the witness list, suggesting the documents were given about the same time.

107

Mid-eleventh century

Bernard of Beaumont and his late nephew Richard made a gift at Lux, consisting of a manse and two serfs.

Cartulary, fol. 97r–v.
Bougaud-Garnier, pp. 348–349.

Karta de Lu

Noticia quam Bernardus Belmontis[1] et nepos eius defunctus, nomine Richardus, fecerunt Sancto Petro Besuensi de terra quadam coniacente in fine uillulae quę uocatur Lu Sancti Martini.[2] In ipsius finibus dedit mansum unum, nouem iornales habens de terra arabili, cum duobus seruis.

For Richard of Beaumont, see also document 103.

108

Mid-eleventh century

The knight Stephen, very ill, gives Bèze for his soul a manse, along with fields and a serf. His wife and sons agree; the land came from her dowry.

Cartulary, fol. 97v.
Bougaud-Garnier, p. 349.

1 Beaumont, 7 km east of Bèze.
2 Lux, 5 km northwest of Bèze.

Karta de uilla Curte

Quidam miles nomine Stephanus, in graui infirmitate decidens, adiuit monasterium quod in honore principis apostolorum est consecratum quod dicitur Besua, ibique ob remedium animę suę tradidit ad ipsum locum unum mansum qui est in uilla quę Curtis dicitur[1] et quattuor iornales de terra in campum qui appellatur Festilliacus, cum seruo nomine Gaudio, et est de ambabus partibus terra Gislerii. Cuius cooperatores sunt filii sui, Wido, Walterius, Hugo, et uxor sua nomine Fera, in cuius dotalitio erat ipsa terra quam reddidit ei.

Et ut hęc donatio eius nota fiat posteris, hanc kartulam fieri iussit et super altare Sancti Petri posuit, testibus quę roborandam tradidit. Ego Stephanus subscripsi. Signum Widonis filii mei. Signum Walterii filii mei. Signum Hugonis filii mei. Signum Aymonis. Signum Widonis. Signum Milonis.

109

Bèze, c. 1055–c. 1065

Two knights, Aduinus and Milo, brothers, along with their sister Tetburgis, give Bèze a woman.

Cartulary, fols. 97v–98r.
Bougaud-Garnier, pp. 349–350.

Item alia

Alii uero duo milites, Aduinus et Milo frater eius, et Teburgis soror eorum tradiderunt Deo et Sancto Petro Girbergam cum infantibus suis. Et ut hęc donatio eorum nulli calumpnię pateat, in conuentu publico statuerunt decretum, ut nullus heredum eorum in ullam partem iure hereditario uiolentiam inferat. Quod si fecerit, excommunicationis uindictam soluat.

Aduinus et frater eius firmauerunt hanc cartulam. Signum Sophie. Signum Teburgis. Signum Widonis archipresbiteri. Signum Lezelini. Signum Hugonis prepositi et tocius familię. Actum publice monasterio Besuensi, presente domno Oddono abbate.[1]

Aduin and Milo were sons of the noble lady Altrudis; see document 115. Their father may have been Milo of Beire; see document 56.

---

1 A number of villages in the region have "-court" in their name; it is impossible to tell to which locality Stephen refers. Garnier suggests Curtil-St-Seine, 26 km west of Bèze.

1 Odo, abbot of Bèze (c. 1055–c. 1065).

110

Mid-eleventh century

Humbert gives a serf with his family, acting with his wife and sons. They free the serfs from any obligation to them.

Cartulary, fol. 98r.
Bougaud-Garnier, p. 350.

Item alia

Similiter et Humbertus et coniunx eius et filii, qui iniuste conabantur detinere seruum Sancti Petri, Fuldradum scilicet, et coniugem eius nomine Richeldem et filios eorum, dimiserunt eos liberos, quatinus ad proprium dominum cęlestem clauigerum redeant.

111

Mid-eleventh century

Samson of Vosne and his wife give Bèze several vineyards.

Cartulary, fol. 98r.
Bougaud-Garnier, p. 350.

Carta de quadam uinea

Item Samson de Vadona[1] et uxor eius dederunt Deo et Sancto Petro unum iugerum de uinea in loco qui dicitur Adalechassanna. Item in alio loco ad Austiuacca dicto, duo.[2] Testes donationis hii sunt, Siluester monachus suscepit, Grimaldus uillicus, Harbertus.

112

Mid-eleventh century

Doda of Marey gives Bèze a meadow next to the Marey millpond, with her husband Joceran's consent.

Cartulary, fol. 98r.
Bougaud-Garnier, p. 350.

1 Vosne, 19 km south-southwest of Dijon.
2 These places are not identified.

Carta de Mariaco

Doda etiam de Mariaco,[1] consentiente uiro suo Iocero, dedit unum pratum habentem ad summum exclusam molendini eiusdem uille Sancto Petro, necnon monachis ibidem Deo seruientibus. Huius autem donationis, quam uiua uoce fecit, uiuos testes adhibuit, quorum nomina hęc sunt, Folradus, Nero, Grimaldus, Lambertus.

113

Mid-eleventh century

Hildeberga, sister of the cleric Herleus, makes gift of a manse at Is-sur-Tille. It comes with a freeman who will pay the monks an annual rent. She also gives a female serf.

Cartulary, fol. 98r.
Bougaud-Garnier, p. 351.

Carta de Icio

Notificamus modernis et successuris quod Hildeberga soror Ærleii sapientis clerici delegauit Sancto Petro mansum unum in uilla cui nomen Ycio[1] et unus diei arationem in fines eiusdem uille ad eundem pertinentem, eo tenore ut in eo consistens homo et excolens eum cui nomen Iordanius, liber tamen, ut censum quod sibi reddere consueuerat monachis persoluat. Insuper etiam unam ancillam quę uocatur Raimburgis, solitum capitis sui duorum denariorum omni anno reddituram debitum. Testes huius donationis sunt hii, Robertus, Widricus, Iohannes, Hugo.

Hildeberga's brother was a canon at Langres; see document 119.

114

Mid-eleventh century

Hildesendis, a nun, gives Bèze a girl.

Cartulary, fol. 98r–v.
Bougaud-Garnier, p. 351.

1 Marey-sur-Tille, 21 km northwest of Bèze.
1 Is-sur-Tille, 14 km northwest of Bèze.

Item alia

Hildesendis sanctimonialis dedit Sancto Petro puellam quandam, nomine Osannam, filiam Humberti et Retrudis.

115

Mid-eleventh century

The noble lady Altrudis, the mother of Aduin and Milo, gives Bèze the wife of the priest of Grenant.

Cartulary, fol. 98v.
Bougaud-Garnier, p. 351.

Item alia

Altrudis etiam nobilissima femina, mater Aduini et Milonis, dedit Sancto Petro uxorem Vlrici presbiteri Granantis uille,[1] Girbergam nomine, cum infantibus suis.

For the brothers Aduin and Milo, see also documents 109 and 136.

116

Mid-eleventh century

Betta, wife of the knight Hermuin, gives a manse for his soul, with her sons. It is located at Bussières.

Cartulary, fol. 98v.
Bougaud-Garnier, pp. 351–352.

Karta de Buxiaco

Notum sit omnibus tam presentibus quam futuris quod Betta uxor Hermuini militis, cum filiis suis, tradidit unum mansum pro redemptione animę prescripti mariti Sancto Petro Besuensi, in uilla cui uocabulum est Buxiacus[1] ad integrum, sicuit tenuit Lambertus maior, cum omnibus quę ad ipsum mansum pertinent, tam in terris quam in siluis, et in pratis uel in pascuis, siue in aquis.

Et ut hęc donatio in perpetuum firma sit et stabilis, his subscriptis testibus firmauit. Hii sunt Wido, Aldo, Gonterius, Otbertus.

1 Grenant, 31 km north-northeast of Bèze.

1 Bussières was the name of a now-ruined village near Lux.

117

Mid-eleventh century

Seiwold and his wife Ida give Bèze a manse at Prauthoy.

Cartulary, fol. 98v.
Bougaud-Garnier, p. 352.

Karta de Pruncethel

Similiter Seiuuoldus et Ida coniunx eius dederunt Sancto Petro Besuensis cęnobii mansum unum, cui terrę arabilis viiii iugera adiacent, et pratum i, ex quo duę carratę feni possunt per singulos annos colligi, in loco qui Pruncethel[1] uocatur. Ea uidelicet ratione ut quicquid exinde facere monachi eiusdem loci uoluerint, libero in omnibus potiantur arbitrio faciendi.

Testes uero huius donationis hic sunt subnotati, Albertus monachus, Oddo, Rotbertus sacerdos, Dares, Iohannes cocus.

118

c. 1055–c. 1065

Aymo of Viévigne, brother of Gui and of the monk Waro, gives Bèze an allod there. His son and daughter agree.

Cartulary, fols. 98v–99r.
Bougaud-Garnier, p. 352.

Karta de Vetus Vineis

Aymo etiam de Vetusuineis[1] natus, frater Widonis et Waroni monachi, alodum suum in ipsa uilla existentem Sancto Petro dedit, et cum filio suo Widone super altare Sancti Petri posuit, et filiam suam Gertrudam laudare fecit.

Signum domni Oddonis abbatis.[2] Signum Gyrardi. Signum Vlrici.

---

1 Prauthoy, 24 km north of Bèze.

1 Viévigne, 4 km southwest of Bèze.

2 Odo, abbot of Bèze (c. 1055–c. 1065).

119

c. 1055–c. 1065

Herleus, archdeacon of Langres, gives Bèze a manse at Flacey, a serf, and some tapestries. He does so for the soul of his brother Milo.

Cartulary, fol. 99r.
Bougaud-Garnier, pp. 352–353.

Karta de Flaciaco

Quidam archidiaconus, Ærleius nomine, canonicus Sancti Mammetis, dedit Sancto Petro unum mansum in uilla quę Flaciacus dicitur,[1] cum suis appenditiis, pro remedio anime fratris sui Milonis. Addidit etiam unum seruum, binaque tapecia mirifici operis et enormis magnitudinis. Ne uero per succedentia temporala ab aliqua obposita persona quiuisset frustrari, rogauit propinquos et circumstantes huius donationis cartam manu propria testimonioque firmari.

Signum Ærleii. Signum Oddonis. Signum Iohannis prioris. Signum Widonis decani.

For his sister, see document 113. The dates I have given assume that the "Oddo" of the witnesses was the abbot.

120

Mid-eleventh century

The canon Hugh, who has established a monastery at Losne, now gives Bèze some allodial land of his father's, with the consent of his brothers and nephews.

Cartulary, fol. 99r.
Bougaud-Garnier, p. 353.

Carta de Dalaima

Notum facimus presentibus et futuris quod Hugo, summe probitatis canonicus, ędificator monasterii Sanctę Marię Lagonniacensis, dedit Sancto Petro suam partem de omni alodo patris sui apud Dalaimam uillam[1] situm, laudantibus fratribus suis et nepotibus.

---

1 Flacey, 10 km west-southwest of Bèze.

1 Damalix is now the name of a farm near Lux.

Signum Hugonis. Signum Ottonis. Signum Radaldi. Signum Petri.

The monastery which the canon Hugh had founded was Notre-Dame of Losne, a small house associated with the house of canons of St-Étienne of Dijon. The more common spelling was "Latonensis." For Hugh, see also document 93.

121

Mid-eleventh century

Elizabeth, daughter of Willer, gives Bèze a manse at Lux for her recently deceased husband Ozilin. Agreeing are her mother and two brothers, both monks.

Cartulary, fol. 99r.
Bougaud-Garnier, p. 353.

Carta de Luco

Notificamus quibusque modernis et successuris quod quedam mulier nomine Helisabet filia Willerii, ex Campanis uilla,[1] nuperrima uiri sui Ozilini morte destituta, adierit Besuense monasterium tradideritque Sancto Petro unum mansum in uilla cui uocabulum est Luco,[2] congruum ualde et oportunum cum suis appenditiis.

Signum Helisabet. Signum Eziline matris eius. Signum Hugonis et Kadalonis fratrum eius monachorum.

122

Mid-eleventh century

Rainard of Véronnes makes a gift of his allod at Blagny to Bèze, to make amends for his crimes. His brothers, the cleric Sewin and Alberic, agree, and bring his body to the monastery to reconfirm after his death.

Cartulary, fol. 99r–v.
Bougaud-Garnier, p. 354.

1 Champagne, 10 km southeast of Bèze.
2 Lux, 5 km northwest of Bèze.

Karta de Blaniaco

Manifestum iri cupimus quod quidam nomine Rainardus ex uilla Varona[1] natus concessit Sancto Petro alodum quod ipse dudum in Blaniaco[2] uilla conparauerat, pro abolicione suorum criminum. Cuius donationem elemosine fratres ipsius, Seuuinus clericus et Albericus, benigne annuentes, et feretro impositum corpus eius deducentes ad monasterium, firmiter stabilierunt et ad altare uice ipsius sancto et fratribus delegauerunt, et subnixis testimoniis coram omnibus roborauerunt.

Signum Seuuini. Signum Alberici. Signum Vlrici militis.

123

Mid-eleventh century

Elizabeth, mother of the monk Hugh, gives Bèze property at Bussières and Lux and nearby. Her sons and brothers agree.

Cartulary, fol. 99v.
Bougaud-Garnier, p. 354.

Karta de Busciaco, Luiato, Luco

Scripto etiam uolumus digerere quod Helisabet, quę etiam Liezilina cognominata est, mater Hugonis monachi, dederit Sancto Petro in uilla Busciaco[1] dicta unum mansum cum colonica sua, et ceteros mansos ad ipsum pertinentes cum colonicis suis et omnibus appendiciis suis, in campis, in siluis, in pratis, in aquis, in aquarum decursibus, in piscatoriis, siue in eadem uilla siue inaniis eidem adiacentibus, id est Luiato, Luco,[2] Dalaima, uel ubicumque ipsa terra coniacet ex integro, cum consensu filiorum suorum atque fratrum suorum, tradidit Deo et Sancto Petro in presentia uniuersorum monachorum. Signum Hugonis monachi filii eius, Richardi filii eius, Bernardi fratris eius, Ottonis fratris eius.[3]

The same woman appears in document 121.

---

1 Véronnes, 7 km north-northwest of Bèze.
2 Blagny, 8 km east-southeast of Bèze.
1 Bussières was the name of a now-ruined village near Lux.
2 Lux is 5 km northwest of Bèze. Garnier identifies the other two places as “little Lux” and Damalix.
3 The identifications of witnesses as Elizabeth’s sons and brothers are given interlinearly.

124

Langres, 1059

Bishop Harduin of Langres makes Bèze a gift of two prebends in the church of St-Gengoux, recalling that his predecessor, Bishop Hugh, had given the monks the church. Harduin also restores the village of Bannes to the monks, which Hugh had originally given but canons of Langres had taken back.

Cartulary, fols. 99v–101r.
Bougaud-Garnier, pp. 355–357.
Summarized in Brequigny, *Table* 2:70.

Carta de duabus prebendis Sancti Gengulfi

Heinricus igitur rex Francorum, cum iam morbo et senectute premeretur, Philippum filium suum, congregatis Francorum primoribus, cunctorum consilio consortem sibi tocius regni constituit,[1] inpositoque capiti eius diademate, regem iussit appellari.

Anno autem primo regni eius domnus Arduinus Lingonensis episcopus,[2] pro solo orationum, premio dedit Sancto Petro ac Besuensi congregationi, laudantibus cunctis canonicis, duas prebendas, quantum accipitur a duobus canonicis, sicut hic demonstrabimus.

Priscorum felix sollertia hoc salutiferum remedium prouidere studuit succedentibus sibi, ut quod non poterant tempora meantia mandare posteris, allegare et apicibus auctoritate fultus illius principis, sub cuius presentia firmatio foret, cum scriptione cartis aut inpressione siggilli. Quod et nos prouidentes, ecclesię nostrę filiis et Sancti Mammetis[3] sacrę concioni fore commodi, qualiter unanimes sint effecti, litteris adnotamus iuxta tenorem utriusque partis.

Largitione itaque famosi Hugonis presulis Lingonensis[4] ecclesię Besuensi adtributa est ecclesia Sancti Gengulfi martiris,[5] pariterque stipendium quem cum consequebatur is qui famulabatur in loco deseruiens liminaribus sacris. Non hęc solummodo uenerabilis episcopus contradidit, quę prediximus, uerum etiam uillam quę uocatur Bannus[6] iure perpetuo concessit. Quod postea quidam indigne ferentes exemplum rebus humanis, antequam uenerabilis Arduinus decoraretur

1 King Henry of France (1031–1060) made his son Philip (1060–1108) king with him shortly before his death.

2 Harduin of Tonnerre, bishop of Langres (1049–1065).

3 The cathedral of Langres.

4 Hugh of Verdun, bishop of Langres (1031–1049).

5 The church of St-Gengoux of Langres.

6 Bannes is 50 km north of Bèze, past Langres from the monastery.

sede pontificali, auxilio fulti Gyrardi prepositi sua procurantes, non que Ihesu Christi redegerunt in potestatem, ut possessum fuerat prius ab eis. Quod uenerabilis Arduinus infula pontificali iam insignitus ut cognouit compati cepit, pietateque qua affluebat, uniuersam congregationem rogare cepit, ut qui uillam abstulerant quam de precessor contulerat, saltem misererentur Deo seruientibus inibi et aliquam rem prouiderent, ex quo sustentari possent ecclesię alumpni. Exegit denique ab eis in presentia Alberonis abbatis Diuionensis,[7] laudantibus cunctis canonicis ut bis edentibus supradictis canonicis. Quantum percipiebatur a duobus ex illis, tantum susciperent et ipsi monachi, uidelicet mane et sero, et si semel cybum sumpserint, eodem modo quo et supra quantitas tribuatur panis et uini, ut accipitur a duobus canonicis.

Quia uero peccunia tunc defuit, qua debeatur consuetudinaria lege cybus preberi uniuersis ecclesię filiis, conditione usi sunt tali, ratumque uisum est cunctis, ut susciperent societatem quę offerebatur illis pro commutatione cibi, eo tenore ut si aliquis nuntiaretur exuisse hominem, taliter celebraretur dies depositionis a monachis, sicut consueuerant pro cunctis congregationibus sibi coniunctis. Insuper et nomina eorum inscriberentur cum nominibus fratrum, quo agnosci posset dies eorum anniuersarii et cęlebrari a cunctis. Et ut hęc quę diximus firmius teneantur, a nostris eadem et ipsi laudauere agere pro nostris.

Ne quando ergo aboleatur in succedentibus sedis quę conscripsimus, presente uiro uenerabili Arduino episcopo huius sanctę sedis subter adnotamus eiusdem iussione presulis nomina uiuorum qui interfuerunt, conditione tali. Signum eiusdem Arduini episcopi. Signum Wilenci archidiaconi. Signum Rainardi qui cognominatus est Hugo.[8] Signum Rogeri thesaurarii. Signum Euuardi decanis. Signum Ærlei archidiaconi. Signum Gyrardi archidiaconi. Signum Warneri. Signum Gybuini. Signum Hildigari. Signum Milonis de Sancti Lupi. Signum Emmarrici. Signum insuper omnium canonicorum qui unanimiter laudauerunt in capitulo.

Actum Lingonis, anno incarnationis Dominice MLVIIII, indictione xii, epacta iiii. Quicumque autem hoc uiolare preseumpserint uel aliquid abstulerint uel Sancto Petro rectoribusque Besuensis cęnobii contraire conati fuerint, auctoritate omnipotentis Dei, Patris et Filii et Spiritus Sancti, Beati quoque Petri omniumque sanctorum et nostra sint excommunicati, anathematizati, et a sorte iustorum expulsi et ęternaliter, nisi digne satisfaciendo emendauerint, dampnati. Signum Oddonis abbatis[9] et omnium monachorum ipsius cęnobii.

7 Adalbero, abbot of St-Bénigne of Dijon (1056–1076).

8 Hugh-Rainard of Tonnerre, Bishop Harduin's cousin, who succeeded him in the see of Langres (1065–1084). For the family, see Bouchard, *Sword, Miter, and Cloister*, pp. 369–372.

9 Odo, abbot of Bèze (c. 1055–c. 1065).

125

Mid-eleventh century

Berno of Genlis gives Bèze an allod. He shall keep the usufruct for his lifetime.

Cartulary, fol. 101r.
Bougaud-Garnier, p. 357.

Karta de uilla Coriaut

Notum sit omnibus presentibus et futuris quod Berno uillicus Ianlint[1] uillę quoddam alodum iuris sui, quod iacet in uilla Coriaut dicta, ea condictione dedit Sancto Petro et propria manu super altare misit, ut ipsius alodi usuarium fructum retineret tempore uitę suę. Post discessum uero uitę suę ad locum Sancti Petri rediret cum omni integritate.

Huius donationis quam uiua uoce fecit uiuos testes adhibuit, quorum nomina hęc sunt, Odilo prepositus, Rodulfus, Dado, Aldo, Euuardus.

126

Mid-eleventh century

Albordis makes Bèze a gift of a vineyard at Bressey, for the soul of her recently deceased husband Erembert. Agreeing is his brother Ozelin.

Cartulary, fol. 101r.
Bougaud-Garnier, pp. 357–358.

Karta de uinea que est in Briscona

Albordis matrona pro remedio anime quondam senioris sui, nomine Æremberti, consentiente fratre eius Ozelino nomine, tradidit Sancto Petro Besuensis cęnobii unam uineam quę appellatur Clausmors, in uilla quę Briscona uocatur.[1]

Ozelin may be the same man as the recently deceased husband of Elizabeth in document 121.

1 Genlis, 16 km southeast of Dijon. "Coriaut" is unidentified.
1 Bressey-sur-Tille, 19 km south-southwest of Bèze.

127

Mid-eleventh century

Alburgis, daughter of Willenc, gives Bèze property at Viévigne along with male and female serfs. Her husband, Ponce, agrees.

Cartulary, fol. 101r–v.
Bougaud-Garnier, p. 358.

Karta de Vetus Vineis

Item Alburgis filia Wilenci fratris Hugonis senioris castri Belmontis[1] quicquid in uilla Vetusuineas[2] habebat in pratis, campis, siluis, pariterque seruos Widonem, Theodericum, Bilinamque sororem eorum, tresque alias ancillas, Heldegardam, Euizaidam, et Teodradam, Sancto Petro dedit perpetualiter possidendas.

Signum Pontii senioris eius, Widonis militis, Walterii militis.

Alburgis is most likely the same person as the Alburga, wife of the knight Poncius, in document 82.

128

Mid-eleventh century

Wilenc gives Bèze a serf with his family and and two mansi at "Moringis."

Cartulary, fol. 101v.
Bougaud-Garnier, p. 358.

Carta de Moringis

Adnotandum credimus futuris quod Wilencus dedit Deo et Sancto Petro duos mansos in Moringis uico[1] cum omnibus appendiciis suis et seruum nomine Vlricum cum uxore et infantibus suis.

Et ut hęc donatio perpetuam firmitatem obtineat, signatorum nomina subter demonstrat sceda. Signum Pontii filii eius, Fulconis, Odilonis, Bernonis clerici.

1 Alburgis's father, Willenc, was younger brother of Hugh III of Beaumont. For the family, see Bouchard, *Sword, Miter, and Cloister*, pp. 320–322.

2 Viévigne, 4 km southwest of Bèze.

1 This place is unidentified.

From the placement in the cartulary, the scribe seems to have assumed this was the same Willenc as Hugh III's brother, which is, however, far from certain. Ponce would be his son-in-law, for example, not his son, though the "filii eius" is added interlinearly.

129

Mid-eleventh century

Lady Heluindis makes Bèze a gift of a manse at Choilley, along with a serf, for her husband Walter the White. Her sons sign.

Cartulary, fol. 101v.
Bougaud-Garnier, p. 358.

Carta de Condilico

Notificamus modernis quibusque et futuris quod Heluindis quedam matrona dederit Sancto Petro pro Walterio marito suo, qui uocabatur Albus, unum mansum apud Condiliacum[1] et seruum nomine Ermenbertum.

Signum Gysleberti, Hugonis, Willerii, Mauricii filii eiusdem domine.

See also the following charter.

130

Mid-eleventh century

Lady Heluindis gives another manse, at Vosne, for her son Maurice, as well as a serf. She specifies that this manse pays no customary dues to the duke.

Cartulary, fol. 101v.
Bougaud-Garnier, p. 359.

Carta de Vaunna

Eadem uidelicet Heluidis tradidit post primam donationem Sancto Petro unum mansum apud Vaunnam[1] pro ipso Mauricio filio suo, quem ex prefato Walterio habuerat. Qui scilicet mansus ita liber est ab omni consuetudine alicuius

---

1 Choilley, 22 km north-northeast of Bèze.

1 Vosne, 19 km south-southwest of Dijon.

hominis, ut non dux uel ministeriales sui in eo aliquid requirere possint ab aliorum etiam principum uel hominum exactione, id est demandatione,[2] omnino extraneus sit. Dedit quoque seruum nomine Richardum.

Signum Haymonis, filii eius Gisleberti.

See also the preceding charter.

131

Mid-eleventh century

Rainard of Autrey gives Bèze a manse. The man living there pays a penny a year for woods usage.

Cartulary, fols. 101v–102r.
Bougaud-Garnier, p. 359.

Karta de Creponensi uilla

Volmus quosque presentes et futuros scire quod Rainardus de Autriaco[1] delegauerit Sancto Petro unum mansum apud Creponensem uicum cum omnibus appendiciis suis, qui debet ministeriali Fontanę potestatis[2] singulis annis unum denarium, si tamen homo in ipso manens siluam ipsius potestatis frequentauerit.

Signum Rainardi, Odilonis, Oddonis.

See also the following charter.

132

Mid-eleventh century

Odo the dwarf, inspired by his cousin Rainard, gives an allod at Fontenelle.

Cartulary, fol. 102r.
Bougaud-Garnier, p. 359.

2 This phrase is interlinear.

1 Autrey, 17 km east-northeast of Bèze. The location of the manse he gives is unidentified.

2 Fontaine-Française, 10 km northeast of Bèze.

Karta de Fontanellis

Eiusdem Rainardi consilio et exemplo prouocatus, quiddam sobrinus eius Oddo, qui appellabatur Gibbosus, id est Bozardus,[1] dedit et ipse Sancto Petro quicquid alodi in uico Fontanellas[2] uocitato habebat.

Signum Oddonis, Odilonis, Rainardi.

See also the preceding charter.

133

c. 1055–c. 1065

Arlebald and his brother Odo give Bèze a field at Bussières.

Cartulary, fol. 102r.
Bougaud-Garnier, p. 360.

Carta de Buciaco uico

Clarum esse cupimus omnibus quod Arlebaldus et Oddo fratres concesserunt Sancto Petro unum campum quindecim iugerum in Buciaco[1] uico.

Signum domni Oddonis abbatis,[2] Moroni, Benedicti.

The two signatories with Abbot Odo were officers of the monastery.

134

Mid-eleventh century

Odilina, mother of Ponce of Bézouotte, gives Bèze a manse at Flacey.

Cartulary, fol. 102r.
Bougaud-Garnier, p. 360.

Carta de Flaciaco

Manifestum iri optamus tam presentibus quam futuris quod Odilina, mater Pontii de Besoeta,[1] attribuit Sancto Petro unum mansum in Flaciaco.[2]

Signum Pontii, Hugonis prepositi, Iohannis.

---

1 This phrase is interlinear.
2 Fontenelle, 9 km northeast of Bèze.
1 Bussières was the name of a now-ruined village near Lux.
2 Odo, abbot of Bèze (c. 1055–c. 1065).
1 Bézouotte, 11 km southeast of Bèze.
2 Flacey, 10 km west-southwest of Bèze.

135

Mid-eleventh century

Gui of Licey gives Bèze a manse, the place to construct a mill, and a serf. He also repeats his gift of another serf whom he had earlier given for the good of his brother.

Cartulary, fol. 102r.
Bougaud-Garnier, p. 360.

Carta de Lisciaco

Patere uolumus cunctis presentibus et futuris quod Wido de Lisciaco[1] dedit Sancto Petro apud eundem uicum Lisciacum unum mansum cum omnibus appenditiis suis. Dedit etiam sedem molini, ubi ipse molinus construeretur, cum uno seruo nomine Drogone. Reddidit quoque seruum quem ante pro fratre suo Anserico dederat, cui nomen Oddo.

Signum Odilonis, Anserici, Hugonis prepositi.

136

Mid-eleventh century

Aduin gives Bèze part of an allod for his brother, Milo the White. The rest of it will go to the monks on his death. Earlier he had given a priest's wife for his mother.

Cartulary, fol. 102r–v.
Bougaud-Garnier, pp. 360–361.

Carta de Moringis

Cognitio quod Aduinus tradidit Sancto Petro pro Milone fratre suo, qui uocabatur Albus, quandam partem alodi quem habebat in uico Moringas nominato,[1] eo tenore ut post excessum suum alia pars in dominicatum monachorum deueniret. Dedit quoque seruum nomine Ærbertum. Necnon ante donauerat pro matre sua, Altrudi nominata, uxorem Vlrici presbiteri Granantis uille,[2] cum omnibus infantibus suis.

Signum Aduini, Heinrici filii eius, Æremberti.

See also document 115. The donor is most likely identical with Aduin of Beire; see document 139.

1 Licey, 8 km east-northeast of Bèze.

1 This place is unidentified.

2 Grenant, 31 km north-northeast of Bèze.

137

Mid-eleventh century

Hugh of "Lanfredi curtis" gives Bèze a manse at Dampierre, as well as a serf with his wife and children.

Cartulary, fol. 102v.
Bougaud-Garnier, p. 361.

Carta de Donno Apro

Notum iri uolumus omnibus quod Hugo Lanfredi curtis concessit Sancto Petro unum mansum in uilla quę uocatur ad Domnum Aprum,[1] propter ęcclesiam quę in eadem uilla constructa est in honore Sancti Apri. Dedit quoque seruum in eo manentem cum uxore et infantibus suis.

Signum Landrici filii eis, Hugonis filii eius,[2] Oddonis.

138

Mid-eleventh century

Odo, a cleric of Gemeaux, gives Bèze a vineyard at Arçon for his brother Dodo.

Cartulary, fol. 102v.
Bougaud-Garnier, p. 361.

Carta Arciaco uilla

Tradimus litteris ad posterorum memoriam quod Oddo clericus de Gimellis[1] concessit Sancto Petro unam uineam in Arciaco uilla,[2] pro Dodone fratre suo.

Signum Oddonis, Bernardi, Beraldi.

139

Mid-eleventh century

Aduin of Beire gives Bèze a manse and a serf.

Cartulary, fol. 102v.
Bougaud-Garnier, p. 361.

---

1 Dampierre, 7 km east-northeast of Bèze. "Lanfredi curtis" is not identified.
2 For both signatories, the words "filii eius" are added interlinearly.
1 Gemeaux, 10 km west of Bèze.
2 Arçon, 13 km south of Bèze.

Carta de Beria

Apertum esse desideramus omnibus secuturis quod Aduinus de Beria[1] tradidit Sancto Petro unum mansum apud eandem Berię uillam, cum omnibus appendiciis suis, et unum seruum nomine Algrimum.

Signum Walonis, Warnerii, Milonis.

The Milo of the witnesses was doubtless Aduin's brother. See documents 56 and 136, and also the following document.

140

Mid-eleventh century

Walo gives Bèze a manse at Beire along with a serf.

Cartulary, fol. 102v.
Bougaud-Garnier, p. 362.

Item alia

Scire uolumus quoque tam modernos quam futuros quod Walo concessit Sancto Petro unum mansum in Beria,[1] cum appendiciis suis, et unum seruum nomine Hugonem de Vado, cum uxore et infantibus suis.

Signum Aldonis, cuius nomen Rusticellus, Milonis, Maioli cognomento Mazilinus.[2]

This is doubtless the same Walo as the first witness in the preceding document. Milo was most likely the same Milo as the twin brother of Maiolus Mazilinus of document 92.

141

Mid-eleventh century

Hildelerius gives Bèze a manse at Noidant for his son Gui, killed at St-Julien. He also gives two female serfs, sisters.

Cartulary, fol. 102v.
Bougaud-Garnier, p. 362.

---

1 Beire, 8 km southwest of Bèze.

1 Beire, 8 km southwest of Bèze.

2 The cognomina for Aldo and Maiolus are given interlineārly.

Carta de Nogdanti uilla

Omnibus cognitum iri cupimus quod Hildelerius delegauit Sancto Petro pro filio suo Widone, apud Sanctum Iulianum[1] a balistario occiso, unum mansum in Gnodanti uilla[2] cum appendiciis suis et consuetudinibus, pariterque duas ancillas quę erant sorores.

Signum Oddonis, Walterii, Bernardi, Beraldi.

See also the following document and document 150.

142

Mid-eleventh century

Hildelerius gives Bèze two mansi at Aubigny for his wife.

Cartulary, fols. 102v–103r.
Bougaud-Garnier, p. 362.

Carta de Albiniaco uilla

Isdem quoque Hildelerius concessit Sancto Petro in uilla Albiniacensi, quę est in comitatu Diuionensi,[1] pro uxore sua, duos mansos cum appendiciis suis, in terris, campis, pratis, siluis, pascuis.

Signum Oddonis, Walterii.

See also the preceding document and document 150.

143

Mid-eleventh century

Milo of Beaumont gives Bèze a manse for his wife, along with a serf and his sister.

Cartulary, fol. 103r.
Bougaud-Garnier, pp. 362–363.

1 St-Julien, 12 km southwest of Bèze.
2 Noidant, 40 km north of Bèze.
1 Aubigny, 22 km north of Bèze, in the county of Dijon.

Carta de Priniaco

Clarescere uolumus cunctis quod Milo de Bellomonte[1] concessit Sancto Petro pro uxore sua unum mansum in Pinriaco uico[2] cum appendiciis suis, et unum seruum nomine Euuardum cum sorore sua.

Signum Milonis, Hugonis, Fulconis.

144

Mid-eleventh century

Hugh of Jancigny gives Bèze a manse at Lux for his wife, sister of the monk Hugh.

Cartulary, fol. 103r.

Carta de Luco

Litteris allegare dignum est quod Hugo de Gencinniaco[1] delegauit Sancto Petro pro uxore sua, quę fuit soror Hugonis monachi, in Luco[2] unum mansum cum appendiciis suis.

Signum Hugonis, Hugonis prepositi, Iohannis.

This document was mistakenly skipped in previous editions.

145

Mid-eleventh century

Walo of Beire gives Bèze two mansi for his wife, along with a serf and his sister.

Cartulary, fol. 103r.

Carta de Beria

Opere precium est scribere quod Walo de Beria[1] attribuit Sancto Petro pro uxore sua duos mansos cum appendiciis suis et consuetudinibus, pariterque seruum nomine …[2] cum sorore sua.

Signum Milonis, Fulconis, Odilonis.

---

1 Beaumont, 7 km east of Bèze.

2 Garnier identifies this place as Preigny, which he locates near Gemeaux.

1 Jancigny, 14 km southeast of Bèze.

2 Lux, 5 km northwest of Bèze.

1 Beire, 8 km southwest of Bèze.

2 The scribe left a blank for the name.

This document was mistakenly skipped in previous editions. Walo was probably lord of Beire; see document 96.

146

Mid-eleventh century

Gislebert of La Rochette gives Bèze a manse at Champagne for his wife. He also gives a serf.

Cartulary, fol. 103r.
Bougaud-Garnier, p. 363.

Carta de Campanis uilla

Hoc etiam ad monimentum futurorum pandere uolumus quod Gyslebertus de Rescia[1] concessit Sancto Petro pro uxore sua unum mansum in Campanis uilla[2] cum omnibus appendiciis suis, simulque seruum nomine Lotzelinum.

Signum Frodonis, Widrici.

Gislebert was lord of La Rochette; see document 96.

147

Mid-eleventh century

Lord Odo of Montsaugeon gives Bèze a manse at Champagne for his brother Hugh. He also gives a serf.

Cartulary, fol. 103r.
Bougaud-Garnier, p. 363.

Item alia

Cunctorum noticię patere uolumus quod Oddo Montis Salionis[1] senior dedit Sancto Petro pro Hugone fratre suo unum mansum in eadem Campanis uilla[2] cum appendiciis suis, pariterque seruum nomine Lozuinum.

Signum Pontii, Hugonis, Arlebaldi.

---

1 Garnier identifies this place as La Rochette, near Oisilly.
2 Champagne, 10 km southeast of Bèze.
1 Montsaugeon, 22 km north of Bèze.
2 Champagne, 10 km southeast of Bèze.

148

c. 1055–c. 1065

Walo of Equivilley gives Bèze a manse at Jancigny, for his ancestors. He adds a serf and his sister.

Cartulary, fol. 103r.
Bougaud-Garnier, p. 363.

Karta de Genciniaco

Manifestare iustum duximus quod Walo de Scuuiliaco[1] dederit Sancto Petro pro predecessoribus suis unum mansum cum appendiciis suis in Gencinniaco uilla,[2] et seruum nomine Isembardum cum sorore sua.

Signum domni Oddonis abbatis,[3] Moroni, Benedicti.

The two men who signed after Abbot Odo in this and the following document were the provost and the prior of the monastery.

149

c. 1055–c. 1065

Bernard of "Veslono" gives Bèze a manse.

Cartulary, fol. 103v.

Karta de Veslono

Ratum, id est firmum,[1] nouimus constare ad insinuandum posteris litteris tradere quod Bernardus de Veslono[2] qui erat pomilio dederit Sancto Petro in eadem uilla unum mansum amplissimum cum appendiciis suis, in terris, campis, pratis, siluis, pascuis.

Signum Bernardi. Signum domni Oddonis abbatis,[3] Moroni, Benedicti.

1 Garnier identifies this place as Equevilley, 17 km north of Vesoul.
2 Jancigny, 14 km southeast of Bèze.
3 Odo, abbot of Bèze (c. 1055–c. 1065).
1 This phrase is written interlinearly.
2 This place is unidentified.
3 Odo, abbot of Bèze (c. 1055–c. 1065).

This document was mistakenly skipped in previous editions. Bernard seems to have been an orchard grower.

150

Mid-eleventh century

Hildelerius makes a gift of a manse at Noidant to Bèze for his daughter, wife of Odo Vetulus. He also gives a female serf.

Cartulary, fol. 103v.
Bougaud-Garnier, p. 364.

Karta de Nogdanti

Opere precium duximus litteris tradere quod Hildelerius, quem superius prefati sumus, dederit Sancto Petro pro filia sua, uxore uidelicet Oddonis qui dicebatur Vetulus, unum mansum in uilla prenominata Nogdanti,[1] cum una ancilla.

Signum Oddonis, Bernardi, Beraldi, Walterii.

See also documents 141, 142, and 166.

151

Mid-eleventh century

Hugh Rufus gives two mansi at Vesvres to Bèze for his father Humbert, son of Hildebrand. He also gives a serf.

Cartulary, fol. 103v.
Bougaud-Garnier, p. 364.

Karta de Vaura

Pandi uolumus modernis et futuris quod Hugo Rufus tradidit Sancto Petro, pro Humberto patre suo, filio Hildebranni, duos mansos cum appendiciis suis in uilla quę dicitur Vaura,[1] cum seruo nomine.[2]

Signum Formaldi, Theoderici, Bernardi, Beraldi.

1 Noidant, 40 km north of Bèze.

1 Vesvres, 26 km north-northwest of Bèze.

2 The serf's name is not given. What may have been intended as a space left to fill in the name later was used by the rubricator for the rubric of the following document.

152

Mid-eleventh century

The wife of the knight Gislerius makes a gift to Bèze for him, consisting of a manse at Vesvres.

Cartulary, fol. 103v.
Bougaud-Garnier, p. 364.

Item alia

Hoc quoque in causto diplomati inseri uolumus quod pro Gislerio milite delegauerit uxor sua Sancto Petro in prescripto uico Vaura[1] unum mansum cum appendiciis suis.

Signum Milonis, Rotberti presbiteri, Hugonis prepositi.

153

Mid-eleventh century

Robert, a knight of Montsaugeon, is dying and becomes a monk. He gives Bèze a manse and a serf.

Cartulary, fols. 103v–104r.
Bougaud-Garnier, pp. 364–365.

Karta de Curte Salonis

Censemus apicibus notificandum presentibus et futuris quod Rotbertus Montis Salionis[1] miles, frater Widonis Magni, concesserit Sancto Petro ad exitum ueniens et monachicum indumentum capiens, unum mansum in uico Curtis Salonis, in parręchia Ruciacensis[2] uillę amplissimum, cum uno seruo nomine Alberico.

Signum Widonis fratris eius, Oddonis senioris Montis Salionis, Hugonis fratris eius, item Hugonis Lanfredi curtis.[3]

Hugh of "Lanfredi curtis," whose loconym is added interlinearly, also appears in document 137, and Lord Odo of Montsaugeon also appears in document 147.

---

1 Vesvres, 26 km north-northwest of Bèze.
1 Montsaugeon, 22 km north of Bèze.
2 Unidentified.
3 Unidentified.

154

Mid-eleventh century

The knight Milo the Bald of Tilchâtel gives Bèze a manse at Véronnes for his wife.

Cartulary, fol. 104r.
Bougaud-Garnier, p. 365.

Karta de Verona uilla

Cunctorum noticię patere cupimus quod Milo Balbus Tilecastri[1] miles delegauerit Sancto Petro unum mansum in Verona uilla[2] pro uxore sua, cum appendiciis suis.

Signum Formaldi, Aldonis priuigni, id est filiastri,[3] ipsius Milonis.

155

Mid-eleventh century

Said Milo also gives Bèze land at Lux after St Peter helped settle his quarrel with his niece's husband, Odo the provost of Dijon.

Cartulary, fol. 104r.
Bougaud-Garnier, p. 365.

Karta de Luco

Isdem quoque Milo cum Oddone Diuionensi preposito, qui neptam eius in coniugio habebat, monomachi certaturus pugna, adtribuit Sancto Petro terram quam habebat in Luco[1] prope atrium ecclesię, quo sibi adiutor in disposito bello existeret.

Signum Lamberti, Oddonis, Formaldi.

156

c. 1055–c. 1065

Ponce of Bézouotte gives Bèze a manse at Lux to make up for his violence in seizing a man of the abbey.

---

1 Tilchâtel, 9 km northwest of Bèze.
2 Véronnes, 7 km north-northwest of Bèze.
3 This phrase is added interlinearly.
1 Lux, 5 km northwest of Bèze.

Cartulary, fol. 104r.
Bougaud-Garnier, p. 365.

Item alia

Omnium cognitioni clarum esse uolumus quod Pontius de Besoeta[1] pro uiolentia quam irrogauit asylis, id est templi,[2] Sancti Petri, adita, id est secreta,[3] uiolando, quando quendam Harduinum inde abstraxit, dederit ipsi sancto unum mansum amplissimum cum appendiciis suis in Luco.[4]

Signum domni Oddonis abbatis,[5] Moroni, Benedicti.

See also the following charter, doubtless done at the same time, and for Ponce's mother, document 134.

157

c. 1055–c. 1065

Ponce of Bézouotte, penitent for his violent behaviour, also gives Bèze another manse at Lux and a serf.

Cartulary, fol. 104r.
Bougaud-Garnier, pp. 365–366.

Item alia

Hoc etiam de eo gramis[1] allegare congruum duximus, quia pro multis tortitudinibus, sceleribus, siue depredationibus in loco sancto, uel in pauperibus eiusdem loci, ab eo commissis quodammodo penitens, delegauerit Sancto Petro alium mansum in eadem uilla cum appendiciis suis et unum seruum nomine Iosbertum, qui etiam Babilinus appellabatur.

Signum domni Oddonis abbatis,[2] Moroni, Benedicti.

1 Bézouotte, 11 km southeast of Bèze.
2 This phrase is added interlinearly.
3 This phrase is also added interlinearly.
4 Lux, 5 km northwest of Bèze.
5 Odo, abbot of Bèze (c. 1055–c. 1065).
1 The word "litteris" is added interlinearly, over "gramis."
2 Odo, abbot of Bèze (c. 1055–c. 1065).

158

c. 1055–c. 1065

Hugh the provost gives Bèze a manse at Velet for his wife. He also gives a serf.

Cartulary, fol. 104r.
Bougaud-Garnier, p. 366.

Karta de Villari uico

Congruum ducimus litteris notificare omnibus quod Hugo prepositus pro uxore sua concesserit Sancto Petro unum mansum in uico Villari nominato, prope Gradicum castellum,[1] et unum seruum uocabulo Lambertus.

Signum domni Oddonis abbatis.[2] Signum Benedicti, Tetbaldi.

159

c. 1055–c. 1065

Willerius of Crecy gives Bèze a manse at Oisilly, along with a serf.

Cartulary, fol. 104r–v.
Bougaud-Garnier, p. 366.

Karta de Auxiliaco

Necessarium remur pro utilitate sequentium scripturę tradere quod Willerius de Criciaco[1] dederit Sancto Petro unum mansum in uilla Auxiliacensi[2] cum appendiciis suis, et seruum nomine Humbertum.

Signum domni Oddonis abbatis,[4] Benedicti, Girardi leuiri eius, id est fratris uxoris eius,[4] Humberti exactoris cauponum, id est tabernariorum.[5]

1 Velet, 23 km east-southeast of Bèze, is 3 km southwest of Gray.
2 Odo, abbot of Bèze (c. 1055–c. 1065).
1 Crecey, 14 km northwest of Bèze.
2 Oisilly, 9 km southeast of Bèze.
3 Odo, abbot of Bèze (c. 1055–c. 1065).
4 This phrase is added interlinearly.
5 This phrase is also added interlinearly.

160

Mid-eleventh century

Agano of Gissey, dying, gives Bèze a manse and a serf with his family at Betoncourt, for the good of his soul.

Cartulary, fol. 104v.
Bougaud-Garnier, pp. 366–367.

Karta Bettonis Curtis

Notum esse uolumus presentibus et futuris quod Hagano de Iussiaco[1] ueniens ad mortem dedit Sancto Petro pro redemptione animę suę unum mansum apud uillam Betthonis Curtis[2] et unum seruum nomine Dominicum, cum uxore sua et filiabus.

Et ut hęc carta perpetuam firmitatem obtineat, nomina testium subter adscribi rogauit. Signum Gysleberti, Hugonis, Willerii, Rotberti.

161

Mid-eleventh century

The knight Humbert, dying, makes gifts to Bèze at "Marciacum" and Renaucourt for the remission of his sins. His gift includes half a manse, of which his brother Girard earlier gave the other half, some serfs, and fishing rights. His wife Adelaide signs.

Cartulary, fol. 104v.
Bougaud-Garnier, p. 367.

Carta de Rainaldi Curte

Quidam miles Humbertus, in extremo uitę constitutus, pro remissione peccatorum suorum dedit Sancto Petro apud Marceacum uillam[1] dimidium mansum,

1 Gissey-sur-Ouche, 20 km west-southwest of Dijon. The Bougaud-Garnier edition mistakenly gives "Vissiaco."
2 Betoncourt, 47 km northeast of Bèze.
1 This place is not identified. Neither is "Rainaldi Curtis," although Garnier calls it Renaucourt.

iam pridem a fratre suo Gyrardo, alterius medietatis donatione facta ipsi Sancto Petro. Tradidit etiam seruum nomine Constantium cum uxore et infantibus suis, pariter etiam unum mansum apud Rainaldi Curtem, in quo habitabat Dauid, cum omnibus appendiciis suis, in campis, in pratis, in siluis, in aquis, in aquarum decursibus. Piscatoriam etiam predicti Constantii, sicut uiuente eo tenuerat, attribuit monachis loci.

Et ut hęc donatio obtineat firmitatem uigoris perpetui, litteris sollempniter adnotauit. Signum Gyrardi fratris eius, Oddonis, Hugonis. Signum Adelaidis uxoris ipsius Humberti.

162

Mid-eleventh century

The lady Raimodis gives Bèze money, land, and a female serf at St-Seine, as she is dying. Her children sign.

Cartulary, fols. 104v–105r.
Bougaud-Garnier, p. 367.

Karta de Sancto Sequano

Scire uolumus quosque futuros quod Raimodis quędam matrona spectabilis ad exitum ueniens et multę quantitatis pecuniam diuersarum specierum Sancto Petro relinquens, dimidiam coloniam apud Sanctum Sequanum Helpricurtis[1] dedit, cum una ancilla.

Ne uero per succedentia tempora hanc elemosinam ulla obliuio ualeat delere, menbranis deprecata est ad confirmationem tradere. Signum Hugonis filii eius, Gertrudis filie eius, Regine filie eius, Landrici generi eius.[2]

163

Mid-eleventh century

Hugh makes Bèze a gift of seven mansi and some serfs at Pichanges, for his soul and that of his son Gui, who has been killed.

Cartulary, fol. 105r.
Bougaud-Garnier, p. 368.

1 St-Seine-sur-Vingeanne, 13 km northeast of Bèze.
2 The phrases identifying the witnesses' relationship to Raimodis are all given interlinearly.

Carta de Picangiis

Notum iri uolumus omnibus presentibus et futuris quod hac spe animatus Hugo, qui pro saluamento Crilliacensis uillę[1] Saluator dicebatur, pro anima sua et filii sui Widonis dudum interfecti, dedit Sancto Petro septem mansos apud Pitiangias uillam,[2] et seruum nomine Halinardum conductorem suum, ancillamque nomine Addetam cum filio uocabulo Gyraldo et sorore ipsius.

Signum Hugonis, Formaldi, Halinardi, Oddonis filii ipsius Hugonis.

164

Mid-eleventh century

Rismodis, wife of Otbert, dying, makes Bèze a gift of two mansi along with several serfs.

Cartulary, fol. 105r.
Bougaud-Garnier, p. 368.

Carta de Euualdi Curte

Notum esse uolumus presentibus et futuris quod Rismodis uxor Otberti, ad exitum ueniens et diuina inspiratione tacta, dedit Sancto Petro apud Euualdi Curtem unum mansum cum seruo nomine Haymone in eo habitante, et uxorem eius et infantes, et in uilla quę Fontanas dicitur proxima Tilecastro,[1] unum mansum cum uno cliente, qui Christianus dicitur.

Signum Otberti, Humberti filii eius, Aldonis filii eius.

165

Mid-eleventh century

Henry makes Bèze a gift at Viévigne, consisting of half a manse and a serf with his family, for his brother Ulric.

Cartulary, fol. 105r.
Bougaud-Garnier, p. 369.

---

1 This place is not identified.

2 Pichanges, 9 km west of Bèze.

1 Fontenotte is now the name of a farm, 7 km northwest of Bèze, close to Tilchâtel. Ewaldi Curtis is not identified.

Carta de Vetus Vineis

Notum iri uolumus tam presentibus quam futuris quod Heinricus, pro fratre suo Vlrico, dedit Sancto Petro dimidium mansum apud Vetusuineas,[1] et seruum nomine Gyraldum cum uxore sua, eo tenore ut quos ex hoc tempore genuerint infantes, in seruitium monachorum cedant.

Signum Heinrici, Humberti Rufi.

166

Mid-eleventh century

Odo Vetulus, dying, gives Bèze a manse, some additional land, and a serf with his son, all at Is-sur-Tille.

Cartulary, fol. 105v.
Bougaud-Garnier, p. 369.

Carta de Icio

Patere uolumus modernis et successuris quod Oddo, qui dicebatur Vetulus, ad extrema perductus tradidit Sancto Petro in uilla Ycio[1] unum mansum et tria iugera terrę in finibus eiusdem uillę cum uno seruo, nomine Erberto, et filium eius cum eo.

Signum Formaldi, Walterii, Bernardi.

See also document 150 for the wife of Odo Vetulus.

167

Mid-eleventh century

Gui of Le Fossé gives Bèze two mansi at Is-sur-Tille and Véronnes, along with a serf, for his brother Aldo.

Cartulary, fol. 105v.
Bougaud-Garnier, p. 369.

Carta de Icio et Verona

Cognitum esse optamus omnibus quod Wido de Fossato[1] delegauit Sancto Petro pro fratre suo Aldone pincerna duos mansos, unum in uilla Ycio, alterum in uilla Verona,[2] cum uno seruo nomine Aldone.

Signum Widonis, Amalrici, Aldonis.

1 Viévigne, 4 km southwest of Bèze.

1 Is-sur-Tille, 14 km northwest of Bèze.

1 Le Fossé is now the name of a farm, 12 km northwest of Bèze.

2 Is-sur-Tille, 14 km northwest of Bèze; and Véronnes, 7 km north-northwest of Bèze.

168

Mid-eleventh century

The knight Gui gives Bèze a manse and some additional property at St-Seine-sur-Vingeanne for the remission of his sins. He adds a female serf with her daughters.

Cartulary, fol. 105v.
Bougaud-Garnier, pp. 369–370.

Karta de Sancto Sequano

Noticia quomodo quidam miles nomine Wido, pro remissione peccatorum suorum, apud Sanctum Sequanum Helpricurtis[1] attribuit Sancto Petro mansum unum et unum curtile in ipsa uilla et quartam partem Vachiriacensis siluę, et unam ancillam nomine Annam cum duabus filiabus suis.

Signum Pontii, Widrici, Bilini.

169

Mid-eleventh century

Formald of Is-sur-Tille gives Bèze a manse at Pouilly for his wife, sister of Willenc. Their relatives witness.

Cartulary, fol. 105v.
Bougaud-Garnier, p. 370.

Karta de Pauliaco

Omnibus presenti uita ingentibus et futura fruituris manifestum esse uolumus quod Formaldus de Ycio[1] dederit Sancto Petro pro anima uxoris suę, quę fuit soror Wilenci, mansum unum apud Pauliacum,[2] sub testimonio utrorumque parentum.

Signum Formaldi, Bernardi, Beraldi.

Formald appears frequently as a witness in this section of the cartulary. For Willenc, see also document 171.

1 St-Seine-sur-Vingeanne, 13 km northeast of Bèze.

1 Is-sur-Tille, 14 km northwest of Bèze.

2 Pouilly, 15 km northeast of Bèze.

170

Mid-eleventh century

Emma, wife of Hildemodus, gives a manse at Pouilly.

Cartulary, fol. 105v.
Bougaud-Garnier, p. 370.

Item alia

Quia labilis est huius uitę status, notum iri uolumus mortalibus quod quędam matrona uxor Hildemodi, Emma nomine, tradidit Sancto Petro unum mansum apud Pauliacum,[1] cum una cortina, sub testimonio presentium fratrum.

Signum Widonis, Æremberti, Alelmi.

171

Mid-eleventh century

The knight Lambert gives Bèze a manse for the good of his soul. He is father-in-law of Willenc.

Cartulary, fols. 105v–106r.
Bougaud-Garnier, p. 370.

Karta de Lalandi Curte

Quidam etiam miles Lambertus nomine, uitricus, id est patraster,[1] Willenci, pro remedio animę suę concessit Sancto Petro unum mansum apud Lalandi Curtem.[2]

Signum Wilenci priuigni, id est filiastri,[3] Formaldi, Pontii.

172

Mid-eleventh century

Gui of Porta, dying, gives Bèze two mansi at Savigny and Grancey, as well as a serf living at Véronnes.

Cartulary, fol. 106r.
Bougaud-Garnier, pp. 370–371.

---

1 Pouilly, 15 km northeast of Bèze.

1 This phrase is given interlinearly.

2 This place is unidentified.

3 These last four words are given interlinearly

Karta de Sauiniaco

Scire quosque uolumus quod Wido de Porta ad exitum ueniens concesserit Sancto Petro duos mansos, unum in Sauiniaco, alterum in Granciaco in regione Diuionensi,[1] et unum seruum nomine Tedonem habitantem in uilla Verona.[2]

Signum Tetbaldi,[3] Widonis, Humberti.

173

Mid-eleventh century

Tetbald, son of Gui of Porta, gives Bèze a manse and a serf at Arçon, as well as the serf's sister.

Cartulary, fol. 106r.
Bougaud-Garnier, p. 371.

Carta de Arciaco

Manifestum iri uolumus omnibus quod Tetbaldus filius ipsius Widonis tradiderit Sancto Petro unum mansum in Arciaco uilla[1] et unum seruum nomine Mauricium, sororemque eius quam Euurardus Recaluester de Acetis uilla[2] in coniugium habebat.

Signum Widonis fratris eius,[3] Humberti, Gunzonis.

174

Mid-eleventh century

Moran's wife and son give Bèze a manse and a serf at Oisilly for him.

Cartulary, fol. 106r.
Bougaud-Garnier, p. 371.

---

1 Savigny and Grancey are both in the region of Dijon, Savigny 39 km northeast of Bèze and Grancey 29 km northwest of Bèze.
2 Véronnes, 7 km north-northwest of Bèze.
3 He was Gui's son, as was doubtless the Wido who signed next; see the following document.
1 Arçon, 13 km south of Bèze.
2 Arcelot, 12 km south-southwest of Bèze.
3 This identification is added interlinearly.

Carta de Auxiliaco

Pandi uolumus quibuscumque quod pro Moranno uxor eius et filius dederint Sancto Petro unum mansum apud Auxiliacum,[1] simulque seruum nomine Waldricum.

Signum uxoris eius, Ioffredi filii eius, Heinrici.

See also the following document.

175

c. 1055–c. 1065

Moran's brother Gui gives Bèze a manse at Oisilly and another nearby, as well as the property he holds from the monks.

Cartulary, fol. 106r.
Bougaud-Garnier, p. 371.

Carta de Ponto

Cognitio quod Wido frater Moranni delegauerit Sancto Petro unum mansum in Auxiliaco et alium in uilla quę dicitur Pontus,[1] et beneficium quod a monachis tenebat reddiderit, et manu miserit.

Signum Widonis, domni Oddonis abbatis,[2] Moroni, Benedicti.

176

Mid-eleventh century

Mainfred makes Bèze a gift of two mansi at Oisilly and some allodial property at Charmes, for his son Maurice.

Cartulary, fol. 106r.
Bougaud-Garnier, pp. 371–372.

Karta de Calmis

Manifestum esse uolumus omnibus presentibus et futuris quod Mainfredus, pro Mauricio filio suo, dederit Sancto Petro duos mansos apud Auxiliacum, et

1 Oisilly, 9 km southeast of Bèze.

1 Oisilly, 9 km southeast of Bèze; and Pont, which no longer exists but seems to have been located at a bridge over the Venelle, between Bèze and Véronnes.

2 Odo, abbot of Bèze (c. 1055–c. 1065).

quicquid alodi in uilla Calmis, quę propinqua est Miribello castello,[1] habebat concessit.

Signum Mainfredi, Leutbranni filii eius, Arlebaldi.

See also the following two documents.

177

Mid-eleventh century

Mainfred gives Bèze a manse for his first wife, sister of Abbot Tetbald.

Cartulary, fol. 106r–v.
Bougaud-Garnier, p. 372.

Carta de Ponto

Isdem quoque Mainfredus, pro uxore sua priori, quę fuit soror Tetbaldi abbatis, dedit ipsi Sancto Petro unum mansum in uilla Ponto.[1]

Signum Mainfredi, Mauricii, Leutbranni.

The most likely identification of Abbot Tetbald is Abbot Theobald of St-Bénigne (1020–1032). The two men who signed after Mainfred were his sons; see the preceding document. The Mainfred of the following document was doubtless the same man.

178

Mid-eleventh century

Mainfred gives Bèze allodial property at Cusey for his second wife. Her brothers agree.

Cartulary, fol. 106v.
Bougaud-Garnier, p. 372.

Item alia

Apud Cuciacum[1] etiam dedit pro secunda uxore quicquid alodi ex eius parte in eadem uilla tenebat, laudantibus fratribus eiusdem domine.

Signum Mainfredi, Theoderici, Widonis.

---

1 Oisilly, 9 km southeast of Bèze; and Charmes, 12 km south-southeast of Bèze and 3 km southeast of Mirebeau.

1 Pont no longer exists but seems to have been located at a bridge over the Venelle, between Bèze and Véronnes.

1 Cusey, 19 km north-northwest of Bèze.

179

Mid-eleventh century

Odo and Hugh give Bèze a manse at Choilley for their brother Gui, who was killed. They also give a female serf.

Cartulary, fol. 106v.
Bougaud-Garnier, p. 372.

Karta de uico Chimiscensi

Scire uolumus quosque quod Oddo et Hugo tradiderint Sancto Petro, pro fratre suo Widone interfecto, unum mansum cum appendiciis suis, in uico Chimiscensi,[1] cum una ancilla nomine Helgardi.

Signum Oddonis, Hugonis, Milonis.

180

Mid-eleventh century

Hildemod gives Bèze all of his allodial property at Vandalenecourt, along with a serf, in return for a rent of two pennies' worth of wax.

Cartulary, fol. 106v.
Bougaud-Garnier, pp. 372–373.

Carta Wandaleni curtis

Vniuersorum noticię cupimus patere quod Hildemodus delegauerit Sancto Petro omnem alodum quem habebat in uico Wandaleni curtis,[1] qui est in potestate Hortesis, cum uno seruo nomine Theoderico, sub censu precii duorum denariorum cerę.

Signum Oddonis, Pontii, Hugonis.

181

Mid-eleventh century

Arlebald, a knight of Montsaugeon, gives Bèze a manse and a serf at Noidant.

Cartulary, fol. 106v.
Bougaud-Garnier, p. 373.

---

1 Choilley, 22 km north-northeast of Bèze.

1 Garnier identifies this place as Vandalenecourt, a destroyed village near Hortes, which is 17 km east of Langres.

Carta de Nogdanti uilla

Limitis uitę uelocitas cogit ut memoranda quęque grammis, id est litteris,[1] kartarum imprimantur, ne longitudine temporum intercurrente a memoria hominum deleantur. Quapropter notificare optamus omnibus quod Arlebaldus Montis Salionis[2] miles tradidit Sancto Petro unum mansum in uilla Nogdanti,[3] cum uno seruo.

Signum Oddonis, Hugonis, Pontii.

Because the witnesses here are the same as the witnesses in the previous document, the two were probably issued at the same time.

182

Mid-eleventh century

Aymo the Hairy gives Bèze a manse at Velet as well as a serf.

Cartulary, fol. 106v.
Bougaud-Garnier, p. 373.

Carta de uico Villari

Omnium nouerit industria quod Aymo, qui erat glabrio, id est pilo siue barba,[1] concesserit Sancto Petro unum mansum in uico Villari uocabulo,[2] cum seruo nomine Raimbaldo.

Signum Heinrici, Oddonis, Widonis.

183

Mid-eleventh century

Geoffrey gives Bèze some land at Oisilly.

Cartulary, fol. 106v.
Bougaud-Garnier, p. 373.

1 This phrase is added interlinearly.
2 Montsaugeon, 22 km north of Bèze.
3 Noidant, 40 km north of Bèze.
1 This phrase is added interlinearly.
2 Velet, 23 km east-southeast of Bèze.

Karta de Auxiliaco

Hoc etiam simili modo intimare curauimus quod Ioffredus dederit Sancto Petro in uilla Auxiliacensi[1] decem iugera terrę.

Signum Oddonis, Heinrici, Willerii.

De obitu Arduini episcopi

Defuncto autem uenerabili Arduino episcopo, Rainardus adeptus est kathedram.[2] Obeunte itidem Oddone abbate, successit in locum eius Wido, ex monasterio Areomarensi monachus.[3] Hic paucis annis in regimine peractis, repedauit ad suum monasterium, dimissa huius loci gubernatione, cui successit ad regimen animarum Gausbertus, in monasterio Sancti Benigni Diuionensis prioris gerens officium.[4]

184

Langres, 1080

Bishop Hugh-Rainard of Langres grants the church of St-Remi freedom from the customary dues spelled out in a polyptyque, specifically what the priest of the church was supposed to pay when attending a synod.

Cartulary, fol. 107r.
Bougaud-Garnier, p. 374.
Summarized in Brequigny, *Table* 2:183.

Karta de ecclesia Sancti Remigii

In nomine sancte Trinitatis et unice Deitatis. Nouerit omnis seculorum tam presentium quam futurorum successio quod domnus Rainardus Lingonensis episcopus,[1] petente abbate Gausberto[2] et eiusdem loci monachis, fecerit liberam Sancti Remigii ęcclesiam ab omnibus consuetudinibus quę in polyptico continentur, paratas siue debitum quod in synodo debebat presbiter remittens,

1 Oisilly, 9 km southeast of Bèze.
2 Bishop Harduin of Langres (1049–1065) was succeeded by Bishop Hugh-Rainard (1065–1084), his cousin.
3 Abbot Odo (c. 1055–c. 1065) was succeeded by Abbot Gui (c. 1065–c. 1070), originally a monk at Montiéramey.
4 Before Gausbert became abbot of Bèze (c. 1070–1088), he had been prior of St-Bénigne of Dijon.
1 Hugh-Rainard of Tonnerre, bishop of Langres (1065–1084).
2 Gausbert, abbot of Bèze (c. 1070–1088).

itam tamen ut presbiter quidem ad synodum consuetudinaliter conceteris pergat, censum uero alium nullum persoluat. Quod ut immobile perseueraret, iam dictus pontifex exemplar huius subscriptionis firmitatisque fieri iussit, ne quisquam suorum successorum hanc donationem euacuare presumeret. In terminationem dampnationis perpetue ab omnipotente Deo sustituens, qui huic notioni infracturam temptauerit inferre.

Actum Lingonis in plenaria synodo, anno ab incarnatione dominica MLXXX, indictione iii. Signum Rainardi episcopi qui hanc noticiam fieri iussit tocius sui synodalis conuentus archidiaconorum suorum seu decanorum. Signum Gyrardi archidiaconi. Ærleii archidiaconi. Walterii decani. Hugonis de Burgiaco[3] canonici.

The church of St-Remi was located in the village of Bèze and was dependent on the abbey.

185

c. 1080

Bishop Hugh-Rainard of Langres returns a man and his family that he had claimed from the monks, in return for one hundred solidi.

Cartulary, fol. 107r–v.
Bougaud-Garnier, pp. 374–375.

Item alia

Isdem etiam episcopus reclamabat quendam hominem uocabulo Rotbertum de Gurziaco,[1] cum uxore sua, et unica filia, pariterque ipsius filie infantes, quos ex Lamberto seruo Sancti Petri habebat. Sed acceptis centum solidis, quicquid in eis rectitudinis sibi habere uidebatur, fratribus concessit, et ex suo iure in eorum dominicatum transfudit.

Signum Walterii, Rainerii, Richardi, Gysleberti, Aymonis.

Although this document cannot be dated more precisely than by the years of Hugh-Rainard's episcopacy, it most likely was given at the same time as the previous document.

3 This loconym is added interlinearly.
1 Gurgy, 29 km west of Langres.

186

Beaujeu, 1083

Lord Ponce of Beaujeu makes Bèze a gift of his hereditary property, a chapel dedicated to St Valerian with its appurtenances. His brother agrees. In addition, Ponce and his brother give the monks market, pasture, and woods rights around Beaujeu, as well as tithes. They also grant the monks judicial rights.

Cartulary, fols. 107v–108v.
Bougaud-Garnier, pp. 375–377.
Summarized by Duchesne, *Histoire généalogique des ducs de Bourgonge*, instr. p. 25; from the cartulary.

Karta de ecclesia Sancti Waleriani et uilla

Constat omnes perfectionis summam uolentes arripere, dominici precepti regulam mentis oculis anteponere, quo suum quemque pro ipso sua distrahere et pauperibus mandat deuote distribuere. Quia talium iusticia per cuncta manebit seculorum uolumina et cornu ipsorum, id est remuneratio certaminis eorum cęlesti exaltabitur in gloria, cum ad cęlestes thesauros translata terrena patrimonia, dantibus proderunt in perhenni uita. Hac ergo spei fiducia confortatus, ego Pontius castelli Belliioci[1] dominus Redemptori omnium uolo tradere de meis rebus quę mihi iure hereditario relictę sunt a parentibus. Do itaque Deo et Sancto Petro Besuensi capellam constructam in honore Sancti Valeriani cum honore et libere sicut actenus uisus sum habere, fratre meo Ermuino laudante, cum uinea et campum usque ad petrosam et usque ad fontem, et quicquid de silua quę est iuxta uineam monachi uel homines illorum ad culturam agri poterunt trahere. Necnon etiam de illa silua quę inter ęcclesiam et Sagonnam flumen[2] est, quicquid ad usum prati ipsi et homines eorum uoluerint adquirere.

Concedo etiam mercatum cum omni libertate et omnes consuetudines quas ego et frater meus uidebamur habere, aliamque consuetudinem pastionis quam nos et homines nostri in cunctis siluis quę in circuitu castelli Belliioci sunt habent monachi, et homines illorum similiter habeant, ita ut homines illorum nostrę partis pastionaticum ipsis monachis soluant, et materiam edificandi domos ipsis et hominibus eorum, qui illic uoluerint remanere, concedimus ex siluis nostris sine precio, et inuentionem uenationis siue apum, quę nostrę partis est et quam homines illorum inuenerint, monachis concedimus et totius cuturę terrę quam eis damus, decimas et tercias monachi habeant,

1 Beaujeu, 31 km east-northeast of Bèze, and not the better-known castellany of Beaujeu located in the Mâconnais.
2 The river Saône.

et ubicumque carruca illorum cuiuscumque hominis terram infra parręchiam exercuerit, damus eis decimas.

De latrocinio uero uel qualicumque proclamatione ex delicto in ipsa terra conmisso, monachis concedimus legem et errantem et uetitum legaliter habeant, et nullius districtione iudicabitur deprehensus, nisi iudicio monachi. Si autem homo monachorum delictum conmiserit, nullius uiolentia constringetur, antequam proclamatio ad monachos facta fuerit, et si monachi rectitudinem executi non fuerint, ad abbatem prius ipsa proclamatio referatur.

Actum publice Belloioco, uigilia ascensionis Domini, anno ab incarnatione Domini MLXXXIII, Hugone ex notario archiepiscopatum Bisonticensis ecclesię gubernante, Philippo Francorum rege existente, Oddone ducatum Burgundie regente, Rotberto fratre eius Lingonensis ecclesię presulatum moderante, Willelmo comite in rebus prospere agente, Gausberto Besuensis abbatie moderamina prouidente.[3] Signum Pontii, Hermuyni, Herluyni, Walterii uicecomitis, Heurelmi, et Pontii alterius.

Either the date is off or else the cartulary scribe added the detail that Robert was bishop of Langres, because he had not yet succeeded in 1083.

187

Bèze, 31 May 1076

Fulk of Beaumont and his son Geoffrey agree to cease their violent activities at Noiron.

Cartulary, fols. 108v–109r.

Duchesne, *Histoire généalogique des ducs de Bourgonge*, instr. p. 21; from the cartulary.

Bougaud-Garnier, pp. 377–378.

Summarized in Brequigny, *Table* 2:152.

Summarized in Petit, *Histoire des ducs de Bourgogne*, 1:388, no. 45.

Karta de saluamento Neronti uille

Notum esse uolumus presentibus et futuris quod Fulco et Ioffredus filus eius[1] saluamentum siue commendationem quam in Nerontis uilla[2] accipiebant,

3 Hugh II, archbishop of Besançon (1067–1085); Philip I, king of France (1060–1108); Odo I, duke of Burgundy (1078–1102); his brother Robert, bishop of Langres (1084–1111); Count William Tête-Hardi of Burgundy (1057–1087); and Gausbert, abbot of Bèze (c. 1070–1088).

1 Fulk, son-in-law and successor to Hugh III as lord of Beaumont, with his son Geoffrey. For the family, see Bouchard, *Sword, Miter, and Cloister*, pp. 321–323.

2 Noiron, 4 km southeast of Bèze.

proclamatione facta a fratribus, apud ducem Hugonem et comitem Willelmum[3] in generali placito ipsis presidentibus Besuę et ceteris quibusque nobilibus uiris instantibus, Sancto Petro et monachis eo tenore dimiserint, ut quicquid sibi iuste preteritis temporibus monachi poterant in causa uiolentię et tortitudinis, preter fundum terrę et caput hominis, ullo modo imputare, id totum remitteretur et predictę uillę habitatores a suprascripta calumpnia et omnibus iniuriis uel tortitudinibus perpetuo liberi manerent.

Quę remissio ut perpetuę firmitatis obtineret uigorem et nullus de eorum heredibus ullo modo supradictam uiolentiam posset repetere, rogauerunt eam annotari litteris et ad futurorum memoriam artius retinendam, signatorum uel testium nominibus confirmari. Signum Hugonis ducis, Willelmi comitis, Widonis comitis Matasconensis,[4] Gyrardi Fontisuenne, Widonis Wangionisriui,[5] Pontii Glane, Aldonis Tilecastri,[6] Seuuini, Vuldenaii, Gysleberti. Actum publicę Besuę in publico conuentu, anno ab incarnatione Domini MLXXVI, indictione quarta decima, imperante Philippo Francorum rege,[7] Hugone duce presente et Willelmo comite Burgundię, ii kalendas Iunii, die Martis.

Igitur postquam Rainardus episcopus[8] huius diei lucem clausit, ute presentis finem faciens, secundum quod scriptum est, "Plures facti sunt sacerdotes, eo quod morte prohiberentur permanere" [Hebr. 7:23], necessarium fuit loco ipsius alium substituere. Et quoniam ipse Rainardus satis clare et gloriose Lingonensem rexerat sedem, omnium quotquot eum pastorem habuerant animos in desiderium et emulationem hanc accenderat, ut Deo fauente, immo Deo donante, talis sibi constitueretur pastor, qui domni Rainardi, sicut successor, ita foret etiam imitator. Quid plura?

De domno Rotberto episcopo

Domnus Rotbertus eligitur, satis et ipse clarus in omnibus, ex Francorum regum prosapia editus, frater autem ducis Oddonis cognomento Borel.[9] Fuit statura non nimium longus, nec tamen breui, sed medie temperata. Et quamuis gemine scientię eloquentia floreret, uerba eius rarissima, nisi forent necessaria.

---

3 Hugh I, duke of Burgundy (1075–1078); and Count William Tête-Hardi of Burgundy (1057–1087).

4 Gui II, count of Mâcon and William Tête-Hardi's cousin; he retired to Cluny in 1078.

5 Girard of Fouvent and Gui III of Vignory (c. 1060–c. 1100); for the latter's family, see Bouchard, *Sword, Miter, and Cloister*, pp. 380–382. Fouvent is 35 km northeast of Bèze, and Vignory is north of Langres.

6 Aldo III of Tilchâtel; see Bouchard, *Sword, Miter, and Cloister*, pp. 366–367.

7 Philip I, king of France (1060–1108).

8 Hugh-Rainard of Tonnerre, bishop of Langres (1065–1084).

9 Robert, bishop of Langres (1084–1111), was brother of Duke Odo I, nicknamed Borel (1078–1102), and great-grandson of King Robert II.

Vt ergo dignum erat, communi uoto tam cleri quam populi Rotbertus eligitur, et pontificali decoratus infula, ecclesię Lingonensi pontifex preficitur.

Ingrati uideremur si eorum quę huic ecclesię contulit beneficiorum inmemores, silencio contegi pateremur. Primo itaque dicamus qualiter ipse capellam castri, qui Fonsuenne dicitur, Deo et Sancto Petro ecclesię Besuensis contradidit.

188

Langres, 1084–1087

Bishop Robert of Langres gives the chapel at Fouvent to Bèze. Humbert, a vassal of the church of Langres, was killed in his service and buried at the monastery.

Cartulary, fol. 109r–v.
Bougaud-Garnier, pp. 378–379.

Karta capelle de Fonuent

Quoniam genus humanum carnis mole corruptibili preoccupatum, labilis ac defectiue memorię contraxit uitium bene uisum est predecessoribus nostris ut quicquid ratum et insolubile teneri uellent, fideli litterarum custodie commendarent. Nos igitur eadem usi ratione, ea quę subtitulantur ne quandoque delerentur obliuione, retinere studimus litterarum traditione.

Ego itaque Rotbertus Lingonensis episcopus,[1] Humberto de Fonuenz[2] Lingonensis ecclesię casato pro seruitio eiusdem ecclesię interfecto, capellam prenominati castri ecclesię Besuensi, in cuius cimiterio eum sepeliuimus, laude et consilio coniugis suę fratrumque suorum eiusdem castri omnium casatorum, perpetualiter tenendam concedimus, quatinus per interuentionem Beati Petri principis apostolorum et orationes monachorum ibi Deo seruientium suorum optinere[3] ualeat ueniam delictorum. Ita etiam hoc donum Lingonis in plenaria synodo tenendum diuidicamus, et si quis clericus uel laicus de beneficiis ad capellam premissam pertinentibus preter uoluntatem monachorum Besuensium aliquid facere presumat, ordinis sui periculo si clericus sit, si laicus excommunicationi donec resipuerit subiaceat.

Huius dationis testes sunt Willelmus comes Burgundiorum, Rainaldus filius eius,[4] Humbertus Rufus et frater eius Wido, Wido Rufus et ceteri casati.

1 Robert, bishop of Langres (1084–1111).
2 Fouvent, 35 km northeast of Bèze.
3 This word should probably read "obtinere."
4 Count William Tête-Hardi of Burgundy (1057–1087) and his son Raynald II, count of Mâcon (1087–1095).

Facta sunt hęc regnante Philippo,[5] episcopante Rotberto, Stephano dictante cancellario.

This document is dated by Bishop Robert and Count William. Although Humbert is here referred to only as a dependent of the church of Langres, in fact he was lord of Fouvent; see document 255. The brothers Humbertus Rufus and Wido were his sons; see document 193.

In illo tempore huic cęnobio preerat domnus Iosbertus abbas,[6] uir totius simplicitatis et religionis, sed quia in ecclesia Dei alii sunt murus ędificati cum propugnaculis, alii ostium conpinctum tabulis cedrinis, hic uir, quia non poterat sicut murus expugnare domus Dei inimicos, exterius existentibus innumeris raptoribus, interius periculis in falsis fratribus erat tamen ad aperiendum, et claudendum ostium conpinctum tabulis cedrinis, quia habebat os ad loquendum et tacendum, defloratum diuersorum excelsorum, et inputribilium patrum sententiis. Prospiciens igitur animę suę bonum esse in superni inspectoris oculos habitare secum, optimam partem elegit quę non auferetur ab eo. Cluniacum[7] namque expeciit, et ibi reliquum uitę suę exegit, pacem querens et pacem inueniens, ei qui pax est angelorum et hominum Christo consociatus. Amen.

Interea domnus Rotberts prefatus Lingonensium episcopus bene sollicitus animo uoluebat quem huic ecclesię loco domni Iosberti abbatem substitueret. Vertebat circumquaque cordis oculum, querens cui committeret huius ecclesię baculum. Nec passus est eum Deus pro uoto defraudari, sed nec in querendo longius fatigari. Est namque cella Sancti Eugendi non multum distans ab urbe Lingonensi, in eodem episcopio, in comitatu uero Trecassino, ecclesia in honore Beati Stephani protomartyris dedicata, in eminenti quodam monte qui Barrus dicitur, decentissime fundata.[8] Factum est autem ut hic inueniretur quod querendum diu longeque fuerat, ut haberetur.

De domno abbate Stephano

Preerat namque illi loco domnus Stephanus,[9] quamuis etatę non multum maturus, pietate tamen et religione circumfultus, in Dei timore et amore et

5 Philip I, king of France (1060–1108).

6 Gausbert, abbot of Bèze (c. 1070–1088).

7 The monastery of Cluny.

8 The cell which Abbot Stephen headed before coming to Bèze was located at Bar-sur-Aube, in the diocese of Langres and county of Troyes; it was dependent on St-Oyend, in the Jura (in the town now known as St-Claude). For this priory, given to St-Oyend by the ancestors of the counts of Champagne, see *Recueil des actes d'Henri le Libéral*, pp. 3–6, no. 3.

9 Stephen, abbot of Bèze (1088–1120).

secundum apostolum in caritate radicatus et fundatus. Videtur haud incongruum lineam generis ipsius paululum adtingere, quoniam solet plerumque nobilitas et sibi ad conseruandam humilitatem, et ecclesiis Dei ad resistendum raptoribus plurimum prodesse. Extitit itaque patre nobilissimo progenitus, Ioffredo nomine, qui et ipse non solum consul sed etiam a patre et auo consulibus originem duxit. De matre uero prefati domni Stephani quid dixerim, nisi quod ex utraque parte, patris uidelicet et matris, ex progenie consulum, immo ab ipsis consulibus est generata. Fuit namque Arnulfi nobilissimi et audacissimi consulis de Risnel filia, matrem habens clarissimi consulis Gerardi de Fonuenz filiam.[10] Quod autem iste leonum catulus, in agnum primo mutatus, postea ut aries ad defendendum eam cornibus, et ad generandum in ea spirituales agnos in ecclesia sit constitutus, fuit hoc gratia Dei, fuit hęc mutatio dextere excelsi. Volo si possim quamuis non faceto, uero tamen sermone percurrere, qualiter iste leonem rugientem reliquerit, et leonem de tribu Iuda secutus sit [cf. Rev. 5:5], et qualiter ab agno inmaculato agnus effectus sit, ut sequatur eum quocumque ierit. In diebus illis uocauit sponsus ad se sponsam suam, Christus uidelicet ecclesiam, uenire a cubilibus leonum et montibus leopardorum [Song 4:8], per montem myrre et colles libani. Principes enim qui prius fuerant similes leonibus propter crudelitatem et terrorem, et leopardis propter diuersarum iniquitatum uarietatem, ysopina humili scilicet confessione mundati, per mirream mortificationem libanino candore sunt super niuem de albati.

Horum uero extitit caput et dux quidam comes Francorum nobilissimus, Symon nomine, Rodulfi comitis.[11] Hic diuina respectus misericordia, mundum fugientem fugit, et Christum uocantem se secutus est. Expetiit autem cenobium Sancti Eugendi Iurensis, ibi Christo se ipsum sacrificaturus. Premiserat ante se duos illustrissimos uiros, domnum Rodulfum et domnum Franconem, secum uero duxit domnum Rotbertum, domnum Arnulfum, et domnum Warnerium. Hi omnes et secundum genus seculi clarissimi, et secundum Deum nobilissimi, postea se holocaustum Deo obtulerunt.

Erat adhuc domnus Stephanus, de quo nobis sermo, tenellus, militaribus tamen armis decoratus. Sed saniori usus consilio, immo Deo inspirante, patres predictos secutus, seculari balteo abrenuncians, Christique iugum suscipiens, in prefato cęnobio monachilem uitam arripuit, ibique sub domno Hunaudo abbate per decem annos se in Dei seruitio mactauit. Deinde Cluniacum expeciit, ubi

10 Stephen was son of Geoffrey, lord of Beaumont, descended from counts; see Bouchard, *Sword, Miter, and Cloister*, p. 323. His mother Gertrude was daughter of Count Arnulf of Reynel and of the daughter of Count Gerard of Fouvent.

11 Garnier identifies Simon as count of Crespy.

cum auunculo suo domno Widone priore magno, per annum demoratus est.[12] Quo Widone postea pro religione et sanctitate uite facto abbate, ipse eum Pictauis secutus, semper se ipso melior efficiebatur. Nouissime ad monasterium suum regressus, apud Barrum cellam Sancti Eugendi missus est. Fiebant hęc omnia Dei dispositione, sine cuius nutu nec passer cadit super terram [Matt. 10:29]. Hic igitur inuentus est domnus Stephanus ac uenerabili prefato Rotberto Lingonensi episcopo, et ab abbate suo huic loco concessus, quamuis renitens abbas effectus est, anno incarnationis Dominice MLXXXVIII, indictione xi, epacta xxv.

Iam uero quanta cura, quanto studio hunc locum emendare et augmentare studuerit, et si cessent uerba ipsa testantur opera. Nam quamuis monasterium istud a quingentis aut eo amplius annis primitus fuerit constuctum, a tempore domni Stephani abbatis uidetur sumpsisse principium, ita omnia innouata, omnia sunt in melius inmutata. Nam quocumque gradiebatur, hoc illi erat desiderium, hęc illi mentis cupiditas, ut si alicubi aliquid uidissset honestum, aut ecclesię suę necessarium, aut illud ipse asportaret aut simile in ecclesia sua ipse construere. In religione uero ita refloruit locus iste in diebus illius, ut usque ad mundi dominam Romam famosum nomen haberet Besua, et per totam Galliam usque ad maris littora. Vnde factum est ut cum primum hic ueniret, uix uiginti essent monach, in diebus uero ipsius quinquaginta seu sexaginta deo seruientes, et uictus ac uestitus necessaria accipientes. Si uero cumputemus eos qui in cellis nostris extra Besuam habitant, numerus usque ad centenarium consurget.

Sed et illud est ei a Deo prestitum quod in diebus eius aliqui conuersi ad Dominum, et ab eo in hoc loco accipientes religionis habitum, postea facti sunt et ipsi lumen ecclesiarum. Preficitur namque ecclesię Sancti Michaelis Ternoderensi domnus Wido abbas. Preficitur ęcclesię Sancti Sequani domnus Heinricus abbas. Preficitur domnus Eustasius ecclesię Nouiomensi Sancti Eligii. Preficitur ecclesię Sancti Iohannis domnus Godefredus.[13] Et quamuis ipse non fuisset noster monachus, de nostro tamen monasterio est assumptus. Sed et alii quamplures sub eo emulatione paterna ducti, in edificando et adquirendo eum imitabantur patrem, et hanc ecclesiam dilatauerunt, exornauerunt, et munierunt ut matrem.

De edificiis et adquisitionibus tam inta Besuam quam extra de instauratione corporis ipsius monasterii, seu officinarum, de bibliotheca tam ueteris quam noui

12 Before he headed the cell at Bar-sur-Aube, Stephen had spent ten years at St-Oyend and a year at Cluny, where his uncle Gui was prior.

13 Abbots Gui of St-Michel of Tonnerre, Henry of St-Seine, Eustace of St-Eloi of Noyen, and Geoffrey of Moûtier-St-Jean.

testamenti, de ornamento ęcclesiastico in tabulis, in capsis, in calicibus, in crucibus, in turibulis, in uestimentis ad officium ecclesiasticum pertinentibus, de cappis et cortinis, de palliis et signis ab eo et ab aliis fratribus et filiis huius ecclesię ipsius tempore comparatis, et huic loco collatis, aliquantulum latius in sequentibus disseremus. Nunc interim dicamus de ecclesiis quę huic loci in diebus ipsius collate sunt, tam in hoc episcopatu, quam in aliis. Ecclesia Sancti Synphoriani de Albiniaco. Ecclesia Sancti Benigni. Ecclesia Sancti Christofori Canlintensis.[14] In episcopatu Tullensi, ecclesia sancti Willegaudi apud Romonem castrum.[15] Et hęc qualiter et a quibus sint collata, carte huic ipsi libello inserte ostendunt.

189

Langres, 1088–1105

Robert, bishop of Langres, gives Bèze the churches of Aubigny and St-Broing.

Cartulary, fol. 112r–v.
Bougaud-Garnier, p. 384.

Karta de Albiniaco et de ecclesia Sancti Benigni

In nomine sanctę et indiuidue Trinitatis, Patris et Filii et Spiritus Sancti. Quoniam antecessores nostri quicquid ratum et indissolubile teneri uoluerunt, literarum custodię commendauerunt, ut uidelicet quod segnis deleret obliuio, litterarum aperiret representatio, dignum duximus litteris cummendare ea quę perpetualiter uolumus permanere. Ego igitur Rotbertus Lingonensis episcopus[1] ecclesiam de Albiniaco et atrium eius, paratas etiam et eulogias quę ad episcopum pertinent, et ecclesiam Sancti Benigni et atrium eius,[2] consensu et consilio fratrum Lingonensium, ecclesię Besuensi tenendam concedo et in plenaria synodo Lingonis habita Stephano premissę ecclesię abbati,[3] de manu in manum trado, et successoribus eius perpetualiter habendam instituo. Hoc etiam donum ita tenendum et permanendum diuidicamus, ut si quis clericus uel laicus auferre eis presumpserit uel inde eos iniuste inquietauerit, si sit clericus ordinis sui periculo, si laicus anathemati donec resipuerit subiaceat.

---

14 The churches were at Aubigny, 22 km north of Bèze; St-Broing, 28 km north of Bèze, and Champlitte, 24 km north-northeast of Bèze.

15 According to the "Annales" of Bèze, Bishop Pibo of Toul gave the monks the church at Romont in 1103; MGH SS 2:250.

1 Robert, bishop of Langres (1084–1111).

2 Aubigny, 22 km north of Bèze; and St-Broing, 28 km north of Bèze.

3 Stephen, abbot of Bèze (1088–1120).

Signum Gozelmi archidiaconi, Hugonis archidiaconi, Guarnerii archidiaconi, Norgaudi archidiaconi, Gyrardi archipresbiteri, Guidrici archipresbiteri. Facta sunt hęc Philippo regnante,[4] episcopante Rotberto, Stephano dictante cancellario.

This charter is dated by Abbot Stephen and by the papal privilege of 1105 (document 238), which refers to it. Most likely it can be dated more closely, to the late 1080s or the 1090s, because the chancellor of Langres was named Stephen then (see documents 188 and 191).

190

1093

Abbot Stephen of Bèze acquires half of the church of Savoyeux, which had been subject to the nobleman Hermuin. Hermuin gives it to Bèze for the good of his soul, after offering hospitality to Abbot Stephen.

Cartulary, fols. 112v–113r.
Bougaud-Garnier, p. 385.
Summarized in Brequigny, *Table* 2:256.

Karta de Siuoio

In nomine sanctę et indiuidue Trinitatis. Notum sit omnibus fidelibus Christi qualiter media pars ecclesię de Siuoio[1] subnixa est ecclesię Besuensi. Abbas Stephanus[2] uir religosus dum remigando per Segunnam ad ecclesiam Besuensem remearet, a Hermuino orto nobili progenie in eadem uilla hospicio susceptus est. Benignissimo amore eum suscepit atque omnem humanitatem hospitalitatis ei exhibiuit, et in crastino die pro ęternis peritura commutans in portu Prantenensi mediam partem ecclesię de Siuoio et ecclesiam Sancti Dionisii in eadem uilla, sicut erat sibi in patrimonio, pro anima sua antecessorumque suorum sub testimonio legali per manus supradicti abbatis tradidit apostolis, scilicet Petro et Paulo ecclesię Besuensis.

Acta sunt hęc anno ab incarnatione Domini MXCIII, indictione i, epacta xx, luna octaua, regnante imperatore Heinrico anno xxxiiii, principante Stephano comite, Hugone archiepiscopo[3] archiepiscopalem cathedram tenente. Si quis

4 Philip I, king of France (1060–1108).

1 Savoyeux is 37 km east-northeast of Bèze, on the Saône.

2 Stephen, abbot of Bèze (1088–1120).

3 Emperor Henry IV (1056–1106); Count Stephen of Burgundy (1087–1102); and Archbishop Hugh III of Besançon (1085–1101), brother of Count Stephen. For the brothers, see Bouchard, *Sword, Miter, and Cloister*, pp. 273–274.

hanc kartam uiolauerit, separetur ab angelorum choris, societurque Datan et Abiron, hic et in ęternum in inferno inferiori. Signum testium nostrorum. Signum Hermuini, Aymonis la Venche, Gyraldi, Albrici, Teberti, Stigandi. Ego Godefredus cancellarius abbatis dictaui et bene subscripsi.

191

Langres, 1088–1099

Robert, bishop of Langres, gives Bèze authority over the priests of the churches of Champlitte and Maâtz.

Cartulary, fol. 113r–v.
Bougaud-Garnier, p. 386.

Karta de Camlintensi ecclesia et de Maiasco

In nomine sancte et indiuidue Trinitatis, Patris et Filii et Spiritus Sancti. Quoniam consuetudinarium est, et ab antecessorum nostrorum industria ductum, ut ea quę memorię commendanda uidentur, litterali tradantur custodie dignum duximus, ea quę subinferuntur ne obliuione dispereant, ne uel quod inde actum est quando quę aliqua inmutetur fraudulentia, in huius cartę sinu fideliter recondere. Ego igitur Rotbertus sanctę Lingonensis ecclesię episcopus,[1] precibus Stephani abbatis Besuensis ecclesię[2] sepius ammonitus, uoluntati illius tandem adquiescens cum in ecclesia Lingonensi synodum celebraremus, et de ecclesiasticis negotiis pro posse diligenter tractaremus, consilio et assensu archidiaconorum consedentium, duos presbiteratus, Camlintensis uidelicet ecclesię et ecclesię de Maiascho,[3] Beato Petro Besuensis cęnobii et fratribus ibi Deo seruientibus deinceps habendos concedimus, ita ut presbiteri parroechiales qui in eis decantauerint medietatem omnium ad eosdem presbiteratus pertinentium per manus Besuensis abbatis obtineant, archidiachonibus aliisque ministris debita seruitia exhibeant, paratas et eulogias suo tempore communiter persoluant. Facta sunt hęc Lingonis in plenaria synodo, Vrbano papa existente, Philippo in Galliis regnante.[4] Signum Wilenci archidiaconi, Gocelmi archidiaconi, Garnerii archidiaconi, Norgaudi archidiaconi, Gosberti archipresbiteri, Stephanus cancellarius dictauit, Durannus notarius scripsit.

1 Robert, bishop of Langres (1084–1111).
2 Stephen, abbot of Bèze (1088–1120).
3 Champlitte, 24 km north-northeast of Bèze; and Maâtz, 30 km north-northeast of Bèze.
4 Pope Urban II (1088–1099); and Philip, king of France (1060–1108).

This document is dated by the pope. The witness list has considerable overlap with that of document 189, suggesting the documents were done about the same time.

192

1101

Odo, lord of Montsaugeon, confirms his earlier gifts as he buries his brother Hugh. Specifically, he confirms that he has given them the churches of Aubigny, St-Broing, Montsaugeon, and Is-sur-Tille. Odo's uncle Peter confirms. They put a copy of the Gospels covered in silver on the altar to mark this gift, for their souls and Hugh's.

Cartulary, fols. 113v–114v.
Bougaud-Garnier, pp. 387–388.
Summarized in Brequigny, *Table* 2:339.

Karta de Albiniaco

In nomine Patris et Filii et Spiritus Sancti. Presentis eui scire uolentibus futurisque deinceps clarificetur hominibus quod Oddo Montis Salionis[1] dominus, poenam ęterni supplicii cupiens euadere et paradisi premia percipere, in die sepulturę fratris sui Hugonis, sua spontanea uoluntate, partem non minimam militum de Monte Saluionis et clientum necnon amicorum et uicinorum suorum in Besuensi capitulo antequam corpus defuncti ad tumulum deferretur conuocauit, ibique dona quę antea fecerat de ecclesiis, scilicet de Albiniaco, de Sancto Benigno, de capella Montis Saluionis, de Ycioma,[2] hoc modo confirmauit.

In presentia namque domni Stephani abbatis et monachorum et eorum quos ipse conuocauerat, predictus Oddo et domnus Petrus auunculus eius[3] iterum donationem supradictarum ecclesiarum ex toto fecerunt et confirmauerunt Deo et Sancto Petro Besuensis ecclesię, possidendam in perpetuum. Textum etiam Euuangelii coopertum de argento ad donationem confirmandam super altare posuerunt, pro anima supradicti Hugonis et pro animabus omnium suorum antecessorum et pro semetipsis. Addiderunt etiam huic elemosine unum mansum in Albiniaco et unum seruum et unam ancillam. Rogatu itaque eorum pro confirmatione huius rei

1 Montsaugeon, 22 km north of Bèze.
2 Aubigny, 22 km north of Bèze and 2 km west of Montsaugeon; St-Broing, 28 km north of Bèze; Montsaugeon; and Is-sur-Tille, 14 km northwest of Bèze.
3 Peter was lord of Mirebeau; see document 203.

domnus abbas Stephanus, ab episcopo Roberto[4] in synodo supradictum Hugonem et patrem eius et antecessores suos defunctos absolui fecit.

Vt uero donatio ista inconuulsa permaneat, adsignamus testes. Signum Stephani abbatis. Signum Widonis prioris, Wilenci. Signum Oddonis et Petri qui hoc donum fecerunt. Acta sunt hęc tempore quo Pascalis summum pontificatum tenebat in Roma, Philippus regimen in Francia,[5] Robertus cathedram episcopalem in Lingonis, Stephanus abbas pastoralem curam in Besua. Anno ab incarnatione Domini MCI, indictione viiii, epacta xviii. Signum Teboldi, Teoderici, Landrici Lanfricurtis, Lamberti de Domarim, Widrici prepositi, Ricardi de Vircillis, Rodulfi, Oddonis de Bellomonte, Haymonis de Fontanis, Oddonis, Walonis de Calmis,[6] clericorum uero Humberti archipresbiteri, Wilenci sacerdotis, Iohannis sacerdotis.

193

Besançon, 1098

The brothers Humbert Rufus and Gui, sons of Humbert of Fouvent, give Bèze shares of churches at Motey, Champlitte, Savoyeux, Fouvent, and Lavoncourt for their souls.

Cartulary, fols. 114v–115r.
Bougaud-Garnier, pp. 388–389.
Summarized in Brequigny, *Table* 2:310.

Karta de ecclesis quas dederunt nobis Humbertus et Wido

Agnoscat hoc uita credentium quod res nulla melius in factis hominum quam elemosina quę bono fit animo reddit placabilem Deum, dicente Scriptura, "Sicut aqua mortificat ignem, sic elemosina occidit peccatum" [Ecc. 3:33]. Ergo de hac sententia non surdi sed fideles auditores fuere duo fratres, Humbertus Rufus et Wido, filii Humberti Fontisuenne.[1] Hii in flore iuuentutis sue pro remedio suarum animarum suorumque maiorum fidelium ecclesias quas de proprio iure retinebant, cithra aquam quę Asmantia[2] dicitur, Deo et Sancto Petro et Besuensi cęnobio concesserunt, ut caritas altius firmaretur, apud Bisonticam ciuitatem,

4 Stephen, abbot of Bèze (1088–1120); and Robert, bishop of Langres (1084–1111).

5 Pope Paschal II (1099–1118); and Philip I, king of France (1060–1108).

6 The laymen are from Dommarien, 25 km north of Bèze and 4 km northeast of Montsaugeon; Verseilles, 33 km north of Bèze; Fontaine-Française, 10 km northeast of Bèze; Beaumont, 7 km east of Bèze; and Chaume, 13 km north-northeast of Bèze.

1 Fouvent, 35 km northeast of Bèze.

2 The river Amance. The locations named, however, are not in the valley of the Amance but rather in the valley of the Saône and of the Salon, a tributary.

secus basilicam Sancti Vincentii, in presentia Hugonis archiepiscopi, supradictas ecclesias Stephano abbati[3] et Besuensi ecclesię perpetualiter tradiderunt. Licet scire quartam partem basilicę Sancti Martini de Monasterio et quicquid habebat ecclesia Sancti Christophori Canlintensis, et quartam partem ecclesię Sancti Mauricii de Siuoio,[4] medietatem ecclesię Fontisuennę uillę, similiter capellam de castro, simul modo ecclesiam de Luuocurte[5] sub tali testimonio.

Signum Hugonis archiepiscopi, Mainerii archidiaconi, Bernardi magistri, Ermuini, Seuuini. In ipsa die predictus episcopus annuit Stephano abbati omnes ecclesias licenter habere, quas posset aquirere in diocesi sua. Acta sunt hęc anno ab incarnatione Domini MXCVIII, indictione vi, epacta xv, Vrbano papa presidente Romę, Henrico imperante in Romano imperio.[6]

194

1099

Odo, son of Lord Hugh of Montsaugeon, gives Bishop Robert of Langres the church of Aubigny, asking him in turn to give it to Bèze, which Robert does.

Cartulary, fol. 115r.

Bougaud-Garnier, pp. 389–390.

Summarized by Duchesne, *Histoire généalogique des ducs de Bourgonge*, instr. 25–26.

Summarized in Brequigny, *Table* 2:309; dated 1098.

Summarized in Petit, *Histoire des ducs de Bourgogne*, 1:414, no. 95.

Karta de Albiniaco

Firmissime sciat omnis ordo fidelium quod Oddo, filius Hugonis senior Montis Salionis,[1] postquam suscepit honorem suum a Roberto Lingonensi episcopo[2] in calma de Perciaco, reddidit supradicto Rotberto ecclesiam de Albiniaco,[3]

3 Archbishop Hugh III of Besançon (1085–1101); and Stephen, abbot of Bèze (1088–1120).

4 Motey-sur-Saône, 36 km east-northeast of Bèze; Champlitte, 24 km north-northeast of Bèze; and Savoyeux, 37 km east-northeast of Bèze.

5 Lavoncourt, 42 km northeast of Bèze.

6 Pope Urban II (1088–1099) and Emperor Henry IV (1054–1106). During the time in the 1090s when King Philip I was excommunicated for his marital problems, Burgundian monasteries tended to date their documents by the emperor instead of the king.

1 Montsaugeon, 22 km north of Bèze. Odo became lord of Montsaugeon within a few years (see document 79).

2 Robert, bishop of Langres (1084–1111).

3 Percey-le-Grand, 18 km northeast of Bèze; and Aubigny, 22 km north of Bèze and 2 km west of Montsaugeon.

tali modo ut eam suo rogatu et suo concessu traderet Sancto Petro et Besuensi ecclesię perpetualiter possidendam. Hoc audiens pontifex, alacri animo suscepit donum que abbati Stephano[4] et ecclesię Besuensi, ut supradictus Oddo subgesserat, firmiter concessit sub testibus istis.

Signum Rotberti episcopi, Stephani abbatis, Albrici monachi, Warnerii archidiaconi, Humberti archipresbiteri, Willelmi Fontisuenne, Widonis de Radiaco,[5] Seuuini filii eius, Oddonis qui donum fecit, Widrici praepositi, Tetboldi, Landrici, Walonis,[6] Alelmi et fratris eius, Pagani de Icioma.[7] Acta sunt hęc anno ab incarnatione Domini MXCVIIII, indictione vii, epacta xxvi, regnante Philippo rege Francorum, Oddone ducatum tenente, Rotberto fratre eius episcopalem cathedram regente.[8] Si quis hanc cartam uiolauerit, separetur ab angelorum choris, societurque Datan et Abiron hic et in ęternum in inferno.

See also documents 192 and 200.

195

Late eleventh century (?)

Odilo, a knight of Licey, gives Bèze what he has there as he dies. He orders his nephew and heir, Anseric, to make sure this donation takes place.

Cartulary, fol. 115r–v.
Bougaud-Garnier, p. 390.

Karta de Lisseiaco

In nomine sanctę et indiuidue Trinitatis, Patris et Filii et Spiritus Sancti. Notum sit omnibus presentibus et futuris Odilonem Lisseiacensem[1] militem Deo Sanctoque Petro liberrime dedisse quicquid apud eandem uillam Lisseiacum habebat cum seruis et ancillis. Qui etiam cum morti esset proximus, Anxiricum nepotem suum substituens heredem sibi precepit ei ut nisi predictam seruaret dationem, sua nullomodo retentaret.

4 Stephen, abbot of Bèze (1088–1120).

5 Fouvent, 35 km northeast of Bèze; and Ray-sur-Saône, 43 km east-northeast of Bèze.

6 Although not identified as such, it seems most likely that these are the Landricus of "Lanfricurtis" and the Walo of Chaume of document 192.

7 Is-sur-Tille, 14 km northwest of Bèze.

8 Philip I, king of France (1060–1108); Odo I, duke of Burgundy (1078–1102); and his brother Robert, bishop of Langres (1084–1111).

1 Licey, 8 km east-northeast of Bèze.

Signum Ioffredi Belmontis,[2] Signum Hugonis Magni, Signum Gybuini, Signum Hugonis Columbe.

This document, as well as others in this section, certainly dates from the reign of Abbot Stephen, most likely from the 1090s, like the dated documents with which they are associated.

196

Late eleventh century (?)

The lady Facies, cousin of the monk Alberic, gives Bèze whatever property she had at Arçon, along with two serfs and their families. Later, the dues the serfs paid were assigned to the sacristan to pay for lighting.

Cartulary, fol. 115v.
Bougaud-Garnier, pp. 390–391.

Item alia

Quedam etiam mulier generosissima, Facies uulgo dicta, cunsobrina Albrici Arcionensis[1] monachi, quęcumque in antefata uilla possidebat Besuensibus contradidit monachis, una cum duobus seruis Gyrardo et Willelmo, cum uxoribus eorum et filiis, eo tenore ut ab eisdem alimonia donaretur monasterii quoad uiueret. Quę tamen possessiuncula sachristę ad luminaria ecclesię postmodum data est, precatibus et pia inportunitate prememorati Ansirici.

Signum predicti Ansirici. Signum Odilonis fratris eius. Signum Albrici monachi. Signum Vlrici monachi.

The Anseric who assigned the income to the sacristan was the nephew and heir of Odilo of Licey in the previous document.

197

Early twelfth century

Odo Chaterius of Spoy gives up his claims to part of a woods at Viévigne, which his mother-in-law, Elisabeth, had given. A monk in the cell at Spoy shall have free usage of the woods, fields, meadows, and fishing there.

2 Beaumont, 7 km east of Bèze.
1 Arçon, 13 km south of Bèze.

Cartulary, fols. 115v–116r.
Bougaud-Garnier, p. 391.

Karta de Cypeto

Opere precium uisum est ac necessarium posteris commendare memorie quod Oddo Chaterius de Cypeto[1] elemosinam socrus suę Elisabez, quę et Karitas appellata fuerat, uideliet partem suam de silua quę adiacet uillę quam dicitur Veteres Vineas,[2] licet iniuste calumpnians postmodum resipuit, et priorem donationem sicut facta fuerat Sancto Petro et ęcclesię Besuensi liberrime concessit. Addidit etiam ut monachus qui Cypeto manebit habeat usuarium liberrimum in siluis, campis, pratis, et in omnibus aquis piscatione, excepto uiuario domnidato, sed et in ipso si abbas in ipsa uilla Cypeto uenerit.

Testes huius rei: Signum Oddonis qui hoc donum fecit. Signum Oddonis Viridis. Signum Stephani abbatis.[3] Signum Wilenci. Et de familia Sancti Petri signum Otberti cocci, signum Hugonis et aliorum multorum.

Elisabeth Karitas had made gifts at Viévigne when dying; see document 273. For Odo Chaterius, see also document 252, and for Odo Viridis, see also document 271.

198

Late eleventh century (?)

Hugh junior of Fontaine-Française becomes a monk while dying and, for his soul, gives Bèze a manse there.

Cartulary, fol. 116r.
Bougaud-Garnier, pp. 391–392.

Carta de Fontanis

Clarificetur cunctis uiuentius postque futuris quod Hugo iuuenis de Fontanis[1] miles, ueniens ad obitum suum, quesiuit habitum monachi et deuote suscepit. Factusque monachus, pro remedio animę suę suorumque antecessorum fidelium dedit Deo et Sancto Petro Besuensi ęcclesię in supradictis Fontanis unum mansum liberum cum omni libertate et vii iugera terrę et iii facces de prato.

---

1 Spoy, 6 km southwest of Bèze.
2 Viévigne, 4 km southwest of Bèze.
3 Stephen, abbot of Bèze (1088–1120).
1 Fontaine-Française, 10 km northeast of Bèze.

Vt hae donatio inconuulsa permaneat, adsignamus ei testes ueraces. Signum Bertranni militis de Fontanis. Signum Teoderici filii eius. Signum Hugonis Carruce. Signum Widrici filii eius. Signum Wilenci militis. Signum Walonis Columbę de Bellomonte.[2] Signum Rodulfi militis de Aquis.[3] Signum Rodulfi rustici de Fontanis. De monachis, Signum Wilenci, Signum Warnerii, Signum Oddilonis, et aliorum multorum.

199

Late eleventh century (?)

Gui, a knight of "Insula Bollini," leaving for Jerusalem, gives Bèze all he has at Licey for his soul and his ancestors'. Dying on the trip, he has his companions add six ounces of gold to his gift.

Cartulary, fol. 116r–v.
Bougaud-Garnier, p. 392.

Inter ceteras elemosinas quę factę sunt ecclesię Besuensi, notum sit omnibus fidelibus quod Wido miles de Insula Bollini[1] dedit Deo et Sancto Petro et Besuensi ecclesie quidquid habebat uel habere existimabat ab antecessoribus suis in Lixiaco,[2] pro remedio anime sue suorumque antecessorum fidelium. Et hoc factum est antequam pergeret Iherusalem. Postquam hoc iter cepit et obbitum suum cognouit, remisit Sancto Petro et Besuensi ecclesie, per socios suos Hugonem militem de Excuuiliaco et per Constancium de Diniaco,[3] sex uncias auri, et elemosinam suam quam fecerat de Lixiaco et elemosinam matris suae de Flexo[4] concessit Sancto Petro et Besuensi ecclesię habere in perpetuum.

Signum Widonis militis qui hoc donum fecit. Signum Hugonis militis. Signum Constantii. Signum Stephani abbatis.[5] Signum Wilenchi prioris. Signum Albrici Captiui et aliorum multorum.

This document is written in a different though contemporary hand, heavier and not as neat. After it, the documents are written in the same hand as before. It has no rubric, although the initial letter is in red. It is most likely that Gui was on the First Crusade, but he may have gone later.

---

2 Beaumont, 7 km east of Bèze.
3 Achey, 28 km northeast of Bèze. Rodulfus also appears in document 231.
1 Unidentified.
2 Licey, 8 km east-northeast of Bèze.
3 Equevilley, 17 km north of Vesoul; and Diénay, 16 km northwest of Bèze.
4 Flée, 8 km east of Bèze.
5 Stephen, abbot of Bèze (1088–1120).

200

Langres, 1099–1108

Robert, bishop of Langres, gives Bèze the chapel of Montsaugeon that is dependent on the church of Aubigny, at the request of Abbot Stephen.

Cartulary, fols. 116v–117r.
Bougaud-Garnier, pp. 393–394.

Karta de capella Montis Saluionis

In nomine summe et indiuidue Trinitatis, Patris et Filii et Spiritus Sancti. Quoniam consuetudinarium est et ab predecessorum nostrorum ductum industria ut ea quę perpetuę memorie comendanda uidentur, litterarum tradantur custodie, dignum duximus ea quę subinferuntur ne obliuione dispereant, ne uel quod inde legitime actum est, quandoque aliqua immutetur fraudulentia, in huius carte sinu fideliter recondere.

Ego igitur Robertus alme sedis Lingonice Dei nutu episcopus,[1] dum in matris basilicę gremio, nobis a Christo collatę degeremus et secundum nostrum dogma una cum fidelibus prefatę ecclesię de statu et profectu illius, cum consilio et uoluntate eorum unanimiter tractaremus, affuit etiam inter eos amicus noster Besuensis ecclesię abbas domnus Stephanus,[2] nostram benignitatem humiliter expetens quatenus capellam quę est in castello Montis Saluionis sita, ad ecclesiam de Albiniaco[3] pertinentem, in honore sanctę Dei genitricis dedicatam, Sancto Petro Besuensis ecclesię per instrumenta apicum concedere et misericorditer largiri non dedignaremur. Cuius nos iustam et racionabilem peticionem libenter suscipientes, hoc quod pie et racionabiliter postulauit, per consilium fidelium nostrorum recto ordine ad effectum perducere curauimus, dantes et concedentes suprascriptam capellam, saluis omnibus Lingonensis ecclesię consuetudinibus. Ea tamen conditione ut capellanus eidem capelle inseruiat et beneficiarios usus ab ipso abbate Besuensi habeat et possideat. Vt autem huius nostrę concessionis testamentum futuris temporibus conseruetur et absque diminutione aut immutatione aliqua custodiatur, manu propria eam firmamus et archidiaconorum nostrorum firmandam tradimus.

Signum Gocelmi archidiaconi, Wilenci archidiaconi, Hugonis archidiaconi, Amalrici archidiaconi, Warnerii archidiaconi. Acta sunt hęc Lingonis plenaria synodo, Romanę sedis Paschali apostolatum gubernante, Philippo regnante,[4] Rotberto episcopo Lingonensem ęcclesiam regente, Stephano cancellario, Duranno notario, suas uices utroque exhibente.

---

1 Robert, bishop of Langres (1084–1111).
2 Stephen, abbot of Bèze (1088–1120).
3 Montsaugeon, 22 km north of Bèze; and Aubigny, 22 km north of Bèze and 2 km west of Montsaugeon.
4 Pope Paschal II (1099–1118); and Philip I, king of France (1060–1108).

The bishop had obtained the church of Aubigny in 1099; see document 194. This document is dated by the pope and the king but most likely dates to 1099 or 1100.

201

Early twelfth century

Abbot Stephen of Bèze gives Widric of Orgeux half the chapel of Montsaugeon for his lifetime. This Widric is nephew of the provost Widric of Montsaugeon.

Cartulary, fol. 117r–v.
Bougaud-Garnier, p. 394.

Item de eadem capella

Notificetur cunctis qui has legerint uel audierint litteras quod domnus Stephanus Besuensis abbas[1] Widrico clerico de Orgis,[2] scilicet nepoti Widrici prepositi, dedit medietatem capellę de Monte Salionis[3] tempore sue uitę, tali pacto et tali ratione ut per hanc partem ex toto seruitium faciat et fidelis Sancto Petro et Besuensi ecclesię et supradicto abbati exsistat. Si autem ipse uel presbiter capellanus qui ibi pro eo uicarius fuerit de nostra diuisione aliquid male subripuerit uel defraudauerit, ammonitus inde se et presbiterum apud Besuam representet coram abbate propter iusticiam faciendam, sicut suus homo. Si quoque domnus abbas in longinquo itinere ire uoluerit, supradictus clericus paratus cum suo equo ad sibi seruiendum existat. Hoc ut supradiximus tempore sue uite agat, post mortem uero eius in manu abbatis et in potestate redigatur.

Huic subscriptioni adsignamus testes. Signum Stephani abbatis, Widonis prioris, Wilenci, Iohannis, Warnerii, Landrici, Albrici, Ioffredi. De laicis, Widrici prepositi de Monte Salionis, Gyrberti de Miribello,[4] Oberti cocci, Hugonis famuli.

This document was doubtless issued shortly after the preceding one. The seven signatories after Abbot Stephen were almost certainly monks of Bèze.

202

Bèze, June 29, early twelfth century

Odo junior, lord of Montsaugeon, gives Bèze the tenement of the priest Germanus for his soul and those of his ancestors. He symbolizes this by putting a

1 Stephen, abbot of Bèze (1088–1120).
2 Orgeux, 15 km south-southwest of Bèze.
3 Montsaugeon, 22 km north of Bèze.
4 Mirebeau, 9 km south-southeast of Bèze.

copy of the Gospels on the altar. He also gives up his quarrels over the cemetery of Aubigny.

Cartulary, fols. 117v–118r.
Bougaud-Garnier, pp. 394–395.

Karta de tenimentum Germani presbiteri

Fidelis contio tam presentium quam futurorum pleniter agnoscat quod domnus Oddo iuuenis de Monte Salione[1] dominus in sollempnitate sanctorum apostolorum Petri et Pauli apud Besuam uenit, ibique oblationem Deo et Sancto Petro et Besuensi ecclesię pro sua anima suorumque antecessorum fidelium, per textum euuangelii supra sanctum altare supradictorum apostolorum, tenimentum Germani presbiteri dedit, pertinentem et adiacentem altari Sancti Simphoriani de Albiniaco,[2] scilicet decimationem de propria uinea domni Montis Salionis, et terciam partem de decimis quę pertinent ad dominicationem episcopi, de uineis, de coruatis, de tertiis, et omnem decimationem de terra Sancti Petri. Necnon et querimoniam quam iniuste querelabat super cimiterium de Albiniaco, de cellariis et de omnibus rebus postposuit et concessit, iure perpetuo tenendum Besuensi ecclesię et monachis cum omni libertate.

Hoc totum factum est rogatu Germani presbiteri filiorumque eius, qui post inde noster effectus est monachus. Huic rationi adsignamus testes. Signum Oddonis qui hoc concessit, Teboldi militis, Richardi de Vircillis, Widrici prepositi, Lamberti militis de Domarim, Calonis de Siluiniaco, Gyrardi Crispi militis, Humberti militis de Bigorna, Hugonis militis de Torciniaco, Theoderici de Diuione militis,[3] aliorumque multorum.

For the church of Aubigny, where the priest collects the tithes, see also documents 194 and 200. For Odo of Montsaugeon, see also the following document.

203

1088–1114

Peter, lord of Mirebeau, and his nephew Odo, lord of Montsaugeon, give up their quarrels with Bèze over fishing rights.

Cartulary, fol. 118r–v.
Bougaud-Garnier, pp. 395–396.

1 Montsaugeon, 22 km north of Bèze.
2 Aubigny, 22 km north of Bèze and 2 km west of Montsaugeon.
3 The laymen are from Verseilles, 33 km north of Bèze; Dommarien, 25 km north of Bèze; Savigny, 39 km northeast of Bèze; Bigorna, unidentified; Torcenay, 41 km north-northeast of Bèze; and Dijon. Theoderic of Dijon's father was named Stephen; see the following document.

Karta de Petro domno Miribelli

Omnis fidelis sexus tam de laicis quam de clericis plane sciat et agnoscat quod domnus Petrus de Monte Salionis, senior de Miribello,[1] propter quoddam infortunium quod sibi contigit quadam die ueniens ad Besuensę monasterium, in presentia domni Stephani abbatis[2] et monachorum necnon et laicorum multorum, supradictus Petrus et domnus Oddo nepos eius de Monte Salionis domnus ambo omnem calumpniam de piscatione quam habebant super aquam nostram, que est a molendino quod est ultra Neronem[3] uillulam nostram usque ad Besuam, ex toto postposuerunt, et si quid iuris inibi ex parte sua uel suorum antecessorum umquam fuit, Deo et Besuensi ecclesię in illa die ęternaliter condonauerunt.

De hac re supradictus Petrus et de suis malefactis quę antea malę egerat aduersus ecclesiam satisfaciens in presentia domni Stephani abbatis de omnibus quęrimoniis finem fecit. Et ut pax firmius teneretur et bonus finis omnibus diebus uitę suę, manu sua coram omnibus finem et pacem supra sanctas reliquias iurauit, necnon et Rainaldus prepositus eius de Miribello, et Hugo clericus, et Lambertus de Iergeiaco hoc iurauerunt perpetualiter tenendum. Necnon et milites quorum auctoritate hoc fecit. Dedit fideiussores domnum Ioffredum cum suis filiis, Hugonem et Fulchonem;[4] Hugonem Columbam cum suo filio Walone; Milonem cum suo filio Euuino; domnum Oddonem nepotem suum; Theodericum de Diuioni, filium Stephani; Aymonem de Diuioni cognomento Chag; Odilonem de Lisiaco.[5] Signum domni Stephani abbatis, Widonis prioris, Wilenci, Albrici, Landrici, et aliorum multorum.

This document is dated by Abbot Stephen and by the 1114 death of young Fulk of Beaumont (document 261). See also the preceding document.

204

Early twelfth century

The men of Bourberain want their payments to Bèze reduced when they rebuild after a fire. They reach an agreement so that they will pay at least some of what they had previously owed.

---

1 Montsaugeon, 22 km north of Bèze; and Mirebeau, 9 km south-southeast of Bèze. In 1120/1124 Peter Malus Respectus, lord of Mirebeau, gave up his quarrels with the canons of St-Étienne of Dijon; his wife was named Eva. *Chartes de l'abbaye de Saint-Étienne de Dijon de 1098 à 1140*, p. 43, no. 34.

2 Stephen, abbot of Bèze (1088–1120).

3 Noiron, 4 km southeast of Bèze.

4 Geoffrey, lord of Beaumont, with his sons Hugh and Fulk.

5 Licey, 8 km east-northeast of Bèze.

Cartulary, fols. 118v–119r.
Bougaud-Garnier, pp. 396–397.

Karta de Burbureno

Notum sit omnibus hominibus qualiter homines natiui de uilla quę dicitur Burburena[1] commanentes in Besua post conbustionem domorum quas in nostra terra primitus habuerant, alias reedificare cupientes, ad abbatem loci isius, nomine Stephanum,[2] conuenerunt, reędificandi licentiam querentes. Quibus ipse ait, "Absit ut umquam deinceps in nostro fundo ita mansiones habeatis sicuti actenus habuistis nisi consuetudinaria seruitia reddideritis, sicut nostri et alii faciunt qui in nostra potestate consistunt. Si autem nolueritis, construendi ulterius licentiam a me non conseqemini."

Hęc autem uerba abbatis uidelicet illi audientes, inter se consilium inierunt, et cum eo pactum firmiter statuerunt, ut deinceps unusquisque de generali placito tantummodo xii nummos persolueret, alias uero consuetudines facerent, excepto carritum uini de Gibriaco,[3] nisi per suam bonitatem aliquis ex eis uellet facere. Constituit etiam ipsis idem abbas Stephanus ut nec ipse nec aliquis in posterum super eos talliam faceret, alias uero consuetudines ab eis exigeret. Et hoc etiam statuerunt ut siquis illorum iniuriam a monachis uel a seruis Sancti Petri pateretur, nullam proclamationem neque alienam iusticiam quereret, donec iusticia abbatis et prepositi monasterii ei deficeret.

Signum Stephani abbatis, Landrici prepositi. Ex familia uero Sancti Petri fuerunt illic tunc multi. Signum Aydulfi, Gyraldi, Albrici uillici de Burburena uilla, et aliorum multorum.

205

1088–1102

Gui, a knight of Frettes, became a monk when ill. Now his relatives make gifts to Bèze, consisting of allodial property at Maâtz. The monks make the donors small counter-gifts.

Cartulary, fols. 119r–v.
Bougaud-Garnier, pp. 397–398.

1 Bourberain, 4 km north-northeast of Bèze.
2 Stephen, abbot of Bèze (1088–1120).
3 Gevrey, 12 km southwest of Dijon; in 1101 the duke gave Gevrey to Cluny; *Recueil des chartes de l'abbaye de Cluny*, 5:156–159, no. 3809.

Karta de Maiasco

Agnoscat firmiter omnis ordo fidelium quod Wido miles de uilla quę Fretas[1] nuncupatur, decidens in infirmitate, noster effectus est monachus, ipse et frater eius Teodericus et uxor cum filiis et filiabus ipsius Teoderici totum alodium ex parte generis sui et ex parte Gybuini de Bellomonte[2] et eius uxoris, quod habebant in uilla quę Maiascus dicitur,[3] in mansis, in agris, in pratis, in siluis, in elemosina deuote obtulerunt Deo et sanctis apostolis Petro et Paulo et Besuensi ecclesię, pro remedio sui suorumque antecessorum pro uiuis siue defunctis.

Vt donum istud firmius teneretur, uxor Theoderici inde pro signo habuit unum anulum de auro, et Richardus filius eius unum cyphum de refectorio. Supradictus quoque Wido post hoc dedi omnem partem ad se pertinentem de proprio fundo quem possidebat ultra Sagunnam fluuium,[4] scilicet in uilla quę Vallarius uocatur, et in alia uilla deserta quę Arcensis appellatur, et in alia uilla quę Luuinensis nuncupatur,[5] in mansis, in agris, in pratis, in siluis, in seruis et ancillis.

Signum Hugonis de Cunuulensi castro,[6] Heinrici, Rainaldi, Widonis, Bernonis, domni Stephani abbatis,[7] Gyrardi monachi, Warnerii, Wilenci, Albrici, Aymonis. Acta sunt hęc tempore illo quo Philippus rex regnabat in Francia, Robertus episcopus in Linguonis, Stephanus abbas in Besua, Oddo dux in ducatu.[8]

This document is dated by Abbot Stephen and Duke Odo I.

206

Dijon, 1088–1102

The duke's provost settles a quarrel with the monastery over dues totaling five solidi, demanded at Belleneuve. Duke Odo and his wife agree when Abbot Stephen confronts them with charters and testimony. Because the provost did

1 Frettes, 31 km northeast of Bèze.
2 Beaumont, 7 km east of Bèze.
3 Maâtz, 30 km north-northeast of Bèze.
4 The river Saône. The next two villages are not identified.
5 Lavoncourt, 42 km northeast of Bèze.
6 Coublanc, 28 km north-northeast of Bèze.
7 Stephen, abbot of Bèze (1088–1120).
8 Philip, king of France (1060–1108); Robert, bishop of Langres (1084–1111); and Robert's brother, Duke Odo I of Burgundy (1078–1102).

not have five solidi on hand, he gave the abbot his furs to keep until he repaid the money.

Cartulary, fol. 119v.
Bougaud-Garnier, pp. 398–399.

Karta de Balenauo

Notum sit omnibus fidelibus tam laicis quam clericis necnon monachis quod ministri ducis Odonis,[1] prepositus et alii, super terram nostram quam Sanctus Petrus et ecclesia Besuensis habet in Baleneua[2] querelabant consuetudines malas, scilicet talliam pro cibo ducis, pro qua re acceperunt v solidos de hominibus. Pro hac iniuria domnus abbas Stephanus[3] proclamationem faciens ad ducem supradictum et ad ducissam uxorem eius inde ex utraque parte terminauerunt placitum apud Diuionem, ad quod pergens domnus abbas Stephanus armatus suis cartis, suisque testimoniis, liberaliter disseruit quod supradicta terra penitus duci neque suis ministris nullam debebat consuetudinem, nec alicui uiuenti nisi Sancto Petro et Besuensi ecclesię. Hoc audiens dux et uxor eius statim fecerunt restituere supradicto abbati illos v solidos suprascriptos per Erueium prepositum. Ille quoque non habens in promptu nummos, absulit pellas suas de collo suo, reddidit eas fideiussori, scilicet Ioscelmo. Ille nempe illas reddidit abbati Stephano, abbas quoque secum eas detulit et tandiu ipsas pelles habuit donec uellet nollet Erueius prepositus illo v solidos reddidit.

This document is dated by the abbot and the duke. It was not noted by Petit.

207

1100

The lady Alburgis Pagana, while dying, gives Bèze land at Pichanges, along with her husband, Walter of Minot. Her sons agree.

Cartulary, fols. 119v–120r.
Bougaud-Garnier, p. 399.

1 Odo I, duke of Burgundy (1078–1102).
2 Belleneuve, 12 km south of Bèze.
3 Stephen, abbot of Bèze (1088–1120).

Karta de Picangiis

Quedam matrona Alburgis, cognomine Pagana, Walterii de Minoio[1] coniux honestissima, ab hoc seculo discessura, Beato Petro et abbati Stephano[2] cęterisque fratribus apud Besuense monasterium in Dei seruitio persistentibus distribuit terram apud uillam quę Picantias[3] uocatur uel prata, nemusque cum aqua, ueluti ea in uita sua possederat, Waltero et Raimundo filiis suis, presente Seualdo fratre suo et coram plurimis testibus gratanter concedentibus.

Signum Landrici monachi, Theoderici atque Albrici monachi, Petri Granceiacensis canonici, Oddonis Iciacensis militis.[4] MC anno ab incarnatione Domini, regnante Philippo rege in Galliam et Roberto episcopo exsistente apud Lingonas,[5] et cum eo regentibus Wilenco atque Goscelmo Lingonensem ecclesiam archidiaconibus.

See also document 230.

208

Early twelfth century (?)

Hugh Barba had given Bèze land in the deserted villa "Vallarium," but Richard, son of Milo, seized and held it for two years. He now gives up his false claims.

Cartulary, fol. 120r.
Bougaud-Garnier, p. 400.

Karta de Villarium

Notum sit omnibus qui has legerint uel audierint litteras quod terram Hugonis cognomento Barbe quam dedit Sancto Petro in uilla deserta quę uocatur Villarium, hanc Richardus filius Milonis, successor et gener Hugonis Magni, qui noster effectus est monachus, iniuste inuasit et per duos anno eam super calumpniam abbatis Stephani[1] ac monachorum eius tenuit, dehinc resiput et terram et fructum ex toto Sancto Petro et domno abbati Stephano cum satisfactione reddidit. Ipse quoque abbas eum uidelicet Richardum tali cunditione de

1 Minot, 37 km northwest of Bèze.
2 Stephen, abbot of Bèze (1088–1120).
3 Pichanges, 9 km west of Bèze.
4 Grancey, 29 km northwest of Bèze; and Is-sur-Tille, 14 km northwest of Bèze.
5 Philip, king of France (1060–1108); and Robert, bishop of Langres (1084–1111).
1 Stephen, abbot of Bèze (1088–1120).

preterito delicto ita absoluit ut si ille aut aliquis successor eius illud repetere uellet, sub anathema maledictionis permaneret.

Signum huius rei Stephani abbatis, Wilenci, Ioffredi, Aymonis, Ricardi. Signumque Milonis patris eius, Hugonis uillici, Oberti, Gyraldi de Virduno, Hugonis famuli, Gysleberti famuli, Gyraldi filii Gunterii, et aliorum multorum.

For this property, see also document 205. The documents in this section most likely date to shortly after the year 1100.

209

Early twelfth century (?)

Aluidis, a noble lady of Beaujeu, makes gifts to Bèze for her soul while dying. Her gift is of a manse and a new vineyard at Beaujeu, along with a servile family. Her sons agree.

Cartulary, fol. 120r–v.
Bougaud-Garnier, pp. 400–401.

Karta de Belloioco

Notificamus modernis quibusque et futuris quod Aluuidis nobilis matrona de Belloioco,[1] soror Ermuini et uxor Vlrici de Trevia[2] castro, in suo obitu pro remedio animę suę suorumque antecessorum dedit fideliter Deo et Sancto Petro et Besuensi ecclesię unum mansum in Belloioco cum seruo nomine Rotberto in illo manso habitante, cum uxore eius et uno filio nomine Tebaldo et una filia quę uocatur Grimoeldis, et simul dedit unam uineam nouellam scilicet nuper plantatam. Hoc totum et mansum et uineam et seruos et ancillas, sicuti ipsa de proprio iure possidebat, honorifice et cum omni libertate dedit Deo et Sancto Petro et Besuensi ecclesię, ut supra dictum est, ipsa et filii eius omnes.

Ne aliquis infidelis falsum hoc existimet, adsignamus testes. Signum Teoderici filii eius, Pontii similiter filii eius, Teoderici pueri, Oddonis de Bellomonte[3] et uxoris eius, Hugonis Columbę, Oddonis de Scia,[4] Milonis de Belloioco, Fulconis, Hugonis, Herberti uuillici, Gyraldi coriarii. De clericis Acilini sacerdotis, Rainaldi diaconi, Tebaldi de Agiliaco. De nostris monachis, Widonis prioris, Wilenci, Warnerii, Landrici, et aliorum multorum.

1 Beaujeu, 31 km east-northeast of Bèze.
2 Most likely Traves, 25 km northeast of Beaujeu.
3 Beaumont, 7 km east of Bèze.
4 Scey-sur-Saône, 28 km northeast of Beaujeu.

210

Early twelfth century (?)

Oltrudis, daughter of Gui of Viévigne and niece of the monk Waro, gives Bèze all her hereditary property at Viévigne.

Cartulary, fols. 120v–121r.
Bougaud-Garnier, p. 401.

Carta de Vetus Vineis

Notum sit omnibus modo uiuentibus post nosque futuris quod Oltrudis filia Widonis de Vetusuineis,[1] neptis Waronis monachi, dedit omnem hereditatem suam Deo et Sancto Petro et Besuensi ecclesię quam possidebat in supradictis Vetusuineis, in mansis, in terris, in pratis, in siluis, et domnus Oddilo monachus noster, qui tunc regebat obedientiam, dedit ei pro signo medietatem emine frumenti et aliam mensuram de milio.

Vt hęc donatio firma teneatur, assignamus testes. Signum Widonis prioris, Wilenci, Iohanni, Ioffredi, Poncii, Oddilonis. De laicis, Rotberti uuillici de Vetusuineis, Bernardi, Rotgerii, Petri, Hugonis famuli, Rainaldi.

For Oltrudis's family, see also document 118.

211

Early twelfth century (?)

Raymond, a knight of Grancey, is dying and gives Bèze mansi at Lux and Rivière, along with some serfs. His wife, sons, and brother all agree.

Cartulary, fol. 121r.
Bougaud-Garnier, pp. 401–402.

Carta de Luco

Audiant omnes tam presentes quam futuri quod Raymundus de Granciaco miles, qui apud Saliuam[1] uulneratus fuit, antequam obisset coram multis testibus, pro sua anima suorumque antecessorum dedit Sancto Petro et Besuensi ecclesię duos mansos, unum apud Lucum cum suis appendiciis et alium

1 Viévigne, 4 km southwest of Bèze.

1 Grancey, 29 km northwest of Bèze; and Salives, 10 km southwest of Bèze.

apud Rariacum,[2] et duos seruos, Waldricum et Humbertum, et duas ancillas, Aluuidem et Ermessendem.

Huic rei assignamus testes. Signum uxoris eius et filii. Signum fratris eius Walterii, Artaldi militis, Pontii militis, Heinrici de Ycio,[3] et aliorum multorum.

212

Early twelfth century

Odo, a knight of Is-sur-Tille, is dying and gives Bèze a manse at Sacquenay for his soul and his ancestors'. His wife and son agree.

Cartulary, fol. 121r.
Bougaud-Garnier, p. 402.

Carta de Secuniaco

Clarum fiat omnibus qui has litteras uiderint uel audierint quod Oddo miles de uilla quę Ycius[1] uocatur, ueniens ad obitum suum, dederit Deo et Sancto Petro et Besuensi ecclesię, pro sua anima suorumque antecessorum, unum mansum in uilla quę dicitur Secuniacus[2] cum appendiciis suis, tam liberum et tam bonum quod partem in se retineat de pastionibus et de terciis, et libertatem per omnes fines illius uillę.

Huic dationi subscribamus testes. Signum Oddonis et uxoris eius et filii ipsius Pontii militis, qui elemosinam fecerunt. Signum Seualdi Balbi, Raymundi, Aymonis militis, Pagani prepositi, Martini Barbati et aliorum multorum.

This document must date to after 1100, when Odo was still alive and witnessed document 207.

213

Early twelfth century (?)

Gui, a knight of Oisilly, is dying and gives Bèze a manse at Chevigny for his soul. After his death, his son, also named Gui, confirms, as do his brothers.

---

2 Lux, 5 km northwest of Bèze. Garnier identifies "Rariacum" as Rivière-les-Fosses, 21 km north of Bèze.

3 Is-sur-Tille, 14 km northwest of Bèze.

1 Is-sur-Tille, 14 km northwest of Bèze.

2 Sacquenay, 14 km north-northeast of Bèze.

Cartulary, fol. 121v.
Bougaud-Garnier, pp. 402–403.

Karta de Cauiniaco et Auxiliaco

Sciant omnes tam presentes quam futuri quod Wido miles de Auxiliaco,[1] ueniens ad obitum suum, pro anima sua dedit Deo et Sancto Petro et Besuensi ecclesię unum mansum cum omnibus appendiciis suis et omni libertate apud Cauiniacum.[2] Dedit etiam uiridarium de Ponto cum appendiciis suis, cum omni libertate, necnon et terciam partem molendini de Auxiliaco cum piscibus, si ibi capti fuerint.

Vt hęc elemosina inconuulsa permaneat, subscribamus ei testes. Signum Widonis filii supradicti defuncti, qui elemosinam loco patris sui super altare posuit sanctorum apostolorum Petri et Pauli. Signum fratris eius Rainaldi, Hugonis militis de Bellomonte, Ioffredi militis, Walonis militis cognomento Columbi, Gysleberti, Warnerii, Hugonis fratris eius, et aliorum multorum. De monachis Warnerii, Wilenci, Landrici.

214

Early twelfth century (?)

Hugh Rufus and his wife Regina give Bèze land at Romagne, with all its appurtenances, including serfs. They also give the church at Véronnes. If Regina, when widowed, wants to join the house, the monks will accept her.

Cartulary, fols. 121v–122r.
Bougaud-Garnier, pp. 403–404.

Karta de Romanisca

Dignum duximus memorie tradere quod Hugo cognomento Rubeus et uxor eius, cognomento Regina, per manum Stephani abbatis[1] dederunt Deo et Sancto Petro et Besuensi ecclesię terram quae dicitur de Romanisca[2] ad integrum, cum omnibus appendiciis suis, in quocumque loco iaceret cum seruis et ancillis, necnon et ecclesiam de Verona.[3] Tali pacto si supradicta matrona uiuens uellet ire ad Besuam post obitum uiri sui, susciperent eam monachi cum

1 Oisilly, 9 km southeast of Bèze.
2 Chevigny, 3 km southeast of Bèze.
1 Stephen, abbot of Bèze (1088–1120).
2 La Romagne, 16 km northeast of Bèze.
3 Véronnes, 7 km north-northwest of Bèze.

terra procurandam. Sin autem nollet usque ad mortem, post obitum suum reciperet ecclesia terram suam cum omni libertate et cum seruis et ancillis, sicut supra taxatum est. Pro hac quoque elemosina dedit domnus abbas Stephanus et uiro et mulieri societatem et omne bonum quod factum fuerit in Besuensi ęcclesia, usque ad finem mundi, pro remedio animarum suarum suorumque antecessorum fidelium.

Vt hęc traditio firma permaneat, assignamus ei testes. Vlrici militis qui fuit frater Hugonis. Widonis militis filii eius. Richardi militis de Vircillis.[4] Widonis fratris ipsius. Widonis capellani. Petri presbiteri. Rogerii qui fuit filius Hugonis. Duranni de Maiasco.[5] Fanuelis et aliorum multorum. De monachis autem Stephani abbatis, Warnerii prioris, Wilenci, Widonis capalani, Albrici.

215

Early twelfth century (?)

Gerberge, the wife of Marcel, gives herself to Bèze along with her five children.

Cartulary, fol. 122r.
Bougaud-Garnier, p. 404.

Item alia

Notum esse uolumus presentibus et futuris quod Girberga, uxor Marcelli sutoris, dederit semetipsam Sancto Petro apostolo cum filiis suis, id est Martino, Ermengarde, Maria, Richilde, Ada.

Presente Godefrido priore, Gyrardo, Walterio, Rotberto, Drogone preposito, Tebaldo, Ingelranno, Stephano, Lamberto preposito, Iohanne filio Iohannis maioris, Willelmo sutore, Marcello sutore, et ceteris.

216

Early twelfth century

The knight Hugh of Choilley, dying, gives Bèze four mansi at Cusey, Choilley, and Rivière for his soul and those of his ancestors.

Cartulary, fol. 122r–v.
Bougaud-Garnier, pp. 404–405.

4 Verseilles, 33 km north of Bèze.
5 Maâtz, 30 km north-northeast of Bèze.

Carta de Cusiaco et de Chimissin

Sacra scriptura testatur quod elemosina liberat animam de morte ęterna [Tob. 4:11] et cunducit eam ad uitam perpetuam. De qua re non inmemor Hugo miles, cognomento de Chimissins, ipse ueniens ad obitum suum, pro sua anima suorumque antecessorum fidelium dedit Deo et Sancto Petro et Besuensi ecclesię quattuor mansos, duos apud Riuuriacam,[1] que est uilla deserta, cum omnibus appendiciis suis. Alium apud Cusiacum[2] cum appendiciis suis. Alterum apud Chimissins cum quattuor iugeribus terrę et unam falcem de prato. Et hos mansos liberos dedit cum omni libertate suprascriptus Hugo.

Vt hęc elemosina inconuulsa permaneat, adsignamus ei testes. Signum Hugonis, Widonis filii eius, Walonis, Aymonis, Hugonis nepotis ipsius, Auuini de Beria, Mainfridi militis de Arco,[3] Walterii de Beria, Nerduini militis, Andree presbiteri, Richardi, Constantini, et aliorum multorum.

217

Early twelfth century

Hugh, son of Wilenc of Rosey, and his uncles make gifts to Bèze for his father's soul. They give mansi at Ferrières and Noiron along with several serfs.

Cartulary, fol. 122v.
Bougaud-Garnier, p. 405.

Carta de Nogdantium Ferrosum

Notum sit omnibus uiuentibus post nosque futuris quod Hugo puer, filius Wilenci de uilla quę Roseius dicitur, et auunculi eius, Walo monachus et Wido miles, fratres supradicti Wilenci, pro anima ipsius Wilenci et pro animabus fratrum suorum et omnium antecessorum suorum, tam pro uiuis quam pro defunctis, tradiderunt Deo et Besuensi ecclesię duos mansos, unum apud

1 Garnier identifies this place as Rivière-les-Fosses, 21 km north of Bèze.

2 Cusey, 19 km north-northwest of Bèze; and Choilley, 4 km northwest of there.

3 Beire, 8 km southwest of Bèze; and Arc-sur-Tille, 15 km south-southwest of Bèze. Manfred of Arc also made gifts to St-Étienne of Dijon, with his brother Walter, between 1113 and 1117 (*Chartes de l'abbaye de Saint-Étienne de Dijon de 1098 à 1140*, 27, pp. 36–37). By the 1130s he had appeared with a brother named Walter and wife Bonadomina (108, pp. 121–122). A son became a canon at St-Etienne (80, pp. 89–90). Initially his sons wouldn't recognize Manfred's gifts but confirmed with their mother, Bonadomina (96, pp. 105–106).

Nogdantium Ferrosum,[1] scilicet mansum Arnulfi cum suis appendicis, et alium in uilla quę dicitur Neronis iuxta Gradiacum castrum,[2] cum duobus seruis, Letbaldo et Widone fratre eius, et cum appendiciis suis.

Vt hęc carta inconuulsa permaneat, adsignamus testes. Signum Widonis, Walonis, Widonis, Willelmi filii eius, Hugonis, Raimodis de Longocampo,[3] Hugonis de Nerone.

218

Early twelfth century

Henry, a knight of La Ferté, makes Bèze a gift while dying, a manse at Bourguignon, along with the serfs living there. His wife and sons agree, as do members of their household.

Cartulary, fols. 122v–123r.
Bougaud-Garnier, pp. 405–406.

Karta de Burgundion

Fiat clarum cunctis uiuentibus modo postque uenturis quod Henricus miles de Firmitate[1] decubans in lecto, ueniensque ad suum obitum, consensu et consilio uxoris sue et filiorum et omnium domesticorum suorum, dedit Deo et Sancto Petro et Besuensi ecclesie, pro sua anima suorumque antecessorum fidelium, unum mansum apud uillam quę dicitur Burgundion,[2] cum omnibus appendiciis suis, liberum cum omni libertate, et tres seruos manentes in ipso manso, scilicet Arnulfum, Henricum, Gyslebertum, et medietatem de filiis uel filiabus supradicti Arnulfi, et de alia parte unam ancillam.

Huic carte adsignamus testes. Signum Leogardis quę donum fecit, Hugonis de Conulensi castro, Richardi de Vircillis,[3] Widonis fratris ipsius. De clientibus Henrici, Vlrici, Iulonis filii eius, Rotberti uillici, Bernardi, Arnaldi clerici, Widonis presbiteri, et aliorum multorum.

---

1 Ferrières, 57 km northeast of Bèze, 3 km southeast of Scey-sur-Saône; and Rosoy, 46 km north-northeast of Bèze.

2 Noiron, 7 km south-southeast of Gray, 24 km east of Bèze, rather than the Noiron much closer to Bèze.

3 Longchamp, 23 km south of Bèze.

1 La Ferté-sur-Amance, 51 km northeast of Bèze.

2 Bourguignon, 14 km south of La Ferté.

3 Coublanc, 28 km north-northeast of Bèze; and Verseilles, 33 km north of Bèze.

219

Early twelfth century

Aluidis, wife of Wilenc of "Altason," gives Bèze mansi located at St-Seine and elsewhere for his soul and for their late son Rainald.

Cartulary, fol. 123r.
Bougaud-Garnier, p. 406.

Carta de Sancto Sequano

In nomine Patris et Filii et Spiritus Sancti. Fiat notum cunctis fidelibus quot Aluuidis, uxor Wilenci de uilla quę Altason[1] uocatur, dedit Deo et Sancto Petro et Besuensi ecclesię duos mansos liberos cum omni libertate pro anima uiri sui Wilenci, necnon et pro anima filii sui Rainaldi qui iuuenis mortuus est, et pro sua anima suorumque fidelium antecessorum. Vnum in uilla quę Sanctus Sequanus[2] nuncupatur cum appendiciis suis, et alterum apud Viriniacum cum suis appendiciis.

Vt hęc carta firma et inconuulsa permaneat, adsignamus ei testes. Signum Aluuidis qui donum dedit, Humberti de Bellomonte, Widonis, Eldeberti, Hugonis. De monachis Stephani abbatis,[3] Warnerii prioris, Willenci, et aliorum monachorum. Si quis huic donationi instigante diabolo contraire uoluerit aut diminuere, cum Datan et Abiron anathema sit.

See also the following document.

220

Early twelfth century

The knight Fulk of Rivière, along with his brother Wizard, gives Bèze mansi at "Viriniacus." They also give usage rights at Montigny and several serfs.

Cartulary, fol. 123r–v.
Bougaud-Garnier, pp. 406–407.

Carta de Viriaco

Habet etiam alium mansum Sanctus Petrus et Besuensis ecclesia apud Viriniacum[1] quem dedit pro sua anima Falco miles de Riueria[2] et Wicardus frater

---

1 This place is not identified.
2 St-Seine-sur-Vingeanne, 13 km northeast of Bèze. "Viriniacus" is not identified.
3 Stephen, abbot of Bèze (1088–1120).
1 This place is unidentified.
2 Rivière-les-Fosses, 21 km north of Bèze.

ipsius, cum omnibus appendiciis suis, et habet usum et communitatem per omnem potestatem de Montiniaco,[3] in siluis et in pratis et in pascuis et ubique, et Petrum qui mansum tenet, quantum eis suppetit, tradiderunt suprascripti milites. Et[4] alius mansus in supradicta uilla, scilicet Viriniaco, quem dedit pro remedio anime sue Sancto Petro et Besuensi ecclesię, Petrus uillicus et Tebertus frater eius, uillicus de Montiniaco, cum suis appendiciis. Et sunt ibi in supradicta uilla alii quattuor mansi cum suis appendiciis, quos tradiderunt alii benefactores pro animabus suis, Deo et Sancto Petro et Besuensi ecclesię cum omni libertate, sicuti Hismahel de Grancicaco[5] et alii fideles, sub testimonio Christi.

221

Early twelfth century

The knight Rayner of Cusey, while dying, gives Bèze three mansi for his soul, along with a female serf and her sons.

Cartulary, fol. 123v.
Bougaud-Garnier, p. 407.

Carta de Cusiaco

Liqueat cunctis modo uiuentibus et futuris post nos quod quidam miles Rainerius de uilla quę Cusiacus[1] dicitur, ueniens ad mortem, pro remedio animę suę parentumque suorum cum magna deuotione tribuit Sancto Petro et Besuensi ecclesię tres mansos, sicuti ipse eos possidebat in ipsa supradicta uilla Cusiaco. Duo ex his debent duo sextaria uini et panem et carnem, et tercius quia minor est medietatem sextarii et panem et carnem. Deditque unam ancillam inibi manentem cum tribus filiis, quę Rolendis nuncupatur, sub tali testimonio.

Signum Oddonis senioris Montis Salionis,[2] Teodeboldi, Odilonis fratris ipsius mortui cum filiis suis.

222

Early twelfth century

Ponce of "Bigorna," a knight of Montsaugeon, is dying and gives Bèze two mansi for his soul, located at Fontenelle and near Fouvent. He also gives a serf with his children.

3 Montigny, 17 km northeast of Bèze.
4 The manuscript reads, "Et &."
5 Grancey, 29 km northwest of Bèze.
1 Cusey, 19 km north-northwest of Bèze.
2 Montsaugeon, 22 km north of Bèze.

Cartulary, fols. 123v–124r.
Bougaud-Garnier, p. 408.

Carta de Fontanelliis

Notum permaneat omnibus legentibus hęc quod miles quidam de Monte Salione,[1] nomine Pontius de Bigorna, in die sue dormitionis, pro sua anima suorumque antecessorum fidelium, Deo et Sancto Petro et Besuensi ecclesię perpetualiter habendos duos mansos tribuit, unum in uilla quę Fontinellas[2] nuncupatur cum suis appenditiis, et alterum in uilla quę Curcellas uocatur, iuxta Fontemuennam,[3] et unum seruum cum filiis et filiabus suis in uilla Campanię.[4]

Signum Humberti filii eius cum sua matre, Walonis de Calmis, Alelmi de Icioma.[5]

223

1088–1108

Milo, a knight of Beaumont, makes gifts to Bèze for his dead son Hugh, consisting of two mansi at Fontenelle and a serf with his children.

Cartulary, fol. 124r.
Bougaud-Garnier, p. 408.

Item alia

Fideliter retineant omnes qui has audierint uel legerint litteras, quod miles quidam de Bellomonte,[1] Milo nomine, pro remedio anime filii sui defuncti Hugonis adita sua suorumque antecessorum sanctis apostolis Petro et Paulo et Besuensi cęnobio duos mansos tradidit in uilla, quę Fontinellas[2] nuncupatur, cum appendiciis suis ex toto liberaliter, et unum seruum comparem terrę, nomine Widonem, et filium eius Albertum et filiam eius Alixem.

---

1 Montsaugeon, 22 km north of Bèze. Birgorna is uidentified.
2 Fontenelle, 9 km northeast of Bèze.
3 Fouvent, 35 km northeast of Bèze. Garnier indicates that Curcellas has now disappeared.
4 Champagne, 10 km southeast of Bèze.
5 Chaume, 12 km north-northeast of Bèze; and Isômes, 20 km north of Bèze and 2 km south of Montsaugeon.
1 Beaumont, 7 km east of Bèze.
2 Fontenelle, 9 km northeast of Bèze.

Signum Milonis qui donum fecit, Richardi filii eius, Ęuuini, Walonis, Aymonis de Fontanas,[3] Widonis filii eius, Stephani abbatis,[4] Wilenci, Ioffredi, Albrici. Acta sunt hęc tempore Philippi regis.[5]

This document is dated by the king and the abbot.

224

Early twelfth century (?)

Hugh Troaudus and his younger brother give Bèze half a villa for their father's and mother's souls. In return they receive a counter-gift of eleven solidi.

Cartulary, fol. 124r–v.
Bougaud-Garnier, p. 409.

Carta de Vachiriaco

Sciant omnes tam presentes quam futuri quod Hugo, cognomento Troaudus, et frater eius iunior Waldinus donauerunt Deo et Sancto Petro et ecclesię medietatem uille quę Vachiriacus[1] uocatur, pro anima patris sui Rainaldi et matris suę et omnium fidelium antecessorum suorum, sicuti illi tenebant et antecessores illorum tenuerunt, in terris cultis et incultis, in pratis et in siluis et in usus aquarum omnino totum cum omni libertate. Et pro signo dedit illis duobus fratribus Wido monachus qui Pauliacum[2] tenebat xi solidos nummorum.

Vt hęc carta inconuulsa permaneat, adsignamus ei testes. Signum Oddonis militis de Bellomonte.[3] Signum uxoris eius, Ailadis uocate, Widonis militis cognomento Margot, Rodulfi militis fratris eius, Hugonis uillici de Pauliaco, Widonis monachi, et aliorum multorum.

3 Fontenotte, 7 km northwest of Bèze.
4 Stephen, abbot of Bèze (1088–1120).
5 Philip I, king of France (1060–1108).
1 Garnier says this place has now disappeared but was near Fontaine-Française. It appears in document 92, from the first half of the eleventh century, as an unpopulated former vicus.
2 Pouilly, 15 km northeast of Bèze.
3 Beaumont, 7 km east of Bèze.

225

Early twelfth century (?)

The brothers Achard and Pagan, knights of St-Julien, make Bèze a gift for their souls.

Cartulary, fol. 124v.
Bougaud-Garnier, p. 409.

Item alia

Simili modo per aliud tempus duo milites fratres, scilicet Achardus et Paganus de Sancto Iuliano,[1] delegauerunt Deo et Sancto Petro et Besuensi ęcclesię, pro remedio animarum suarum, quicquid de proprio fundo habebant in illa uilla deserta quę Vachiriacus nuncupatur, in terris, in pratis, et in siluis, et in decursus aquarum.

Signum Warnerii, Vlgerii, Widonis, Walterii, Humberti, et aliorm multorum.

This is the same deserted villa as in the preceding document.

226

Early twelfth century

Sewin, a knight of Ray, makes Bèze gifts for his father's soul, consisting of a manse at Vauconcourt.

Cartulary, fol. 124v.
Bougaud-Garnier, p. 410.

Carta de Wascum curtis

Notum sit omnibus tam presentibus quam futuris quod Seuuinus miles de Raico,[1] pro anima patris sui Widonis et pro anima sua suorumque fidelium antecessorum, dedit Deo et Sancto Petro et Besuensi ecclesię in presentia domni Stephanis abbatis[2] et monachorum unum mansum de suo proprio fundo cum omnibus appendiciis suis, in uilla de agris quę Wascumcurtis[3] dicitur, de siluis, de pratis, cum omni libertate, sub tali testimonio.

---

1 St-Julien, 12 km southwest of Bèze.

1 Ray-sur-Saône, 43 km east-northeast of Bèze.

2 Stephen, abbot of Bèze (1088–1120).

3 Vauconcourt, 8 km north of Ray.

Signum Seuuini et uxoris eius, Widonis qui est dominus Fontisuenne, Oddonis de Bellomonte, Hugonis de uilla quę Geniperias dicitur, Beraldi fratris eius, Kalonis de Siluiniaco,[4] et aliorum multorum.

This document can be dated to the early twelfth century because Wido of Ray was still alive in 1099 (document 194).

227

Early twelfth century (?)

The knight Sewin of Ray gives Bèze two mansi, with their serfs, at Fedry and Vauconcourt, acting with his wife.

Cartulary, fols. 124v–125r.
Bougaud-Garnier, p. 410.

Carta de Firdriaco

Ratum et cognitum permaneat modo uiuentibus post nosque futuris quod Seuuinus miles et eius uxor de loco quę Villesons[1] dicitur Sancto Petro et Besuensi ecclesię, pro remedio anime suę et suorum parentum, in elemosina duos mansos concessit, unum in uilla quę nuncupatur Firdriacus[2] cum seruo, Bisontico nomine, manente, et alium in uilla quę Wascumcurtis appellatur,[3] cum seruo ad eundem mansum pertinente.

Signum Widonis de Raiaco, Seuuini, Hermuini, Teoderici de Treuia,[4] Fulconis, Oddonis, Moranni archipresbiteri.

This is the same knight as the previous document. It was perhaps done a little earlier than that one because Sewin's father is still alive.

4 Fouvent, 35 km northeast of Bèze; Beaumont, 7 km east of Bèze; Genevrières, 38 km north-northeast of Bèze; and Savigny, 2 km east of Genevrières and 39 km northeast of Bèze.

1 Vellexon, 4 km southwest of Ray.

2 Garnier identifies this place as Fedry, near Dampierre.

3 Vauconcourt, 8 km north of Ray.

4 Traves, 56 km northeast of Bèze.

228

Early twelfth century (?)

The knight Ponce of St-Seine gives Bèze a serf and land at "Morengis."

Cartulary, fol. 125r.
Bougaud-Garnier, p. 411.

Carta de Morengis

Summopere curandum est omnibus quibus Deus dedit feliciter frui de presenti uita, ut sint semper solliciti de perpetua. Sed de hoc bene fuit memor in uita sua quidam miles Pontius de uilla quę numcupatur Sanctus Sequanus iuxta Polliacum,[1] qui pro remedio animę sui filii, scilicet Widonis, sua adita et parentum suorum tradidit principibus apostolorum Petro et Paulo et Besuensi ecclesię seruum unum, Teuuinum, et terram de Morengis[2] et nemus quod uocatur Noaino ex totum sicut possidebat.

Signum Poncii qui hoc dedit, Nerduini fratris eius, Widrici de Arco, Oddonis Bellimontis,[3] Aymonis, Hugonis Columbe, Hugonis uillici de Palliaco, Lamberti filii eius, Iohannis filii eius.

229

Early twelfth century (?)

Gertrude, wife of Henri of Neuvelle, with her daughter and son-in-law, makes a gift to Bèze for Henri's soul, consisting of half a manse and two serfs.

Cartulary, fol. 125r–v.
Bougaud-Garnier, p. 411.

Carta de Vetus Vineis

Per has cognitum fiat litteras quod Gertrudis, uxor Henrici de Nouauilla,[1] et Warnerius gener eius et filia eius uxor Warnerii, cognomine Kara, pro remedio animę supradicti Henrici et suarum suorumque antecessorum, obtulerunt Deo et Sancto Petro et Besuensi ecclesię super altare in Vetusuineis[2] uilla

1 St-Seine-sur-Vingeanne, 13 km northeast of Bèze; it is 3 km south of Pouilly.
2 This place is unidentified, but it also appears in documents 103, 128, and 136.
3 Arc-sur-Tille, 15 km south-southwest of Bèze; and Beaumont, 7 km east of Bèze.
1 Neuvelle, 24 km northeast of Bèze.
2 Viévigne, 4 km southwest of Bèze.

medietatem mansi, cum sex iugeribus terrę, de proprio fundo, et simul unum seruum nomine Tetbertum et unam ancillam, istius sororem, nomine Oltrudem. Vterque et seruus et ancilla nati sunt de Petro rustico de Vetusuineis.

Signum illorum qui fecerunt donum, Oddonis, Richardi fratris eius, Hugonis de Conulensi castro,[3] Rainaldi. Rainaldi serui eius de Vetusuineis. Signum domni Stephani abbatis,[4] Wilenci monachi, Iohannis cantoris, et aliorum monachorum.

230

c. 1100

Alburgis Pagana, wife of Walter of Minot, is dying and makes Bèze a gift of all she had at Pichanges for her soul. Her two sons agree, along with their uncle, her brother.

Cartulary, fol. 125v.
Bougaud-Garnier, p. 412.

Carta de Pichangiis

Pro certo sciant omnes tam futuri quam presentes quod Alburgis cognomine Pagana, uxor Walterii de Mignoio,[1] ueniens ad obitum suum, pro sua anima dedit Deo et Sancto Petro et Besuensi ecclesię partem suam, scilicet quicquid habebat uel possidebat in uita sua, in uilla quę Picangias[2] uocatur, in terris, in pratis, in siluis, omnino totum. Hanc elemosinam confirmauerunt filii supradicte matrone, Raimundus uidelicet et Walterius, necnon et Seuualdus auunculus illorum, cognomento Balbus.

Vt hęc carta inconuulsa permaneat, assignamus ei testes. Signum Oddonis militis de Itio,[3] Pontii filii eius, Haymonis militis, Heinrici qui erat minister et cliens ipsius dominę, Widonis sacerdotis, Petri canonici de Granciaco.[4] De monachis, signum domni Stephani abbatis,[5] Wilenci, Iohannis, Albrici, et

3 Coublanc, 28 km north-northeast of Bèze.
4 Stephen, abbot of Bèze (1088–1120).
1 Minot, 37 km northwest of Bèze.
2 Pichanges, 9 km west of Bèze.
3 Is-sur-Tille, 14 km northwest of Bèze.
4 Grancey, 29 km northwest of Bèze.
5 Stephen, abbot of Bèze (1088–1120).

de familia Sancti Petri quamplures adfuerunt, Otbertus, Hugo, Gyslebertus, Iohannes, Aydulfus.[6]

For Alburgis and her dying gift, see also document 207, given in 1100. Many of the witnesses are the same, suggesting this document was given at about the same time.

231

Early twelfth century (?)

Lord Peter of Montsaugeon and his wife Eva give Bèze a house plot, which they had held from the abbot. They do so for the good of their souls.

Cartulary, fols. 125v–126r.
Bougaud-Garnier, pp. 412–413.

Karta de quadam plastro domus in Besua sito

Sciant omnes tam presentes quam futuri quod Domnus Petrus, Montis Salionis[1] dominus, et uxor eius Eua quandam sedem domus uacuam, quam plastrum uocant, quod tenebat ipse et antecessores eius de abbatibus Besuensibus et de monachis, conpunctus corde pro remedio anime suę suorumque antecessorum reddidit illud Sancto Petro et Besuensi ecclesię et monachis penitus liberum, tali modo ut si aliquis de heredibus suis deinceps aliquam calumpniam super hoc facere uoluerit, anathema sit, maranata in perpetuum.

Vt hęc redditio inconuulsa permaneat, subscribamus ei testes. Signum Petri, Hugonis de Varua, Rodulfi militis de Aquis, Hugonis clerici de Miribello,[2] de familia Sancti Petri Rotberti prepositi, Otberti cocci, Hugonis, Willelmi, Lamberti, Tebaldi, Iohannis cocci, et aliorum multorm. De monachis, Signum Domni Stephani abbatis,[3] Warnerii prioris, Wilenci, Iohannis, Philippi, Widrici, Roffredi et aliorum.

6 Of these household servants of the abbey, Otbertus and Iohannes were most likely the cooks by those names found in nearby documents.

1 Montsaugeon, 22 km north of Bèze.

2 Vesvres, 26 km north-northwest of Bèze; Achey, 28 km northeast of Bèze; and Mirebeau, 9 km south-southeast of Bèze.

3 Stephen, abbot of Bèze (1088–1120).

232

Early twelfth century (?)

The brothers Henry and Bernard of Framont had an allod in the woods of the monks of Bèze. Henry, reduced to poverty, gave away all his property to Hugh of Beire for his support. Hugh in turn gave Henry's allodial land in the woods to Bèze for his late son's soul. Bernard's son made a similar gift. They receive five solidi as a counter-gift.

Cartulary, fol. 126r–v.
Bougaud-Garnier, p. 413.

Carta de nemore Valle Victoris dicto

Hoc ad memoriam reducatur quod duo fratres fuerunt, Henricus scilicet et Bernardus de Fracto Monte.[1] Hi dicebant se habere quoddam alodium infra terram nostram in Valle Victoris. Supradictus quoque Henricus ueniens ad paupertatem dedit Domno Hugoni de Beria[2] omnem suam hereditatem, et ipse tutauit eum usque ad mortem. Et partem supradicti alodii Henrici dedit supradictus Hugo Deo et Sancto Petro et Besuensi ecclesię pro anima filii sui defuncti Warnerii pueri. Partem quoque Bernardi de ipso alodio dedit Ęuuinus filius Bernardi, et mater eius Poncia et sororius eius Milo et Richardus frater Euuini dederunt et confirmauerunt utramque donationem, pro anima patris sui Bernardi et pro animabus suis suormque antecessorum. Domnus Oddilo monachus noster dedit illis pro signo quinque solidos nummorum.

Vt hęc carta inconuulsa permaneat, adnotamus testes. Signum Stephani abbatis,[3] Widonis prioris, Albrici, Oddilonis. De laicis, Ęuuini, Milonis, Hugonis famuli, Gysleberti, Rotberti de Vetusuineis,[4] Bernardi, Rainaldi. Et in ipso die supradictus Euuinus iunctis manibus effectus est homo Domni Stephani abbatis pro quibusdam quas super eum habebat calumpniis.

233

Early twelfth century

The knight Ponce, son of Henry of La Ferté, makes Bèze a gift for his father, consisting of three men and two women. He signifies the gift by putting the Rule of St Benedict on the altar.

1 Framont, 25 km northeast of Bèze.
2 Beire, 8 km southwest of Bèze.
3 Stephen, abbot of Bèze (1088–1120).
4 Viévigne, 4 km southwest of Bèze.

Cartulary, fols. 126v–127r.
Bougaud-Garnier, p. 414.

Carta de hominibus Sancto Petro a Poncio datis

Clarificetur cunctis modo uiuentibus post nosque futuris quod Pontius miles, filius Heinrici de Firmitate quę dicitur Anrosiacus,[1] pro anima patris sui suorumque antecessorum et pro sua anima, per consilium suorum fidelium, dedit Deo et Sancto Petro et Besuensi ecclesię liberaliter et perpetualiter quinque homines, tres mares et duas feminas, scilicet Gandradam cum tribus filiis suis, quorum hęc sunt nomina, primus Petrus, secundus Albricus, tercius Teodoricus. Altera de feminis uocatur Helisabeth, uxor Petri desuper nominati. Hoc donum fecit supradictus Pontius in festiuitate Sancti Petri, et propria manu donum roborauit super altare per librum qui uocatur Regula Sancti Benedicti, coram multis testibus, tali pacto ut si umquam aliquis de parentibus suis, siue aliquis instigante diabolo, huic carte contraire aut calumpniare uoluerit, anathema sit.

Huic carte assignamus testes. Signum ipsius Pontii qui hoc donum fecit. Signum Richardi et Widonis fratris eius de Vircillis,[2] Iulonis de Granando, Widonis filii Rainaldi Conulensis, Willelmi de Fossato, Oddilonis de Lissiaco,[3] Hugonis de Torcennaco,[4] et aliorum nobilium qui presentes fuerunt. De monachis uero, Signum Stephani abbatis,[5] Wilenci, Albrici Captiui, Antonii fratris ipsius Poncii, et multorum aliorum.

See also document 218, Henry of La Ferté's own gift. There is some overlap of the witness list for the two documents.

234

Early twelfth century (?)

Girald of Lux, a dependent villager, has damaged the monk's property, but the quarrel is now settled when the abbot releases him from certain dues for his lifetime.

1 La Ferté-sur-Amance, 51 km northeast of Bèze; and Anrosey, 2 km west of there.
2 Verseilles, 33 km north of Bèze.
3 Grenant, 31 km north-northeast of Bèze; Coublanc, 28 km north-northeast of Bèze; Le Fossé, 12 km northwest of Bèze; and Licey, 8 km east-northeast of Bèze.
4 Torcenay, 41 km north-northeast of Bèze.
5 Stephen, abbot of Bèze (1088–1120).

Cartulary, fol. 127r–v.
Bougaud-Garnier, pp. 414–415.

Carta de feodo Gyraldi de Luco

Notum sit omnibus modo uiuentibus post nosque futuris quod Gyraldus noster uillicus de Luco,[1] multociens discordatus est a nostro seruitio propter quasdam iniurias quas faciebat de terris nostris, que non pertinebant ad suum foedum. De qua re domnus abbas Stephanus[2] per consilium fratrum uolens terminare ex utraque parte pacem et concordiam, suo iussu et iussu Giraldi per monachos et per laicos fecit inquirere ad purum feodum Gyraldi de uillicatione. Inquisitione facta inuenti sunt quinquaginta duo iugera terrę et quattuor falces de prato. Hęc iugera suprascripta et has falces de prato concessit domnus abbas Stephanus et monachi nostri supradicto Giraldo, decimum de uiciis ad suum foedum, medietatem quoque illius annone quę uocatur Vngranus, de qua erat contentio inter illum et monachos quam ibi ex toto dimist, scilicet in supradicto placito domnus abbas et monachi concesserunt ei illam supradictam medietatem Vngrani tempore uitę suę et non amplius, propter misericordiam et bonum finem. Et in uno quoque anno examen de horreo monachorum uel unum becharium, hoc est medietatem emine de frumento uel de sigilo. Hoc concessit domnus abbas Stephanus per consilium fratrum Giraldo, ut fidelis permaneret Sancto Petro et Besuensi ecclesię melius quam antea fuerat ipse et frater eius Olardus.

Huius rei adsignamus testes. Signum Stephani abbatis, Widonis prioris, Wilenci, Albrici, Landrici, Teoderici. De laicis Giraldi, Olardi de Luco, Hugonis uillici, Euurardi, Gyraldi, Giraldi filii Gunterii, Giraldi, Hugonis famuli, et aliorum multorum.

See also document 236.

235

Early twelfth century (?)

Alisendis, wife of Aymo of Fontaine, is dying and makes Bèze the gift of half a mill for the good of her soul. Her husband and son agree.

Cartulary, fol. 127v.
Bougaud-Garnier, pp. 415–416.

1 Lux, 5 km northwest of Bèze.
2 Stephen, abbot of Bèze (1088–1120).

Karta de molendino apud Fontanas

Opere precium duximus adnotare litteris quod Alisendis uxor Aymonis de Fontanis,[1] ueniens ad mortem, dedit pro sua anima Deo et Sancto Petro et Besuensi ęcclesię, cum omni honore et omni libertate, medietatem molendini de prato Hayrardi, laude et concessione Aymonis uiri sui et Widonis filii sui.

Vt hęc donatio firma et inconuulsa persistat, adsignamus testes. Signum Aymonis de Fontanis qui hoc donum fecit, Widonis filii eius, Hugonis Carruce, Wilenci militis, Hugonis de Porta, Bertranni militis de Fontanis, Herberti uillịci et Oddonis fratris eius, Hildemari presbiteri, et aliorum multorum. Et de monachis nostris, Signum Domni Stephani abbatis,[2] Wilenci, Girardi, Iohannis, Albrici.

236

Early twelfth century (?)

Girald of Lux and Humbert of Spoy give up claims to tithes at Lux that should rightfully go to Bèze.

Cartulary, fol. 127v.
Bougaud-Garnier, p. 416.

Carta de Luco

Memoria et recognicio sit omnibus modo uiuentibus postque futuris quod Giraldus de Luco[1] uillicus noster et Humbertus, cognomento Ingelricus, de Cipeto[2] quandam partem decimę de terra quę dicitur Sancti Vincentii de Luco, quam per aliquot annos male subripuerant et sub anathemate et furto retinuerant, agnoscentes reatum suum et culpam clamantes, restituerunt Sancto Petro et Besuensi ecclesię, in presentia domni Stephani abbatis[3] et monachorum, promittentes nunquam per se neque per aliquem successorum suorum tam execrabilem rapinam repetere.

See also document 234 for Girald of Lux; this agreement appears to be part of the settlement of the same long-standing quarrel.

1 Fontaine-Française, 10 km northeast of Bèze.
2 Stephen, abbot of Bèze (1088–1120).
1 Lux, 5 km northwest of Bèze.
2 Spoy, 6 km southwest of Bèze.
3 Stephen, abbot of Bèze (1088–1120).

237

Cirey, 28 October 1109

The monks of Bèze reach a settlement with the monks of St-Léger over tithes at Drambon, as well as a woods and a field. The agreement is reached by the respective abbots as well as by the abbots of St-Bénigne and of St-Germain of Auxerre, under the direction of the bishop of Langres.

Cartulary, fols. 127v–129r.
Bougaud-Garnier, pp. 416–418.
Summarized in Brequigny, *Table* 2:402.

Carta de pertinentibus ad Arcionem

In nomine Patris et Filii et Spiritus Sancti. Cum precedentium patrum statuta a posteris cotidie uideamus dissolui, et ea quę in mundo firmius stare uidebantur aut iam cediderint aut casum minitentur ne dum uerba, quę cum formari ceperint, iam non sunt, litterarum tenaci memorie, conmendare studuimus qualiter inter monachos Besuenses et monachos Sancti Leodegarii[1] ex diutina contentione pax et concordia firmata sit. Hęc uero contentio fuerat de decimis duarum ecclesiarum Sancti Petri, uidelicet Danblin et Danbrun,[2] et de una silua quam Ferrerarias uocant, et de uno campo.

Placuit itaque Rotberto uenerabili Lingonicę sedis episcopo Stephanum Besuensem abbatem et Hugonem Autisiodorensem illius loci, uidelicet Sancti Leodegarii, abbatem, Ierentonem quoque Diuionensem[3] conuocare, ac demum predicta contentio hoc modo terminata est. Laudatum est atque sanccitum ab abbatibus Stephano Besuensi et predicto Hugone Autisiodorensi et Rotberto tunc temporis priore Sancti Leodegarii et ab utriusque partis hominibus quod parrochiani Sancti Leodegarii ex eo quod in ipsis parrechiis, uidelicet Danblin et Danbrun, laborauerint, medietatem decimarum secum deferent et medietatem ecclesiis relinquent, in predicta silua quam Ferrarias uocari diximus communitatem nostri homines et illorum habebunt. De tribus siluis Sancti Leodegarii, quarum hęc sunt nomina, Granzuuaure, Chalmes, Droul, faciet monachus qui

1 The priory of St-Léger-de-Champeaux, dependent on St-Germain of Auxerre, located 19 km south-southeast of Bèze.

2 Drambon, 17 km south-southeast of Bèze. The two twelfth-century places have been united into one modern village.

3 Robert, bishop of Langres (1084–1111); Stephen, abbot of Bèze (1088–1120); Hugh of Montaigu, abbot of St-Germain of Auxerre (1100–1115); and Jarenton, abbot of St-Bénigne of Dijon (1076–1113).

Arcioni[4] erit, domum suam et ut uulgaliter dicitur aasimentum domus sue. In predictam siluam quam Ferrarias uocari diximus, si laboratum fuerit, cuius erit fundus terre ipsius erit et tercia. Pasturam in nostris et illorum terris communem habebunt utrumque sine dampno tamen. Et si dampnum factum fuerit, si sine clamore redditum fuerit, pax erit. Quod si clamor ad Dominum peruenerit, dampnum restaurabit et legem Domino persoluet ipse qui dampnum fecerit. Campum illum qui est intra terram uille quę dicitur Trescasas,[5] sicut fuerat monstratus et aratus, dimisit domnus abbot Stephanus Besuensis Sancto Leodegario et domno Hugoni Autisiodorensi abbati.

Facta est hęc concordia in uno campo super Cyriacum[6] ab abbatibus Stephano Besuensi et Hugone Autisiodorensi. Ex monachis Besuensibus affuerunt Warnerius prior, Lebaldus, Albericus qui Arcioni morabatur, Landricus frater Hugonis cognomento Columbe. De monachis Autisiodorensibus affuerunt Rotbertus prior de Sancto Leodegario, Itherius secretarius, Ænielbertus, Artaldus prior de Sancto Marcello.[7] Ex militibus Humbertus de Lissei[8] et Oddilo frater eius, et Hugo Columba, Wido de Agullun, Wido de Danbrun et Humbertus frater eius, et Hugo prepositus de Sancto Leodegario. Emelbertus prepositus Autisiodorensis. De familia Sancti Petri, Arlebaldus de Balenaua[9] prepositus, Otbertus coccus, Gislebertus famulus. De familia Sancti Leodegarii, Hugo de Balenaua uillicus et Oddilo, Paganus prepositus de Magnei,[10] et Humbertus et Hugo fratres eius. Petrus de Mosteriolo.[11]

Acta sunt hęc anno ab incarnatione Domini MCVIIII, indictione ii, epacta xvii, concurrente iv, Hlucdouuico rege filio Philippi regnante,[12] anno ii imperii eius, episcopali cathedrę Lingonensium presidente domno Rotberto, qui hoc placitum tenuit et hanc concordiam laudauit, die uicesima viii mensis Octobris.

Considerans etiam domnus Stephanus abbas karitatem refrigescere, ueritatem a filiis hominum diminui, nec solum largitiones quę olim fiebant ecclesiis Dei maxima ex parte remanere uerum etiam largita auferri, Romam peciit, et

4 Arçon, 13 km south of Bèze.
5 Trochères, 14 km south-southeast of Bèze.
6 Cirey, 18 km south of Bèze and 5 km west of St-Léger.
7 Artald, prior of St-Marcel of Chalon (c. 1108–c. 1120).
8 Licey, 8 km east-northeast of Bèze.
9 Belleneuve, 12 km south of Bèze.
10 Magny, 10 km south-southwest of Bèze.
11 Mitreuil, 15 km south of Bèze.
12 Louis VI (1108–1137), son of King Philip.

ad eum qui tunc apostolice cathedre sedebat papam, domnum uidelicet Paschalem, accessit et Beati Petri auctoritate, necnon et illius qui tunc loco ipsius uniuersalis atque catholicę ecclesię curam habebat, predicti pape priuilegio inuiolabili confirmari fecit, queumque istud Besuense cenobium possidebat, siue in futurum concessione pontificum, liberalite principum, uel oblatione fidelium, iuste atque canonice posset adipisci. Potitus autem eo quod quesierat, ea quę retro sunt obliuiscens et in anterioribus se extendens, pericula et labores uie, hyemps enim erat, parui pendens non reminiscebatur pressure propter gaudium subsecutum. Nos uero exemplum priuilegii illius, curauimus subscribere infra.

238

Lateran, 1 January 1105

Pope Paschal II issues a privilege for Bèze.

Cartulary, fols. 129r–130v.
Cocquelines, *Bullarum privilegiorum ac diplomatum Romanorum pontificum*, 2:125–126, no. 19.
Mansi, *Sacrorum conciliorum collectio*, vol. 20, 1033–1035.
Labbe and Cossart, *Sacrosancta concilia*, vol. 10, 677–679, no. 62.
PL 163:142–144, no. 137, from Mansi, *Sacrorum conciliorum collectio.*
Bougaud-Garnier, pp. 419–422.
Summarized in Brequigny, *Table* 2:368.
Summarized in Jaffe, *Regesta pontificum Romanorum*, 1:719, no. 6004 (4483).

Priuilegium domni Paschalis pape

Paschalis episcopus seruus seruorum Dei,[1] dilecto filio Stephano Besuensi abbati[2] eiusque successoribus regulariter promouendis in perpetuum.

Religiosis desideriis dignum est facilem prebere consensum, ut fidelis deuotio çelerem sortiatur effectum. Proinde nos religioni uestrę desideria confouentes, uestro Besuensi monasterio in honore beatorum apostolorum Petri et Pauli edificato, eorundem apostolorum ex apostolice sedis benignitate munimen inpendimus. Constituentes et presentis decreti pagina sancientes ut ecclesia de Albiniaco, et ecclesia Sancti Benigni, et capella Sancte Marie quę

1 Pope Paschal II (1099–1118).
2 Stephen, abbot of Bèze (1088–1120).

castello Montis Saluionis sita est,[3] ad supradictam Albinaci ecclesiam pertinens, ecclesia etiam Camlintensis, et ecclesia de Maiasch cum appenditiis suis, capella de Fonuenz[4] uestro semper cenobio ita firme, ita libere, quieteque permaneant, sicut a fratre nostro Rotberto Lingonensi episcopo cum tocius Lingonensis cleri conuientia tradite sunt.

Idipsum etiam de duabus prebendis statuimus quas bone memorie Harduinus et Hugo Lingonenses episcopi fratribus in ecclesia Sancti Gengulfi apud Lingonas Domino seruientibus tradiderunt.[5] Idipsum etiam statuimus super ecclesia de Siuoio cum pertinentiis suis, super capella Sancti Mauricii seu Sancti Dionisii, capella Sancti Valeriani, et ecclesia de Raiol, et parte quarta ecclesię Sancti Martini de Monasterio, seu ceteris rebus quas bone memorie Hugo Bisontinus episcopus uestro monasterio contradidit.[6] Porro ecclesia Sancti Remigii, que est in burgo Besue, et ecclesia de Belenauo cum appendiciis suis, ita in possessione uestra liberas, ita ab omnibus consuetudinalibus inmunes semper manere censemus, sicut a bone memorię Alberico quondam Lingonensi episcopo seu successore eius Rainardo eiusdem ecclesię uenerabilii episcopo libertate, ac inmunitate donatę sunt.[7]

Preterea confirmamus uobis ecclesiam Sancti Saluatoris de Veteribus Vineis, ecclesiam Sancti Martini de Luco, ecclesiam Sancti Laurentii de Beria, ecclesiam Sancti Benigni de Boensis uilla, ecclesiam Sancti Sequani que est parrochialis, ecclesiam Sancti Valerii de Talemaro, ecclesiam Sancto Leodegarii de Genziniaco, ecclesiam Sancti Martini Belmontis,[8] capellam quoque Sancti

3 Aubigny is 2 km west of Montsaugeon, itself 22 km north of Bèze. St-Broing is 28 km north of Bèze. These churches were given to the monks by Bishop Robert of Langres (1084–1111); see document 189.

4 Champlitte, 24 km north-northeast of Bèze; Maâtz, 30 km north-northeast of Bèze; and Fouvent, 35 km northeast of Bèze. Bishop Robert had given Bèze these churches in 1084–1087 and 1088–1099; see documents 188 and 191.

5 This gift was made in 1059; see document 124. The bishops of Langres mentioned here are Hugh of Verdun (1031–1049) and Harduin of Tonnerre (1049–1065).

6 The relevant charter of the archbishop of Besançon, doubtless Hugh III (1085–1101), does not exist. The places referred to are Savoyeux, 37 km east-northeast of Bèze; unidentified; and Motey-sur-Saône, 36 km east-northeast of Bèze. Hugh III had confirmed the donation of the first and third of these places to Bèze; see document 193.

7 The chapel of St-Remi of Bèze was freed from dues by Bishop Hugh-Rainard of Langres (1065–1084); see document 184. Belleneuve, 12 km south of Bèze, was originally given to the monks in the ninth century, when Alberic was bishop of Langres (821–838); see document 8.

8 Viévigne, 4 km southwest of Bèze; Lux, 5 km northwest of Bèze; Beire, 8 km southwest of Bèze; Bouhans, 18 km east-northeast of Bèze; St-Seine-sur-Vingeanne, 13 km northeast of Bèze; Talmay, 18 km southeast of Bèze; Jancigny, 14 km southeast of Bèze; and Beaumont, 7 km east of Bèze.

Marcellini quam bone memorię Geilo Lingonensis episcopus ad luminaria altaris ecclesię uestrę contulisse donoscitur, cum Beati Prudentii martyris sub eodem altari reliquias collocauit,[9] cum appendiciis et mancipiis utriusque sexus, sicut ea supradictus episcopus Virdunensi episcopo conmutauit. Ecclesiam quoque Sancti Ypoliti de Pontiliaco cum appendiciis suis, ecclesiam de Casoto Sancti Symphoriani,[10] ecclesiam Sanctę Marię de Fonuenz, a Lamberto Lingonensi episcopo datam cum pertinentiis suis.[11] Ecclesiam quoque Sancti Gengulfi superius nominatam, infra muros Lingonice ciuitatis. Porro uillam Besue sanctorum apostolorum Petri et Pauli monasterio adiacentem cum omnibus pertinentiis suis, ab omnium hominum uexationibus liberam, sicut hodie est, uobis in perpetuum manere sancimus. Piscariam quoque a Fontis loco[12] usque ad princianum in iure ac possessione uestra semper seruari libere, quieteque sancimus.

Preterea quęcumque in presentarum nunc idem monasterium possidet siue in futurum concessione pontificum, liberalitate principum, uel oblatione fidelium, iuste atque canonice poterit adipisci, firma tibi tuisque successoribus et illibata permaneant.

Decernimus ergo ut nulli omnino hominum liceat idem cenobium temere perturbare aut eius possessiones auferre, uel ablatas retinere, minuere, uel temarariis uexationibus fatigare, sed omnia integra conseruentur eorum pro quorum sustentatione et gubernatione concessa sunt, usibus omnimodis profutura, salua Lingonensis episcopi canonica retinentia. Et episcopo tamen et episcopi ministris omnino non liceat monasterium ipsum aut eius loca grauare, nec ornamenta ecclesię qualibet occasione diripere, nec exactiones aliquas aut consuetudines quę fratrum quieti noceant irrogare. Interdicimus etiam ne quis idem Besuense cenobium in cellam redigere audeat, quandiu monastici ordinis obseruantia illic Domino prestante uiguerit.

Si quis sane in crastinum archiepiscopus uel episcopus, imperator, aut rex, princeps, aut dux, comes, uicecomes, aut iudex, uel qualibet ecclesiastica, secularisue persona, hanc nostrę constitutionis paginam sciens contra eam temere uenire temptauerit, secundo tercioue conmonita, si non satisfactione congrua emendauerit, potestatis, honorisque sui dignitate careat, reumque se diuino iudicio existere de perpetrata iniquitate cognoscat, et a sacratissimo corpore ac sanguine Dei et Domini redemptoris nostri Ihesu Christi aliena fiat, atque

9 This gift from Bishop Geilo of Langres (880–889) took place in 883; see document 21.

10 Pontailler-sur-Saône, 21 km southeast of Bèze; and Chazeuil, 10 km north of Bèze. These churches were also included in document 21.

11 Bishop Lambert of Langres (1016–1031) gave the monks the church at Fouvent in 1019; see document 59.

12 Fontaine-Française, 10 km northeast of Bèze.

in extremo examine districte ultioni subiaceat. Cunctis autem eidem loco iusta seruantibus, sit pax Domini nostri Ihesu Christi quatinus et hic fructum bone actionis percipiant, et apud districtum iudicem premia eternę pacis inueniant. Amen.

Scriptum per manum Rainerii scriniarii et notarii sacri palacii. Datum Laterani per manum Iohannis sanctę Romanę ecclesię diaconi cardinalis. Kalendas Ianuarii, indictione xiii, incarnationis Dominice anno MCV, pontificatus autem domni Paschalis II pape vi.

Ego Paschalis catholice ecclesię subscripsi.

The monks of St-Bénigne also received a privilege from Pope Paschal, issued the same day; theirs, which still exists as an original; it listed much more extensive property than Bèze's. The pope also consecrated the church of St-Bénigne two days before he consecrated the church of Bèze, a detail omitted in the following.[13]

Euolutis igitur annis duobus contigit eundem papam Paschalem Galliarum partes inuisere. Deueniens autem usque ad nos, a domno Stephano abbate et a nobis aliis cum copioso cardinalium tam episcoporum quam presbiterorum ac clericorum suorum comitatu, necnon et aliorum episcoporum, abbatum diuersorumque graduum ecclesiastici ordinis in hoc monasterio Besuense deuote susceptus est. Vbi usque in tercium diem demoratus, cum situs huius loci multum, fratrumque conuentus et ordo plurimum ei placuisset, omnia laudans, omnia benedicens, ad ultimum in capitulum ueniens consedit, ubi sermonem faciens, ab eo loco incepit, ubi dicitur, "Fratres, quecumque scripta sunt, ad nostram doctrinam scripta sunt, ut per pacientiam et consolationem scripturarum spem habeamus" [Rom. 15:4]. Et quia monachis loquebatur, quibus maxime pacientia necessaria est, eam posuit quasi fundamentum. Deinde ostendans quod pacientia spem operetur, de spe disserens peruenit ad fidem. Fidem autem nos docens tenere non fictam, de ea etiam multa nos edocens tandem ad karitatem, quę Deus est [1 John 4:8], conscendit. Dixit et de ea, immo de eo, ut tempus et ratio expetebat. Cumque sermonem terminasset, rogatus a domno abbate, et ab aliis fratribus, ut pote qui locum tenebat eius, cui data est potestas ligandi et soluendi in celo et in terra [Matt. 18:18], ut nobis et fratribus nostris tam uiuis quam defunctis absolutionem daret et benedictionem annuit, et incipiens L Psalmum, cum oratione dominica, et collecta uti rogatus fuerat, nos absoluit et benedixit.

13 *Chartes et documents de Saint-Bénigne de Dijon,* 2:188–191, 196–198, nos. 411, 419.

Nec illud pretermittendum, quod altare sanctorum apostolorum Petri et Pauli ipse in honore eorumdem consecrcrauit, ibique messam sollempniter celebrauit, et eum diem sicut diem natalis Domini quot annis celebrari precepit.

Nomina uero eorum cardinalium, episcoporum, abbatum, presbiterorum, seu clericorum qui cum eo adfuere, quantum memorie occurrere potuit, subter scripsimus. Richardus cardinalis episcopus Albanensis,[14] Diuizo cardinalis Sancti Martini, Risus cardinalis Sancti Laurentii, Gregorius cardinalis Sanctorum Apostolorum, Iohannes diaconus cardinalis Sanctę Romane ecclesię, episcopus Lingonensis Rotbertus ad cuius peticionem hęc aucta sunt,[15] episcopus Placentinus, episcopus Vivariensis, episcopus Cameracensis, Henricus abbas Angeriacensis, Lambertus Pultariensis abbas, Henricus abbas Sancti Sequani, Wido abbas Sancti Michaelis,[16] et alii multi. Inferioris uero ordinis clericorum seu laicorum fere innumera multitudo.

Quoniam uero Dei dispositione ab ętemo cuncta sequuntur, suisque quando et quomodo uult, miseretur gratuita pietate nos uoluit apostolica benedictione releuari. Aucta sunt hęc anno ab incarnatione Domini MCVII, indictione xv, epacta xxv, die xii kalendas Marcii.

239

Early twelfth century (?)

John settles a quarrel with Bèze over a vineyard. He recounts the history of this vineyard, going back two generations.

Cartulary, fols. 131v–132r.
Bougaud-Garnier, p. 424.

Carta de uinea sacriste in Besua

Euuangelice auctoritatis exemplo didicimus quod seruus fidelis et prudens in modico a Domino Ihesu supra multa constituetur [Matt. 25:21]. Studui igitur ego Iohannes terram quę circa basilicam Sancte Marie iacet ecclesię sanctorum

14 The attendees included Richard, cardinal bishop of Albano; Aldo, bishop of Piacenza; and Leodegar, bishop of Viviers (1097–1119), who were also present at the consecration of the church of St-Bénigne.

15 Robert, bishop of Langres (1084–1111).

16 Garnier identifies these as Eodo, bishop of Cambrai (1105–1113), and Henry, abbot of St-Jean d'Angély (1104–1131). Others include Lambert, abbot of Pouthières (1104–1114), Henry, abbot of St-Seine (c. 1100–1116), and Guy, abbot of St-Michel of Tonnerre (1096–1134).

apostolorum Petri et Pauli reuocare, quę iam diu aliquomodo distracta steterat, sicut infra docebimus.

Domnus namque abbas Oddo[17] dederat eam Warnerio, patri Vlgerii, excolendam et ad plantandam uineam, ut in uita sua illam teneret, post decessum uero ecclesię redderetur. Sed eo mortuo, haud ita euenit. Cum enim filio eius Vlgerio predicto pecunias deberet ecclesia, concessit ei domnus abbas Stephanus[18] terram illam, eo modo quo pater eius habuerat. Ego uero cupiens talentum mihi creditum ampliare, donaui Vlgerio cxx solidos, id est vi libras, et ipse ac filii eius quicquid in terra illa clamabant Deo et Sancto Petro in manu domni abbatis Stephani reddiderunt. Domnus autem abbas Stephanus donauit et concessit eam secretario monasterii per manum meam, in perpetuum habendam libere absque censu et omni consuetudines quę de aliis uineis persoluitur. Concessit etiam eam consuetudinem quam Warnerius et Vlgerius habuerant, scilicet ut de silua illa quam Castanetum uocamus, liceret in uinea illa fieri perticas, furcas, paxellos, et quicquid in ea opus fuerit.

Et ut hęc carta inconuulsa permaneat, adsignamus etiam testes. Signum domni Stephani abbatis, Warnerii priori, Iohannis secretarii, Theoderici prepositi, Landrici, Gyraldi. De laicis uero Otberti cocci, Martini clerici, Vlgerii, Amalberti, Gyraldi, Stephani de Beria,[19] Formati, Petri, Humberti et Warnerii filiorum Vlgerii.

The John who issued this document was secretary of the monastery; see the following document. This agreement was also mentioned in the "Annales" of Bèze.[20]

240

Early twelfth century (?)

Abbot Stephen of Bèze makes an agreement over vineyards at Givrey and Marsannay with John.

Cartulary, fol. 132r–v.

Bougaud-Garnier, p. 425.

17 Odo, abbot of Bèze (c. 1055–c. 1065).

18 Stephen, abbot of Bèze (1088–1120).

19 Beire, 8 km southwest of Bèze.

20 "Annales Besuenses" 1105, MGH SS 2:249.

Carta de Mercennaco

Sanctorum patrum exemplis pie considerationis oculum ad imitationem infigentes, nos qui regimen sancte ecclesię suscepimus, necessarium inmo equum et salubre esse cognoscimus, eam fidelier ordinare et in ea quicquid boni ordinate disponimus, ne citius destruatur aut pereat, sapienter prouidere.

Notum igitur facimus omnibus tam presentibus quam futuris nostris successoribus ego Stephanus abbas Besuensis ecclesię[1] ceterique qui mecum sunt eiusdem cenobii prouisores quandam uineam quam apud Gibriacum[2] frater Iohannes secretarius emerat, nos cum uineas de quibus uinum ad commune deportatur cellarium terminasse. Sibi etiam cunctisque post eum uenturis quicquid terrę siue uinearum atque consuetudinum apud Mercenniacum[3] habebamus id concessisse, quatenus ex reditibus earum, ea quę sunt in nostrę ecclesię ministerio apta comparentur, et insuper altare Sancti Martini in sinistra parte situm monasterii, exinde iugiter illuminetur. Quod statutum litteris inprimentes, auctoritate qua debemus inuiolatum permanere precipimus.

Domni Stephani abbatis, Warnerii prioris, Wilenci, Iohannis, et ceterorum monachorum.

Based on the placement of this charter, it involved the same people and places as the preceding document.

241

Early twelfth century (?)

Theobold of St-Prudent gives Bèze vineyards for twenty-five solidi and another piece of land.

Cartulary, fols. 132v–133r.
Bougaud-Garnier, pp. 425–426.

Item alia

Sciant omnes presentes et futuri quod Thebaldus qui nuncupatur de Sancto Prudentio quicquid ędificii habuit super campum qui cappelle Sancte Marie adiacet, scilicet de uinea, reddidit Beato Petro et Stephano abbati[1] et secretario Iohanni

1 Stephen, abbot of Bèze (1088–1120).
2 Gevrey, 12 km southwest of Dijon.
3 Marsannay, 7 km southwest of Dijon.
1 Stephen, abbot of Bèze (1088–1120).

in perpetuum possidendum, et pro tali commercio dedit illi Iohannes secretarius xxv solidos et unam combam quam plantauerat. Communicauit ei taliter ut per medium excolat et per medium fructum capiat. Eo tenore si fidelis cultor extiterit, habeat eam cum honore tempore uitę suę absque censu. Post eius obitum si quis legalis heres eius supradictam uineam habere uoluerit, cum secretario qui dominus et socius inde est inprimis eam offerat. Si ipse eam sibi retinuerit, bene, sin autem noluerit, per consilium abbatis et monachorum uendat eam alicui de seruis Sancti Petri qui eam fideliter excolat, et censum et consuetudines secretario reddat.

Huic carte assignamus testes. Signum Stephai abbatis, Wilenci, Iohannis secretarii qui hoc fecit, Gyrardi, Albrici, Thebaldi, Hugonis uillici, Haydulfi, Hugonis famuli, Berengarii, Baldi, et aliorum multorum de familia ecclesię.

De obitu Rotberti episcopi

Cum per multorum annorum curricula domnus Rotbertus ęcclesiam rexixet Lingonensem,[2] grauissimo correptus morbo ad extreme propinquans, apud castellum quod Castellion dicitur,[3] abbates suos, Stephanum Besuensem, Widonem Molimensem, item Widonem Ternoderensem,[4] ad se mandans, humiliter se in conspectum Dei accusans, et ueniam peccatorum exposcens, a domno Widone Molimense abbate monachilem habitum suscepit, deinde non post multum, uiaticum ipsum corpus Christi accipiens, uitam finiuit. Sepultusque est apud Molimense monasterium in capitulo decenter ut decuit. Cuius loco substituitur domnus Iocerannus[5] Lingonensem sedem gubernaturus.

242

1113

Duke Hugh II of Burgundy frees Bèze from paying tolls at Dijon.

Cartulary, fols. 133r–134r.

Duchesne, *Histoire généalogique des ducs de Bourgonge*, instr. pp. 33–34, from the chronicle.

Bougaud-Garnier, pp. 427–428.

Summarized in Brequigny, *Table* 2:434.[1]

2 Robert, bishop of Langres (1084–1111).

3 Châtillon-sur-Seine.

4 Stephen, abbot of Bèze (1088–1120); Gui, abbot of Molesme (1111–1132); and Gui, abbot of St-Michel of Tonnerre (1096–1134).

5 Joceran, bishop of Langres (1113–1125).

1 Ernest Petit's catalogue of ducal acts mistakenly omits this one.

Karta Hugonis ducis de karris apud Diuionem

In nomine sanctę et indiuidue Trinitatis. Quantam animi deuotionem erga sanctam Dei ecclesiam habere debeamus, diuina sanctarum scripturarum demonstrant testimonia, quę siquidem eam et muneribus precipiunt fieri locupletem, et omnimoda ueneratione testantur, et commendant effici gloriosam. Hac igitur animaduersione compunctus, et a Sancto Spiritu spiritualiter instinctus, ego Hugo dux Burgundie[2] notum facio omnibus tam modernis quam futuris fidelibus quod redemptionem carrorum quam in porta Diuionensi capere consueueram, Deo et Sancto Petro et abbati Stephano[3] omnibusque Besuensis ecclesię monachis donuerim, ut amodo quibuscumque annis uel temporibus Diuionem uenerint ipsi denominate ecclesie monachi, tam claustrales quam in cellis manentes. Hanc sibi libertatem a me meisque successoribus obtineant, ut sine omni inpedimento et absque alicuius redemptionis exactione cum suis carris indubitanter pertranseant. Cuius si quidem doni largitionem zelo Dei succensus, huius gratia rei pro anime patris mei remedio Besuensi ecclesię contuli, ut uidelicet singulis annis apud eandem ecclesiam ipse in memoriam sit omnium, et sicut mos est Catholicus anniuersarium ei a filiis ecclesię celebretur omnibus, quatenus orationibus fidelium Dei famulorum, sibi meisque omnibus antecessoribus remissio omnium concedatur peccatorum. Proinde quoniam multa et maxima parentum nostrorum instituta, eos qui modo sunt in silentio et obliuione conspicio preterire, autentico placuit hoc donum commendare priuilegio, et subscripto approbatorum uirorum roborare testimonio.

Signum Hugonis ducis, Heinrici fratris ducis,[4] Walonis abbatis,[5] Hugonis dapiferi, Waleranni militis, Hugonis prepositi, Euurardi prepositi, Dominici iuuenis. Signum Stephani abbatis Besuensis, Warnerii priori, Albrici. De laicis Othberti, Euurardi, Gyraldi, Arnaldi uillici Lingonensis.

Acta sunt hec anno ab incarnatione Domini MCXIII, indictione vi, epacta i, regnante Hlugdouuico rege Francorum, episcopante Ioceranno in urbe Lingonensium.[6]

2 Duke Hugh II of Burgundy (1102–1143).

3 Stephen, abbot of Bèze (1088–1120).

4 Henry is sometimes erroneously said to have become a Cistercian monk, perhaps due to confusion with Prince Henry, brother of Louis VI, who did do so. Garnier mistakenly identifies this Henry with his Uncle Henry, prince of Portugal.

5 Walo, abbot of Losne, often appeared in ducal charters. See, for example, *Chartes de l'abbaye de Saint-Étienne de Dijon de 1098 à 1140*, pp. 17–19, 21–22, nos. 13, 15, 17.

6 Louis VI, king of France (1108–1137); and Joceran, bishop of Langres (1113–1125).

243

Early twelfth century

Richard, nephew of Isembert of Chazeuil, gives up his claims to the tithes of Chazeuil. Abbot Stephen in return will give him four measures of grain a year.

Cartulary, fol. 134r.
Bougaud-Garnier, p. 428.

Carta de decima Casoti

Opere precium duximus litteris adnotare quod Richardus qui nepos Esemberti de Casoto[1] fuit omnem calumpniam quam habebat super decimam de suprataxata uilla postposuit et omnino dimisit in presentia Stephani abbatis[2] et monachorum necnon et laicorum. Qua propter ut de hac re firma pax teneretur ex utraque parte, dedit ei supradictus Stephanus abbas quattuor eminas de annona in supradicto Casoto annuatim, duas de tritico et duas de ordeo qualiscumque ibi erit per fedum, tali pacto et tali ratione si supradicta uilla ad illam destructionem peruenerit, ut ibi capere non ualeat supradictam mensuram, scilicet de iiii eminis, tandiu pacienter expectet donec uilla melioretur, et quod sibi competit iterum recipere possit. Hoc laudauerunt frater eius Seuuinus et soror.

Huic rei adsignamus testes. Signum Richardi qui hoc fecit, Thetbaldi militis de Casoto, Pagani prepositi de Tilecastro.[3] De familia Sancti Petri, Otberti, Amalberti, Gysleberti, Hugonis, Gyrardi.

244

Early twelfth century (?)

Besueta, daughter of Ponce, along with her son Odo, a knight, give up claims to a certain Girard's children, for the good of her soul and her ancestors'.

Cartulary, fol. 134r–v.
Bougaud-Garnier, p. 429.

Item alia

Sciant omnes tam presentes quam futuri quod filia Pontii, quę cognominata est Besueta, et Oddo miles filius eius quicquid iuris uel proclamationis habebant super pueros Gyrardi, qui cognominatus est Aligrinus, dederunt Deo et Sancto

1 Chazeuil, 10 km north of Bèze. Isembert of Chazeuil is also mentioned in document 272.
2 Stephen, abbot of Bèze (1088–1120).
3 Tilchâtel, 9 km northwest of Bèze.

Petro et Besuensi ecclesię ęternaliter, pro suo remedio suorumque antecessorum, ante aram sanctorum apostolorum Petri et Pauli, et in presentia Stephanis abbatis[1] et monachorum.

Vt hęc carta inconuulsa permaneat, adsignamus ei testes: Signum Oddonis militis et matris eius, qui hoc fecerunt, Benzonis sacerdotis de Tilecastro,[2] Humberti qui cognominatur Angelricus, Viviani, Hugonis uillici, Iohannis, et aliorum multorum.

See also document 252.

245

Dijon, 1112/1113

Peter, who has just succeeded his nephew Odo as lord of Montsaugeon, settles his quarrels with Bèze over churches that Odo had given the monks, an agreement reached before the bishops of Lyon, Chalon, and Autun.

Cartulary, fols. 134v–135r.
Bougaud-Garnier, pp. 429–430.

Carta de ecclesiis datis ad nostris Montis Salionis

In nomine Patris et Filii et Spiritus Sancti. Notificamus omnibus fidelibus quorum usque ad aures cartula ista peuenerit quod Domnus Petrus, cum nepoti suo Domno Oddoni in honore et dominio Montis Salionis[1] successisset, dona quę ipse Oddo et auunculus eius Rainaldus contulerant Deo et ecclesię Sancti Petri Besuensis, de ecclesiis uidelicet, calumpniari cepit. Accidit interim archiepiscopum Iocerannum Lugdunensem et episcopum Cabilonensem et episcopum Augustidunensem[2] Diuionem aduenire. Ibique ratione consilii immo racionabili consilio suo commonitus domnus ipse Petrus quicquid in rebus prefatis calumpniatus fuerat in manu domni Ioceranni archiepiscopi Lugdunensis reddidit. Archiepiscopus autem ipse donum illud in manu domni Stephani abbatis[3] posuit, et ecclesiam Besuensem inde reuestiuit.

Adsignamus testes. Signum Ioceranni archiepiscopi, Stephani Eduensis episcopi, Walterii Cabilonensis episcopi, Wilenci archidiaconi, domni

1 Stephen, abbot of Bèze (1088–1120).
2 Tilchâtel, 9 km northwest of Bèze.
1 Montsaugeon, 22 km north of Bèze.
2 Joceran, archbishop of Lyon (1107–1118); Walter, bishop of Chalon (1080–1123); and Stephen, bishop of Autun (1112–1139).
3 Stephen, abbot of Bèze (1088–1120).

Ioceranni archidiaconi, Stephani abbatis, Gerentonis abbatis, Stephani Noui Monasterii abbatis,[4] Warnerii prioris, Iohannis, Albrici. De militibus, Willelmi Fontisuenne,[5] Hugonis dapiferi, Petri qui hoc donum fecit, Widrici, Othberti cocci, Hugonis famuli.

This document is dated by Bishop Stephen and Abbot Jarenton. For Odo's original gift of the churches, which Peter had confirmed, see document 192.

246

Early twelfth century (?)

Arlebald, provost of the church of Belleneuve, returns to Bèze the fief he held from the monastery at Arçon, consisting of mansi. He does so for his soul and those of his wife and sons. In return, he receives two measures of grain and a cow.

Cartulary, fol. 135r.
Bougaud-Garnier, p. 430.

Carta de Arcione

In nomine sancte ac indiuidue Trinitatis. Dignum duximus litteris adnotare quod Arlebaldus prepositus Sancti Petri de Belenaua reddidit Deo et Sancto Petro et Besuensi ecclesię omne fedum quod habebat de abbate et de monachis super mansos de Arcione,[1] sicut supradiximus, omnem consuetudinem et quicquid calumpnii uel iuris habebat super supradictos, super altare in dono posuit, pro sua anima suorumque antecessorum, ipse et uxor eius et filii eius ęternaliter. Et propter hoc, ut hec datio inconuulsa permaneat, dedit illi Albricus monachus qui tunc temporis Arcionem regebat duas eminas frumenti et unam uaccam, et redemit illi de Ranaldo de Miribel quinque eminas annone quas perdiderat apud Cuseriacum,[2] cum quadraginta solidis.

Huic rei adsignamus testes: Signum Stephani abbatis, Wilenci, Iohannis, Ioffredi. Et de familia Sancti Petri, Othberti, Hugonis, Gisleberti, Nerduini, Iohannis, et aliorum multorum.

4 Jarenton, abbot of St-Bénigne of Dijon (1076–1113); and Stephen Harding, abbot of Cîteaux (1108–1133).

5 Fouvent, 35 km northeast of Bèze.

1 Belleneuve, 12 km south of Bèze; and Arçon 1 km east of there.

2 Mirebeau, 9 km south-southeast of Bèze; and Cuiserey, 3 km south of there.

247

Early twelfth century

Suffisia, wife of Ponce of St-Seine, along with her son-in-law, the knight Humbert of Liey, makes a gift for Ponce, who died going to Jerusalem. The gift consists of a manse at Chivigny, as well as a serf at St-Seine with half his children.

Cartulary, fol. 135r–v.
Bougaud-Garnier, p. 431.

Cara de Cauiniaco

Clarescat hoc cunctis modo uiuentibus post nosque futuris quod Suffisia uxor Pontii de uilla quę Sanctus Sequanus nuncupatur et Humbertus gener eius de Lisiaco,[1] pro anima supradicti Pontii qui in Hierosolimitano itinere mortuus est, pro sua requie suorumque antecessorum fidelium, dederunt Deo et Sancto Petro et Besuensi ecclesię unum mansum cum suis terris et suis appendiciis in nostra uilla quę Cauiniacus[2] dicitur, et unum seruum cum medietate suorum infantum in supradicta uilla Sancti Sequani, Vlricum nomine.

Ne talis memoria deleatur adsignamus testes: Humberti militis de Lisiaco qui donum fecit cum socru sua, Widrici de Sancto Sequano, Theoderici de Campocurto.[3] De clericis Wilenci archidiaconi, Humberti canonici, Iohannis presbiteri. De monachis Widonis prioris, Wilenci, Heinrici, Iohannis, Ioffredi, et aliorum. De familia nostra Hugonis famuli, Aidulfi, Arnulfi uillici de Cauiniaco, Rotberti filii Girberti.

"Going to Jerusalem" was the original term for going on Crusade. Many Burgundian knights headed to the Holy Land after the 1100 establishment of the Kingdom of Jerusalem.

248

Early twelfth century (?)

Deodatus of Neuvelle and his wife agree that they owe Bèze the head-tax required of the monks' other serfs, four pennies for a man and two for a woman. Their children shall not be able to deny this obligation.

1 St-Seine-sur-Vingeanne, 13 km northeast of Bèze; and Licey, 8 km east-northeast of Bèze.
2 Chevigny, 3 km southeast of Bèze.
3 Courchamp, 16 km north-northeast of Bèze.

Cartulary, fol. 135v.
Bougaud-Garnier, p. 431.

Carta de hominibus Noueuille

Notum sit omnibus qui modo sunt postque futuri quod Deodatus de Nouauilla[1] et uxor eius censum de capitibus suis reddiderunt Sancto Petro et Besuensi ecclesię et Stephano abbati, ut alii serui Sancti Petri et ancille, uir quattuor nummos et mulier duos. Hoc adnotamus litteris ne filii et filię eorum uel posteritas si negare uoluerint hoc umquam negare possint. Nempe hę litterę de hoc scriptę, testimonium ueritatis semper habebunt.

249

Early twelfth century (?)

Gui, son of Aymo, a knight of Fontaine-Française, is dying and gives Bèze a manse at Fontenelle, along with four serfs. His brother Robert, a boy, confirms.

Cartulary, fols. 135v–136r.
Bougaud-Garnier, p. 432.

Carta de Fontinellis

Clarificetur cunctis modo uiuentibus post nosque futuris quod Wido miles de Fontanis,[1] filius Haymonis, decumbens in infirmitate ueniens ad obitum suum, ipse et manipulares eius et Rotbertus frater eius puer dederunt Deo et Sancto Petro et cęnobio Besuensi mansum unum in uilla quę Fontanellas[2] dicitur, cum appendiciis suis, qui nuncupatur mansus Hugonis prepositi, et quattuor seruos, Constantium qui uocatur miles cum filiis suis, sub tali testimonio.

Signum Richardi de Vircillis,[3] Hugonis Carruce, Wilenci militis de Fontanis. Signum Herberti uillici, Hugonis de Conuulensi castro domini,[4] Rotberti pueri qui donum fecit and laudauit, et aliorum multorum.

1 Neuvelle, 24 km northeast of Bèze.

1 Fontaine-Française, 10 km northeast of Bèze.

2 Fontenelle, 9 km northeast of Bèze.

3 Verseilles, 33 km north of Bèze.

4 Coublanc, 28 km north-northeast of Bèze.

250

Early twelfth century (?)

Humbert, son of Arlebald, gives Bèze a manse at Beire for his soul and those of his ancestors. The manse comes with two serfs, brother and sister.

Cartulary, fol. 136r.
Bougaud-Garnier, p. 432.

Carta de Beria

Agnoscat pleniter et retineat memoriter fidelis natio, tam de presentibus quam de futuris, quod Humbertus cognomento Solitarius, filius Arlebaldi, dedit Deo et Sancto Petro et Besuensi ecclesię unum mansum pro sua anima suorumque antecessorum fidelium in Beria uilla,[1] cum omnibus appendiciis suis, de pratis et de terris cultis et incultis, ornatum omni libertate. Dedit etiam supradictus Humbertus unum seruum et unam ancillam, fratrem et sororem, Humbertum et Rotrudem, pertinentibus ad supradictum mansum iure perpetuo.

Huic rei adsignamus testes. Signum Hugonis militis de Chimissiaco,[2] Leterii et filiorum eius, Stephani, Richardi, Iohannis presbiteri, Andreę presbiteri, et aliorum multorum de Beria. Si quis peruersus huic elemosinę contraire uoluerit, aut aliquid demere uoluerit, anathema sit.

251

Early twelfth century

Milo, a knight of of Beaumont, along with his wife, gives Bèze a manse at Beire. They do so on the day that their son Geoffrey, a monk, first celebrates mass.

Cartulary, fol. 136r.
Bougaud-Garnier, p. 433.

Item alia

Est in eadem uilla Beria[1] mansus quem honorifice et cum omni libertate dedit Deo et Sancto Petro Milo miles de Bellomonte[2] et uxor eius Adilina, in die quando primum Ioffredus filius eorum celebrauit missam, sub tali testimonio.

1 Beire, 8 km southwest of Bèze.
2 Choilley, 22 km north-northeast of Bèze.
1 Beire, 8 km southwest of Bèze.
2 Beaumont, 7 km east of Bèze.

Signum Milonis. Signum Ioffredi monachi qui per cultellum suum donum recepit, Odonis, Stephani, Rotberti, et aliorum multorum.

For Milo of Beaumont, see also document 223.

252

Early twelfth century

Odo, a knight of Spoy, makes gifts to Bèze for his parents. He gives up customary dues he had collected at Maâtz as well as some farmland there.

Cartulary, fol. 136r–v.
Bougaud-Garnier, p. 433.

Carta de Maiasco

Omnis fidelis homo pleniter agnoscat quod elemosina fideles uiuos ad uitam dirigit et animas defunctorum a morte liberat. De qua re non immemor Oddo miles de Cipeto,[1] qui Caterius cognominatur, fideliter pro anima matris suę, quę Besueta nuncupata est, patrisque sui sorumque fidelium antecessorum, dedit Deo et Sancto Petro et Besuensi ecclesię in elemosina coruatam apud Maiascum[2] cum omnibus consuetudinibus, quę illi succedebat liberaliter de proprio iure, et quinque iugera terrę necnon et partem suam de campo qui supra castellum iacet qui Vinea nuncupatur. Nos quoque Besuenses monachi pro signo recompensauimus illi suisque fidelibus orationes et benefacta ecclesię, tam uiuis quam defunctis in sempiternum.

Huic carte adsignamus testes. Signum Odonis qui elemosinam fecit, Willelmi Fontisuenne,[3] Humberti de Cipeto, Benzonis sacerdotis de Tilecastro,[4] Pagani prepositi, Willelmi de Fossato,[5] et de nostra familia quam plurimorum.

For Odo and his mother, see also documents 197 and 244.

1 Spoy, 6 km southwest of Bèze.
2 Maâtz, 30 km north-northeast of Bèze.
3 Fouvent, 35 km northeast of Bèze.
4 Tilchâtel, 9 km northwest of Bèze.
5 Le Fossé, 12 km northwest of Bèze.

253

Early twelfth century (?)

Odo, a knight of Beaumont, gives up his claims to the children of one Lambert, nicknamed Big Penny.

Cartulary, fol. 136v.
Bougaud-Garnier, p. 434.

Item alia

Notum sit omnibus tam presentibus quam futuris quod Oddo miles de Bellomonte[1] concessit et ex toto donauit Deo et Sancto Petro et Besuensi ecclesię quicquid umquam habuit, uel ipse uel antecessores sui, calumpnii super infantes Lamberti, qui Grossus-denarius nuncupatus est, siue iuste siue iniuste.

Huic noticie adsignamus testes. Signum Oddonis qui hoc fecit ex sua parte et omnium antecessorum suorum. Signum Seuuini de Reiaco, Oddilonis militis de Lissiaco,[2] Hugonis Columbe de Bellomonte, Lamberti, Otberti filii eius, Widrici. De monachis, Warnerii prioris, Landrici, Theoderici, et aliorum multorum.

254

Early twelfth century

Men of Bourberain, who had received land from Abbot Stephen to establish a vineyard, make an agreement about their sons marrying female serfs of the abbey. If the sons do so and continue to serve the monastery, they may have the land and a house, but will forfeit these if they do not do so.

Cartulary, fols. 136v–137r.
Bougaud-Garnier, p. 434.

Carta de hominibus Burbureni

Sciant omnes per noticiam istarum litterarum quod homines natiui de Burbureno,[1] qui terram acceperunt Sancti Petri ad plantandas uineas de manu

1 Beaumont, 7 km east of Bèze.
2 Ray-sur-Saône, 43 km east-northeast of Bèze; and Licey, 8 km east-northeast of Bèze.
1 Bourberain, 4 km north-northeast of Bèze.

Stephani abbatis,[2] scilicet Albricus, Warnerius, et Nerduinus cum fratribus suis, tali pacto concessa est eis predicta terra ut si quis ex filiis eorum acceperit ancillam Sancti Petri in uxorem et in seruitio ecclesię remanere uoluerit, ipse habeat edificium et terram supranominatam. Et qui hoc non fecerit, post mortem eius recipiet ecclesia et edificium et terram in suo proprio iure.

The men of Bourberain pushed hard against their lords, the monks of Bèze; see also document 204.

255

1084–1087

Humbert Brunus, lord of Fouvent, is buried at the abbey. His wife establishes his anniversary, giving Bèze the chapel of the castle of Fouvent.

Cartulary, fol. 137r–v.
Bougaud-Garnier, pp. 434–435.

Carta de ecclesiis pro Humberto Bruno datis

In nomine sanctę et indiuidue Trinitatis, Patris et Filii et Spiritus Sancti. Omnibus qui has legerint uel audierint notulas certum fiat quod in die illa quando corpus Humberti Bruni, Fontisuenne[1] senioris, apud Besue monasterium traditum fuit sepulturę, consilio et laude Rotberti Lingonensis episcopi[2] et fratrum et militum et clientum suprataxati Humberti, uxor eius pro eius anima in illa die dedit Deo et Sancto Petro et Besuensi ecclesię capellam de castro Fontisuenne et illam partem quam habebat in ecclesia Sancti Valentini de Luuocurte,[3] habendum et possidendum iure perpetuo, necnon et duos cyphos argenteos, tali pacto ut annuatim in suo anniuersario eius memoria et antecessorum suorum fideliter celebraretur in conuentu monachorum.

Vt hęc carta inconuulsa permaneat, subscribamus ei testes idoneos. Signum Rotberti episcopi, Willelmi comitis Burgundię, Rainaldi filii eius,[4] Widonis de Raiaco, Widonis de Burgundione uilla, Hugonis de Bellomonte, Lebaldi

2 Stephen, abbot of Bèze (1088–1120).
1 Fouvent, 35 km northeast of Bèze.
2 Robert, bishop of Langres (1084–1111).
3 Lavoncourt, 42 km northeast of Bèze.
4 Count William Tête-Hardi of Burgundy (1057–1087); and his son, Count Raynald II of Mâcon (1087–1095).

de Domnopetro, Heinrici de Nouauilla, Heinrici de Firmitate,[5] Rotberti capellani, et aliorum multorum. De monachis signum Gausberti abbatis,[6] Warnerii prepositi, Benedicti prioris Fontisuenne, Constantii. Facta sunt hęc regnante Philippo,[7] episcopante Rotberto.

This document is dated by Bishop Robert and Count William. It was doubtless done at the same time as document 188, in which the bishop confirms the chapel of Fouvent to the monks. Because all the other documents in this section date from the reign of Abbot Stephen, it seems most likely that this one was discovered late.

256

Late eleventh century (?)

Odo, son of the Hugh who was brother of Abbot Odo, offers himself to Bèze. He will remain free but will permanently serve the monks, in return for a vineyard which Abbot Stephen gave him after his father's death. If he dies without an heir born to a female serf of the monastery, the vineyard will revert to the monks.

Cartulary, fol. 137v.
Bougaud-Garnier, pp. 435–436.

Item alia

Notum sit omnibus tam presentibus quam futuris quod Oddo filius Hugonis, qui frater fuit Abbatis Oddonis, propter quandam uineam quam sibi cuncessit habere domnus Abbas Stephanus[1] post obitum patris sui, scilicet supradicti Hugonis, seipsum spopondit permanere in seruicio et in fidelitate Sancti Petri et monachorum sicuti liber. Et tali modo, si ipse absque proprio herede moriatur qui non sit de ancilla Sancti Petri, ipsa supradicta uinea et quicquid ibi edificatum fuerit ueniat in iure et in proprietate Sancti Petri et monachorum pro anima eius. Sin autem ancillam Sancti Petri acceperit, infantes eius uineam possideant quamdiu bene seruierint, et per istam pactionem si circa nos morte preoccupatus fuerit, quasi nostrum commissum obtinebimus.

5 Ray-sur-Saône, 43 km east-northeast of Bèze; Bourguignon, 40 km northeast of Bèze; Beaumont, 7 km east of Bèze; Dampierre, 32 km east-northeast of Bèze; Neuvelle, 24 km northeast of Bèze; and La Ferté-sur-Amance, 51 km northeast of Bèze.

6 Gausbert, abbot of Bèze (c. 1070–1088).

7 Philip I, king of France (1060–1108).

1 These abbots of Bèze are Odo (c. 1055–c. 1065) and Stephen (1088–1120).

257

Late eleventh century (?)

Theobald, chaplain of Vergy, makes an agreement over Bèze's land at Vosne. He shall be able to plant there but shall pay twelve pennies a year for it, and it shall revert to the monastery on his death.

Cartulary, fols. 137v–138r.
Bougaud-Garnier, p. 436.

Carta de Veona

Ad memoriam reducatur modo uiuentibus post nosque uicturis quod Thebaldus capellanus de Verziaco[1] pactum fecit et confirmauit cum Stephano Besuensi abbate[2] super duo iugera de terra Sancti Petri que est in Veona,[3] quę ad plantadum quesiuit tali ratione, ut annuatim tempore uitę suę duodecim nummos Besuensi ecclesię pro signo persoluat. Post obitum uero eius supradicta ęcclesia terram suam cum omni ediffìcio liberam et edificatam recipiat.

Huic rationi subscripsimus testes. Signum Stephani abbatis, Guilenci, Albrici, Ioffredi Diuionensis prioris, Rotberti presbiteri de Gibriaco,[4] Humberti clerici de Diuione, necnon et aliorum multorum.

258

Early twelfth century (?)

A description of Lambert's land at Neuvelle.

Cartulary, fol. 138v.
Bougaud-Garnier, p. 436.

Carta de terra Lamberti apud Nouemuillam

Descriptio terrę Lamberti de Poliaco, quę est apud Nouam Villam.[1] Super fontem, diurnalem et dimidium, in uillenas, duos in Campanolas, iiii in cumba de uilla Marcelli ab ea parte, ubi fuit capella Sancti Langisi, iiii ad campum iuxta pratum qui appellatur Campus Natorie. Et in miliario duos in campo Del Challo, et in campo Del Fimuuz iii. De prato ad iiii falces et dimidiam.

1 Vergy, 20 km southwest of Dijon.
2 Stephen, abbot of Bèze (1088–1120).
3 Vosne, 19 km south-southwest of Dijon.
4 Gevrey, 12 km southwest of Dijon.
1 Pouilly, 15 km northeast of Bèze; and Neuvelle, 24 km northeast of Bèze.

259

Early twelfth century (?)

Humbert, son of Humbert of Spoy, gives Bèze a women for the soul of his father.

Cartulary, fol. 138r.
Bougaud-Garnier, p. 437.

Carta de uxore Euuardi

Clarificetur cunctis modo uiuentibus post hosque futuris quod Humbertus puer, filius Humberti de Cipeto,[1] pro anima patris sui suorumque antecessorum dedit Deo et Sancto Petro et Besuensi ecclesię Helisabeth filiam Warnerii de Burburano, sponsam Euurardi filii Gysleberti de Fonte.[2]

Ne aliquis infidelis hoc mendatium existimet, adsignamus testes. Humberti qui donum fecit, Pagani prepositi de Tilecastro,[3] Walterii, Hugonis fratris eius de Tilecastro, Otberti de Picangis, Tebaldi de Casoto,[4] Humberti Engelrici, Albrici de Burburano. De familia Sancti Petri, Euurardi, Gunterii, Gyraldi, Albuini, Gyraldi, Otberti, Hugonis famuli.

The woman Helisabeth was daughter of one of the three men who had earlier made an agreement with the monks; see document 254. Albricus, one of the witnesses, was another one of the men.

260

Early twelfth century (?)

Abbot Stephen decides to build a church at Coublanc, next to the castle. He asks Itier, lord of the castle, for usage rights there. Itier agrees, along with his mother and brothers and sisters.

Cartulary, fol. 138r–v.
Bougaud-Garnier, pp. 437–438.

1 Spoy, 6 km southwest of Bèze.
2 Bourberain, 4 km north-northeast of Bèze; and Fontaine-Française, 10 km northeast of Bèze.
3 Tilchâtel, 9 km northwest of Bèze.
4 Pichanges, 9 km west of Bèze; and Chazeuil, 10 km north of Bèze.

Carta de Maiasco

Religiosorum fides ac deuotio uirorum eo maxime semper fuit laudabilis quo non solum ecclesiis Dei acquisita retinere, uerum etiam alia undecumque studuerunt adquirere. Quorum formam prout potui imitatus, ego Stephanus ecclesię Besuensis licet indignus abbas[1] et ecclesiam iuxta castrum quod dicitur Confluentum[2] construere cupiens, quesiui ab Iterio, qui tunc dominus ipsius castri fuerat, quatinus Deo et ecclesię Sancti Petri Besuensis concederet quodcumque usuarium habebat in pratis, in siluis, in aquis, seu in campis. Qui peticionem nostram intelligens, de fonte pietatis descendere, annuit quod petebam, ipse cum matre sua et fratribus ac sororibus suis.

Annuit hoc ipsum Warnerius de Fulcherolis[3] quantum ad se pertinebat. Item Poncius de castello quod Firmitas[4] dicitur ubicumque ad se pertinebat eodem modo Deo et ecclesię Besuensi concessit.

The rubric refers to Maâtz, not Coublanc, and must have been written in error.

261

1114

Geoffrey, lord of Beaumont, and his wife, Gertrude, make gifts for their son Fulk, consisting of property at Nantilly.

Cartulary, fol. 138v–139r.
Bougaud-Garnier, pp. 438–439.
Summarized in Brequigny, *Table* 2:444.

Karta de Lentiliaco

In nomine Patris et Filii et Spiritus Sancti. Religiosa fidelium rebus sanctę ecclesię inuigilans industria sic sue possessioni oportet ut prouideat, ut quicquid tenet inconcusse teneatur, et quecumque ex propriis laboribus uel ex piorum oblationibus adipiscitur, cuncta se perhenniter obtinere in futurum gratuletur. Quamplures etenim huius temporis homines crudeles et seuissimi sponsam Christi, uidelicet ecclesiam, non solum non curant augmentare, uerum etiam eam omnimodis moliuntur de propriis annullare. Proinde notum

---

1 Stephen, abbot of Bèze (1088–1120).
2 Coublanc, 28 km north-northeast of Bèze.
3 Garnier suggests Fougerolles, near Lure, in Haute-Saône.
4 La Ferté-sur-Amance, 51 km northeast of Bèze.

sit omnibus et presentis et futuri seculi fidelibus domnus Ioffredum dominum Bellimontis,[1] cum Gertrudi sua coniuge suoque filio Hugone, pro anime filii sui Fulchonis antecessorumque suorum remedio, in loco elemosine, Deo et Sancto Petro fratribusque Besuensis cenobii unanimiter cuncessisse quicquid apud Lentiliacum[2] in terris, in aquis, in siluis possidebat, id est quicquid prorsus in reditibus uel appendiciis aliquibus proprio iure ibidem obtinebat.

Quod donum a se suisque heredibus collaudatum, ne pro cursu temporis uel aliquo obliuionis dissoluatur dispondio, oportunum esse cognoscitur solidari priuilegio, uirorumque qui adfuerunt roborari testimonio. Signum Ioffredi qui donum fecit, Hugonis filii eius, Widonis qui Fontisuenne est dominus, Willelmi auunculi eius, Hugonis de Poliaco, Seuuini de Raiaco, Odilonis de Lixiaco, Humberti de Faberniaco, Mayfredi de Arco, Audonis de Fontinellis.[3] De familia domni Ioffredi afuerunt Wido prepositus, Warnerius cognomento Pirdix, et Hugo frater eius, Gyslebertus de Alteriaco prepositus, et Rodulfus de Alteriaco, Gyslebertus de Poliaco, Warnerius de Solario,[4] et alii quamplures. Aucta sunt hęc anno ab incarnatione Domini MCXIIII, indictione vii, epacta xii, Hlucdouuico rege regnante in Francia, Ioceranno episcopo presidente in Lingonis, et Stephano abbate in Besua.[5]

See also the following document.

262

1114–1120

Geoffrey of Beaumont, along with his wife and son Hugh, adds to his gift to Bèze of property at Nantilly.

Cartulary, fol. 139r–v.
Bougaud-Garnier, pp. 439–440.

---

1 Geoffrey, lord of Beaumont, which is 7 km east of Bèze. Geoffrey was son of Ermengard, daughter and heiress of Hugh III of Beaumont, and Geoffrey's wife Gertrude was most likely from Fouvent. See Bouchard, *Sword, Miter, and Cloister*, pp. 319–323.

2 Nantilly, 20 km east of Bèze.

3 Fouvent, 35 km northeast of Bèze; Pouilly, 15 km northeast of Bèze; Ray-sur-Saône, 43 km east-northeast of Bèze; Licey, 8 km east-northeast of Bèze; Fauverney, 25 km south-southwest of Bèze; Arc-sur-Tille, 15 km south-southwest of Bèze; and Fontenelle, 9 km northeast of Bèze.

4 Autrey, 17 km east-northeast of Bèze; Pouilly; and Saulles, 34 km north-northeast of Bèze.

5 Louis VI, king of France (1108–1137); Joceran, bishop of Langres (1113–1125); and Stephen, abbot of Bèze (1088–1120).

Item carta de eodem postea facta propter contentionem de illa prima donatione habitam

Omnipotentis edoctus consilio simulque illud considerans quod pro omnibus quę in hac uita geruntur aut puniatur quisque aut remuneretur a Christo, deliberaui ego Ioffredus[1] cum uxore mea Gertrudi et Hugone filio meo uite meę tempus et dies quoniam mali sunt redimere.

Concedo igitur cum uxore mea et filio ecclesię Sancti Petri Besuensis quidquid apud Lentiliacum[2] habeo in ipsa uilla et in campis et in pratis et in aliis appenditiis, ita ex toto liberrimum sicut umquam liberius ab antecessoribus meis, seu a me possessum est. De silua illa quę uocatur Broulz medietatem a parte uille Lentiliaci, omnino ab omni consuetudine liberrimam possideat. In alia medietate mea, monachi et homines ac mulieres qui apud Lentiliacum manebunt libere et consuetudinaliter sibi et bestiis suis procursum habeant. Ingressus usque in eam partem silue que mea est erit ab ea parte quę Angulus Lirratus dicitur, et eo tenore ut si in eundo dampnum nescienter factum fuerit, simpliciter reddatur, si uero scienter aut expectando, dampnum cum lege restituetur. Quod si guerra mihi aut heredibus meis superuenerit, a castello Fontisuenne aut ab Aquato aut a Chargeiaco,[3] ingressus usque in meam partem silue erit mihi et meis per antiquas et originales uias. Et iterum eo tenore ut si dampnum in eundo factum fuerit nescienter, simpliciter reddatur, si uero scienter dampnum cum lege restituetur.

Huic donationi adsignamus testes, Iocerannum episcopum Lingonensem, Stephanum abbatem Besuensem,[4] Warnerium priorem, Lebaldum, Theodericum prepositum, Albricum. De clericis Iosbertum decanum, Lambertum. De militibus Ioffredum cum uxore sua Gertrude et Hugone filio suo, Humbertum de Lisseio cum Odilone fratre suo, Widonem uillicum de Gradeio, Rocilinum, Rotbertum de Furt, Richardum de Poiens, Wirricum de Altreio, Gyslebertum, Rodulfum, Humbertum uillicum Sancto Petri, Widonem fratrem eius, Hugonem de Pauliaco.[5]

See also the preceding document.

At this point, at the bottom of fol. 139v, the ink changes, to a lighter brown. The hand stays the same for the next few documents, but one can assume that

1 Geoffrey of Beaumont, 7 km east of Bèze.

2 Nantilly, 20 km east of Bèze.

3 Fouvent, 35 km northeast of Bèze; Achey, 28 km northeast of Bèze; and Chargey, 23 km east of Bèze.

4 Joceran, bishop of Langres (1113–1125); and Stephen, abbot of Bèze (1088–1120).

5 Licey, 8 km east-northeast of Bèze; Gray, 24 km east of Bèze; Feurg, 3 km southeast of Autrey; Poyans, 16 km east of Bèze; Autrey, 17 km east-northeast of Bèze; and Pouilly, 15 km northeast of Bèze.

document 262 was the last document John had intended for the codex, especially since he had completed it with a four-folio gathering, and that the rest were an addition to the original cartulary-chronicle. There was only room for the first line of the next charter at the bottom of folio 139v. The following gatherings are not numbered. Yet because the hand initially stays the same, even if apparently after a period during which John did not copy anything into the cartulary, it seems most likely that the first few charters in the next gathering were also written by John.

263

Early twelfth century (?)

Girard, archdeacon of Langres, gives Bèze all he has in the church of Beaumont, for his soul and those of his ancestors.

Cartulary, fols. 139v–139^{bis}r.
Bougaud-Garnier, pp. 440–441.

Carta de ecclesia Sancti Martini

Presentis eui futurique deinceps hominibus clarificetur quod domnus Gyrardus ecclesię Lingonensis archidiaconus dedit ecclesię Besuensi pro quiete suę anime suorumque antecessorum quicquid habebat in ecclesia Sancti Martini castri qui dicitur Bellimons,[1] scilicet medietatem ecclesię et presbiteratum, laudante idipsum donno episcopo Rotberto[2] et omni capitulo Lingonensi. Nos uero contuentes pene cuncta a memoriis hominum dilabi cartis hoc placuit inseri ut si quis deinceps huic donationi contraire uoluerit, harum auctoritate litterarum retineatur.

Huius autem testes rei quamplurimi extitere, ex quibus nobis quosdam placuit hic nominatim subtexere. Domnus Rotbertus episcopus, Abbas Stephanus.[3] Warnerius. Constantius. Et de militibus Rainaldus de Monte Salionis[4] et frater eius Petrus.

Domnus uero Stephanus abbas cum Gibuino sacerdote et fratre eius, filiis Berengarii, ex eadem re huiusmodi pactum firmauerunt. Terciam partem decime de omnibus annonis sibi retinuit, excepto Canabo. De oblationibus uero iiii festiuitatum, Natiuitatis, Purificationis Sancte Marię, Pasche, et Omnium Sanctorum quartam partem et candelarum et oblationum pro defunctis.

1 Beaumont, 7 km east of Bèze.
2 Robert, bishop of Langres (1084–1111).
3 Stephen, abbot of Bèze (1088–1120).
4 Montsaugeon, 22 km north of Bèze.

Vt vero pax utriumque teneretur, Gybuinus presbiter dedit fideiussores Warnerium Perdicem et Warnerium de Solario,[5] taliter ut si isti defecerint, alii ab eo restituantur. Hoc etiam statutum est ut si domnus abbas seu quislibet ex monachis Besuensibus uenerit in domo presbiteri libenter suscipiat et seruiat ei. Illud etiam additum est quod si presbiter quid ex nostra portionem interceperit, si domno abbati uel monacho seu ministro rem requirenti reddiderit, in pace erit. Sin alias, semel et iterum per fideiussores ammonitus, nisi reddiderit postea summam et legem persoluet.

264

Early twelfth century (?)

Alfred, a knight of Vaite, is dying and gives Bèze all his hereditary possessions, that is his manse with its house, the place for a mill, and meadows and fields.

Cartulary, fol. 139^{bis}r–v.
Bougaud-Garnier, pp. 441–442.

Karta de Vactis

Cunctorum noticie patere uolumus quod Alefridus miles de Vactis[1] ueniens ad obitum dedit Sancto Petro et Besuensi ęcclesię omnem hereditatem quam possidebat de proprio fundo, scilicet mansum proprium cum domo et sedem molendini cum prato, omnemque possessionem alodii sui, ut supradiximus, in agris, in siluis, in pratis ubicumque.

Et ut hęc carta inconuulsa permaneat, adsignamus testes. Signum Andreę presbiteri de Beria. Signum Walterii presbiteri de Ecellis.[2] Signum Stephani prepositi de Beria. Signum Hugonis de Chimissiaco.[3] Signum Humberti qui fuit nepos eius. Signum Walterii de Vactis qui fuit filius Laifini. De monachis nostris, Signum Warnerii, Signum Haymonis, Signum Ogdilonis, et aliorum multorum.

265

Palm Sunday, early twelfth century

Hugh, lord of Beire, is leaving for Jerusalem and gives Bèze two mansi at Beire and Lavoncourt, asking the monks for their prayers for his soul.

Cartulary, fol. 139^{bis}v.
Bougaud-Garnier, p. 442.

---

5 Saulles, 34 km north-northeast of Bèze.
1 Vaite, 37 km northeast of Bèze.
2 Beire, 8 km southwest of Bèze; and Arcelot, 12 km south-southwest of Bèze.
3 Choilley, 22 km north-northeast of Bèze.

Karta de Beria

Pateat cunctis modo uiuentibus postmodumque futuris quod domnus Hugo miles et dominus de Beria,[1] in die qua peram assumpsit ad Hierosolimitanum iter faciendum, scilicet in die Ramis palmarum, ueniens in Besuensi capitulo, misit se ad pedes monachorum, orans et petens ut sui misererentur et in suis orationibus memoriam illius habere dignarentur. In ipsa die et in ipso presenti capitulo coram testibus dedit Deo et Sancto Petro et Besuensi ecclesię duos mansos optimos pro se et pro anima sua et pro animabus antecessorum suorum fidelium, unum in uilla quę Beria dicitur, cum omnibus appendiciis suis, scilicet mansum Ogerii quem tenet Walterius filius eius uetulus, frater Stephani prepositi qui uocatur Albus, alium in uilla que dicitur Luecurtis,[2] cum omnibus appendiciis suis, quem nominauit mansum Otberti de Arbore.

Ne aliquis peruersus hoc friuolum existimet, adsignamus testes. Signum Hugonis qui donum fecit. Signum Nerduini qui habet filiam eius. Signum Hugonis Columbe de Bellomonte.[3] Signum Milonis de eodem castro. Signum omnium monachorum qui ibi presentes affuerunt.

See also the following document.

266

Early twelfth century

Nerduin, a knight of Pin, and his wife Ermengard, daughter of Hugh of Beire, give Bèze a manse at Beire. He also renews an earlier gift of some serfs. These gifts are for the soul of his son Walo.

Cartulary, fols. 139[bis]v–140r.
Bougaud-Garnier, p. 443.

Item alia

Per has ergo litteras agnoscant omnes tam presentes quam futuri quod Nerduinus miles de uilla quę Pinus dicitur et uxor eius Hermengardis, quę filia Hugonis de Beria[1] fuit, donauerunt Deo et Sancto Petro et Besuensi ecclesię unum mansum in Beria uilla, scilicet mansum Gunterii, cum omnibus appendiciis suis in pratis et in terris, et unum seruum nomine Stephanum quem supradictus Hugo antea concesserat, et unam ancillam quę Osanna uocatur, necnon et sororem eius. Hoc totum tradiderunt Deo et Sancto Petro, ut supra diximus,

1 Beire, 8 km southwest of Bèze.
2 Lavoncourt, 42 km northeast of Bèze.
3 Beaumont, 7 km east of Bèze.
1 Pin, 48 km east-southeast of Bèze; and Beire, 8 km southwest of Bèze.

Nerduinus et uxor eius, pro anima Walonis pueri et pro anima patris sui suprataxati Hugonis, necnon et pro remedio animarum omnium antecessorum suorum fidelium, tam pro uiuis quam pro defunctis.

Huic rei adsignamus testes. Signum Nerduini qui elemosinam fecit. Signum Milonis de Bellomonte. Signum Richardi filii eius. Signum Hilberti militis de Salice.[2] Signum Walonis fratris eius. Signum Hugonis militis de Chimissiaco.[3] Signum Andreę presbiteri. De nostra familia quamplurimi. Hoc donum et hęc elemosina tradita est per manus Nerduini et uxoris eius per frustum lapidis super altare apostolorum Petri et Pauli, cum omni honore et omni libertate eternaliter possidendum.

See also the preceding document.

At this point, in the middle of the page (fol. 140r), the ink changes again, becoming much blacker. The hand, however, is the same or at least very similar. The following is the first document clearly given after the death of Abbot Stephen, and if John is still the scribe, it must be a later addition.

267

1125–1130

Peter, lord of Montsaugeon, gives Bèze allodial property at Nantilly, as well as serfs at Trochères.

Cartulary, fol. 140r–v.
Bougaud-Garnier, pp. 443–444.

Karta Domni Petri

In nomine sancte et indiuidue Trinitatis, Patris et Filii et Spiritus Sancti. Ecclesię Dei fidelium donatione collata ob id sine dubio litteralibus traduntur monumentis, ne temporum longo succedentium uoluente curriculo a memoria mortalium aboleantur. Quapropter non inutile fore uenturis arbitramur si nuper ecclesię nostre concessa tenacibus apicum scriptis commendemus. Quę ita sese habent. Petrus dominus castri Montis Salionensis, agnomine Malusrespectus,[1] Deo et sanctis apostolis Petro et Paulo Besuensique ęcclesiae concessit, laudantibus

2 Beaumont, 7 km east of Bèze; and Saulx, 21 km northwest of Bèze.

3 Choilley, 22 km north-northeast of Bèze.

1 Lord Peter of Montsaugeon, 22 km north of Bèze, was said to have urged his sons, in a post-mortem vision, to establish the Cistercian house of Theuley; GC 4, instr. cols. 163–164, no. 40. According to Theuley's documents, Peter was also lord of Mirebeau and Ahuy.

coniuge et filiis, alodium quod quondam apud Lentiliacum[2] dederat, liberrime in posterum possidendum. Addidit quoque in capitulo, abbate assidente cum monachis, seruum nomine Walterium et ancillam dictam Aluidem in uilla quę Trescasę[3] appellaur habitantes.

De quibus ne qua in superuenientibus temporibus nascatur controuersia, idoneos assignamus testes. Signum eiusdem Petri. Signum uxoris eius. Signum Odtonis et Rainaldi filiorum eius. Signum Rodulfi militis. Signum Gaudini militis. Signum Walterii prepositi. Signum Humberti filii Olgerii. Signum Gyrardi abbatis.[4] Signum Wilenci prioris et tocius conuentus.

This was given before 1130, when the Cistercian house of Theuley was founded, for Peter "Malusrespectus" had recently died at that time.

268

c. 1130

Hugh, a knight of Renève, gives Bèze all his allodial property at Oisilly for his soul.

Cartulary, fol. 140v.
Bougaud-Garnier, pp. 444–445.

Karta[1] *Hugonis Herli*

In nomine Domini.[2] Sciant omnes tam presentes quam futuri quod Hugo miles de Renauis,[3] cognomento Herlus, gratis et cum magno affectu dedit Deo et Sancto Petro et Besuensi ęcclesię alodium suum totum cum omni libertate quod habebat et possidebat in uilla quę dicitur Ausiliacus,[4] pro anima sua et pro animabus antecessorum suorum, in campis, in pratis, in mansis, in siluis, in aquis.

Et ut elemosina ista et donum firmum persistant, adsignamus testes idoneos. Signum Hugonis de Bellomonte. Signum Walonis et Haymonis Columbe. Signum Ricardi. Signum Milonis de Poiens.[5] Signum Vrrici de Rænauis. Signum

2 Nantilly, 20 km east of Bèze.
3 Trochères, 14 km south-southeast of Bèze.
4 Girard, abbot of Bèze (1125–1142).
1 The manuscript reads "Kartha."
2 This invocation is in red ink.
3 Renève, 13 km south-southeast of Bèze.
4 Oisilly, 9 km southeast of Bèze.
5 Beaumont, 7 km east of Bèze; and Poyans, 16 km east of Bèze.

Rodulphi[6] fratris eius. Signum Rodulfi filii Vrrici. Signum Widonis cognomento Chiminal.[7] De monachis signum Gyrardi abbatis,[8] signum Teoderici, signum Widonis de Renauis, signum Lebaldi, signum Remigii presbiteri et aliorum multorum.

In tempore illo Rodulfus filius Vrrici de supradicto alodio concessit Sancto Petro et Besuensi ęcclesię unum mansum quod ei contulit auia sua post obitum suum, ubicumque obisset.

This document was probably given at roughly the same time as the preceding one.

At this point the ink becomes less black, more brown, and the hand changes. There are also several lines left blank before the next document. From this point on, there are a variety of hands, some copying several documents, others just one.

269

c. 1130–c. 1140

The knight Walter of Courternon, while dying, gives Bèze a manse at Sacquenay. He and his nephew, also named Walter, add the gift of a female serf. His sons, Milo, Walo, and Hilbert, agree.

Cartulary, fols. 140v–141r.
Bougaud-Garnier, p. 445.

Karta de Secuniaco

Sciant omnes tam presentes quam futuri quod Galterius miles de Chortoson,[1] ueniens ad obitum suum, Deo et Sancto Petro et Besuensi ecclesię, pro sua anima suorumque antecessorum, dedit unum mansum liberum cum omni libertate apud uillam quę uocatur Secuniacus,[2] cum nemore et terris et omnibus appendiciis quę ad ipsum mansum pertinent. Omnia quę ibi uidebatur habere, ipse et Galterius nepos eius in terris et in siluis tradiderunt Santo Petro et Besuensi ecclesie iure perpetuo, et unam ancillam quę uocatur Doda.

---

6 The cartulary reads "Rodulphus."
7 He should probably be identified with Wido of Choilley, 22 km north-northeast of Bèze.
8 Girard, abbot of Bèze (1125–1142).
1 Courternon, 17 km southwest of Bèze.
2 Sacquenay, 14 km north-northeast of Bèze.

Et ut nullus falsator possit contraire huic helemosine, adsignamus ei testes. Signum Milonis militis. Signum Walonis. Signum Hilberti filiorum eius qui donum fecerunt cum matre illorum. Signum Galterii nepotis eius qui similiter donum fecit. Et de militibus de Beria, signum Walonis, signum Hilberti, signum Pagani fratris illorum. Signum Mainfredi de Archo.[3] Signum Andree presbiteri de Beria.

This document would have been given after the preceding ones.

270

c. 1120

Odilo of Licey gives Bèze all he has there, in return for property at Bressey, for his lifetime. He marks this offering by putting a copy of the Gospels on the monastery altar. Odilo's brother Hugh gives additional property at Licey.

Cartulary, fol. 141r–v.
Bougaud-Garnier, pp. 445–446.

Karta de Lisseiaco

Notum fiat fidelibus quod Odilo de Lisseiaco[1] ecclesie Dei et Sancti Petri et Besuensis contulit in elemosina quicquid habebat apud Lisseiacum ubique, tam in terra quam in aquis, in pratis, in pascuis, in siluis, ita honorifice sicut ipse tenebat ea. Sed et ipsi monachi Besuenses concesserunt ei Odiloni ea quę ipsi habeant apud Bruceiacum,[2] eo tenore ut ipso ex hac uita exeunte, cum omnibus quę ibi edificauisset ecclesię Besuensi remaneret. Obtulit autem super altare Sancti Petri per textum Euangelii deauratum et hoc ipsum, sicut diximus, de Bruceiaco coram testibus tam monachis quam laicis.

Quorum quędam nomina hęc sunt. Signum Odilonis qui hoc donum fecit. Signum Mauricii militis de Probato. Signum Otberti. Signum Hugonis. Signum Giberti. Signum Euuardi. Signum domni Stephani abbatis.[3] Signum Wilenci, Lebaldi, Albrici.

Similem donationem fecit Hugo senior, frater Odilonis, de Insula Bollina,[4] de sua parte de Lissiaco, ipse et filius eius Wido puer et uxor eius et

3 Beire, 8 km southwest of Bèze; and Arc-sur-Tille, 15 km south-southwest of Bèze.

1 Licey, 8 km east-northeast of Bèze.

2 Bressey-sur-Tille, 19 km south-southwest of Bèze.

3 Stephen, abbot of Bèze (1088–1120).

4 This place is unidentified, but it was presumably near Licey; see document 199.

filia eius Aia, ad integrum cum omni libertate tenendum et possidendum Beato Petro et Besuensi ecclesię in perpetuum, pro sua anima suorumque antecessorum fidelium. Signum Hugonis, Widonis filii eius. Signum Humberti de Lissiaco. Signum Odilonis fratris eius. Signum Gysleberti sacerdotis de Malliaco.[5] Signum Humberti prouisoris uel ministralis et aliorum multorum.

271

c. 1120

Robert of Rigny gives up his claim to property at Maâtz, in return for two horses which Abbot Stephen and the monks of Bèze give him.

Cartulary, fol. 141v.
Bougaud-Garnier, pp. 446–447.

Karta de Maiasco

Sapientum uirorum consuetudinem esse cognoscimus presentia litteris adsignata futuris ęternaliter reseruare temporibus. Scribere igitur dignum duximus quod Robertus de Rinei[1] calumpniam quam faciebat de terra quę apud Maiascum[2] sita est in finem et pacem posuit, pro duobus equis quos ab abbate Stephano[3] et fratribus Besuensis ecclesię accepit. Quapropter quicquid in predicta terra iuste uel iniuste habere se dicebat, Deo et Sancto Petro et predictis fratribus libere concessit in ęternum possidere.

Quod ut firmius permaneat, testes qui adfuerunt subsequens scriptura demonstrat. Signum Roberti militis de Fontanis et uxoris eius Auiline. Signum Richardi militis de Vircillis. Signum Oddonis Viridi. Signum Haymonis de Monte Salione.[4] Signum Bertranni militis de Fontanis. Signum Wilenci militis de Fontanis. De familia Sancti Petri, signum Otberti, signum Hugonis, signum alterius Hugonis, signum Aygulfi, et aliorum multorum.

5 Mailly-le-Château, 37 km south of Bèze.

1 Rigny, 26 km east of Bèze.

2 Maâtz, 30 km north-northeast of Bèze.

3 Stephen, abbot of Bèze (1088–1120).

4 Fontaine-Française, 10 km northeast of Bèze; Verseilles, 33 km north of Bèze; and Montsaugeon, 22 km north of Bèze.

272

c. 1070–1088

The knight Otbert of Tilchâtel, lord of Spoy, converts to the monastic life at Bèze and gives a manse at Lux, along with a serf, a mule, and anything he had claimed. His sons sign.

Cartulary, fols. 141v–142r.
Bougaud-Garnier, pp. 447–448.

Karta de Luat

In nomine Patris et Filii et Spiritus Sancti. Dominus dicit in euangelio, "Date elemosinam, et ecce omnia munda sunt uobis" [Luke 11:41]. De qua re non surdus auditor fuit miles quidam, Otbertus scilicet de Tilecastro, senior de Cypeto,[1] ut de suis propriis liberius elemosinam faceret, seipsum in primis elemosinam fecit. Qui ueniens ad conuersionem ad Besuense monasterium, dedit Deo et Sancto Petro et Besuensi ecclesię unum mansum in uillula quę uocatur Luat,[2] cum adiacentiis suis, cum terris et pratis, sic libere et sic honorifice ut iste mansus, qui uocatur mansus Letaldi, habeat procursum et consuetudines per omnia nemora quę sunt de Cypetho citra Tilam[3] et ultra, et seruum unum Bricionem, cum omni suppellectili sua, qui erat ministralis de terris suis, et unum mulum optimum quem habebat, et quicquid calumpnii habebat super terram Sancti Petri et super homines postposuit.

Vt haec karta inconuulsa permaneat, supponamus ei testes idoneos. Signum Humberti de Cypeto filii eius. Signum Aymonis filii eius. Signum Widonis clerici filii eius. Signum Iohannis prepositi. Signum Walterii prepositi eius. Signum Iniulrici. Signum Humberti filii eius de Tilocastro. Signum Aldonis senioris. Signum Oldilerii militis. Signum Widonis de Fossato[4] militis, et aliorum multorum. De monachis signum Iosberti abbatis,[5] signum Benedicti, signum Constantii, signum Roberti prepositi. De familia Sancti Petri, signum Iohannis uillici, signum Humberti cocci, signum Gyraldi clerici.

Habet Sanctus Petrus et nostra Besuensis ęcclesia plurimam terram in ipsa uillula, quę uocatur Luat, infra et per confinia ipsius. Terram scilicet Isemberti

---

1 Tilchâtel, 9 km northwest of Bèze; and Spoy, 6 km southwest of Bèze.
2 Lux, 5 km northwest of Bèze.
3 The river Tille, on which Spoy is located.
4 Le Fossé, 12 km northwest of Bèze.
5 Gausbert, abbot of Bèze (c. 1070–1088).

de Casoto cum adiacentiis suis, terram Walterii de Bellomonte pincerne,[6] cum adiacentiis suis, terram Landrici cum adiacentiis suis.

This document, earlier than others in this section, had doubtless been accidentally omitted when the cartulary was compiled.

EPITAPHIUM

Omnibus ostendit monachi pia cura Iohannis,
Qualis in ęcclesia fuit a puerilibus annis,
Abbatis Stephani studium querens imitari,
Plus studuit reliquis ea quę bona sunt operari,
Abbas ecclesiam uenerabiliter renoauit,
Desertasque domos ueluti patet edificauit.
Hic partem cupiens ipsius habere laboris,
Libris scribendis operam dedit omnibus horis.
Stephanus ęcclesię possessa sue duplicauit,
Dum reditus, fundos, et predia multiplicauit.
Hic rerum custos sibi credita dum bene seruat,
Multiplici studio libros studiosus aceruat,
Stephanus ecclesię thesauros amplificauit,
Omnia septa fere melius mutando locauit,
Hic rerum custos dum curis inuigilauit,
Plus in ea reliquis custodibus ędificauit.
Stephanus ecclesiam ditem de paupere fecit,
Quam melius statuendo, superflua quęque reiecit.
Cuius et iste sequens factum non degenerauit.
Dum res ecclesię pro posse suo decorauit.
Stephanus ecclesię caput extendit super amnem.
Nouimus auxilium simul impendisse Iohannem.
Quisque modo famulando suo dat plurima, perque
Fine sui cursus brauio sit dignus uterque.
Ecclesie Domini dilexit uterque decorem,
Dum pro posse sui famulatus prestat honorem.
Fidus uterque cliens Domini sepelire talentum
Noluit, ex uno dum querit reddere centum.

6 Chazeuil, 10 km north of Bèze; and Beaumont, 7 km east of Bèze.

Vita patris Stephani pastoribus est imitanda,
Vita Iohannis erit non inmerito memoranda.
Hic erit exemplo prelatis, iste sequendus,
Quisque in officio suus est successor habendus.
Nos igitur qui tot tanti bona patris habemus,
Quique Iohannis opus tot florida scripta uidemus.
Expansis regi manibus qui regnat ubique,
Conferat, oremus, meritum pietatis utrique,
Vt qui iustificat maiores atque pusillos,
Cum numeret patrię cęlestis ciuibus illos.

Hic sunt libri pretitulati quos Iohannes fecit describi, uidelicet magnam partem Iosephi, Augustinum etiam super quinquaginta Psalmos ultimos, a "Domine exaudi" usque "Omnis spiritus laudet Dominum." Exameron Ambrosii, Ambrosium De Officiis et De Sacramentis, et de morte Satiri fratris sui. Ambrosium De Virginitate et Hystoriam Wandalorum, Ystoriam Orosii, Ystoriam Iustini, Ystoriam de Iherusalem, Homelias Origenis, Confessiones Augustini, Collectaneum Nouum, Musicam Widonis, duos antiphonarios optimos de musica, gradalem et nocturnalem, Vitam Sancte Fidis, et Pastoralem Beati Gregorii. Gregorium De Miraculis. Vitam S. Galli et alias multas uitas et passiones sanctorum. Vitam Sancti Leonis et Iheronimum super Sophoniam, Aggeum, Iohelem, et Malachiam. Decem collationes patrum et alias septem. Vitas patrum beati Iheronimi. Librum Scintiarum. Questiones Bede in Libros Regum. Istum etiam librum de diuersis rebus et kartis composuit.

This "epitaph" and list of books John copied is written in the same hand as documents 269–272, an additional indication that John's role in the cartuary ended with document 268. The "epitaph" is written continuously rather than as a poem, even though it is obviously a poem.

273

c. 1125–1130

Milo, a knight of Montsaugeon, is dying and takes the habit, while making gifts to Bèze. He and his nephew Ascherius give land at Piépape and Percey.

Cartulary, fol. 143r.
Bougaud-Garnier, p. 450.

Karta de Preopa

Sciant omnes tam presentes quam futuri quod Milo quidam miles de Monte Salionis,[1] cognomento[2] Paganus, ueniens ad obitum suum, cum magno affectu suscipiens habitum monachi pro remedio animę suę, ipse et Ascherius miles, nepos ipsius, tradiderunt Deo et Sancto Petro et Besuensi ecclesię in uilla quę nuncupatur Preopapa tres falces de prato et quartam apud uillam quę dicitur Perciacus[3] et unum mansum cum sex iugeribus terrę, et de silua quę pertinet ad uillam superius nominatam Preopapa dederunt monachis de Albiniaco[4] procursum et consuetudinem de pastione, et si ibi miserint porcos suos et omnia quę necessaria illis erunt de illa silua a domos faciendas et ad omnia habitacula sua, et ad omnia utensilia sua quę de ligno fieri possunt, tradiderunt illis iure perpetuo cum omni honore. Ille quoque rusticus qui in supradicto manso habitauerit habeat similiter cum honore omnes consuetudines de uilla supradicta, de siluis, de aquis, de pratis, de pascuis, et nulli umquam seruiat nisi Sancto Petro et monachis. Et dederunt adhuc in hac elemosina unum plastrum iuxtra capellam de Monte Salione. Si quis falsator huic elemosine contraire uoluerit, anathema sit.

Vt hęc karta inconuulsa permaneat, subponamus ei testes. Signum Ascherii qui hoc donum fecit. Signum Lamberti de Domarim.[5] Signum Hugonis militis de Torciniaco.[6] Signum Oddonis Viridis. Signm Aymonis militis. Signum Rotberti presbiteri. Signum Dominici. De monachis, signum Constantii, signum Iohannis, signum Vlgerii.

Although this document is in the same hand as the "epitaph," from here on the hands change frequently, sometimes every document. The nephew Ascherius of this document is also found in document 287, making a deathbed gift of his own.

274

Early twelfth century

Elisabeth of Neuvelle is dying and gives Bèze what she has at Viévigne, including woods and houses and two serfs. Her sons agree, including one who is a monk.

1 Montsaugeon, 22 km north of Bèze.
2 The cartulary reads "quognomento."
3 Piépape, 29 km north of Bèze; and Percey-le-Grand, 18 km northeast of Bèze.
4 Aubigny, 22 km north of Bèze and 2 km west of Montsaugeon.
5 Dommarien, 3 km northeast of Montsaugeon.
6 Torcenay, 41 km north-northeast of Bèze. Hugo later became a monk; see document 285.

Cartulary, fols. 143r–v.
Bougaud-Garnier, p. 451.

Karta de silua Vetus Vinearum et mansilis quod appellatur domos
Quoniam inuidia diaboli mors intrauit in orbem terrarum, eo ipso adnitente ut nemo ad uitam possit redire, uix est qui faciat bonum uix est usque ad unum. Necessarium remur ut si quis aliquid ecclesie contulerit litterali memoria futurorum fidelium noticię transmittere. Quedam mulier et ortu et actu satis in seculo clara, filia Heinrici de Nouauilla[1] nomine Elisabeth, cognomento autem Karitas dicta, dum ad obitum propinquaret, ecclesię sanctorum apostolorum Petri et Pauli contulit in elemosina pro remissione peccatorum suorum et antecessorum suorum quidquid habebat in silua Veterum Vinearum[2] et eius mansilis, quod apellant domos. Dedit etiam seruum nomine Iohannem et ancillam nomine Emmam, ita omnino libere et honorifice habendum ut melius sciuit et potuit, landantibus filiis suis, Widone et Philippo.

Testibus uero Alinardo clerico, Oddone de Bellomonte, Seuuino de Raiaco,[3] Gerardo Crispo, Hugone de Voslun, Theoderico ministro, Pagano capellano. De monachis, Gerardo priore, Vlgerio Caluo, Albrico Captiuo, Gerardo filio eiusdem mulieris.[4]

Elisabeth's son-in-law later disputed her gift; see document 197.

275

1 June 1119

Humbert of Licey gives Bèze all he has there, specifying that he will not vex or injure anyone in the village or cemetery. His wife and sons agree. This was done at the same time that Bishop Joceran of Langres consecrated the church. Humbert of Cecey gave Bèze twelve denarii from the church of Mantoche and a manse at the same time.

Cartulary, fols. 143v–144r.
Bougaud-Garnier, pp. 451–452.
Summarized in Brequigny, *Table* 2:475.

1 Neuvelle, 24 km northeast of Bèze.
2 Viévigne, 4 km southwest of Bèze.
3 Beaumont, 7 km east of Bèze; and Ray-sur-Saône, 43 km east-northeast of Bèze.
4 The cartulary reads "muelieris."

Karta de Lixiaco

Perspicientes huius seculi casus et mutationes opere precium duximus ea quę nostris temporibus ęcclesię Besuensi collata sunt, memorię commendare perhenni. Notum itaque fiat quod Humbertus de Lisseum[1] quidquid in eadem uilla habebat seu habuerat ipse et antecessores eius Deo et Sancto Petro Besuensi, ita omnino liberrime contulit, ut deinceps neque in cymiterio neque in ipsa uilla cuiquam homini, neque suo neque alterius, liceat ei seu heredibus eius aut alicui loco eius persone iniuriam, uexationem, seu exactionem inferre. Et ut pretulimus in tota uilla illa non solum hominem sed nec quidquam omnino uiolenter capere.

Data ab Humberto prefato cum uxore et filiis suis coram testibus annotatis infra: Albrico fratre eius, Theoderico monacho, Balduino, Lecilino, Pontio militibus, eo die quo ecclesia consecrata est a domno Ioceranno Lingonensi episcopo,[2] anno ab Incarnatione Verbi Dei MCXVIIII, indictione xii, epacta vii, concurrente ii, kalendas Iunii, die Dominico.

Eodem tempore et eadem ebdomada feria iiii quidam miles, Humbertus de Cynciaco,[3] dedit Sancto Petro pro anima filii sui Widonis et antecessorum suorum xii denarios de ęcclesia cuiusdam uille quę dicitur Mentusca,[4] et unum mansum apud Cynciacum uillam, ad portum cum pontinatico et piscaria, quę omnia obtulit ad altare, imponens librum super illud coram testibus, Letbaldo, Wilenco, ceterisque quamplurimis monachis et Widone fratre eius, Walterio de Beria,[5] cum aliis multis.

See also document 277.

276

Fouvent, 1113–1120

Bishop Joceran of Langres gives the churches of Spoy and Tanay to Bèze, where Stephen is abbot.

Cartulary, fol. 144r.
Bougaud-Garnier, pp. 452–453.

1 Licey, 8 km east-northeast of Bèze.
2 Joceran, bishop of Langres (1113–1125).
3 Cecey, 18 km east-southeast of Bèze.
4 Mantoche, 21 km east-southeast of Bèze.
5 Beire, 8 km southwest of Bèze.

Karta de ecclesiis Cypeto et Tasneto

Non minimum successoribus nostris credimus profuturum si iuxta nostrorum maiorum consuetudinem nos quoque de rebus huic ecclesię collatis memoriam, etsi non luculenta uera tamen narratione, posteris relinquamus. Notum sit igitur quod domnus Iocerannus Lingonensis episcopus[1] ecclesiam de Cypeto[2] donauerit ecclesię Sancti Petri Besuensis, per manum domni Stephani abbatis,[3] in capitulo Sanctę Marię Fontisuenne castelli,[4] coram archidiaconis suis, et laudantibus Wilenco archidiacono et Ayrardo archidiacono, Humberto canonico. Signum Stephani abbatis, Vlgerii, Rodulfi monachis.

Dedit etiam ecclesiam de Tasneto[5] predicte Besuensi ecclesię, in silua quę uocatur Volort,[6] coram Warnerio archidiacono, laudante eo et donante quidquid in ea habebat, coram pluribus, Rotberto preposito et aliis.

This document is dated by the bishop and the abbot.

277

1119

Bishop Joceran of Langres gives Bèze property at Mantoche, including the church there, at the request of Abbot Stephen. The archdeacons of Langres agree.

Cartulary, fol. 144v.
Bougaud-Garnier, pp. 453–454.
Summarized in Brequigny, *Table* 2:483.

Karta Ioceranni episcopi de Mentusca

Ego Iocerannus nutu Dei Lingonensis episcopus,[1] cum pro possibilitate mea una cum fidelibus et filiis nostris, de negociis et commodis Lingonensis ecclesie fideliter agendo disponeremus, uenit ad nos Besuensis monasterii uenerabilis abbas domnus Stephanus,[2] humiliter et deuote postulans quatenus

1 Joceran, bishop of Langres (1113–1125).
2 Spoy, 6 km southwest of Bèze.
3 Stephen, abbot of Bèze (1088–1120).
4 Fouvent, 35 km northeast of Bèze.
5 Tanay, 7 km south of Bèze.
6 The forest of Velours lies immediately west of Bèze.
1 Joceran, bishop of Langres (1113–1125).
2 Stephen, abbot of Bèze (1088–1120).

deserta cuiusdam solitudinis in territorio Attoarensium iuxta flumen Ararim posita,[3] nostrę tantum episcopali dominationi proprię pertinentia, Deo et fratribus Besuensis monasterii donaremus, et supradicte possessionis heredes illos constitueremus. Ciuius iustę et racionabili peticioni citissime consentientes, laude et consilio fidelium nostrorum Lingonensis ecclesię archidiaconorum, quicquid in uilla quę uocatur Mentusca[4] episcopali iure possidere debemus, ecclesiam quoque ipsam cum omnibus appendiciis suis, supradicto abbati et successoribus eius in posterum, saluis Lingonensis ęcclesię consuetudinibus, libere donamus et episcopali auctoritate donata confirmamus.

Signum Guilenci archidiaconi.[5] Signum Garnerii archidiaconi. Signum Ayrardi archidiaconi. Signum Widonis archidiaconi. Huius rei testes sunt domnus Gualo canonicus regularium, Ioczaudus decanus Cabilonensis,[6] Guilencus monachus, Albericus monachus, Rodulfus. Acta sunt hęc anno ab incarnatione Domini MCXVIIII, indictione xii, epacta vii, concurrente ii, apostolice sedis Kalixto anno primo pontificatum regente, Lucdouuico Francorum rege,[7] Ioceranno Lingonensis ecclesię episcopatum gubernante, Duranno notario dictante.

This document was doubtless given at the same time as document 275, when the bishop consecrated the abbey church.

278

c. 1119

Walo of Ruffey and his brother-in-law give Bèze whatever they have in the church of Mantoche.

Cartulary, fols. 144v–145r.
Bougaud-Garnier, p. 454.

Item de Mentusca

Audiat omnis homo quod Gualo de Ruphiaco castro,[1] filius Vlgerii de Coloniis,[2] et Gualo sororius eius cum Haimone fratre suo, donauerunt Deo et

3 Attuyer, once a county, was the region north of Dijon. The river is the Saône.
4 Mantoche, 21 km east-southeast of Bèze.
5 Willenc succeeded Joceran as bishop of Langres (1125–1136).
6 Jotsald, dean of Chalon-sur-Saône, who later became bishop of that see (1123–1126).
7 Pope Calixtus II (1119–1124); and Louis VI, king of France (1108–1137).
1 Ruffey-le-Château, 46 km southeast of Bèze.
2 Colonge, 13 km southeast of Bèze.

Sancto Petro Besuensis ecclesię quicquid habebant seu tenebant in ecclesia de Mentusche uilla,[3] uidelicet cymiterium et presbiteratum ipsius ecclesię, cum omnibus ad ipsum presbiteratum pertinentibus in mansis et pratis et terris, sed etiam terciam partem de decima eiusdem uille et usuarias consuetudines in omnibus terris et pratis et siluis et aquis ipsius potestatis.

Signum Stephani abbatis,[4] signum Wilenci, signum Iohannis monachorum. Signum Walonis qui hoc donum fecit. Signum Walonis. Signum Haymonis fratris eius. Item signum Walonis de Vilar.[5] Signum Henrici. Signum Roberti prepositi. Et de familia nostra signum Thebaldi hospitiarii, signum Humberti pistoris, et aliorum plurimorum.

This document was doubtless given about the same time as the preceding.

279

Bèze, 1125–1136

Hugh IV, lord of Beaumont, gives up holding a disputed fair after the monks of Bèze complained to the bishop of Langres.

Cartulary, fol. 145r–v.
Bougaud-Garnier, pp. 454–456.

De foro Bellimontis falso

Ex diuini paginis didicimus testamenti condempnationis ęternę maledicto debere cum subici, qui ecclesiam Dei persequi, et contra ministros eius nititur altercari. Pacem enim quam angelus in Redemptoris cecinit natiuitate hominibus bonę uoluntatis [Luke 2:14], inpium est exturbare. Ego igitur Hugo Bellimontis dominus,[1] penitentia ductus quod mea Besuensis cęnobii fratres tociens uexauerit inperitia, animum apposui iam ab eorum iniuriis cessare, et eis amodo perhenni dulcedine concordare. Ad sopiendam ergo fori, quod eis abstuleram, calumpniam, ante Lingonensem episcopum cui clamor ab abbate predicti loci factus super hoc fuerat ueni, et quia pro eo qui siquidem abbatias sui episcopatus tueri ac defendere deberet, iusticiari rationemque facere nolueram, rectum feci et de cetero me emendaturum promisi.

3 Mantoche, 21 km east-southeast of Bèze.
4 Stephen, abbot of Bèze (1088–1120).
5 Villiers, 31 km north-northwest of Bèze.
1 Hugh IV, lord of Beaumont. His son, Hugh V, is mentioned below. For the family, see Bouchard, *Sword, Miter, and Cloister*, p. 323.

Quadam itaque sollempni die cum aput Besuam dedicaretur ecclesia Beati Remigii, ac pro tantę celebritatis deuotione innumerabiles undecumque confluxissent populi, in monasterio beatorum apostolorum Petri et Pauli fratribus adstantibus cum predicto pontifice quamplurimis nobilibus, clericis, ac militibus, adstiti et quod eis forum amplius non auferrem, nec in castro meo, nec in tota terra mea, neque in toto posse meo forum uenale constituerem, nec homines mee terre a mercato Besuensi prohiberem promisi, filiumque meum Hugonem promittere et iurare feci. Ego ipse Hugo dexterę manus meę iuramento firmaui et insuper ne successorum aliqua redeat in futurum calumpnia, Deo et Sancto Petro et fratribus Besuensis ęcclesie quicquid est, uel erat, quod meum ius iuste aut iniuste possederat de hoc mercato, totum super altare posui et ipsum mercatum dono donaui.

Ne autem alicuius longeuitatis hoc factum dispereat obliuione, uirorum subscriptorum testimonio placuit hanc cartam roborare. Signum Guilenci episcopi.[2] Signum Gocelini archidiaconi. Signum Fulconis archidiaconi. Signum Garneri Rufi archidiaconi. Signum Poncii de Riuel. Signum Gerardi abbatis.[3] Signum Wilenci prioris. Signum Rodulfi sacristę. Signum Iosberti prepositi. Signum Albrici de Arcione. Signum Lebaldi de Ganibreris.[4] Signum Rainaldi de Granceio. Signum Milonis de Poens. Signum Odelrici de Renauis.[5] Signum Guidonis Raniuel. Signum Oberti. Signum Hugonis dapiferi. Signum Constancii Giroardi et filii eius.

This document is dated by the bishop.

280

1125–1142

Abbot Girard establishes an annual income for the cantor to take care of the books, now that John is gone.

Cartulary, fols. 145v–146r.
Bougaud-Garnier, p. 456.

Carta de reditibus annuis cantoris

Fideles quique aut oracionibus aut donariis se inuicem debent sustentare, ut et hi qui quietam agunt uitam, eos qui circa multa occupantur precibus iuuent,

2 Willenc, bishop of Langres (1125–1136).
3 Girard, abbot of Bèze (1125–1142).
4 Arçon, 13 km south of Bèze; and Genevrières, 38 km north-northeast of Bèze.
5 Grancey, 29 km northwest of Bèze; Poyans, 16 km east of Bèze; and Renève, 13 km south-southeast of Bèze.

et illi cum karitate ad utilitatem ipsorum necessaria administrent. Necesse est enim ut sic transitoria peragant, quatinus pro his premia ęterna consequi ualeant.

Igitur domnus abbas Gerardus[1] audiens quod ex quo uenerabilis Iohannes cantor[2] ex hac uita migrauit, monumenta librorum nemo condidisset, instituit ut omni anno cantori de unaquaque obediencia emina frumenti daretur, nolens quamuis maiora uellet aliquem grauare, quo libencius diciores et pauperiores preberent assensum, et futuris non esset honoerosum. Omnes uero obedienciarum prepositi huic decreto, quod eis in remissionem peccatorum[3] iniungebatur, assenserunt et libenter se hoc acturos promiserunt. Sanccitum est hoc a predicto abbate omnibus laudantibus, die festiuitatis apostolorum Petri et Pauli, atque statutum ut a kalendis Octobribus usque in Kalendas Nouembris idem donum unusquisque cantori solutum habeat.

Signum Wilenchi prioris. Signum Warnerii precentoris. Signum Rodulfi sacriste. Signum Albrici de Arcione.[4] Signum Iosberti prepositi. Signum Bartholomei subcentoris, et omnium monachorum.

The lists of monks who signed this and the following two documents are very similar, suggesting they were all given at about the same time.

281

1125–1142

Abbot Girard establishes that one Haymo shall be toll-taker at the fair, and his sons after him.

Cartulary, fol. 146r.
Bougaud-Garnier, p. 457.

De Haymone et filiis eius

Presentibus futurisque fratribus nostris clarificetur quod domnus abbas Gerardus[1] omnisque conuentus Haymonem et eius filios post obitum illius thelonearios fori esse constituit, quamdiu illud ministerium fideliter et sine fraude seruauerint. Si uero inde aliquis eorum fraudator deprehendatur, perpetuo caret predicto ministerio.

---

1 Girard, abbot of Bèze (1125–1142).
2 This is the John who was responsible for most of the cartulary.
3 The scribe first wrote "in remissi" again here, then cancelled it.
4 Arçon, 13 km south of Bèze.
1 Girard, abbot of Bèze (1125–1142).

Signum Wilenchi prioris. Signum Rodulfi sacriste. Signum Warnerii precentoris. Signum Tigerii cellerarii. Signum Iosberti prepositi. Signum Otberti famuli. Signum Willelmi. Signum Hugonis de Vlmis.

282

1125–1142

Aywin, lord of Beire, gives Bèze a manse there, some allodial land, and two female serfs with the first one's sons, on the day that his mother is buried. Aywin's brother Gui confirms.

Cartulary, fol. 146r–v.
Bougaud-Garnier, pp. 457–458.

Carta de Beria

Omnium cognicioni clarum esse uolumus quod Ewinus dominus de Beria,[1] in die deposicionis matris suę, dedit ipse et uxor eius Annilina Deo et Sancto Petro ac Besuensi ecclesie unum mansum in uilla Berie et quinque iugera alodii, necnon eciam unam ancillam quę uocatur Gocia cum tribus filiis suis, quorum hec sunt nomina, Ogdierius, Gyrardus, Hugo, alteram quoque ancillam uocabulo Hodiernam et medietatem cuiusdam prati, siquidem alia pars a priscis temporibus nostra esse dinoscitur.

Vt uero insolubilem firmitatem presens carta contineat, adsignamus ei testes. Signum Haymonis Borgni.[2] Signum Heberti Auxissi. Signum Widonis de Perciaco.[3] Signum Roberti Gastulli. Signum Humberti filii Regnardi. Signum Lamberti Falsardi. Signum Gunterii fratris Hodierne supradicte mulieris. Signum Warnerii clerici et Bartholomei fratris eius. De monachis, signum Gerardi abbatis,[4] signum Wilenchi prioris, Rodulfi sacriste, Warnerii precentoris, Iosberti prepositi. Hanc elemosinam in foro Besue laudauit et concessit Wido frater Ewini, coram Mainfredo de Archo.[5]

See also the following document.

1 Beire, 8 km southwest of Bèze.
2 The *cognomina* and clerical offices of the witnesses are written interlinearly.
3 Percey-le-Grand, 18 km northeast of Bèze.
4 Girard, abbot of Bèze (1125–1142).
5 Arc-sur-Tille, 15 km south-southwest of Bèze.

283

1125–1142

Aywin, lord of Beire, acting with his wife and son, gives Bèze some property at Beire.

Cartulary, fol. 146v.
Bougaud-Garnier, p. 458.

Item de quodam plastra sita in hac Besuensi uilla

Fiat notum filiis ecclesie quod Ayuinus miles, de Beria[1] dominus, quoddam plastrum quod possidebat in uilla Besue siue per ius siue iniuste dedit Sancto Petro et Besuensi ecclesie perpetualiter, et uxor eius et filius eius Wilermus puer.

Vt hec elemosina firma permaneat, asygnamus ei testes. Signum Gyrardi abbatis,[2] Wilenchi, Rodulfi.[3] De laicis signum Ayuini, Widonis de Chimisim, Roberti Castul. Signum Ilberti militis de Salice.[4] Signum Lamberti Falsarii et filii eius. S. Raynardi prepositi de Beria. S. Humberti filii eius. S. Gunterii. Signum Ricaldi Caprarii. Signum Heinrici filii eius. Signum Heinrici de Fracto Monte,[5] et aliorum multorum.

Aywin of Beire gave up claims against St-Étienne of Dijon in 1128, before the duke.[6] See also the preceding document.

284

1125–1142

Galo Columba of Beaumont takes the habit at Bèze and gives tithes at Nantilly, as well as a manse with land and half a mill. His son, brother, and wife all agree.

Cartulary, fols. 146v–147r.
Bougaud-Garnier, pp. 458 459.

1 Beire, 8 km southwest of Bèze.
2 Girard, abbot of Bèze (1125–1142).
3 These two were most likely the prior and the sacristan of the abbey, identified as such in the preceding documents.
4 Choilley, 22 km north-northeast of Bèze; and Saulx, 21 km northwest of Bèze.
5 Framont, 25 km northeast of Bèze. This loconym is added interlinearly, as are the identifiers for Robert, Ilbert, Lamberti, Raynard, and Ricald earlier in the witness list.
6 *Chartes de l'abbaye de Saint-Étienne de Dijon de 1098 à 1140*, pp. 65–66, no. 58.

Carta doni Galonis Columbę

Omne quod est natum tendit ad interitum, secundum Salomonem, ne dum uerba quę cum prolata sint, iam non sunt. Idcirco hic assignamus Galonem Bellimontis,[1] cognomine dictum Columbam, habitum sanctę religionis suscipientem, Sancto Petro Besuensi ęcclesię dedisse in uilla Lentiliaco[2] medietatem decimarum ad se pertinentium, de propriis scilicet bubus monachorum, et mansum cum terra et pratis pertinentibus ad ipsum, in uilla Sancti Benigni Diuionensis Casneto,[3] atque medietatem molendini apud uillam Perceium,[4] simulque medietatem plastri siti in hac uilla Besensi. Addidit etiam mansum apud Lisseium cum terra quę Montis Salionis[5] dicitur pertinenti ad ipsum, ibidemque in pratis, paniciariis dictis, quicquid eximi potest a nemore in pratum.

Laudante hoc et concedente domino Montis Salionis Oddone, domno Girardo abbate,[6] testibus assistentibus Alberto Tullensi et Guidone de Vircillis.[7] Hanc donationem a predicto Galone factam Hugo filius, Haymo frater, et uxor eius propriis manibus librum super altare ponentes, laudauerunt. Quam roboramus testimonio proborum uirorum, domni Girardi abbatis, Guilenci prioris, Alberti Tullensis, Bartholomei et reliquorum monachorum. Laicorum, Milonis de Poiens, Hugonis de Roife,[8] Humberti Salomonis, Humberti Diuitis, Roberti prepositi, et aliorum multorum.

Galo Columba also appears in St-Étienne's charters, with his brother Aymo.[9]

285

1125–1142

Hugh, a knight of Torcenay, takes the habit and gives Bèze a manse at Rosoy and his part of the woods of Montigy.

Cartulary, fol. 147r.
Bougaud-Garnier, p. 459.

1 Beaumont, 7 km east of Bèze.
2 Nantilly, 20 km east of Bèze.
3 Chaignay, 15 km west of Bèze, was dependent on St-Bénigne of Dijon. The monks of St-Bénigne acquired the rights there around the year 1100; *Chartes et documents de Saint-Bénigne de Dijon*, 2:154–156, no. 375.
4 Percey-le-Grand, 18 km northeast of Bèze.
5 Licey, 8 km east-northeast of Bèze; and Montsaugeon, 22 km north of Bèze.
6 Girard, abbot of Bèze (1125–1142).
7 Verseilles, 33 km north of Bèze.
8 Poyans, 16 km east of Bèze; and Ruffey-le-Château, 46 km southeast of Bèze.
9 *Chartes de l'abbaye de Saint-Étienne de Dijon de 1098 à 1140*, p. 61, no. 52, dated 1125–1136.

Carta Hugonis de Torcennaco

Memorie posterorum litteris imprimimus quod Hugo miles de Torcennaco,[1] habitum religionis suscipiens, dedit Sancto Petro et Besuensi ecclesię quoddam mansum apud Rosecium,[2] partemque suam nemoris Montaniaci,[3] laudantibus filiis suis, testibus Roberto capellano Montis Salionis, et Widone milite de Ortis, fratreque eius Hugone Rufo, cum aliis multis.

Although Abbot Girard is not mentioned, it is most likely that this document was given during his abbacy, like the other documents in this section.

286

1125–1142

Odo, a knight of Pichanges, gives Bèze rights in a mill at Lux as he takes the habit. He had previously claimed it. His four brothers all witness his gift.

Cartulary, fol. 147v.
Bougaud-Garnier, pp. 459–460.

Noscant omnes qui hos legerint apices quod Oddo miles de Pichangiis,[1] cognomine dictus Saxo, monachus ad finem factus, quicquid in molendino apud uillam Lucum[2] calumpniabatur, Sancto Petro concessit, ipsumque molendinum fratribus suis laudantibus, Besuensi ecclesię perpetuo habendum deuote tradidit.

Et ne hoc quisquam in posterum irritare presumat, subponimus signa testium qui presentes adfuerunt. Signum Gerardi abbatis,[3] Rodulfi sacriste, Hugonis de Belloioco, Lebaldi de Geneureris.[4] De laicis, signum Hugonis, Walterii, Milonis, Humberti fratrum predicti Oddonis. Signum Roberti prepositi, Humberti Diuitis, Otberti cocci, Gyraldi uillici.

287

1125–1142

Ascher, a knight of Montsaugeon, is dying and gives Bèze a manse, along with land and two brothers with their niece.

Cartulary, fol. 147v.
Bougaud-Garnier, p. 460.

---

1 Torcenay, 41 km north-northeast of Bèze.
2 Rosoy, 5 km northeast of Torcenay.
3 Montigny, 17 km northeast of Bèze.
1 Pichanges, 9 km west of Bèze.
2 Lux, 5 km northwest of Bèze.
3 Girard, abbot of Bèze (1125–1142).
4 Beaujeu, 31 km east-northeast of Bèze; and Genevrières, 38 km north-northeast of Bèze.

Carta doni Ascherii Montis Salionis

Idcirco elemosinę fidelium litteris adnotantur ut hi qui post futuri sunt legendo quod non uiderunt agnoscant, et si hinc aliqua forte calumpnia prauorum hominum orta fuerit, auctoritate priorum resistere ualent. Notificandum ergo posteris censemus quod Ascherius quidam miles Montis Salionis,[1] ad obitum ueniens, dedit Deo et Sancto Petro Besuensi, in terra quę Craias dicitur, mansum quoddam ita libere ut ipse habebat, cum hominibus scilicet et pratis, ceterisque appendiciis suis, duos eciam fratres uillę Albiniaci[2] incolas, Albricum, Stephanum, neptemque eorum Auilinam.

Testes huius elemosinę sunt Gerardus abbas,[3] Guilencius prior, Rodulfus sacrista, Heinricus, Garnerius precentor, et Gunterius. De militibus, Hugo et Oddo fratres predicti Ascherii, Paganus de Buiris,[4] aliique quamplurimi.

288

1125–1142

Lord William of Fouvent gives Bèze fishing rights at Champlitte. Later he becomes a monk and adds to his gift with mansi at Courtesoult. On the day of his burial, his son gives up what he characterizes as unjust claims.

Cartulary, fols. 147v–148v.
Bougaud-Garnier, pp. 460–462.

Karta domni Willermi Fontisuenne

Quia presens uita ad malum procliua est, oportet ut elemosinis uel bonis operibus quisque mala admissa a conspectu Domini abscondat, quoniam et apostolus tempus redimi precipit, eo quod dies mali sint. Quod Guillelmus Fontisuenne[1] gratia Dei adimplens, piscatoriam quandam cum manso appendenti ad ipsam, piscatoremque Albricum nomine cum uxore et filiis, Besuensi ęcclesię in uilla Camlintensi[2] tribuit, cum adhuc in seculari milicia positus esset.

Postquam uero diuino respectu monachus effectus est, delegauit in uilla quę Cortesours[3] uocatur Deo ac Sancto Petro Besuensi duos mansos cum appendiciis

1 Montsaugeon, 22 km north of Bèze.
2 Aubigny, 22 km north of Bèze and 2 km west of Montsaugeon.
3 Girard, abbot of Bèze (1125–1142).
4 Bure-lès-Templiers, 40 km northwest of Bèze.
1 Fouvent, 35 km northeast of Bèze.
2 Champlitte, 24 km north-northeast of Bèze.
3 Courtesoult, 4 km southwest of Fouvent.

suis, duosque homines Stephanum et Teodericum, habitatores eorum, cum uxoribus et filiis omnibusque ad se pertinentibus, atque omnes usuarios fructus quos tercias nominant, duarum uillarum de Cortesour et de Lare,[4] excepto quod duo fratres Nerduinus et Amalricus, uillici domni Gyrardi filii eiusdem Guillelmi, pro manso maiorali lx iugera retinuerunt. Hęc ut predictum est Besuensi ecclesie concesserunt Guillelmus et Gyrardus filius eius, landantibus Guidone domino Fontisuenne, cum filio suo Teoderico et Guidone domino Iouisuille.

Preterea in die sepulture predicti Guillelmi, Gyrardus et Guido domini Montaniaci[5] reliquerunt iniustam consuetudinem quam erga homines nostros de Pauliaco[6] habebant, decreueruntque ut si aliquis eorum de aliquo homine Sancti Petri iusticiam pro aliquo forfacto appeteret, alter nullomodo tale ab eodem exigeret. Nam antea uterque ab uno ex uno forfacto duplex rectum exigebat.

De his omnibus testes adhibemus domnum Gyrardum abbatem,[7] Guilencum priorem, Rodulfus sacristam, Garnerium precentorem, Widricum priorem Fontisuenne, Albertum Tullensem. Item Hugonem dominum Bellimontis filiumque eius Hugonem,[8] Haymonem de Tilecastro, Hugonem de Belloioco, Milonem de Poiens, Oddonem iuuenem de Domna Petra, Widricum de Monz,[9] Vlgerium de Burgo Walterii, Oddilonem prepositum Camlintensis, Otbertum coccum, Hugonem dapiferum, fratresque prememoratos Nerduinum et Amalricum.

289

1125–1142

Milo, a knight of Tilchâtel, frees a female serf and her descendants from his service, phrased as a gift to Bèze. His brothers agree.

Cartulary, fol. 148v.
Bougaud-Garnier, p. 462.

Carta Milonis cognomento Pautenerii

Secundum Prophetam monentem, "Dissolue colligationes impietatis, solue fasciculos deprimentes" [Isa. 58:6], Milo Tilecastri[1] miles dictus, agnomine

4 Larrey, near Champlitte according to Garnier.

5 Montigny, 17 km northeast of Bèze.

6 Pouilly, 15 km northeast of Bèze.

7 Girard, abbot of Bèze (1125–1142).

8 Hugh IV, lord of Beaumont, 7 km east of Bèze, and his son, Hugh V.

9 Tilchâtel, 9 km northwest of Bèze; Beaujeu, 31 km east-northeast of Bèze; Poyans, 16 km east of Bèze; Dampierre, 32 km east-northeast of Bèze; and Mont (now Mont-le-Frânois), 26 km northeast of Bèze.

1 Tilchâtel, 9 km northwest of Bèze.

Gyrouagus, Humberti Vetule filiam, uxorem scilicet Oddonis Maleth filii Eurardi Diuionensis, Oddilinam uocatam, a seruitute et famulatu suo, et progenitorum suorum absoluit, et super altare Sancti Petri Besuensis liberam proclamans posuit, audientibus, uidentibus, et laudantibus suis fratribus Humberto et Willelmo Delfosse, et filiis suis.

Hanc donationem confirmamus subscriptis testibus, Gyrardo abbate Besuensi,[2] Guilenco priore, Roberto preposito, Oberto cocco, Gyrardo filio Aydulfi, Drogone filio Girberti, Hugone de Vlmis, Lamberto Falsart, Aldone et Oddone fratribus de Fontanis,[3] aliisque multis.

290

1125–1142

Rudolf, a knight of St-Michel, gives up his claims to a serf of Bèze.

Cartulary, fols. 148v–149r.
Bougaud-Garnier, pp. 462–463.

De Dominico Malner

Memoriali digno his litteris adnotamus, Rodulfum militem Sancti Michaelis[1] quicquid super Dominicum Malenigrum quem sicutti seruum ab antecessoribus iuste uel iniuste habuerat ac possederat Sancto Petro Besuensi donasse et super altare posuisse, testibus assistentibus multis, Gyrardo abbate,[2] Heinrico, Lebaldo, Ricardo, Hugone monachis. Laicorum uero affuerunt milites, Wido Rauines, maritus sororis datoris, Euuinus de Excelso, Walterius Malsualez Granciaci, Oddo de Furno.[3] Familie nostre, Humbertus Salomon, Guilelmus, Petrus Pauliaci, Petrus etiam, et Robertus Monte Salionis.[4]

291

c. 1125–1142

Nerduin, lord of Aprey, and Galo of Villiers, with their sons, give Bèze land at Orcevaux for their souls.

Cartulary, fol. 149r.
Bougaud-Garnier, p. 463.

---

2 Girard, abbot of Bèze (1125–1142).
3 Fontaine-Française, 10 km northeast of Bèze.
1 St-Michel, 29 km north of Bèze.
2 Girard, abbot of Bèze (1125–1142).
3 Occey, 16 km north of Bèze; Grancey, 29 km northwest of Bèze; and Feurg, 18 km east of Bèze.
4 Pouilly, 15 km northeast of Bèze; and Montsaugeon, 22 km north of Bèze.

De Orceual

Sciant omnes tam presentes quam futuri quod Nerduinus dominus Aspermontis et Hugo filius eius miles et Galo de Willer[1] et Haymo filius eius, pro animabus suis et antecessorum suorum, tradiderunt Deo et Sancto Petro ac Besuensi ęcclesię in locum qui Orceuallis[2] dicitur xl iugera terre.

Huic dono assignamus testes. Signum Hugonis Francigene. Signum Rodulfi de Renauis,[3] Hugonis Conitensis, Euuini Spinelli.

292

1125–1142

Mainfred of Arc gave Bèze the wife of the carpenter Theoderic, along with her children, when Stephen was abbot and received twenty solidi as a counter-gift. Although he later claimed that he had not given her children, he does so now, when Girard is abbot; Girard gives him ten solidi and Humbert of Belleneuve two.

Cartulary, fol. 149r–v.
Bougaud-Garnier, p. 463.

De uxore Teoderici carpentarii

Fideliter retineat quisquis has legerit literas quod Mainfredus de Arco[1] uxorem Teoderici cum liberis suis Deo Sanctoque Petro Besuensi pro anima sua concessit. Ipsique Mainfredo domnus abbas Stephanus[2] ob hanc causam immo magis gratia amicicie, xx tunc solidos dedit. Sed quoniam mens humana sepe a bono deuiat, idem Mainfredus post obitum Teoderici cum coram domno G[irardo] abbate[3] de hac re quasi non gratis uel libere filios eius dedisset, queritando placitaret, conuictus racione, eos se libere concessisse recognouit atque eandem elemosinam confirmans, denuo liberrime huic ecclesie perpetuo contulit, et uxori sue ac filiis laudari fecit. Abbas uero G[irardus] ob pacem uel memoriam huius pacti dedit ei x solidos et Humberto de Baleneua[4] duos.

Huic carte testes idoneos qui afuerunt subponimus. Signum Girardi abbatis, Guilenchi prioris, Heinrici, Albrici, Lebaldi. Signum Hugonis Bellimontis,[5]

1 Aprey, 33 km north-northwest of Bèze; and Villiers, 2 km south of Aprey.
2 Orcevaux, 4 km northeast of Aprey and 34 km north of Bèze.
3 Renève, 13 km south-southeast of Bèze.
1 Arc-sur-Tille, 15 km south-southwest of Bèze.
2 Stephen, abbot of Bèze (1088–1120).
3 Girard, abbot of Bèze (1125–1142).
4 Belleneuve, 12 km south of Bèze.
5 Hugh IV, lord of Beaumont, 7 km east of Bèze. His son and heir, also witnessing, was Hugh V.

Euini et Hugonis filii eius, Guidonis prepositi Sancti Iuliani, Humberti uillici de Baleneua, Valeth, Oberti cocci, Giraudi uillici.

The following document includes almost all the same people and was doubtless done at the same time.

293

1125–1142

Hugh, a villager of Belleneuve, and his sons give up a claim to some of Bèze's land at Trochères.

Cartulary, fol. 149v.
Bougaud-Garnier, p. 464.

De uilla que dicitur Trescase

Presencium ac futurorum memorie clarescat quod Hugo uillicus de Baleneua[1] et filii eius Humberrtus, Iohannes, Petrus, terram Sancti Petri apud Trescasas,[2] quam per multos annos calumpniati fuerant, reddiderunt in pace Sancto Petro et Besuensi ecclesię atque se peccasse quod eam inuaserant, cognoscentes absolucionem delicti sui a domno Gyrardo abbate[3] et omnibus fratribus in capitulo pecierunt et acceperunt.

De hoc facto assignamus testes, Gyrardum abbatem, Guilenchum priorem, Albricum Alcionis, et reliquos capituli. Mainfredum etiam de Arco,[4] Guidonem prepositum Sancti Iuliani, Valeth de Baleneua, et Otbertum.

294

1125–1142

Geoffrey, lord of Beaumont, and his wife Gertrude give Bèze the villa St-Seine-en-Bâche. His nephew Geoffrey Martel later claimed justice rights there but gives them up.

Cartulary, fol. 150r.
Bougaud-Garnier, pp. 464–465.

1 Belleneuve, 12 km south of Bèze.
2 Trochères, 14 km south-southeast of Bèze.
3 Girard, abbot of Bèze (1125–1142).
4 Arçon, 13 km south of Bèze; and Arc-sur-Tille, 15 km south-southwest of Bèze.

Quoniam facta precedentia per litterarum annotationem cognouimus, placuit et nobis scribendo posteris relinquere, ut inuiolabile in eternum permaneat quod Ioffredus Bellimontis dominus cum Gertrude uxore sua,[5] pro salute animarum suarum, Sancto Petro et abbati Gyrardo[6] et monachis Besuensibus uillam quandam, que uocatur Sanctus Sequanus in Baascha,[7] sicut ipsi eam libere tenebant concesserunt, laudante Hugone filio et nepote Ioffredo agnomine Martello, omnibusque qui hoc donum in postremo perturbare uidebantur.

Contigit autem instigante diabolo ut successor Martellus post mortem predictorum antecessorum suorum uiolari non erubesceret quod prius laudauerat, uidelicet ut iusticiam et latrocinium in predicta uilla clamaret. Postea uero animante Domino qui ecclesiam suam elemosinis fidelium priuari non patitur, et donno Gyrardo abbate hoc ei ammonente ad seipsum reuersus, deuotus capitulo fratrum adiit, fraternitatem accepit, et pro requie anime sue et antecessorum suorum gratis quicquid in uilla clamabat uel quecumque habebat libere concessit, excepto manso Odilonis et fratris eius Galonis, seruorum suorum.

Signum Gyrardi abbatis. Signum Lebaldi. Signum Ricardi monachi. De militibus, Martelli, Welfonis, Elluini, Haymonis filii Vuidrici. Signum Sauarini. Signum Odilonis. Signum Wiberti. De familia Sancti Petri, Signum Otberti cocci. Signum Widonis. Signum Humberti Diuitis, Humberti Salomonis.

Although this document does not have a rubric, there is some red ink highlighting the signatures of important people. This is the last red ink for the charters. Presumably the scribes were going to get back to it but never did.

295

Mantoche, 1125–1142

The knight Aymo, son of Galo of Villiers, claimed justice rights but gives them up, on the advice of his mother.

Cartulary, fol. 150v.
Bougaud-Garnier, pp. 165–166.

[A]rbitramur[1] rectum fore fidelium memorie tradere census ęcclesię ne quando per incuriam nostram a prauis hominibus minuantur. Ideoque assignamus hic

5 For Geoffrey, see Bouchard, *Sword, Miter, and Cloister*, pp. 321–323. Their son was Hugh IV of Beaumont.

6 Girard, abbot of Bèze (1125–1142).

7 St-Seine-en-Bâche, 40 km south-southeast of Bèze.

1 The initial *A* was never filled in. The same is the case with many subsequent documents.

quendam militem, Haymonem nomine, filium uidelicet Galonis de Viler,[2] clamantem in atrio Sancti Martyni de Montusca[3] iusticiam et latrocinium. Nam ob huiuscemodi causam predam abduxit et alia multa mala ecclesie Besuensi irrogauit. Cui cum in hac pertinacia diu permaneret, placitum terminauit abbas Gyrardus[4] in eadem uilla. Conuenerunt igitur utrique die terminato, consultus a matre que secum placitatura uenerat, et a reliquis amicis suis querimoniam quam super familiam monachorum nostrorum ibi degencium faciebat, in pace abbati proclamauit. Insuper de duobus hominibus quos monachus foris atrium habitare faceret. Ita tamen ut si aliquod seclus a suis uel ab aliis hominibus illuc committeretur, isdem ad abbatem Besuensem clamationem faceret et pro ullo patatro scelere, si etiam homicidium aut adulterium esset, quorum lex maior esse dinoscitur aliis sceleribus, ultra quintos[5] solidos lege rectitudinis inde quippiam haberet.

This doubtless took place after Aymo's father had died; see document 291.

296

1134

Hugh of Beaumont with his sons makes a gift to Bèze of whatever the priest Remigius had in the parish St-Martin. He also gives a place to fish.

Cartulary, fol. 151r–v.
Bougaud-Garnier, pp. 466–467.
Summarized in Brequigny, *Table* 2:617.

In nomine sancte et indiuidue Trinitatis. Vniuersi fidei Christianę domestici sanctam Dei ecclesiam animi deuocione gloriosam, et muneribus in quantum possunt largissimis, facere debent locupletem. Qua si quidem animaduersione compunctus et a Sancto Spiritu spiritualiter instinctus, ego Hugo de Bellomonte cum filiis meis Hugone et Ioffredo,[1] pro remedio animę meę[2] antecessorumque meorum, Deo et Sancto Petro Besuensi abbatique Gerardo[3] monachisque Besuensibus in parrochia Sancti Martyni Deo seruire uolentibus, dono concessi quicquid domnus Remigius eiusdem loci presbiter in ecclesiis,

2 Villiers, 31 km north-northwest of Bèze.
3 Mantoche, 21 km east-southeast of Bèze.
4 Girard, abbot of Bèze (1125–1142).
5 The cartulary reads "quinos."
1 Hugh IV of Beaumont, 7 km east of Bèze, with his sons, Hugh V and Geoffrey.
2 The cartulary reads "męę."
3 Girard, abbot of Bèze (1125–1142).

in agris, in pratis, in siluis, in domibus et uniuersis humane uite usibus tenebat. Et insuper quicquid uademoniorum que predictis monachis aut iam dederit aut in futurum dare uoluerit possidebat.

Placuit etiam huic dono adnectere quod homines qui apud Sanctum Martynum hospitati erunt et circa monachos habitabunt in terris castri Belmontensis omne usuarium libere habeant in siluis, in pratis, in pascuis, et in omnibus quibus uiuunt homines usibus, ita scilicet quod si homines dampnum nescienter fecerint, dampnum sine lege reddant. Monachi uero quoquomodo aut ipsi aut sui famuli scienter uel nescienter dampnum fecerint, dampnum sine lege prorsus restituant. Piscariam etiam ipsis donaui a Belmonte desuper, ubi uel quando uel quomodo eis placuerit piscari, subtus uero Belmontem pede tenus piscari tantum concessi.

Quod donum ne qua tegatur obliuionis nebula, placuit litteris commendare, approbatorumque qui adfuerunt uirorum testimonio roborare. Signum Gyrardi abbatis. Signum Ricardi de Vircillis. Signum Lebaldi de Geneureris,[4] Iosberti prepositi, Heinrici capellani. Signum Humberti negociatoris. Petrus Rufus, Iohannes famulus, Christianus, Hugo Bellimontis dominus, Hugo filius eius, Remigius presbiter, Milo de Poiens,[5] Hugo de Aces, Euurardus de Rolens, Fredericus de Campaneio, Wido de Renauis,[6] Rodulfus filius Odolrici, Erbertus capicium. Acta sunt hec anno ab incarnacione Domini Millesimo Centesimo XXXIV, indictione xii, epacta xxiii, concurrente vii.

This is a confirmation of one of the churches the bishop gave to Bèze in this same year; see document 333. One can perhaps conclude that the documents from Abbot Girard's rule that were copied before this one took place before 1134, given that the hands had been changing with nearly every document, suggesting that they were copied into the cartulary as they were given.

297

c. 1125–1142

Aymo of Tilchâtel gives up his claims to property at Lux, for his soul.

Cartulary, fols. 151v–152r.
Bougaud-Garnier, pp. 467–468.

4 Verseilles, 33 km north of Bèze; and Genevrières, 38 km north-northeast of Bèze.

5 Poyans, 16 km east of Bèze.

6 Occey, 16 km north of Bèze; unidentified; Champagne, 10 km southeast of Bèze; and Renève, 13 km south-southeast of Bèze.

[O]mnium hominum est qui nominis censentur uocabulo Christiani, in lege Domini die ac nocte iugiter meditari. Lex enim Domini inreprehensibilis, cum conuertat animas et testimonium sit fidele, sapientiam prestat paruulis. Ego igitur Haymo de Tiricastro[1] paruulus scientia, multorumque malorum que egeram honeratus insipientia, cum ante meum obitum longa depressus fuissem egritudine, ad meipsum rediens et insuper cogitans quod ante Deum nullum ferrem manipulum iustitie, pro remedio anime mee parentumque meorum, Deo et Sancto Petro et monachis Besuensis cenobii atrium Sancti Martyni de Luco[2] concessi, et quidquid ibidem iuste uel iniuste possederam totum eis dimisi.

Testes adfuerunt Ricardus capellanus, Petrus capellanus eiusdem Ricardi, Hugo de Conulent,[3] Iohannes clericus, Thebaldus de Chasoto,[4] Wido Talauat.

See also the following document.

298

Tilchâtel, 1129–1142

Agnes, widow of Aymo of Tilchâtel, confirms his gifts at Lux as he is buried in the cemetery of St-Florent.

Cartulary, fol. 152r–v.
Bougaud-Garnier, p. 268.

Ego Agnes uxor donni Haymonis de Tiricastel, cum ipse Haymo maritus meus in paradiso Sancti Florentii[1] fuisset tumulatus, assistentibus clericis, parentibus, et amicis, cum insimul in claustrum regressi fuissemus et cum de elemosina eius tractaremus, uisum nobis est esse bonum ut donum quod donnus Haymo fecerat ecclesie Besuensi de atrio Sancti Martini de Luco,[2] cum liberis meis facerem, et quoram eis bonis ac pluribus uiris qui adfuerunt illud confirmarem.

1 Aymo II, lord of Tilchâtel, which is 9 km northwest of Bèze; his wife Agnes is mentioned in the following document. For the family, see Bouchard, *Sword, Miter, and Cloister*, pp. 366–368.
2 Lux, 5 km northwest of Bèze.
3 Coublanc, 28 km north-northeast of Bèze.
4 Chazeuil, 10 km north of Bèze.
1 Lord Aymo I of Tilchâtel had made his chapel of St-Florent a dependency of St-Étienne of Dijon in 1033; *Chartes de l'abbaye de Saint-Étienne de Dijon (VIIIe, IXe, Xe et XIe siècles)*, pp. 86–87, no. 64.
2 Lux, 5 km northwest of Bèze.

Dedi igitur et confirmaui donum quod fecerat, atrium uidelicet sancti Martyni de Luco monachis Besuensibus, quietum et cum omni libertate et pace pro anima mariti mei in eternum possidendum.

Quod ne deleatur aut obliuioni tradatur temporum interuallo, uirorum subscriptorum roboramus testimonio. Petrus abbas Sancti Benigni Diuionensis, Herbertus abbas Sancti Stephani Diuionensis,[3] Thebaldus decanus, Ricardus presbiter, Dominicus prior Sancti Florentii, Bonet de Mare,[4] Iohannes clericus, Petrus capellanus, Haymo de Mimire, Wido de Saut,[5] Nocherus, Wido Talauat, Thebaldus de Casoto,[6] Vaslerus, Rollannus, Wido marscalcus, Malueslot, Tebaldus Excotex, Robertus filius eius.

Hoc[7] factum est et recognitum quod donum quod fecerant de atrio non ideo fecerant quod atrium suum esset, sed ideo quia in atrio quod Sancti Petri erat rapiebant, et ablactiones faciebant et ea que iure uel rectitudine in ipso atrio non habebant iniuria et uiolentia rapiebant.

299

Good Friday, 1125–1142

The brothers Rudolf and Milo give Bèze two mansi at Montigny for the souls of their brothers and parents.

Cartulary, fol. 152v.
Bougaud-Garnier, p. 469.

[C]um transeant cuncta et ea que in hoc mundo sunt nunquam in eodem statu sint diu permanentia, litteris adnotamus quod Rodulfus et Milo frater eius, qui suo agnomine dicti sunt Bigornenses, pro animabus fratrum suorum Guidonis et Rotgeri et pro animabus patris et matris sue antecessorumque suorum remedio, Deo et Sancto Petro et monachis Besuensis ecclesie dederunt duos mansos apud Montiniacum,[1] unum mansum qui dicitur mansus Oddonis Euruini et alterum

3 Abbot Peter of St-Bénigne (1129–1142) and Abbot Herbert of St-Étienne of Dijon (1125–1157), the first abbot there once the house acquired regular canons. The Bougaud-Garnier edition mistakenly jumps from the first "abbas" to the second, making Peter abbot of St-Étienne.

4 Marey-sur-Tille, 21 km northwest of Bèze.

5 Saulx, 21 km northwest of Bèze.

6 Chazeuil, 10 km north of Bèze.

7 This final comment is added in a different hand.

1 Montigny, 17 km northeast of Bèze.

qui dicitur mansus Widonis Malę filie. Hoc donum apud Besuam fecerunt in Parasceuen, id est in die Passionis Domini, tenentes ambo librum per quem hanc donationem in presentia donni abbatis Gyrardi[2] super altare posuerunt.

Signum ipsius abbatis Gyrardi. Signum Widrici prioris Fontisuenne. Signum Albrici de Arcione.[3] Signum Alberti de Tullo. Signum Girberti de Alteriaco.[4] Signum Iohannis presbiteri de Besua.

300

1134–1142

Bishop Willenc of Langres had given Bèze the church of St-Martin and authority over the priest of Dampierre, but Humbert of Licey and his sons claimed it. Now Theoderic, one of the sons, has died, and Humbert and his other sons give up their claims and make additional gifts of property to the monks for Theoderic's soul.

Cartulary, fols. 152v–153r.
Bougaud-Garnier, pp. 469–470.

[P]atet quod genus humanum ad finem semper defluat, cum profecto honor et potentia hominis labatur, decorque iuuentutis cito marcens euanescat. Quapropter necesse est ut homo elemosinarum remedia querat, quoniam elemosina faciem Domini placat et misericordiam impetrat. Ne uero dona fidelium obliuioni tradantur, litteris ea intimare debemus. Igitur tempore quo a domno Wilenco Lingonensi episcopo[1] ecclesia Sancti Martyni Sancto Petro Besuensi data est, presbiteratum etiam ęcclesię de Donnapetra[2] idem episcopus nobis concesserat. Sed hunc Humbertus de Lissei[3] et filii eius, quia tunc in eorum dominio erat, calumpniabantur, uique illum retinebant. Theoderico autem filio predicti Humberti uita decedente, fratres ipsius Teoderici, Wido scilicet cum tribus aliis, patre eorum laudante, ipsum presbiteratum et atrium ęcclesię Sancto Petro Besuensi libere tradiderunt, iusticias tantum atrii retinentes. Ita sane ut si homo Sancti Petri in eodem atrio aliquod forfactum fecerit, clamatio

2 Girard, abbot of Bèze (1125–1142).
3 Fouvent, 35 km northeast of Bèze; and Arçon, 13 km south of Bèze.
4 Autrey, 17 km east-northeast of Bèze.
1 Willenc, bishop of Langres (1125–1136).
2 Dampierre, 7 km east-northeast of Bèze.
3 Licey, 8 km east-northeast of Bèze.

ad abbatem Besuensem fiat, rectumque faciens non amplius quam quod uiuens lex eius fuerit, soluat.

Dederunt etiam quattuor falces prati in suo broulo Sancti Sequani[4] et hominem Albricum nomine cum uxore et filiis, suisque tenimentis, sororemque eius uxorem cuiusdam Elluini. Addiderunt et terciam partem terciarum de Blaniaco[5] et alodum et omnia quę illic habebant, excepto manso cuiusdam Walterii, cum appendiciis suis.

Hanc ergo elemosinam fratres supradicti defuncti Wido, et Humbertus pro remedio anime eius Sancto Petro et Besuensi ęcclesię per impositionem libri super altare confirmauerunt, testibus coram adstantibus quos hic assignabimus. Signum Gerardi abbatis,[6] signum Rodulfi prioris, Heinrici, Alberti, Ricardi, Ansirici, Bartholomei, Ricardi. De militibus, signum Hugonis Bellimontis et filiorum eius Hugonis et Ioffredi,[7] Ottonis de Miribel, Hugonis Asperimontis, Euuini de Aces, Milonis de Poiens, Haymonis Columbe, Vrrici de Renauis[8] et filii eius Milonis.

See also documents 296 and 333.

301

c. 1125–1142

Walo of Ruffey, for his wife's soul, gave Bèze tithes at Mantoche and Cecey. He later tried to claim them, but now gives up his claim. His sons agree, including one who is a monk.

Cartulary, fol. 153r–v.
Bougaud-Garnier, pp. 470–471.

[C]onstat multimoda uarietate mundi negotia pretergredi, ideoque necesse est quę memorię digna sunt scriptis adnotari. Notificamus ergo posteris quod Galo de Rofei,[1] pro anima uxoris suę, Annilina nomine, et animabus antecessorum

---

4 St-Seine-sur-Vingeanne, 13 km northeast of Bèze.
5 Blagny, 8 km east-southeast of Bèze.
6 Girard, abbot of Bèze (1125–1142).
7 Hugh IV of Beaumont, 7 km east of Bèze, with his sons, Hugh V and Geoffrey.
8 Mirebeau, 9 km south-southeast of Bèze; Aprey, 33 km north-northwest of Bèze; Occey, 16 km north of Bèze; Poyans, 16 km east of Bèze; and Renève, 13 km south-southeast of Bèze.
1 Ruffey-le-Château, 46 km southeast of Bèze.

suorum, dedit Sancto Petro et Besuensi ecclesię minutas decimas uillę que Mentusca dicitur, omnesque decimas de uilla Cincei,[2] libere uti possederat. Accidit autem ut postea subripiente auaritia, donum quod fecerat calumpniaretur. De qua re monachus qui preerat Mentusche cum eo locutionem habuit, in qua idem Galo se errasse cognoscens, deuote predictam elemosinam ęcclesię Besuensi in pace habendam concessit.

Signum Ricardi monachi de Mentuscha, Alelmi sotii eius. Signum Vlgerii monachi, filii Galonis qui donum fecit. Signum Ricardi prepositi. Item signum Hugonis et Willermi filii predicti Galonis. Signum Notberti capellani, Ricardi conuersi Moliniensis.[3] Signum Widonis et Ermenfredi, et aliorum multorum.

Walo of Ruffey had given the monks the church of Mantoche somewhat earlier; see document 278.

302

1125–1142

Milo of Fontaine-Française and his mother, Petronilla, give Bèze a manse at Cusey with the family living there, for the soul of his brother Aymo. Milo also gives some land at Fontenelle and an annual income of five solidi.

Cartulary, fols. 153v–154r.
Bougaud-Garnier, pp. 471–472.

De Cusuo

[F]idelium elemosinas recensere dignum est, qui iuxta quod Dominus precipit, in cęlo sibi thesaurizare student [cf. Matt. 12:21]. Omnibus ergo scire uolentibus clarum fiat quod Milo de Fontanis,[1] Haymone fratre suo defuncto, pro eius anima dedit ipse et mater sua, Petronilla nomine, Sancto Petro Besuensis ęcclesię mansum unum apud Cusiacum[2] cum appendiciis suis, hominemque nomine Benignum cum uxore ac familia. Habebamus autem ex eisdem apud Fontanellas[3] tria iugera terrę, cum quibus alia tria libere sicut possederant,

2 Mantoche, 21 km east-southeast of Bèze; and Cecey, 18 km east-southeast of Bèze.
3 The monastery of Molesme.
1 Fontaine-Française, 10 km northeast of Bèze.
2 Cusey, 19 km north-northwest of Bèze.
3 Fontenelle, 9 km northeast of Bèze.

nobis dederunt, et eciam minister illius terrę ministracionem suam ęcclesię Besuensi reliquit. Dederunt quoque apud Fontanas v solidos singulis annis in uigilia Omnium Sanctorum ad refectionem fratrum. Hęc supradictus Milo cum matre sua Petronilla deuote Sancto Petro Besuensi contulit, Euuino cum ceteris fratribus, et Gybuino sororio eius cum uxore laudantibus.

Signum Gyrardi abbatis.[4] Signum Rodulfi prioris. Signum Widrici prioris Fontisuenne,[5] Ricardi prepositi, Bartholomei, Ricardi, Poncii, signum Widrici presbiteri. De laicis, signum Teoderici, Signum Widrici et Humberti fratrum. Signum Lebaldi et Hugonis.

303

c. 1142

Geoffrey, bishop of Langres, attests that the monks of Bèze have given one tenth of their allod at Colonge and the parish church to the nuns there, by the bishop's hand. In return, the nuns promise to give the abbot six pounds of wax a year. The abbot also gives the nuns the tithes of Colonge, which his men had taken.

Cartulary, fol. 154r.
Bougaud-Garnier, p. 472.

De Colongis

In nomine summe et indiuidue Trinitatis. Ego Gothefredus Dei gratia Lingonensium humilis episcopus[1] omnibus sanctę matris ecclesię filiis, in perpetuum. Notum facimus tam presentium ętati quam future posteritati domnum Gerardum[2] Besuensem abbatem eiusdemque loci monachos decimam partem alodii, quam habebant in Colungiis,[3] et omnem parrochiam et ad ipsam pertinentia per manum nostram sanctimonialibus de Colungiis dedisse et concessisse. Ita tamen quod singulis annis ab ipsis sanctionialibus abbas Besuensis ęcclesię sex libras de cera usque ad octauas Natalis Domini pro alodio et parrochia haberet. Concessit etiam idem abbas consenciente suo capitulo sanctimonialibus

4 Girard, abbot of Bèze (1125–1142).
5 Fouvent, 35 km northeast of Bèze.
1 Geoffrey of La Roche, bishop of Langres (1139–1163).
2 Girard, abbot of Bèze (1125–1142).
3 Colonge, 13 km southeast of Bèze.

de Colungiis decimam eiusdem loci, quam quidam homines sibi usurpauerant. Pro qua decima mulieres ibidem Deo deuotae reddant eis octo minas bladi per medium annuatim.

The charter must have been given during the short period (1139–1142) when Girard was still abbot and Geoffrey had become bishop. The traditional date for the foundation of the house of Cistercian nuns at Colonge, as given by GC, is 1142.

304

Mailly, 1127–1142

Robert of Billey, going to Jerusalem, gives Bèze all his allodial property at Licey, along with a man and his family. If he returns from Jerusalem and any of his sons or nephews wish to become monks, the monastery shall receive them. His brother Peter agrees and receives seventy solidi from the abbot.

Cartulary, fol. 154v.
Bougaud-Garnier, pp. 472–473.

De Lisseiaco

Litterarum memorię tradere censemus quod Robertus Billeiaci,[1] Ierusalem ire disponens, omnem terram allodii quam habebat Lisseiaco[2] dedit Sancto Petro ac Besuensi ęcclesię, hominemque Bernardum nomine cum uxore et filiis. Eo pacto ut si gratia Dei rediret Iherosolimis et de se ipso uel de fratre suo seu de aliquo filiorum ac nepotum suorum monachum facere uellet, libenter susciperetur. Hoc etiam Petro fratri suo fecit laudare coram comite Guillelmo,[3] multisque militibus, Malleiaco.[4] Quapropter domnus abbas Gerardus[5] dedit ei lxx solidos.

Huic carte idoneos testes adsignamus, Guillelmum comitem, Martellum de Malleiaco, Widonem Trosellum, Haymonem Columbam. Signum Gerardi abbatis. Signum Richardi prepositi, Alberti, Pontii, Girberti.

1 Billey, 38 km south-southeast of Bèze.
2 Licey, 8 km east-northeast of Bèze.
3 William IV, count of Mâcon (1127–1156).
4 Mailly-le-Château, 37 km south of Bèze.
5 Girard, abbot of Bèze (1125–1142).

305

1125–1142

Gui of Percey gives Bèze all his allodial property at Percey and Noidant. If he wishes to become a monk, the monastery shall receive him.

Cartulary, fols. 154v–155r.
Bougaud-Garnier, p. 473.

[G]ratia sacri flaminis tactus Guido de Perciaco seminare studuit in benedictione ut meteret benedictionem [cf. Gal. 6:7]. Dedit namque in uita sua Deo et Sancto Petro Besuensi cuncta alodia sua quę apud Perciacum maiorem ac minorem[1] et apud Noidant,[2] et eciam ubicumque habebat tam in mansis quam in pratis, et campis et terris ac siluis, cum quodam molendino ea interposito. Rogauit eciam ut si quando monachus effici uellet, in eodem monasterio reciperetur, quod actore Deo ad finem consequi meruit.

Huic carte subscribimus idoneos testes, qui predictam elemosinam coram altare Sancti Petri laudando confirmauerunt: Eguinum de Beria,[3] Guidonem Taleuar cum uxoribus eorum, sororibus supradicti Guidonis de Perciaco, Paganum Busun, Erluinum, Iohannem clericum, Hugonem Falsarium. Signum Gerardi abbatis.[4] Signum Rodulfi sacriste, Ricardi prepositi.

306

1125–1142

Girard, abbot of Bèze, gives the priesthood of St-Remi to the priest Theoderic Brutin. His brother and brothers-in-law agree and promise to restore any damages.

Cartulary, fol. 155r.
Bougaud-Garnier, p. 474.

Carta Brutini presbiteri

Omnibus filiis ęcclesię perpatescat quod domnus abbas Gerardus[1] tali pacto presbiteratum ęcclesię Sancti Remigii Teoderico presbitero, cognomento

1 Percey-le-Grand, 18 km northeast of Bèze; and Percey-le-Petit (now Percey-sous-Montormentier), 2 km west of there. The two Perceys are now in different départements.
2 Noidant, 40 km north of Bèze.
3 Beire, 8 km southwest of Bèze.
4 Girard, abbot of Bèze (1125–1142).
1 Girard, abbot of Bèze (1125–1142).

Brutino, dedit, ut quamdiu res ęcclesię fideliter ad profectum monachorum tractaret, eandem ęcclesiam uoluntate fratrum haberet. Sin uero bona fratrum adimere aut eos inhonorare probaretur, nisi ad eorum uoluntatem emendaret, ipsam ęcclesiam amitteret.

Testes huius rei designamus Humbertum Diuitem et Garnerium fratrem eius, Geraudum et Bernonem, Symonem et Galterium sororios eiusdem presbiteri, Iohannem quoque fratrem eius qui eciam ipso die matriculariam ęcclesię reliquit. Hii omnes in capitulo cum fidei sacramento in manu domni Gerardi abbatis in re predicta se fideles erga monachos, dampna eorum restituendo, fore promiserunt.

307

1125–1142

The priest Aymo of St-Broing gives up baptismal and other offerings as well as three-quarters of the tithes to the current priest there.

Cartulary, fol. 155r–v.
Bougaud-Garnier, pp. 474–475.

De Sancto Benigno

Notificamus his litteris quod Haymo presbiter uille Sancti Benigni,[1] cum magis quam ius erat aut predecessores eius acceperant in decimis eiusdem uillę uellet accipere, cum Garnerio qui tunc eidem loco preerat, coram domno Gerardo abbate[2] uenit, statutumque est ut quartam partem solummodo de decimis frumenti et auene acciperet. Porro media pars baptisterii mediaque pars sperarum eidem presbitero concessa est, quatinus monacho fidelis existeret. Hęc idem presbiter laudauit et spopondit nil ultra quam sui iuris esset accipere.

Domno Gerardo abbate, Garnerio priore Sancti Benigni, Ricardo preposito, et Poncio ceterisque nonnullis presentibus.

308

c. 1125–1142

Robert of Feurg becomes a monk at Bèze and gives land and a share of a mill, as well as mansi at Nantilly. His wife and daughter agree. His son agrees initially, raises claims, but then gives them up.

1 St-Broing, 28 km north of Bèze.
2 Girard, abbot of Bèze (1125–1142).

Cartulary, fols. 155v–156r.
Bougaud-Garnier, p. 475.

[Q]uę a fidelibus ęcclesię Christi donantur, litteris tradi necesse constat, ne quod deuotio Deo parat, auaricię cupido subtrahat. Pateat itaque quod Robertus de uilla quę Furt[1] uocatur, ad monachatum ueniens, dedit Sancto Petro Besuensi pratum quod in eadem uilla possederat, eo pacto ut x solidis quibus in uadimonio erat redimeretur. Dedit quoque quartam partem molendini, mediamque pasturam eiusdem uillę, et duos mansos cum appendiciis suis iuxta fontem uillę Lentilliaci.[2] Hoc donum uxor eius laudauit cum filio suo Hugone et filia Boillot uocata, testibus Mathaeo monacho Lentilliaci, Ricardo, Roberto. De laicis Bernone, Humberto Diuite, Rodulfo, Guilelmo famulo.

Accidit autem ut Hugo de Furt, predicti Roberti filius, hanc elemosinam quam laudauerat calumpniaretur, pro qua re cum a monacho qui Lentilliaci preerat argueretur, tandem ratione constrictus, super altare Sancti Petri hoc idem donum per impositionem libri optulit, nec umquam deinceps calumpniari uel adimi spopondit.

Signum Mathei Lentilliaci. Signum Ricardi, Poncii, Bartholomei, Gyrardi. De laicis, signum Humberti Diuitis, Bernonis, Petri Pauliaci,[3] Iohannis cocci.

309

Arc-sur-Tille, 14 September 1125–1142

Severin of Fauverney and his brother give up claims to serfs of Bèze, excepting only one priest's son. This is called a manumission. Severin does so for his parents' souls and for his brother, who is becoming a monk.

Cartulary, fol. 156r.
Bougaud-Garnier, pp. 475–476.

De Sancto Apolinari

[O]mnibus in Christo fidelibus manifestum iri uolumus quod Seuerinus de Fauerneiaco[1] et Guiardus frater eius domno Gyrardo Besuensis ecclesię abbati[2] Petrum de Sancto Apollinari ac fratrem eius, omnesque eorum heredes,

---

1 Feurg, 18 km east of Bèze.
2 Nantilly, 1 km southeast of Feurg.
3 Pouilly, 15 km northeast of Bèze.
1 Fauverney, 25 km south-southwest of Bèze.
2 Girard, abbot of Bèze (1125–1142).

simulque sacerdotis Belenauie[3] filios et nepotes illius, quos omnes diu calumpniati fuerant, liberos et solutos manumiserunt, uno excepto ex prefati sacerdotis filiis qui eis seruiebat, quem ad seruiendum sibi retinuerunt. Hanc uero predictam manumissionem tam pro salute sua quam pro animarum parentum suorum remedio, et etiam pro eo quod eorum frater nomine Petrus in ęcclesia supradicta iam erat factus monachus, facere decreuerunt.

Huius rei testes sunt de parte illorum Humbertus de Vuchi,[4] Stephanus Fauerneiaci prepositus, ac Meifridus de Arcu.[5] De parte uero abbatis, Narduinus de Asperomonte et Poncius de Siluenneiaco[6] monachi, Humbertus de Gillens qui eo tempore Arcioni[7] manebat, Humbertus quoque Belenauię uillicus et Vaslo de eodem uilla. Hoc autem factum est in campus illius uillę quae Arcus dicitur ante canonicorum horreum, in loco qui uulgo Corbiton nuncupatur, die quadam Dominica in qua festum Sancte Crucis celebratur. In nomine Domini, amen.

310

1138

Count Raynald of Burgundy gives Bèze property at Champlitte that had been held in fief from him, for his soul and his ancestors'. He also has his provost restore the money he stole from the monks' men at Neuvelle.

Cartulary, fols. 156r–157r.
Bougaud-Garnier, pp. 476–478.

De Camllenten uilla

[Q]uoniam maiorum nostrorum ac sanctorum aliorum autoritas cyrografa beneficiorum nostrorum ecclesiasticorum redituumque institutorum priuilegia scripta in usibus nostris ad preteritorum memoriam reuocandam habere nos instituit, suorumque institutorum quamplurima nobis exempla reliquerit, omnia beneficia a nobilibus fidelibus nostris uel innobilibus clericis uel laicis pro Christi nomine nobis collata memorie sanctę scriptis comendare consueuimus,

3 Belleneuve, 12 km south of Bèze.
4 Garnier suggests Uchey, southeast of Dijon.
5 Arc-sur-Tille, 15 km south-southwest of Bèze.
6 Aprey, 33 km north-northwest of Bèze; and Savigny, 39 km northeast of Bèze.
7 Arçon, 13 km south of Bèze.

ut ostensis beneficiorum nostrorum frequentissime cedulis, benefactorum nostrorum animarum in orationibus frequens memoria habeatur, illaque beneficia memoriter teneantur, ne pro deleta eorum memoria inportunus error sequatur. Non ergo inter alia pleraque beneficia nostra unum speciale et magnum beneficium a Burgundiorum consule Renaldo[1] nobis illatum, opere precium sub silentio oculere existimauimus, tum quia tanta res intitulatione est digna, tum quia a tanta et tam digna persona est acta.

Omnibus itaque catholicis notificare hac presenti scriptura satagimus quod Renaldus comes potissimus Deo et Sancto Petro eius apostolo, Besuensis basilice patrono, Sanctoque Dei martyris Christophoro, Camllentensis[2] cęllę nostre aduocato, instinctu diuino nulla coactus offensa, sed uoluntate pia et bona libere et absolute donauit quicquid de feodo suo unusquisque de eadem uilla tam nobilis quam ignobilis clericus uel laicus pro se uel predecessorum[3] suorum animarum requie, predicte cęllę nostre fratribus dederat uel daturus fuerat, dum tatummodo ex hoc totum foedum suum ipse non omittat, assumpta huius rei occasione ex hoc quod Odo prepositus suus tirannide sua, vii marchas argenti hominibus de Nouauilla[4] abstulerat, quas ipse domno Gyrardo abbati[5] statim ut iniuriam presentit redituram se firmiter edixit. Huius etiam redditionis fideiussores domnum Hugonem de Belliioco[6] et domnum Gyrardum de Strabona, nec non Othone de Durnecto et Humbertum de Trimolario[7] predicto abbati dedit. Quo toto beneficio diffinito, ecclesiam Sancti Dei et martyris Christophori se comitantibus multis, festinus intrauit ac ibi ante altare flexo poplite coram omnibus adstantibus de iniuria supradicta manu etiam sua super ipsum altar imposita, Deo ac Sancto Christophoro et abbati Gyrardo fecit rectum. Et hoc faciendo quod nullum ius nullamque calumpniam eiusdem iniurie in supradicta hominibus faciende habuisset, recognouit.

Hoc autem factum est die quadam Dominica diliculo, cum etiam diuina missa in supradicta ecclesia celebraretur. Qua die etiam ad colloquium contra episcopum Lingonensem proficiscebatur. Huius rei testes sunt quatuor supradicti argenti fideiussores, Hugo uidelicet de Belliioco, Gyrardus de Strabona, Otho de Durnecto, et Humbertus de Trimolario, et Odo suus prepositus et

1 Raynald III, count of Burgundy (d. 1148).
2 Champlitte, 24 km north-northeast of Bèze.
3 The cartulary reads "prodecessorum."
4 Neuvelle, 24 km northeast of Bèze.
5 Girard, abbot of Bèze (1125–1142).
6 Beaujeu, 31 km east-northeast of Bèze.
7 These places are not identified; they were presumably located outside Bèze's region.

Guillermus Siluestris, Odo Albus et Hugo frater eius. Isti de parte consulis. De parte abbatis, Guirricus prior de Fonteuenne,[8] Gothifridus prior Camllentensis, Poncius de Siluenneiaco.[9] In Christo Ihesu Domino nostro, amen.

This was almost certainly done in 1138, at the time of the deposition of Bishop William of Langres.[10]

Epitaphium[11]

[Q]ui decreta decreuerunt,
Ex decretis hoc sanxerunt,
Quod scriptura notaretur,
Quicquid iam definiretur,
Aut sigillis insignirent
Quicquid omnes stabilirent,
Ne periret uetustate,
Vel dierum quantitate,
Hoc maiores statuerunt,
Et statutum reliquerunt.
Tales usus antiquorum
Cura seruat modernorum.
Sua namque per scripturas
Instituta uel figuras;
Semper solent designare,
Vel signando demonstrare.
Sed cum tales uigens usus
Aput omnes sit diffusus,
Nos sequentes usuale,
Donum quoddam speciale,
Donum dico donum tale,
Magnum uel memoriale
Dignum satis annotari
Scriptis et astipulari
Diligenter studeamus,
Vt perfecte describamus.
Ergo cunctis innotescat,
Nec ab ullis euanescat.
Noscat omnis litteratus
Simul et illiteratus,
Quod Hugo de Bellomonte
Donauit de sua sponte,
Corde bonę uoluntatis,
Et affectu pietatis,
Deo simul et fratribus
In Christo confidelibus
Besuensis ęcclesię,
Pro defunctorum requie,
Pro se et Iofredo filio
Pro parentum remedio
Tam pro cunctis fidelibus
Quam pro suis heredibus,
Inter prima coloniam
Vel si mauis coeueiam,
Simul et quandam terrulam,
Dictam uulgo Rupeculam,[12]

8 Fouvent, 35 km northeast of Bèze.

9 Savigny, 39 km northeast of Bèze.

10 For Bishop William's election and deposition, see Giles Constable, "The Disputed Election at Langres in 1138," *Traditio* 13 (1957): 119–152.

11 This epitaph of Hugh of Beaumont is on fols. 157r–158r. Although it is obviously a poem, it is written in prose format.

12 Lœuilley, 9 km east of Bèze.

Bis binis prati falcibus
Accumulata grandibus.
Hec supradictis fratribus
Donauit Besuensibus
Qui deseruirent sedule
Sancti Martini cellule.
Hec sunt in territorio
Bellimontis sub predio.
Hec preter per iniuriam
Suamque uiolenciam
Quendam facta calumpnia
Male fugarat patria,
Et sine rectitudine
Carbonem dictum nomine,
Qui iuxta dictam cellulam
Construxerat domunculam,
Seruire uolens fratribus
Inibi famulantibus,
Quem mox liberum credidit,
Et absolutum reddidit.
Ad hec totam iusticiam
Suam dedit per gratiam,
De Boiens[13] rebus omnibus,
Simul dictis et actibus.
Post hec sibi collibuit,
Quod saluimentum tribuit
De Cauennei[14] predio
Quod tenebat in proprio,
Postremo querimoniam
De Blegne[15] uel calumpniam
Iustam, uel non exposuit,
Ita quod nil retinuit.
Rursus unam filiolam,
Quam domi nutrit paruolam,
De concubina genuit,
Quod sancta lex prohibuit.
Hanc quidam sibi garcio
Legali matrimonio
Querebat semper iungere,
Tali decreto fędere
Quod Hugonis presidio,
De Besuano predio
Sibi foret redditio,
Prefecture uel racio,
De qua fecit calumpniam
Nec iustam querimoniam.
Sed quicquid sic disposuit,
Garcio non obtinuit.
Hugo namque supplicibus
Monachorum clamoribus,
Et dare natura renuit,
Et opem ferre noluit.
Hec predicta donaria
Facta sunt in ecclesia
Besuensis cenobii
Super gradus altarii,
Per textum Euangelicum.
Nota res est in publicum.
Quod pater fecit, filius
Hugo gessit libencius.

This refers to Hugh IV of Beaumont. Document 312 spells out the agreement by which Hugh made many of these gifts to Bèze.

13 Bouhans, 18 km east-northeast of Bèze.

14 Chevigny, 3 km southeast of Bèze.

15 Blagny, 8 km east-southeast of Bèze.

311

c. 1142

Robert the provost, who was born to servile parents but rose to his position, grossly misused his power but came to repentance and resigned at the time of Abbot Stephen. But later Humbert of Belleneuve and his brothers declared themselves Robert's heirs for the office of provost. Robert denied this, and Humbert did not come to court for the arranged trial by battle, thus losing. But after Robert died as a monk, the brothers of Belleneuve reopened their claims. These were settled, but then Urric of Renève, whose daughter married Robert's brother, raised his own claims, now settled before the duke.

Cartulary, fols. 158r–159r.
Bougaud-Garnier, pp. 481–483.

[C]atholica mater ecclesia gaudens de suorum profectibus filiorum et merens pro defectibus, quos patitur a priuignis insurgentibus, loco filiorum Dauitica uoce proclamat, dicens, "Retribuebant michi mala pro bonis" [1 Sam. 25:21]. Et per Isaiam, "Filios enutriui et exaltaui, ipsi autem contempnentes spreuerunt me" [Isa. 1:2]. De quibus profecto exstitit quidam Robertus, natus ex seruis et ancillis huius Besuensis ecclesie et exaltatus ab ea ministerio prepos iture, sepe numero ipsam exaltatricem plagis, placitis, rapinis, incendiis deuastauit. Postmodum itaque respectu clementie Dei de tantis malis penitens, et nullo alio modo se posse saluari credens, ministerium ipsum, id est prepositur am, cum omnibus pertinentibus ad ipsam reliquid ecclesie Besuensi et concessit in presentia domni Stephani abbatis[1] et aliorum multorum, quorum hec sunt nomina, Rodulfus et Tigerius monachi, Obertus cocus, Hugo dapifer, Berno. Die uero depositionis uxoris sue, idem donum iterando confirmauit in capitulo nostro. Hanc donationem multis diebus in pace et quiete et sine calumpnia tenuit ecclesia, donec quadam die Humbertus de Baleneua[2] adiens abbatem Gyrardum,[3] proclamauit eundem Robertum eiusdem preposi ture se suosque fratres heredes statuisse.

Vnde Robertus nimium exacerbatus, et istud uiriliter abnegans protestatus est se quondam in captione positum fuisse, et si in illa captione moreretur,

1 Stephen, abbot of Bèze (1088–1120).
2 Belleneuve, 12 km south of Bèze.
3 Girard, abbot of Bèze (1125–1142).

ius sue prepositure eis dedisse. Quid multa? Duellum inde firmauerunt, sed statuto die pugne Roberto conuenienter adstante, Humbertus et sui non aduenerunt, neque contra mandauerunt. Sic ista sopita calumpnia, post dies aliquot supradictus Robertus monachatum expeciit, accepit, eandemque concessionem et donum quod fecerat et iterauerat reiterans, totius capituli nostri testimonio roborari fecit.

Eo autem uiam uniuerse carnis ingresso, insurrexerunt contra nos obloquentes pro ipsa prefectura, uidelicet fratres de Baleneua, Humbertus, Petrus, et Iohannes. Prepositus etiam de Sancto Iuliano, cum nepotibus, quorum causa in curia ducis Hugonis[4] per manum ipsius et uxoris eius et obtimatum curie ita terminata est. Nam uicti ratione et donorum largitione, quicquid iuste uel iniuste uel parentela uel dono alicuius in prefectura proclamabant, totum abnegauerunt et deuouerunt, fide data, contra omne genus suum et contra omnes homines guarantiam portaturos.

Hoc adsignamus uidisse et audisse Hugonem ducem Burgundie et uxorem eius, Widricum Besuensem abbatem,[5] Petrum abbatem Diuionensem,[6] Guidonem priorem, Nerduinum de Asperomonte, Pontium de Siluiniaco,[7] Humbertum de Virzeiaco,[8] monachos Besuenses.

Vrricus uero de Renauis[9] et filii sui nancta occasione quod Haymo frater Roberti defuncti filiam ipsius Vrrici uxorem duxerat, contra nos insurrexerunt calumpniantes eandem preposituram, sed resipiscentes ipsam cum omnibus pertinentibus suis agnegantes abiurauerunt. Ipse quoque Vrricus et filii sui, Rodulfus, Milo, Wido, et Hugo, et filia, pro qua clamabant, annuerunt et laudauerunt ecclesie Besuensi quiete et liberrimę in perpetuum possidendam. Quod roboramus testimonio proborum uirorum, domni Guidrici abbatis, Rodulfi prioris, Alberti Tullensis, Nerduini de Asperomonte, Poncii de Siluiniaco et reliquorum, militum uero Euuini d'Alcels, Haymonis Columbe, Milonis de Poiens,[10] Mainfredi.

This document is dated by the abbots.

4 Duke Hugh II of Burgundy (1102–1143).
5 Widric, abbot of Bèze (1142–c. 1145).
6 Peter, abbot of St-Bénigne of Dijon (1129–1142).
7 Aprey, 33 km north-northwest of Bèze; and Savigny, 39 km northeast of Bèze.
8 Vergy, 20 km southwest of Dijon.
9 Renève, 13 km south-southeast of Bèze.
10 Arcelot, 12 km south-southwest of Bèze; and Poyans, 16 km east of Bèze.

312

1142–c. 1145

Young Geoffrey of Beaumont, dead in a tournament, was excommunicated and unburied for a year. But Bishop Geoffrey of Langres successfully petitioned the pope for the right to lift the excommunication and bury him. The dead knight's father and brother, both named Hugh, confirm the gifts they made to Bèze in attempting to get the excommunication lifted, and they and the count of Burgundy promise to maintain the peace.

Cartulary, fols. 159v–160r.
Bougaud-Garnier, pp. 483–485.

Carta Ioffredi Bellimontis iuuenis

Cuncti fideles in corpore sancte ecclesie compaginati, qui ueri capitis Christi menbra se esse cognoscunt, perpendant qualiter inualida menbra sua refouere debeant, iuxta quod ait Apostolus, "Si compatitur unum menbrum, compatiuntur omnia menbra" [1 Cor. 12:26]. Sancta enim ecclesia more sagene misse in mare, sinu sue pietatis cunctos aduenientes colligit, alios solido cybo reficiens, aliis lac potum dulcedinis infundens, nonnullos uero de naufragio mortis liberans. Hoc igitur naufragium instigante diabolo Ioffredus miles, Hugonis domini Bellimontis filius,[1] incurrens, in exercicio militari morte deprehensus, litus orationum fidelium euasurus expeciit, et elemosinis sua malefacta redimere studuit. Que elemosina quanta memoria sit digna, in subsequentibus demonstrabimus. Pro tanti igitur criminis execratione, mortuum corpus illius anno et amplius sepultura caruit, donec Deo disponente qui neminem uult perire, uenerabilis Gothefredus, qui tunc Lingonensis ęcclesię preerat episcopus,[2] Romam iret.

Expletis uero prospere cunctis, pro quibus ierat, cum apostolica auctoritate et licentia rediens, eundem Ioffredum a sue excommunicationis nodo absoluit, et pro eo hostiam salutarem offerens, inhumata eius menbra honorifice tumulauit. Aderat tunc Besue cum episcopo consul Burgundie Renaldus,[3] cum

1 Geoffrey, son of Lord Hugh IV of Beaumont, 7 km east of Bèze. His brother, mentioned below, became Hugh V. For the family, see Bouchard, *Sword, Miter, and Cloister*, pp. 321–323.

2 Geoffrey of La Roche, bishop of Langres (1139–1163).

3 Raynald III, count of Burgundy (d. 1148).

multa militum caterua qui eo die coram cunctis iurauit tenere pacem ecclesie et omnes eam depredantes manu bellicosa expugnare. Ante quorum presentiam deuotus Hugo, pater Ioffredi defuncti, cum Hugone filio suo adueniens domno Widrico abbati[4] et Besuensi ecclesie promisit pacem tenere, et contra omnes qui de rebus monasterii aliquid usurparent, quasi propriam terram depopularentur, auxilium ferre. Post hec autem uterque Hugo pater cum Hugone filio elemosinam, quam prius pro Ioffredo fecerat, per manum Godefredi episcopi coram multis testibus confirmauit.

Dedit igitur Deo et Sancto Petro et Besuensi ęcclesie, pro anima filii sui et pro animabus antecessorum suorum, adstante et laudante Hugone filio suo, corueiam propriam quam Remigius presbiter in uadimonio ab ipsis habebat, et quandam terram quam dicunt Rupeculam, a uia que ducit Luille usque ad uia que uadit Fleix,[5] et quatuor falces prati iuxtam cellulam nostram Sancti Martyni, et hominem nomine Carbonem, quem ob multis iniuriis de patria fugauerat. Preterea dedit iusticiam et corueias quas proclamabat, liberrime et absque consuetudine in uilla nostra que Boens dicitur. Dedit et saluimentum Cauaneiaci uillę nostrę et calumpniam quam faciebat in terra nostra apud uillam que Blaineis[6] nuncupatur, siue iustam siue iniustam libere concessit.

Hanc autem donationem roborari uolumus proborum uirorum testimonio, quorum ista sunt nomina. Signum Hugonis qui hanc elemosinam fecit et Hugonis filii eius. Signum Euuini de Acels[7] et Hugonis filii eius. Die uero sepulture ipsius Ioffredi, quando hec elemosina iterum confirmata est per manum episcopi, fuerunt et alii quamplures quorum ista sunt nomina. Signum Godfredi episcopi. Signum Rainaldi comitis. Signum Widonis abbatis.[8] Signum Haymonis Columbe. Signum Mainfredi d'Arc.[9] Signum Richardi de Fretis. Signum Milonis de Poiens.[10] Signum Hugonis Chaine. Signum Vrrici de Renauis[11] et filiorum eius. De monachis, Signum Widrici abbatis,

4 Widric, abbot of Bèze (1142–c. 1145).

5 Lœuilley, 9 km east of Bèze; and Flée, 2 km northwest of Lœuilley.

6 Bouhans, 18 km east-northeast of Bèze; Chevigny, 3 km southeast of Bèze; and Blagny, 8 km east-southeast of Bèze.

7 Arcelot, 12 km south-southwest of Bèze.

8 This abbot is unidentified.

9 Arc-sur-Tille, 15 km south-southwest of Bèze.

10 Frettes, 31 km northeast of Bèze; and Poyans, 16 km east of Bèze.

11 Renève, 13 km south-southeast of Bèze. For Urric, see also document 311.

Signum Pontii, Signum Nerduini de Asperomonte,[12] Signum Warnerii, Signum Alberti, Signum Mathei. Signum Rodulfi carte istius dictatoris, et aliorum multorum.

The list of witnesses is very similar to that of the preceding charter. See also, above, the epitaph of Hugh IV of Beaumont, which gives further detail on the sometimes tumultuous relationship between Bèze and the lords of Beaumont.

Ciuitatis[13] et regis Iherusalem frequens recordatio, dulcis est nobis est solatio, religiose exercitationis gratia occasio, onerosę sarcine nostrę necessaria subleuato. Dicam ergo aliquid breuiter utinam et utiliter de ciuitate Ierusalem ad edificationem eiusdem ciuitatis et ad gloriam regni regis. Dicam et audiam uobiscum quid loquatur Dominus Deus in me de se et de sua ciuitate. Mittam modicum oleum in ignem quem misit Deus in corda nostra ut anima uestra igne caritatis, et oleo exhortationis parit succensa robustius exurgat, seruentius ardeat altius ascendat uidelicet una deferat, mundum transeat, celum et cęlestia transcendat, Deum in spiritu uidendo et amando tangat, et in ipso paululum respiret re et quiescat. Sicut ergo fides hunc catholica et sacra docet scriptura, pater est summa rerum origo, filius est perfectissima pulchritudo, spiritus sanctus est beatissima delectatio. Pater est causa constitutę uniuersitatis, filius est lux percipiendę ueritatis, spiritus sanctus est fons bibendę felicitatis. Pater potentus cuncta creauit ex nichilo, filius potentus creata sapienter ordinauit, spiritus sanctus sic creata sic ordinata benigne multiplicauit. Filius in uia facit discipulos, spiritus sanctus desolatos consolatur amicos, pater in patria suscipit uictores, et efficit gloriosos. Summa et beata trinitas sibi est comprehensibilis angelis et hominibus incomprehensibilis. Et quod hic creditur ibi uidetur, quomodo unum diuisibiliter tria et tria indiuisibiliter unum. Ciuitas autem Ierusalem in sublimi posita est, artifex eius Deus est. Vnum est fundamentum huius ciuitatis, quod est ipse Deus. Vnus est fundator quia ipse fundauit eam altissimus.

Vna est uita omnium uiuentium in ea, una est lux uidentium, una est pax quiescentium, unus est panis quo omnes reficiuntur, unus est fons de quo omnes hauriunt sine fine felices. Et hec omnia ipse Deus est qui est omnia in omnibus, scilicet honor et gloria, uirtus et copia, pax et omnia bona, et sufficit omnibus

12 Aprey, 33 km north-northwest of Bèze.

13 On fols. 160v–162v is a description of the city of New Jerusalem, not indicated in any previous printed editions. It perhaps was intended to be a poem, though written out as prose.

unus. Ciuitas illa poterit firmata stat ęternaliter, et hoc per patrem, luce lucet prefulgidi, et hoc per filium qui splendor est patris gaudet, et amat, et hoc per spiritum sanctum, qui amor est patris et filii. Subsistens modificatur, circeplans illustratur, inherens incundatur. Est, uidet, et amat. Est quia in uirtute patris iuget, uidet quia in sapientia Dei lucet, amat quia in bonitate Dei gaudet.

Beata ista patria quę nulla formidat aduersa, nil nouit nisi gaudia, plena Dei noticia. Et nunc quidem singuli singulas habent stolas, sed in etatę octaua florebant duplici palma beatorum agmina, omnes scient omnia cessabunt uerba loquentur cordi. Corpora erunt inmortalia et spiritalia, sicut sol fulgidi pro uelle agilia, et ad quęcumquę uoluerint potencia. Tunc erit mersis ex merse et sabbatum ex sabbato. Tunc erit lux lunę sicut lux solis, et lux solis splendebit septempliciter, et unaquęque facies sancti fulgebit sicut sol in regno patris sui. Ciuitas illa non egebit lumine solis, sed Deus omnipotens illuminabit eam, et lucerna eius est agnus. Hic est agnus Dei, agnus sine macula, quem ad salutare uictimam pater misit in mundum, qui sine peccato uiuens, et pro peccatoribus moriens, abstulit peccata mundi, soluit dolores inferni, et eduxit uinctos de lacu in quo non erat aqua, palam triumphans illos in semet ipso, et resticuens regno suo. Ipse est pulcherrimus aspectu uisu desiderabilis, in quem desiderant angeli prospicere. Ipse est rex pacificus, cuius uultum desiderat uniuersa terra. Ipse est propiciatorium penitentium, ipse est amicus miserorum merentium, consolator custos paruulorum, doctor simplicium, ductor peregrinorum, redemptor mortuorum, pugnantium fortis adiutor, austorum uictorum pius remunerator. Ipse est altare aureum infra sancta sanctorum, dulce reclinatorium filiorum, iocundum spectaculum angelorum. Ipse est summę trinitatis solum excelsum et eleuatum super omnia, qui est Deus benedictus in secula, corona sanctorum omnium lux, et uita angelorum. O quid retribuemus illi pro omnibus quę retribuit nobis? Quando liberabimur de corpore mortis huius? Quando inebriabimur ab ubertate domus Dei, uidentes lumen in lumine eius? Quando apparebit Christus uita nostra et nos cum eo in gloria? Quando uidebimus Dominum Domini in terra uiuentium remuneratorem pium hominem pacis, et habitatorem quietis, consolatorem dolentium, primogenitum ex mortuis? Gaudium resurrectionis, uirum dextere Dei quem confirmauit sibi pater.

Hic est filius Dei dilectus, et electus ex milibus ipsum audiamus, ad ipsum curramus, ipsum sitiamus, ad ipsum stilent oculi nostri, donec transferamur de hac misera plorationis ualle, et collocemur in sinu Abrahe. Sed quid est sinus Abrahe? Quid habent, quid agunt, hi qui sunt in sinu Abrahe? Quis intellectu comprehendit, quis uerbo explicet, quis affectu sentiat, quid uirtutis, et pulchritudinis, quid glorię et honoris, quid suauitatis et pacis contineat iste sinus Abrahe? Ille ille nouit de his archanis quantulum cumque proferre, qui cotidie accipit in corde, stillantem rorem gratię de largo sinu Abrahę. Sinus Abrahę secreta requies est patris. Ibi manifeste declaratur uirtus patris, splendor filii, suauitas spiritus sancti. Ibi epulantur sancti, et exultant in conspectu Dei. Ibi sunt mansiones lucidissime, ibi requiescunt sanctorum animę, et inebriantur ab ubertate laudis diuine. Gaudium et leticia inuenitur in illis, gratię actio et uox laudis. Ibi est sollempnitas preclara, requies opulenta, lux inaccessibilis, pax interminabilis. Magnus et paruus ibi sunt, et seruus liber a domino suo. Ibi uiuit Lazarus, quondam ulcerosus ante ianuam diuitis, nunc sine fine felix in gloria patris. Ibi gaudent chori angelorum et sanctorum omnium. O quam largus et iocundus est iste sinus Abrahę, quia secretus et quietus, quam liber et lucidus. O Israel quam bonus est sinus Abrahę non gloriantibus in se, sed his qui recto sunt corde, et his precipuę quos continet in se, et reficit ex se. Oculis non uidit Deus absque te, quę parata sunt in sinu Abrahe, expectantibus te. Nescit homo secretum hoc, nec apparet in terra suauiter uiuentibus. Hoc est illud secretum quid oculus non uidit, nec auris audiuit, nec inhocor hominis ascendit. Hoc est quod promittitur fidelibus pro Christo certantibus, et daturibus uictoribus cum Christo regnantibus. Quid ergo nobiscum perituris, quibus tanta promittuntur in cęlis? Quid in terrenis gaudemus cum peccore, qui uocati sumus ad curiam cęlestis iudicię? Quid nobiscum oblectamento carnis qui portare debemus imaginem celestis? Quid nobiscum concupiscentia oculorum qui uidere desideramus iocundum spectaculum angelorum? Quid nobiscum ambitione seculi quibus promissa est tota possessio celi? Dum ergo hospites sumus et aduene, sicut omnes patres nostri dum transeunt dies nostri sicut umbra super terram, et nulla est mora, dum transit per mundum angelus exterminans, et nubes exercans, uentus turbinis et ignis inuoluens, fugiamus ab umbra Ęgypta ad umbram alarum Domini, et ibi maneamus donec transeat iniquitas, donec aspiret dies, et inclinentur umbrę, et collocari mereamur in sinu Abrahę. Ibi sunt uere diuitię, ibi sunt thesauri sapientię, longiturnitas et iocunditas uitę. Ibi est plena potentia, ubi nichil inest debilitatis, nichil deest fortitudinis. Ibi est plena sapientia, ubi nichil inest ignorantię, nichil deest cognitionis uere. Ibi est summa felicitas, ubi nichil inest aduersitatis, nichil deest bonitatis. Ibi est plena sanitas, quia plena caritas. Ibi est plena beatitudo, que plena Dei uisio, uisio in quam incognicione cognicio in amore, amor cum laude, laus cum securitate, et hec sine fine.

Quis dabit nobis pennas sicut columbe, et trans uolabimus omnia regna mundi, et penetrabimus interiora austri? Quis deducet nos in ciuitatem regis magni, ut quod nunc in paginis legimus, quod per speculum ineminathe uidemus, tunc per presentem Dei faciem uideamus, et gaudeamus? O ciuitas Dei, quam gloriosa dicta sunt de te, sicut letancium omnium habithacione in te. Lux et uita omnium super te. Fundamentum tuum lapis est unus, lapis angularis et uiuus, et singulariter preciosus. Porte tue nitent margaritis optimis, aditis patentibus, lapides preciosi omnes muri tui. Et turres tue geminis edificabuntur. Plathee tue Ierualsem sternentur auro mundo, similes uitro perspicuo, et uidebitur uite uisio glorie, et cantabitur in te canthicum lethicie, et audietur ab omnibus suauis celi cunceret, synphonia et corus, et ab uniuersis dicetur uox una alleluia. Vox uiua, uox dulcissima. Vox laude plena. In hac ciuithiathe uiuunt parentes nostri, et amici carissimi, ut inpellant pro nobis Dominum, expectant auentum nostrum, et quantum possit accelerant cursum nostrum. Leuemus igitur corda nostra cum manibus ad eos, transcendamus omnia transitoria, stillent iugiter oculi nostri ad gaudia promissa. Lethemur in his quę iam cumpleta sunt in fidelibus heri pro Christo certantibus. Hodie cum Christo regnantibus, letemur et in his quę uere dicta sunt nobisque in terram uiuencium ibimus, terram dico egregiam super omnes terras terram inclitam cui benedixit Dominus, terram lacte et mello manentem, terram desiderabilem, quam pro nichilo habet carnalis Israel proquarisque ad mortem certat omnis uerus Israelita. Felix hora in qua intrabimus in terram hanc, transeunte Domino et ministrante nobis. Letantibus angelis, est gaudentibus sanctis. Illo die Deus manifeste manifestabit se ipsum nobis et omnibus amicis suis, et absterget omnem lacrimam ab oculis sanctorum restituens eis pro modicis magna, pro perituris leticia. Tunc omnibus omnia patebunt, tunc omnium omnia erunt, tunc manifeste uidebitur quomodo Deus est trinus et unus, et in omnibus omnia, et super omnia. Tunc pleno gaudio gaudebit cor nostrum, et gaudium nostrum nemo collet a nobis, quia quod non sumus in spe, tunc erimus in re filii scilicet regni angelorum confortes perpetui, heredes Dei, coheredes autem Christi, per eumdem Christum Dominum nostrum qui cum patre ipsum Deo. Viuit et regnat Deus per omnia secula seculorum, Amen.

313

1125–1142

Bartholomew of Maâtz becomes a monk at Bèze against his parents' wishes. His father eventually gives the monastery half the tithes of Maâtz, which he had received in pawn, doing so for Bartholomew.

Cartulary, fol. 162v.
Bougaud-Garnier, pp. 485–486.

Cum quedam patrum nostrorum instituta erroribus succedentium obliuioni perpetuę tradita uideantur, adiudicamus de presentibus institutis magnopere fore curandum, ut ea serie litterarum semper memorata teneantur. Nos igitur quantum est possibilitatis nostrę stili officio commendamus, quod Bartholomeus filius Rodulfi uillici de Maiasco,[1] patre ac matre eius nescientibus, ecclesię Besuensis a domno Girardo abbate,[2] laudante conuentu, monachus effectus est. Illis uero temporibus predicti Bartholomei pater in uilla quę dicitur Maiascus de minimis decimis medietatem a Guidone capellano pro xv solidis in uademonio habebat, tali scilicet conditione, nisi uiuente eo redimeret, Guidone defuncto ipse Rodulfus et filii eius super eam hereditarent. Illam siquidem decimarum medietatem, de qua superius sermonem fecimus, donauit Rodulfus pro filio Bartholomeo beatis apostolis Petro et Paulo et sanctę Besuensi ecclesię, in presentia domni Girardi abbatis, uxore sua cum filiis laudantibus. Quo facto petiit uxor eius a domno Girardo abbate, ut quod de decimis illis sua pars in canabo sibi conferebat, ea uiuente retinere concederet, eius peticioni domnus abbas Girardus coram cunctis qui aderant fauit.

The monk Bartholomew witnessed several documents in this section of the cartulary. The name was unusual in the region, so presumably these mentions were of the convert of this document.

314

1142–c. 1145

Lord Hugh of Beire gave a man with his heirs to Bèze. But Hugh's grandsons dispute his gift, claiming the donated man's children until they are ruled against. Now they formally give up their claim.

Cartulary, fol. 163r.
Bougaud-Garnier, pp. 486–487.

Karta de duobus fratribus de Beria, scilicet Roberto et Walterio

Presentibus litteris notificamus quod domnus Hugo de Beria[1] Stephanum, cum suis heredibus, Sancto Petro et Besuensi ecclesie dederit. Post cuius mortem Hugo de Magne[2] cum Aldone fratre suo, qui de filia ipsius Hugonis de Beria orti fuerant, ceperunt predicti Stephani filios proclamare, nolentes adquiescere, nec laudare, quod auus eorum Hugo eos dedisset. Quapropter cognitum examen quod sibi iudicatum fuerat, manu tulerunt, quod domnus Hugo auus

1 Maâtz, 30 km north-northeast of Bèze.
2 Girard, abbot of Bèze (1125–1142).
1 Beire, 8 km southwest of Bèze.
2 Magny, 10 km south-southwest of Bèze.

eorum totum quod in patre suo et in heredibus suis habebat, Deo et Sancto Petro dedisset. Predictus uero Hugo, qui calumpniabatur eos, uidens querimoniam suam adnullatam, iniuste eos proclamasse, concessit Deo et Sancto Petro, ponens per librum super altare in Besuensi ecclesia.

Presentes qui adfuerunt huius rei testes idonei sunt, Haimo, Odo Malenutritus, Haymo Strabus. Et de nostris, Widricus abbas,[3] Nerduinus de Asperomonte, Poncius de Siluinne, Vlricus de Renauis.[4] De laicis, Berno, Petrus de Paulis,[5] Humbertus Diues. Cum hoc laudassent apud Besuam predictus Hugo cum Aldone fratre suo, statuerunt diem quo hec matri sue et uxore facerent laudare, quo die affuit Poncius de Siluinne monachus apud Magne et laudauit coram eo mater Hugonis et uxor et unicus eius iuxta capellam ligneam, presentibus Hugone et Aldone et Haymone Columba et Odone Malenutrito, Hugone Columba et Vlrico de Angele.[6]

The Robert and Walter of the rubric do not appear in the document; presumably these were the names of Stephen's sons.

315

27 August, c. 1145

Ponce and Humbert of St-Seine give Bèze whatever they have in the woods called Rotard. They do so as part of their peace agreement over someone who was killed at St-Seine.

Cartulary, fol. 163r–v.
Bougaud-Garnier, pp. 487–488.

De nemore qui Rotardus dicitur

Notum sit omnibus quod Pontius de Sancto Sequano[1] et Humbertus frater suus, pro pace et fine quam fecerunt cum Gisleberto d'Auenne de morte fratris sui Willelmi, qui apud uillam Sancti Sequani fuit occisus, et auunculis ipsius Widone et Renaldo, dederunt Deo et Sancto Petro quicquid habebant in nemore qui dicitur Rotardus. Item pro hac eadem pace et fine, Hugo Belmontis

3 Widric, abbot of Bèze (1142–c. 1145).

4 Aprey, 33 km north-northwest of Bèze; Savigny, 39 km northeast of Bèze; and Renève, 13 km south-southeast of Bèze.

5 Pouilly, 15 km northeast of Bèze.

6 Garner suggests Angély, near Isle-sur-Serein..

1 St-Seine-sur-Vingeanne, 13 km northeast of Bèze.

dominus[2] v solidos censuales apud Montaniacum[3] in manso de siligne Sancte Marie de Fonuenz,[4] ubi corpus defuncti iacebat, dari constituit tertia die post natale Sancti Bartholomei, quo anniuersaria dies eius agitur.

Quod etiam testimonio proborum uirorum roborari uolumus. Signum abbatis de Tusleio.[5] Signum abbatis de Karitate, Rotgero de Abens monachi Belleuallis,[6] Odonis de Furno. De monachis nostris, signum Richardi prepositi, Poncii, Nerduini. De militibus, signum Haymonis Columbe, Hugonis Channe.

The witnesses suggest this document dates to roughly the same time as the preceding. See also document 328.

316

1142–c. 1145

Humbert of Bigorne becomes a monk at Bèze in his old age. He gives several pieces of land with the consent of his brothers and nephew.

Cartulary, fols. 163v–164r.
Bougaud-Garnier, p. 488.

[C]lemens pater familias conditor noster non solum eos qui a puericia fideliter in sua uinea, sancta scilicet ęcclesia, laborant, mercede non priuat, uerum etiam eos qui sero uenientes, hoc est iam senio grauati in eadem deuote uiuere student, denario beatitudinis ęterne remunerat [cf. Matt. 20:1–10]. Diuino itaque respectu Humbertus de Bigorna,[1] in senectute mundo renuncians, Besuense monasterium deuota mente petiit ac eidem cenobio quatuor falces prati, tres aput Sanctum Martinum Bellimontis et unam aput Lisseiacum[2] contulit. Dedit etiam mansum apud uillam Casotum[3] et campum trium iugerum inter

2 Either Hugh IV or Hugh V, lord of Beaumont, which is 7 km east of Bèze.

3 Montigny, 17 km northeast of Bèze.

4 Fouvent, 35 km northeast of Bèze.

5 The Cistercian monastery of Theuley, 20 km northeast of Bèze. Without a date for the charter, it is impossible to say which abbot this was. Nicholas was the first abbot when Theuley was founded in 1130 and was abbot into the 1140s, but at least five different men held the office from the late 1140s until the early 1160s. Bouchard, *Holy Entrepreneurs*, p. 225.

6 Garnier identifies these as La Charité and Bellevaux, Cistercian monasteries in the diocese of Besançon.

1 This place is not identified, but it seems to have been located close to Montsaugeon. Humbert of Bigorna is also found in document 202, and his brothers in document 299.

2 Beaumont, 7 km east of Bèze; and Licey, 8 km east-northeast of Bèze.

3 Chazeuil, 10 km north of Bèze.

Albiniacum et castrum Montis Sialionis.[4] Hanc elemosinam ipse Humbertus et fratres eius Rodulfus et Milo et Poncius nepos eorum Sancto Petro Besuensi super altare librum ponentes, dederunt.

Signum Widrici abbatis,[5] Gunterii capellani, Ricardi prepositi. Signum Willelmi famuli, Petri Pauliaci.[6] Signum Widonis et Petri cocci.

317

c. 1145

Urric of Renève gives Bèze a manse at Oisilly for the soul of his son Hugh. He also gives his half of the corvée at Jancigny. His sons and nephew agree.

Cartulary, fol. 164r.
Bougaud-Garnier, p. 488.

[F]idelium memorie tradimus quod Vrricus de Ranauis,[1] pro anima filii sui Hugonis, dedit Sancto Petro Besuensi mansum apud Osiliacum,[2] singulis annis nummos duodecim duoque menbra, siue duas gallinas in Natale Domini, iure personuentem. Addidit et medietatem quam possederat corueię nostrę Genciniaci,[3] quatinus ipsa corueia Besuensi ecclesię maneat.

Signum Rodulfi, Milonis, et Widonis filiorum predicti Vrrici. Signum Widonis Rufi nepotis ipsius Vrrici.

318

1142–c. 1145

Milo of Poyans gives Bèze a field for his young son Odo, who has just died. He does so with the consent of his wife, his sons, and his relatives.

Cartulary, fol. 164r.
Bougaud-Garnier, p. 489.

[P]resens uita, ut Beatus ait Papa Gregorius, uia est qua ad patriam pergimus. Qui ergo ad patriam uitę peruenire desiderat, dum in uia est, ante mortem

4 Montsaugeon, 22 km north of Bèze. Aubigny is 2 km west of there.
5 Widric, abbot of Bèze (1142–c. 1145).
6 Pouilly, 15 km northeast of Bèze.
1 Renève, 13 km south-southeast of Bèze.
2 Oisilly, 9 km southeast of Bèze.
3 Jancigny, 14 km southeast of Bèze.

legationem bonorum operum aut elemosinarum ad Dominum premittere studeat. Assignamus itaque Oddonem inmatura morte hac de uita sublatum, pro cuius anima pater eius Milo de Podiens[1] ecclesię Besuensi dedit campum x iugerum, uxore cum filiis et propinquis eius laudantibus.

Signum Widrici abbatis.[2] Signum Mathaei, Alberti. Signum Bartholomei et Richardi fratrum. De militibus, signum Hugonis domini Bellimontis.[3]

319

1088–1120

Lord Simon of Beaujeu and his brother Hugh, both as yet unmarried, give the daughter of Gerald the Rich to Peter of Pouilly as his wife. Abbot Stephen of Bèze agrees as she is granted freely to his monastery.

Cartulary, fol. 164r–v.
Bougaud-Garnier, pp. 489–490.

In nomine sancte et indiuidue Trinitatis, amen. Ecclesia Dei, que ex piorum largitatibus ampliari gratulatur, eorumque gaudet adipisci, propter obliuionis incommodum deuitandum debet semper reminisci. Nam quia morte prohibente unusquisque pastor non potest in ęternum permanere, quicquid agit uel cognoscit ad commodum sue esse ęcclesię, litteris et scripto suis debet successoribus demonstrare. Ego igitur Stephanus abbas[1] notifico omnibus tam presentis quam futuri seculi fidelibus domnum Symonem de Belioco[2] et domnum Hugonem fratrem eius, antequam fuissent uxorati, filiam Geraldi Diuitis quam parentes et amici Petro filio Lamberti de Pauliaco[3] in matrimonium dare disponebant, Sancto Petro et michi, qui preesse uidebar, et monachis Besuensis ęcclesię liberam, et sicut Sancti Petri feminam absque omni retractacione autentica concessione coram multis concessisse. Quod ne alicuius maliuoli inuidia uel inprobitate possit in calumpniam suscitari, iustum mihi uisum est hanc cartam subscriptorum qui adfuerunt uirorum testimonio debere roborari.

---

1 Poyans, 16 km east of Bèze.
2 Widric, abbot of Bèze (1142–c. 1145).
3 Hugh V, lord of Beaumont, 7 km east of Bèze.
1 Stephen, abbot of Bèze (1088–1120).
2 Beaujeu, 31 km east-northeast of Bèze.
3 Pouilly, 15 km northeast of Bèze.

Signum Symonis. Signum Hugonis fratris eius. Signum Poncii de Siluiniaco.[4] Signum Fulchonis de Vore. Signum Rainaldi presbiteri. Signum Bernardi fratris eius. Signum Geraldi Diuitis. Signum Gaulteri filii eius. Signum Stephani abbatis. Signum Gerardi prioris de Fonsuenz.[5] Signum Guilenci. Signum Alberti Tullensis, prioris Sancti Valeriani. Signum Lamberti de Pauliaco. Signum Iohannis fratris eius. Signum Gisleberti famuli.

This document, dated by Abbot Stephen, was given a generation before the others copied here. For Lambert of Pouilly and his son, see also the following document.

320

1125–1142

After Lambert of Pouilly died, his son Audo demanded of his own brother Peter a share of Lambert's market stall. Peter responded that it was his, given to him by their father when he married. The case was adjudicated at Bèze, before Abbot Girard, in Peter's favour.

Cartulary, fols. 164v–165r.
Bougaud-Garnier, p. 490.

Sciendum uero est quod post mortem Lamberti Pauliaci[1] quesiuit Audo fratri suo Petro partem de domo quę erat in mercato. Cui respondens, Petrus dixit se ei de hac re nullo modo respondere, quia Lambertus pater suus sine parte ceterorum filiorum suorum et filiarum dedit ipsi, quando uxorem duxit. Hoc Audo se ignorare respondit. Venerunt itaque ambo ad iudicium, et iudicatum est in curia Girardi abbatis,[2] ut si isdem Petrus de hac re legales testes haberet, in pace esse deberet. Die autem placiti uento, affuit etiam Petrus cum testibus suis, Roberto scilicet preposito et Hugone dapifero, cum matre eius, hoc afirmantibus, et ita domo libera atque in pace Petro reddita. Audo fideiussores pacis tenende dedit supradictos.

Isti sunt qui ad iudicium fuerunt, Iosbertus prepositus, Lebaldus, Albricus, Albertus. Hec domus Petro dampnum intulit, scilicet xxx libras.

4 Savigny, 39 km northeast of Bèze.
5 Fouvent, 35 km northeast of Bèze.
1 Pouilly, 15 km northeast of Bèze.
2 Girard, abbot of Bèze (1125–1142).

321

1142–c. 1145

Richard, a knight of Beaumont, made his son a monk at Bèze, giving half a corvée he held by heredity along with the boy. Abbot Girard bought the other half of the corvée from him. Richard's brother Theoderic tried to reclaim his gift and sale but gave up his claim when the abbot gave him thirty solidi. Now, under Abbot Widric, Richard has attempted to reclaim his gift but now yields and promises not to do so again.

Cartulary, fol. 165r–v.
Bougaud-Garnier, pp. 491–492.

Quoniam rerum mutatione pluraque melius stare uidebantur destructa et quasi non fuissent uideantur esse abolita, litteris commendare ratum fore ducimus ea quibus ecclesia Christi in exterioribus augetur, quo uel earum auctoritate defendatur uel futuris clarificetur. Et ideo annotamus quod quidam miles Belmontensis[1] nomine Richardus, cognomento Truta, habuit filium nomine Haymonem quem in ecclesia Besuensi monachum fieri deliberauit. Qui accessit ad domnum Gyrardum,[2] qui tunc ecclesiam Besuensem regebat, et ad fratres ipsius monasterii, filium ipsum coram multis testibus abbati et fratribus tradidit et pro eo ecclesiam ipsam ex propriis amplificari decreuit. Dedit ergo huic ecclesię apud Sanctum Martynum in confinio Belmontensi medietatem corueie quam hereditario iure possidebat, et pratum de Roseros[3] quod similiter habebat.

Consuetudinem etiam quam in nostris hominibus habebat apud Artasiam[4] manentibus, scilicet corueiam et cetera que habebat, concessit. Nec multo post medietatem corueie de Sancto Martyno quam retinuit uendere sibi placuit. Qui cum ex hoc supradictum abbatem Gyrardum prius conuenisset, emit ab eo isdem abbas ipsam medietatem, laudante hoc uxore sua et filiis in capitulo Besuensi.

Postea uero quidam frater eius nomine Teodericus, Ierusalem iturus, omnia que a fratre suo nobis data fuerant uel uendita, cepit calumpniari, consentiente fratre suo Richardo, ut postea res innotuit. Abbas uero Gyrardus triginta solidos eis dedit et super sanctum altare in capella Sancti Bartholomei coram multis testibus, adstante et laudante uxore sua et filiis, uterque superposuit.

1 Beaumont, 7 km east of Bèze.
2 Girard, abbot of Bèze (1125–1142).
3 Most likely Rosières, 11 km northeast of Bèze.
4 According to Garnier this is Vars, 20 km northeast of Bèze.

Euolutis uero aliquantis annorum curriculis, et de medio exempto bone memorie Gyrardo, et succedente in loco eius uenerabili Widrico,[5] Richardus, de quo agimus, abbati Widrico, quasi rudi et nescienti, et monachis apud Sanctum Martynum manentibus totum abdicauit et contradixit. Cui abbas Widricus quasi pastor bonus lupo rapienti obstitit, placitumque cum eo terminauit. Qui cum uterque ad diem uenisset, abbas supradictus sapienti consilio fultus, testes idoneos qui hoc uiderunt et audierunt secum adduxit. Quibus cum non posset contraire, cognouit iniuste et necessitate urgente se hoc calumpniasse. Promisit etiam numquam amplius molestiam inferre, sed fidelem se in hoc et in aliis quibus posset exsistere.

Que res ne amplius inquietetur, proborum uirorum testimonio roboramus. Signum Hugonis Belmontis domini. Signum Widonis de Sauz.[6] Signum Nocherii. Signum Euuini d'Aces[7] et Hugonis filii eius, Milonis de Poiens[8] et Hugonis fratris eius. Signum Pontii Crassi, Widonis Rauinel, Widonis Rufi, et Wiardi. Et de clientibus, Humberti de Soleri[9] et Warnerii fratris, Alberti, Christiani, Warnerii Crassi, Dominici ministri.

322

1139–c. 1145

Lord Hugh IV of Beaumont gives Bèze a mill for the good of his soul. He does so in the hand of Bishop Geoffrey of Langres.

Cartulary, fols. 165v–166r.
Bougaud-Garnier, pp. 492–493.

Carta domni Hugonis Belmontis domini

Ad omnipotentis Dei laudem prouidentes futurorum utilitatem, monimentis tradimus litterarum ne aliqua obliuionis obfuscetur nebula, uel malorum aliquando perturbetur audatia. Presentibus igitur cunctis fidelibus notificamus quod domnus Hugo Bellimontis dominus,[1] diuino igne succensus, et de salute anime sue sollicitus, dederit Deo et Sancto Petro et huic Besuensi ecclesie molendinum quod Petrus Rufus tenebat, ante ecclesiam Sancti Martyni situm, cum molendinario et eius domo et prato et omnibus appendiciis suis, laudante

5 Widric, abbot of Bèze (1142–c. 1145).

6 Hugh V, lord of Beaumont; and Gui III, the future lord of Saulx, 21 km northwest of Bèze.

7 Arcelot, 12 km south-southwest of Bèze.

8 Poyans, 16 km east of Bèze.

9 Saulles, 34 km north-northeast of Bèze.

1 Hugh IV, lord of Beaumont, 7 km east of Bèze. His wife Mathilda and son, Hugh V, are noted below.

filio suo Hugone, qui tunc predicto castro dominabatur, ex uxore sua Mathilde, per manum Domini Gotefredi Lingonensis ecclesie pontificis,[2] die qua predictam ecclesiam consecrauit.

Huius donationis testes idoneos adsignamus. Signum Gotefredi episcopi. Signum Euuini d'Acels[3] et filiorum eius, Hugonis et Hugonis cognomento Werra et Milonis. Signum Milonis de Poiens et Hugonis fratris eius.[4] Signum Hugonis Chaine et filii eius. Et de clientibus, Humberti de Soleri[5] et Warnerii fratris eius, Christiani et Alberti et aliorum multorum.

Although this document can only be dated definitively by Bishop Geoffrey, it most likely was given very early in this span, while Hugh IV was still lord of Beaumont. The similarity of witnesses between this document and the previous one suggests they were given about the same time.

323

1139–c. 1150

Hugh V of Beaumont is preparing to go to Jerusalem. He gives Bèze what he had at Pouilly, half of the rights of justice, land, and men, with his father's consent. Frederick of Champagne is also going to Jerusalem and gives Bèze a mill at Blagny.

Cartulary, fol. 166r–v.
Bougaud-Garnier, pp. 493–494.

Post[1] non multum temporis cum superna Prouidentia incitasset fideles ad confutandam paganorum perfidiam, conpunctus Hugo, filius supradicti Hugonis,[2] cum in expedicione Hierosoliminana profisci deberet, incertus quid de se rei euentus daret, deuotus capitulo fratrum uale dicturus eis adiit, de malis a se ęcclesięe Besuensi irrogatis ueniam postulauit, fratrumque orationibus se commendans, elemosinam fecit. Habebat namque in uilla Sancti Petri quę Pauliacus[3] dicitur medietatem iusticiarum et terram et homines ipsam tenentes, quę cuncta eis concessit, presente et laudante patre suo Hugone.

2 Geoffrey of La Roche, bishop of Langres (1139–1163).
3 Garnier identifies this as Arcelot, 12 km south-southwest of Bèze.
4 Poyans, 16 km east of Bèze.
5 Saulles, 34 km north-northeast of Bèze.
1 This document is run into the previous one in the cartulary, without a break.
2 Hugh V, son of Hugh IV of Beaumont, 7 km east of Bèze.
3 Pouilly, 15 km northeast of Bèze.

Testes huius rei sunt qui adfuerunt in capitulo, cum eo penę omnis Besuensium hominum et monachorum multitudo, et de militibus Hugo pater eius, Iosbertus Gloseius, Wido d'Essartinis, Viardus de Renauis,[4] Wido Rufus, Hugo Chaine, Wido Rauinellus, et alii multi.

Adiungimus etiam quod alius quidam miles Fredericus nomine de Campaniis,[5] Hierusalem iturus, in eodem capitulo concessit Sancto Petro et fratribus Besuensis cenobii molendinum cum appendiciis suis apud Blainiset[6] et terram et cuncta quę habebat in eadem uilla, adstantibus et laudantibus Hugone domino Belmontensi et Hugone Carne fratre suo, et ceteris supradictis.

This document, like the preceding (with which it shares a number of witnesses), can be dated only by Bishop Geoffrey, but it seems most likely that it dates to the 1140s, perhaps the time of the Second Crusade.

324

1142–c. 1145

Geoffrey, bishop of Langres, gives churches to Bèze, where Widric is abbot. Bishop Willenc had earlier given them to Abbot Girard. The churches, which the priest Remigius of Beaumont had held, are at Beaumont, Oisilly, Champagne, and Dampierre.

Original, Chaumont, Archives départementales de la Haute-Marne, 2 G 1171.[1]
Cartulary, fols. 166v–167r.
Chaumont, Archives départementales de la Haute-Marne, 2 G 921, thirteenth-century cartulary of the bishopric of Langres, fol. 26r–v; from the original.[2]
Bougaud-Garnier, pp. 494–495.
Cartulaire du chapitre cathédral de Langres, pp. 64–65, no. 24; from the original.

---

4 Essertenne, 17 km southeast of Bèze; and Renève, 13 km south-southeast of Bèze.
5 Champagne, 10 km southeast of Bèze.
6 Blagny, 8 km east-southeast of Bèze.
1 Parchment, written in brown ink, 32.5 cm tall, with a fold at the bottom measuring 2.5 cm, and 32.5 cm wide. Originally sealed. This is not exactly the original that the monks of Bèze had, because this copy was kept by the bishop, but presumably he made a copy for himself and a copy for them. There is however no sign of it being a chirograph.
2 Has the rubric "Karta Godefridi Lingonensis episcopi ut ecclesias quas Villencus Lingonensis episcopus dederat Girardo abbati Besuensis Vidrico abbati iterato donaret." This copy does not have the e-cedilla found in the original or the Bèze copy.

Rerum mundanarum uarietas quam multimoda sequitur defectio sapientem ducit ad consilium ut ad cautelam prouidentię ne / si quid boni fecerit, pereat, mentis oculum extendat in futurum. Quicquid enim in humanis agitur aut transcursu temporis / aut obliuionis nebula citius aboletur nisi sit quod in exemplis patrum et in usu sanctę cognoscimus ęcclesię elemosinas et / bona quę sancti uiri operantur opera litteris propter memoriam studeamus annotare. Quapropter ego Gotefrdus,[3] Dei gratia Lin- / gonensium episcopus[4] notum facio omnibus tam presentis quam futuri seculi fidelibus uenerabilem fratrem nostrum Widricum Besuensem / abbatem[5] presentiam nostram adiisse et deuotę supplicationis precibus postulasse ut ęcclesias quas tenuit domnus Remigius / Belmontensis castri[6] presbiter quas siquidem bonę memorię antecessor noster domnus Wilencus Lingonensis ęcclesię presul domno / Girardo[7] abbati Besuensium[8] antea dederat ut firmior esset donatio iterato donarem et auctoritate nostra roborarem, ac / propter euitandas malorum hominum calumpnias quas ęcclesiastica semper nititur euitare,[9] prudentia, sigillo nostro sigillarem. Dono igitur / saluo iure Lingonensis ęcclesię Deo et Sancto Petro et uenerabili fratri nostro Widrico abbati monachisque Besuensis cęnobii ęcclesias quas / sicut dictum est Remigius presbiter tenuit, ęcclesiam uidelicet Sancti Martini,[10] cum capella Sancti Bartolomei, et ecclesiam de Auxiliaco, / et ęcclesias de Campaniis Sancti uidelicet Iuliani et Sancti Hylarii et ęcclesiam de Domna Petra[11] auctoritate confirmans pontificali, ne quis / amplius abbatem uel fratres Besuensis cenobii de tenore harum ęcclesiarum exturbet aut audeat inquietare, aut alicuius con- / trouersię fraudibus usurpare. Quod siquis presumpserit, proprio reatu exigente sententia anathematis se cognoscat / subiacere.

For the original gift from Bishop Willenc, see document 333.

3 The Bèze cartulary reads "Gothefredus."
4 Geoffrey of La Roche, bishop of Langres (1139–1163).
5 Widric, abbot of Bèze (1142–c. 1145).
6 Beaumont, 7 km east of Bèze.
7 The Bèze cartulary reads "Gyrardo," both here and below.
8 Willenc, bishop of Langres (1125–1136); and Girard, abbot of Bèze (1125–1142).
9 The Bèze cartulary reads "deuitare."
10 The Bèze cartulary reads "Martyni." This church was located at Beaumont.
11 Oisilly, 9 km southeast of Bèze; Champagne, 10 km southeast of Bèze; and Dampierre, 7 km east-northeast of Bèze.

325

c. 1145

Wido of Licey, dying, makes Bèze gifts of whatever he has at Noiron, for his soul. His wife, son, and brothers confirm his gift.

Cartulary, fol. 167r.
Bougaud-Garnier, pp. 495–496.

De Nerone

Ecclesie Dei filiis etsi simplicitas auctoritate diuina teneri precipitur, serpentina tamen calliditas eodem precepto adhibenda cognoscitur [Matt. 10:16], quatinus et innocentes ad malum non festinemus, et ea que uidentur utilia exercere studeamus. Cum etenim mundus secundum Prophetam ollam succensam, id est humanam conscientiam, ad faciem extendat aquilonis et moderni quampluribus pro cupiditate mali uiciorum inmergantur procellis, iustum est ut ecclesiastica prouidentia et sua innocenter teneat, et sapienter quod tenuerit in futurum non amittat. Proinde ad excitandam futurorum memoriam et obstruendam obliuionis nebulam, scripto commendamus domnus Widonem de Lyseio,[1] cum ueniret ad obitum, pro anime sue antecessorumque remedio, Deo et monachis Besuensibus in elemosinam dedisse quicquid apud Neronem[2] habebat et quicquid iure hereditario uel quolibet alio modo debere esse suum inibi reclamabat. Quę siquidem elemosina super altare Sancti Petri per manum uxoris sue Chartei et filii sui Wilenchi posita est, assistentibus fratribus ipsius Widonis, Poncio, et Willelmo, qui et ipsi hoc donum fecerunt, audientibus et uidentibus quampluribus approbatis uiris, monachis, clericis, et laicis subscriptis, qui adfuerunt.

Dedit etiam tunc querimoniam et reclamationem prati quod tenebat Albricus. Signum Widonis prioris, Alberti subprioris, Alberti Tullensis, Ricardi monachi.[3]

326

c. 1145

Cecelia makes a gift to Bèze for her husband, Evrard of Rollens, consisting of a servant. She symbolizes this by putting a copy of the Gospels on the monastery altar, with the consent of her son and daughter.

1 Licey, 8 km east-northeast of Bèze.
2 Noiron, 4 km southeast of Bèze.
3 These final two sentences are in a different, darker ink. The identification of the monastery officers is done interlinearly.

Cartulary, fol. 167v.
Bougaud-Garnier, p. 496.

[B]eatudinem quam uniuersalis ęcclesia de oratione intellegit Dominica, "Adueniat regnum tuum" [Matt. 6:10], omni nisu mentis et corporis assequi debemus, ut cum sanctis postmodum qui cum eo regnabunt gaudere ualeamus. Qua animaduersione ducta ego Cecilia, uxor Eurardi de Rollens,[1] cum filio meo Willelmo, quendam seruientem meum Widonem Deo et Sancto Petro et monachis Besuensis ecclesię, pro remedio animę meę et animę maritis mei antecessorumque salute, dedi et hoc donum tenens librum Euangelii cum predicto filio meo super altare posui, et filiam meam Helisabeth laudare hanc ipsam donationem feci. Quod ne irritum fiat uel obliuionis nebula depereat, testes qui adfuerunt assignari benigne concessi.

Signum Guidonis prioris. Signum Alberti Tullensis. Signum Widonis. Signum Lamberti de Raeio.[2] Signum Bartholomei de Arcu.[3] Signum Petri cellerarii de coquina. Signum Humberti Diuitis, Signum Giraldi, Signum Chalueth Febri, Signum Humberti sacrisinarii, Signum Stephani nepotis abbatis Widrici,[4] Signum Petri ministri de Bassei.[5]

327

Bèze, 1142–c. 1145

Lord William of Tilchâtel gives up his claim to one Aldric, a man of St Peter, after Aldric gives him four and a half pounds. William's wife confirms.

Cartulary, fols. 167v–168r.
Bougaud-Garnier, pp. 496–497.

Ecclesia Dei uariis et crebis tribulationum procellis, sicut maris insula sepius percutitur, uento turbinis flante, id est inimici suasione pestifera, fidelium qui nocte ac die seruitio Dei uidentur mancipati quietem perturbante. Quapropter ipsis sollerter inuigilandum est ut que habent et possident pacifice queant retinere, ne malorum aliquorum uersucia perdant quod debent conseruare.

Memoriale igitur et eternale esse uolumus scripto commendantes qualiter calunnia, quam domnus Guillelmus de Tricastel[1] de Aldrico homine Sancti Petri faciebat, fuerat terminata. Ipse Guillelmus dicebat predictum Aldricum

1 Garnier suggests Roulans, in the Jura. Evrard is also found in document 296.
2 Ray-sur-Saône, 43 km east-northeast of Bèze.
3 Arc-sur-Tille, 15 km south-southwest of Bèze.
4 Widric, abbot of Bèze (c. 1140–c. 1145).
5 Baissey, 31 km north of Bèze.
1 William, lord of Tilchâtel, 9 km northwest of Bèze.

apud Veronam[2] mansisse et pecuniam fratris sui qui mortuus fuerat ipsum Aldricum habuisse. Aldricus dicebat e contrario se nunquam in terra Domni Guillelmi mansum accepisse, nec pecuniam defuncti fratris habuisse. Medi-antibus igitur bonis qui adfuerunt uiris, Aldricus Domno Guillelmo quatuor libras et decem solidos dedit, et ipse Guillelmus quicquid clamabat super eum dimisit. Et ita calunniam suam et hominem in pace dereliquit.

Quod ut inconuulsum permaneat et obliuionis nebula non deleatur, uirorum qui adfuerunt testimonio roborare, et eorum nomina opus est singillatim nominare. Signum Widrici abbatis,[3] Alberti Tullensis. Signum Widonis capellani. Signum Humberti Diuitis. Signum Warnerii. Signum Petri de Pauliaco.[4] Signum Audonis. Signum Iohannis. Signum Haymonis. Signum[5] Bardulfi, Walterii de Pichangi,[6] Wasleri Maluasloth, Lamberti de Marcelliaco,[7] Serianth, Milonis Falsart, Warnerii de Veronna, Warnerii de Solunge.[8]

Hec facta sunt apud Besuam. Postea uero apud Tricastel ipsius uxor domni Guillelmi laudauit et benigne concessit pacem, quam de Aldrico fecerat Guillelmus maritus eius. Testes adfuerunt ipse Guillelmus, Vlricus capellanus de Claromonte,[9] Richardus presbiter, Warnerus nepos eius, Iohannes clericus, Nocherus miles, Willelmus de Casoto,[10] Bardulfus, Walterus, Wido Checeuath, Paganus, Willelmus filius Miribelli, Waruadus, Hugo, Wido, uuillici de Luco.[11]

328

1142–c. 1145

Abbot Widric tries to settle the turmoil that has marked the Rotard woods, near Beaumont. One Brutinus was accidentally killed there and died without confession or absolution, and now he cannot be buried. His brothers and sons make peace now with Bèze, and the monks give them small payments.

Cartulary, fols. 168v–169r.
Bougaud-Garnier, pp. 498–500.

---

2 Véronnes, 7 km north-northwest of Bèze.
3 Widric, abbot of Bèze (1142–c. 1145).
4 Pouilly, 15 km northeast of Bèze.
5 Starting here, to the end of this witness list, the names seem to have been mistakenly skipped and are given in the bottom margin.
6 Pichanges, 9 km west of Bèze.
7 Marcilly, 13 km northwest of Bèze.
8 Garnier identifies this as Selongey, in the Dijon region.
9 Unidentified.
10 Chazeuil, 10 km north of Bèze.
11 Lux, 5 km northwest of Bèze.

Carta de nemore Rothart

Ecclesiastice dispensationis prudentia etsi pro precepto Domini serpentina calliditate debeat augmentari, columbina tamen simplicitate iubentur temperari [Matt. 10:16], ut sic a nobis teneatur ne plus iusto temperata inprudenter dissoluatur. Cui considerationi inuigilans, ego Widricus abbas[1] notum facio meis omnibus in perpetuum successoribus quomodo Besuensis ęcclesia, cui preesse uideor, de uexationibus et doloribus quos diu sustinuerat pro calumpnia, que erat de nemore Rotart, tandem fuerit liberata. Quidam enim Belmontenses,[2] qui prepositales dicuntur, in predicto nemore partem hereditario iure proclamabant, et infestatione non modica malis quampluribus illatis nobis insurgebant.

Cuius doloris uehementia cum multo tempore percrebesceret, Deo ut credimus uolente accidit quod quidam ex ipsis, nomine Brutinus, quadam die cum in fabrica fabri cultellum emoleret et eum ad terram incaute deponeret, ipso cultello uulneratus cecidit, et absque uiatico et confessione quantocius expirauit. Cum igitur tali morte defuncto parentes et amici condolerent et excommunicatum fuisse cognoscerent, ceperunt inquirere quomodo ín terra cimiterii adhibito Christianitatis officio potuisset tumulari. Quod non posse fieri uisum est, nisi a malis absolutus esset, quepropter nemoris calumpniam ecclesię fecerat, pro quibus excommunicatus apparebat. Clarino igitur fratre eius agente, qui sapientior erat, cum Widrico alio fratre actum est, quod uxor ipsius Brutini, quem[3] Baldulfum uocant, et pueri eius Petrus et Willelmus et omnis familia calumpniam predicti nemoris dimiserunt, et eminam milii que tunc cara erat pro tempore, a nobis suscipientes, Deo et Sancto Petro et monachis Besuensis ęcclesię pro absolutione illius concesserunt, testibus appositis, Haymone monacho, Clarino, Widrico, Christiano, Humberto Loir, qui uidentes et audientes affuerunt.

Proinde periculosam mortem illius adducentes sibi in exemplum fratres et consanguinei, Clarino agente, qui melioris sicut dictum est fuerat scientie, omnes in hoc conuenerunt, ut predicte ęcclesię pacem facerent, et ne ante Deum rei pro calumpnia nemoris apparerent, omnes concorditer ipsum nemus Deo et Sancto Petro dimiserunt. Insuper benedictionem temporalem a monachis susceperunt, Widricus xl solidos et eminam milii, Clarinus et Willelmus frater eius xl solidos. Hugo prepositus, pro eo quod nemus ipsum Deo et Sancto Petro guilpiuit, filium suum in ęcclesia nostra fieri monachum obtinuit. Dimissa sic nemoris calumpnia omnes pacem bonam et concordiam fecerunt, et super altare Sancti Petri quicquid in predicto nemore et appendiciis eius seu

1 Widric, abbot of Bèze (1142–c. 1145).

2 Beaumont is 7 km east of Bèze. The "Rotart" forest presumably lay close by. For this woods, see also document 315.

3 The cartulary reads "quam."

iuste uel iniuste proclamabant, totum Deo et Sancto Petro dederunt, guilpiuerunt, et insuper iurauerunt quod amplius non repeterent. Et si calumpnia exinde ueniret aliqua, fideli enarratione guarantiam portantes legitimam nobis contra omnes calumpniatores enarrarent.

Que pax ne temporum interuallo uel obliuionis depereat incommodo, legitimorum qui affuerunt uirorum roboranda est testimonio. Haymo Columba, Willelmus de Sancto Sequano, Petrus, Aldo frater eius de Pauliaco,[4] Malet, Humbertus, Warnerius, Christianus, Humbertus de Solio,[5] Clarinus, Widricus, Guillelmus. Sibilla uxor Hugonis laudauit pacem et donum nemoris quod fecit maritus suus Hugo et pueri eius, Milo et alii. Maluaslet cum moreretur predictum nemus guilpiuit presente abbate, Poncio capellano Fineta, Gisleberto filio eius et Christiano. Hugo de Aquato[6] iterum cum moreretur hoc nemus guilpiuit, presente uxore sua. Testes affuerunt, Christianus, Maluaslet, Amalricus, Garnerius siluestris.

See also document 315. This document has both a rubric and a red initial letter. The following document, in a different hand, has neither.

329

1127–1142

Martel of Mailly, going to Jerusalem, gives Bèze fishing rights, a meadow, and woods at St-Seine-en-Bâche. He also gives tithes at Flagey. In addition, he grants the monks the right to pasture their pigs freely in his woods. Count William of Mâcon shall protect Martel's land while he is gone.

Cartulary, fols. 169v–170r.
Bougaud-Garnier, pp. 500–502.

[Q]uantę pietatis desiderio debeamus ęterna meditari, labentis mundi casus indicat, qui cotidianis defectibus uidetur annullari. Presens etenim uita, quę in suis stipendiis erumpnosa conspicitur, quicquid confert infirmum est et fragile, et quod sui amatorem tandem reddat miserrimum euidenter conprobatur. In cuius siquidem dispendiis, quia multiplex pro inbecillitate carnis patimur detrimentum, ipsa mors per quam omnis caro destituitur, doloris et timoris nobis est argumentum. Pro respectu huiusmodi, nolens iam amplius adquiescere carni et

4 St-Seine-sur-Vingeanne, 13 km northeast of Bèze; and Pouilly, 15 km northeast of Bèze.

5 Most likely Saulles, 34 km north-northeast of Bèze, even though it is here spelled slightly differently than typical. A Humbertus of Saulles also appears in documents 321 and 322.

6 Achey, 28 km northeast of Bèze.

sanguini, sed maiestatem cęli propiciam promereri, ego Martellus de Malleio,[1] uolensque de peccatis agere penitentiam, que per meę iuuentutis commisi laciuiam, animo proposui sepulchrum Domini Iherusalem inuisere, ac Besuensem ęcclesiam, quę mea est parrochia, prout patris antecessorumque meorum testatur sepultura, largiori bonorum meorum erogatione, consilio caritatis placuit augmentare. Deo itaque et Sancto Petro fratribusque Besuensis cęnobii, in presencia domni abbatis Gerardi,[2] concedente et laudante comite Guillelmo,[3] cui in custodia et proptectione terram meam dimisi, donaui duas in Sagonna[4] piscarias, unam quam ante dederam, aliam quam dedi cum hoc iter arripui. Dedi autem hoc tenore ut si opus fuerit, piscator seruientem habeat, qui ad gubernandam nauem eum adiuuet, et ea quę in arte uel officio piscandi sunt necessaria ei famulando subministret. Hominem enim qui solus nititur operari, cum parum aut nichil proficiat, opportet adiuuari.

Dedi eciam pratum unum quod dicitur Brachium Lamberti. Dedique nemus quod iusta Sagonnam Weura appellatur, et omnia memora quę habeo circa uillam quę Beesca[5] uocatur, dedi monachis ibidem manentibus ex illis omne quodcumque fuerit necessarium monachis et hominibus ipsorum in asimentum.

Dedi etiam decimas de Flagei[6] et parrochiaticum, et omnem usum et consuetudinem in nemoribus et in siluis ipsius uille cum omni libertate. Ad hanc donacionem addici decimam quarte partis de portu. Dedi eciam paagium Sancti Sequani, quod meum erat, concessique et donaui monachis Besuensibus ut porcos suos[7] indominicales in nemora mea ubicumque habuero mittant et sine pastionatico per omnia libere currant. Monachi[8] uero qui apud Beescam manebunt similiter faciant, per omnia nemora mea porcos suos indominicales sine pastionatico mittant, et centum desuper si adtrahere porcos uoluerint. Qui siquidem Beescenses monachi, quia pro remedio antecessorum meorum ibi sunt mancipati, nolo quod aliqua uexacione mala per meos homines uideantur fatigari. Quapropter concessi et in loco elemosine mihi constitui, ut uillam illam, Beescam uidelicet, in qua habitant, cum omni libertate habitent ipsi monachi, et precepi ut homines mei qui terras habent in uilla illas claudant et sepes oportunas apponant, ne animalia

1 Mailly-le-Château, 37 km south of Bèze. Martel was a cousin of the lords of Beaumont; Bouchard, *Sword, Miter, and Cloister*, pp. 321–323.
2 Girard, abbot of Bèze (1125–1142).
3 William IV, count of Mâcon (1127–1156).
4 The river Saône, which flows between Mailly and St-Seine-en-Bâche.
5 St-Seine-en-Bâche, 40 km south-southeast of Bèze.
6 Flagey, 3 km east of Mailly-le-Château, on the opposite side of the Saône.
7 The cartulary reads "suo."
8 The cartulary reads "Monachis."

uille quod intus fuerit deuastare preualeant. Quod si claudere noluerint et aliquod dampnum euenerit, homo uille in causam non trahatur, et nemini inde respondeat, nec dampnum, nec legem inde persoluat. Et si homo predicte uille dampnum per clausuram malefactam susceperit, comiti Guillelmo ostendat clamorem, et ipse comes plenariam super hoc faciat iusticiam.

Et ut hec donacio autentico roboretur priuilegio, subscriptorum uirorum firmamus testimonio. Signum Martelli qui hoc donum fecit. Signum Wilelmi comitis. Signum Gyrardi abbatis. Signum Constantii de Derneyi abbatis.[9] Signum Poncii de Silium.[10] Signum Gyleberti prioris Beesce. Signum Parisii canonici de Masenot. Signum Roberti militis de Bille,[11] Wido Trosellus, Walo de terre Diuionensis.[12]

Martel of Mailly and Count William also appear together in document 304, from roughly the same time.

330

1159–1164

Humbert makes a gift to Bèze of a manse at Belleneuve, so that his son William can be buried at the monastery. He also remits the rent that the monks at Arçon pay him each year for his mill and adds some other pieces of land. He acts with his wife, other sons, and brothers.

Cartulary, fol. 170v.
Bougaud-Garnier, pp. 502–503.

… uolumus memorie … puli quod … pro sua suorumque eterna salute … filii sui Guilelmi nomine nuper defuncti et honorifice Besue sepulti, dedit liberrime Deo et ecclesie Besuensi hec subtus annotata perpetuo iure possidenda, uolentibus atque laudantibus uxore cum filiis, necnon et fratribus, Richardo scilicet et Girardo. Mansum unum uidelicet apud Balenauam,[1] eo tenore ut habitator ipsius usus consuetudinales habeat, sicut prius, in aquis in terris in pascuis et in siluis eiusdem Humberti et successorum ipsius. Dimisit quoque nummos quatuor quos monachus Arcionensis[2] ei debebat annuatim pro ripa molendini

9 I have not identified this abbey. It is not Montier-en-Der.
10 Savigny, 39 km northeast of Bèze.
11 Billey, 38 km south-southeast of Bèze.
12 Dijon.
1 Belleneuve, 12 km south of Bèze.
2 Arçon, 13 km south of Bèze.

sui in festiuitate Sancti Martini. Dedit etiam quatuor iugera terre, que habentur prope arborem ulmum, que de Mulmis dicitur. Addidit his et falcem prati prope pontem Arcionensem siti.

Cuius donationis testes idoneos etiam subscribere curauimus. Quorum nomina sunt hec. De monachis abbas Ioffredus,[3] Poncius prior, Guido sacrista. Bartolomeus frater eiusdem Humberti, Robertus Verna. Milites, Hugo de Asperomonte,[4] Aimo Columba, Aimo de Mimire, Aimo Bornus. Burgenes Petrus de Pauliaco,[5] Maletus, Iohannes coquus, et alii quamplures.

In the previous printed editions this document is run in with the previous one, even though it is in a new hand. The top of the folio, the last in the codex, is badly worn and hard to read, as it apparently was even in the seventeenth century.

331

1159–1164

Hugh, a knight of Fontaine, makes a gift for his brother Aymo, who was killed and buried at Bèze. Hugh's sister and nephews agree. The gift consists of a manse at Fontenelle, with meadow and tithes.

Cartulary, fol. 170v.
Bougaud-Garnier, p. 503.

Carta de Fontanellis

Mansuris est imprimendum litteris quod Hugo miles de Fontanis[1] pro anima fratris sui Haymonis nuper interfecti, et apud Besuam honorifice sepulti, laudante sorore cum nepotibus et ceteris ad quos res pertinere uidebatur, dedit Deo et ecclesie Besuensi apud Fontinellas[2] mansum unum cum falce prati, et terciam partem medietatis minute decime.

Hoc autem fieri fecerunt Milo miles dominus de Fossato,[3] cum fratre Roberto ad quos maxime attinebat, in die sepulture ipsius Besue, multis presentibus, quorum nomina partim subnotantur. Abbas Ioffredus,[4] Haimo prior, Vido sacrista, Bartolomeus, Gybuinus monachi. Milo de Fossato et Robertus frater eius milites.

3 Geoffrey, abbot of Bèze (1159–1164).
4 Aprey, 33 km north-northwest of Bèze.
5 Pouilly, 15 km northeast of Bèze.
1 Fontaine-Française, 10 km northeast of Bèze.
2 Fontenelle, 9 km northeast of Bèze.
3 Le Fossé, 12 km northwest of Bèze.
4 Geoffrey, abbot of Bèze (1159–1164).

APPENDIX

The following two documents are the only documents preserved at Bèze for which the originals still exist from the time period covered by the cartulary-chronicle. Neither one is included in the cartulary, suggesting that they were stored in a different place, missed by John's continuators but also missed by the mass destruction of Bèze's archives. Neither has been previously printed.

332

Langres, 1131

John, papal legate, writes to Abbots Hugh of Luxeuil and Girard of Bèze in order to make peace between them over the church of Pressigny. Both abbots claim that the church was given to them by the bishop of Langres. The legate rules that they shall hold it in common.

Original, Arch. Côte-d'Or, 3 H 518.[1]
Arch. Côte-d'Or, 3 H 1 (cart. 130), pp. 1–2; copy made in 1772.

Frater Iohannes sancte Romane ecclesię presbiter cardinalis et apostolice sedis legatus, uenerabilibus fratribus Hugoni Luxouiensi et Gerardo Besu- / ensi abbatibus,[2] eorumque successoribus in perpetuum. Notum omnibus fieri uolumus qualiter questio quę inter uos super ecclesiam Sancti Petri / de Prissinniaco[3] dudum agitata, Lingonis in presentia nostra nuper mota est et concordia

1 The document measures 37 cm tall by 28 cm wide, written in brown ink on parchment.

2 Abbots Hugh of Luxeuil (1123–1136) and Girard of Bèze (1125–1142).

3 Pressigny is roughly halfway between Bèze and Luxeuil, being 46 km northeast of the former and 54 km west-southwest of the latter.

terminata. Siquidem tu frater Hugo / Luxouiensis abbas dicebas predictam ęcclesiam monasterio uestro per Lingonenses episcopos fuisse concessam, cuiusdam firmamentum / duas cartas Roberti quondam episcopi unam Guilenci uero presentis pontificis[4] alteram ostendebas. E contra uero tu frater Gerarde Besuensis / abbas eandem ecclesia cenobio tuo a Lingonensi episcopo donatam asseuerebas. Ad cuius rei confirmationem supranominati Roberti quondam / episcopi cartam unam similiter demonstrabas. Nos uero inspectis utriusque monumentis et allegationibus pleniter auditis in partem sece- / dentes, una cum domino Guilenco uenerabili episcopo, Petro Diuionensi et Herberto Sancti Stephani abbatibus,[5] necnon Iocelino archidiacono et magistro Anselmo, / concordia inter uos conposuimus ut predicta ecclesia Sancti Petri de Prissiniaco cum omnibus ad eam pertinentibus, tam his que in presenti possidet quam que / in futuro poterit adipisci, uestre Luxouiensis et Besuensis ecclesie in commune possideant, cum decimis siue quę ad presbiterium pertinent, / siue duas porciones decimarum quas quisque uestrum prius adquisieratis, cum oblationibus, cum sepulturis et omni ecclesie eiusdem introitu, cimiterium quoque / quod foris est et ad ecclesiam Luxouiensem specialiter pertinebat commune deinceps utrique erit monasterio. Pro cuius recompensatione a te Gerar- / de Besuensi abbas ad maiorem ipsius unitatis firmamentum mansus unus quod Ayaldi quondam medici fuerat Luxouiensis monasterio collatus est, / similiter et capellanus qui nunc in presenti eidem deseruit ecclesie seu in posterum pro tempore seruiet per uos et successores uestros sepe nominatam / capellam suscipiet et communia uobis utriusque successoribus pro eadem ecclesia exhibebit seruitia. Pro uos eciam et uestros successores tam iste quam qui / in futuro in eadem ministrabit ecclesia presbiter iudicabitur, saluo nimirum in omnibus iure et consuetudinibus Lingonensis ecclesię, preterea si que / iusticiae prefate ecclesie seu cimiterio acciderint communes uobis erunt per omnia. Hanc concordiam suscepit Hugo prescriptus abbas Luxouiensis abbas consensu et / comuentia Widonis prioris, Vuilelmi camerarii, Gerardi sacristae, Henrici prioris de Claromonte monachorum uidelicet Luxouiensium, et magistri / Warini, similiter et Gerardus Besuensis abbas consensu monachorum suorum, Widrici prioris Fontisuene, Godefredi Calentensi prioris, Lebaldi de Gene- / brariis,[6] Haimonis Tullensis. Actum et hoc Lingonis in claustro Sancti Mammetis anno ab incarnatione dominica MCXXXI, indictione viiii, pontificatus autem

4 Bishops Robert (1084–1111) and Willenc (1125–1136) of Langres. The bishops' charters do not survive. Bishop Robert gave Bèze a number of churches at the end of the eleventh century (see documents 188, 189, and 191), but this one was not among them.

5 Abbots Peter of St-Bénigne (1129–1142) and Herbert of St-Étienne of Dijon (1125–1157), the first abbot there once the house acquired regular canons.

6 Genevrières, 38 km north-northeast of Bèze.

Domni / Innocencii secundi pape[7] anno secundo. Testes fuerunt huius Fulco et Vuarnerius archidiaconi, Wido presbiter, Gibuinus, Pontius, Teodericus subdiaconi, Guido, item Teodericus presbiter, omnes isti Lingonenses canonici. /

+ Ego Iohannes tituli Sancti Grisogoni presbiter cardinalis et apostolicę sedis legatus hanc concordiam feci, et SS. Signum W. episcopi.

"Signum W. Episcopi" is in a different hand, doubtless the hand of Bishop Willenc.

333

1134

Willenc, bishop of Langres, grants Bèze some churches that the priest Remigius had held, at the request of Abbot Girard and of Remigius. The churches are at Beaumont, Dampierre, Oisilly, and Champagne.

Original, Arch. Côte-d'Or, 3 H 47.[1]

Arch. Côte-d'Or, 3 H 1 (cart 130), pp. 3–4; copy made in 1772.

Summarized in Petit, *Histoire des ducs de Bourgogne*, 2:220, no. 258.

In nomine sancte et indiuidue trinitatis, patris et filii et spiritus sancti. /

Sanctorum precedentium patrum laudabilibus instrumentum exemplis queque digna memorie, litterarum monimentis fideliter / annotare ad omnipotentis Dei laudem et honorem, qui actor est et amator ueritatis et ad refellendas uersutias diabolice pra- / uitatis. Ego igitur Guilencus Dei misericordia Linguonensis ęcclesię episcopus[2] notificare studui omnibus tam futuris / quam presentibus dominum Gerardum uenerabilem Be[suensis e]cclesię abbatem[3] presentiam nostram adille et ut ęcclesias / quas Remigius sacerdos tenebat eodem intercedente ... sibi et prefate [Besuensi eccle]sie concederemus, humiliter / postulasse. Cuius peticioni assensum nostrum prebenter [prefate] ęcclesias, illam [scilicet de] Sancto Martino cum ca- / pella Sancti Bartolomei de castro Bellimontis, et [aliam] de Domnapetra in honore Beatri Petri

7 Pope Innocent II (1130–1143).

1 Written in brown ink on parchment, now with a number of holes, apparently nibbled by rats along the fold lines. It measures 58 cm tall, now 55 because there is a 3 cm fold at the bottom (previously sealed), and 43 cm wide. I have filled in text from 3 H 1 (in brackets) in a few places where it seems to have not been quite so badly disintegrated in 1772, although the copyist also gave ellipses in a few places, indicating the damage had already begun.

2 Bishop Willenc of Langres (1125–1136).

3 Abbot Girard of Bèze (1125–1142).

apostolorum / principis fundatum, et aliam apud Osillei uillam in ho[nore] Sancti Leodegarii dicatam, et illas duas apud / Campanias uillam in honore Sancti Iuliani martiris et Sancti Hylarii confessoris consecratas,[4] laudante Fulcone archi- / diacono, in cuius litę sunt archidiaconatu, concedentibus ceteris fidelibus nostris, cum et eundem ęcclesiarum appen- / diciis, saluo iure Linguonensis ęcclesię benigne concessimus et prefato abbati Gerardo eiusque in eadem ęcclesia suc- / cessoribus perpetualiter possidendas confirmamus. Huius rei testes sunt, Bernardus abbas Clariuallis[5] et / frater eius Girardus, Godefridus prior, Gozelmus, Pontius, Rotbertus, Garnerius archidiaconi. De Besuensibus / monachis Iosbertus prepositus, Henricus capellanus … Albricus. De laicis … Gerardus de Robro, Hugo / prepositus Linguonensis, et Guillelmus camerarius. Quicumque [huic nostr]ę scedulę ausu temerario obuiare presumpersit, anathe- / matis iaculo illum percutimus et a sancte matris ęcclesię [premio] actoritate Dei et nostra sequestramus, donec resipiscat et ad / satisfaccionem ueniat. /

Acta sunt hęc anno ab incarnatione Domini MCXXXIIII, Innocentio papa secundo, Ludouico Francorum rege regnante,[6] / Guilenco Linguonis feliciter pontificante, indictione xii, epacta xxiii, concurrente vii.

4 Beaumont, 7 km east of Bèze; Dampierre, 7 km east-northeast of Bèze; Oisilly, 9 km southeast of Bèze; and Champagne, 10 km southeast of Bèze.

5 Bernard, abbot of Clairvaux (1115–1153).

6 Pope Innocent II (1130–1143) and King Louis VI (1108–1137).

LIST OF ABBOTS

This list of abbots has several large gaps, corresponding to the times that the monastery was abandoned. The cartulary-chronicle itself is the major source of information on the abbots; the late twelfth-century "Annales" of the house provides additional detail on the twelfth-century abbots.

Waldalenus
: Considered to be the first abbot of the house in the mid-seventh century.

Bercangus
: He and his two successors' names are known only from the chronicle.

Ferreolus

Sirannus

Seraphim
: Abbot in 827 and 830.

Walcaud
: Abbot in c. 840 and c. 850.

Warin
: Abbot in c. 860. Possibly the same Warin as acted as rector of Flavigny in the 850s.

Theodebert
: Abbot in c. 870.

Walcaud II
: Abbot in c. 890.

Walcaud III
: Abbot in c. 915.

Walcaud IV
: One can doubt whether Walcaud III and IV, known only from the chronicle, were real, or whether the chronicler multiplied one abbot (Walcaud II) to account for the tenth century, although he also said the monastery was devastated by Huns during this time and did not regain regularity until 981.

Milo
Became bishop of Mâcon (981–993).
William (991–1031)
Abbot of St-Bénigne as well as Bèze.
Ulger (1031–c. 1055)
Had been prior under Abbot William.
Odo (c. 1055–c. 1065)
Gui (c. 1065–c. 1070)
Originally a monk at Montiéramey, to which he returned when he resigned.
Gausbert (c. 1070–1088)
Had been prior of St-Bénigne. Resigned to become a monk at Cluny.
Stephen of Beaumont (1088–1120)[1]
Of the family of the lords of Beaumont. Had served in a cell at Bar-sur-Aube, dependent of St-Oyend, before becoming abbot of Bèze. His uncle was prior of Cluny.
Robert (1120–1125)
Girard (1125–1142)
He may be identical with the Girard who had been prior of Fouvent, one of the monastery's cells (document 319).
Widric (1142–c. 1145)
He may be identical with the Widric who had been prior of Fouvent.
Hugh (c. 1145–1157)
Gui (1157–1158)
Geoffrey (1159–1164)

1 The dates for most of the abbots from this point forward are given by the late twelfth-century "Annales Besuenses," MGH SS 2:247–250.

WORKS CITED

Abbo. *Bella Parisiae urbis: Le siège de Paris par les Normands.* Ed. Henri Waquet. Paris: Les Belles Lettres, 1942.

"Annales Besuenses." MGH SS 2, pp. 247–250.

Bautier, Robert-Henri. *Chartes, sceaux, et chancelleries: Études de diplomatique et de sigillographie médiévales.* 2 vols. Paris: École de Chartes, 1990.

Böhmer, J.F. *Regesta imperii*, vol. 1. Innsbruck, 1908; rpt. Hildesheim: G. Olms, 1966.

Bouchard, Constance B. "Childeric III and the Emperors Drogo Magnus and Pippin the Pious." *Medieval Prosopography* 28 (2013): pp. 1–16.

–. "High Medieval Monks Contemplate Their Merovingian Past." *Journal of Medieval Monastic Studies* 1 (2012): pp. 41–62.

–. *Holy Entrepreneurs: Cistercians, Knights, and Economic Exchange in Twelfth-Century Burgundy.* Ithaca, NY: Cornell University Press, 1991.

–. *Rewriting Saints and Ancestors: Memory and Forgetting in France, 500–1200.* Philadelphia: University of Pennsylvania Press, 2015.

–. *Sword, Miter, and Cloister: Nobility and the Church in Burgundy, 980–1198.* Ithaca, NY: Cornell University Press, 1987.

–. *"Those of My Blood": Constructing Noble Families in Medieval Francia.* Philadelphia: University of Pennsylvania Press, 2001.

Brequigny, M. de. *Table chronologique des diplômes, chartes, titres et actes imprimés concernant l'histoire de France.* 3 vols. Paris, 1769, 1775, 1783.

Bulst, Neithard. *Untersuchungen zu den Klosterreform Wilhelms von Dijon (962–1031).* Pariser historische Studien 11. Bonn: L. Röhrscheid, 1973.

Cartulaire du chapitre cathédral de Langres. Ed. Hubert Flammarion. Rev. ed. Turnhout: Brepols, 2004.

The Cartulary of Flavigny, 717–1113. Ed. Constance Brittain Bouchard. Medieval Academy Books 99. Cambridge, MA: Medieval Academy of America, 1991.

The Cartulary of Saint-Marcel-les-Chalon, 779–1126. Ed. Constance Brittain Bouchard. Medieval Academy Books 102. Cambridge, MA: Medieval Academy of America, 1998.

Chartae Latinae Antiquiores, vol. 13 [France 1]. Ed. Hartmut Atsma and Jean Vezin. Zurich: Graf, 1981.

Chartes de l'abbaye de Saint-Étienne de Dijon (VIIIe, IXe, Xe et XIe siècles). Ed. J. Courtois. Paris: Picard, 1908.

Chartes de l'abbaye de Saint-Étienne de Dijon de 1098 à 1140. Ed. Adrien Bièvre Poulalier. Dijon: J. Bernigaud, 1912.

Chartes et documents de Saint-Bénigne de Dijon, vol. 1. Ed. Robert Folz and Jean Marilier. Dijon: Société des Annales de Bourgogne, 1986.

Chartes et documents de Saint-Bénigne de Dijon, vol. 2. Ed. Georges Chevrier and Maurice Chaume. Dijon: Société des Annales de Bourgogne, 1943.

Chronique de l'abbaye de Saint-Bénigne de Dijon, suivie de la Chronique de Saint-Pierre de Bèze. Ed. E. Bougaud and Joseph Garnier. Analecta Divionensia 9. Dijon: Darantière, 1875.

Chronique des abbés de Fontenelle (Saint-Wandrille). Ed. Pascal Pradié. Paris: Les Belles Lettres, 1999.

Cocquelines, Charles. *Bullarum privilegiorum ac diplomatum Romanorum pontificum amplissima collectio*, vol. 2. Rome, 1739; rpt. Graz: Akademische Druck- u. Verlagsanstalt, 1964.

Collins, Roger. *Die Fredegar-Chroniken.* MGH Studien und Texte 44. Hanover: Hahnsche Buchhandlung, 2007.

Columbanus. "Epistolae." MGH Epp. 3, 2nd ed. [Epistolae Merowingici et Karolini, vol. 1], ed. Wilhelm Gundlach, pp. 154–190.

d'Achery, Luc. *Spicilegium: Sive collectio veterum aliquot scriptorum qui in galliae bibliothecis delituerant*, vol. 2. Ed. Etienne Baluze, Edmund Martène, and Louis-François-Joseph de la Barre. Paris: Montalant, 1723; rpt. Farnborough, UK: Gregg, 1968.

Deflou-Leca, Noëlle. *Saint-Germain d'Auxerre et ses dépendances (Ve–XIIIe siècle).* Saint-Étienne: Publications de l'Université de Saint-Étienne, 2010.

Duchesne, André. *Histoire généalogique des ducs de Bourgonge de la maison de France.* Paris: Sabastien Cramoisy, 1628.

–. *Preuves de l'histoire de la maison de Vergy.* Paris, 1625.

Einhard. *Vie de Charlemagne.* Ed. Louis Halphen. Paris: Les Belles Lettres, 1981.

Fassler, Margot E. *The Virgin of Chartres: Making History Through Liturgy and the Arts.* New Haven, CT: Yale University Press, 2010.

Fox, Yaniv. *Power and Religion in Merovingian Gaul: Columbanian Monasticism and the Frankish Elites.* Cambridge: Cambridge University Press, 2014.

Fredegar. *Chronica.* Ed. Bruno Krusch. MGH SSRM 2, pp. 1–193. Hanover: Hahn, 1888.

–. *The Fourth Book of the Chronicle with Its Continuations.* Ed. J.M. Wallace-Hadrill. London: Nelson, 1960.

Geary, Patrick J. *Furta Sacra: Thefts of Relics in the Central Middle Ages.* Princeton, NJ: Princeton University Press, 1978.

Gerberding, Richard A. *The Rise of the Carolingians and the "Liber Historiae Francorum."* Oxford: Clarendon Press, 1987.

Gervers, Michael, ed. *Dating Undated Medieval Charters.* Woodbridge, UK: Boydell Press, 2000.

Gregory the Great. *Dialogues.* Ed. Adalbert de Vogüé. Sources chrétiennes 260. Paris: Éditions du Cerf, 1979.

Hugh of Flavigny. "Chronicon." MGH SS 8, pp. 280–502.

Hummer, Hans J. *Politics and Power in Early Medieval Europe: Alsace and the Frankish Realm, 600–1000.* Cambridge: Cambridge University Press, 2005.

Jaffe, Philip. *Regesta pontificum Romanorum ab condita ecclesia ad annum post Christum natum MCXCVIII.* 2 vols. Ed. Wilhelm Wattenbach. Leipzig, 1885–1888.

Joch, Waltraud. *Legitimität und Integration: Undersuchungen zu den Anfängen Karl Martells.* Husum, Germany: Matthiesen, 1999.

Jonas of Bobbio. "Vita Columbani." MGH SSRM 4, pp. 64–108.

Kölzer, Theo. *Merowingerstudien.* 2 vols. MGH Studien und Texte 21, 26. Hanover: Hahnsche Buchhandlung, 1998–1999.

Kreiner, Jamie. *The Social Life of Hagiography in the Merovingian Kingdom.* Cambridge: Cambridge University Press, 2014.

Labbe, Philippe, and Gabriel Cossart, eds. *Sacrosancta concilia*, vols. 7, 10. Paris, 1671.

Le liber pontificalis, vol. 2. Ed. L. Duchesne. Paris: E. de Boccard, 1955.

Leo IX. "Epistolae et diplomata pontificia." PL 143, pp. 591–794.

Les miracles de Saint Benoît. Ed. E. de Certain. Paris: Renouard, 1858.

"Liber Historiae Francorum." MGH SSRM 2, pp. 215–328.

Louis the Pious. "Diplomata." RHGF 6, pp. 452–632.

Louis the Pious. "Diplomata ecclesiastica." PL 104, pp. 979–1310.

Mansi, J.D., ed. *Sacrorum conciliorum nova et amplissima collectio*, vols. 14, 20. Venice, 1769, 1775; rpt. Paris: Welter, 1902.

Marculf. "Formulae." MGH Formulae, pp. 36–112.

Martène, Edmund, and Ursin Durand, eds. *Thesaurus novus anecdotorum*, vol. 4. Paris, 1717; rpt. New York: Burt Franklin, 1968.

Mathieu, Jean-Noël. "A propos d'une généalogie mâconnaise du XIe siècle: Un second mariage du comte de Troyes Robert de Vermandois (Xe siècle)?" *Annales de Bourgogne* 79 (2007): pp. 193–210.

Mathisen, Ralph W., and Danuta Shanzer, eds. *The Battle of Vouillé, 507 CE: Where France Began.* Boston: De Gruyter, 2012.

MGH DD imperii. Ed. Georg Heinrich Pertz. Hanover, 1872; rpt. Vaduz, Lichtenstein: Kraus Reprint, 1965.

MGH DD regum francorum e stirpe Merovingica. Ed. Theo Kölzer. Hanover: Hahnsche Buchhandlung, 2001.

Pardessus, Jean Marie, ed. *Diplomata, chartae, epistolae, leges aliaque instrumenta ad res Gallo-francicas spectantia*, vol. 2. Paris, 1849; rpt. Aalen: Scientia, 1969.

Paschal II. "Epistolae et privilegia." PL 163, pp. 31–448.

Peter Damian. *Vita Beati Romualdi.* Ed. Giovanni Tabacco. Fonti per la storia d'Italia 94. Rome: Tipografia del Senato, 1957.

Petit, Ernest, ed. *Histoire des ducs de Bourgogne de la race capétienne*, vols. 1–2. Dijon, 1885, 1888.

Prinz, Friedrich. *Frühes Mönchtum in Frankenreich.* Vienna: Oldenbourg, 1965.

Raoul Glaber. *The Five Books of the Histories.* Ed. John France. Oxford: Oxford University Press, 1989.

Recueil des actes d'Henri le Libéral, comte de Champagne (1152–1181). Ed. John Benton and Michel Bur, vol. 1. Paris: Boccard, 2009.

Recueil des chartes de l'abbaye de Cluny. Vol.5. Ed. Auguste Bernard and Alexandre Bruel. Paris, 1890.

Rosenwein, Barbara H. *Rhinoceros Bound: Cluny in the Tenth Century.* Philadelphia: University of Pennsylvania Press, 1982.

Roserot, Alphonse. *Dictionnaire topographique du département de la Côte-d'Or.* Paris: Imprimerie Nationale, 1924.Symes, Carol. "The Middle Ages between Nationalism and Colonialism." *French Historical Studies* 34 (2011): pp. 37–46.

Teobaudus. "Acta, translationes, et miracula S. Prudentii martyris." AASS October 3: pp. 348–377.

Vollmer, Franz. "Die Etichonen: Ein Beitrag zur Frage des Kontinuität früher Adelsfamilien." In *Studien und Vorarbeiten zur Geschichte des grossfränkischen und frühdeutschen Adels.* Ed. Gerd Tellenbach, pp. 137–84. Freiburg: Eberhard Albert, 1957.

Weidemann, Margarete, ed. *Geschichte des Bistums Le Mans von der Spätantike bis zur Karolingerzeit: Actus Pontificum Cenomannis in Urbe Degentium und Gesta Aldrici.* 3 vols. Mainz: Verlag des Römisch-Germanischen Zentralmuseums, 2002.

White, Stephen D. "Proposing the Ordeal and Avoiding It: Strategy and Power in Western French Litigation, 1050–1110." In *Cultures of Power: Lordship, Status, and Process in Twelfth-century Europe*, ed. Thomas N. Bisson, pp. 89–123. Philadelphia: University of Pennsylvania Press, 1995.

Wilsdorf, Christian. "Les Etichonides aux temps carolingiens et ottoniens." *Bulletin philologique et historique du Comité des travaux historiques et scientifiques*, 1964, pp. 1–33.

Wood, Ian. *The Merovingian Kingdoms, 450–751.* London: Longman, 1994.

Wood, Susan. *The Proprietary Church in the Medieval West.* Oxford: Oxford University Press, 2006.

INDEX OF PEOPLE

This index references, by document number, the people mentioned in the cartulary. It does not include the introduction or the chronicle portions of the cartulary-chronicle. When a name appears in several different forms, as it may even for the same person in the same document, I have normalized it to the most common spelling. If there are a number of people with the same name, I give the normalized name in boldface, the people with their various names arranged beneath, and cross-reference. (I have not bothered to distinguish extremely minor spelling variants, such as Adalsindis versus Adalsinda.) In alphabetizing different people with the same name, I have put ecclesiastics before laymen, more important dignitaries before less important ones, and people unidentified except by name at the end. For the most common names (Hugo and Guido), exactly how to alphabetize has been something of a challenge.

INDEX OF PLACES

This index references, by document number, the places mentioned in the cartulary. It does not include the introduction or the chronicle portions of the cartulary-chronicle. The principal entry is for the modern name of a place, if it is known; Latin names are cross-referenced, unless the reference would be to an immediately adjacent entry. Bèze itself, mentioned in nearly every document, is not listed in this index. For places in the region of the monastery, I generally give the distance and direction from there, or occasionally from Dijon or Langres.

INDEX OF TOPICS

This index lists topics by English words, rather than Latin. Thus someone interested in finding documents referring to woods usage, for example, can look for "woods usage," without having to think of the different Latin terms that might be used. There is no entry for "gifts" because that would have required listing well over half the documents in the cartulary.

www.ingramcontent.com/pod-product-compliance
Lightning Source LLC
LaVergne TN
LVHW040154080826
844660LV00014B/954/J